# COMPUTER FUNDAMENTALS
## Concepts, Systems & Applications

**Third Edition**

# COMPUTER FUNDAMENTALS
## Concepts, Systems & Applications

### Third Edition

Pradeep K. Sinha

Priti Sinha

**BPB PUBLICATIONS**
B-14, CONNAUGHT PLACE, NEW DELHI-110001

*FIRST INDIAN EDITION 2003*

Distributors:

**MICRO BOOK CENTRE**
2, City Centre, CG Road,
Near Swastic Char Rasta,
**AHMEDABAD-380009** Phone: 26421611

**COMPUTER BOOK CENTRE**
12, Shrungar Shopping Centre, M.G. Road,
**BANGALORE-560001** Phone: 25587923, 25584641

**MICRO BOOKS**
Shanti Niketan Building, 8, Camac Street,
**KOLKATTA-700017** Phone: 2826518, 2826519

**BUSINESS PROMOTION BUREAU**
8/1, Ritchie Street, Mount Road,
**CHENNAI-600002** Phone: 28534796, 28550491

**DECCAN AGENCIES**
4-3-329, Bank Street,
**HYDERABAD-500195** Phone: 24756400, 24756967

**MICRO MEDIA**
Shop No. 5, Mahendra Chambers, 150 D.N. Road,
Next to Capital Cinema V.T. (C.S.T.) Station,
**MUMBAI-400001**
Ph.: 22078296, 22078297, 22002732

**BPB PUBLICATIONS**
B-14, Connaught Place, **NEW DELHI-110001**
Phone: 23325760, 23723393, 23737742

**INFOTECH**
G-2, Sidhartha Building, 96 Nehru Place,
**NEW DELHI-110019**
Phone: 26438245, 26415092, 26234208

**INFOTECH**
Shop No. 2, F-38, South Extension Part-1
**NEW DELHI-110049**
Phone: 24691288, 24641941

**BPB BOOK CENTRE**
376, Old Lajpat Rai Market,
**DELHI-110006 PHONE:** 23861747

Price : Rs. 150/-

ISBN 81-7656-752-3

Published by Manish Jain for BPB Publications, B-14, Connaught Place, New Delhi-110 001 and Printed by Kwality Offset Printing Press.

*Dedicated to our parents*

*whose sacrifices, love, and affection made us*

*capable of carrying out such work.*

# Table of Contents

# CHAPTER 14:  OPERATING SYSTEMS                    237

# CHAPTER 15:  APPLICATION SOFTWARE PACKAGES          262

## CHAPTER 16: BUSINESS DATA PROCESSING     279

## CHAPTER 17: DATA COMMUNICATIONS AND COMPUTER NETWORKS     305

# CHAPTER 18:  THE INTERNET     341

# CHAPTER 19:  MULTIMEDIA     349

# CHAPTER 20:  CLASSIFICATION OF COMPUTERS     362

# Preface

## Audience

This book is intended for anyone, who is interested in knowing about computers. In today's information age, computers are being used in every occupation. They are being used by people of all age and profession, in their work as well as in their leisure. This new social revolution has changed the basic concept of 'Computing'. Computing, in today's information age, is no more limited to computer programmers and computer engineers. It has become an activity of a common man. Rather than knowing how to program a computer, most computer users simply need to understand how a computer functions, and what all it can do. Even those who need to program a computer, can do their job more effectively, with a better understanding of how computers function, and their capabilities and limitations. This book has been written to address this requirement of a wide variety of computer users. Rather than focusing on how to program a computer, it explains how a computer functions, what are its various components, and what are its capabilities and limitations.

The book has been thoughtfully structured to serve as an ideal textbook for various introductory courses offered in Computer Science, Information Technology, and other related areas. More specifically, different types of readers can benefit from this book in the following manner:

- It can be used as a textbook for the first course in computers taught in diploma, bachelor's and master's programmes in computer science, computer applications and information technology (for example, DCA, PGDCA, BCA, BCS, B.Sc. (IT), MCA, MCS, M.Sc. (IT), DOEACC 'O' Level, etc.).

- It can be used as a textbook for the first course in computers taught to the engineering students of all branches of engineering.

- It can be used as a textbook for the first course in computers taught to B.Sc. and B.Com. students.

- It can be used as a textbook for the first course in computers taught to management students (for example, BBA, MBA, and MCM students).

- The book can also serve as a good course material for participants of short-term courses, which are conducted by various training organizations.

- As the book explains the computer jargons in a simple language, it can also be used by various types of computer users, as a self-study material, for obtaining a basic understanding of the various hardware and software components of computers.

Knowledge of computers is not prerequisite to follow the contents of the book. It assumes no background in computers or computer programming.

## Overview

The layout and organization of the book, and its contents are designed to present the fundamental concepts of computers in an interesting, logical, and informative manner. The book does not concentrate on any particular computer system or hardware. Instead, it discusses, in a general setting, the organization, functions, and usage principles, which are applicable to all types of modern computer systems.

All the concepts presented in the book are illustrated with suitable examples, as and when required. The book also contains numerous diagrams for better illustration. These features will enable the readers to grasp the presented concepts easily, and to use the book effectively for self-study.

Each chapter contains a section on 'Points to Remember', which highlights the important points covered in the chapter.

Each chapter also contains a large number of carefully designed review questions, which are meant to test the understanding of the materials presented in the chapter.

To make the text easy to read and understand, the style of presentation used throughout the book is motivational, non-mathematical and explanatory in nature.

## Contents

The book begins with an introduction to computers. Chapter 1 explains what this versatile tool is, why is it so powerful and useful, what are its limitations, and how it has evolved from its early days, to become a powerful and useful tool for all types of users in today's society.

Chapter 2 presents the basic organization of a computer system. It briefly explains about the five main units present in any computer system, which correspond to the five basic operations performed by all computer systems.

Chapter 3 introduces the fundamentals of number system, and some of the number systems commonly used by computer professionals. Chapter 4 describes how binary numbers are coded to represent characters in computers, and some of the most commonly used computer codes. Chapter 5 describes how the basic arithmetic operations are performed inside the computer, by using binary numbers.

Chapter 6 introduces Boolean algebra, which is an algebra to deal with the binary number system. This chapter also describes logic gates, which are used for building logic circuits, which are used by the processors of computer systems.

Chapter 7 deals with the internal structure and working of the Central Processing Unit (popularly known as CPU or processor), and the primary storage (popularly known as main memory or simply memory). Chapters 8 and 9, respectively, deal with the structure and working of the secondary storage devices and input/output devices.

Chapter 10 introduces the software of computers. It explains why both hardware and software are necessary for a computer to do useful job, what are the various types of software, and how to acquire or develop software.

Chapter 11 deals with the commonly used tools for planning computer programs, before starting to write them. Chapter 12 deals with the commonly used programming languages for writing computer programs. Chapter 13 deals with the main activities of the implementation and operation phase, which include testing and debugging of programs, complete documentation of the system, changeover from an existing system to the new system, and system modification and maintenance.

Chapter 14 presents the important concepts of operating systems, which is a system software present in all computer systems. Chapter 15 describes some of the most commonly used application software packages. They are word-processing package, spreadsheet package, graphics package, and personal assistance package.

Chapter 16 deals with business data processing. It describes the basic concepts of database systems. Chapter 17 presents the important concepts of data communications, computer networks, and distributed computing systems.

Chapter 18 presents a description of the Internet, and Chapter 19 deals with multimedia computing systems.

Chapter 20 explains how computers are classified as notebook computers, personal computers, workstations, mainframe systems, and supercomputers. It also describes client-server computing, and explains what is a client computer and a server computer.

## Features of the Third Edition

Readers will find this edition of the book to be much more informative and useful than its previous edition because:

- It has been extensively revised to reflect the current state-of-the-art in computing.
- The layout has been considerably improved to make the contents attractive and easier to read.
- A section on 'Points to Remember' has been added at the end of each chapter to highlight the important points covered in the chapter.
- An index has been added at the end of the book to enable the readers to quickly search a topic of interest.

## For Additional Information

Several of the topics covered in this book have been covered in greater detail in the book titled *Foundations of Computing* by us. We have consciously done this, to avoid over-loading a reader, who is interested in introductory concepts, with unwanted details. Readers, who are interested in a more comprehensive coverage of the topics presented in this book, should refer to our *Foundations of Computing* book.

## Acknowledgement

A book of this type naturally gained a number of ideas from previous books dealing with the subject matter presented in this book. The authors express their thanks to all these authors, too numerous to acknowledge individually.

We would like to thank Ms. Sushma Pawar for her support activities. Her hard work, and cheerful devotion to the project, has helped us in bringing out the book in a timely manner.

We are also thankful to Mr. Manish Jain and other members of BPB Publications for their support and help in publishing the work.

Finally, we would like to thank our eight years old son, Deeptansu, for his loving support and understanding, during the entire period of this long project.

Pradeep K. Sinha<br>Priti Sinha

May, 2003.

# List of Abbreviations

| | | | | |
|---|---|---|---|---|
| A/D | Analog-to-Digital | CPU | Central Processing Unit |
| ABC | Atanasoff-Berry Computer | CRT | Cathode-Ray Tube |
| AI | Artificial Intelligence | CSCW | Computer Supported Cooperative Working |
| ALGOL | ALGOrithmic Language | | |
| ALU | Arithmetic Logic Unit | D/A | Digital-to-Analog |
| AM | Amplitude Modulation | DAT | Digital Audio Tape |
| ANSI | American National Standards Institute | DBMS | DataBase Management System |
| ASCII | American Standard Code for Information Interchange | DDL | Data Definition Language |
| | | DDS | Digital Data Storage |
| ATM | Automatic Teller Machine; Asynchronous Transfer Mode | DEC | Digital Equipment Corporation |
| | | DML | Data Manipulation Language |
| BARC | Bhabha Atomic Research Centre | DNA | Digital Network Architecture |
| BASIC | Beginners All-purpose Symbolic Instruction Code | DPI | Dots Per Inch |
| | | DRDO | Defense Research and Development Organization |
| BCD | Binary Coded Decimal | | |
| B-ISDN | Broad band ISDN | DSN | Distributed Systems Network |
| BNA | Burroughs Network Architecture | EBCDIC | Extended Binary-Coded Decimal Interchange Code |
| BPI | Bytes Per Inch | | |
| BSNL | Bharat Sanchar Nigam Limited | EDSAC | Electronic Delay Storage Automatic Calculator |
| CAD | Computer-Aided Design | | |
| CAE | Computer-Aided Engineering | EDVAC | Electronic Discrete Variable Automatic Computer |
| CAM | Computer-Aided Manufacturing | | |
| CASE | Computer-Aided Software Engineering | EEPROM | Electrically EPROM |
| | | ENIAC | Electronic Numerical Integrator And Calculator |
| CD | Compact Disk | | |
| C-DAC | Centre for Development of Advanced Computing | EPIC | Explicitly Parallel Instruction Computing |
| | | | |
| CDC | Control Data Corporation | EPROM | Erasable Programmable Read-Only Memory |
| CD-R | CD-Recordable | | |
| CD-ROM | Compact Disk-Read Only Memory | ERNET | Education and Research NETwork |
| CISC | Complex Instruction Set Computer | FAT | File Allocation Table |
| CL | Command Language | FDM | Frequency-Division Multiplexing |
| COBOL | COmmon Business Oriented Language | FEP | Front-End Processor |
| | | FM | Frequency Modulation |
| CODASYL | Conference On DAta SYstems Languages | FMS | File Management System |
| | | FORTRAN | FORmula TRANslation |
| CPS | Characters Per Second | FSK | Frequency Shift Keying |

| | | | |
|---|---|---|---|
| FTP | File Transfer Protocol | OMR | Optical Mark Reader |
| GB | Giga Bytes | OOP | Object-Oriented Programming |
| GIGO | Garbage-In-Garbage-Out | OS | Operating System |
| GIS | Geographical Information System | OSI | Open System Interconnection |
| GUI | Graphical User Interface | PC | Personal Computer |
| HP | Hewlett Packard | PCB | Process Control Block |
| HTML | HypterText Markup Language | PDA | Personal Digital Assistant |
| HTTP | HyperText Transport Protocol | PDL | Program Design Language |
| Hz | Hertz | PDP | Programmed Data Processor |
| I/O | Input and Output | PL/1 | Programming Language One |
| IBG | Inter-Block Gap | PM | Phase Modulation |
| IBM | International Business Machines | POS | Point-Of-Sale |
| IC | Integrated Circuit | POTS | Plain Old Telephone Service |
| IDN | Integrated Digital Networks | PPM | Pages Per Minute |
| IEEE | Institute of Electrical and Electronics Engineers | PRIMENET | PRIME Computers NETwork |
| | | PROM | Programmable Read-Only Memory |
| IP | Internet Protocol | PSTN | Public Switched Telephone Network |
| IRG | Inter-Record Gap | QBE | Query By Example |
| ISAM | Indexed Sequential Access Method | QIC | Quarter Inch Cartridge |
| ISDN | Integrated Services Digital Network | QoS | Quality of Service |
| ISO | International Standards Organization | RAID | Redundant Array of Inexpensive Disks |
| ISP | Internet Service Provider | RAM | Random Access Memory |
| JCL | Job Control Language | RGB | Red, Green and Blue |
| KB | Kilo Bytes | RISC | Reduced Instruction Set Computer |
| LAN | Local Area Network | ROM | Read Only Memory |
| LCD | Liquid Crystal Display | RPG | Report Program Generator |
| LED | Light-Emitting Diode | SEQUEL | Structured English QUEry Language |
| LISP | LISt Processing | SGML | Standard Generalized Markup Language |
| LPM | Lines Per Minute | | |
| LSD | Least Significant Digit | SIMM | Single In-line Memory Module |
| LSI | Large Scale Integration | SNA | Systems Network Architecture |
| MAN | Metropolitan Area Network | SNOBOL | StriNg Oriented symBOlic Language |
| MAR | Memory Address Register | SSI | Small Scale Integration |
| MB | Mega Bytes | TB | Tera Bytes |
| MBR | Memory Buffer Register | TCP | Transport Control Protocol |
| MFT | Multiprogramming with Fixed Tasks | TCP/IP | Transmission Control Protocol/Internet Protocol |
| MHz | Mega Hertz | | |
| MICR | Magnetic-Ink Character Recognition | TDM | Time-Division Multiplexing |
| MIDI | Musical Instrument Digital Interface | UDP | User Datagram Protocol |
| MODEM | MOdulator/DEModulator | ULSI | Ultra Large Scale Integration |
| MSD | Most Significant Digit | UNIVAC | UNIVersal Automatic Computer |
| MS-DOS | MicroSoft Disk Operating System | UPC | Universal Product Code |
| MSI | Medium Scale Integration | URL | Uniform Resource Locator |
| MTNL | Mahanagar Telephone Nigam Limited | UTP | Unshielded Twisted-Pair |
| MVT | Multiprogramming with Variable Tasks | UVEPROM | Ultra Violet EPROM |
| | | VAN | Value Added Network |
| NIC | Network Interface Card | VCR | Video Cassette Recorder |
| NICNET | National Informatics Center NETwork | VDT | Video Display Terminal |
| OCR | Optical Character Recognition | VLSI | Very Large Scale Integration |

| | |
|---|---|
| VSAT | Very Small Aperture Terminals |
| VSNL | Videsh Sanchar Nigam Limited |
| WAN | Wide Area Network |
| WORM | Write-Once Read Many |
| WYSIWYG | What You See Is What You Get |
| WWW | Word Wide Web |
| X.400 | Electronic Mail Protocol |
| X.500 | Directory Server Protocol |
| XHTML | eXtensible HyperText Markup Language |
| XML | eXtensible Markup Language |

# Chapter 1

# Introduction

The word "computer" comes from the word "compute", which means to calculate. Hence, a computer is normally considered to be a calculating device, which can perform arithmetic operations at enormous speed.

In fact, the original objective for inventing the computer was to create a fast calculating machine. However, more than 80% of the work done by computers today is of non-mathematical or non-numerical nature. Hence, to define a computer merely as a calculating device is to ignore over 80% of its functions.

More accurately, a computer may be defined as a device, which operates upon data. Data can be anything like bio-data of various applicants when the computer is used for recruiting personnel, or the marks obtained by various students in various subjects when the computer is used to prepare results, or the details (name, age, sex, etc.) of various passengers when the computer is employed for making airline or railway reservations, or numbers of different types in case of use of computers for solving scientific research problems, etc.

Hence, data comes in various shapes and sizes, depending upon the type of computer application. A computer can store, process, and retrieve data as and when desired. The fact that computers process data is so fundamental that many people have started calling it a *data processor*.

The name data processor is more inclusive because modern computers not only compute in the usual sense, but also perform other functions with the data, which flow to and from them. For example, data processors may gather data from various incoming sources, merge (process of mixing or putting together) them all, sort (process of arranging in some sequence – ascending or descending) them in the desired order, and finally print them in the desired format. None of these operations involve the arithmetic operations normally associated with the computing device, but the term computer is often applied anyway.

The activity of processing data using a computer is called *data processing*. Data processing consists of three sub-activities: capturing the input data, manipulating the data, and managing the output results. As used in data processing, information is data arranged in an order and form, which is useful to the people who receive it.

Hence, *data* is the raw material used as input to data processing, and *information* is the processed data obtained as the output of data processing.

# CHARACTERISTICS OF COMPUTERS

The increasing popularity of computers has proved that it is a very powerful and useful tool. The power and usefulness of this popular tool are mainly due to its following characteristics:

1. **Automatic.** A machine is said to be automatic, if it works by itself without human intervention. Computers are automatic machines because once started on a job, they carry on, until the job is finished, normally without any human assistance. However, computers being machines cannot start themselves. They cannot go out and find their own problems and solutions. They have to be instructed. That is, a computer works from a program of coded instructions, which specify exactly how a particular job is to be done. Some of the other characteristics of computers, such as speed and accuracy, are due to the fact that they are automatic, and work on a problem without any human intervention.

2. **Speed.** A computer is a very fast device. It can perform in a few seconds, the amount of work that a human being can do in an entire year – if he worked day and night and did nothing else. To put it in a different manner, a computer does in one minute what would take a man his entire lifetime.

   While talking about the speed of a computer, we do not talk in terms of seconds or even milliseconds ($10^{-3}$). Our units of speed are the microseconds ($10^{-6}$), the nanoseconds ($10^{-9}$), and even the picoseconds ($10^{-12}$). A powerful computer is capable of performing several billion ($10^9$) simple arithmetic operations per second.

3. **Accuracy.** In addition to being very fast, computers are very accurate. The accuracy of a computer is consistently high, and the degree of accuracy of a particular computer depends upon its design. However, for a particular computer, every calculation is performed with the same accuracy.

   Errors can occur in a computer. However, these are mainly due to human rather than technological weaknesses. For example, errors may occur due to imprecise thinking by the programmer (a person who writes instructions for a computer to solve a particular problem) or incorrect input data. Computer errors caused due to incorrect input data or unreliable programs are often referred to as *garbage-in-garbage-out* (*GIGO*).

4. **Diligence.** Unlike human beings, a computer is free from monotony, tiredness and lack of concentration. It can continuously work for hours, without creating any error and without grumbling. Hence, computers score over human beings in doing routine type of jobs, which require great accuracy. If ten million calculations have to be performed, a computer will perform the ten millionth calculation with exactly the same accuracy and speed as the first one.

5. **Versatility.** Versatility is one of the most wonderful things about the computer. One moment, it is preparing the results of an examination, the next moment, it is busy preparing electricity bills, and in between, it may be helping an office secretary to trace an important letter in seconds. All that is required to change its talent is to slip in a new program (a sequence of instructions for the computer) into it. Briefly, a computer is capable of performing almost any task, if the task can be reduced to a series of logical steps.

6. **Power of Remembering.** As a human being acquires new knowledge, the brain subconsciously selects what it feels to be important and worth retaining in its memory, and relegates unimportant details to the back of the mind or just forgets them. This is not the case with computers. A computer can store and recall any amount of information because of its secondary storage (a type of detachable

memory) capability. Every piece of information can be retained as long as desired by the user, and can be recalled, as and when required. Even after several years, the information recalled would be as accurate as on the day when it was fed to the computer. A computer forgets or looses certain information only when it is asked to do so. Hence, it is entirely up to the user, to make a computer retain or forget a particular information.

7. **No I. Q.** A computer is not a magical device. It possesses no intelligence of its own. Its I. Q. is zero, at least untill today. It has to be told what to do and in what sequence. Hence, only the user can determine what tasks a computer will perform. A computer cannot take its own decision in this regard.

8. **No Feelings.** Computers are devoid of emotions. They have no feelings and no instincts because they are machines. Although men have succeeded in building a memory for the computer, but no computer possesses the equivalent of a human heart and soul. Based on our feelings, taste, knowledge, and experience, we often make certain judgements in our day-to-day life. However, computers cannot make such judgements on their own. Their judgement is based on the instructions given to them in the form of programs that are written by us.

# THE EVOLUTION OF COMPUTERS

Necessity is the mother of invention. The saying holds true for computers also, because computers were invented because of man's search for fast and accurate calculating devices.

The first mechanical adding machine was invented by Blaise Pascal in 1642. Later, in the year 1671, Baron Gottfried Wilhelm von Leibniz of Germany invented the first calculator for multiplication. Keyboard machines originated in the United States around 1880 and are extensively used even today. Around this period only, Herman Hollerith came up with the concept of punched cards, which were extensively used as input medium in computers even in late 1970s. Business machines and calculators made their appearance in Europe and America towards the end of the nineteenth century.

Charles Babbage, a nineteenth century Professor at Cambridge University, is considered the father of modern digital computers. During his period, mathematical and statistical tables were prepared by a group of clerks. Even the utmost care and precautions could not eliminate human errors. Babbage had to spend several hours checking these tables. Soon he became dissatisfied and exasperated with this type of monotonous job. The result was that he started thinking to build a machine, which could compute tables guaranteed to be error-free. In this process, Babbage designed a "Difference Engine" in the year 1822, which could produce reliable tables. In 1842, Babbage came out with his new idea of Analytical Engine, which was intended to be completely automatic. It was to be capable of performing the basic arithmetic functions for any mathematical problem, and it was to do so at an average speed of 60 additions per minute. Unfortunately, he was unable to produce a working model of this machine, because the precision engineering required to manufacture the machine was not available during that period. However, his efforts established a number of principles, which have been shown to be fundamental to the design of any digital computer. In order to have a better idea of the evolution of computers, let us now briefly discuss about some of the well-known early computers. These are as follows:

1. **The Mark I Computer (1937-44).** Also known as Automatic Sequence Controlled calculator, this was the first fully automatic calculating machine designed by Howard A. Aiken of Harvard University, in collaboration with IBM (International Business Machines) Corporation. Its design was based on the techniques already developed for punched card machinery. It was an electro-mechanical device, since both mechanical and electronic components were used in its design.

Although this machine proved to be extremely reliable, it was very complex in design and huge in size. It used over 3000 electrically actuated switches to control its operations, and was approximately 50 feet long and 8 feet high. It was capable of performing five basic arithmetic operations: addition, subtraction, multiplication, division and table reference. A number as big as 23 decimal digits could be used in this machine. It took approximately 0.3 second to add two numbers and 4.5 seconds for multiplication of two numbers. Hence, the machine was very slow as compared to today's computers.

2. **The Atanasoff-Berry Computer (1939-42).** This electronic machine was developed by Dr. John Atanasoff to solve certain mathematical equations. It was called the Atanasoff-Berry Computer, or ABC, after its inventor's name and his assistant, Clifford Berry. It used 45 vacuum tubes for internal logic and capacitors for storage.

3. **The ENIAC (1943-46).** The Electronic Numerical Integrator And Calculator (ENIAC) was the first all electronic computer. It was constructed at the Moore School of Engineering of the University of Pennsylvania, U.S.A. by a design team led by Professors J. Presper Eckert and John Mauchly.

ENIAC was developed because of military need, and was used for many years to solve ballistic problems. It took up the wall space in a 20 x 40 square feet room and used 18,000 vacuum tubes. The addition of two numbers was achieved in 200 microseconds, and multiplication in 2000 microseconds.

4. **The EDVAC (1946-52).** A major drawback of ENIAC was that its programs were wired on boards, which made it difficult to change the programs. This problem was later overcome by the "stored program" concept introduced by Dr. John Von Neumann. The basic idea behind this concept is that a sequence of instructions, as well as data, can be stored in the memory of the computer, for automatically directing the flow of operations. This feature considerably influenced the development of modern digital computers because of the ease with which different programs can be loaded and executed on the same computer. Due to this feature, we often refer to modern digital computers as stored program digital computers. The Electronic Discrete Variable Automatic Computer (EDVAC) was designed on stored program concept. Von Neumann also has a share of the credit for introducing the idea of storing both instructions and data in the binary form (a system that uses only two digits – 0 & 1 to represent all characters), instead of the decimal numbers or human readable words.

5. **The EDSAC (1947-49).** Almost simultaneously with EDVAC of U.S.A., the Britishers developed the Electronic Delay Storage Automatic Calculator (EDSAC). The machine executed its first program in May 1949. In this machine, addition operation was accomplished in 1500 microseconds, and multiplication operation in 4000 microseconds. The machine was developed by a group of scientists, headed by Professor Maurice Wilkes, at the Cambridge University Mathematical Laboratory.

6. **The UNIVAC I (1951).** The Universal Automatic Computer (UNIVAC) was the first digital computer, which was not "one of a kind". Many UNIVAC machines were produced, the first of which was installed in the Census Bureau in 1951 and was used continuously for 10 years. The first business use of a computer, a UNIVAC I, was by General Electric Corporation in 1954.

In 1952, the International Business Machines (IBM) Corporation introduced the 701 commercial computer. In rapid succession, improved models of the UNIVAC I and other 700-series machines were introduced. In 1953, IBM produced the IBM-650, and sold over 1000 of these computers.

The commercially available digital computers, which could be used for business and scientific applications, had arrived.

# THE COMPUTER GENERATIONS

"Generation" in computer talk is a step in technology. It provides a framework for the growth of the computer industry. Originally, the term "generation" was used to distinguish between varying hardware technologies. However, nowadays, it has been extended to include both hardware and software, which together make up an entire computer system.

The custom of referring to the computer era in terms of generations came into wide use only after 1964. There are totally five computer generations known untill today. Each generation has been discussed below in detail along with its identifying characteristics. Although there is a certain amount of overlapping between the generations, the approximate dates shown against each are normally accepted.

During the description of the various computer generations, you will come across several terminologies and computer jargons, which you might not be aware of, and may not be able to understand properly. However, the idea here is to just give you an overview of the major developments and technologies during the five generations of computers. These developments and technologies will be described in detail in subsequent chapters. Moreover, remember that the objective of this book is also the same – to introduce you to the various concepts about computers. Hence, you will have a better understanding of the terminologies introduced in this section, only after you have completed reading this entire book. The objective of this section is mainly to provide an overview of what all you are going to learn in this entire book.

## First Generation (1942-1955)

We have already discussed about some of the early computers – ENIAC, EDVAC, EDSAC, UNIVAC I, and IBM 701. These machines and others of their time were built by using thousands of vacuum tubes. A vacuum tube [see Figure 1.1(a)] was a fragile glass device, which used filaments as a source of electronics, and could control and amplify electronic signals. It was the only high-speed electronic switching device available in those days. These vacuum tube computers could perform computations in milliseconds, and were referred to as first-generation computers.

The memory of these computers was constructed using electromagnetic relays, and all data and instructions were fed into the system from punched cards. The instructions were written in machine and assembly languages because high-level programming languages were introduced much later (computer languages are covered in Chapter 12). Because machine and assembly languages are very difficult to work with, only a few specialists understood how to program these early computers.

The characteristic features of first-generation computers are as follows:

1. They were the fastest calculating devices of their time.

2. They were too bulky in size, requiring large rooms for installation.

3. Thousands of vacuum tubes, which were used, emitted large amount of heat and burnt out frequently. Hence, the rooms/areas in which these computers were located had to be properly air-conditioned.

4. Each vacuum tube consumed about half a watt of power. Since a computer typically used more than ten thousand vacuum tubes, the power consumption of these computers was very high.

5. As vacuum tubes used filaments, they had a limited life. Since thousands of vacuum tubes were used in making one computer, these computers were prone to frequent hardware failures.

6. Due to low mean time between failures, these computers required almost constant maintenance.

7. In these computers, thousands of individual components had to be assembled manually by hand into functioning circuits. Hence, commercial production of these computers was difficult and costly.

8. Since these computers were difficult to program and use, they had limited commercial use.

# Second Generation (1955-1964)

A new electronic switching device, called transistor [see Figure 1.1(b)], was invented at Bell Laboratories in 1947 by John Bardeen, Willian Shockley, and Walter Brattain. Transistors soon proved to be a better electronic switching device than the vacuum tubes, due to their following properties:

1. They were more rugged and easier to handle than tubes, since they were made of germanium semiconductor material rather than glass.

2. They were highly reliable as compared to tubes, since they had no part like a filament, which could burn out.

3. They could switch much faster (almost ten times faster) than tubes. Hence, switching circuits made of transistors could operate much faster than their counterparts made of tubes.

4. They consumed almost one-tenth the power consumed by a tube.

5. They were much smaller than a tube.

6. They were less expensive to produce.

7. They dissipated much less heat as compared to vacuum tubes.

The second-generation computers were manufactured using transistors, instead of vacuum tubes. Due to the properties of transistors listed above, the second-generation computers were more powerful, more reliable, less expensive, smaller, and cooler to operate than the first-generation computers.

The memory of the second-generation computers was composed of magnetic cores. Magnetic disk and magnetic tape were the main secondary storage media used in second-generation computers. Punched cards were still popular and widely used for preparing programs and data to be fed to these computers.

On the software front, the second generation saw the emergence of high-level programming languages and batch operating systems. High-level programming languages like FORTRAN, COBOL, ALGOL and SNOBOL were developed during the second-generation period, which were much easier for people to understand and work with than assembly or machine languages. Hence, second-generation computers were easier to program and use than first-generation computers. The introduction of batch operating system allowed multiple jobs to be batched together and submitted at a time, and automatic transition from one job to another, as soon as the former job finished. This concept helped in reducing human intervention while processing multiple jobs, resulting in faster processing, enhanced throughput, and easier operation of second-generation computers.

The first-generation computers were mainly used for scientific computations. However, in the second generation, an increasing usage of computers was seen in business and industry for commercial data processing applications like payroll, inventory control, marketing, and production planning.

The characteristic features of second-generation computers are as follows:

1. They were more than ten times faster than the first-generation computers.

2. They were much smaller than first-generation computers, requiring smaller space.

3. Although the heat dissipation was much less than first-generation computers, the rooms/areas in which the second-generation computers were located had to be properly air-conditioned.

4. They consumed much less power than the first-generation computers.

5. They were more reliable and less prone to hardware failures than the first-generation computers.

6. They had faster and larger primary and secondary storage as compared to first-generation computers.

7. They were much easier to program and use than the first-generation computers. Hence, they had wider commercial use.

8. In these computers, thousands of individual transistors had to be assembled manually by hand into functioning circuits. Hence, commercial production of these computers was difficult and costly.

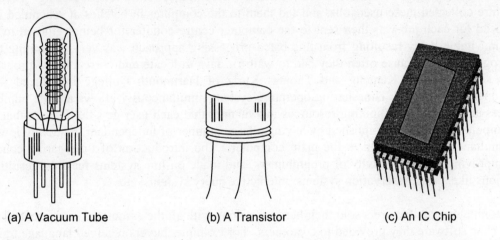

(a) A Vacuum Tube                (b) A Transistor                (c) An IC Chip

**Figure 1.1.** Electronics devices used for manufacturing computers of different generations.

# Third Generation (1964-1975)

In 1958, Jack St. Clair Kilby and Robert Noyce invented the first integrated circuit. *Integrated circuits* (called *ICs*) are circuits consisting of several electronic components like transistors, resistors, and capacitors grown on a single chip of silicon, eliminating wired interconnection between components. The IC technology was also known as "microelectronics" technology because it made it possible to integrate larger number of circuit components into very small (less than 5 mm square) surface of silicon, known as "chip" [see Figure 1.1(c)]. Initially, the integrated circuits contained only about ten to twenty components. This technology was named *small scale integration* (SSI). Later, with the advancement in technology for manufacturing ICs, it became possible to integrate up to about hundred components on a single chip. This technology came to be known as *medium scale integration* (MSI). The third generation was characterized by computers built using integrated circuits. The earlier ones used SSI technology and the later ones used MSI technology. ICs were much smaller, less expensive to produce, more rugged and reliable, faster in operation, dissipated less heat, and consumed much less power than circuits built by wiring electronic components manually. Hence, third-generation computers were more powerful, more reliable, less expensive, smaller, and cooler to operate than the second-generation computers.

Parallel advancements in storage technologies allowed the construction of larger magnetic cores based random access memory, and larger capacity magnetic disks and magnetic tapes. Hence, the third-generation computers typically had few megabytes (less than 5 Megabytes) of main memory, and magnetic disks capable of storing few tens of megabytes of data per disk drive.

On the software front, the third generation saw the emergence of standardization of high-level programming languages, timesharing operating systems, unbundling of software from hardware, and the creation of an independent software industry. FORTRAN and COBOL, which were the most popular high-level programming languages in those days, were standardized by the American National Standards Institute (ANSI) in 1966 and 1968 respectively. They were referred to as ANSI FORTRAN and ANSI COBOL. The idea was that as long as these standards are followed in program writing, a FORTRAN or a COBOL program could be run on any computer with an ANSI FORTRAN or ANSI COBOL compiler (see Chapter 12 for details). Additionally, some more high-level programming languages were introduced during the third-generation period. Notable among these were PL/1, PASCAL and BASIC.

We saw that in second-generation computers, batch operating system was used. In these systems, users had to prepare their data and programs, and then submit them to the computer centre for processing. The operator at the computer centre collected these user jobs, and fed them to the computer in batches at scheduled intervals. The output produced for each job was then sent to the computer centre counter for being returned to the respective users. The inevitable delay resulting from this batch processing approach was very frustrating to some users, especially programmers, because often they had to wait for days to locate and correct a few program errors. To remedy this situation, John Kemeny and Thomas Kurtz of Dartmouth College introduced the concept of timesharing operating system. Timesharing operating system simultaneously allows a large number of users to directly access and share the computing resources in a manner that each user gets the illusion that no one else is using the computer. This is accomplished by having a large number of independent, relatively low-speed, online terminals simultaneously connected to the main computer. The introduction of timesharing concept helped in drastically improving the productivity of programmers, and made on-line systems feasible, resulting in new on-line applications like airline reservation systems, interactive query systems, etc.

Until 1965, computer manufacturers sold their hardware along with all the associated software, and did not charge separately for the software they provided to customers. For example, buyers received language translators for all the languages, which could run on the computers they purchased. From the user's standpoint, all this software was free. However, the situation changed in 1969 when IBM and other computer manufacturers began to price their hardware and software products separately. This unbundling of software from hardware gave users an opportunity to invest only in software of their need and value. For example, now buyers could purchase only the language translators they needed and not all the language translators supported on the computer they purchased. This led to the creation of many new software houses, and the beginning of an independent software industry.

The development and introduction of minicomputers also took place during the third-generation period. The computers built until the early 1960s were mainframe systems, which only very large companies could afford to purchase and use. Clearly, a need existed for low-cost smaller computers, to fill the gaps left by the bigger, faster, and costlier mainframe systems. Several innovators recognized this need and formed new firms in the 1960s to produce smaller computers. The first commercially available minicomputer, the PDP-8 (Programmed Data Processor), was introduced in 1965 by Digital Equipment Corporation (DEC). It could easily fit in the corner of a room, and did not require the attention of a full-time computer operator. It was based on timesharing operating system, and could be accessed simultaneously by a number of users from different locations in the same building. Its cost was about one-fourth of the cost of a traditional mainframe system, making it possible for smaller companies to afford computers. It confirmed the tremendous demand for small computers for business and scientific applications, and by 1971, there were more than 25 computer manufacturers who had entered the minicomputer market.

The characteristic features of third-generation computers are as follows:

1. They were much more powerful than the second-generation computers. They were capable of performing about 1 million instructions per second.

2. They were much smaller than second-generation computers, requiring smaller space.

3. Although the heat dissipation was much less than second-generation computers, the rooms/areas in which the third-generation computers were located had to be properly air-conditioned.

4. They consumed much less power than the second-generation computers.

5. They were more reliable and less prone to hardware failures than the second-generation computers. Hence, the maintenance cost was much lower.

6. They had faster and larger primary and secondary storage as compared to second-generation computers.

7. They were totally general-purpose machines suitable for both scientific and commercial applications.

8. Their manufacturing did not require manual assembly of individual components into electronic circuits, resulting in reduced human labor and cost involved at assembly stage. Hence, commercial production of these systems was easier and cheaper. However, highly sophisticated technology and expensive setup was required for the manufacture of IC chips.

9. Standardization of high-level programming languages allowed programs written for one computer to be easily ported to and executed on another computer.

10. Timesharing operating system allowed interactive usage and simultaneous use of these systems by a large number of users.

11. Timesharing operating system helped in drastically improving the productivity of programmers, cutting down the time and cost of program development by several fold.

12. Timesharing operating system also made on-line systems feasible, resulting in the usage of these systems for new on-line applications.

13. Unbundling of software from hardware gave users of these systems an opportunity to invest only in software of their need and value.

14. The minicomputers of the third-generation made computers affordable even by smaller companies.

# Fourth Generation (1975-1989)

The average number of electronic components packed on a silicon chip doubled each year after 1965. This progress soon led to the era of *large scale integration* (*LSI*) when it was possible to integrate over 30,000 electronic components on a single chip, followed by *very large scale integration* (*VLSI*) when it was possible to integrate about one million electronic components on a single chip. This progress led to a dramatic development – the creation of a microprocessor. A *microprocessor* contains all the circuits needed to perform arithmetic logic and control functions, the core activities of all computers, on a single chip. Hence, it became possible to build a complete computer with a microprocessor, a few additional primary storage chips, and other support circuitry. It started a new social revolution – the *personal computer* (*PC*) revolution. Overnight, computers became incredibly compact. They became inexpensive to make, and suddenly it became possible for anyone to own a computer.

During the fourth generation, magnetic core memories were replaced by semiconductor memories, resulting in large random access memories with very fast access time. On the other hand, hard disks became cheaper, smaller, and larger in capacity. Parallely, in addition to magnetic tapes, floppy disks became very popular as a portable medium for porting programs and data from one computer system to another.

Another significant development during the fourth-generation period was the spread of high-speed computer networking, which enabled multiple computers to be connected together, to enable them to communicate and share data. Local area networks (LANs) became popular for connecting several dozen or even several hundred computers within an organization or within a campus, and wide area networks (WANs) became popular for connecting computers located at larger distances. This gave rise to network of computers and distributed systems.

On the software front, there were several new developments, which emerged to match the new technologies of the fourth generation. For example, several new operating systems were developed for PCs. Notable among these were MS-DOS, MS-Windows, and Apple's propriety OS. Because PCs were to be used by individuals who were not computer professionals, to make computers more user friendly (easier to use), companies developed graphical user interfaces. A *graphical user interface* (*GUI*) provides icons (pictures) and menus (list of choices), which users can select with a mouse. This enables new computer users to learn to use a PC quickly. Several new PC-based applications were also developed to make the PCs a powerful tool. Notable among these were powerful word processing packages, which allowed easy development of documents, spreadsheet package, which allowed easy manipulation and analysis of data organized in columns and rows, and graphics packages, which allowed easy drawing of pictures and diagrams. Another very useful concept, which became popular during the fourth-generation period, was that of multiple windows on a single terminal screen. This feature allowed users to simultaneously see the current status of several applications, in separate windows, on the same terminal screen. During the fourth-generation period, the UNIX operating system and the C programming language also became very popular.

The characteristic features of fourth-generation computers are as follows:

1.  The PCs were smaller and cheaper than the mainframes or minicomputers of the third generation.

2.  The mainframes were much more powerful than the third-generation systems.

3.  Although the mainframes required proper air-conditioning of the rooms/areas in which they were located, no air-conditioning was required for the PCs.

4.  They consumed much less power than the third-generation computers.

5.  They were more reliable and less prone to hardware failures than the third-generation computers. Hence, the maintenance cost was negligible.

6.  They had faster and larger primary and secondary storage as compared to third-generation computers.

7.  They were totally general-purpose machines.

8.  Their manufacturing did not require manual assembly of individual components into electronic circuits, resulting in reduced human labor and cost involved at assembly stage. Hence, commercial production of these systems was easier and cheaper. However, highly sophisticated technology and expensive setup was required for the manufacture of LSI and VLSI chips.

9.  Use of standard high-level programming languages allowed programs written for one computer to be easily ported to and executed on another computer.

10. Graphical user interface (GUI) enabled new users to quickly learn how to use computers.

11. PC-based applications made the PCs a powerful tool for both office and home usage.

12. Network of computers enabled sharing of resources like disks, printers, etc. among multiple computers and their users. They also enabled several new types of applications involving interaction among computer users at geographically distant locations. *Computer Supported Cooperative Working* (*CSCW*), or *groupware* is one such application, in which multiple members working on a single project and located at distant locations, cooperate with each other, by using a network of computers.

13. In addition to unbundled software, these systems also used add-on hardware feature, which allowed users to invest only in the hardware configuration and software of their need and value.

14. The PCs of the fourth-generation made computers affordable even by individuals, for their personal use at home.

# Fifth Generation (1989-Present)

The trend of further miniaturization of electronic components, the dramatic increase in the power of microprocessor chips, and the capacity of main memory and hard disk continued in the fifth generation. The VLSI technology became *ULSI* (*Ultra Large Scale Integration*) technology in the fifth generation, resulting in the production of microprocessor chips, having ten million electronic components. In fact, the speed of microprocessors and the size of main memory and hard disk doubled almost every eighteen months. As a result, many of the features found in the CPUs of large mainframe systems of the third and fourth generations, became part of the microprocessor architecture in the fifth generation. This ultimately resulted in the availability of very powerful and compact computers becoming available at cheaper rates, and the death of traditional large mainframe systems.

Due to this fast pace of advancement in computer technology, we see more compact and more powerful computers being introduced almost every year, at more or less the same price or even cheaper. Notable among these are portable notebook computers, which give the power of a PC to their users even while travelling, powerful desktop PCs and workstations, powerful servers, and very powerful supercomputers (see Chapter 20 for a detailed description of these types of computers).

Storage technology also advanced very fast, making larger and larger main memory and disk storage available in newly introduced systems. During the fifth generation, optical disks also emerged as a popular portable mass storage media. They are more commonly known as *CD-ROM* (*Compact Disk - Read Only Memory*), because they are mainly used for storing programs and data, which are only read (not written/modified).

During the fifth-generation period, there was tremendous outgrowth of computer networks. Communication technologies became faster day-by-day, and more and more computers were networked together. This trend resulted in the emergence and popularity of the Internet and associated technologies and applications. The Internet made it possible for computer users sitting across the globe to communicate with each other within minutes, by the use of *electronic mail* (known as *e-mail*) facility. A vast ocean of information became readily available to the computer users through the *World Wide Web* (known as *WWW*). Moreover, several new types of exciting applications, like electronic commerce, virtual libraries, virtual classrooms, distance education, etc., emerged during the period.

The tremendous processing power and the massive storage capacity of the fifth-generation computers also made them a very useful and popular tool for a wide range of multimedia applications, which deal with information containing text, graphics, animation, audio, and video data. In general, the data size for multimedia information is much larger than textual information, because representation of graphics, animation, audio, or video media in digital form requires much larger number of bits than that required for representation of textual information.

The characteristic features of fifth-generation computers are as follows:

1. Portable PCs (called notebook computers) are much more smaller and handy than the PCs of the fourth generation, allowing users to use computing facility even while travelling.

2. The desktop PCs and workstations are several times more powerful than the PCs of the fourth generation.

3. The mainframes are several times more powerful than the mainframe systems of the fourth generation.

4. Although the mainframes require proper air-conditioning of the rooms/areas in which they are located, no air-conditioning is normally required for the notebook computers, desktop PCs, and workstations.

5. They consume much less power than their predecessors.

6. They are more reliable and less prone to hardware failures than their predecessors. Hence, the maintenance cost is negligible.

7. Many of the large-scale systems of fifth generation have hot-pluggable feature. This feature enables, a failed component to be replaced with a new one, without the need to shutdown the system, allowing the uptime of the system to be very high.

8. They have faster and larger primary and secondary storage as compared to their predecessors.

9. They are totally general-purpose machines.

10. Their manufacturing does not require manual assembly of individual components into electronic circuits, resulting in reduced human labor and cost involved at assembly stage. Hence, commercial production of these systems is easier and cheaper. However, highly sophisticated technology and expensive setup (affordable only by a few organizations in the world) is required for the manufacture of ULSI chips.

11. Use of standard high-level programming languages allows programs written for one computer to be easily ported to and executed on another computer.

12. More user-friendly interfaces with multimedia features make the systems easier to learn and use by anyone, including small children.

13. Newer and more powerful applications, including multimedia applications, make the systems more useful in every occupation.

14. The explosion in the size of the Internet, coupled with Internet-based tools and applications, have made these systems influence the life of even common men and women.

15. These systems also use the concept of unbundled software and add-on hardware, allowing the users to invest only in the hardware configuration and software of their need and value.

16. With so many types of computers in all price ranges, today we have a computer for almost any type of user, whether the user is a small child or a scientist of world-fame.

Figure 1.2 summarizes the key technologies and features of the various generations of computers discussed above.

We have looked at the history of computing divided into five generations, and we have seen how quickly things have changed in the last few decades. However, the rate of technological progress in this area is not slowing down at all. As we enter into the 21$^{st}$ century, future generations of computers will evolve with higher capability and user friendliness. In fact, the fastest-growth period in the history of computing may be still ahead.

# Points to Remember

1. A computer is normally considered to be a calculating device, which can perform arithmetic operations at enormous speed. It is also known as a data processor since it not only computes in the usual sense, but also performs other functions with the data.

2. The activity of processing data using a computer is called data processing. Data is the raw material used as input to data processing, and information is the processed data obtained as the output of data processing.

| Generation (Period) | Key hardware Technologies | Key software technologies | Key characteristics | Some representative systems |
|---|---|---|---|---|
| First (1942-1955) | Vacuum tubes; electromagnetic relay memory; punched cards secondary storage | Machine and assembly languages; stored program concept; mostly scientific applications | Bulky in size; highly unreliable; limited commercial use; commercial production difficult and costly; difficult to use | ENIAC, EDVAC, EDSAC, UNIVAC 1, IBM 701 |
| Second (1955-1964) | Transistors; magnetic cores memory; magnetic tapes and disks secondary storage | Batch operating system; high-level programming languages; scientific and commercial applications | Faster, smaller, more reliable and easier to program than previous generation systems; commercial production was still difficult and costly | Honeywell 400, IBM 7030, CDC 1604, UNIVAC LARC |
| Third (1964-1975) | ICs with SSI and MSI technologies; larger magnetic cores memory; larger capacity disks and magnetic tapes secondary storage; minicomputers | Timesharing operating system; standardization of high-level programming languages; unbundling of software from hardware | Faster, smaller, more reliable, easier and cheaper to produce commercially, easier to use, and easier to upgrade than previous generation systems; scientific, commercial and interactive on-line applications | IBM 360/370, PDP-8, PDP-11, CDC 6600 |
| Fourth (1975-1989) | ICs with VLSI technology; microprocessors; semiconductor memory; larger capacity hard disks as in-built secondary storage; magnetic tapes and floppy disks as portable storage media; personal computers; spread of high-speed computer networks | Operating systems for PCs; GUI; multiple windows on a single terminal screen; UNIX operating system; C programming language; PC-based applications; network-based applications | Small, affordable, reliable, and easy to use PCs; more powerful and reliable mainframe systems; totally general purpose machines; easier to produce commercially | IBM PC and its clones, Apple II, TRS-80, VAX 9000, CRAY-1, CRAY-2, CRAY-X/MP |
| Fifth (1989-Present) | ICs with ULSI technology; larger capacity main memory; larger capacity hard disks; optical disks as portable read-only storage media; powerful notebook computers; powerful desktop PCs and workstations; very powerful mainframes; internet | World Wide Web; multimedia applications; internet-based applications | Portable computers; more powerful, cheaper, reliable, and easier to use desktop machines; very powerful mainframes; very high uptime due to hot-pluggable components; totally general purpose machines; easier to produce commercially | IBM notebooks, Pentium PCs, SUN Workstations, IBM SP/2, SGI Origin 2000, PARAM 10000 |

**Figure 1.2.** Computer generations – A summary.

3. Computers are characterized by their being automatic, speed and accuracy of computing, diligence, versatility, power of remembering, and lack of intelligence and feelings.

4. Charles Babbage is considered the father of modern digital computers.

5. Some of the well known early computers are the MARK I (1937-44), the ATANASOFF-BERRY (1939-42), the ENIAC (1943-46), the EDVAC (1946-52), the EDSAC (1947-49) and the UNIVAC I (1951).

6. Dr. John Von Neumann introduced the "stored program" concept, which considerably influenced the development of modern digital computers. Due to this feature, we often refer to modern digital computers as stored program digital computers.

7. "Generation" in computer talk is a step in technology. It provides a framework for the growth of the computer industry. Originally, it was used to distinguish between various hardware technologies, but now it has been extended to include both hardware and software.

8. Until today, there are totally five computer generations, namely, first, second, third, fourth and fifth generation.

9. The key hardware and software technologies and the key characteristics of the computers of the five different generations are summarized in Figure 1.2.

# Questions

1. What is a computer? Why is it also known as a data processor?

2. What is data processing? Differentiate between data and information. Which is more useful to the people and why?

3. List out and explain some of the important characteristics of a computer.

4. What is meant by garbage-in-garbage-out?

5. Who is known as the father of modern digital computers and why?

6. Who invented the concept of stored program? Why is this concept so important?

7. Why are modern digital computers often referred to as stored program digital computers?

8. Which was the first commercially produced computer? When and where was it first installed?

9. Give the full form of the following abbreviations used in computer terminology: IBM, ENIAC, EDVAC, EDSAC, UNIVAC.

10. What is meant by "generation" in computer terminology? How many computer generations are there until now?

11. List out the various computer generations along with the key characteristics of the computers of each generation.

12. List out the key hardware technologies used in building the computers of each of the five generations.

13. List out the key software technologies used in building the computers of each of the five generations.

14. What are the advantages of transistors over vacuum tubes?

15. What is an IC? How does it help in reducing the size of computers?

16. List out some of the advantages of IC technology over transistor technology.

17. Give the full form of the following abbreviations used in computer terminology: GIGO, IC, SSI, MSI, LSI, VLSI, ULSI.

18. Why were first and second generation computers more difficult and costlier to produce commercially than the computers of subsequent generations?

19. Name the technologies used for constructing main memory in the computers of first, second, third, and fourth generations.

20. Name the secondary storage media popularly used in the computers of first, second, third, fourth, and fifth generations.

21. What is a microprocessor? How did it revolutionize the computer industry?

22. Name some applications that emerged due to the emergence of computer networks.

23. Name some of the representative computer systems of each of the five computer generations.

# Chapter 2

# Basic Computer Organization

Even though the size, shape, performance, reliability, and cost of computers have been changing over the years, the basic logical structure (based on the stored program concept), as proposed by Von Neumann, has not changed. No matter what shape and size of computer we are talking about, all computer systems perform the following five basic operations, for converting raw input data into information, which is useful to their users:

1. **Inputting.** The process of entering data and instructions into the computer system.

2. **Storing.** Saving data and instructions to make them readily available for initial or additional processing, as and when required.

3. **Processing.** Performing arithmetic operations (add, subtract, multiply, divide, etc.), or logical operations (comparisons like equal to, less than, greater than, etc.) on data, to convert them into useful information.

4. **Outputting.** The process of producing useful information or results for the user, such as a printed report or visual display.

5. **Controlling.** Directing the manner and sequence in which all of the above operations are performed.

The goal of this chapter is to familiarize you with the computer system units, which perform these functions. It will provide you with an overview of computer systems, as they are viewed by computer system architects.

The internal architecture of computers differs from one system model to another. However, the basic organization remains the same for all computer systems. A block diagram of the basic computer organization is shown in Figure 2.1. In this figure, the solid lines indicate the flow of instruction and data, and the dotted lines represent the control exercised by the control unit. It displays the five major building blocks (functional units) of a digital computer system. These five units correspond to the five basic operations, performed by all computer systems. The functions of each of these units are described below.

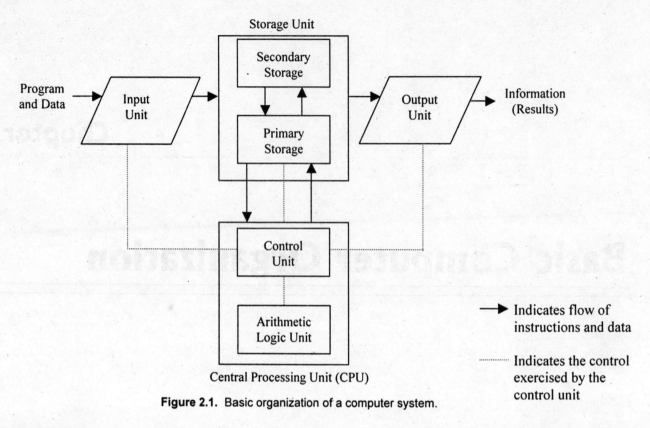

**Figure 2.1.** Basic organization of a computer system.

# INPUT UNIT

Data and instructions must enter the computer system, before any computation can be performed on the supplied data. This task is performed by the input unit, which links the external environment with the computer system. Data and instructions enter input units in forms, which depend upon the particular device used. For example, data are entered from a keyboard in a manner similar to typing, and this differs from the way in which data are entered through a scanner, which is another type of input device. However, regardless of the form in which they receive their inputs, all input devices must transform the input data into the binary codes, which the primary memory of a computer is designed to accept. This transformation is accomplished by units called *input interfaces*. Input interfaces are designed to match the unique physical or electrical characteristics of input devices, to the requirements of the computer system.

In short, the following functions are performed by an input unit:

1. It accepts (or reads) the instructions and data from the outside world.

2. It converts these instructions and data in computer acceptable form.

3. It supplies the converted instructions and data to the computer system for further processing.

# OUTPUT UNIT

The job of an output unit is just the reverse of that of an input unit. It supplies the information obtained from data processing, to the outside world. Hence, it links the computer with the external environment. As computers work with binary code, the results produced are also in the binary form. Hence, before supplying the results to the outside world, they must be converted to human acceptable (readable) form. This task is accomplished by units called *output interfaces*. Output interfaces are designed to match the unique physical or electrical characteristics of output devices (terminals, printers, etc.), to the requirements of the external environment.

In short, the following functions are performed by an output unit:

1. It accepts the results produced by the computer, which are in coded form, and hence, cannot be easily understood by us.

2. It converts these coded results to human acceptable (readable) form.

3. It supplies the converted results to the outside world.

# STORAGE UNIT

The data and instructions, which are entered into the computer system through input units, have to be stored inside the computer, before the actual processing starts. Similarly, the results produced by the computer after processing, must also be kept somewhere inside the computer system, before being passed on to the output units. Moreover, the intermediate results produced by the computer, must also be preserved for ongoing processing. The storage unit of a computer system is designed to cater to all these needs. It provides space for storing data and instructions, space for intermediate results, and space for the final results.

In short, the specific functions of the storage unit are to hold (store):

1. The data and instructions required for processing (received from input devices).

2. Intermediate results of processing.

3. Final results of processing, before these results are released to an output device.

The storage unit of all computers is comprised of the following two types of storage:

1. **Primary storage**. The primary storage, also known as *main memory*, is used to hold pieces of program instructions and data, intermediate results of processing, and recently produced results of processing, of the job(s), which the computer system is currently working on. These pieces of information are represented electronically in the main memory chip's circuitry, and while it remains in the main memory, the central processing unit can access it directly at a very fast speed. However, the primary storage can hold information only while the computer system is on. As soon as the computer system is switched off or reset, the information held in the primary storage disappears. Moreover, the primary storage normally has limited storage capacity, because it is very expensive. The primary storage of modern computer systems is made up of semiconductor devices.

2. **Secondary storage**. The secondary storage, also known as *auxiliary storage*, is used to take care of the limitations of the primary storage. That is, it is used to supplement the limited storage capacity and the volatile characteristic of primary storage. This is because secondary storage is much cheaper than primary storage, and it can retain information even when the computer system is switched off or reset. The secondary storage is normally used to hold the program instructions, data, and information of those jobs, on which the computer system is not working on currently, but needs to hold them for processing later. The most commonly used secondary storage medium is the magnetic disk.

# ARITHMETIC LOGIC UNIT

The arithmetic logic unit (ALU) of a computer system is the place, where the actual execution of the instructions takes place, during the processing operation. To be more precise, calculations are performed, and all comparisons (decisions) are made in the ALU. The data and instructions, stored in the primary storage before processing, are transferred as and when needed to the ALU, where processing takes place. No processing is done in the primary storage unit. Intermediate results generated in the ALU are temporarily transferred back to the primary storage, until needed later. Hence, data may move from primary storage to ALU, and back again to storage, many times, before the processing is over.

The type and number of arithmetic and logic operations, which a computer can perform, is determined by the engineering design of the ALU. However, almost all ALUs are designed to perform the four basic arithmetic operations (add, subtract, multiply and divide), and logic operations or comparisons, such as less than, equal to, and greater than.

# CONTROL UNIT

How does the input device know that it is time for it to feed data into the storage unit? How does the ALU know, what should be done with the data once they are received? Moreover, how is it that only the final results are sent to the output device, and not the intermediate results? All this is possible due to the control unit of the computer system. Although, it does not perform any actual processing on the data, the control unit acts as a central nervous system, for the other components of the computer system. It manages and coordinates the entire computer system. It obtains instructions from the program stored in main memory, interprets the instructions, and issues signals, which cause other units of the system to execute them.

# CENTRAL PROCESSING UNIT

The control unit and the arithmetic logic unit of a computer system are jointly known as the Central Processing Unit (CPU). The CPU is the brain of a computer system. In a human body, all major decisions are taken by the brain, and the other parts of the body function as directed by the brain. Similarly, in a computer system, all major calculations and comparisons are made inside the CPU, and the CPU is responsible for activating and controlling the operations of other units of the computer system.

# THE SYSTEM CONCEPT

You might have observed that we have been referring to a computer as a system (computer system). What can be the reason behind this? To know the answer, let us first understand the definition of a system.

A system is a group of integrated parts, which have the common purpose of achieving some objective(s). Hence, the following three characteristics are key to a system:

1. A system has more than one element.

2. All the elements of a system are logically related.

3. All the elements of a system are controlled in a manner to achieve the system goal.

Since a computer is made up of integrated components (input, output, storage, and CPU), which work together to perform the steps called for in the program being executed, it is a system. The input or output units cannot function, until they receive signals from the CPU. Similarly, the storage unit or the CPU alone is of no use. Hence, the usefulness of each unit depends on other units, and can be realized only when all units are put together (integrated) to form a system.

# Points to Remember

1. All computer systems perform the following five basic operations, for converting raw input data into useful information – inputting, storing, processing, outputting, and controlling.

2. The main components of a computer system are shown in Figure 2.1.

3. The *input unit* allows data and instructions to be fed to the computer system from the outside world, in computer acceptable form.

4. The *input interfaces* transform the input data and instructions fed to the computer, through its input devices, into the binary codes, which are acceptable to the computer.

5. The *output unit* allows the computer system to supply the information, obtained from data processing, to the outside world, in human acceptable (readable) form.

6. The *output interfaces* transform the information, obtained from data processing, from binary form to human acceptable (readable) form.

7. The *storage unit* of a computer system holds the data and instructions to be processed, and the intermediate and final results of processing. The two types of storage are – primary and secondary storage. As compared to primary storage, secondary storage is slower in operation, larger in capacity, cheaper in price, and can retain information even when the computer system is switched off or reset.

8. During data processing, the actual execution of the instructions takes place in the *Arithmetic Logic Unit* (ALU) of a computer system.

9. The *control unit* of a computer system manages and coordinates the operations of all the other components of the computer system.

10. The control unit and the arithmetic logic unit of a computer system are jointly known as the *Central Processing Unit* (CPU), which serves as the brain of the computer system, and is responsible for controlling the operations of all other units of the system.

11. A computer is often referred to as a *computer system,* because it is made up of integrated components (input, output, storage, and CPU), which work together to perform the steps called for, in the program being executed.

# Questions

1. What are the five basic operations performed by any computer system?

2. Draw a block diagram to illustrate the basic organization of a computer system, and explain the functions of the various units.

3. What is an input interface? How does it differ from an output interface?

4. How many types of storage are normally there in the storage unit of a computer system? Justify the need for each storage type.

5. Differentiate between the characteristics of primary and secondary storage of a computer system.

6. What are the basic components of the CPU of a computer system? Describe the roles of each of the components in the functioning of a computer system.

7. List out the logical steps taken by a computer system, along with the roles of its main units in each step, while transforming input data to useful information, for presentation to the user.

8. What is a system? Why is a computer often referred to as a computer system?

# Chapter 3

# Number Systems

In the previous chapter, we saw that inside a computer system, data are stored in a format, which cannot be easily read by human beings. This is the reason why input and output (I/O) interfaces are required. Every computer stores numbers, letters, and other special characters in coded form. Before going into the details of these codes, it is essential to have a basic understanding of the number system. Hence, the goal of this chapter is to familiarize you with the fundamentals of number system. It also introduces some of the commonly used number systems by computer professionals, and the relationship among them.

## NON-POSITIONAL NUMBER SYSTEMS

Number systems are basically of two types: non-positional and positional. In early days, human beings counted on fingers. When ten fingers were not adequate, stones, pebbles, or sticks were used to indicate values. This method of counting uses an additive approach or the *non-positional number system*. In this system, we have symbols, such as I for 1, II for 2, III for 3, IIII for 4, IIIII for 5, etc. Each symbol represents the same value, regardless of its position in the number, and the symbols are simply added to find out the value of a particular number. Since it is very difficult to perform arithmetic with such a number system, positional number systems were developed, as the centuries passed.

## POSITIONAL NUMBER SYSTEMS

In a *positional number system*, there are only a few symbols, called digits, and these symbols represent different values, depending on the position, they occupy in the number. The value of each digit in such a number is determined by three considerations:

1. The digit itself,

2. The position of the digit in the number, and

3. The base of the number system (where *base* is defined as the total number of digits available in the number system).

The number system, which we use in our day-to-day life is called the *decimal number system*. In this system, the base is equal to 10, because there are altogether ten symbols or digits (0, 1, 2, 3, 4, 5, 6, 7, 8, 9). You know that in the decimal system, the successive positions to the left of the decimal point represent units, tens, hundreds, thousands, etc. However, you may not have given much attention to the fact that each position represents a specific power of the base (10). For example, the decimal number 2586 (written as $2586_{10}$) consists of the digit 6 in the units position, 8 in the tens position, 5 in the hundreds position, and 2 in the thousands position, and its value can be written as:

$$(2 \times 1000) + (5 \times 100) + (8 \times 10) + (6 \times 1) = 2000 + 500 + 80 + 6 = 2586$$

It may also be observed that the same digit signifies different values, depending on the position it occupies in the number. For example,

In $2586_{10}$ the digit 6 signifies $6 \times 10^0 = 6$
In $2568_{10}$ the digit 6 signifies $6 \times 10^1 = 60$
In $2658_{10}$ the digit 6 signifies $6 \times 10^2 = 600$
In $6258_{10}$ the digit 6 signifies $6 \times 10^3 = 6000$

Hence, any number can be represented by using the available digits and arranging them in various positions.

The principles, which apply to the decimal number system, also apply to any other positional number system. It is important only to keep track of the base of the number system, in which we are working.

The following characteristics are suggested by the value of the base, in all positional number systems:

1. The value of the base determines the total number of different symbols or digits available in the number system. The first of these choices is always zero.

2. The maximum value of a single digit is always equal to one less than the value of the base.

Some of the positional number systems, which are used in computer design and by computer professionals, are discussed below.

# Binary Number System

The binary number system is exactly like the decimal number system, except that the base is 2, instead of 10. We have only two symbols or digits (0 and 1), which can be used in this number system. Note that the largest single digit is 1 (one less than the base). Each position in a binary number represents a power of the base (2). Hence, in this system, the rightmost position is the units ($2^0$) position, the second position from the right is the 2's ($2^1$) position, and proceeding in this way, we have 4's ($2^2$) position, 8's ($2^3$) position, 16's ($2^4$) position, and so on. Therefore, the decimal equivalent of the binary number 10101 (written as $10101_2$) is:

$$(1 \times 2^4) + (0 \times 2^3) + (1 \times 2^2) + (0 \times 2^1) + (1 \times 2^0) = 16 + 0 + 4 + 0 + 1 = 21$$

In order to be specific about which system we are referring to, it is common practice to indicate the base as a subscript. Hence, we write:

$$10101_2 = 21_{10}$$

"Binary digit" is often referred to by the common abbreviation *bit*. Hence, a "bit" in computer terminology means either a 0 or a 1. A binary number consisting of 'n' bits is called an n-bit number. Figure 3.1 lists all the 3-bit numbers, along with their decimal equivalent. Remember that we have only two digits, 0 and 1, in the binary system, and hence, the binary equivalent of the decimal number 2 has to be stated as 10 (read as one, zero). Another important point to note is that with 3 bits (positions), only 8 ($2^3$) different patterns of 0s and 1s are possible, and from Figure 3.1, it may be seen that a 3-bit number can have one of the 8 values in the range 0 to 7. In fact, it can be shown that any decimal number in the range 0 to $2^{n-1}$ can be represented in the binary form as an n-bit number.

| Binary | Decimal Equivalent |
|--------|--------------------|
| 000 | 0 |
| 001 | 1 |
| 010 | 2 |
| 011 | 3 |
| 100 | 4 |
| 101 | 5 |
| 110 | 6 |
| 111 | 7 |

**Figure 3.1**. 3-bit numbers with their decimal values.

Every computer stores numbers, letters, and other special characters in binary form. There are several occasions when computer professionals need to know the raw data contained in a computer's memory. A commonly used way of doing this is to print out the memory contents on a printer. This printout is called a *memory dump*. Memory dumps, which use binary numbers, would have many pages of 0s and 1s. Working with these numbers would also be very difficult and error prone for computer professionals. Hence, two number systems, octal and hexadecimal, are often used as shortcut notations for binary. These number systems, and their relationship with the binary number system, are explained below.

## Octal Number System

In the octal number system, the base is 8. Hence, there are only eight symbols or digits: 0, 1, 2, 3, 4, 5, 6, and 7 (8 and 9 do not exist in this system). The largest single digit is 7 (one less than the base). Each position in an octal number represents a power of the base (8). Therefore, the decimal equivalent of the octal number 2057 (written as $2057_8$) is:

$$(2 \times 8^3) + (0 \times 8^2) + (5 \times 8^1) + (7 \times 8^0) = 1024 + 0 + 40 + 7 = 1071$$

Hence, $2057_8 = 1071_{10}$

Observe that since there are only 8 digits in the octal number system, 3 bits ($2^3 = 8$) are sufficient to represent any octal number in binary (see Figure 3.1).

## Hexadecimal Number System

The hexadecimal number system is one with a base of 16, having 16 single-character digits or symbols. The first 10 digits are the digits of the decimal number system – 0, 1, 2, 3, 4, 5, 6, 7, 8, 9. The remaining six digits are denoted by the symbols A, B, C, D, E, and F, representing the decimal values 10, 11, 12, 13, 14, and 15, respectively. Hence, the largest single digit is F or 15 (one less than the base). Each position in the hexadecimal system represents a power of the base (16). Therefore, the decimal equivalent of the hexadecimal number 1AF (written as $1AF_{16}$) is:

$$(1 \times 16^2) + (A \times 16^1) + (F \times 16^0) = (1 \times 256) + (10 \times 16) + (15 \times 1) = 256 + 160 + 15 = 431$$

Hence, $1AF_{16} = 431_{10}$

Observe that since there are only 16 digits in the hexadecimal number system, 4 bits ($2^4 = 16$) are sufficient to represent any hexadecimal number in binary.

# CONVERTING FROM ONE NUMBER SYSTEM TO ANOTHER

Numbers expressed in decimal number system are much more meaningful to us, than are numbers expressed in any other number system. This is because we have been using decimal numbers in our day-to-day life, right from childhood. However, any number in one number system can be represented in any other number system. Because the input and the final output values are to be in decimal, computer professionals are often required to convert numbers in other number systems to decimal and vice-versa. There are many methods, which can be used to convert numbers from one base to another. One method of converting to base 10 from any other base, and a second method of converting from base 10 to any other base, are described below.

## Converting to Decimal from Another Base

The following steps are used to convert a number to a base 10 value from any other number system:

Step 1: Determine the column (positional) value of each digit (this depends on the position of the digit and the base of the number system).

Step 2: Multiply the obtained column values (in Step 1) by the digits in the corresponding columns.

Step 3: Sum the products calculated in Step 2. The total is the equivalent value in decimal.

*Example 3.1.*

$$11001_2 = ?_{10}$$

*Solution:*

Step 1: Determine column values

| Column Number (from right) | Column Value |
|---|---|
| 1 | $2^0 = 1$ |
| 2 | $2^1 = 2$ |
| 3 | $2^2 = 4$ |
| 4 | $2^3 = 8$ |
| 5 | $2^4 = 16$ |

Step 2: Multiply column values by corresponding column digits

```
16   8   4   2   1
x1  x1  x0  x0  x1
------------------
16   8   0   0   1
```

Step 3: Sum the products

$$16 + 8 + 0 + 0 + 1 = 25$$

Hence, $11001_2 = 25_{10}$

*Example 3.2.*

$$4706_8 = ?_{10}$$

*Solution:*

Step 1: Determine column values

| Column Number (from right) | Column Value |
|---|---|
| 1 | $8^0 = 1$ |
| 2 | $8^1 = 8$ |
| 3 | $8^2 = 64$ |
| 4 | $8^3 = 512$ |

Step 2: Multiply column values by corresponding column digits

```
512   64   8   1
x4   x7  x0  x6
-----------------
2048  448   0   6
```

Step 3: Sum the products

$$2048 + 448 + 0 + 6 = 2502$$

Hence, $4706_8 = 2502_{10}$

*Example 3.3.*

$$1AC_{16} = ?_{10}$$

*Solution:*

$$
\begin{aligned}
1AC_{16} &= 1 \times 16^2 + A \times 16^1 + C \times 16^0 \\
&= 1 \times 256 + 10 \times 16 + 12 \times 1 \\
&= 256 + 160 + 12 \\
&= 428_{10}
\end{aligned}
$$

*Example 3.4.*

$$4052_7 = ?_{10}$$

*Solution:*

$$
\begin{aligned}
4052_7 &= 4 \times 7^3 + 0 \times 7^2 + 5 \times 7^1 + 2 \times 7^0 \\
&= 4 \times 343 + 0 \times 49 + 5 \times 7 + 2 \times 1 \\
&= 1372 + 0 + 35 + 2 \\
&= 1409_{10}
\end{aligned}
$$

*Example 3.5.*

$$4052_6 = ?_{10}$$

*Solution:*

$$
\begin{aligned}
4052_6 &= 4 \times 6^3 + 0 \times 6^2 + 5 \times 6^1 + 2 \times 6^0 \\
&= 4 \times 216 + 0 \times 36 + 5 \times 6 + 2 \times 1 \\
&= 864 + 0 + 30 + 2 \\
&= 896_{10}
\end{aligned}
$$

Comparing this result with the result obtained in Example 3.4, we find that although the digits (4052) are same for both the numbers, their decimal equivalents are different. This is because the number in Example 3.4 is represented in base 7 number system, whereas the number in Example 3.5 is represented in base 6 number system.

*Example 3.6.*

$$11001_4 = ?_{10}$$

*Solution:*

$$
\begin{aligned}
11001_4 &= 1 \times 4^4 + 1 \times 4^3 + 0 \times 4^2 + 0 \times 4^1 + \\
&\quad\; 1 \times 4^0 \\
&= 1 \times 256 + 1 \times 64 + 0 \times 16 + 0 \times 4 + \\
&\quad\; 1 \times 1 \\
&= 256 + 64 + 0 + 0 + 1 \\
&= 321_{10}
\end{aligned}
$$

Compare the result with Example 3.1.

*Example 3.7.*

$$1AC_{13} = ?_{10}$$

*Solution:*

$$
\begin{aligned}
1AC_{13} &= 1 \times 13^2 + A \times 13^1 + C \times 13^0 \\
&= 1 \times 169 + 10 \times 13 + 12 \times 1 \\
&= 311_{10}
\end{aligned}
$$

Compare the result with Example 3.3.

# Converting from Decimal to Another Base (Division–Remainder Technique)

The following steps are used to convert a number from decimal to another base:

Step 1:  Divide the decimal number to be converted by the value of the new base.

Step 2:  Record the remainder from Step 1 as the rightmost digit (least significant digit) of the new base number.

Step 3:  Divide the quotient of the previous divide by the new base.

Step 4:  Record the remainder from Step 3 as the next digit (to the left) of the new base number.

Repeat Steps 3 and 4, recording remainders from right to left, until the quotient becomes zero in Step 3. Note that the last remainder, thus obtained, will be the most significant digit of the new base number.

**Example 3.8.**

$$25_{10} = ?_2$$

*Solution:*

Steps 1 and 2:  25/2 = 12 and remainder 1
Steps 3 and 4:  12/2 =  6 and remainder 0
Steps 3 and 4:   6/2 =  3 and remainder 0
Steps 3 and 4:   3/2 =  1 and remainder 1
Steps 3 and 4:   1/2 =  0 and remainder 1

As mentioned in Steps 2 and 4, the remainders have to be arranged in the reverse order, making the first remainder the least significant digit (LSD), and the last remainder the most significant digit (MSD).

Hence, $25_{10} = 11001_2$

Compare the result with Example 3.1.

**Example 3.9.**

$$42_{10} = ?_2$$

*Solution:*

| 2 | 42 | Remainders |
|---|---|---|
|   | 21 | 0 |
|   | 10 | 1 |
|   | 5 | 0 |
|   | 2 | 1 |
|   | 1 | 0 |
|   | 0 | 1 |

Hence, $42_{10} = 101010_2$

**Example 3.10.**

$$952_{10} = ?_8$$

*Solution:*

| 8 | 952 | Remainders |
|---|---|---|
|   | 119 | 0 |
|   | 14 | 7 |
|   | 1 | 6 |
|   | 0 | 1 |

Hence, $952_{10} = 1670_8$

*Example 3.11.*

$$428_{10} = ?_{16}$$

*Solution:*

| 16 | 428 | Remainders in hexadecimal |
|----|-----|---------------------------|
|    | 26  | 12 = C |
|    | 1   | 10 = A |
|    | 0   | 1 = 1 |

Hence, $428_{10} = 1AC_{16}$

Compare the result with Example 3.3.

*Example 3.12.*

$$100_{10} = ?_5$$

*Solution:*

| 5 | 100 | Remainders |
|---|-----|------------|
|   | 20  | 0 |
|   | 4   | 0 |
|   | 0   | 4 |

Hence, $100_{10} = 400_5$

*Example 3.13.*

$$100_{10} = ?_4$$

*Solution:*

| 4 | 100 | Remainders |
|---|-----|------------|
|   | 25  | 0 |
|   | 6   | 1 |
|   | 1   | 2 |
|   | 0   | 1 |

Hence, $100_{10} = 1210_4$

Compare this result with the result obtained in Example 3.12.

*Example 3.14.*

$$1715_{10} = ?_{12}$$

*Solution:*

| 12 | 1715 | Remainders in base 12 |
|----|------|-----------------------|
|    | 142  | 11 = B |
|    | 11   | 10 = A |
|    | 0    | 11 = B |

Hence, $1715_{10} = BAB_{12}$

# Converting from a Base Other Than 10 to a Base Other Than 10

The following steps are used to convert a number from a base other than 10, to a base other than 10:

Step 1: Convert the original number to a decimal number (base 10).

Step 2: Convert the decimal number obtained in Step 1 to the new base number.

**Example 3.15.**

$545_6 = ?_4$

*Solution:*

    Step 1: Convert from base 6 to base 10

$$545 = 5 \times 6^2 + 4 \times 6^1 + 5 \times 6^0$$
$$= 5 \times 36 + 4 \times 6 + 5 \times 1$$
$$= 180 + 24 + 5$$
$$= 209_{10}$$

    Step 2: Convert $209_{10}$ to base 4

| 4 | 209 | Remainders |
|---|-----|-----------|
|   | 52  | 1 |
|   | 13  | 0 |
|   | 3   | 1 |
|   | 0   | 3 |

$209_{10} = 3101_4$

Therefore, $545_6 = 209_{10} = 3101_4$

Hence, $545_6 = 3101_4$

**Example 3.16.**

$101110_2 = ?_8$

*Solution:*

    Step 1: Convert $101110_2$ to base 10

$$101110_2 = 1 \times 2^5 + 0 \times 2^4 + 1 \times 2^3 +$$
$$1 \times 2^2 + 1 \times 2^1 + 0 \times 2^0$$
$$= 32 + 0 + 8 + 4 + 2 + 0$$
$$= 46_{10}$$

    Step 2: Convert $46_{10}$ to base 8

| 8 | 46 | Remainders |
|---|-----|-----------|
|   | 5   | 6 |
|   | 0   | 5 |

$46_{10} = 56_8$

Therefore, $101110_2 = 46_{10} = 56_8$

Hence, $101110_2 = 56_8$

**Example 3.17.**

$11010011_2 = ?_{16}$

*Solution:*

    Step 1: Convert $11010011_2$ to base 10

$$11010011_2 = 1 \times 2^7 + 1 \times 2^6 + 0 \times 2^5 + 1 \times 2^4 + 0 \times 2^3 + 0 \times 2^2 + 1 \times 2^1 + 1 \times 2^0$$
$$= 1 \times 128 + 1 \times 64 + 0 \times 32 + 1 \times 16 + 0 \times 8 + 0 \times 4 + 1 \times 2 + 1 \times 1$$
$$= 128 + 64 + 0 + 16 + 0 + 0 + 2 + 1$$
$$= 211_{10}$$

    Step 2: Convert $211_{10}$ to base 16

| 16 | 211 | Remainders |
|----|-----|-----------|
|    | 13  | 3 = 3 in Hexadecimal |
|    | 0   | 13 = D in Hexadecimal |

Therefore, $11010011_2 = 211_{10} = D3_{16}$

Hence, $11010011_2 = D3_{16}$

Example 3.16 illustrates the method of converting a number from binary to octal. Similarly, Example 3.17 shows how to convert a number from binary to hexadecimal. However, these are lengthy procedures, and shortcut methods can be used when we desire such conversions. These shortcut methods are described below.

## Shortcut Method for Binary to Octal Conversion

The following steps are used in this method:

Step 1: Divide the binary digits into groups of three (starting from the right).

Step 2: Convert each group of three binary digits to one octal digit. Since there are only 8 digits (0 to 7) in the octal number system (refer to Figure 3.1), 3 bits ($2^3 = 8$) are sufficient to represent any octal number in binary. Moreover, since decimal digits 0 to 7 are equal to octal digits 0 to 7, binary to decimal conversion can be used in this step.

**Example 3.18.**

$$101110_2 = ?_8$$

*Solution:*

Step 1: Divide the binary digits into groups of 3, starting from right (LSD).

$$\underline{101} \quad \underline{110}$$

Step 2: Convert each group into one digit of octal (use binary-to-decimal conversion).

$$101_2 = 1 \times 2^2 + 0 \times 2^1 + 1 \times 2^0 \qquad\qquad 110_2 = 1 \times 2^2 + 1 \times 2^1 + 0 \times 2^0$$
$$= 4 + 0 + 1 \qquad\qquad\qquad\qquad\qquad = 4 + 2 + 0$$
$$= 5_8 \qquad\qquad\qquad\qquad\qquad\qquad\quad = 6_8$$

Hence, $101110_2 = 56_8$

Compare the result with the result of Example 3.16.

**Example 3.19.**

$$1101010_2 = ?_8$$

*Solution:*

$$1101010_2 = \underline{001} \quad \underline{101} \quad \underline{010} \text{ (Group of 3 digits from right)}$$
$$= 152_8 \text{ (Convert each group to an octal digit)}$$

Hence, $1101010_2 = 152_8$

## Shortcut Method for Octal to Binary Conversion

The following steps are used in this method:

Step 1: Convert each octal digit to a 3 digit binary number (the octal digits may be treated as decimal for this conversion).

Step 2: Combine all the resulting binary groups (of 3 digits each) into a single binary number.

*Example 3.20.*

$$562_8 = ?_2$$

*Solution:*

Step 1:  Convert each octal digit to 3 binary digits.

$$5_8 = 101_2$$
$$6_8 = 110_2$$
$$2_8 = 010_2$$

Step 2:  Combine the binary groups.

$$562_8 = \underline{101} \quad \underline{110} \quad \underline{010}$$
$$\quad\quad\quad\quad 5 \quad\quad 6 \quad\quad 2$$

Hence, $562_8 = 101110010_2$

*Example 3.21.*

$$6751_8 = ?_2$$

*Solution:*

$$6751_8 = \underline{110} \quad \underline{111} \quad \underline{101} \quad \underline{001}$$
$$\quad\quad\quad\quad 6 \quad\quad 7 \quad\quad 5 \quad\quad 1$$
$$= 110111101001_2$$

Hence, $6751_8 = 110111101001_2$

## Shortcut Method for Binary to Hexadecimal Conversion

The following steps are used in this method:

Step 1:  Divide the binary digits into groups of four (starting from the right).

Step 2:  Convert each group of four binary digits to one hexadecimal digit.  Remember that hexadecimal digits 0 to 9 are equal to decimal digits 0 to 9, and hexadecimal digits A to F are equal to decimal values 10 to 15.  Hence, for this step, the binary to decimal conversion procedure can be used, but the decimal values 10 to 15 must be represented as hexadecimal A to F.

*Example 3.22.*

$$11010011_2 = ?_{16}$$

*Solution:*

Step 1:  Divide the binary digits into groups of 4, starting from the right (LSD).

$$\underline{1101} \quad \underline{0011}$$

Step 2:  Convert each group of 4 binary digits to 1 hexadecimal digit.

$$1101_2 = 1 \times 2^3 + 1 \times 2^2 + 0 \times 2^1 + 1 \times 2^0 \quad\quad 0011_2 = 0 \times 2^3 + 0 \times 2^2 + 1 \times 2^1 + 1 \times 2^0$$
$$= 8 + 4 + 0 + 1 \quad\quad\quad\quad\quad\quad\quad\quad\quad\quad = 0 + 0 + 2 + 1$$
$$= 13_{10} \quad\quad\quad\quad\quad\quad\quad\quad\quad\quad\quad\quad\quad = 3_{16}$$
$$= D_{16}$$

Hence, $11010011_2 = D3_{16}$

Compare the result with the result of Example 3.17.

*Example 3.23.*

$10110101100_2 = ?_{16}$

*Solution:*

$10110101100_2 = \underline{0101} \quad \underline{1010} \quad \underline{1100}$  (Group 4 digits from right)

$= 5AC$  (Convert each group to a hexadecimal digit)

Hence, $10110101100_2 = 5AC_{16}$

# Shortcut Method for Hexadecimal to Binary Conversion

The following steps are used in this method:

Step 1:  Convert the decimal equivalent of each hexadecimal digit to 4 binary digits.

Step 2:  Combine all the resulting binary groups (of 4 digits each) into a single binary number.

*Example 3.24.*

$2AB_{16} = ?_2$

*Solution:*

Step 1:  Convert the decimal equivalent of each hexadecimal digit to 4 binary digits.

$2_{16} = 2_{10} = 0010_2$
$A_{16} = 10_{10} = 1010_2$
$B_{16} = 11_{10} = 1011_2$

Step 2:  Combine the binary groups.

$2AB_{16} = \underline{0010} \quad \underline{1010} \quad \underline{1011}$
$\qquad\qquad 2 \qquad A \qquad B$

Hence, $2AB_{16} = 001010101011_2$

*Example 3.25.*

$ABC_{16} = ?_2$

*Solution:*

$ABC_{16} = \underline{1010} \quad \underline{1011} \quad \underline{1100}$
$\qquad\qquad A \qquad B \qquad C$
$= 101010111100_2$

Hence, $ABC_{16} = 101010111100_2$

Figure 3.2 summarizes the relationship among the decimal, binary, hexadecimal, and octal number systems. Note that the maximum value for a single digit of octal (7) is equal to the maximum value of three digits of binary. The value range of one digit of octal duplicates the value range of three digits of binary. If octal digits are substituted for binary digits, the substitution is on a one-to-three basis. Hence, computers that print octal numbers instead of binary, while taking memory dump, save one-third of the printing space and time.

Similarly, note that the maximum value of one digit in hexadecimal is equal to the maximum value of four digits in binary. Hence, the value range of one digit of hexadecimal is equivalent to the value range of four digits of binary. Therefore, hexadecimal shortcut notation is a one-to-four reduction in the space and time required for memory dump.

| Decimal | Hexadecimal | Binary | Octal |
|---------|-------------|--------|-------|
| 0 | 0 | 0 | 0 |
| 1 | 1 | 1 | 1 |
| 2 | 2 | 10 | 2 |
| 3 | 3 | 11 | 3 |
| 4 | 4 | 100 | 4 |
| 5 | 5 | 101 | 5 |
| 6 | 6 | 110 | 6 |
| 7 | 7 | 111 | 7 |
| 8 | 8 | 1000 | 10 |
| 9 | 9 | 1001 | |
| 10 | A | 1010 | |
| 11 | B | 1011 | |
| 12 | C | 1100 | |
| 13 | D | 1101 | |
| 14 | E | 1110 | |
| 15 | F | 1111 | |
| 16 | 10 | 10000 | |

**Figure 3.2.** Relationship among Decimal, Binary, Hexadecimal and Octal number systems.

# FRACTIONAL NUMBERS

In binary number system, fractional numbers are formed in the same general way as in the decimal number system. For example, in the decimal number system,

$$0.235 = (2 \times 10^{-1}) + (3 \times 10^{-2}) + (5 \times 10^{-3}) \quad \text{and} \quad 68.53 = (6 \times 10^{1}) + (8 \times 10^{0}) + (5 \times 10^{-1}) + (3 \times 10^{-2})$$

Similarly, in the binary number system,

$$0.101 = (1 \times 2^{-1}) + (0 \times 2^{-2}) + (1 \times 2^{-3}) \quad \text{and} \quad 10.01 = (1 \times 2^{1}) + (0 \times 2^{0}) + (0 \times 2^{-1}) + (1 \times 2^{-2})$$

Hence, the binary point serves the same purpose as the decimal point. Some of the positional values in the binary number system are given below.

|  |  |  |  |  | Binary Point ↓ |  |  |  |  |
|--|--|--|--|--|--|--|--|--|--|
| Position | 4 | 3 | 2 | 1 | 0 | -1 | -2 | -3 | -4 |
| Position Value | $2^4$ | $2^3$ | $2^2$ | $2^1$ | $2^0$ | $2^{-1}$ | $2^{-2}$ | $2^{-3}$ | $2^{-4}$ |
| Quantity Represented | 16 | 8 | 4 | 2 | 1 | $\frac{1}{2}$ | $\frac{1}{4}$ | $\frac{1}{8}$ | $\frac{1}{16}$ |

In general, a number in a number system with base $b$ would be written as:

$$a_n a_{n-1} \ldots a_0 . a_{-1} a_{-2} \ldots a_{-m}$$

and would be interpreted to mean

$$a_n \times b^n + a_{n-1} \times b^{n-1} + \ldots + a_0 \times b^0 + a_{-1} \times b^{-1} + a_{-2} \times b^{-2} + \ldots + a_{-m} \times b^{-m}$$

The symbols $a_n$, $a_{n-1}$, ..., $a_{-m}$ used in the above representation should be one of the $b$ symbols allowed in the number system.

Hence, as per the above mentioned general rule,

$$46.32_8 = (4 \times 8^1) + (6 \times 8^0) + (3 \times 8^{-1}) + (2 \times 8^{-2}) \quad \text{and} \quad 5A.3C_{16} = (5 \times 16^1) + (A \times 16^0) + (3 \times 16^{-1}) + (C \times 16^{-2})$$

**Example 3.26.**

Find the decimal equivalent of the binary number 110.101

*Solution:*

$$\begin{aligned}
110.101_2 &= 1 \times 2^2 + 1 \times 2^1 + 0 \times 2^0 + 1 \times 2^{-1} + \\
&\quad 0 \times 2^{-2} + 1 \times 2^{-3} \\
&= 4 + 2 + 0 + 0.5 + 0 + 0.125 \\
&= 6 + 0.5 + 0.125 \\
&= 6.625_{10}
\end{aligned}$$

**Example 3.27.**

Find the decimal equivalent of the octal number 127.54

*Solution:*

$$\begin{aligned}
127.54_8 &= 1 \times 8^2 + 2 \times 8^1 + 7 \times 8^0 + \\
&\quad 5 \times 8^{-1} + 4 \times 8^{-2} \\
&= 64 + 16 + 7 + 5/8 + 4/64 \\
&= 87 + 0.625 + 0.0625 \\
&= 87.6875_{10}
\end{aligned}$$

**Example 3.28.**

Find the decimal equivalent of the hexadecimal number 2B.C4

*Solution:*

$$\begin{aligned}
2B.C4_{16} &= 2 \times 16^1 + B \times 16^0 + C \times 16^{-1} + 4 \times 16^{-2} \\
&= 32 + B + C/16 + 4/256 \\
&= 32 + 11 + 12/16 + 4/256 \\
&= 43 + 0.75 + 0.015625 \\
&= 43.765652_{10}
\end{aligned}$$

# Points to Remember

1. Number systems are basically of two types: non-positional and positional.

2. In a *non-positional number system*, each symbol represents the same value, regardless of its position in the number, and the symbols are simply added to find out the value of a particular number. It is very difficult to perform arithmetic with such a number system.

3. In a *positional number system*, there are only a few symbols, called digits, and these symbols represent different values, depending on the position, they occupy in the number. The value of each digit in such a number is determined by three considerations:
   - The digit itself,
   - The position of the digit in the number, and

   - The base of the number system (where base is defined as the total number of digits available in the number system).

4. The number system that we use in our day-to-day life is called the *decimal number system*. In this system, the base is equal to 10, because there are altogether ten symbols or digits (0, 1, 2, 3, 4, 5, 6, 7, 8, 9).

5. Some of the positional number systems, which are used in computer design and by computer professionals, are *binary* (for which base is 2), *octal* (for which base is 8), and *hexadecimal* (for which base is 16).

6. The relationship among decimal, binary, hexadecimal and octal number systems is given in Figure 3.2.

7. Readers must know the techniques for the following types of conversions to convert numbers from one base to another:

- Converting to decimal from another base
- Converting from decimal to another base
- Converting from a base other than 10, to a base other than 10
- Shortcut method for binary to octal conversion
- Shortcut method for octal to binary conversion
- Shortcut method for binary to hexadecimal conversion
- Shortcut method for hexadecimal to binary conversion

8. *Fractional numbers* are formed in the same way as in the decimal number system. In general, a number in a number system with base $b$ would be written as:

$$a_n \, a_{n-1} \ldots a_0 \, . \, a_{-1} \, a_{-2} \ldots a_{-m}$$

and would be interpreted to mean

$$a_n \times b^n + a_{n-1} \times b^{n-1} + \ldots + a_0 \times b^0 + a_{-1} \times b^{-1} + a_{-2} \times b^{-2} + \ldots + a_{-m} \times b^{-m}$$

The symbols $a_n$, $a_{n-1}$, $\ldots$, $a_{-m}$ used in the above representation should be one of the $b$ symbols allowed in the number system.

# Questions

1. What is the difference between positional and non-positional number systems? Give examples of both types of number systems.

2. What is meant by the base of a number system? Give examples to illustrate the role of base in positional number systems.

3. What is the value of the base for decimal, hexadecimal, binary and octal number systems?

4. Give an example for octal number system to show that the same digit may signify different values, depending on the position it occupies in the number.

5. What will be the total number of different symbols or digits, and the maximum value of a single digit, for the following number systems:
   - (a) Number system with base 5
   - (b) Number system with base 20
   - (c) Number system with base 9
   - (d) Number system with base 12

6. What is a 'bit' in computer terminology? How many different patterns of bits are possible with
   - (a) 6 bits    (b) 7 bits    (c) 8 bits

7. Explain the meaning of the term "memory dump".

8. Why are octal and/or hexadecimal number systems used as shortcut notations?

9. Find out the decimal equivalent of the following binary numbers:
   - (a) 1101011
   - (b) 11010
   - (c) 10110011
   - (d) 11011101
   - (e) 1110101
   - (f) 1000
   - (g) 10110001100
   - (h) 110001
   - (i) 1010101100
   - (j) 111

10. Find out the octal equivalent of the binary numbers of Question 9.

11. Find out the hexadecimal equivalent of the binary numbers of Question 9.

12. Convert the following numbers to decimal numbers:
   - (a) $110110_2$
   - (b) $2573_6$
   - (c) $2A3B_{16}$
   - (d) $1234_9$

13. Convert the following decimal numbers to binary numbers:
   - (a) $435_{10}$
   - (b) $1694_{10}$
   - (c) $32_{10}$
   - (d) $135_{10}$

14. Convert the decimal numbers of Question 13 to octal numbers.

15. Convert the decimal numbers of Question 13 to hexadecimal numbers.

16. Carry out the following conversions:
   - (a) $125_6 = ?_4$    (b) $24_9 = ?_3$    (c) $ABC_{16} = ?_8$

17. Convert the following numbers to their binary equivalent:
   - (a) $2AC_{16}$
   - (b) $FAB_{16}$
   - (c) $2614_8$
   - (d) $562_8$

18. Find the decimal equivalent of the following numbers:
   - (a) $111.01_2$
   - (b) $1001.011_2$
   - (c) $247.65_8$
   - (d) $A2B.D4_{16}$

# Chapter 4

# Computer Codes

In the previous chapter, we have discussed about true or "pure" binary numbers. In this chapter, we will see how these binary numbers are coded to represent characters in computers. Although, many coding schemes have been developed over the years, we will be discussing only the most commonly used computer codes.

Numeric data is not the only form of data, which is handled by a computer. We often require to process alphanumeric data also. An *alphanumeric data* is a string of symbols, where a symbol may be one of the letters A, B, C, ..., Z, or one of the digits 0, 1, 2, ..., 9, or a special character, such as + - * / , . ( ) = (space or blank) etc. An *alphabetic data* consists of only the letters A, B, C, ..., Z and the blank character. Similarly, *numeric data* consists of only numbers 0, 1, 2, ..., 9. However, any data must be represented internally by the bits 0 and 1. Hence, binary coding schemes are used in computers to represent data internally. In binary coding, every symbol, which appears in the data, is represented by a group of bits. The group of bits used to represent a symbol is called a *byte*. To indicate the number of bits in a group, sometimes, a byte is referred to as "n-bit byte", where the group contains *n* bits. However, the term byte is commonly used to mean an 8-bit byte (a group of 8 bits), because most of the modern computers use 8 bits to represent a symbol.

## BCD CODE

The *Binary Coded Decimal* (BCD) code is one of the early computer codes. It is based on the idea of converting each digit of a decimal number into its binary equivalent, rather than converting the entire decimal value into a pure binary form. This makes the conversion process easier.

The BCD equivalent of each decimal digit is shown in Figure 4.1. Since 8 and 9 require 4 bits, all decimal digits are represented in BCD by 4 bits. In Example 3.9, we saw that $42_{10}$ is equal to $101010_2$ in a pure binary form. Converting $42_{10}$ into BCD, however, produces the following result:

$$42_{10} = \underset{4}{\underline{0100}} \quad \underset{2}{\underline{0010}} \qquad \text{or} \qquad 01000010 \text{ in BCD}$$

Note that each decimal digit is independently converted to a 4 bit binary number, and hence, the conversion process is very easy. Also note that when 4 bits are used, altogether 16 $(2^4)$ configurations are possible (refer to hexadecimal number system). However, from Figure 4.1 you can see that only the first 10 of these combinations are used to represent decimal digits. The remaining 6 arrangements (1010, 1011, 1100, 1101, 1110 and 1111) have decimal values from 10 to 15. These arrangements are not used in BCD coding. That is, 1010 does not represent $10_{10}$ in BCD. Instead,

| Decimal Digits | BCD Equivalent |
|:---:|:---:|
| 0 | 0000 |
| 1 | 0001 |
| 2 | 0010 |
| 3 | 0011 |
| 4 | 0100 |
| 5 | 0101 |
| 6 | 0110 |
| 7 | 0111 |
| 8 | 1000 |
| 9 | 1001 |

**Figure 4.1.** BCD equivalent of decimal digits.

$$10_{10} = \underset{1}{\underline{0001}} \quad \underset{0}{\underline{0000}} \quad \text{or} \quad 00010000 \text{ in BCD}$$

Similarly,

$$15_{10} = \underset{1}{\underline{0001}} \quad \underset{5}{\underline{0101}} \quad \text{or} \quad 00010101 \text{ in BCD}$$

In the discussion above, we have used a group of 4 bits to represent a digit (character) in BCD. 4-bit BCD coding system can be used to represent only decimal numbers, because 4 bits are insufficient to represent the various characters used by a computer. Hence, instead of using 4 bits with only 16 possible characters, computer designers commonly use 6 bits to represent characters in BCD code. In the 6-bit BCD code, the four BCD numeric place positions are retained, but two additional *zone* positions are added. With 6 bits, it is possible to represent 64 $(2^6)$ different characters. This is a sufficient number to code the decimal digits (10), alphabetic letters (26), and other special characters (28). Figure 4.2 illustrates the coding of alphabetic and numeric characters in BCD.

In Chapter 3, we have seen the use of octal and hexadecimal number systems, as shortcut notations for binary. Since BCD is a 6-bit code, it can be easily divided into two 3-bit groups. Each of these 3-bit groups can be represented by 1 octal digit. Hence, octal number system is used as shortcut notation for memory dump by computers, which use BCD code for internal representation of characters. This results in a one-to-three reduction in the volume of memory dump. Figure 4.2 also shows the octal equivalent of the alphabetic and numeric characters coded in BCD.

*Example 4.1.*

Show the binary digits used to record the word BASE in BCD.

*Solution:*

B = 110010 in BCD binary notation
A = 110001 in BCD binary notation
S = 010010 in BCD binary notation
E = 110101 in BCD binary notation

Hence, the binary digits

$$\underset{B}{\underline{110010}} \quad \underset{A}{\underline{110001}} \quad \underset{S}{\underline{010010}} \quad \underset{E}{\underline{110101}}$$

will record the word BASE in BCD.

*Example 4.2.*

Using octal notation, show the BCD coding for the word DIGIT.

*Solution:*

D = 64 in BCD octal notation
I = 71 in BCD octal notation
G = 67 in BCD octal notation
I = 71 in BCD octal notation
T = 23 in BCD octal notation

Hence, the BCD coding for the word DIGIT in octal notation will be

$$\underset{D}{\underline{64}} \quad \underset{I}{\underline{71}} \quad \underset{G}{\underline{67}} \quad \underset{I}{\underline{71}} \quad \underset{T}{\underline{23}}$$

| Character | BCD Code | | Octal Equivalent |
| --- | --- | --- | --- |
| | Zone | Digit | |
| A | 11 | 0001 | 61 |
| B | 11 | 0010 | 62 |
| C | 11 | 0011 | 63 |
| D | 11 | 0100 | 64 |
| E | 11 | 0101 | 65 |
| F | 11 | 0110 | 66 |
| G | 11 | 0111 | 67 |
| H | 11 | 1000 | 70 |
| I | 11 | 1001 | 71 |
| | | | |
| J | 10 | 0001 | 41 |
| K | 10 | 0010 | 42 |
| L | 10 | 0011 | 43 |
| M | 10 | 0100 | 44 |
| N | 10 | 0101 | 45 |
| O | 10 | 0110 | 46 |
| P | 10 | 0111 | 47 |
| Q | 10 | 1000 | 50 |
| R | 10 | 1001 | 51 |
| | | | |
| S | 01 | 0010 | 22 |
| T | 01 | 0011 | 23 |
| U | 01 | 0100 | 24 |
| V | 01 | 0101 | 25 |
| W | 01 | 0110 | 26 |
| X | 01 | 0111 | 27 |
| Y | 01 | 1000 | 30 |
| Z | 01 | 1001 | 31 |
| | | | |
| 1 | 00 | 0001 | 01 |
| 2 | 00 | 0010 | 02 |
| 3 | 00 | 0011 | 03 |
| 4 | 00 | 0100 | 04 |
| 5 | 00 | 0101 | 05 |
| 6 | 00 | 0110 | 06 |
| 7 | 00 | 0111 | 07 |
| 8 | 00 | 1000 | 10 |
| 9 | 00 | 1001 | 11 |
| 0 | 00 | 1010 | 12 |

**Figure 4.2.** Alphabetic and numeric characters in BCD, along with their Octal equivalent.

# EBCDIC

The major problem with BCD code is that only 64 ($2^6$) different characters can be represented in it. This is not sufficient for providing decimal numbers (10), lower-case letters (26), capital letters (26), and a large number of other special characters (28+).

Hence, the BCD code was extended from a 6-bit code to an 8-bit code. The added 2 bits are used as additional zone bits, expanding the zone to 4 bits. The resulting code is called the *Extended Binary-Coded Decimal Interchange Code (EBCDIC)*. In this code, it is possible to represent 256 ($2^8$) different characters, instead of 64 ($2^6$). In addition to the various character requirements mentioned above, this also allows a large variety of printable characters and several nonprintable control characters. The *control characters* are used to control such activities as printer vertical spacing, movement of cursor on the terminal screen, etc. All of the 256 bit combinations have not yet been assigned characters. Hence, the code can still grow, as new requirements develop.

Since EBCDIC is an 8-bit code, it can be easily divided into two 4-bit groups. Each of these 4-bit groups can be represented by 1 hexadecimal digit (refer to Chapter 3). Hence, hexadecimal number system is used as shortcut notation for memory dump by computers, which use EBCDIC for internal representation of characters. This results in a one-to-four reduction in the volume of memory dump. Figure 4.3 shows the alphabetic and numeric characters in EBCDIC, along with their hexadecimal equivalent.

Developed by IBM, EBCDIC code is used in most IBM models, and in many other computers.

## Zoned and Packed Decimal Numbers

From Figure 4.3, it can be observed that in the EBCDIC code, the digit values are the same as the numeric characters – 0 through 9 (0000 – 1001). However, numeric values need some special consideration, because we must have a way of indicating whether the number is positive, negative, or unsigned (implies positive). Hence, when a numeric value is represented in EBCDIC, a sign indicator is used in the zone position of the rightmost digit. A sign indicator of hexadecimal C is a plus sign, hexadecimal D is a minus sign, and hexadecimal F means the number is unsigned. Figure 4.4 illustrates the representation of numeric values in EBCDIC. Note that the only zone affected by the sign is the zone of the rightmost digit. All other zones remain as F, the zone value for numeric characters in EBCDIC. Since each decimal digit has a zone with it, numbers coded in EBCDIC are called *zoned decimal numbers*. Numeric data input into the computer are usually zoned decimal numbers. Printers can print only those numeric characters, which are in a zoned-decimal format.

Most computers cannot perform arithmetic operations on zoned-decimal data. Hence, before any arithmetic operation can be performed, the data must be converted to a format on which arithmetic operations are possible. One such acceptable format is the *packed decimal* format. The following steps are used to convert a zoned decimal number to a packed decimal number:

Step 1: The zone half and the digit half of the rightmost byte are reversed. This moves the sign to the extreme right of the number.

Step 2: All remaining zones are dropped out.

Figure 4.5 illustrates the conversion process of zoned decimal data to packed data. It may be observed that packed data requires less number of bytes (group of 8 bits) as compared to zoned data. In the zoned format, there is only one digit per byte (each digit along with the zone requires 8 bits). However, there are two digits in each byte in the packed format (each digit requires 4 bits). If the packing process does not completely fill a byte, it is filled with a zero. For example, the zoned data F3F4F5F6 will convert to packed data 03456F. Observe that in this example, the zoned data requires 4 bytes, and the packed data requires only 3 bytes.

| Character | EBCDIC Code | | Hexadecimal Equivalent |
|-----------|-------------|-------|------------------------|
|           | Zone        | Digit |                        |
| A         | 1100        | 0001  | C1                     |
| B         | 1100        | 0010  | C2                     |
| C         | 1100        | 0011  | C3                     |
| D         | 1100        | 0100  | C4                     |
| E         | 1100        | 0101  | C5                     |
| F         | 1100        | 0110  | C6                     |
| G         | 1100        | 0111  | C7                     |
| H         | 1100        | 1000  | C8                     |
| I         | 1100        | 1001  | C9                     |
| J         | 1101        | 0001  | D1                     |
| K         | 1101        | 0010  | D2                     |
| L         | 1101        | 0011  | D3                     |
| M         | 1101        | 0100  | D4                     |
| N         | 1101        | 0101  | D5                     |
| O         | 1101        | 0110  | D6                     |
| P         | 1101        | 0111  | D7                     |
| Q         | 1101        | 1000  | D8                     |
| R         | 1101        | 1001  | D9                     |
| S         | 1110        | 0010  | E2                     |
| T         | 1110        | 0011  | E3                     |
| U         | 1110        | 0100  | E4                     |
| V         | 1110        | 0101  | E5                     |
| W         | 1110        | 0110  | E6                     |
| X         | 1110        | 0111  | E7                     |
| Y         | 1110        | 1000  | E8                     |
| Z         | 1110        | 1001  | E9                     |
| 0         | 1111        | 0000  | F0                     |
| 1         | 1111        | 0001  | F1                     |
| 2         | 1111        | 0010  | F2                     |
| 3         | 1111        | 0011  | F3                     |
| 4         | 1111        | 0100  | F4                     |
| 5         | 1111        | 0101  | F5                     |
| 6         | 1111        | 0110  | F6                     |
| 7         | 1111        | 0111  | F7                     |
| 8         | 1111        | 1000  | F8                     |
| 9         | 1111        | 1001  | F9                     |

**Figure 4.3.** Alphabetic and numeric characters in EBCDIC, along with their Hexadecimal equivalent.

| Numeric Value | EBCDIC | Sign Indicator   |
|---------------|--------|------------------|
| 345           | F3F4F5 | F for unsigned   |
| +345          | F3F4C5 | C for positive   |
| -345          | F3F4D5 | D for negative   |

**Figure 4.4.** Numeric values in EBCDIC in Hexadecimal notation.

| Numeric Value | Zoned Format | Packed Format |
|---------------|--------------|---------------|
| 345           | F3F4F5       | 345F          |
| +345          | F3F4C5       | 345C          |
| -345          | F3F4D5       | 345D          |
| 3456          | F3F4F5F6     | 03456F        |

**Figure 4.5.** Zoned and packed decimal numbers.

*Example 4.3.*

Using binary notation, write the EBCDIC coding for the word BIT. How many bytes are required for this representation?

*Solution:*

B = 1100 0010 in EBCDIC binary notation
I = 1100 1001 in EBCDIC binary notation
T = 1110 0011 in EBCDIC binary notation

Hence, the EBCDIC coding for the word BIT in binary notation will be

<u>11000010</u>  <u>11001001</u>  <u>11100011</u>
   B          I          T

3 bytes will be required for this representation, because each letter requires 1 byte (or 8 bits).

*Example 4.4.*

Write the EBCDIC coding for the word ZONE (use hexadecimal notation). How many bytes will be required for this representation?

*Solution:*

Z = E9 in EBCDIC hexadecimal notation
O = D6 in EBCDIC hexadecimal notation
N = D5 in EBCDIC hexadecimal notation
E = C5 in EBCDIC hexadecimal notation

Hence, the EBCDIC coding for the word ZONE in hexadecimal notation will be

<u>E9</u>  <u>D6</u>  <u>D5</u>  <u>C5</u>
Z   O   N   E

Each hexadecimal digit requires 4 bits, and there are altogether 8 hexadecimal digits. Therefore, 8 x 4 = 32 bits or 4 bytes (8 bits = 1 byte) will be required for this representation. We may also write directly that, since each letter requires 1 byte for its representation in EBCDIC, and there are 4 letters in the word ZONE, 4 bytes will be required for this representation.

*Example 4.5.*

Write the EBCDIC zoned-decimal coding for the value +256 (use hexadecimal). How many bytes will be required for this representation?

*Solution:*

+256 = F2F5C6 in EBCDIC

Each hexadecimal digit requires 4 bits, and there are altogether 6 hexadecimal digits. Therefore, 6 x 4 = 24 bits or 3 bytes (8 bits = 1 byte) will be required for this representation. We may also write directly that, since each digit requires 1 byte for its representation in the EBCDIC zoned decimal coding, and there are 3 digits in the given number, 3 bytes will be required for this representation.

*Example 4.6.*

Write -128 as packed decimal number (use hexadecimal). How many bytes will be required for this representation?

*Solution:*

-128 = F1F2D8 in EBCDIC
      = 128D in packed format

Each hexadecimal digit requires 4 bits, and there are altogether 4 hexadecimal digits. Therefore, 4 x 4 = 16 bits or 2 bytes (1 byte = 8 bits) will be required for this representation.

# ASCII

Another computer code, which is widely used, is the *American Standard Code for Information Interchange* (ASCII). ASCII has been adopted by several American computer manufacturers as their computers' internal code. This code is popular in data communications, is used almost exclusively to represent data internally in microcomputers, and is frequently found in the larger computers produced by some vendors.

ASCII is of two types – ASCII-7 and ASCII-8. ASCII-7 is a 7-bit code, which allows 128 ($2^7$) different characters. The first 3 bits are used as zone bits, and the last 4 bits indicate the digit. Microcomputers using 8-bit byte (group of 8 bits for 1 byte) use the 7-bit ASCII by leaving the leftmost first bit of each byte as a zero. Figure 4.6 shows the alphabetic and numeric characters in ASCII-7 notation.

ASCII-8 is an extended version of ASCII-7. It is an 8-bit code, which allows 256 ($2^8$) different characters, rather than 128. The additional bit is added to the zone bits. Figure 4.7 shows the alphabetic and numeric characters in ASCII-8 notation. Observe that, other than the zone-value differences, ASCII-7 and ASCII-8 are identical. ASCII also uses hexadecimal as its four-to-one shortcut notation for memory dump. Figures 4.6 and 4.7 also show the hexadecimal equivalent of the ASCII notations.

*Example 4.7.*

Write the binary coding for the word BOY in ASCII-7. How many bytes are required for this representation?

*Solution:*

B = 1000010 in ASCII-7 binary notation
O = 1001111 in ASCII-7 binary notation
Y = 1011001 in ASCII-7 binary notation

Hence, the binary coding for the word BOY in ASCII-7 will be

<u>1000010</u>  <u>1001111</u>  <u>1011001</u>
   B        O        Y

Since each character in ASCII-7 requires one byte for its representation, and there are 3 characters in the word BOY, 3 bytes will be required for this representation.

*Example 4.8.*

Write the hexadecimal coding for the word GIRL in ASCII-7. How many bytes are required for this representation?

*Solution:*

G = 47 in ASCII-7 hexadecimal notation
I = 49 in ASCII-7 hexadecimal notation
R = 52 in ASCII-7 hexadecimal notation
L = 4C in ASCII-7 hexadecimal notation

Hence, the hexadecimal coding for the word GIRL in ASCII-7 will be

<u>47</u>  <u>49</u>  <u>52</u>  <u>4C</u>
G   I   R  L

Since each character in ASCII-7 requires one byte for its representation, and there are 4 characters in the word GIRL, 4 bytes will be required for this representation.

*Example 4.9.*

Write the binary coding for the word SKY in ASCII-8. How many bytes are required for this representation?

*Solution:*

S = 10110011 in ASCII-8 binary notation
K = 10101011 in ASCII-8 binary notation
Y = 10111001 in ASCII-8 binary notation

Hence, the binary coding for the word SKY in ASCII-8 will be

<u>10110011</u>   <u>10101011</u>   <u>10111001</u>
   S          K          Y

Since each character in ASCII-8 requires one byte for its representation, and there are 3 characters in the word SKY, 3 bytes will be required for this representation.

| Character | ASCII-7 Code | | Hexadecimal Equivalent |
|:---:|:---:|:---:|:---:|
| | Zone | Digit | |
| 0 | 011 | 0000 | 30 |
| 1 | 011 | 0001 | 31 |
| 2 | 011 | 0010 | 32 |
| 3 | 011 | 0011 | 33 |
| 4 | 011 | 0100 | 34 |
| 5 | 011 | 0101 | 35 |
| 6 | 011 | 0110 | 36 |
| 7 | 011 | 0111 | 37 |
| 8 | 011 | 1000 | 38 |
| 9 | 011 | 1001 | 39 |
| | | | |
| A | 100 | 0001 | 41 |
| B | 100 | 0010 | 42 |
| C | 100 | 0011 | 43 |
| D | 100 | 0100 | 44 |
| E | 100 | 0101 | 45 |
| F | 100 | 0110 | 46 |
| G | 100 | 0111 | 47 |
| H | 100 | 1000 | 48 |
| I | 100 | 1001 | 49 |
| J | 100 | 1010 | 4A |
| K | 100 | 1011 | 4B |
| L | 100 | 1100 | 4C |
| M | 100 | 1101 | 4D |
| N | 100 | 1110 | 4E |
| O | 100 | 1111 | 4F |
| | | | |
| P | 101 | 0000 | 50 |
| Q | 101 | 0001 | 51 |
| R | 101 | 0010 | 52 |
| S | 101 | 0011 | 53 |
| T | 101 | 0100 | 54 |
| U | 101 | 0101 | 55 |
| V | 101 | 0110 | 56 |
| W | 101 | 0111 | 57 |
| X | 101 | 1000 | 58 |
| Y | 101 | 1001 | 59 |
| Z | 101 | 1010 | 5A |

**Figure 4.6.** Numeric and alphabetic characters in ASCII-7 notation, along with their Hexadecimal equivalent.

| Character | ASCII-8 Code | | Hexadecimal Equivalent |
|-----------|------|-------|------------------------|
|           | Zone | Digit |                        |
| 0 | 0101 | 0000 | 50 |
| 1 | 0101 | 0001 | 51 |
| 2 | 0101 | 0010 | 52 |
| 3 | 0101 | 0011 | 53 |
| 4 | 0101 | 0100 | 54 |
| 5 | 0101 | 0101 | 55 |
| 6 | 0101 | 0110 | 56 |
| 7 | 0101 | 0111 | 57 |
| 8 | 0101 | 1000 | 58 |
| 9 | 0101 | 1001 | 59 |
|   |      |      |    |
| A | 1010 | 0001 | A1 |
| B | 1010 | 0010 | A2 |
| C | 1010 | 0011 | A3 |
| D | 1010 | 0100 | A4 |
| E | 1010 | 0101 | A5 |
| F | 1010 | 0110 | A6 |
| G | 1010 | 0111 | A7 |
| H | 1010 | 1000 | A8 |
| I | 1010 | 1001 | A9 |
| J | 1010 | 1010 | AA |
| K | 1010 | 1011 | AB |
| L | 1010 | 1100 | AC |
| M | 1010 | 1101 | AD |
| N | 1010 | 1110 | AE |
| O | 1010 | 1111 | AF |
|   |      |      |    |
| P | 1011 | 0000 | B0 |
| Q | 1011 | 0001 | B1 |
| R | 1011 | 0010 | B2 |
| S | 1011 | 0011 | B3 |
| T | 1011 | 0100 | B4 |
| U | 1011 | 0101 | B5 |
| V | 1011 | 0110 | B6 |
| W | 1011 | 0111 | B7 |
| X | 1011 | 1000 | B8 |
| Y | 1011 | 1001 | B9 |
| Z | 1011 | 1010 | BA |

**Figure 4.7.** Numeric and alphabetic characters in ASCII-8 notation, along with their Hexadecimal equivalent.

*Example 4.10.*

Write the hexadecimal coding for the word STAR in ASCII-8. How many bytes are required for this representation?

*Solution:*

S = B3 in ASCII-8 hexadecimal notation
T = B4 in ASCII-8 hexadecimal notation

A = A1 in ASCII-8 hexadecimal notation

R = B2 in ASCII-8 hexadecimal notation

Hence, the hexadecimal coding for the word STAR in ASCII-8 will be

| B3 | B4 | A1 | B2 |
| --- | --- | --- | --- |
| S | T | A | R |

Since each character in ASCII-8 requires one byte for its representation, and there are 4 characters in the word STAR, 4 bytes will be required for this representation.

## COLLATING SEQUENCE

The value of an alphanumeric or alphabetic data element is usually the name of some object. Obviously, one would not like to perform any arithmetic on such data, but one may like to compare them, for arranging them in some desired sequence. Now, if we compare the alphabetic values A and B, which one will be treated as greater by the computer? For an answer to such questions, it is necessary to have some assigned ordering among the characters used by the computer. This ordering is known as the *collating sequence*.

Collating sequence may vary from one computer system to another, depending on the type of computer code used by a particular computer. To illustrate this, let us consider the computer codes already discussed in this chapter. Observe from Figures 4.2 and 4.3 that the zone values of the characters A through 9 decrease in BCD code from the equivalent of decimal 3 down to 0, while the zone values of the characters A through 9 increases in EBCDIC from the equivalent of decimal 12 to 15. This means that a computer, which uses BCD code for its internal representation of characters, will treat alphabetic characters (A, B, ..., Z) to be greater than numeric characters (0, 1, ..., 9). On the other hand, a computer, which uses EBCDIC for its internal representation of characters, will treat numeric characters to be greater than alphabetic characters. Similarly, observe from Figures 4.6 and 4.7 that a computer, which uses ASCII for its internal representation of characters, will place numbers ahead of letters during a sort (ascending), because the number characters have a zone value, which is less than the zone value for letters.

However, whatever may be the type of computer code used, in most (not all – in BCD 0 > 9) collating sequences, the following rules are observed:

1.  Letters are considered in alphabetic order (A < B < C < ... < Z)

2.  Digits are considered in numeric order (0 < 1 < 2 < ... < 9)

### Example 4.11.

A computer uses EBCDIC as its internal representation of characters. In which order will this computer sort the strings 23, A1, 1A?

*Solution:*

In EBCDIC, numeric characters are treated to be greater than alphabetic characters. Hence, in the said computer, the numeric characters will be placed after the alphabetic characters, and the given string will be treated as:

A1 < 1A < 23

Therefore, the sorted sequence will be: A1, 1A, 23.

*Example 4.12.*

A computer uses ASCII for its internal representation of characters. In which order will this computer sort the strings 23, A1, 1A?

*Solution:*

In ASCII, numeric characters are treated to be less than alphabetic characters. Hence, in the said computer, the numeric characters will be placed before the alphabetic characters, and the given string will be treated as:

$$23 < 1A < A1$$

Therefore, the sorted sequence will be: 23, 1A, A1.

# Points To Remember

1. Binary coding schemes are used in computers to represent data internally. In binary coding, every symbol, which appears in the data, is represented by a group of bits. The group of bits used to represent a symbol is called a byte. Most modern computers use 8 bits to represent a symbol. Hence, the term *byte* is commonly used to mean a group of 8 bits.

2. The commonly used computer codes for internal representation of data are BCD, EBCDIC and ASCII.

3. *BCD (Binary Coded Decimal)* is a 6-bit code, which can represent 64 different characters.

4. *EBCDIC (Extended Binary-Coded Decimal Interchange Code)* is an 8-bit code, which can represent 256 different characters.

5. *ASCII (American Standard Code for Information Interchange)* is one of the most popular computer codes. It is of two types – ASCII-7 and ASCII-8. ASCII-7 is a 7-bit code, which can represent 128 different characters, and ASCII-8 is an 8-bit code, which can represent 256 different characters.

# Questions

1. Define the term 'byte'. What is the difference between a bit and a byte?

2. Write the 4-bit BCD code for the following numbers:
   (a) $25_{10}$      (c) $128_{10}$
   (b) $64_{10}$      (d) $1024_{10}$

3. Using binary notation, show the BCD coding for the following words:
   (a) BIT      (c) CODE
   (b) BYTE      (d) ZERO

4. Using octal notation, show the BCD coding for the following words:
   (a) COMPUTER    (c) VIDEO
   (b) INPUT      (d) OUTPUT

5. Why was BCD code extended to EBCDIC?

6. How many different characters are possible for the following codes:
   (a) BCD      (b) EBCDIC

   (c) ASCII-7      (d) ASCII-8

7. Why are octal and hexadecimal shortcut notations used? Identify the shortcut notations used for each of these computer codes:
   (a) BCD      (c) ASCII-7
   (b) EBCDIC      (d) ASCII-8

8. Why do we have a packed decimal format? How does it differ from a zoned decimal format?

9. A new computer code is designed, which uses 9 bits. How many different characters are possible in this code?

10. Using binary notation, write the EBCDIC coding for the following words:
    (a) SUN      (c) CAT
    (b) MOON      (d) DOG
    How many bytes are required for each of these representations?

11. Using hexadecimal notation, write the EBCDIC coding for the following words:
    (a) PROGRAM     (c) BYTE
    (b) OUTPUT     (d) OCTAL
    How many bytes are required for each of these representations?

12. Using hexadecimal notation, write the zoned-decimal coding for the following numbers:
    (a) 1256     (c) -63
    (b) +439     (d) -786
    How many bytes are required for each of these representations?

13. Using hexadecimal notation, write the packed-decimal coding for the following numbers:
    (a) 12915     (c) 872
    (b) +9876     (d) -256
    How many bytes are required for each of these representations?

14. List out the similarities and differences between 7-bit and 8-bit ASCII.

15. Using binary notation, write the ASCII-7 and ASCII-8 codes for the following words:
    (a) DRY     (c) DAMP
    (b) WET     (d) TERM

How many bytes are required for each of these representations?

16. Using hexadecimal notation, write the ASCII-7 and ASCII-8 codes for the following words:
    (a) PRINT     (c) RUB
    (b) TYPE     (d) GIVE
    How many bytes are required for each of these representations?

17. Explain the meaning of the term "collating sequence".

18. A computer uses EBCDIC as its internal representation of characters. In which order will this computer sort the following strings?
    (a) ABC     (c) 245
    (b) 123     (d) ADD

19. A computer uses ASCII. In which order will this computer sort the following strings?
    (a) BED     (d) 128
    (b) 512     (e) BAD
    (c) ADD

20. Give the full form of the following abbreviations:
    (a) BCD
    (b) EBCDIC
    (c) ASCII

# Chapter 5

# Computer Arithmetic

In Chapter 4, we saw that computers store numbers, letters, and other characters in coded form, in binary number system. In this chapter, you will learn why computers use binary numbers instead of decimal numbers, and how the basic arithmetic operations are performed inside the computer by using binary numbers.

## WHY BINARY?

In Chapter 3, we saw that the use of a smaller base often requires more positions to represent a given value (recall the reason for using octal and hexadecimal notations). For example, $9_{10} = 1001_2$. Here, four positions are required, instead of one, to represent the decimal number 9 in binary form. In spite of this, almost all computers use binary numbers. Hence, the obvious question that arises is 'Why do we use binary numbers, instead of decimal numbers?' The reasons are as follows:

1. Information is handled in a computer by electronic/electrical components, such as transistors, semiconductors, wires, etc., all of which can only indicate two states or conditions – on(1) or off(0). Transistors are either conducting(1) or nonconducting(0); magnetic materials are either magnetized(1) or nonmagnetized(0) in one direction or in the opposite direction; a pulse or voltage is present(1) or absent(0) in wire. All information are represented within the computer by the presence or absence of these types of signals. The binary number system, which has only two digits (0 and 1), is most suitable for expressing the two possible states. The concept of binary components is illustrated in Figure 5.1.

2. By using binary numbers, computer circuits only have to handle two binary digits, rather than ten decimal digits. This greatly simplifies the internal circuit design of computers, resulting in less expensive and more reliable circuits.

3. Finally, everything that can be done in decimal number system can also be done in binary number system. How this is achieved has been discussed below.

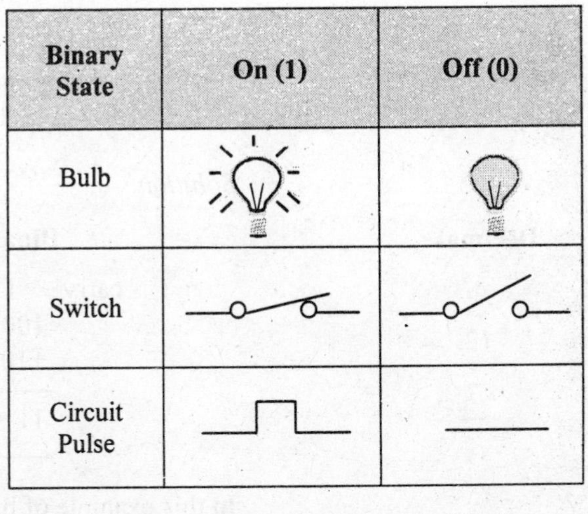

| Binary State | On (1) | Off (0) |
|---|---|---|
| Bulb | | |
| Switch | | |
| Circuit Pulse | | |

**Figure 5.1.** Examples of devices that work in binary mode. These devices can only represent two states – on or off, which can represent 1 (yes) or 0 (no).

# BINARY ARITHMETIC

In this section, you will see how the four basic arithmetic operations are performed inside a computer by using binary numbers. Actually, binary arithmetic is much simpler to learn, because binary number system deals with only two digits – 0 and 1. Therefore, all binary numbers are made up of only 0s and 1s, and when arithmetic operations are performed on these numbers, the results are also in 0s and 1s only.

## Addition

Binary addition is performed in the same manner as decimal addition. However, since binary number system has only two digits, the addition table for binary arithmetic is very simple, consisting of only four entries. The complete table for binary addition is as follows:

$0 + 0 = 0$
$0 + 1 = 1$
$1 + 0 = 1$
$1 + 1 = 0$ plus a carry of 1 to next higher column

Carry-overs are performed in the same manner as in decimal arithmetic. Since 1 is the largest digit in the binary number system, any sum greater than 1 requires a digit to be carried over. For instance, 10 plus 10 binary requires the addition of two 1s in the second position. Since $1 + 1 = 0$ plus a carry-over of 1, the sum of 10 + 10 is 100 in binary.

By repeated use of the above rules, any two binary numbers can be added together by adding two bits at a time. The exact procedure is illustrated with the examples given below.

*Example 5.1.*

Add the binary numbers 101 and
10 in both decimal and binary forms.

*Solution:*

| Binary | Decimal |
|--------|---------|
| 101    | 5       |
| +10    | +2      |
| 111    | 7       |

*Example 5.2.*

Add the binary numbers 10011 and
1001 in both decimal and binary forms.

*Solution:*

| | Binary | | Decimal |
|------|--------|-------|---------|
| carry | 11     | carry | 1       |
|       | 10011  |       | 19      |
|       | +1001  |       | +9      |
|       | 11100  |       | 28      |

In this example of binary addition, a carry is
generated for first and second columns.

*Example 5.3.*

Add the binary numbers 100111 and 11011 in both decimal and binary forms.

*Solution:*

| | Binary | | Decimal |
|-------|---------|-------|---------|
| carry | 11111   | carry | 1       |
|       | 100111  |       | 39      |
|       | +11011  |       | +27     |
|       | 1000010 |       | 66      |

In this example, we face a new situation $(1 + 1 + 1)$,
brought about by the carry-over of 1 in the second column.
This can also be handled using the same four rules for
binary addition. The addition of three 1s can be broken up
into two steps. First, we add only two 1s giving 10 $(1 + 1 =
10)$. The third 1 is now added to this result to obtain 11 (a 1
sum with a 1 carry). Hence, $1 + 1 + 1 = 1$, plus a carry of 1
to next higher column.

# Subtraction

The principles of decimal subtraction can as well be applied to subtraction of numbers in other number systems.
It consists of two steps, which are repeated for each column of the numbers. The first step is to determine if it is
necessary to borrow. If the subtrahend (the lower digit) is larger than the minuend (the upper digit), it is necessary
to borrow from the column to the left. It is important to note here that the value borrowed depends upon the base
of the number system, and is always the decimal equivalent of the base. Hence, in decimal, 10 is borrowed; in
binary, 2 is borrowed; in octal, 8 is borrowed; in hexadecimal, 16 is borrowed. The second step is simply to
subtract the lower value from the upper value. The complete table for binary subtraction is as follows:

$0 - 0 = 0$
$1 - 0 = 1$
$1 - 1 = 0$
$0 - 1 = 1$ with a borrow from the next column

Observe that, the only case in which it is necessary to borrow is when 1 is subtracted from 0. The exact procedure
is illustrated with the examples given below.

*Example 5.4.*

Subtract $01110_2$ from $10101_2$.

*Solution:*

$$\text{Borrow} \left\{ \begin{array}{l} 12 \\ 0202 \end{array} \right.$$

$$\begin{array}{r} 10101 \\ -01110 \\ \hline 00111 \\ \hline \end{array}$$

In the first column, 0 is subtracted from 1. No borrow is required in this case, and the result is 1. In the second column, we have to subtract 1 from 0. A borrow is necessary to perform this subtraction. Hence, a 1 is borrowed from the third column, which becomes 2 in the second column, because the base is 2. A 1 in the 4's column is equal to 2 in the 2's column. Now, in the second column, we subtract 1 from 2 giving 1. The borrow performed in the second column reduces the 1 in the third column to 0. Hence, in the third column, once again we have to subtract 1 from 0 for which borrow is required. The fourth column contains a 0, and hence, has nothing to borrow. Therefore, we have to borrow from the fifth column. Borrowing 1 from the fifth column gives 2 in the fourth column. A 1 in the 16's column equals 2 in the 8's column. Now, the fourth column has something to borrow. When 1 of the 2 in the fourth column is borrowed, it becomes 2 in the third column. Now, in the third column, we subtract 1 from 2, giving 1. The borrow performed in the third column, reduces the 1 in the fifth column to 0, and the 2 in the fourth column to 1. Therefore, subtraction of the fourth column is now 1 from 1, giving 0 and in the fifth column, subtraction is 0 from 0, giving 0. Hence, the result of subtraction is $00111_2$. The result may be verified by subtracting $14_{10}$ (= $01110_2$) from $21_{10}$ ($10101_2$), which gives $7_{10}$ (= $00111_2$).

*Example 5.5.*

Subtract $0111000_2$ from $1011100_2$.

*Solution:*

$$\text{Borrow} \quad 2$$

$$\begin{array}{r} 1011100 \\ -0111000 \\ \hline 0100100 \\ \hline \end{array}$$

The result may be verified by subtracting $56_{10}$ (= $0111000_2$) from $92_{10}$ (= $1011100_2$), which gives $36_{10}$ (= $0100100_2$).

## Additive Method of Subtraction

The direct method of subtraction by using the borrow concept, seems to be easiest when we perform subtraction with paper and pencil. However, when subtraction is implemented by means of digital components, this method is found to be less efficient than the additive method of subtraction. It may sound surprising that even subtraction is performed, by using an additive method. The additive method of subtraction is known as *complementary subtraction*.

In order to understand complementary subtraction, it is necessary to know what is meant by the complement of a number. For a number, which has *n* digits in it, a *complement* is defined as the difference between the number and the base raised to the $n^{th}$ power minus one. The definition is illustrated with the following examples:

*Example 5.6.*

Find the complement of $37_{10}$.

*Solution:*

Since the number has 2 digits, and the value of base is 10,
$(Base)^n - 1 = 10^2 - 1 = 99$
Now, $99 - 37 = 62$
Hence, the complement of $37_{10} = 62_{10}$.

*Example 5.7.*

Find the complement of $6_8$.

*Solution:*

Since the number has 1 digit, and the value of base is 8,
$(Base)^n - 1 = 8^1 - 1 = 7_{10}$
Also, $6_8 = 6_{10}$
Now, $7_{10} - 6_{10} = 1_{10} = 1_8$
Hence, the complement of $6_8 = 1_8$.

*Example 5.8.*

Find the complement of $10101_2$.

*Solution:*

Since the number has 5 digits, and the value of base is 2,
$(Base)^n - 1 = 2^5 - 1 = 31_{10}$
Also, $10101_2 = 21_{10}$
Now, $31_{10} - 21_{10} = 10_{10} = 1010_2$
Hence, the complement of $10101_2 = 01010_2$.

In case of binary numbers, it is not necessary to go through the usual process of obtaining complement. Instead, a quick way to obtain the complement of a binary number is to transform all its 0s to 1s, and all its 1s to 0s. For example, the complement of 1011010 is 0100101. This may also be observed in case of Example 5.8. Hence, the circuit for obtaining the complement of a number in binary number system can be easily designed at very less expense.

After having seen how to obtain the complement of a number, we will now see how subtraction is performed by using the complementary method.

Subtraction by the complementary method involves the following steps:

Step 1: Find the complement of the number you are subtracting (subtrahend);

Step 2: Add this to the number from which you are taking away (minuend);

Step 3: If there is a carry of 1, add it to obtain the result; if there is no carry, recomplement the sum and attach a negative sign to cbtain the result.

To illustrate the procedure, let us first consider few examples for decimal numbers.

*Example 5.9.*

Subtract $56_{10}$ from $92_{10}$ using complementary method.

*Solution:*

Step 1:  Complement of $56_{10}$
$$= 10^2 - 1 - 56$$
$$= 99 - 56$$
$$= 43_{10}$$

Step 2:   92
        +43  (complement of 56)

        135

Step 3:  ↳1 (add the carry of 1)

Result = 36

The result may be verified by using the method of normal subtraction:

$$92 - 56 = 36.$$

*Example 5.10.*

Subtract $35_{10}$ from $18_{10}$ using complementary method.

*Solution:*

Step 1:  Complement of $35_{10}$
$$= 10^2 - 1 - 35$$
$$= 99 - 35$$
$$= 64_{10}$$

Step 2:   18
        +64  (complement of 35)

        82

Step 3:  Since there is no carry, recomplement the sum and attach a negative sign to obtain the result.

Result   $= -(99 - 82)$
         $= -17$

The result may be verified by using the method of normal subtraction:

$$18 - 35 = -17$$

Let us re-work these examples, by using binary numbers.

*Example 5.11.*

Subtract $0111000_2$ ($56_{10}$) from $1011100_2$ ($92_{10}$) using complementary method.

*Solution:*

   1011100
 +1000111  (complement of 0111000)

 10100011

        └───→ 1 (add the carry of 1)

  0100100

Result = $0100100_2 = 36_{10}$

Verify the result with the results of Example 5.5 and Example 5.9.

*Example 5.12.*

Subtract $100011_2$ ($35_{10}$) from $010010_2$ ($18_{10}$) using complementary method.

*Solution:*

   010010
 +011100  (complement of 100011)

  101110

Since there is no carry, we have to complement the sum and attach a negative sign to it.  Hence,

Result = $-010001_2$ (complement of $101110_2$)
       = $-17_{10}$

Verify the result with the result of Example 5.10.

*Example 5.13.*

Subtract $01110_2$ from $10101_2$ using complementary method.

*Solution:*

$$10101$$
$$+10001 \quad \text{(complement of 01110)}$$

$$100110$$

$$\longrightarrow 1 \quad \text{(add the carry of 1)}$$

$$00111$$

Result = $00111_2$

Verify the result with the result of Example 5.4.

# Multiplication

Multiplication in the binary number system also follows the same general rules as multiplication in decimal number system. However, learning the binary multiplication is a trivial task, because the table for binary multiplication is very short, with only four entries, instead of the 100 necessary for decimal multiplication. The complete table for binary multiplication is as follows:

$0 \times 0 = 0$      The method of binary multiplication is illustrated with the example given below. It is
$0 \times 1 = 0$      only necessary to copy the multiplicand, if the digit in the multiplier is 1, and to copy
$1 \times 0 = 0$      all 0s, if the digit in the multiplier is 0. The ease with which each step of the
$1 \times 1 = 1$      operation is performed is apparent.

*Example 5.14.*

Multiply the binary numbers 1010 and 1001.

*Solution:*

```
    1010    Multiplicand
   x1001    Multiplier

    1010    Partial Product
    0000    Partial Product
    0000    Partial Product
    1010    Partial Product

 1011010    Final Product
```

Note that the multiplicand is simply copied when multiplier digit is 1, and when the multiplier digit is 0, the partial product is only a string of 0s. As in decimal multiplication, each partial product is shifted one place to the left from the previous partial product. Finally, all the partial products obtained in this manner are added according to the binary addition rules to obtain the final product.

In actual practice, whenever a 0 appears in the multiplier, a separate partial product consisting of a string of 0s need not be generated. Instead, only a left shift will do. As a result, Example 5.14 may be reduced to

```
   1010
  x1001
  _____
   1010
  1010SS   (S = left shift)
  _____
 1011010
```

A computer would also follow this procedure in performing multiplication. The result of this multiplication may be verified by multiplying $10_{10}$ ($1010_2$) by $9_{10}$ ($1001_2$), which produces a result of $90_{10}$ ($1011010_2$).

It may not be obvious how to handle the addition, if the result of the multiplication gives columns with more than two 1s. They can be handled as pairs, or by adjusting the column to which the carry is placed, as shown in Example 5.15.

*Example 5.15.*

Multiply the binary numbers 1111 and 111.

*Solution:*

```
          1 | 1 | 1   1
          x | 1 | 1   1
         _____
          1 | 1 | 1   1
      1   1 | 1 | 1
  1   1   1 | 1 |
 _____
  1   1   0 | 1 | 0   0   1
```

As shown below, the addition in column 3 above can be handled in any one of the following two ways:

Addition handled as pairs (Column 3)                    Addition handled as single carry (Column 3)

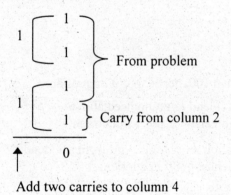

Add two carries to column 4

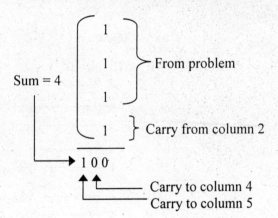

## Additive Method of Multiplication

Most computers perform multiplication operation by the way of addition only. This can be easily seen by considering an example, say 4 x 8. The result for this multiplication can be obtained simply by adding the digit 8 four times $(8 + 8 + 8 + 8)$. Similarly, the computer performs all multiplication operations in binary by using the additive approach.

The idea of repeated addition may seem to be a longer way of doing things, but remember that the computer is well suited to carry out the operations at great speed. The internal circuit design of computer systems is also simplified to a great extent by using this method of multiplication.

## Division

Once again, division in binary number system is very simple. As in the decimal number system (or in any other number system), division by zero is meaningless. Hence, the complete table for binary division is as follows:

$$0 \div 1 = 0$$
$$1 \div 1 = 1$$

The division process is performed in a manner similar to decimal division. The rules for binary division are:

1.  Start from the left of the dividend.

2.  Perform a series of subtractions, in which the divisor is subtracted from the dividend.

3.  If subtraction is possible, put a 1 in the quotient and subtract the divisor from the corresponding digits of dividend.

4.  If subtraction is not possible (divisor greater than remainder), record a 0 in the quotient.

5.  Bring down the next digit to add to the remainder digits. Proceed as before in a manner similar to long division.

The method is illustrated with Example 5.16.

### Example 5.16.

Divide $100001_2$ by $110_2$.

*Solution:*

```
        0101    (Quotient)
  110 ) 100001  (Dividend)
        110   1 ◄────────── Divisor greater than 100, hence, put 0 in quotient
        1000  2 ◄────────── Add digit from dividend to group used above
        110   3 ◄────────── Subtraction possible, hence, put 1 in quotient
        100   4 ◄────────── Remainder from subtraction plus digit from dividend
        110   5 ◄────────── Divisor greater, hence, put 0 in quotient
        1001  6 ◄────────── Add digit from dividend to group used above
        110   7 ◄────────── Subtraction possible, hence, put 1 in quotient
        11      (Remainder)
```

The result may be verified by dividing $33_{10}$ ($100001_2$) by $6_{10}$ ($110_2$), which gives a quotient of $5_{10}$ ($101_2$) and a remainder of $3_{10}$ ($11_2$).

## Additive Method of Division

Even division operation is performed inside most computers by the process of addition only. This may again sound surprising, but it is true. The computer performs the division operation essentially by repeating the complementary subtraction method. For example, $35 \div 5$ may be thought of as:

| | |
|---|---|
| $35 - 5 = 30$ | That is, the divisor is subtracted repeatedly from the dividend, until the result of |
| $30 - 5 = 25$ | subtraction becomes less than or equal to zero. The total number of times |
| $25 - 5 = 20$ | subtraction was performed gives the value of the quotient. In this case, the value |
| $20 - 5 = 15$ | of quotient is 7, because the divisor (5) was subtracted 7 times from the dividend |
| $15 - 5 = 10$ | (35), until the result of subtraction became zero. If the result of last subtraction |
| $10 - 5 = \phantom{0}5$ | is zero, then there is no remainder for the division. However, if it is less than |
| $5 - 5 = \phantom{0}0$ | zero, then the last subtraction is ignored, and the result of the previous |

subtraction is taken as the value of the remainder. In this case, the last subtraction operation is not counted for evaluating the value of the quotient. The process is illustrated below with an example.

*Example 5.17.*

Divide $33_{10}$ by $6_{10}$ using the method of addition.

*Solution:*

| | |
|---|---|
| $33 - 6 = 27$ | Total number of subtractions = 6. |
| $27 - 6 = 21$ | Since the result of the last subtraction is less than zero, |
| $21 - 6 = 15$ | |
| $15 - 6 = \phantom{0}9$ | Quotient = 6 - 1 (ignore last subtraction) = 5 |
| $9 - 6 = \phantom{0}3$ | Remainder = 3 (result of previous subtraction) |
| $3 - 6 = -3$ | Hence, $33 \div 6 = 5$ with a remainder 3. |

It has been assumed here that all the subtraction operations are carried out by using the complementary subtraction method (additive method).

Once again, performing division inside a computer by the way of addition is desirable, because the addition and complementation operations are easily performed in a computer, and usually save the labour and expense of designing complicated circuits.

We have demonstrated how computer arithmetic is based on addition. Exactly how this simplifies matter can only be understood in the context of binary (not in decimal). The number of individual steps may indeed be increased because all computer arithmetic is reduced to addition. However, but the computer can carry out binary additions at such great speed that this is not a disadvantage.

# Points to Remember

1. Almost all computers use binary numbers for internal computations, because electronic circuits for performing arithmetic operations in binary mode can be designed and implemented more easily, reliably, and at a much lesser cost than those required for performing arithmetic operations in decimal mode.

2. The rules for *binary addition* are as follows:
   $0 + 0 = 0$
   $0 + 1 = 1$
   $1 + 0 = 1$
   $1 + 1 = 0$ plus a carry of 1 to next higher column

3. The rules for *binary subtraction* are as follows:
   $0 - 0 = 0$
   $1 - 0 = 1$
   $1 - 1 = 0$
   $0 - 1 = 1$ with a borrow from the next column

4. The *complement* of a number, which has $n$ digits in it, is defined as the difference between the number and the base raised to the $n^{th}$ power minus one.

5. A quick way to obtain the *complement of a binary number* is to transform all its 0s to 1s, and all its 1s to 0s.

6. *Complementary subtraction* is an additive approach of subtraction.

7. The rules for *binary multiplication* are as follows:
   $0 \times 0 = 0$
   $0 \times 1 = 0$
   $1 \times 0 = 0$
   $1 \times 1 = 1$

8. The rules for *binary division* are as follows:
   $0 \div 1 = 0$
   $1 \div 1 = 1$

9. Most computers use the *additive approach* for performing multiplication and division operations.

# Questions

1. Why have computers been designed to use the binary number system?

2. Add the binary numbers 1011 and 101 in both decimal and binary forms.

3. Add the binary numbers 1010110 and 1011010.

4. Add the binary numbers 10111 and 1011.

5. Find the complement of the following numbers:
   (a) $495_{10}$       (d) $C_{16}$
   (b) $29_{10}$        (e) $2_5$
   (c) $4_8$            (f) $32_4$

6. Find the complement of the following binary numbers:
   (a) 10         (d) 011011
   (b) 101        (e) 10110001
   (c) 101101     (f) 001101001110

7. Subtract $0110111_2$ from $1101110_2$.

8. Subtract $01010_2$ from $10000_2$.

9. Subtract $011011_2$ from $110111_2$.

10. Subtract $25_{10}$ from $50_{10}$ using complementary method.

11. Subtract $25_{10}$ from $20_{10}$ using complementary method.

12. Subtract $234_{10}$ from $588_{10}$ using complementary method.

13. Subtract $216_{10}$ from $172_{10}$ using complementary method.

14. Subtract $01010_2$ from $10000_2$ using complementary method.

15. Subtract $110111_2$ from $101110_2$ using complementary method.

16. Subtract $011011_2$ from $110111_2$ using complementary method.

17. Subtract $1111_2$ from $1100_2$ using complementary method.

18. Multiply the binary numbers 1100 and 1010.

19. Multiply the binary numbers 01101 and 1001.

20. Multiply the binary numbers 101111 and 111.

21. Divide $11001_2$ by $101_2$.

22. Divide $0110111_2$ by $0111_2$.

23. Briefly, explain how multiplication and division operations are performed within a computer by using additive approach.

24. What is the primary advantage of performing subtraction by the complementary method in digital computers?

25. Discuss the advantages and disadvantages of performing the various arithmetic operations by additive method in a digital computer.

# Chapter 6

# Boolean Algebra and Logic Circuits

Boolean algebra is an algebra, which deals with the binary number system. It is very useful in designing logic circuits, which are used by the processors of computer systems. In this chapter, you will learn about this algebra, and the elementary logic gates, which are used to build up circuits of different types, for performing the necessary arithmetic operations. These logic gates are the building blocks of all the circuits in a computer. You will also learn how to use Boolean algebra for designing simple logic circuits, which are frequently used by the arithmetic logic unit of almost all computers.

## BOOLEAN ALGEBRA

In the mid-1800's, an algebra, which simplified the representation and manipulation of propositional logic, was developed by the English mathematician, George Boole (1815-1864). It became known as Boolean algebra, after its developer's name. Later, in the year 1938, Claude E. Shannon proposed the use of Boolean algebra in the design of relay switching circuits. The basic techniques described by Shannon were adopted almost universally, for the design and analysis of switching circuits. Because of the analogous relationship between the action of relays and modern electronic circuits, the same techniques, which were developed for the design of relay circuits, are still being used in the design of modern computers.

Boolean algebra provides an economical and straightforward approach to the design of relay, and other types of switching circuits. Just as an ordinary algebraic expression may be simplified by means of the basic theorems, the expression describing a given switching circuit network, may also be reduced or simplified by using Boolean algebra. Today, Boolean algebra is used extensively in designing the circuitry used in computers.

## Fundamental Concepts of Boolean Algebra

Boolean algebra is based on the fundamental concepts described below.

## Use of Binary Digits

In a normal algebraic expression, a variable can take any numerical value. For example, in the expression 3A + 7B = C, the values of A, B, and C may range through the entire field of real numbers. Since, Boolean algebra deals with the binary number system, the variables used in the Boolean equations may have only two possible values (0 or 1). If an equation describing logical circuitry has several variables, it is still understood that each of the variables can assume only the values 0 or 1. For example, in the equation A + B = C, each of the variables A, B and C may have only the values 0 or 1.

## Logical Addition

The symbol '+' is used for logical addition operator. It is also known as 'OR' operator. We can define the + symbol (OR operator) by listing all possible combinations of A and B, and the resulting value of C, in the equation A + B = C. Since, the variables A and B can have only two possible values (0 or 1), only four ($2^2$) combinations of inputs are possible, as shown in Figure 6.1. The resulting output values for each of the four input combinations are given in the table. Such a table is known as a *truth table*. Hence, Figure 6.1 is the truth table for the logical OR operator.

Observe that, the result is 0, only when both the input variables are 0; it is 1, when any of the input variables is 1; and it is also 1, when both the input variables are 1. This is the reason why the + symbol does not have the "normal" meaning, but is a logical addition operator. This concept of logical addition may be extended to any number of variables. For example, in the equation A + B + C + D = E, even if A, B, C, and D, all had the value of 1, the sum of the values (the result E) would be 1 only. The equation A + B = C is normally read as "A or B equals C".

| Inputs | | | Output |
|---|---|---|---|
| A | + | B  =  | C |
| 0 | | 0 | 0 |
| 0 | | 1 | 1 |
| 1 | | 0 | 1 |
| 1 | | 1 | 1 |

**Figure 6.1.** Truth table for logical OR (+) operator.

## Logical Multiplication

The symbol '·' is used for logical multiplication operator. It is also known as 'AND' operator. We can again define the · symbol (AND operator) by listing all possible combinations of A and B, and the resulting value of C, in the equation A · B = C. The truth table for logical AND operator is shown in Figure 6.2. Observe from the truth table that, the result C is equal to 1, only when both the input variables A and B are 1, otherwise it is 0. The equation A · B = C is normally read as "A and B equals C".

| Inputs | | | Output |
|---|---|---|---|
| A | · | B  =  | C |
| 0 | | 0 | 0 |
| 0 | | 1 | 0 |
| 1 | | 0 | 0 |
| 1 | | 1 | 1 |

**Figure 6.2.** Truth table for logical AND (·) operator.

## Complementation

The OR and AND operations are binary operations, because they define an operation on two variables. The complementation operation is a unary operation, which is defined on a single variable.

The symbol '–' is normally used for complementation operator. It is also known as 'NOT' operator. Hence, we write $\overline{A}$, meaning "complement of A", or $\left(\overline{A+B}\right)$, meaning "complement of A + B." The complementation of a variable is the reverse of its value. Hence, if A = 0, then $\overline{A}$ = 1, and if A = 1, then $\overline{A}$ = 0. The truth table for logical NOT (–) operator is shown in Figure 6.3. $\overline{A}$ is read as "complement of A" or "not of A".

| Input | Output |
|-------|--------|
| A | $\overline{A}$ |
| 0 | 1 |
| 1 | 0 |

**Figure 6.3.** Truth table for logical NOT (–) operator.

## Operator Precedence

Does A + B · C mean (A + B) · C or A + (B · C)? The two generate different values for A = 1, B = 0, and C = 0, because we have (1 + 0) · 0 = 0 and 1 + (0 · 0) = 1, which differ. Hence, it is necessary to define operator precedence, to correctly evaluate Boolean expressions. The precedence of Boolean operators is as follows:

1. The expression is scanned from left to right.
2. Expressions enclosed within parentheses are evaluated first.
3. All complement (NOT) operations are performed next.
4. All '·' (AND) operations are performed after that.
5. Finally, all '+' (OR) operations are performed in the end.

According to this precedence rule, A + B · C means A + (B · C). Similarly, for the expression $\overline{A} \cdot \overline{B}$, the complement of A and B are both evaluated first, and the results are then ANDed. Again, for the expression $\left(\overline{A+B}\right)$, the expression inside the parenthesis (A + B) is evaluated first, and the result is then complemented.

## Postulates of Boolean Algebra

*Postulate 1:*
    (a) A = 0, if and only if, A is not equal to 1
    (b) A = 1, if and only if, A is not equal to 0

*Postulate 2:*
    (a) x + 0 = x
    (b) x · 1 = x

*Postulate 3: Commutative Law*
    (a) x + y = y + x
    (b) x · y = y · x

*Postulate 4: Associative Law*
    (a) x + (y + z) = (x + y) + z
    (b) x · (y · z) = (x · y) · z

*Postulate 5: Distributive Law*
    (a) x · (y + z) = x · y + x · z
    (b) x + y · z = (x + y) · (x + z)

*Postulate 6:*
    (a) x + $\overline{x}$ = 1
    (b) x · $\overline{x}$ = 0

These postulates are the basic axioms of the algebraic structure, which need no proof. They are used to prove the theorems of Boolean algebra.

# The Principle of Duality

In Boolean algebra, there is a precise duality between the operators · (AND) and + (OR), and the digits 0 and 1. For instance, let us consider Figure 6.4. We can see that the second row of the table is obtainable from the first row, and vice-versa, simply by interchanging '+' with '·' and '0' with '1'. This important property is known as the principle of duality in Boolean algebra.

|       | Column 1 | Column 2 | Column 3 |
|-------|----------|----------|----------|
| Row 1 | $1 + 1 = 1$ | $1 + 0 = 0 + 1 = 1$ | $0 + 0 = 0$ |
| Row 2 | $0 \cdot 0 = 0$ | $0 \cdot 1 = 1 \cdot 0 = 0$ | $1 \cdot 1 = 1$ |

**Figure 6.4.**  Illustrating the principle of duality in Boolean algebra.

The implication of this principle is that, any theorem in Boolean algebra has its dual obtainable by interchanging '+' with '·' and '0' with '1'. Hence, if a particular theorem is proved, its dual theorem automatically holds, and need not be proved separately.

# Theorems of Boolean Algebra

Some of the important theorems of Boolean algebra are stated below, along with their proof.

*Theorem 1 (Idempotent law)*

    (a)  $x + x = x$

    (b)  $x \cdot x = x$

*Proof of (a)*

    L.H.S.

    $= x + x$

    $= (x + x) \cdot 1$      by postulate 2(b)

    $= (x + x) \cdot (x + \overline{x})$      by postulate 6(a)

    $= x + x \cdot \overline{x}$      by postulate 5(b)

    $= x + 0$      by postulate 6(b)

    $= x$      by postulate 2(a)

    $= $ R.H.S.

*Proof of (b)*

    L.H.S.

    $= x \cdot x$

    $= x \cdot x + 0$      by postulate 2(a)

    $= x \cdot x + x \cdot \overline{x}$      by postulate 6(b)

    $= x \cdot (x + \overline{x})$      by postulate 5(a)

    $= x \cdot 1$      by postulate 6(a)

    $= x$      by postulate 2(b)

    $= $ R.H.S.

Note that Theorem 1(b) is the dual of Theorem 1(a), and each step of the proof in part (b) is the dual of part (a). Any dual theorem can be similarly derived from the proof of its corresponding pair. Hence, from now onwards, the proof of part (a) only will be given. Interested readers can apply the principle of duality to the various steps of the proof of part (a), to obtain the proof of part (b), for any theorem.

*Theorem 2*

    (a) $x + 1 = 1$

    (b) $x \cdot 0 = 0$

*Proof of (a)*

| | |
|---|---|
| L.H.S. | |
| $= x + 1$ | |
| $= (x + 1) \cdot 1$ | by postulate 2(b) |
| $= (x + 1) \cdot (x + \overline{x})$ | by postulate 6(a) |
| $= x + 1 \cdot \overline{x}$ | by postulate 5(b) |
| $= x + \overline{x} \cdot 1$ | by postulate 3(b) |
| $= x + \overline{x}$ | by postulate 2(b) |
| $= 1$ | by postulate 6(a) |
| $= R.H.S.$ | |

Proof of (b) holds by duality.

*Theorem 3 (Absorption law)*

    (a) $x + x \cdot y = x$

    (b) $x \cdot (x + y) = x$

*Proof of (a)*

| | |
|---|---|
| L.H.S. | |
| $= x + x \cdot y$ | |
| $= x \cdot 1 + x \cdot y$ | by postulate 2(b) |
| $= x \cdot (1 + y)$ | by postulate 5(a) |
| $= x \cdot (y + 1)$ | by postulate 3(a) |
| $= x \cdot 1$ | by theorem 2(a) |
| $= x$ | by postulate 2(b) |
| $= R.H.S.$ | |

Proof of (b) holds by duality.

## Proof by the Method of Perfect Induction

The theorems of Boolean algebra can also be proved by means of truth tables. In a truth table, both sides of the relation are checked, to yield identical results, for all possible combinations of variables involved. In principle, it is possible to enumerate all possible combinations of the variables involved, because Boolean algebra deals with variables, which can have only two values. This method of proving theorems is called *exhaustive enumeration* or *perfect induction*.

For example, Figure 6.5 is a truth table for proving Theorem 3(a) by the method of perfect induction. Similarly, Figure 6.6 proves Theorem 3(b) by the method of perfect induction.

| x | y | $x \cdot y$ | $x + x \cdot y$ |
|---|---|---|---|
| 0 | 0 | 0 | 0 |
| 0 | 1 | 0 | 0 |
| 1 | 0 | 0 | 1 |
| 1 | 1 | 1 | 1 |

**Figure 6.5.** Truth table for proving Theorem 3(a) by the method of perfect induction.

| x | y | $x + y$ | $x \cdot (x + y)$ |
|---|---|---|---|
| 0 | 0 | 0 | 0 |
| 0 | 1 | 1 | 0 |
| 1 | 0 | 1 | 1 |
| 1 | 1 | 1 | 1 |

**Figure 6.6.** Truth table for proving Theorem 3(b) by the method of perfect induction.

**Theorem 4** *(Involution Law)*

$$\overline{\overline{x}} = x$$

*Proof*

Figure 6.7 proves this theorem by the method of perfect induction.

| x | $\overline{x}$ | $\overline{\overline{x}}$ |
|---|---|---|
| 0 | 1 | 0 |
| 1 | 0 | 1 |

**Figure 6.7.** Truth table for proving Theorem 4 by the method of perfect induction.

Note that Theorem 4 has no dual, since it deals with the NOT operator, which is unary operator.

**Theorem 5**

(a) $x \cdot (\overline{x} + y) = x \cdot y$

(b) $x + \overline{x} \cdot y = x + y$

*Proof of (a)*

Figure 6.8 proves this theorem by the method of perfect induction.

| x | y | $\overline{x}$ | $\overline{x} + y$ | $x \cdot (\overline{x} + y)$ | $x \cdot y$ |
|---|---|---|---|---|---|
| 0 | 0 | 1 | 1 | 0 | 0 |
| 0 | 1 | 1 | 1 | 0 | 0 |
| 1 | 0 | 0 | 0 | 0 | 0 |
| 1 | 1 | 0 | 1 | 1 | 1 |

**Figure 6.8.** Truth table for proving Theorem 5(a) by the method of perfect induction.

*Proof of (b)*

Figure 6.9 proves this theorem by the method of perfect induction.

| x | y | $\overline{x}$ | $\overline{x} \cdot y$ | $x + \overline{x} \cdot y$ | $x + y$ |
|---|---|---|---|---|---|
| 0 | 0 | 1 | 0 | 0 | 0 |
| 0 | 1 | 1 | 1 | 1 | 1 |
| 1 | 0 | 0 | 0 | 1 | 1 |
| 1 | 1 | 0 | 0 | 1 | 1 |

**Figure 6.9.** Truth table for proving Theorem 5(b) by the method of perfect induction.

### Theorem 6 (De Morgan's Law)

(a) $\overline{x+y} = \overline{x} \cdot \overline{y}$

(b) $\overline{x \cdot y} = \overline{x} + \overline{y}$

*Proof of (a)*

Figure 6.10 proves this theorem by the method of perfect induction.

| x | y | x+y | $\overline{x+y}$ | $\overline{x}$ | $\overline{y}$ | $\overline{x} \cdot \overline{y}$ |
|---|---|-----|------|-----|-----|-------|
| 0 | 0 | 0 | 1 | 1 | 1 | 1 |
| 0 | 1 | 1 | 0 | 1 | 0 | 0 |
| 1 | 0 | 1 | 0 | 0 | 1 | 0 |
| 1 | 1 | 1 | 0 | 0 | 0 | 0 |

**Figure 6.10**. Truth table for proving Theorem 6(a) by the method of perfect induction.

*Proof of (b)*

Figure 6.11 proves this theorem by the method of perfect induction.

| x | y | x · y | $\overline{x \cdot y}$ | $\overline{x}$ | $\overline{y}$ | $\overline{x} + \overline{y}$ |
|---|---|-------|------|-----|-----|-------|
| 0 | 0 | 0 | 1 | 1 | 1 | 1 |
| 0 | 1 | 0 | 1 | 1 | 0 | 1 |
| 1 | 0 | 0 | 1 | 0 | 1 | 1 |
| 1 | 1 | 1 | 0 | 0 | 0 | 0 |

**Figure 6.11.** Truth table for proving Theorem 6(b) by the method of perfect induction.

Theorems 6(a) and 6(b) are important and very useful. They are known as De Morgan's law. They can be extended to *n* variables as given below:

$$\overline{X_1 + X_2 + X_3 + ... + X_n} = \overline{X_1} \cdot \overline{X_2} \cdot \overline{X_3} \cdot ... \cdot \overline{X_n}$$

$$\overline{X_1 \cdot X_2 \cdot X_3 \cdot ... \cdot X_n} = \overline{X_1} + \overline{X_2} + \overline{X_3} + ... + \overline{X_n}$$

The basic Boolean identities are summarized in Figure 6.12. It is suggested that the readers should become well conversant with the identities given in this table, to use the algebra effectively.

| Sr. No. | Identities | Dual identities |
|---------|-----------|-----------------|
| 1 | $A + 0 = A$ | $A \cdot 1 = A$ |
| 2 | $A + 1 = 1$ | $A \cdot 0 = 0$ |
| 3 | $A + A = A$ | $A \cdot A = A$ |
| 4 | $A + \overline{A} = 1$ | $A \cdot \overline{A} = 0$ |
| 5 | $\overline{\overline{A}} = A$ | |
| 6 | $A + B = B + A$ | $A \cdot B = B \cdot A$ |
| 7 | $(A + B) + C = A + (B + C)$ | $(A \cdot B) \cdot C = A \cdot (B \cdot C)$ |
| 8 | $A \cdot (B + C) = A \cdot B + A \cdot C$ | $A + B \cdot C = (A + B) \cdot (A + C)$ |
| 9 | $A + A \cdot B = A$ | $A \cdot (A + B) = A$ |
| 10 | $A + \overline{A} \cdot B = A + B$ | $A \cdot (\overline{A} + B) = A \cdot B$ |
| 11 | $\overline{A + B} = \overline{A} \cdot \overline{B}$ | $\overline{A \cdot B} = \overline{A} + \overline{B}$ |

**Figure 6.12.** Summary of basic Boolean identities.

# BOOLEAN FUNCTIONS

A Boolean function is an expression, which is formed with binary variables, the two binary operators OR and AND, the unary operator NOT, parentheses and equal sign. For a given value of the variables, the value of the function can be either 0 or 1. For example, consider the equation

$$W = X + \overline{Y} \cdot Z$$

Here, the variable W is a function of X, Y and Z. This is written as $W = f(X, Y, Z)$, and the right hand side of the equation is called an *expression*. The symbols X, Y and Z are referred to as *literals* of this function.

The above is an example of a Boolean function, represented as an algebraic expression. A Boolean function may also be represented in the form of a truth table. The number of rows in the table will be equal to $2^n$, where $n$ is the number of literals (binary variables) used in the function. The combinations of 0s and 1s for each row of this table are easily obtained from the binary numbers, by counting from 0 to $2^n - 1$. For each row of the table, there is a value for the function equal to either 0 or 1, which is listed in a separate column of the table. Such a truth table for the function $W = X + \overline{Y} \cdot Z$, is shown in Figure 6.13. Observe that, there are $(2^3)$ possible distinct combinations for assigning bits to three variables. The column labeled W is either a 0 or 1, for each of these combinations. The table shows that out of eight, there are five different combinations, for which $W = 1$.

| X | Y | Z | W |
|---|---|---|---|
| 0 | 0 | 0 | 0 |
| 0 | 0 | 1 | 1 |
| 0 | 1 | 0 | 0 |
| 0 | 1 | 1 | 0 |
| 1 | 0 | 0 | 1 |
| 1 | 0 | 1 | 1 |
| 1 | 1 | 0 | 1 |
| 1 | 1 | 1 | 1 |

**Figure 6.13.** Truth table for the Boolean function $W = X + \overline{Y} \cdot Z$.

The question now arises – is an algebraic expression for a given Boolean function unique? In other words, is it possible to find two algebraic expressions, which specify the same Boolean function? The answer is yes. Actually, the manipulation of Boolean algebra is applied mostly to the problem of finding simpler expressions, for a given expression. For example, let us consider the following two functions:

$$F_1 = \overline{x} \cdot \overline{y} \cdot z + \overline{x} \cdot y \cdot z + x \cdot \overline{y} \quad \text{and}$$

$$F_2 = x \cdot \overline{y} + \overline{x} \cdot z$$

The representation of these two functions in the form of truth table, is shown in Figure 6.14. From the table we find that the function $F_2$ is the same as the function $F_1$, since both have identical 0s and 1s, for each combination of values of the three binary variables x, y and z. In general, two functions of $n$ binary variables are said to be equal, if they have the same value, for all possible $2^n$ combinations of the $n$ literals.

| x | y | z | $F_1$ | $F_2$ |
|---|---|---|---|---|
| 0 | 0 | 0 | 0 | 0 |
| 0 | 0 | 1 | 1 | 1 |
| 0 | 1 | 0 | 0 | 0 |
| 0 | 1 | 1 | 1 | 1 |
| 1 | 0 | 0 | 1 | 1 |
| 1 | 0 | 1 | 1 | 1 |
| 1 | 1 | 0 | 0 | 0 |
| 1 | 1 | 1 | 0 | 0 |

**Figure 6.14.** Truth table for the Boolean functions:
$$F_1 = \overline{x} \cdot \overline{y} \cdot z + \overline{x} \cdot y \cdot z + x \cdot \overline{y} \quad \text{and} \quad F_2 = x \cdot \overline{y} + \overline{x} \cdot z$$

## Minimization of Boolean Functions

When a Boolean function is implemented with logic gates (discussed later in this chapter), each literal in the function designates an input to a gate, and each term is implemented with a gate. Hence, for a given Boolean function, the minimization of the number of literals, and the number of terms, will result in a circuit with less components. For example, since functions $F_1$ and $F_2$ of Figure 6.14 are equal Boolean functions, it is more economical to implement the $F_2$ form than the $F_1$ form, because the $F_2$ form contains fewer terms. To find simpler circuits, one must know how to manipulate Boolean functions, to obtain equal and simpler expressions. What constitutes the best form of Boolean function depends on the particular application. However, we will give consideration only to the criterion of component minimization, which is achieved by literal minimization.

There are several methods used for minimizing the number of literals in a Boolean function. However, a discussion of all these methods is beyond the scope of this book. Hence, here we will consider only the method of algebraic manipulations. Unfortunately, in this method, there are no specific rules or guidelines to be followed, which will guarantee the final answer. The only method available is cut-and-try procedure by employing the postulates, the basic theorems, and any other manipulation method, which becomes familiar with use. The following examples illustrate this procedure.

*Example 6.1.*

Simplify the following Boolean functions to a minimum number of literals.

(a) $x + \overline{x} \cdot y$

(b) $x \cdot (\overline{x} + y)$

(c) $\overline{x} \cdot \overline{y} \cdot z + \overline{x} \cdot y \cdot z + x \cdot \overline{y}$

(d) $x \cdot y + \overline{x} \cdot z + y \cdot z$

(e) $(x + y) \cdot (\overline{x} + z) \cdot (y + z)$

*Solution:*

(a) $x + \overline{x} \cdot y$

    $= (x + \overline{x}) \cdot (x + y)$                 by postulate 5(b)

    $= 1 \cdot (x + y)$                     by postulate 6(a)

    $= (x + y) \cdot 1$                    by postulate 3(b)

    $= x + y$                        by postulate 2(b)

(b) $x \cdot (\overline{x} + y)$

    $= x \cdot \overline{x} + x \cdot y$                by postulate 5(a)

    $= 0 + x \cdot y$                  by postulate 6(b)

    $= x \cdot y + 0$                  by postulate 3(a)

    $= x \cdot y$                      by postulate 2(a)

(c) $\overline{x} \cdot \overline{y} \cdot z + \overline{x} \cdot y \cdot z + x \cdot \overline{y}$

    $= \overline{x} \cdot z \cdot (\overline{y} + y) + x \cdot \overline{y}$        by postulate 5(a)

    $= \overline{x} \cdot z \cdot (y + \overline{y}) + x \cdot \overline{y}$        by postulate 3(a)

    $= \overline{x} \cdot z \cdot 1 + x \cdot \overline{y}$           by postulate 6(a)

    $= \overline{x} \cdot z + x \cdot \overline{y}$              by postulate 2(b)

(d) $x \cdot y + \overline{x} \cdot z + y \cdot z$

    $= x \cdot y + \overline{x} \cdot z + y \cdot z \cdot 1$       by postulate 2(b)

    $= x \cdot y + \overline{x} \cdot z + y \cdot z \cdot (x + \overline{x})$    by postulate 6(a)

    $= x \cdot y + \overline{x} \cdot z + y \cdot z \cdot x + y \cdot z \cdot \overline{x}$   by postulate 5(a)

    $= x \cdot y + \overline{x} \cdot z + x \cdot y \cdot z + \overline{x} \cdot y \cdot z$   by postulate 3(b)

    $= x \cdot y \cdot 1 + \overline{x} \cdot z + x \cdot y \cdot z + \overline{x} \cdot y \cdot z$   by postulate 2(b)

    $= x \cdot y \cdot 1 + x \cdot y \cdot z + \overline{x} \cdot z + \overline{x} \cdot y \cdot z$   by postulate 3(a)

    $= x \cdot y \cdot (1 + z) + \overline{x} \cdot z \cdot (1 + y)$    by postulate 5(a)

    $= x \cdot y \cdot (z + 1) + \overline{x} \cdot z \cdot (y + 1)$    by postulate 3(a)

    $= x \cdot y \cdot 1 + \overline{x} \cdot z \cdot 1$         by theorem 2(a)

    $= x \cdot y + \overline{x} \cdot z$             by postulate 2(b)

(e) $(x + y) \cdot (\overline{x} + z) \cdot (y + z)$

    $= (x + y) \cdot (\overline{x} + z)$           by duality from (d)

Note that, in Example 6.1, functions (a) and (b) are the dual of each other, and use dual expressions in corresponding minimization steps. Function (c) shows the equality of the functions $F_1$ and $F_2$ of Figure 6.14. Function (d) illustrates the fact that an increase in the number of literals, sometimes leads to a final simpler expression. Observe that, function (e) is the dual of function (d). Hence, it is not minimized directly, and can be easily derived from the dual of the steps used to derive function (d).

# Complement of a Function

The complement of a Boolean function F is $\overline{F}$, and is obtained by interchanging 0s for 1s and 1s for 0s in the truth table, which defines the function. For example, Figure 6.15 defines the function $F = x \cdot \overline{y} + \overline{x} \cdot z$ and its complement $\overline{F}$.

| x | y | z | F | $\overline{F}$ |
|---|---|---|---|---|
| 0 | 0 | 0 | 0 | 1 |
| 0 | 0 | 1 | 1 | 0 |
| 0 | 1 | 0 | 0 | 1 |
| 0 | 1 | 1 | 1 | 0 |
| 1 | 0 | 0 | 1 | 0 |
| 1 | 0 | 1 | 1 | 0 |
| 1 | 1 | 0 | 0 | 1 |
| 1 | 1 | 1 | 0 | 1 |

**Figure 6.15.** Truth table for the function $F = x \cdot \overline{y} + \overline{x} \cdot z$ and its complement $\overline{F}$.

Algebraically, the complement of a function may be derived from De Morgan's theorems, whose generalized forms are as follows:

$$\overline{A_1 + A_2 + A_3 + ... + A_n} = \overline{A_1} \cdot \overline{A_2} \cdot \overline{A_3} \cdot ... \cdot \overline{A_n}$$

$$\overline{A_1 \cdot A_2 \cdot A_3 \cdot ... \cdot A_n} = \overline{A_1} + \overline{A_2} + \overline{A_3} + ... + \overline{A_n}$$

These theorems state that the complement of a function is obtained by interchanging the OR and the AND operators, and complementing each literal. The method is illustrated below with an example.

*Example 6.2.*

Find the complement of the following functions:

(a) $F_1 = \overline{x} \cdot y \cdot \overline{z} + \overline{x} \cdot \overline{y} \cdot z$

(b) $F_2 = x \cdot (\overline{y} \cdot \overline{z} + y \cdot z)$

*Solution:*

Applying De Morgan's theorems as many times as necessary, the complements are obtained as follows:

(a) $\overline{F_1} = \overline{\overline{x} \cdot y \cdot \overline{z} + \overline{x} \cdot \overline{y} \cdot z}$

$= \left(\overline{\overline{x} \cdot y \cdot \overline{z}}\right) \cdot \left(\overline{\overline{x} \cdot \overline{y} \cdot z}\right)$

$= \left(\overline{\overline{x}} + \overline{y} + \overline{\overline{z}}\right) \cdot \left(\overline{\overline{x}} + \overline{\overline{y}} + \overline{z}\right)$

$= \left(x + \overline{y} + z\right) \cdot \left(x + y + \overline{z}\right)$

(b) $\overline{F_2} = \overline{x \cdot (\overline{y} \cdot \overline{z} + y \cdot z)}$

$= \overline{x} + \left(\overline{\overline{y} \cdot \overline{z} + y \cdot z}\right)$

$= \overline{x} + \left(\overline{\overline{y} \cdot \overline{z}}\right) \cdot \left(\overline{y \cdot z}\right)$

$= \overline{x} + \left(\overline{\overline{y}} + \overline{\overline{z}}\right) \cdot \left(\overline{y} + \overline{z}\right)$

$= \overline{x} + (y + z) \cdot \left(\overline{y} + \overline{z}\right)$

A simpler procedure for deriving the complement of a function is to take the dual of the function, and then complement each literal. This method follows from the generalized De Morgan's theorems. Remember that the dual of a function is obtained by interchanging OR and AND operators, and 0s and 1s. The method is illustrated below with an example.

*Example 6.3.*

Find the complement of the functions $F_1$ and $F_2$ of Example 6.2 by taking their dual, and complementing each literal.

*Solution:*

(a) $F_1 = \overline{x} \cdot y \cdot \overline{z} + \overline{x} \cdot \overline{y} \cdot z$

The dual of $F_1$ is: $(\overline{x} + y + \overline{z}) \cdot (\overline{x} + \overline{y} + z)$

Complementing each literal, we get

$\overline{F_1} = (x + \overline{y} + z) \cdot (x + y + \overline{z})$

(b) $F_2 = x \cdot (\overline{y} \cdot \overline{z} + y \cdot z)$

The dual of $F_2$ is: $x + (\overline{y} + \overline{z}) \cdot (y + z)$

Complementing each literal we get

$\overline{F_2} = \overline{x} + (y + z) \cdot (\overline{y} + \overline{z})$

# Canonical Forms for Boolean Functions

## Minterms and Maxterms

A binary variable may appear either in its normal form $(x)$, or in its complement form $(\overline{x})$. Now, consider two binary variables, x and y, combined with an AND operator. Since, each variable may appear in either form, there are four possible combinations:

$$\overline{x} \cdot \overline{y}, \qquad \overline{x} \cdot y, \qquad x \cdot \overline{y}, \qquad x \cdot y \qquad$$ Each of these four AND terms is called a *minterm* or a *standard product*.

In a similar manner, $n$ variables can be combined to form $2^n$ minterms. The $2^n$ different minterms may be determined by a method similar to the one shown in Figure 6.16 for three variables. The binary numbers from 0 to $2^n - 1$ are listed under the $n$ variables. Each minterm is obtained from an AND term of the $n$ variables, with each variable being primed, if the corresponding bit of the binary number is 0, and unprimed, if it is a 1.

| Variables | | | Minterms | | Maxterms | |
|---|---|---|---|---|---|---|
| **x** | **y** | **z** | **Term** | **Designation** | **Term** | **Designation** |
| 0 | 0 | 0 | $\overline{x} \cdot \overline{y} \cdot \overline{z}$ | $m_0$ | $x + y + z$ | $M_0$ |
| 0 | 0 | 1 | $\overline{x} \cdot \overline{y} \cdot z$ | $m_1$ | $x + y + \overline{z}$ | $M_1$ |
| 0 | 1 | 0 | $\overline{x} \cdot y \cdot \overline{z}$ | $m_2$ | $x + \overline{y} + z$ | $M_2$ |
| 0 | 1 | 1 | $\overline{x} \cdot y \cdot z$ | $m_3$ | $x + \overline{y} + \overline{z}$ | $M_3$ |
| 1 | 0 | 0 | $x \cdot \overline{y} \cdot \overline{z}$ | $m_4$ | $\overline{x} + y + z$ | $M_4$ |
| 1 | 0 | 1 | $x \cdot \overline{y} \cdot z$ | $m_5$ | $\overline{x} + y + \overline{z}$ | $M_5$ |
| 1 | 1 | 0 | $x \cdot y \cdot \overline{z}$ | $m_6$ | $\overline{x} + \overline{y} + z$ | $M_6$ |
| 1 | 1 | 1 | $x \cdot y \cdot z$ | $m_7$ | $\overline{x} + \overline{y} + \overline{z}$ | $M_7$ |

**Figure 6.16.** Minterms and Maxterms for three variables.

A symbol for each minterm is also shown in the figure, and is of the form $m_j$, where $j$ denotes the decimal equivalent of the binary number of the minterm designated.

Similarly, $n$ variables forming an OR term, with each variable being primed or unprimed, provide $2^n$ possible combinations called *maxterms* or *standard sums*.

The eight maxterms for three variables, together with their symbolic designation, are shown in Figure 6.16. Any $2^n$ maxterms for $n$ variables may be determined similarly. Each maxterm is obtained from an OR term of the $n$ variables, with each variable being unprimed, if the corresponding bit is a 0, and primed, if it is a 1.

Note that, each maxterm is the complement of its corresponding minterm, and vice-versa.

## Sum-of-Products

A sum-of-products expression is a product term (minterm), or several product terms (minterms), logically added (ORed) together. For example, the expression $x \cdot \overline{y} + \overline{x} \cdot y$ is a sum-of-products expression. The following are all sum-of-products expressions:

$x$

$x + y$

$x + y \cdot z$

$x \cdot y + z$

$\overline{x} \cdot \overline{y} + x \cdot \overline{y} \cdot \overline{z}$

The following steps are followed to express a Boolean function in its sum-of-products form:

1. Construct a truth table for the given Boolean function.

2. Form a minterm for each combination of the variables, which produces a 1 in the function.

3. The desired expression is the sum (OR) of all the minterms obtained in Step 2.

For example, in case of function $F_1$ of Figure 6.17, the following three combinations of the variables produce a 1:

001,   100,   and   111

Their corresponding minterms are

$\overline{x} \cdot \overline{y} \cdot z$,   $x \cdot \overline{y} \cdot \overline{z}$,   and   $x \cdot y \cdot z$

Taking the sum (OR) of all these minterms, the function $F_1$ can be expressed in its sum-of-products form as:

$F_1 = \overline{x} \cdot \overline{y} \cdot z + x \cdot \overline{y} \cdot \overline{z} + x \cdot y \cdot z$   or

$F_1 = m_1 + m_4 + m_7$

Similarly, the function $F_2$ of Figure 6.17 can be expressed in its sum-of-products form as:

$F_2 = \overline{x} \cdot y \cdot z + x \cdot \overline{y} \cdot z + x \cdot y \cdot \overline{z} + x \cdot y \cdot z$   or

$F_2 = m_3 + m_5 + m_6 + m_7$

| x | y | z | $F_1$ | $F_2$ |
|---|---|---|---|---|
| 0 | 0 | 0 | 0 | 0 |
| 0 | 0 | 1 | 1 | 0 |
| 0 | 1 | 0 | 0 | 0 |
| 0 | 1 | 1 | 0 | 1 |
| 1 | 0 | 0 | 1 | 0 |
| 1 | 0 | 1 | 0 | 1 |
| 1 | 1 | 0 | 0 | 1 |
| 1 | 1 | 1 | 1 | 1 |

**Figure 6.17.** Truth table for functions $F_1$ and $F_2$.

It is sometimes convenient to express a Boolean function in its sum-of-products form. If it is not in this form, it can be converted into this form by first expanding the expression into a sum of AND terms. Each term is then inspected to see if it contains all the variables. If it misses one or more variables, it is ANDed with an expression of the form $(x + \overline{x})$, where x is one of the missing variables. The following example clarifies this procedure.

*Example 6.4.*

Express the Boolean function $F = A + \overline{B} \cdot C$ in the sum-of-minterms (products) form.

*Solution:*

The function has three variables A, B and C. The first term A is missing two variables, therefore,

$$A = A \cdot (B + \overline{B})$$
$$= A \cdot B + A \cdot \overline{B}$$

This is still missing one variable, therefore,

$$A = A \cdot B \cdot (C + \overline{C}) + A \cdot \overline{B} \cdot (C + \overline{C})$$
$$= A \cdot B \cdot C + A \cdot B \cdot \overline{C} + A \cdot \overline{B} \cdot C + A \cdot \overline{B} \cdot \overline{C}$$

The second term $\overline{B} \cdot C$ is missing one variable, therefore,

$$\overline{B} \cdot C = \overline{B} \cdot C \cdot (A + \overline{A})$$
$$= A \cdot \overline{B} \cdot C + \overline{A} \cdot \overline{B} \cdot C$$

Hence, by combining all the terms we get
$$F = A \cdot B \cdot C + A \cdot B \cdot \overline{C} + A \cdot \overline{B} \cdot C + A \cdot \overline{B} \cdot \overline{C} + A \cdot \overline{B} \cdot C + \overline{A} \cdot \overline{B} \cdot C$$

However, in the above expression, the term $A \cdot \overline{B} \cdot C$ appears twice, and according to Theorem 1(a), we have $x + x = x$. Hence, removing one of them, and rearranging the minterms in ascending order, we obtain:

$$F = \overline{A} \cdot \overline{B} \cdot C + A \cdot \overline{B} \cdot \overline{C} + A \cdot \overline{B} \cdot C + A \cdot B \cdot \overline{C} + A \cdot B \cdot C$$

$$= m_1 + m_4 + m_5 + m_6 + m_7$$

It is sometimes convenient to express the Boolean function, when in its sum-of-minterms, in the following short notation:

$$F(A, B, C) = \sum (1, 4, 5, 6, 7)$$

The summation symbol '$\sum$' stands for the ORing of terms. The numbers following it are the minterms of the function. Finally, the letters in parentheses with F form a list of the variables in the order taken, when the minterm is converted to an AND term.

## Product-of-Sums

A product-of-sums expression is a sum term (maxterm), or several sum terms (maxterms), logically multiplied (ANDed) together. For example, the expression $(\overline{x} + y) \cdot (x + \overline{y})$ is a product of sums expression. The following are all product-of-sums expressions:

x

$(\overline{x} + y)$

$(\overline{x} + \overline{y}) \cdot z$

$(x + \overline{y}) \cdot (\overline{x} + y) \cdot (\overline{x} + \overline{y})$

$(x + y) \cdot (\overline{x} + y + z)$

The following steps are followed to express a Boolean function in its product-of-sums form:

1. Construct a truth table for the given Boolean function.

2. Form a maxterm for each combination of the variables, which produce a 0 in the function.

3. The desired expression is the product (AND) of all the maxterms obtained in Step 2.

For example in case of function $F_1$ of Figure 6.17, the following five combinations of the variables produce a 0:

000, 010, 011, 101, and 110

Their corresponding maxterms are:

$(x + y + z), (x + \overline{y} + z), (x + \overline{y} + \overline{z}), (\overline{x} + y + \overline{z})$, and $(\overline{x} + \overline{y} + z)$

Taking the product (AND) of all these maxterms, the function $F_1$ can be expressed in its product-of-sums form as:

$$F_1 = (x + y + z) \cdot (x + \overline{y} + z) \cdot (x + \overline{y} + \overline{z}) \cdot (\overline{x} + y + \overline{z}) \cdot (\overline{x} + \overline{y} + z) \quad \text{or}$$

$$F_1 = M_0 \cdot M_2 \cdot M_3 \cdot M_5 \cdot M_6$$

Similarly, the function $F_2$ of Figure 6.17 can be expressed in its product-of-sums form as:

$$F_2 = (x + y + z) \cdot (x + y + \overline{z}) \cdot (x + \overline{y} + z) \cdot (\overline{x} + y + z) \quad \text{or}$$

$$F_2 = M_0 \cdot M_1 \cdot M_2 \cdot M_4$$

To express a Boolean function in its product-of-sums form, it must first be brought into a form of OR terms. This may be done by using the distributive law:

$$x + y \cdot z = (x + y) \cdot (x + z)$$

Then any missing variable (say x) in each OR term is ORed with the form $x \cdot \overline{x}$. This procedure is explained with the following example.

*Example 6.5.*

Express the Boolean function $F = x \cdot y + \overline{x} \cdot z$ in the product-of-maxterms (sums) form.

*Solution:*

At first, we convert the function into OR terms by using the distributive law:

$F = x \cdot y + \overline{x} \cdot z$

$= (x \cdot y + \overline{x}) \cdot (x \cdot y + z)$

$= (x + \overline{x}) \cdot (y + \overline{x}) \cdot (x + z) \cdot (y + z)$

$= (\overline{x} + y) \cdot (x + z) \cdot (y + z)$

The function has three variables x, y and z. Each OR term is missing one variable, therefore,

$\overline{x} + y = \overline{x} + y + z \cdot \overline{z} = (\overline{x} + y + z) \cdot (\overline{x} + y + \overline{z})$

$x + z = x + z + y \cdot \overline{y} = (x + z + y) \cdot (x + z + \overline{y}) = (x + y + z) \cdot (x + \overline{y} + z)$

$y + z = x \cdot \overline{x} + y + z = (x + y + z) \cdot (\overline{x} + y + z)$

Combining all the terms, and removing those, which appear more than once, we obtain:

$F = (x + y + z) \cdot (x + \overline{y} + z) \cdot (\overline{x} + y + z) \cdot (\overline{x} + y + \overline{z})$

$= M_0 \cdot M_2 \cdot M_4 \cdot M_5$

A convenient way to express this function is as follows:

$F(x, y, z) = \prod (0, 2, 4, 5)$

The product symbol $\prod$ denotes the ANDing of maxterms. The numbers following it are the maxterms of the function.

The sum-of-products and the product-of-sums forms of Boolean expressions are known as *standard forms*. One prime reason for liking the sum-of-products or the product-of-sums expressions is their straightforward conversion to very nice gating networks, which are more desirable from most implementation points of view. In their purest, nicest form, they go into two-level networks, which are networks, for which the longest path through which the signal must pass from input to output is two gates.

# Conversion Between Canonical Forms

The complement of a function, expressed as the sum-of-minterms, equals the sum-of-minterms missing from the original function. This is because the original function is expressed by those minterms, which make the function equal to 1, while its complement is a 1 for those minterms, for which the function is a 0. For example, the function

$F(A, B, C) = \sum (1, 4, 5, 6, 7) = m_1 + m_4 + m_5 + m_6 + m_7$

has a complement, which can be expressed as:

$\overline{F}(A, B, C) = \sum (0, 2, 3) = m_0 + m_2 + m_3$

Taking the complement of $\overline{F}$ by De Morgan's theorem, we obtain F back in a different form:

$$F = \overline{m_0 + m_2 + m_3}$$
$$= \overline{m}_0 \cdot \overline{m}_2 \cdot \overline{m}_3$$
$$= M_0 \cdot M_2 \cdot M_3$$
$$= \Pi\,(0, 2, 3)$$

The last conversion follows from the definition of minterms and maxterms as shown in Figure 6.16. From the figure, it is clear that the following relation holds true:

$$\overline{m}_j = M_j$$

That is, the maxterm with subscript $j$ is a complement of the minterm with the same subscript $j$, and vice-versa.

The last example has demonstrated the conversion of a function, expressed in sum-of-minterms, to its equivalent function in product-of-maxterms. The conversion between the product-of-maxterms and the sum-of-minterms is similar. We now state a general conversion procedure:

> "To convert from one canonical form to another, interchange the
> symbol, and list those numbers missing from the original form."

For example, the function

$$F\,(x, y, z) = \Pi\,(0, 2, 4, 5)$$

is expressed in the product-of-maxterms form. Its conversion to sum-of-minterms is:

$$F\,(x, y, z) = \Sigma\,(1, 3, 6, 7)$$

To find the missing terms, one must note that the total number of minterms or maxterms is always $2^n$, where n is the number of binary variables in the function.

# LOGIC GATES

All operations within a computer are carried out by means of combinations of signals passing through standard blocks of built-in circuits, which are known as logic gates. In other words, a *logic gate* is an electronic circuit, which operates on one or more input signals, to produce standard output signals. These logic gates are the building blocks of all the circuits in a computer.

Computer circuits are built up using combinations of different types of logic gates to perform the necessary operation. There are several types of gates, but we shall consider here only some of the most important ones. These are sufficient to introduce the concept of circuit design by using logic gates.

## AND Gate

An AND gate is the physical realization of the logical multiplication (AND) operation. It is an electronic circuit, which generates an output signal of 1, only if all input signals are also 1.

To have a conceptual idea, let us consider the case of Figure 6.18. Here, two switches A and B are connected in series. It is obvious that the input current will reach the output point, only when both the switches are in the on(1) state. There will be no output (output = 0), if either one or both the switches are in the off(0) state. Hence, two or more switches connected in series behave as an AND gate.

**Figure 6.18.** Two or more switches connected in series behave as an AND gate.

The behaviour of a logic gate, that is, the state of its output signal, depending on the various combinations of input signals, is conveniently represented by means of a truth table. The truth table and the block diagram symbol for an AND gate, for two input signals, are shown in Figure 6.19. Since there are only two inputs (A and B), only four ($2^2$) combinations of inputs are possible. Also observe from the truth table that an output of 1 is obtained, only when both the inputs are in 1 state, otherwise it is 0.

| Inputs | | Output |
|---|---|---|
| A | B | C = A · B |
| 0 | 0 | 0 |
| 0 | 1 | 0 |
| 1 | 0 | 0 |
| 1 | 1 | 1 |

**Figure 6.19.** Block diagram symbol and truth table for an AND gate.

# OR Gate

An OR gate is the physical realization of the logical addition (OR) operation. It is an electronic circuit, which generates an output signal of 1, if any of the input signals is also 1.

Two or more switches connected in parallel behave as an OR gate. It can be seen from Figure 6.20 that the input current will reach the output point, when any one of the two switches are in the on(1) state. There will be no output, only when both the switches (A and B) are in the off(0) state.

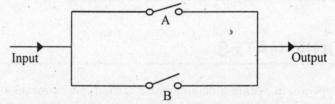

**Figure 6.20.** Two or more switches connected in parallel behave as an OR gate.

The truth table and the block diagram symbol for an OR gate, for two input signals, are shown in Figure 6.21. Observe that, an output of 1 is obtained, when any of the input signals is 1. It is 0, only when both the inputs are 0.

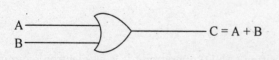

| Inputs | | Output |
|---|---|---|
| A | B | C = A + B |
| 0 | 0 | 0 |
| 0 | 1 | 1 |
| 1 | 0 | 1 |
| 1 | 1 | 1 |

**Figure 6.21.** Block diagram symbol and truth table for an OR gate.

Just as the + and · operations could be extended to several variables by using the associative law, AND gates and OR gates can have more than two inputs. Figure 6.22 shows three input AND and OR gates, and the table of all input combinations for each. As expected, the output of the AND gate with inputs A, B and C is a 1, only if A and B and C are 1, i.e., when all three of the inputs are 1, so that, we write the output as A · B · C. Similarly, the OR gate with inputs A, B, and C has a 1 output, if A or B or C is a 1, so that, we can write A + B + C for its output.

The above argument can be extended. A four-input AND gate has a 1 output, only when all four inputs are 1, and a four-input OR gate has a 1 output, when any of its inputs is a 1.

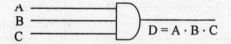

| Inputs | | | Output |
|---|---|---|---|
| A | B | C | D = A · B · C |
| 0 | 0 | 0 | 0 |
| 0 | 0 | 1 | 0 |
| 0 | 1 | 0 | 0 |
| 0 | 1 | 1 | 0 |
| 1 | 0 | 0 | 0 |
| 1 | 0 | 1 | 0 |
| 1 | 1 | 0 | 0 |
| 1 | 1 | 1 | 1 |

(a) Three input AND gate.

| Inputs | | | Output |
|---|---|---|---|
| A | B | C | D = A + B + C |
| 0 | 0 | 0 | 0 |
| 0 | 0 | 1 | 1 |
| 0 | 1 | 0 | 1 |
| 0 | 1 | 1 | 1 |
| 1 | 0 | 0 | 1 |
| 1 | 0 | 1 | 1 |
| 1 | 1 | 0 | 1 |
| 1 | 1 | 1 | 1 |

(b) Three input OR gate.

**Figure 6.22.** Block diagram symbol and truth table for (a) Three input AND gate and (b) Three input OR gate.

# NOT Gate

A NOT gate is the physical realization of the complementation operation. It is an electronic circuit, which generates an output signal, which is the reverse of the input signal. A NOT gate is also known as an *inverter* because it inverts the input.

The truth table and the block diagram symbol for a NOT gate are shown in Figure 6.23. Recall that the complementation operation is unary operation, which is defined on a single variable. Hence, a NOT gate always has a single input. Figure 6.23 also shows that connecting two NOT gates in series gives an output equal to the input, and this is the gating counterpart to the law of the double complementation, $\overline{\overline{A}} = A$.

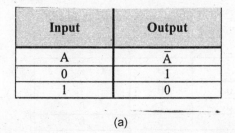

| Input | Output |
|---|---|
| A | $\overline{A}$ |
| 0 | 1 |
| 1 | 0 |

(a)

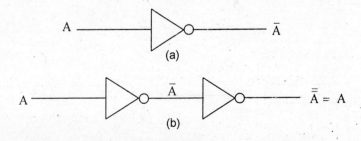

**Figure 6.23.** (a) Block diagram symbol and truth table for NOT gate, and (b) Two NOT gates in series.

## NAND Gate

A NAND gate is a complemented AND gate. That is, the output of NAND gate will be a 1, if any one of the inputs is a 0, and will be a 0, only when all the inputs are 1.

The truth table and the block diagram symbol for a NAND gate are shown in Figure 6.24. The symbol '↑' is usually used to represent a NAND operation in Boolean expressions. Hence, $A \uparrow B = \overline{A \cdot B} = \overline{A} + \overline{B}$.

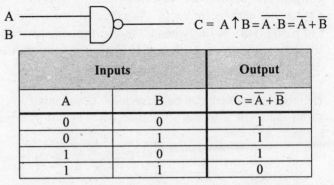

$$C = A \uparrow B = \overline{A \cdot B} = \overline{A} + \overline{B}$$

| Inputs | | Output |
|---|---|---|
| A | B | $C = \overline{A} + \overline{B}$ |
| 0 | 0 | 1 |
| 0 | 1 | 1 |
| 1 | 0 | 1 |
| 1 | 1 | 0 |

**Figure 6.24.** Block diagram symbol and truth table for a NAND gate.

The operation of a NAND gate can be analysed by using the equivalent block diagram circuit shown in Figure 6.25, which has an AND gate followed by a NOT gate . For inputs A and B, the output of the AND gate will be $A \cdot B$, which is fed as input to the NOT gate. Hence, the complement of $A \cdot B$ will be $\overline{A \cdot B}$, which is equal to $\overline{A} + \overline{B}$ or $A \uparrow B$. In fact, the small circle on the output of the NAND gate (see Figure 6.24) represents complementation. The NAND gate can then be seen to be an AND gate, followed by a NOT gate.

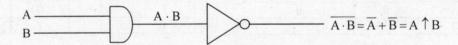

$$\overline{A \cdot B} = \overline{A} + \overline{B} = A \uparrow B$$

**Figure 6.25.** NAND gate realization with an AND gate and a NOT gate.

Multiple-input NAND gates can be analyzed similarly. A three-input NAND gate, with inputs A, B, and C, will have an output equal to $\overline{A \cdot B \cdot C}$ or $\overline{A} + \overline{B} + \overline{C}$, which says that the output will be a 1, if any of the inputs is a 0, and will be a 0, only when all three inputs are 1.

## NOR Gate

A NOR gate is a complemented OR gate. That is, the output of a NOR gate will be a 1, only when all inputs are 0, and it will be a 0, if any input is a 1.

The truth table and the block diagram symbol for a NOR gate are shown in Figure 6.26. The symbol '↓' is usually used to represent a NOR operation in Boolean expressions. Hence, $A \downarrow B = \overline{A + B} = \overline{A} \cdot \overline{B}$.

$$C = A \downarrow B = \overline{A + B} = \overline{A} \cdot \overline{B}$$

| Inputs | | Output |
|---|---|---|
| A | B | $C = \overline{A} \cdot \overline{B}$ |
| 0 | 0 | 1 |
| 0 | 1 | 0 |
| 1 | 0 | 0 |
| 1 | 1 | 0 |

**Figure 6.26.** Block diagram symbol and truth table for a NOR gate.

The operation of a NOR gate can be analyzed by using the equivalent block diagram circuit shown in Figure 6.27, which has an OR gate, followed by a NOT gate. For inputs A and B, the output of the OR gate will be $A+B$, which is fed as input to the NOT gate. Hence, the complement of $A+B$ will be $\overline{A+B}$, which is equal to $\overline{A}\cdot\overline{B}$ or $A\downarrow B$. In fact, the small circle on the output of the NOR gate (see Figure 6.26) represents complementation. The NOR gate can then be seen to be an OR gate, followed by a NOT gate.

Multiple input NOR gates can be analyzed similarly. A three-input NOR gate, with inputs A, B, and C, will have an output equal to $\overline{A+B+C}$ or $\overline{A}\cdot\overline{B}\cdot\overline{C}$, which says that the output will be a 1, only when all the three inputs are 0, and it will be a 0, if any of the three inputs is a 1.

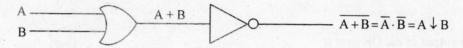

**Figure 6.27.** NOR gate realization with an OR gate and a NOT gate.

# LOGIC CIRCUITS

The logic gates, described in the previous section, are seldom used alone, but are used in combinations. They are interconnected to form gating/logic networks, which are known as *combinational logic circuits*. For these logic circuits, the Boolean algebra expression can be derived by systematically progressing from input to output on the gates. Few examples are given below.

*Example 6.6.*

Find the Boolean expression for the output of the logic circuit given below.

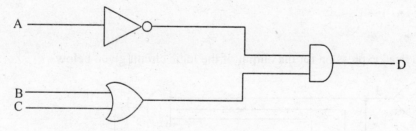

*Solution:*

Input A is fed to the NOT gate, whose output will be $\overline{A}$.

Inputs B and C are fed to the OR gate, whose output will be B + C.

Now, these two outputs ($\overline{A}$ and B + C) are fed as input to the AND gate. The output produced by the AND gate will be $\overline{A}\cdot(B+C)$.

Hence, D = $\overline{A}\cdot(B+C)$, which is the required Boolean expression for the output of the given logic circuit.

## Example 6.7.

Find the logic expression for the output produced by the logic circuit given below.

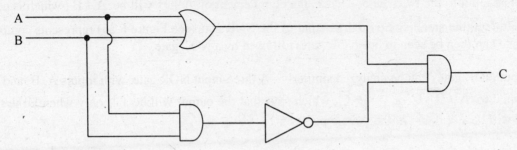

*Solution:*

The output of the OR gate is

$$A + B \qquad \text{------------} \qquad (a)$$

The output of the first AND gate is

$$A \cdot B \qquad \text{------------} \qquad (b)$$

Since, expression (b) is fed as input to the NOT gate, the output of the NOT gate is

$$\overline{A \cdot B} \qquad \text{------------} \qquad (c)$$

Now, expressions (a) and (c) are fed as input to the second AND gate, whose output will be

$$(A + B) \cdot \left( \overline{A \cdot B} \right)$$

Hence, $C = (A + B) \cdot \left( \overline{A \cdot B} \right)$, which is the desired logic expression for the output produced by the given logic circuit.

## Example 6.8.

Find the Boolean expression for the output of the logic circuit given below.

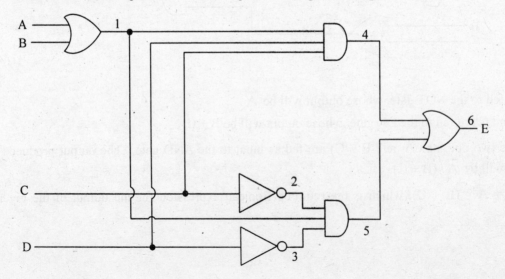

*Solution:*

At point 1, the output of the OR gate is

$A + B$              ------------     (a)

At point 2, the output of the NOT gate is

$\overline{C}$              ------------     (b)

At point 3, the output of the NOT gate is

$\overline{D}$              ------------     (c)

The inputs to the AND gate at point 4 are $(A + B)$, C, and D. Hence, at point 4, the output of the AND gate is

$(A + B) \cdot C \cdot D$              ------------     (d)

The inputs to the AND gate at point 5 are $(A + B)$, $\overline{C}$, and $\overline{D}$. Hence, at point 5, the output of the AND gate is

$(A + B) \cdot \overline{C} \cdot \overline{D}$              ------------     (e)

Finally, the inputs to the OR gate at point 6 are (d) and (e). Hence, at point 6, the output of the OR gate is

$$(A+B) \cdot C \cdot D + (A+B) \cdot \overline{C} \cdot \overline{D}$$

Hence, $E = (A+B) \cdot C \cdot D + (A+B) \cdot \overline{C} \cdot \overline{D}$,

which is the required Boolean expression for the output of the given logic circuit.

## Converting Expressions to Logic Circuits

We just now saw few examples, which illustrate the method of deriving Boolean expression for a given logic circuit. The reverse problem of constructing a logic circuit for a given Boolean expression is also not difficult. The three logic gates – AND, OR, and NOT are said to be logically complete, because any Boolean expression may be realized using only these three gates. The method of constructing logic circuits for Boolean expressions, by using only these three gates, is illustrated below with the help a few examples.

***Example 6.9.***

Construct a logic circuit for the Boolean expression $A \cdot B + C$.

*Solution:*

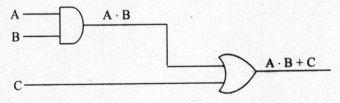

The desired logic circuit is shown above, which is self-explanatory.

*Example 6.10.*

Construct a logic circuit for the Boolean expression $\overline{A \cdot B} + C \cdot D + \overline{E \cdot F}$.

*Solution:*

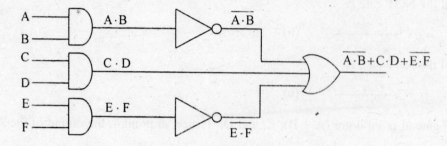

The desired logic circuit is shown above, which is self-explanatory.

*Example 6.11.*

Construct a logic circuit for the Boolean expression $(\overline{x} + y) \cdot (x + z) \cdot (y + z)$.

*Solution:*

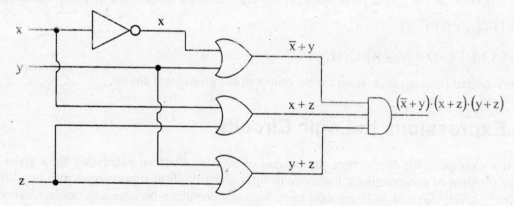

The desired logic circuit is shown above, which is self-explanatory.

*Example 6.12.*

Construct a logic circuit for the Boolean expression $(x + y + z) \cdot (x + \overline{y}) \cdot (\overline{x} + \overline{y})$

*Solution:*

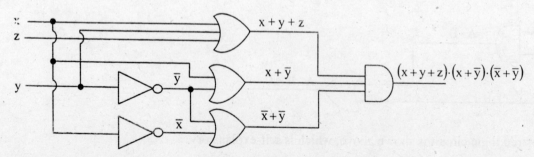

The desired logic circuit is shown above, which is self-explanatory.

# The Universal NAND Gate

We have seen that AND, OR, and NOT gates are logically complete, because any Boolean expression may be realized by using these three gates. However, the NAND gate, which was introduced in the previous section, is said to be an universal gate, because it is alone sufficient to implement any Boolean expression.

To show that any Boolean expression can be implemented with only NAND gates, we need to only show that the logical operations AND, OR, and NOT can be implemented with NAND gates. This is shown in Figure 6.28.

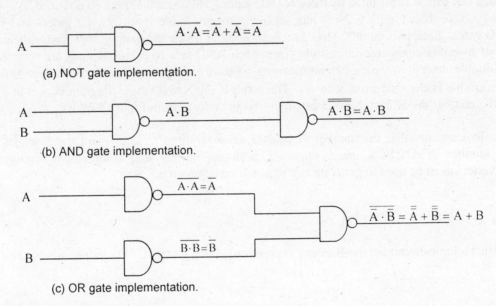

(a) NOT gate implementation.

(b) AND gate implementation.

(c) OR gate implementation.

**Figure 6.28.** Implementation of NOT, AND, and OR gates by NAND gates.

A NOT operation is obtained from a single-input NAND gate, which behaves as an inverter.

The AND operation requires two NAND gates. The first one produces the inverted AND, and the second one, being a single-input NAND gate, acts as an inverter, to obtain the normal AND output.

For the OR operation, the normal inputs A and B are first complemented by using two single-input NAND gates. The complemented variables are then fed to another NAND gate, which produces the normal ORed output.

The implementation of Boolean expressions with NAND gates, may be obtained by means of a simple block diagram manipulation technique. The method requires that two other logic diagrams be drawn, before obtaining the NAND logic diagram. The following steps are to be carried out in sequence:

Step 1: From the given Boolean expression, draw the logic diagram with AND, OR, and NOT gates. Assume that both the normal (A) and complement $\left(\overline{A}\right)$ inputs are available.

Step 2: Draw a second logic diagram with the equivalent NAND logic substituted for each AND, OR, and NOT gate.

Step 3: Remove all pairs of inverters connected in cascade from the diagram, since double inversion does not perform any logical function. Also remove inverters connected to single external inputs, and complement the corresponding input variable. The new logic diagram, so obtained, is the required NAND gate implementation of the Boolean expression.

*Example 6.13.*

Construct a logic circuit for the Boolean expression $A \cdot \overline{B} + C \cdot (A + B \cdot D)$ using only NAND gates.

*Solution:*

The AND/OR implementation for the given Boolean expression is drawn in Figure 6.29(a). Now, each AND gate is substituted by a NAND gate, followed by an inverter, and each OR gate is substituted by two input inverters, followed by a NAND gate. Hence, each AND gate is substituted by two NAND gates, and each OR gate is substituted by three NAND gates. The logic diagram, so obtained, is shown in Figure 6.29(b). Note that, Figure 6.29(b) has seven inverters (single input NAND gates) and five two-input NAND gates. Each two-input NAND gate has a number inside the gate symbol for identification purpose. Pairs of inverters connected in cascade (from each AND box to each OR box) are removed, since they form double inversion, which has no meaning. The inverter connected to input A is removed, and the input variable is changed from A to $\overline{A}$. The result is the NAND logic diagram shown in Figure 6.29(c), with the number inside each NAND gate identifying the gate from Figure 6.29(b).

This example demonstrates that the number of NAND gates required to implement the Boolean expression is equal to the number of AND/OR gates, provided, both the normal and complement inputs are available. Otherwise, inverters must be used to generate any required complemented input.

*Example 6.14.*

Construct a logic circuit for the Boolean expression $(A + \overline{E}) \cdot (B + C \cdot D)$ using only NAND gates.

*Solution:*

The AND/OR implementation for the given Boolean expression is drawn in Figure 6.30(a). Now, the NAND equivalent of each AND and each OR gate is substituted, resulting in Figure 6.30(b). Note that, Figure 6.30(b) has six inverters (single input NAND gates) and four two-input NAND gates. One pair of cascaded inverters may be removed. In addition, the three external inputs A, B, and $\overline{E}$, which go directly to inverters, are complemented, and the corresponding inverters are removed. The final NAND gate implementation, so obtained, is shown in Figure 6.30(c). The number inside each NAND gate of Figure 6.30(c) corresponds to the NAND gate of Figure 6.30(b) having the same number.

For this example, the number of NAND gates required is equal to the number of AND/OR gates, plus an additional inverter at the output (NAND gate number 5). In general, the number of NAND gates required to implement a Boolean function, equals the number of AND/OR gates, except for an occasional inverter. This is true, only when both normal and complemented inputs are available, because the conversion forces certain input variables to be complemented.

# The Universal NOR Gate

The NOR function is the dual of the NAND function. For this reason, all procedures and rules for NOR logic, form a dual of the corresponding procedures and rules developed from NAND logic. Like the NAND gate, the NOR gate is also universal, because it is alone sufficient to implement any Boolean expression.

To show that any Boolean expression can be implemented with only NOR gates, we need to only show that the logical operations AND, OR, and NOT can be implemented with NOR gates. This is shown in Figure 6.31.

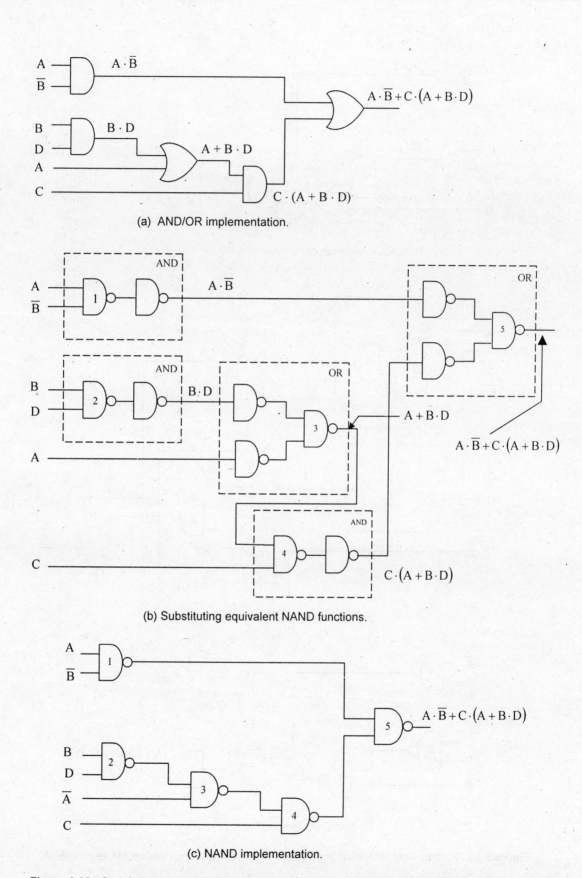

(a) AND/OR implementation.

(b) Substituting equivalent NAND functions.

(c) NAND implementation.

**Figure 6.29.** Step-by-step NAND implementation for the Boolean expression of Example 6.13.

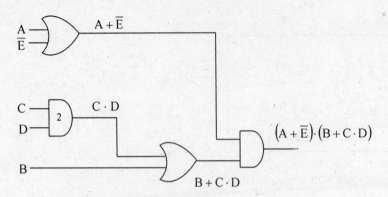

(a) AND/OR implementation.

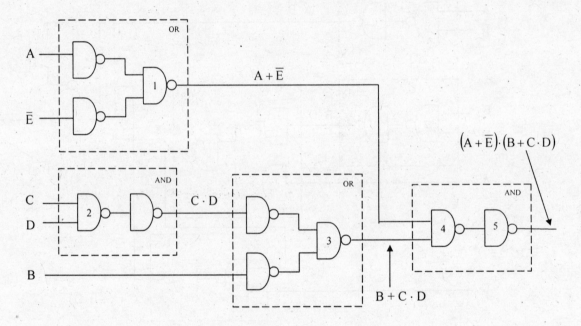

(b) Substituting equivalent NAND functions.

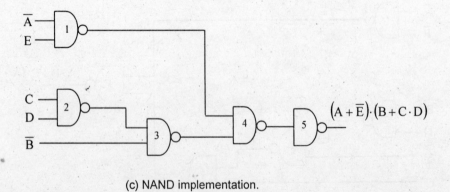

(c) NAND implementation.

**Figure 6.30.** Step-by-step NAND implementation for the Boolean expression of Example 6.14.

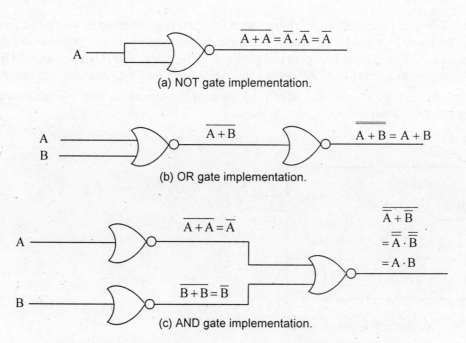

(a) NOT gate implementation.

(b) OR gate implementation.

(c) AND gate implementation.

**Figure 6.31.** Implementation of NOT, OR and AND gates by NOR gates.

The NOT operation is obtained from a single-input NOR gate, which is yet another inverter circuit.

The OR operation requires two NOR gates. The first one produces the inverted OR, and the second one, being a single-input NOT gate, acts as an inverter, to obtain the normal OR output.

The AND operation is achieved through a NOR gate with additional inverters in each input.

Similar to the NAND logic diagram, the implementation of Boolean expressions with NOR gates may be obtained by carrying out the following steps in sequence:

Step 1: For the given Boolean expression, draw the logic diagram with AND, OR, and NOT gates. Assume that both the normal (A) and complement $\left(\overline{A}\right)$ inputs are available.

Step 2: Draw a second logic diagram with equivalent NOR logic substituted for each AND, OR, and NOT gate.

Step 3: Remove all pairs of inverters connected in cascade from the diagram, since double inversion does not perform any logical function. Also remove inverters connected to single external inputs, and complement the corresponding input variable. The new logic diagram, so obtained, is the required NOR gate implementation of the given Boolean expression.

*Example 6.15.*

Construct a logic diagram for the Boolean expression $A \cdot \overline{B} + C \cdot (A + B \cdot D)$ using only NOR gates.

*Solution:*

The AND/OR implementation for the given Boolean expression is shown in Figure 6.32(a). Now, each OR gate is substituted by a NOR gate, followed by an inverter, and each AND gate is substituted by two input inverters, followed by a NOR gate. Hence, each OR gate is substituted by two NOR gates, and each AND gate is substituted by three NOR gates. The logic diagram, so obtained, is shown in Figure 6.32(b). Note that, Figure 6.32(b) has eight inverters (single input NOR gates) and five two-input NOR gates. One pair of cascaded inverters (from the OR box to the AND box) may be removed. In addition, the five external inputs A, $\overline{B}$, B, D and C, which go directly to inverters, are complemented, and the corresponding inverters are removed.

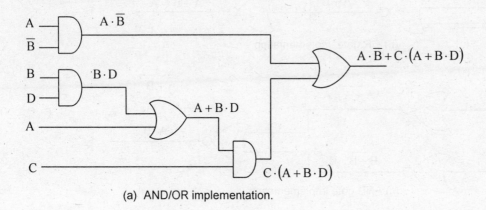

(a)  AND/OR implementation.

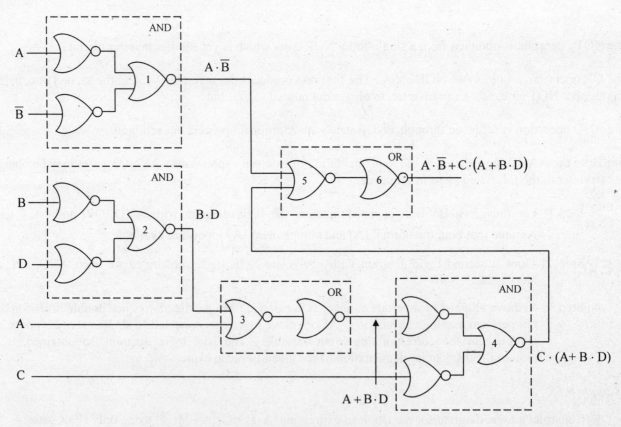

(b) Substituting equivalent NOR functions.

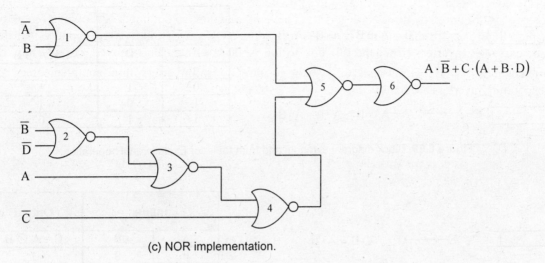

(c) NOR implementation.

**Figure 6.32.** Step-by-step NOR implementation for the Boolean expression of Example 6.15.

The final NOR gate implementation, so obtained, is shown in Figure 6.32(c). The number inside each NOR gate of Figure 6.32(c) corresponds to the NOR gate of Figure 6.32(b) having the same number.

The number of NOR gates in this example equals the number of AND/OR gates, plus an additional inverter in the output (NOR gate number 6). In general, the number of NOR gates required to implement a Boolean expression, equals the number of AND/OR gates, except for an occasional inverter. This is true, only if both normal and complement inputs are available, because the conversion forces certain input variables to be complemented.

Combinational circuits are more frequently constructed with NAND or NOR gates than with AND, OR and NOT gates. NAND and NOR gates are more popular than the AND and OR gates, because NAND and NOR gates are easily constructed with transistor circuits, and Boolean expressions can be easily implemented with them. Moreover, NAND and NOR gates are superior to AND and OR gates from the hardware point of view, because they supply outputs, which maintain the signal value, without loss of amplitude. OR and AND gates sometimes need amplitude restoration, after the signal travels through a few levels of gates.

## Exclusive-OR and Equivalence Functions

Exclusive-OR and equivalence, denoted by $\oplus$ and $\odot$ respectively, are binary operations, which perform the following Boolean functions:

$$A \oplus B = A \cdot \overline{B} + \overline{A} \cdot B$$
$$A \odot B = A \cdot B + \overline{A} \cdot \overline{B}$$

The truth tables and the block diagram symbols for the exclusive-OR and the equivalence operations are shown in Figure 6.33 and Figure 6.34 respectively. Observe that the two operations are the complement of each other. Each is commutative and associative. Because of these two properties, a function of three or more variables can be expressed without parentheses as follows:

$$(A \oplus B) \oplus C = A \oplus (B \oplus C) = A \oplus B \oplus C$$
$$(A \odot B) \odot C = A \odot (B \odot C) = A \odot B \odot C$$

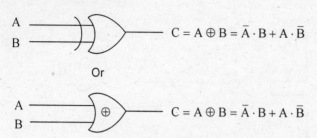

| Inputs | | Output |
|---|---|---|
| A | B | $C = A \oplus B$ |
| 0 | 0 | 0 |
| 0 | 1 | 1 |
| 1 | 0 | 1 |
| 1 | 1 | 0 |

**Figure 6.33.** Block diagram symbols and truth table for Exclusive-OR operation.

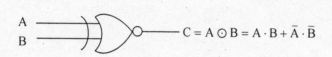

| Inputs | | Output |
|---|---|---|
| A | B | $C = A \odot B$ |
| 0 | 0 | 1 |
| 0 | 1 | 0 |
| 1 | 0 | 0 |
| 1 | 1 | 1 |

**Figure 6.34.** Block diagram symbol and truth table for Equivalence operation.

The exclusive-OR and equivalence operations have many excellent characteristics as candidates for logic gates. However, they are expensive to construct with physical components. They are available as standard logic gates in IC packages, but are usually constructed internally with other standard gates. For example, Figure 6.35(a) shows the implementation of a two-input, exclusive-OR function with AND, OR and NOT gates. Figure 6.35(b) shows its implementation with NAND gates.

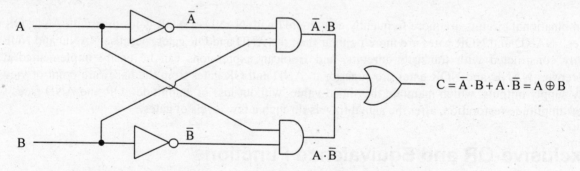

(a) Implementation of Exclusive-OR operation with AND/OR/NOT gates.

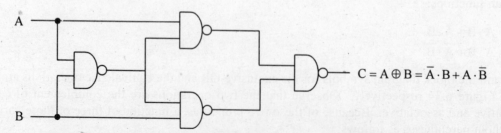

(b) Implementation of Exclusive-OR operation with NAND gates.

**Figure 6.35.** Logic diagrams of Exclusive-OR function.

Only a limited number of Boolean expressions can be expressed exclusively in terms of exclusive-OR or equivalence operations. Nevertheless, these expressions emerge quite often during the design of digital systems. The two functions are particularly useful in arithmetic operations, and error detection and correction.

# DESIGN OF COMBINATIONAL CIRCUITS

The design of combinational circuits starts from the verbal outline of the problem and ends in a logic circuit diagram. The procedure involves the following steps:

1. State the given problem completely and exactly.

2. Interpret the problem, and determine the available input variables and required output variables.

3. Assign a letter symbol to each input and output variables.

4. Design the truth table, which defines the required relations between inputs and outputs.

5. Obtain the simplified Boolean expression for each output.

6. Draw the logic circuit diagram to implement the Boolean expression.

The design procedure is illustrated below with the design of adder circuits, because addition is the most basic arithmetic operation for any computer system.

Addition in binary system can be summarized by the following four rules:

$$0 + 0 = 0$$
$$0 + 1 = 1$$
$$1 + 0 = 1$$
$$1 + 1 = 10$$

The first three operations produce a sum, whose length is one digit, but when both augend and addend bits are equal to 1, the binary sum consists of two digits. The higher significant bit of this result is called a *carry*. When the augend and addend numbers contain more significant digits, the carry obtained from the addition of two bits is added to the next higher order pair of significant bits. A combinational circuit, which performs the addition of two bits, is called a *half-adder*. One that performs the addition of three bits (two significant bits and previous carry), is called a *full-adder*. The name of the former stems from the fact that two half-adders can be employed to implement a full-adder.

# Design of Half-Adder

From the definition of a half-adder, we find that this circuit needs two binary inputs and two binary outputs. The input variables designate the augend and addend bits, whereas the output variables produce the sum and carry bits. Let A and B be the two inputs, and S (for sum) and C (for carry) be the two outputs. The truth table of Figure 6.36 defines the function of the half-adder.

| Inputs | | Outputs | |
|---|---|---|---|
| A | B | C | S |
| 0 | 0 | 0 | 0 |
| 0 | 1 | 0 | 1 |
| 1 | 0 | 0 | 1 |
| 1 | 1 | 1 | 0 |

**Figure 6.36.** Truth table for a half-adder.

The simplified Boolean expressions for the two outputs, directly obtained from the truth table, are:

$$S = \bar{A} \cdot B + A \cdot \bar{B}$$
$$C = A \cdot B$$

The logic circuit diagram to implement this is shown in Figure 6.37.

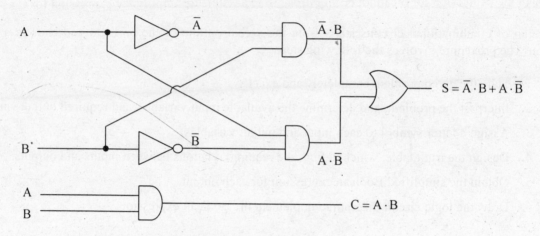

**Figure 6.37.** Logic circuit diagram for a half-adder.

The half-adder is limited in the sense that it can add only two single bits. Although, it generates a carry for the next higher pair of significant bits, it cannot accept a carry generated from the previous pair of lower significant bits. A full-adder solves this problem.

# Design of Full-Adder

A full-adder forms the arithmetic sum of three input bits. Hence, it consists of three inputs and two outputs. Two of the input variables (A and B) represent the augend and the addend bits, and the third input variable (D) represents the carry from the previous lower significant position. Two outputs are necessary, because the sum of three binary digits ranges in value from 0 to 3, and binary 2 and 3 need two digits. These two outputs are designated by the symbols S (for sum) and C (for carry). The truth table of Figure 6.38 defines the function of full-adder. The 1's and 0's for the output variables are determined from the arithmetic sum of the three input variables. When all input variables are 0, the output is 0, for both C and S. The S output is equal to 1, when only one input is equal to 1, or when all three inputs are equal to 1. The C output is 1, if two or three inputs are equal to 1.

| Inputs | | | Outputs | |
|---|---|---|---|---|
| A | B | D | C | S |
| 0 | 0 | 0 | 0 | 0 |
| 0 | 0 | 1 | 0 | 1 |
| 0 | 1 | 0 | 0 | 1 |
| 0 | 1 | 1 | 1 | 0 |
| 1 | 0 | 0 | 0 | 1 |
| 1 | 0 | 1 | 1 | 0 |
| 1 | 1 | 0 | 1 | 0 |
| 1 | 1 | 1 | 1 | 1 |

**Figure 6.38.** Truth table for a full-adder.

The sum-of-products expressions for the two outputs can be directly obtained from the truth table, and are given below:

$$S = \bar{A} \cdot \bar{B} \cdot D + \bar{A} \cdot B \cdot \bar{D} + A \cdot \bar{B} \cdot \bar{D} + A \cdot B \cdot D$$
$$C = \bar{A} \cdot B \cdot D + A \cdot \bar{B} \cdot D + A \cdot B \cdot \bar{D} + A \cdot B \cdot D$$

Although the expression for S cannot be simplified, it is possible to simplify the expression for C as follows:

$$C = \bar{A} \cdot B \cdot D + A \cdot \bar{B} \cdot D + A \cdot B \cdot \bar{D} + A \cdot B \cdot D$$
$$= \bar{A} \cdot B \cdot D + A \cdot \bar{B} \cdot D + A \cdot B \cdot \bar{D} + A \cdot B \cdot D + A \cdot B \cdot D + A \cdot B \cdot D \text{ (since, } x + x = x)$$
$$= \left( \bar{A} \cdot B \cdot D + A \cdot B \cdot D \right) + \left( A \cdot \bar{B} \cdot D + A \cdot B \cdot D \right) + \left( A \cdot B \cdot \bar{D} + A \cdot B \cdot D \right)$$
$$= \left( A + \bar{A} \right) \cdot B \cdot D + \left( B + \bar{B} \right) \cdot A \cdot D + \left( D + \bar{D} \right) \cdot A \cdot B$$
$$= B \cdot D + A \cdot D + A \cdot B \text{ (since, } x + \bar{x} = x)$$
$$= A \cdot B + A \cdot D + B \cdot D$$

Hence, we obtain the following expressions for the two outputs:

$$S = \bar{A} \cdot \bar{B} \cdot D + \bar{A} \cdot B \cdot \bar{D} + A \cdot \bar{B} \cdot \bar{D} + A \cdot B \cdot D$$
$$C = A \cdot B + A \cdot D + B \cdot D$$

The logic circuit diagrams to implement these expressions are shown in Figure 6.39.

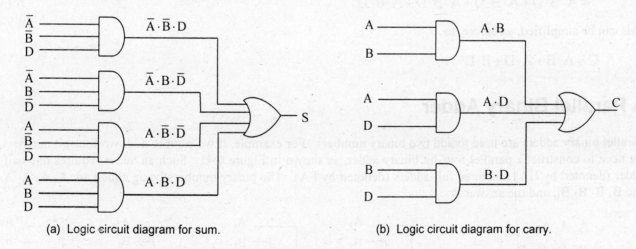

(a) Logic circuit diagram for sum.          (b) Logic circuit diagram for carry.

**Figure 6.39.** Logic circuit diagram for a full-adder.

A full-adder can also be implemented with two half-adders and one OR gate, as shown in Figure 6.40.

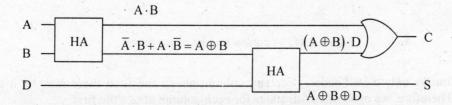

**Figure 6.40.** Implementation of full-adder with two half-adders and one OR gate.

The S output from the second half-adder is the exclusive-OR of D, and the output of the first half-adder giving:

$$S = \left(\overline{A} \cdot B + A \cdot \overline{B}\right) \cdot D + \left(\overline{A} \cdot B + A \cdot \overline{B}\right) \cdot \overline{D}$$

$$= \left(\overline{\overline{A} \cdot B} \cdot \overline{A \cdot \overline{B}}\right) \cdot D + \overline{A} \cdot B \cdot \overline{D} + A \cdot \overline{B} \cdot \overline{D}$$

$$= \left(\overline{\overline{A}} + \overline{B}\right) \cdot \left(\overline{A} + \overline{\overline{B}}\right) \cdot D + \overline{A} \cdot B \cdot \overline{D} + A \cdot \overline{B} \cdot \overline{D}$$

$$= \left(A + \overline{B}\right) \cdot \left(\overline{A} + B\right) \cdot D + \overline{A} \cdot B \cdot \overline{D} + A \cdot \overline{B} \cdot \overline{D}$$

$$= \left(A \cdot \overline{A} + A \cdot B + \overline{A} \cdot \overline{B} + B \cdot \overline{B}\right) \cdot D + \overline{A} \cdot B \cdot \overline{D} + A \cdot \overline{B} \cdot \overline{D}$$

$$= \left(A \cdot B + \overline{A} \cdot \overline{B}\right) \cdot D + \overline{A} \cdot B \cdot \overline{D} + A \cdot \overline{B} \cdot \overline{D}$$

$$= A \cdot B \cdot D + \overline{A} \cdot \overline{B} \cdot D + \overline{A} \cdot B \cdot \overline{D} + A \cdot \overline{B} \cdot \overline{D}$$

$$= \overline{A} \cdot \overline{B} \cdot D + \overline{A} \cdot B \cdot \overline{D} + A \cdot \overline{B} \cdot \overline{D} + A \cdot B \cdot D$$

And, we have the carry output

$$C = \left(\overline{A} \cdot B + A \cdot \overline{B}\right) \cdot D + A \cdot B$$

$$= \overline{A} \cdot B \cdot D + A \cdot \overline{B} \cdot D + A \cdot B \cdot \left(D + \overline{D}\right)$$

$$= \overline{A} \cdot B \cdot D + A \cdot \overline{B} \cdot D + A \cdot B \cdot D + A \cdot B \cdot \overline{D}$$

This can be simplified, as before, to

$$C = A \cdot B + A \cdot D + B \cdot D$$

# A Parallel Binary Adder

Parallel binary adders are used to add two binary numbers.  For example, if we want to add two four-bit numbers, we need to construct a parallel four-bit binary adder, as shown in Figure 6.41.  Such an adder requires one half-adder (denoted by HA) and three full-adders (denoted by FA).  The binary numbers being added are $A_4\,A_3\,A_2\,A_1$ and $B_4\,B_3\,B_2\,B_1$, and the answer is:

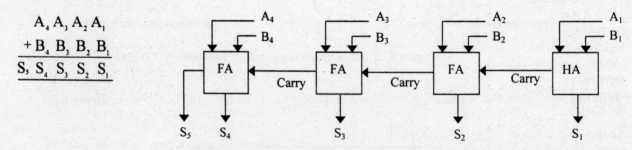

$$\begin{array}{r} A_4\,A_3\,A_2\,A_1 \\ +\ B_4\,B_3\,B_2\,B_1 \\ \hline S_5\,S_4\,S_3\,S_2\,S_1 \end{array}$$

**Figure 6.41.**  A parallel four-bit binary adder.

The first column requires only a half-adder.  For any column above the first, there may be a carry from the preceding column.  Therefore, we must use a full adder for each column above the first.

To illustrate how the adder of Figure 6.41 works, let us see how it will add two numbers say, 9 and 11. The binary equivalent of decimal 9 is 1001, and that of decimal 11 is 1011. Figure 6.42 shows the binary adder with these inputs.

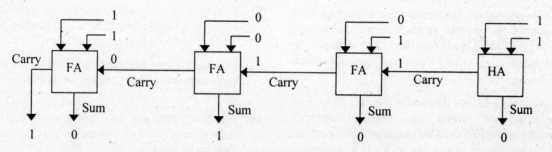

**Figure 6.42.** Example of adding two four-bit numbers using a parallel binary adder.

As shown in the figure, the half-adder adds 1 + 1 to give a sum of 0, and a carry 1. The carry goes into the first full-adder, which adds 0 + 1 + 1 to get a sum of 0, and a carry of 1. This carry goes into the next full-adder, which adds 0 + 0 + 1 to get a sum of 1, and a carry of 0. The last full-adder adds 1 + 1 + 0 to get a sum of 0, and a carry of 1. The final output of the system is 10100. The decimal equivalent of binary 10100 is 20, which is the correct decimal sum of 9 and 11.

The parallel binary adder of Figure 6.41 has limited capacity. The largest binary numbers that can be added, by using it are 1111 and 1111. Hence, its maximum capacity is:

$$
\begin{array}{rr}
15 & 1111 \\
+\ 15 & +\ 1111 \\
\hline
30 & 11110 \\
\end{array}
$$

In order to increase the capacity, more full-adders can be connected to the left end of the system. For instance, to add six bit numbers, two more full-adders must be connected, and for adding eight bit numbers, four more full-adders must be connected to the left end of the full-adder of Figure 6.41.

# Points to Remember

1. *Boolean algebra* deals with the binary number system. That is, the variables used in the Boolean equations may have only two possible values (0 and 1).

2. In Boolean algebra, the 'OR' operator used for logical addition is represented by the symbol '+'; the 'AND' operator used for logical multiplication is represented by the symbol '·'; and the 'NOT' operator used for complementation is represented by the symbol '–'.

3. As regards precedence of Boolean operators, 'NOT' operator takes precedence over 'AND' and 'OR' operators, and 'AND' operator takes precedence over 'OR' operator.

4. The postulates of Boolean algebra are
   (a) $A = 0$, if and only if, A is not equal to 1
   (b) $A = 1$, if and only if, A is not equal to 0
   (c) $x + 0 = x$
   (d) $x \cdot 1 = x$
   (e) $x + y = y + x$
   (f) $x \cdot y = y \cdot x$
   (g) $x + (y + z) = (x + y) + z$
   (h) $x \cdot (y \cdot z) = (x \cdot y) \cdot z$
   (i) $x \cdot (y + z) = x \cdot y + x \cdot z$
   (j) $x + y \cdot z = (x + y) \cdot (x + z)$
   (k) $x + \overline{x} = 1$
   (l) $x \cdot \overline{x} = 0$

5. In Boolean algebra, there is a precise duality between the operators · (AND) and + (OR), and the digits 0 and 1. This property is known as the *principle of duality*.

6. The basic Boolean identities are summarized in Figure 6.12. They are very helpful while dealing with Boolean algebra.

7. A *Boolean function* is an expression formed with binary variables, the two binary operators OR and AND, the unary operator NOT, parentheses, and equal sign.

8. The *complement* of a Boolean function F is $\bar{F}$, and is obtained by interchanging 0s for 1s and 1s for 0s in the truth table, which defines the function.

9. A *sum-of-products expression* is a product term (minterm), or several product terms (minterms), logically added (ORed) together. For example, the expression $x \cdot \bar{y} + \bar{x} \cdot y$ is a sum-of-products expression.

10. *A product-of-sums expression* is a sum term (maxterm), or several sum terms (maxterms), logically multiplied (ANDed) together. For example, the expression $(\bar{x} + y) \cdot (x + \bar{y})$ is a product-of-sums expression.

11. The sum-of-products and the product-of-sums forms of Boolean expressions are known as *standard forms*. One prime reason for liking the sum-of-products or the product-of-sums expressions is their straightforward conversion to very nice gating networks.

12. A *logic gate* is an electronic circuit, which operates on one or more input signals to produce standard output signals. These logic gates are the building blocks of all the circuits in a computer.

13. An *AND gate* is the physical realization of the logical multiplication (AND) operation. It is an electronic circuit, which generates an output signal of 1, only if all input signals are also 1.

14. An *OR gate* is the physical realization of the logical addition (OR) operation. It is an electronic circuit, which generates an output signal of 1, if any of the input signals is also 1.

15. A *NOT gate* is the physical realization of the complementation operation. It is an electronic circuit, which generates an output signal, which is the reverse of the input signal. A NOT gate is also known as an *inverter*, because it inverts the input.

16. A *NAND gate* is a complemented AND gate. That is, the output of NAND gate will be a 1, if any one of the inputs is a 0, and will be a 0, only when all the inputs are 1.

17. A *NOR gate* is a complemented OR gate. That is, the output of a NOR gate will be a 1, only when all inputs are 0, and it will be a 0, if any input is a 1.

18. The logic gates are interconnected to form gating, or logic, networks, which are known as *combinational logic circuits*.

19. The AND, OR, and NOT gates are logically complete, because any Boolean expression may be realized using these three gates.

20. The NAND gate is said to be an *universal gate*, because it is alone sufficient to implement any Boolean expression. Similarly, the NOR gate is also an universal gate.

21. *Exclusive-OR* and *equivalence*, denoted by $\oplus$ and $\odot$ respectively, are binary operations that perform the following Boolean functions:
$$A \oplus B = A \cdot \bar{B} + \bar{A} \cdot B$$
$$A \odot B = A \cdot B + \bar{A} \cdot \bar{B}$$

22. The design of combinational circuits starts from the verbal outline of the problem, and ends in a logic circuit diagram. The procedure involves the following steps:
    (a) State the given problem completely and exactly.
    (b) Interpret the problem, and determine the available input variables and required output variables.
    (c) Assign a letter symbol to each input and output variable.
    (d) Design the truth table, which defines the required relations between inputs and outputs.
    (e) Obtain the simplified Boolean expression for each output.
    (f) Draw the logic circuit diagram to implement the Boolean expression.

# Questions

1. Explain the principle of duality in Boolean algebra. How is it useful?

2. Give the dual of the following Boolean expressions:
    (a) $\bar{A} + \bar{B}$
    (d) $\overline{A + B}$
    (b) $A + \bar{B} + C$
    (e) $A \cdot (A + B)$
    (c) $\bar{A} \cdot B + A \cdot \bar{B}$
    (f) $\bar{A} + A \cdot B$

3. Give the dual of the rule $A + \bar{A} \cdot B = A + B$.

4. Prepare truth tables for the following Boolean expressions:
    (a) $A \cdot B + \bar{A} \cdot B$
    (e) $A \cdot B \cdot \bar{C}$
    (b) $A \cdot \bar{B} \cdot C + \bar{B} \cdot \bar{C}$
    (f) $A \cdot \bar{B} \cdot C + \bar{A} \cdot B \cdot \bar{C}$
    (c) $\bar{A} + \bar{B}$
    (g) $(\bar{A} + \bar{B}) \cdot (A + C) \cdot (B + \bar{C})$
    (d) $\bar{A} + B + \bar{C}$
    (h) $\bar{A} \cdot C + \bar{A} \cdot \bar{C}$

5. State and prove the two basic De Morgan's theorems.

6. Prove the following rules by the method of perfect induction:

   (a) $A \cdot \bar{B} + A \cdot B = A$

   (b) $A + \bar{A} \cdot B = A + B$

   (c) $A \cdot (A + C) = A$

   (d) $(A + B) \cdot (\overline{A \cdot B}) = A \cdot \bar{B} + B \cdot \bar{A}$

   (e) $(A + B) \cdot (\bar{A} + \bar{B}) = \overline{A \cdot B + \bar{A} \cdot \bar{B}}$

7. Simplify the following Boolean expressions, and draw logic circuit diagrams for your simplified expressions by using AND, OR and NOT gates:

   (a) $\bar{x} \cdot y \cdot z + \bar{x} \cdot y \cdot \bar{z} + x \cdot \bar{y} \cdot \bar{z} + x \cdot \bar{y} \cdot z$

   (b) $\bar{x} \cdot y \cdot z + x \cdot \bar{y} \cdot \bar{z} + x \cdot y \cdot z + x \cdot y \cdot \bar{z}$

   (c) $\bar{A} \cdot C + \bar{A} \cdot B + A \cdot \bar{B} \cdot C + B \cdot C$

   (d) $\bar{A} \cdot \bar{B} \cdot \bar{C} + \bar{A} \cdot B \cdot \bar{C} + A \cdot \bar{B} \cdot \bar{C} + A \cdot \bar{B} \cdot C + A \cdot B \cdot \bar{C}$

   (e) $(A + B + C) \cdot (A + \bar{B} + \bar{C}) \cdot (A + B + \bar{C}) \cdot (A + \bar{B} + C)$

   (f) $(A \cdot B \cdot C) \cdot (A \cdot B \cdot \bar{C} + A \cdot \bar{B} \cdot C + \bar{A} \cdot B \cdot C)$

8. Find the complement of the following Boolean expressions:

   (a) $A \cdot B + A \cdot C$

   (b) $\bar{A} \cdot \bar{B} + A \cdot B$

   (c) $A \cdot (B \cdot C + \bar{B} \cdot \bar{C})$

   (d) $A \cdot (\bar{B} + \bar{C})$

   (e) $(A + B) \cdot (B + C) \cdot (A + C)$

   (f) $A \cdot (B + C) \cdot (\bar{C} + \bar{D})$

   (g) $A \cdot B + (\bar{A} \cdot \bar{B}) \cdot (B \cdot C + \bar{B} \cdot \bar{C})$

9. Express the following Boolean expressions in their sum-of-products form. Ensure that each term has all the literals.

   (a) $\bar{A} \cdot (B + \bar{C})$

   (b) $(\bar{A} + B) \cdot (\bar{B} + \bar{C})$

   (c) $(A + B) \cdot \bar{C}$

   (d) $(A \cdot B) \cdot (A \cdot \bar{B} \cdot \bar{C} + \bar{A} \cdot C)$

   (e) $(\bar{A} + C) \cdot (\bar{A} + \bar{B} + \bar{C}) \cdot (A + \bar{B})$

   (f) $(\bar{A} + C) \cdot (A \cdot B + A \cdot C + B \cdot C)$

10. Express the following Boolean expressions in their product-of-sums form. Ensure that each term has all the literals.

    (a) $\bar{A} + B \cdot \bar{C}$

    (b) $A \cdot B + \bar{C}$

    (c) $A + B + C$

    (d) $(\bar{A} \cdot \bar{B}) \cdot (\bar{A} \cdot \bar{C} + \bar{B} \cdot \bar{C})$

    (e) $(A \cdot B) \cdot (\bar{B} + \bar{C})$

    (f) $A + A \cdot \bar{B} + \bar{A} \cdot C$

11. What will be the outputs of the following logic circuits for the specified inputs?

    (a)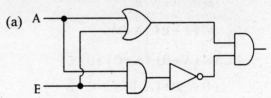

    (b)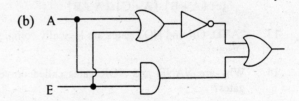

    (c)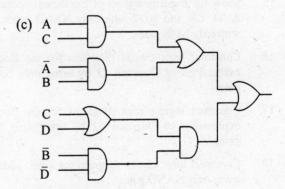

    (d)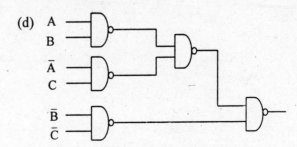

(e)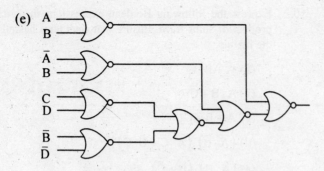

12. Construct logic circuit diagrams for the following Boolean expressions by using AND/OR/NOT gates:

(a) $A \cdot \bar{B} + A \cdot B$

(b) $(A + B) \cdot \overline{(A \cdot B)}$

(c) $(\bar{A} + \bar{B}) \cdot (A + C) \cdot (B + \bar{C})$

(d) $A \cdot B + (\bar{A} \cdot \bar{B}) \cdot (B \cdot C + \bar{B} \cdot \bar{C})$

(e) $(A + B) \cdot (A + C) \cdot (\bar{A} + \bar{B})$

13. "AND, OR and NOT gates are logically complete". Discuss.

14. Why are NAND and NOR gates called universal gates?

15. Show the implementation of the logical operations AND, OR and NOT with only NAND gates, and with only NOR gates.

16. Construct logic circuit diagrams for the Boolean expressions of Question 12 by using only NAND gates.

17. Construct logic circuit diagrams for the Boolean expressions of Question 12 by using only NOR gates.

18. Construct logic circuit diagram for a half-adder by using only NAND gates.

19. Construct logic circuit diagram for a half-adder by using only NOR gates.

20. Why are combinational circuits more frequently constructed with NAND or NOR gates than with AND, OR and NOT gates?

21. Prove that

(a) $(A \oplus B) \oplus C = A \oplus (B \oplus C)$

(b) $(A \odot B) \odot C = A \odot (B \odot C)$

22. Construct a logic circuit diagram for the exclusive-OR function by using only NOR gates.

23. Construct a logic circuit diagram for the equivalence function by using only NAND gates.

24. A logic circuit has three inputs, A, B and C. It generates an output of 1, only when A = 0, B = 1, C = 0, or when A = 1, B = 1, C = 0. Design a combinational circuit for this system.

25. A logic circuit has three inputs, A, B and C. It generates an output of 1, only under the following conditions:
A = 0, B = 0, C = 0
A = 0, B = 1, C = 1
A = 1, B = 0, C = 1
A = 1, B = 1, C = 1
Design a combinational circuit for this system.

26. Design a gating network, which will have outputs 0, only when A = 0, B = 0, C = 0; A = 1, B = 0, C = 0; A = 1, B = 1, C = 0. The outputs are to be 1 for all other cases.

27. A three-bit message is to be transmitted with an odd parity. An odd parity generator generates a parity bit (say P) to make the total number of 1s odd (including P). That is, P = 1, only when the number of 1s in the input string is even. Design a combinational logic circuit for such a parity generator.

28. Design a combinational logic circuit to generate an even parity for hexadecimal digits.

# Chapter 7

# Processor and Memory

In Chapter 2, we saw that the main components of a computer system are input, output, storage, and CPU. We also saw that storage units are basically of two types – primary and secondary. With this background knowledge, we are now ready to learn more about the internal structure and functioning of the various components of a computer system. This and the next two chapters have been devoted to this learning. In this chapter, we will learn about the structure and functioning of the CPU (also known as *processor*) and the primary storage (also known as *main memory* or simply *memory*). Subsequently, the structure and functioning of secondary storage devices and input/output devices will be presented in Chapters 8 and 9, respectively.

The basic processor and memory architecture of a computer system is shown in Figure 7.1.

## THE CENTRAL PROCESSING UNIT (CPU)

The CPU is the brain of a computer system. All major calculations and comparisons performed by a computer are carried out inside its CPU. The CPU is also responsible for activating and controlling the operations of other units of the computer system. Hence, no other single component of a computer determines its overall performance, as much as the CPU. In order to be able to quickly evaluate any computer's capabilities, it is important to know how CPUs are internally structured, how different CPUs differ from each other, and how CPU speed is evaluated. These and other related concepts about CPU are described below.

### The Control Unit

In Chapter 2 (see Figure 2.1), we saw that the two basic components of a CPU are the control unit and the arithmetic logic unit. The control unit of the CPU selects and interprets program instructions, and then sees that they are executed. As shown in Figure 7.1, it has some special purpose registers (whose functions are described in a later subsection), and a decoder to perform these activities. The special purpose registers, namely the *instruction register* and the *program control register*, respectively hold the current instruction and the next instruction to be executed, and in this way help the control unit in instruction selection. On the other hand, the *decoder* has the necessary circuitry to decode and interpret the meaning of every instruction supported by the CPU. Each instruction is accompanied by *microcode* – very basic directions, which tell the CPU how to execute the instruction.

Although, the control unit does not perform any actual processing of the data, it acts as a central nervous system for the other components of the computer. It manages and coordinates the entire computer system, including the input and output units. It obtains instructions from the program stored in the main memory, interprets the instructions, and issues signals, which cause other units of the system to execute them.

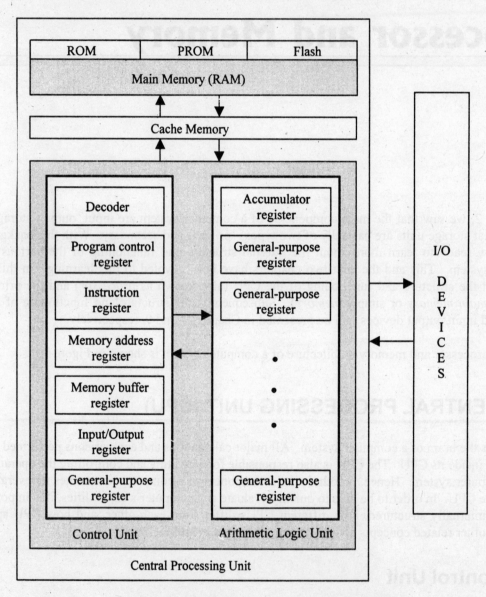

**Figure 7.1.** Processor and memory architecture of a computer system.

# The Arithmetic Logic Unit (ALU)

The ALU of the CPU is the place, where the actual execution of the instructions takes place, during the data processing operation. That is, when the control unit encounters an instruction, which involves an arithmetic operation (such as, add, subtract, multiply, divide), or a logic operation (such as less than, equal to, greater than), it passes control to the ALU. As shown in Figure 7.1, the ALU has some special purpose registers (whose functions are described in a later subsection), and the necessary circuitry, to carry out all the arithmetic and logic operations, which are included in the instructions supported by the CPU. For example, the control unit might load two numbers into the registers in the ALU. Then, it might tell the ALU to add the two numbers (an arithmetic operation), or to check if the two numbers are equal (a logical operation).

In case of a microcomputer, the entire CPU (both the control unit and the ALU) is contained on a single tiny silicon chip, called a *microprocessor*.

# Instruction Set

Every CPU has built-in ability to execute a set of machine instructions, called its *instruction set*. Most CPUs have 200 or more instructions (such as add, subtract, and compare) in their instruction set. The machine language designed for a processor (CPU), is based on the list of instructions supported by the CPU in its instruction set. Since each processor has a unique instruction set, machine language programs written for one computer will generally not run on another computer, with a different CPU.

CPUs made by different manufacturers have different instruction sets. In fact, different CPU models of the same manufacturer also often have different instruction sets. However, manufacturers tend to group their CPUs into "families", which have similar instruction sets. When a new CPU is developed, it is ensured that its instruction set includes all the instructions in the instruction set of its predecessor CPU, plus some new ones. This manufacturing strategy is known as *upward compatibility*, and the new CPU is said to be *upward compatible* with its predecessor. This feature allows software written for a computer with a particular CPU, to work on computers with newer processors of the same family. In turn, it allows the users of these computer systems to easily upgrade their system, without worrying about converting all their existing software.

# Registers

As the instructions are interpreted and executed by the CPU, there is a movement of information between the various units of the computer system. In order to handle this process satisfactorily, and to speed up the rate of information transfer, the computer uses a number of special memory units, called *registers*. These registers are used to hold information on a temporary basis, and are part of the CPU (not main memory).

The length of a register equals the number of bits it can store. Hence, a register that can store 8 bits is normally referred to as an 8-bit register. Most CPUs sold today, have 32-bit or 64-bit registers. The size of the registers is sometimes called the *word size*. The bigger the word size, the faster the computer can process a set of data. With all other parameters being same, a CPU with 32-bit registers, can process data twice as fast as one with 16-bit registers.

Although, the number of registers varies from computer to computer, there are some registers, which are common to all computers. The functions of these registers are described below.

1. **Memory Address Register (MAR).** It holds the address of the active memory location. It is loaded from the program control register, when an instruction is read from memory.

2. **Memory Buffer Register (MBR).** It holds the contents of the memory word read from, or written in, memory. An instruction word placed in this register is transferred to the instruction register. A data word placed in this register is accessible for operation with the accumulator register, or for transfer to the I/O register. A word to be stored in a memory location must first be transferred to the MBR, from where it is written in memory.

3. **Program Control Register (PC).** It holds the address of the next instruction to be executed. Normally, the instructions of a program are stored in consecutive memory locations, and read and executed in sequence, unless a branch instruction is encountered. A *branch instruction* is an operation, which calls for a transfer to a non-consecutive instruction. The address part of a branch instruction is transferred to the PC register, to become the address of the next instruction.

4. **Accumulator Register (A).** It holds the data to be operated upon, the intermediate results, and the results of processing. It is used during the execution of most instructions. The results of arithmetic operations are returned to the accumulator register, for transfer to main memory, through the memory buffer register. In many computers, there are more than one accumulator registers.

5. **Instruction Register (I).** It holds the current instruction, which is being executed. As soon as the instruction is stored in this register, the operation part and the address part of the instruction (see Chapter 12) are separated. The address part of the instruction is sent to the MAR, while its operation part is sent to the control unit, where it is decoded and interpreted, and ultimately command signals are generated to carry out the task specified by the instruction.

6. **Input/Output Register (I/O).** It is used to communicate with the input/output devices. All input information, such as instructions and data, are transferred to this register by an input device. Similarly, all output information, to be transferred to an output device, are found in this register.

Figure 7.2 summarizes the functions of each of these registers.

| Sl. No. | Name of Register | Function |
|---|---|---|
| 1 | Memory Address (MAR) | Holds the address of the active memory location |
| 2 | Memory Buffer (MBR) | Holds information on its way to and from memory |
| 3 | Program Control (PC) | Holds the address of the next instruction to be executed |
| 4 | Accumulator (A) | Accumulates results and data to be operated upon |
| 5 | Instruction (I) | Holds an instruction, while it is being executed |
| 6 | Input/Output (I/O) | Communicates with the I/O devices |

**Figure 7.2.** Functions of various registers.

The execution of an instruction by the CPU, during program execution, normally involves the following steps:

1. The control unit takes the address of the next program instruction to be executed from the program control register, and reads the instruction from the corresponding memory address, into the instruction register of the control unit.

2. The control unit then sends the operation part and the address part of the instruction, to the decoder and the memory address register, respectively.

3. The decoder interprets the instruction, and accordingly the control unit sends signals to the appropriate unit, which needs to be involved in carrying out the task specified in the instruction. For example, if it is an arithmetic or logic operation, the signal is sent to the ALU. In this case, the control unit also ensures that the data corresponding to the address part of the instruction is loaded in

a suitable register in the ALU, before the signal is sent to the ALU. The ALU performs the necessary operation on the data, and signals the control unit as soon as it has finished.

4.  As each instruction is executed, the address of the next instruction to be executed is automatically loaded into the program control register, and Steps 1 to 4 are repeated.

# Processor Speed

The operations of the ALU and control unit are performed at incredible speed. These operations are usually synchronized by a built-in electronic clock (known as *system clock*), which emits millions of regularly spaced electric pulses per second (known as *clock cycles*). Commands are interpreted, and then executed at proper intervals, and the intervals are timed by a specific number of clock cycles. One cycle is the time it takes to perform one operation, such as moving a byte of data from one memory location to another. Normally, several clock cycles are required to fetch, decode, and execute a single program instruction. The shorter the clock cycle, the faster the processor. Hence, the speed with which an instruction is executed is directly related to the computer's built-in *clock speed,* which is the number of pulses, produced per second. This clock speed is measured in *megahertz* (or *MHz*), where *mega* means million, and *hertz* means cycles per second. Over the years, clock speeds of processors have increased steadily. Most of today's popular personal computers have clock speeds in the 500- to 2000-MHz range. However, processors are now being built with even faster ratings. With all other parameters being equal (although they never are), a CPU operating at 500 MHz can process data five times as fast as one operating at 100 MHz.

# Types of Processors

## CISC Processors

One of the earlier goals of CPU designers was to provide more and more instructions in the instruction set of a CPU, to ensure that the CPU directly supports more features, making it easier to translate high-level language programs to machine language, and to ensure that the machine language programs run more effectively. Of course, every additional instruction in the instruction set of a CPU requires the necessary hardware circuitry to handle that instruction, adding more complexity to the CPU's hardware circuitry. Another goal of CPU designers was to optimize the usage of expensive memory. To achieve this, the designers tried to pack more instructions in memory, by introducing the concept of variable-length instructions, such as half word, one and half word, etc. For example, an operand in an immediate instruction needs fewer bits, and can be designed as a half word instruction. Additionally, CPUs were designed to support a variety of addressing modes (discussed later in this chapter during the discussion of memory). CPUs with large instruction set, variable-length instructions, and a variety of addressing modes, are said to employ *CISC (Complex Instruction Set Computer) architecture.* Since CISC processors possess so many processing features, they make the job of machine language programmers easier. However, they are complex and expensive to produce. Most personal computers of today use CISC processors.

## RISC Processors

In early 1980s, some CPU designers discovered that several of the instructions supported by a CISC-based CPU are rarely used. Hence, they came out with an idea that the complexity of CPU design can be greatly reduced, by implementing only a bare minimum basic set of instructions, plus some of the more frequently used instructions in the hardware circuitry of the CPU. Other complex instructions need not be supported in the instruction set of the CPU, because they can always be implemented in software, by using the basic set of instructions. While working on simpler CPU design, these designers also came up with the idea of making all the instructions of uniform length, so that the decoding and execution of all instructions becomes simple and fast. Furthermore, to speed up computation, and to reduce the complexity of handling a number of addressing modes, they decided to design all the instructions in such a way that they retrieve operands stored in registers in CPU, rather than from memory. These design ideas resulted in producing faster and less expensive processors. CPUs with a small instruction set, fixed-length instructions, and reduced references to memory to retrieve operands, are said to employ *RISC* (*Reduced Instruction Set Computer*) *architecture*. Since RISC processors have a small instruction set, they place extra demand on programmers, who must consider how to implement complex computations, by combining simple instructions. However, due to simpler design, RISC processors are faster for most applications, less complex, and less expensive to produce than CISC processors.

## EPIC Processors

The *Explicitly Parallel Instruction Computing (EPIC)* technology breaks through the sequential nature of conventional processor architectures, by allowing the software to communicate explicitly to the processor, when operations can be done in parallel. For this, it uses tighter coupling between the compiler and the processor, and enables the compiler to extract maximum parallelism in the original code, and explicitly describe it to the processor. Processors based on EPIC architecture are simpler and more powerful than traditional CISC or RISC processors. These processors are mainly targeted to next-generation, 64-bit, high-end server and workstation market (not for personal computer market).

# THE MAIN MEMORY

In the discussion above, we saw that the CPU contains the necessary circuitry for data processing and controlling the other components of a computer system. However, one thing it does not have built into it is the place to store programs and data, which are needed during data processing. We also saw that the CPU does contain several registers for storing data and instructions, but these are very small areas, which can hold only a few bytes at a time, and are just sufficient to hold only one or two instructions and the corresponding data. If the instructions and data of a program being executed by the CPU, were to reside in secondary storage like a disk, and fetched and loaded one by one into the registers of the CPU as the program execution proceeded, this would lead to the CPU being idle most of the time, because there is a large speed mismatch between the rate at which CPU can process data and the rate at which data can be transferred from disk to CPU registers. For example, a CPU can process data at a rate of about 5 nanosecond/byte, and a disk reader can read data at a speed of around 5 microsecond/byte. Hence, within the time in which the disk can supply one byte of data, the CPU can process 1000 bytes. This would lead to a very slow overall performance, even if the computer system used a very fast CPU. To overcome this problem, there is a need to have a reasonably large storage space, which can hold the instructions and data of the program(s), on which the CPU is currently working. The time to fetch and load data from this storage space into the CPU registers must also be very small as compared to that for disk storage, to reduce the speed mismatch problem with the CPU speed. Every computer has such a storage space, which is known as *primary storage*, *main memory*, or simply *memory*. It is a temporary storage area, which is built into the computer hardware, and in which instructions and data of a program reside, mainly when the program is being executed by the CPU. Physically, this memory consists of some chips either on the motherboard, or on a small circuit board attached to the motherboard of a computer system. This built-in memory allows the CPU to store and retrieve data very quickly. The rate of fetching data from this memory is typically of the order of 50 nanosecond/byte. Hence, the rate of data fetching from the main memory is about 100 times faster than that from a high-speed secondary storage like disk.

# Storage Evaluation Criteria

Any storage unit of a computer system is characterized and evaluated based on the following properties:

1. **Storage capacity.** It is the amount of data, which can be stored in the storage unit. A large capacity iş desired. As compared to secondary storage units, primary storage units have less storage capacity.

2. **Access time.** This is the time required to locate and retrieve stored data from the storage unit, in response to a program instruction. A fast access time is preferred. As compared to secondary storage units, primary storage units have faster access time.

3. **Cost per bit of storage.** This refers to the cost of a storage unit for a given storage capacity. Obviously, a lower cost is desirable. As compared to secondary storage units, primary storage units have higher cost per bit of storage.

4. **Volatile.** If the storage unit can retain the data stored in it, even when the power is turned off or interrupted, it is called *non-volatile storage*. On the other hand, if the data stored are lost, when the power is turned off or interrupted, it is called *volatile storage*. Obviously, a non-volatile storage is desirable. In almost all computer systems, the primary storage units are volatile and the secondary storage units are non-volatile.

5. **Random access.** If the time taken to access a piece of data from the storage unit is independent of the location of the data in the storage unit, it is called a *random access storage* or *random access memory (RAM)*. Each separate location of a RAM is as easy to access as any other location, and takes the same amount of time. In almost all computer systems, the primary storage units have random access property, and the secondary storage units have either pseudo-random access (access time is nearly same for all locations but not exactly same), or sequential access (access time directly depends on the location of the data) property.

# Main Memory Organization

A primary storage or main memory of a computer system is made up of several small storage areas, called locations or cells. Each of these locations can store a fixed number of bits, called *word length* of that particular memory. Hence, as shown in Figure 7.3, a given memory is divided into $N$ words, where $N$ generally is some power of 2. Each word or location has a built-in and unique number assigned to it. This number is called the *address* of the location, and is used to identify the location. Each location can hold either a data item or an instruction, and its address remains the same, regardless of its contents. The addresses normally start at 0, and the highest address equals the number of words, which can be stored in the memory minus 1. For example, if a memory has 1024 locations, the address ranges between 0 and 1023. Hence, at address 0 we find a word, at address 1 a second word, at address 2 a third word, and so on, up to the final word at the largest address.

## Why More Bits?

You might have heard about 8-bit computers, 16-bit computers, 32-bit computers, etc. This refers to the word length of the memory of a particular computer, in terms of total number of bits per memory word. Word length is an important architectural factor. Small machines have word lengths of 8, 16, or 32 bits, whereas large machines have word lengths of 64 bits or more. The obvious question that arises is, what is the advantage of having more number of bits per word, instead of having more words of smaller size (length).

For an answer to the above question, imagine a highway with eight lanes, and a heavy flow of traffic. If it is expanded to sixteen lanes, the flow of traffic speeds up considerably. "8 bits" refers to the number of "lanes" on a microchip. More bits, means a more rapid flow of electronic signals. In other words, a faster computer. Hence, what an 8-bit computer takes one minute to do, a 32-bit computer may do in few seconds.

There is an important difference between a memory address and its contents. A memory is like a large cabinet containing as many drawers as there are addresses in memory. Each drawer contains a word, and the address of each word is written on the outside of the drawer. If we write or store a word, say 10101010 at address 125, it is like placing the word 10101010 in the drawer labeled 125. Later, reading from address 125, is like looking in that drawer to see its contents, which is now 10101010. We do not remove the word at an address when we read, but change the contents at an address, only when we store or write a new word. Hence, entering data into a storage location is *destructive* of previous contents, but retrieving data from a location is *non-destructive*. The act of entering data into a storage location is called *memory write operation*, and the act of retrieving data from a storage location is called *memory read operation*. Hence, read is a non-destructive operation, and write is a destructive operation.

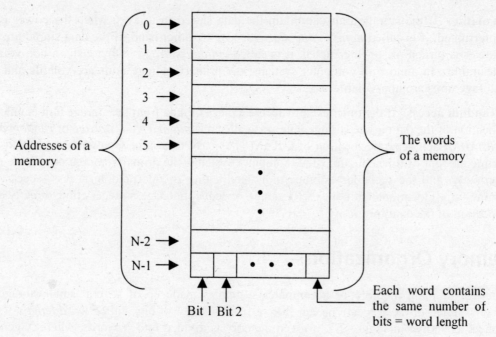

**Figure 7.3.** Organization of a main memory having N words.

Data and instructions are moved, to and from memory, in bunches of word length. Therefore, even if the electronic circuits used are comparable in speed, machines having smaller word length will be slower in operation than machines having larger word length. This difference is analogous to providing the user of a machine having smaller word length with a small data shovel, and the user of a machine having larger word length with a large data shovel. Even though they both may be shoveling at comparable speeds, the user with the smaller shovel will be slower, because more shovelfuls are needed to move the same amount of data.

## Fixed and Variable Word-length Memory

The main memory of some computers is designed to store a fixed number of characters (equal to its word-length in bytes) in each numbered address location. Such computers are said to be *word-addressable*, and they employ a *fixed-word-length* memory approach. In these computers, storage space is always allocated in multiples of word-length. Therefore, if a word-addressable computer has a fixed word-length of 4 bytes (4 characters), this computer will require one word (4 bytes) to store the word "CAT", and two words (8 bytes) to store the word "BOMBAY".

In many computers, the main memory is also designed in a manner that each numbered address can only store a single character (A, B, 1, 2, +, -, etc.). Computers designed in this manner, are said to be *character-addressable*, and they employ a *variable-word-length* memory approach. Hence, in these machines, only 3 bytes will be required to store the word "CAT", and only 6 bytes will be required to store the word "BOMBAY". Figure 7.4 summarizes the difference between the fixed-word-length and variable-word-length memory approaches.

Both the fixed and the variable word-length memory systems have their own merits and demerits. The fixed-word-length approach is normally used in large scientific computers, for gaining speed of calculation. On the other hand, the variable-word-length approach is used in small business computers, for optimizing the use of storage space. For example, let us consider a fixed-word-length memory machine with a word size of eight characters. If most of the data words to be stored are of less than five characters, more than half of the storage space will remain unused. This will not happen in case of a machine with variable-word-length memory, because a character can be placed in every storage cell of this machine. However, word-addressable computers possess faster calculating capability, because they can add two data words in a single operation. If the fixed-length word is eight characters, two eight digit numbers can be added in a single operation. On the other hand, with a character-addressable machine, only one digit in each number is added during a single operation, and eight steps would be needed to add two eight digit numbers.

A computer may be designed to employ either a fixed-word-length or a variable-word-length memory organization. The set of instructions available with these computers allow them to be operated as either variable- or fixed-word-length memory computers. However, with the memory becoming cheaper and larger day-by-day, most modern computers employ fixed-word-length memory organization.

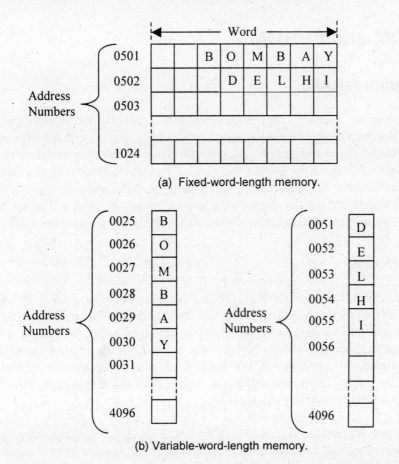

**Figure 7.4.** Fixed-word-length memory compared with variable-word-length memory.

# Main Memory Capacity

The main memory capacity of large computer systems is normally more than that of small systems. This capacity is defined in terms of the number of bytes a computer system can store.

Memory capacity of a computer system is normally stated in terms of *kilobytes* (*KB*), which is equal to 1024 ($2^{10}$) bytes of storage, or in terms of *megabytes* (*MB*), which is equal to 1,048,576 ($2^{20}$) bytes of storage, or in terms of *gigabytes* (*GB*), which is equal to 1,073,741,824 ($2^{30}$) bytes of storage. Notice that 1 KB is about $10^3$ bytes, 1 MB is about $10^6$ bytes, and 1 GB is about $10^9$ bytes, hence, the origin of the prefixes *kilo* (thousand), *mega* (million) and *giga* (billion). Therefore, a computer having 32 MB of memory is capable of storing 32 x 1048576 = 33,554,432 bytes or characters.

Sometimes, the memory capacity of a computer system is also stated in terms of number of words. However, if the memory capacity is stated in terms of words, it is necessary to know the word size in bits or bytes, to determine the actual memory capacity of the computer. Hence, while specifying the memory capacity in terms of words, it is customary to specify the total number of bits per word, along with the total number of words. Therefore, a memory with 4096 locations, with each location storing 16 bits, is called a "16-bit 4096-word memory, or, in the vernacular of the computer trade, a "4 K, 16-bit memory". Similarly, a memory having $2^{15}$ words, with each word of 16 bits, is called a "32 K, 16-bit memory". If the word size of a memory is 8 bits (equal to a byte), it becomes immaterial whether the memory capacity is expressed in terms of bytes or words. Hence, a memory having $2^{16}$ words with each word of 8 bits is simply referred to as 64 K memory (word size of 8-bits is implicit here).

# RAM, ROM, PROM and EPROM

## Random Access Memory (RAM)

When people talk about computer memory, they usually mean the volatile RAM memory. Physically, this memory consists of some integrated circuit chips (IC chips, shown in Figure 1.1), either on the motherboard, or on a small circuit board attached to the motherboard. A computer's motherboard is designed in a manner that its memory capacity can be easily enhanced by adding more memory chips. Hence, if you decide to have more memory than your computer currently has, you can buy more memory chips, and plug them in the empty memory slots on the motherboard. This job is normally done by the service engineers. The additional RAM chips, which plug into special sockets on the motherboard, are also known as *single in-line memory modules* (*SIMMs*).

## Read-Only Memory (ROM)

A special type of RAM, called *read-only memory* (*ROM*), is a non-volatile memory chip, in which data is stored permanently and cannot be altered by the programmer. In fact, storing data permanently into this kind of memory is called "burning in the data", because data in such memory is stored by using fuse-links. Once a fuse-link is burnt, it is permanent. The data stored in a ROM chip can only be read and used – they cannot be changed. This is the reason why it is called read-only memory (ROM). Since ROM chips are non-volatile, the data stored inside a ROM are not lost, when the power supply is switched off, unlike the case of a volatile RAM chip. ROMs are also known as field stores, permanent stores, or dead stores.

ROMs are mainly used to store programs and data, which do not change and are frequently used. For example, the most basic computer operations are carried out by wired electronic circuits. However, several higher-level operations, which are very frequently used, require very complicated electronic circuits for their implementations.

Hence, instead of building electronic circuits for these operations, special programs are written to perform them. These programs are called *microprograms*, because they deal with low-level machine functions, and are essentially substitutes for additional hardware. ROMs are used by computer manufacturers for storing these microprograms, so that they cannot be modified by the users.

A good example of a microprogram is the set of instructions needed to make the computer system ready for use, when its power is switched on. This microprogram, called "system boot program", contains a set of start-up instructions to check if the system hardware like memory, I/O devices, etc. are functioning properly, and looks for an operating system and loads its core part in the volatile RAM of the system, to produce the initial display-screen prompt. Note that this microprogram is used every time the computer is switched on, and needs to be retained when the computer is switched off. Hence, ROM is an ideal storage for storing it.

## Programmable Read-Only Memory (PROM)

There are two types of read-only memory (ROM) – manufacturer-programmed and user-programmed. A *manufacturer-programmed ROM* is one in which data is burnt in by the manufacturer of the electronic equipment in which it is used. For example, a personal computer manufacturer may store the system boot program permanently in the ROM chip used on the motherboard of all the PCs manufactured by it. Similarly, a printer manufacturer may store the printer controller software in the ROM chip used on the circuit board of all the printers manufactured by it. Manufacturer-programmed ROMs are mainly used in those cases, where the demand for such programmed ROMs is large. Note that manufacturer-programmed ROM chips are supplied by the manufacturers of electronic equipment, and it is not possible for a user to modify the programs or data stored inside the ROM chip. On the other hand, *a user-programmed ROM* is one in which the user can load and store "read-only" programs and data. That is, it is possible for a user to "customize" a system by converting his/her own programs to microprograms, and storing them in a user-programmed ROM chip. Such a ROM is commonly known as *Programmable Read-Only Memory* (*PROM*), because a user can program it. Once the user programs are stored in a PROM chip, they can usually be executed in a fraction of the time previously required. PROMs are programmed to record information using a special device, known as PROM-programmer. However, once the chip has been programmed, the recorded information cannot be changed, i.e., the PROM becomes a ROM, and it is only possible to read the stored information. PROM is also non-volatile storage, i.e., the stored information remains intact, even if power is switched off.

## Erasable Programmable Read-Only Memory (EPROM)

Once information is stored in a ROM chip or a PROM chip, it cannot be altered. However, there is another type of memory chip, called *Erasable Programmable Read-Only Memory* (*EPROM*), which overcomes this problem. As the name implies, it is possible to erase information stored in an EPROM chip, and the chip can be reprogrammed to store new information. EPROMs are often used by R&D personnel (experimenters), who frequently change the microprograms to test the efficiency of the computer system with new programs. EPROMs are also useful in case of those applications, where one may like to store a program in a ROM, which would normally not change, but under some unforeseen conditions one may like to alter it. When an EPROM is in use, information stored in it can only be "read", and the information remains in the chip, until it is erased.

EPROM chips are of two types – one in which the stored information is erased by exposing the chip for some time to ultraviolet light, and the other one in which the stored information is erased by using high voltage electric pulses. The former is known as *Ultra Voilet EPROM* (*UVEPROM*), and the latter is known as *Electrically EPROM* (*EEPROM*). It is easier to alter information stored in an EEPROM chip, as compared to an UVEPROM chip. Due to the ease with which stored programs can be altered, EEPROM is also known as *flash memory*. Flash memory is used in many new I/O and storage devices.

# Cache Memory

We saw that the use of main memory helps in minimizing the disk-processor speed mismatch to a large extent because the rate of data fetching by the CPU from the main memory is about 100 times faster than that from a high-speed secondary storage like disk. However, even with the use of main memory, the memory-processor speed mismatch becomes a bottleneck in the speed with which the CPU can process instructions because there is a 1 to 10 speed mismatch between the processor and the memory. That is, the rate at which data can be fetched from memory is about 10 times slower than the rate at which CPU can process data. Hence, in many situations, the performance of processors gets limited due to the slow speed of main memory. Obviously, the overall performance of a processor can be greatly improved by minimizing the memory-processor speed mismatch. Cache memory (pronounced "cash" memory) is commonly used for minimizing the memory-processor speed mismatch. Cache memory is an extremely fast, small memory between CPU and main memory (see Figure 7.1), whose access time is closer to the processing speed of the CPU. It acts as a high-speed buffer between CPU and main memory and is used to temporarily store very active data and instructions during processing. Since the cache memory is faster than main memory, the processing speed is increased by making data and instructions needed in current processing available in the cache.

## Points to Remember

1. The *CPU* is the brain of a computer system. All major calculations and comparisons performed by a computer are carried out inside its CPU. The CPU is also responsible for activating and controlling the operations of other units of the computer system. Hence, no other single component of a computer determines its overall performance, as much as the CPU.

2. The two basic components of a CPU are the control unit and the arithmetic logic unit.

3. The *control unit* of the CPU acts as a central nervous system for the other components of the computer. It manages and coordinates the entire computer system, including the input and output units. It obtains instructions from the program stored in the main memory, interprets the instructions, and issues signals, which cause other units of the system to execute them.

4. The *Arithmetic Logic Unit* (*ALU*) of the CPU is the place, where the actual execution of the instructions takes place, during the data processing operation.

5. Every CPU has built-in ability to execute a set of machine instructions, called its *instruction set*.

6. As the instructions are interpreted and executed by the CPU, there is a movement of information between the various units of the computer system. In order to handle this process satisfactorily, and to speed up the rate of information transfer, the computer uses a number of special memory units, called *registers*. These registers are used to hold information on a temporary basis, and are part of the CPU (not main memory).

7. The speed of a processor is directly related to the computer's *clock speed*, which is the number of pulses, produced per second by the built-in electronic clock. This clock speed is measured in megahertz (or MHz.).

8. The three commonly known processor architectures are *CISC (Complex Instruction Set Computer)*, *RISC (Reduced Instruction Set Computer)* and *EPIC (Explicitly Parallel Instruction Computing)*.

9. Every computer has a temporary storage area, which is built into the computer hardware, and in which instructions and data of a program reside mainly when the program is being executed by the CPU. This storage space is known as *primary storage*, *main memory*, or simply *memory*.

10. Any storage unit of a computer system is characterized and evaluated based on the following properties – storage capacity, access time, cost per bit of storage, volatile, and random access.

11. A primary storage or main memory of a computer system is made up of several small storage areas, called *locations* or *cells*. Each of these locations can store a fixed number of bits, called *word length* of that particular memory.

12. In a word-addressable computer, each numbered address location can store a fixed number of characters (equal to its word-length in bytes). In these computers, storage space is always allocated in multiples of word-length. On the other hand, in a character-addressable computer,

each numbered address can only store a single character (A, B, 1, 2, +, -, etc.).

13. The main memory capacity of large computer systems is normally more than that of small systems. This capacity is defined in terms of the number of bytes a computer system can store. Memory capacity of a computer system is normally stated in terms of *kilobytes* (*KB*), which is equal to 1024 ($2^{10}$) bytes of storage, or in terms of *megabytes* (*MB*), which is equal to 1,048,576 ($2^{20}$) bytes of storage, or in terms of *gigabytes* (*GB*), which is equal to 1,073,741,824 ($2^{30}$) bytes of storage.

14. A computer's main memory is built of volatile RAM chips.

15. A special type of RAM, called *read-only memory* (*ROM*), is a non-volatile memory chip, in which data are stored permanently and cannot be altered by the programmer. There are two types of read-only memory (ROM) – manufacturer-programmed and user-programmed. The latter is commonly known as *Programmable Read-Only Memory* (*PROM*), because a user can program it.

16. Once information is stored in a ROM chip or a PROM chip, it cannot be altered. However, *Erasable Programmable Read-Only Memory* (*EPROM*) chips can be reprogrammed to store new information. EPROM chips are of two types – *Ultra Voilet EPROM* (*UVEPROM*) and *Electrically EPROM* (*EEPROM*). EEPROM is also known as *flash memory*.

17. *Cache memory* is an extremely fast, small memory between CPU and main memory, whose access time is closer to the processing speed of the CPU. It acts as a high-speed buffer between CPU and main memory, and is used to temporarily store very active data and instructions during processing.

# Questions

1. List out the main functions of CPU in a computer system.

2. What are the two main components of CPU of a computer system? List out the main functions of each of these components.

3. Describe the role of the decoder of the control unit of a CPU.

4. What is a microprocessor?

5. What is an instruction set of a computer system? Do computers made by different manufacturers generally have the same or different instruction sets?

6. Machine language programs written for one computer will generally not run on another computer with a different CPU. Explain why?

7. What is meant by a family of CPUs? When do two CPUs belong to the same family?

8. When is a computer said to be upward compatible with another computer? How is this feature useful for the users of these computers?

9. What are registers? Name some of the commonly used registers, and briefly describe the function of each.

10. What is meant by the length of a register? What are the commonly used register-lengths in modern computer systems? Why is a larger register length more desirable?

11. List out the main steps involved in the execution of an instruction by the CPU of a computer system.

12. What is meant by the clock speed of a computer system? How does it influence the overall speed of a computer system?

13. Differentiate between CISC and RISC processors.

14. List out the relative advantages and disadvantages of CISC and RISC processors.

15. List out the key properties used to characterize and evaluate storage units of computer systems.

16. Explain the difference between volatile and non-volatile memory. Give an example of each type of memory.

17. Explain the difference among random access, pseudo-random access, and sequential access storage units. Give an example of each type of storage unit.

18. Differentiate among a bit, a byte, and a word.

19. Explain the difference between an address and the contents of an address.

20. Explain the key difference between memory read and write operations.

21. Explain why is it advantageous to have more number of bits per word, instead of having more words of shorter

length, in the memory architecture of a computer system?

22. Distinguish between word-addressable and character-addressable computers. Discuss their relative advantages and disadvantages.

23. How many bytes will be required to store the word 'MEMORY' in (a) a character-addressable computer, (b) a word-addressable computer having word-length of 64 bits?

24. Name some of the commonly used units for stating memory capacity. How many characters is each unit roughly equivalent to?

25. A computer has 512 MB of memory. How many characters can be stored in its memory at a time?

26. What is a ROM? Why is it so called? Give few typical uses of ROM.

27. What is a microprogram? Give an example of a microprogram, which is a good candidate for storage in the ROM of a computer system.

28. Differentiate between PROM and EPROM.

29. Differentiate between UVEPROM and EEPROM.

30. What is a flash memory? Why is it so called?

31. Differentiate among RAM, ROM, PROM and EPROM.

32. What is a cache memory? How is it different from a primary memory?

33. Explain how a cache memory helps in improving the overall processing speed of a computer system.

34. Write short notes on:
    (a) Central Processing Unit (CPU)
    (b) Arithmetic Logic Unit (ALU)
    (c) Registers
    (d) Storage evaluation criteria
    (e) Memory capacity
    (f) Cache memory
    (g) Volatile and Non-volatile storage
    (h) Fixed and Variable word-length memory
    (i) Processor speed
    (j) Instruction set

35. Write the full form of the following abbreviations:
    (a) KB        (i) UVEPROM
    (b) RAM       (j) EEPROM
    (c) ROM       (k) PROM
    (d) MBR       (l) EPROM
    (e) MB        (m) MAR
    (f) GB        (n) SIMM
    (g) CISC      (o) EPIC
    (h) RISC

# Chapter 8

# Secondary Storage Devices

The primary storage of a computer system has the following limitations:

1. **Limited Capacity.** It is often necessary to store many millions, sometimes billions, and even trillions, of bytes of data in a computer. Unfortunately, the storage capacity of the primary storage of today's computers is not sufficient to store the large volume of data, which needs to be handled by most data processing centres.

2. **Volatile.** The primary storage is volatile, and the data stored in it is lost, when the electric power is turned off or interrupted. However, computer systems need to store data on a permanent basis for several days, several months, or even several years.

As a result, additional memory, called *auxiliary memory* or *secondary storage*, is used with most computer systems. This section of the computer's memory is non-volatile, and has lower cost per bit stored, but it generally has an operating speed far slower than that of the primary storage. This section of the memory is used to store large volume of data on a permanent basis, which can be partially transferred to the primary storage, as and when required for processing.

Over the years, several devices and media have been developed for use as secondary storage in computer systems. Many of them, such as punched paper tape and punched cards, have become obsolete. As shown in Figure 8.1, the popular ones used in today's computer systems are magnetic tape, magnetic disk and optical disk. In this chapter, you will learn about the terminologies, principles of operation, uses, and trade-offs of many different types of secondary storage devices.

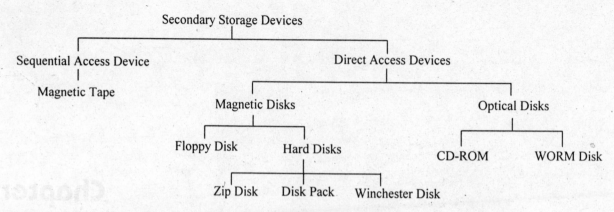

**Figure 8.1.** Commonly used secondary storage devices and their classification.

# SEQUENTIAL AND DIRECT-ACCESS DEVICES

Several different devices can be used as a secondary storage device, but the one selected for a particular application, mainly depends upon how the stored information needs to be accessed. There are two methods of accessing information – sequential or serial access, and direct or random access. A *sequential-access storage device* is one in which the arrival at the location desired may be preceded by sequencing through other locations, so that access time varies according to location. In other words, information on a sequential-access device can only be retrieved in the same sequence in which it is stored. Sequential processing is quite suitable for such applications like preparation of monthly pay slips, or monthly electricity bills, etc., where most, if not all, of the data records need to be processed one after another. In these applications, data records for every employee or customer, needs to be processed at scheduled intervals (in this case monthly). However, while working with a sequential-access device, if an address is required out of order, it can only be reached by searching through all those addresses, which are stored before it. For instance, data stored at the last few locations cannot be accessed, until all preceding locations in the sequence have been traversed. This is analogous to a music tape cassette. If 10 songs are recorded on a music tape, and if you want to listen to (or access) the 8th song, you must listen to the 7 songs, which come before your favorite song, before you can hear it. Although, your player may "fast forward" the tape quickly past the first 7 songs, the first 7 songs are still accessed, although, not fully played. In the same way, to access the 28th data record stored on a sequential-access device, the computer must first access (although not process) the first 27 data records. Magnetic tape is an example of a sequential-access storage device.

In many applications, we need to access information in a more direct manner than sequential-access devices allow. For example, in a computerized bank, at any instance, it is required to determine the exact balance in the savings account of a particular customer. Similarly, in a computerized airline ticket booking system, immediate access may be required to reservation system records, to find out if seats are currently available on a particular flight. In such applications, if we use a sequential-access device for data storage, the time taken to access the desired information may be enormous, causing frustration to the customer. Secondary storage devices exist, which permit access to individual information in a more direct or immediate manner. These direct-access devices are also called random-access devices, because the information is literally available at random, i.e., it is available in any order. Hence, a random-access storage device is one in which any location in the device may be selected at random, access to the information stored is direct, and approximately equal access time is required for each location. This is analogous to a music CD. If 10 songs are recorded on a music CD, and if you want to listen to (or access) the 6th song, you need not listen to or fast-forward the 5 songs, which come before your favorite song. All you have to do is select track number 6 on the player, and the player directly moves the pickup arm across the CD to the groove where the 6th song begins, and starts playing. Magnetic and optical disks of various types are examples of direct-access storage devices.

# MAGNETIC TAPE

Magnetic tape is the most popular storage medium for large data, which are sequentially accessed and processed.

The magnetic tape medium is a plastic ribbon, which is usually ½ inch or ¼ inch wide, and 50 to 2400 feet long. It is coated with a magnetizable recording material, such as iron oxide or chromium dioxide. Data are recorded on the tape in the form of tiny invisible magnetized and non-magnetized spots (representing 1s and 0s) on the coated surface of the tape. The tape ribbon is itself stored in reels or a small cartridge or cassette.

Like audio or videotape, the magnetic tape used in computer systems can also be erased and reused indefinitely. Old data on a tape are automatically erased, as new data are recorded in the same area. However, the information stored can be read many times, without affecting the stored data.

## Basic Principles of Operation

### Storage Organization

The tape of magnetic tape storage is divided into vertical columns, called *frames*, and horizontal rows, called *channels* or *tracks*. As shown in Figure 8.2, older tapes had 7 tracks, and they used the 6-bit BCD code format for data recording. As in BCD code, the letter A is represented on this tape by the code 110001. The first six tracks are used for recording the 6 bits of the BCD code. The seventh track is used for recording the parity bit.

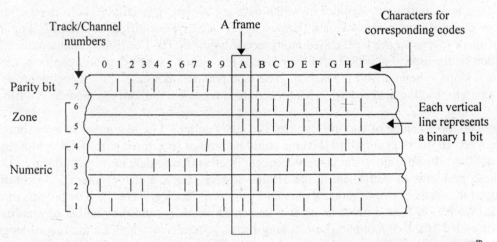

**Figure 8.2.** Data recording on a 7 track magnetic tape, using 6-bit BCD code format. Here the 7th track is used for an even-parity. Hence all frames contain an even number of 1 bits.

A *parity bit* or *check bit* is used to detect errors, which may occur due to the loss of a bit from a string of 6 or 8 bits, during data input or output operations. If the basic code for a character requires an odd number of 1 bits (such as the characters 1, 2, or A in BCD), an additional 1 bit is added to the check bit location, so that there will always be an even number of 1 bits. This is an example of *even-parity*. Similarly, in *odd-parity*, the check bit is used to always produce an odd number of 1 bits. That is, the check bit will be 1, if the total number of 1 bits for representing a particular character is even, and it will be 0, otherwise. The tape shown in Figure 8.2 uses the parity bit for an even parity.

Most modern magnetic tapes have 9 tracks, and they use the 8-bit EBCDIC code format for data recording. As shown in Figure 8.3, in this case, the fourth track is used for parity bit, which produces an odd parity in this example. Notice that, the letter A is represented here by the code 11000001, as in the 8-bit EBCDIC code format.

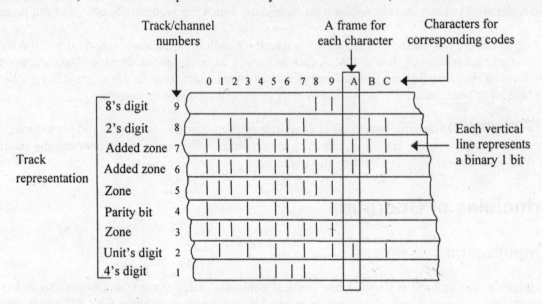

**Figure 8.3.** Data recording on a 9 track magnetic tape, using 8-bit EBCDIC code format. This figure illustrates an odd-parity tape, on which all the frames contain an odd number of 1 bits.

A magnetic tape is a continuous medium in which data are recorded serially. There is no addressing. In this situation, how can different pieces of data (known as *records*) be identified on a tape? For this, records are separated by blank spaces on the tape, called *inter-record gaps* (*IRG*). The IRGs are automatically created when data are written on the tape. Each IRG is of the order of 0.5 inches. When data are read from a moving tape, the tape movement stops, when an IRG is reached. The tape remains motionless, until the record is processed, and then moves again to read the next record. This procedure is repeated, until all the records in a file are processed.

Records stored on tapes can be of varying lengths. If a tape contains a large number of very short records with an IRG after each record, more than half of the tape could be unused (occupied with IRGs). Moreover, the tape I/O operation would also be very slow, due to very frequent interruption in tape movement during I/O operations. To overcome these problems of inefficient usage of tape storage space, and inefficient I/O operation, records are usually grouped in blocks of two or more, separated by an *inter-block gap* (*IBG*). The process of grouping two or more records together, to form a block of data, is known as *blocking*, and the number of records put together in each block, is called *blocking factor*. The blocking factor generally depends on the record length. The rule of thumb for deciding blocking factor is that the block should be at least ten times as long as the IBG, to reduce wastage of tape storage space.

## Storage Capacity

The storage capacity of a tape is a multiple of its length and data recording density. That is,

*Storage capacity of a tape = Data recording density × Length*

Data recording density refers to the amount of data, which can be stored on a given length of tape. It is measured in *bytes per inch* (*bpi*), or the number of bytes (characters), which can be stored per linear inch of tape. Tape density varies from 800 bpi in older systems to 77,000 bpi in some of the most modern systems. Hence, if a 2400 feet tape has a data recording density of 800 bpi, its storage capacity will be 2400 × 12 inches × 800 bpi = 23 × $10^6$ bytes = 23 Giga bytes. Note that, this is the total storage capacity of the tape. Its actual storage capacity (storage available for storing user data) is much less, due to the use of IBGs. In fact, the actual storage capacity of a tape may be anywhere from 35% to 70% of its total storage capacity, depending on the storage organization.

## Data Transfer Rate

*Data transfer rate* refers to the number of characters per second, which can be transmitted to the primary storage from the tape. It is measured in *bytes per second* (*bps*). Its value depends on the data recording density, and the speed with which the tape travels under the read/write head. Tape speed is typically of the order of 100 inches per second. Therefore, a tape having data recording density of 77,000 bpi, and its drive having a tape speed of 100 inches per second, will have a data transfer rate of 77,000 × 100 = 77,00,000 bytes or 7.7 MB per second.

## Tape Drive

A *magnetic tape drive* is used for storage and retrieval of data, which is stored on magnetic tape medium. The tape drive is different for tape reels, tape cartridges, and tape cassettes. However, all of them work on a similar mechanism like the audio tape recorders or videocassette recorders (VCR) found in our homes. That is, the tape drive has read/write heads, and as the tape ribbon passes under the read/write heads, the data can be either read and transmitted to primary storage, or transmitted from primary storage and written to the tape by giving suitable commands to the tape drive. Instead of *play* and *record*, *read* and *write* commands are used with the tape drive. Just as in the case of an audio tape recorder or videocassette recorder, a magnetic tape reel or cartridge or cassette has to be first loaded on to a tape drive for processing. Once loaded, the magnetic tape is said to be *on-line*; that is, it can now be used for storage or retrieval of data by the computer system. When processing is complete, the tape is removed from the tape drive for *off-line* storage; that is, it is stored away from the computer system, and data on it are not accessible to the computer system, until it is loaded again on the tape drive.

## Tape Controller

A magnetic tape must be mounted on a tape drive, before it can be used for reading/writing of information. A tape drive is connected to, and controlled by a tape controller, which interprets the commands for operating the tape drive.

# Types of Magnetic Tapes

The data recording density and data transfer rate of magnetic tapes depend to a large extent on the data organization and principles of operation of various types of magnetic tapes, and their tape drives. The commonly used ones are:

1. ½-inch tape reel
2. ½-inch tape cartridge
3. ¼-inch streamer tape
4. 4-mm digital audio tape (DAT)

They are described below.

## Half-inch Tape Reel

A magnetic tape reel uses ½ inch tape ribbon, which is stored on a tape reel (see Figure 8.4). The magnetic tape drive of a tape reel is shown in Figure 8.5. The tape on a reel moves through a tape drive in much the same way as a videotape moves through a movie projector. During processing, the tape moves from a supply reel to a take-up reel via two vacuum channels, and through a read/write head assembly. The read/write head assembly either reads data, or writes data on the tape. It is a single unit having one read/write head for each tape track. Therefore, the read/write head assembly of a 9-track tape drive will have a set of nine heads. Each head operates independently, and stores information on nine parallel tracks, parallel to the edge of the tape. This method of storing data in adjacent bit configurations is known as *parallel representation*. In parallel representation, data are read or written a byte at a time.

The two vacuum channels of the tape drive are designed to take up slack tape, acting as buffers, to prevent the tapes from snapping or stretching, when starting from a stationary position, or slowing down from full speed. Several methods are used to prevent tape damage from sudden bursts of speed, and different tape drives may use different mechanisms for this purpose.

Magnetic tape reels are fast getting replaced by tape cartridge, streamer tape, and digital audio tape, because these new magnetic tape storage devices are more compact, cheaper, and easier to handle and use.

**Figure 8.4.** Magnetic tape in reel form.

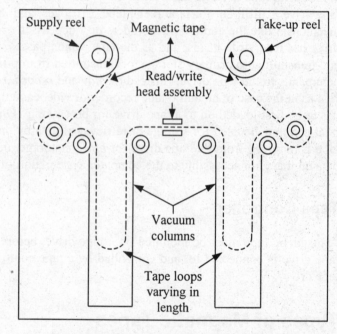

**Figure 8.5.** Tape drive of a magnetic tape reel.

## Half-inch Tape Cartridge

Magnetic tape reels are suitable for use only with large and medium size computers. The same magnetic tape is used in smaller computer systems in the form of tape cartridges. As shown in Figure 8.6, these tape cartridges look very similar to the video cassettes, which are used in the familiar home VCRs (video cassette recorders). The tape drives of these tape cartridges are also very similar in look and mechanical operation to the familiar home VCRs. A tape cartridge can be pushed inside or ejected from the tape drive, just as a videotape cassette is pushed inside or ejected from a VCR unit.

**Figure 8.6.** Magnetic tape cartridge.

These tape cartridges provide a more convenient way to package tape. They also simplify the mounting of tape, which is normally a problem with magnetic tape reels that have to be manually mounted on the tape drive. Moreover, tape cartridges provide protection against dirt and contamination, since the tape is sealed inside the cartridge.

### Quarter-inch Streamer Tape

In addition to the storage of data of those applications, which process data sequentially, one of the primary uses of magnetic tapes is to serve as a backup storage medium for data stored on on-line devices, such as a disk. During backup or recovery process, backup tapes are normally processed continuously from beginning to end, because there is seldom a need for selective access of records. Hence, there is no need to start and stop the backup tape after every few records. Based on these observations, researchers came out with a special type of quarter-inch streamer tape, which eliminates the need for the start/stop operation of traditional tape drives, for half-inch tape reels or tape cartridges. As there is no start/stop mechanism, streamer tape drives can read/write data more efficiently than the traditional tape drives, which stop and restart the tape movement at each IBG. These tapes are ¼ inch wide and are sealed in a cartridge. Their tape drives are very similar in look and mechanical operation to the tape drives of half-inch tape cartridges.

Streamer tapes are so called because they read/write data serially as streams of bits. The data format used in these tapes has been standardized by the industry, and is known as the *QIC standard*. This helps in easy use of these tapes for exchanging data between different computers. That is, data recorded on a streamer tape by one computer can be read by another computer, if both of them use the common QIC standard data format. QIC stands for Quarter Inch Cartridge.

### 4mm Digital Audio Tape (DAT)

This is the most recent type of magnetic tape storage device, which provides a very high data density per inch of tape. It uses a tape ribbon of 4mm width enclosed in a cartridge. The tape length is either 60 meters or 90 meters. Very high data recording density is obtained by using a tape drive, which uses a special technique for data recording.

## Advantages and Limitations of Magnetic Tapes

### Advantages

1. Their storage capacity is virtually unlimited, because as many tapes, as required, can be used for storing very large data sets.

2. With the low cost of tape reels and cartridges, and high data recording densities, the cost per bit of storage is very low for magnetic tapes. An additional cost benefit is that tapes can be erased and reused many times.

3. Since the tape reels and cartridges are compact and light in weight, they are easy to handle and store. Very large amount of data can be stored in a small storage space.

4. Due to their compact size and lightweight, magnetic tape reels and cartridges are also easily portable from one place to another. They are often used for transferring data and programs from one computer to another, which are not linked together.

## Limitations

1. Due to their sequential access nature, they are not suitable for storage of those data, which frequently require to be accessed randomly.

2. They must be stored in a dust-free environment, because specks of dust can cause tape-reading errors.

3. They must also be stored in an environment with properly controlled temperature and humidity levels, otherwise, the tape ribbon may get twisted due to warping, resulting in loss of stored data.

4. They must be properly labeled, so that some useful data stored on a tape is not erased by mistake.

## Uses of Magnetic Tapes

Magnetic tapes are typically used for one or more of the following purposes:

1. For applications, which are based on sequential data processing. For example, as shown in Figure 8.7, the contents of an inventory *master file* (which is the permanent source of inventory data) may be periodically updated using a *transaction file* (which contains data reflecting inventory activities during the period) to create a new inventory master file, which is used in the next processing cycle. Magnetic tapes are the most suitable storage for such applications.

2. Backing up of data stored on an on-line storage device, such as a disk, for its off-line storage, so that, if by accident, the data on the disk is corrupted or lost, it can be retrieved from the backup tape and stored back on the disk.

3. Archiving of data which are not used frequently, but which may be used once in a while.

4. Transferring of data and programs from one computer to another, which are not linked together.

5. Distribution of software by vendors. Originally sold software or software updates are often distributed by vendors on magnetic tapes.

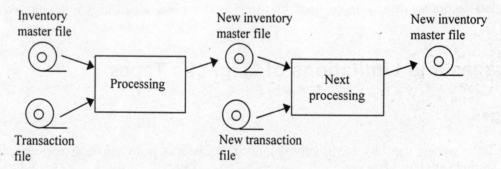

**Figure 8.7.** Illustrating the use of tapes in a sequential application.

## MAGNETIC DISK

Magnetic disk is the most popular storage medium for direct-access secondary storage. Due to their random access capability, magnetic disks are the most popular on-line secondary storage device.

A magnetic disk is a thin, circular plate/platter made of metal or plastic, which is usually coated on both sides with a magnetizable recording material, such as iron oxide. Data are recorded on the disk in the form of tiny invisible magnetized and non-magnetized spots (representing 1s and 0s) on the coated surfaces of the disk. A standard binary code, usually 8-bit EBCDIC, is used for recording data. The disk itself is stored in a specially designed protective envelope or cartridge, or several of them may be stacked together in a sealed, contamination-free container.

Like magnetic tapes, magnetic disks can also be erased and reused indefinitely. Old data on a disk are automatically erased as new data are recorded in the same area. However, the information stored can be read many times, without affecting the stored data.

# Basic Principles of Operation

## Storage Organization

For data recording, the surface of a disk is divided into a number of invisible concentric circles, called *tracks*. As shown in Figure 8.8, the tracks are numbered consecutively from outermost to innermost, starting from zero. The number of tracks varies greatly between disks, from as few as 40 on some small, low capacity disks, to several thousand on large, high-capacity disks.

Each track is further subdivided into sectors. For this, in addition to the concentric circles, the disk surface is also divided into invisible pie-shaped segments (see Figure 8.9). Hence, if there are eight such pie-shaped segments, each track will be divided into eight parts, and each of these eight portions of a track is called a *sector*.

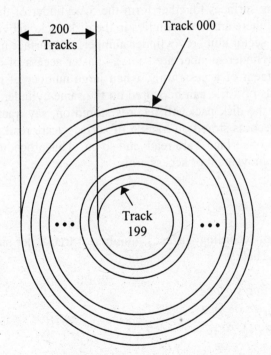

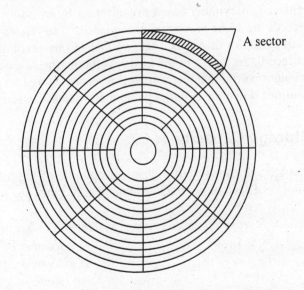

**Figure 8.8.** Tracks on a disk. The outermost track is numbered 000, and the innermost track is numbered one less than the total number of tracks (199 in this example).

**Figure 8.9.** Sectors of a disk. The number varies, but there are often 8 or more sectors per track.

A sector typically contains 512 bytes. A sector is the smallest unit with which any disk can work. That is, disk drives are designed to access (read/write) only whole sectors at a time. Even if the computer needs to change just one byte, out of the 512 bytes stored on a sector, it rewrites the entire sector.

When people refer to the number of sectors a disk has, the unit they use is *sectors per track* – not just sectors. Hence, if a disk has 200 tracks and 8 sectors per track, it has 1600 (200 × 8) sectors – not 8 sectors.

Each sector of a disk is assigned a unique number. Before a disk drive can access a piece of data (a record) stored on a disk, it must specify the record's *disk address*. The disk address is comprised of the *sector number, track number*, and *surface number* (when double-sided disks are used). That is, the disk address represents the physical location of the record on the disk.

Often, multiple disks are stacked and used together to create large capacity disk-storage systems. In this case, a set of magnetic disks is fixed to a central shaft, one below the other, to form a *disk pack* (see Figure 8.10). The disk pack is sealed and mounted on a disk drive, which consists of a motor to rotate the disk pack about its axis. The disk drive also has an access arms assembly, which has separate read/write heads for each surface of the disk pack, on which data can be recorded. Normally, the upper surface of the top disk and the lower surface of the bottom disk, are not used in a disk pack, because these surfaces may be easily scratched. The access arms assembly is designed in a manner that all the access arms (on which the read/write heads are fixed) for all the disk surfaces move together. Hence, if the read/write head, which serves the $0^{th}$ recording surface, is positioned over the $5^{th}$ track, each of the heads on the arms, which serve other recording surfaces, is similarly positioned over the $5^{th}$ track. For faster access of data from disk packs, a concept called *cylinder* is used for data organization on disk packs. As shown in Figure 8.10, a set of corresponding tracks on all the recording surfaces of a disk pack together form a cylinder. For example, the $5^{th}$ tracks of all recording surfaces together form the $5^{th}$ cylinder of the disk pack. Hence, if there are 200 tracks on a single disk surface, there are 200 cylinders in the disk pack. Obviously, in this case, the disk address of a data record is comprised of sector number, cylinder number, and surface number (track number is not required, because track number and cylinder number are same). Faster access of data is achieved in cylinder-based organization by avoiding movement of access arms, when large number of related records are to be processed in sequence. The related records of a file can be stored on the same cylinder of the multiple disks of a disk pack, so that in one revolution of the disk pack, all records stored on, say track 5 of surface 0, are read. In the next revolution, the subsequent records stored on track 5 of surface 1 are read, in the revolution after that, the subsequent records stored on track 5 of surface 2 are read, and so on. This procedure can continue down the cylinder without any delays caused by the movement of access arms.

## Storage Capacity

The storage capacity of a disk is a multiple of the number of recording surfaces, number of tracks per surface, number of sectors per track, and number of bytes per sector. That is,

$$
\begin{aligned}
\textit{Storage capacity of a disk system} &= \textit{Number of recording surfaces} \\
&\times \textit{Number of tracks per surface} \\
&\times \textit{Number of sectors per track} \\
&\times \textit{Number of bytes per sector}
\end{aligned}
$$

For example, let us assume that a disk pack has 10 disk plates, each having 2655 tracks. Also, assume that there are 125 sectors per track, and each sector can store 512 bytes. Since the disk pack has 10 disk plates, it will have 18 recording surfaces (excluding the upper surface of the topmost disk, and the lower surface of the bottommost disk). Hence, the capacity of this disk pack will be = 18 × 2655 × 125 × 512 = 3,05,85,60,000 bytes = $3 \times 10^9$ bytes (approximately) = 3 GB (3 Giga Bytes). As one character can be stored per byte, this disk pack can store 3 billion characters of information.

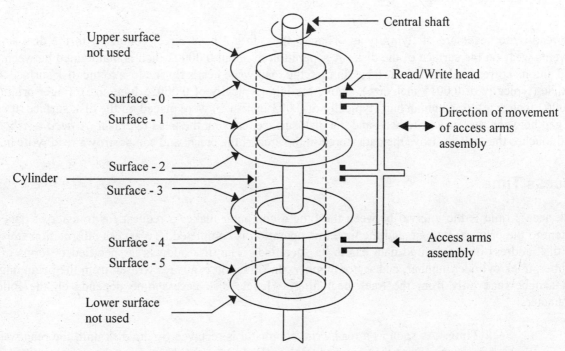

**Figure 8.10.** A disk pack having 4 disk platters. The upper surface of the top plate, and the lower surface of the bottom plate are not used. Hence, altogether there are 6 usable surfaces numbered 0, 1, 2, 3, 4 and 5. As shown, a set of corresponding tracks on all the 6 surfaces is called a cylinder.

## Access Mechanism

Data are recorded on the tracks of a spinning disk surface, and read from the surface by one or more *read/write heads*. As shown in Figure 8.11, the read/write heads are mounted on an access arms assembly. Most disk drives have a single read/write head for each disk surface. However, some faster disk systems use multiple heads on each access arm to service a number of adjacent tracks simultaneously.

The access arms assembly can be moved in and out in the direction shown in the figure, so that the read/write heads can be moved horizontally across the surfaces of the disks. In this manner, the read/write heads can be positioned on any track, on which data are to be recorded, or from which data are to be read. In case of a disk pack, each usable surface has its own read/write head, and all the heads move together. Hence, information stored on the tracks, which constitute a cylindrical shape through the disk pack, is accessed simultaneously. Recall the cylindrical storage arrangement of information in a disk pack.

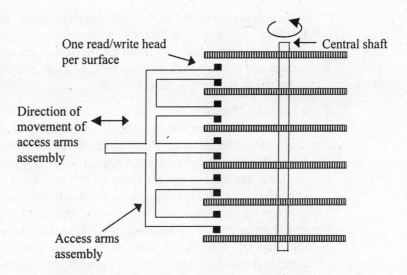

**Figure 8.11.** Vertical cross section of a disk system. There is one read/write head per recording surface.

The read/write heads are of flying type. That is, they do not have direct contact with the disk surfaces. This prevents wear on the surface of the disk. A separation of about 0.00002 inch is maintained between a read/write head and its corresponding disk surface. In fact, the read/write heads fly so close to the disk surface that, if a dust particle (typically of 0.0015 inch size), smoke particle (typically of 0.00025 inch size), finger print (typically of 0.00062 inch size), or a human hair (typically of 0.003 inch size) were placed on the disk surface, it would bridge the gap between the read/write head and the disk surface, causing the head to crash. A *head crash*, in which the head touches the disk, destroys the data stored in the area of the crash, and can destroy a read/write head as well.

## Access Time

Disk access time is the interval between the time a computer makes a request for transfer of data from a disk system to the primary storage, and the time this operation is completed. To access information stored on a disk, the disk address of the desired data has to be specified. The disk address is specified in terms of the surface number, track/cylinder number, and sector number. Information is always written from the beginning of a sector, and can be read only from the track beginning. Hence, disk access time depends on the following three parameters:

1. **Seek Time.** As soon as a read/write command is received by the disk unit, the read/write heads are first positioned on to the specified track (cylinder) number by moving the access arms assembly in the proper direction. The time required to position the read/write head over the desired track is called the *seek time*. The seek time varies, depending on the position of the access arms assembly, when a read/write command is received. If the access arms assembly is positioned on the outer most track, and the track to be reached is the inner most one, the seek time will be maximum. It will be zero, if the access arms assembly already happens to be on the desired track. The average seek time is thus specified for most systems. It is of the order of 10 to 100 milliseconds.

   We also saw that some disk systems have multiple read/write heads on each access arm. This is done to reduce the seek time. For example, a disk system may have two sets of read/write heads for each surface, one for reading/writing on the inside tracks, and another for the outside tracks. This will reduce the average seek time by half, because each read/write head needs to cover and move across only half of the total number of tracks.

2. **Latency.** Once the heads are positioned on the desired track, the head on the specified surface is activated. Since the disk is continuously rotating, this head should wait for the desired data (specified sector) to come under it. This rotational waiting time, i.e., the time required to spin the desired sector under the head is called the *latency*. The latency, also known as the *rotational delay time*, is also a variable, and depends on the distance of the desired sector from the initial position of the head on the specified track. It also depends on the rotational speed of the disk, which may be anywhere from 300 rpm (rotations per minute) to 7200 rpm. An average latency time is thus normally specified, which is of the order of 5 to 80 milliseconds. Note that, the average latency of a disk system is equal to half the time taken by the disk to rotate once. Hence, the average latency of a disk system, whose rotational speed is 3600 rpm, will be 0.5/3600 minutes = 8.3 milliseconds.

3. **Transfer Rate.** Transfer rate refers to the rate at which data are read from or written to the disk. Once the read/write head is positioned over the desired sector, the data are read/written at a speed determined by the rotational speed of the disk. If the rotational speed of a disk is 3600 rpm, and the disk has 125 sectors/track, and 512 bytes/sector, the amount of data transferred in one full revolution of the disk will be $125 \times 512 = 64,000$ bytes = 64K bytes (approximately). Hence, the transfer rate of the disk system will be $64,000 \times 3600/60$ bytes/second = 38,40,000 bytes/second = 3.8 Megabytes/second (approximately). Notice that, the transfer rate of a disk system depends on the density of the stored data and the rotational speed of the disk.

Since the data transfer time is negligible (due to high transfer rate) as compared to seek time and latency, the average access time for a disk system is the sum of its average seek time and average latency. The average access time for different types of disk systems varies over a wide range, and may be anywhere from 10 to 600 milliseconds.

Since the access time for a piece of data stored on a disk depends on the physical location of the data, it is more correct to refer to a disk system as *direct access storage device*, instead of *random access storage device*. Random access refers to a storage device, in which the access time is independent of the physical location of the data. For example, primary storage is a random access storage. However, this distinction is not always observed strictly, and hence, disk systems are often referred to as random access storage devices.

## Disk Formatting

Magnetic disks come in different sizes. The size of a disk is usually referred to by its diameter. Typical disk sizes include those with 14 inch, 9 inch, 8 inch, 5¼ inch, 3½ inch, and 3¼ inch diameter. Obviously, different size disks require different disk drives, so that the dimensions of the mechanical components of the disk drive match with that of the disks to be used with it. Even for disks of the same size, all disk drives are not the same, because different computer systems have different ways of organizing data on the disk surface. Hence, disk drives of different computers may have their own way of defining tracks, sectors, and sector size (number of bytes/sector) to match their own way of organizing data. This implies that computer manufacturers should also manufacture the disks, which can be used in their computer systems. This is a severe limitation, because it prevents the use of disks manufactured by third party vendors into one's own computer system. To overcome this problem, the concept of *disk formatting* was introduced. According to this concept, before a disk can be used with a computer system, it must first be prepared by means of a process, called disk formatting, by the computer system. For this the raw (unformatted) disk is inserted in the disk drive of the computer system, and the disk formatting command is initiated. In this process, the disk drive's read/write head lays down a magnetic pattern on the disk's surface. This pattern enables the disk drive to organize and store the data in the data organization defined for the disk drive. Most computers maintain on the disk, a table with the sector and track locations of data. This table, known as the *File Allocation Table* (*FAT*), enables the computer to locate data easily. The disk formatting command also takes care of creating the FAT, and setting aside sufficient space on the disk for it.

Disk formatting is one of the basic tasks handled by the computer's operating system. If the formatting done by the disk drives of two different computer systems is exactly the same, the two computers are said to have *compatible disk drives*. Compatible disk drives allow disks prepared by one computer to be used by the other computer. This facilitates transfer of data and programs from one computer to another, which are not linked together. Note that, this is not possible by the use of disks between computers having incompatible disk drives.

## Disk Drive

A magnetic disk has to be mounted on a disk drive, before it can be used for reading or writing of information. A disk drive contains all the mechanical, electrical and electronic components for holding one or more disks, and for reading or writing of information on to it. That is, it contains the central shaft on which the disks are mounted, the access arms assembly, the read/write heads, and the motors to rotate the disks and to move the access arms assembly. Although, disk drives vary greatly in their shape, size and disk-formatting pattern, they can be broadly classified into the following two types:

1. **Disk drives with interchangeable magnetic disks.** These disk drives allow the loading and unloading of magnetic disks, as and when they are needed, for reading/writing of data on to them. That is, at one instance, a particular disk might be loaded for use, and at another instance, another disk

might be loaded in the same disk drive. This allows data on disks to be stored off-line, and virtually unlimited capacity of the disk system, because as many disks as required can be used one after another to store very large data sets.

2. **Disk drives with fixed magnetic disks.** These disk drives come along with a set of permanently fixed disks. In this case, the disks along with the read/write heads, and the access mechanisms of the disk drive are permanently housed in a sealed, contamination-free container. The sealed packaging allows the disks to operate in a dust-free environment. This enables the designers to provide increased data density of each square inch of disk surface in these disk drives by reducing the distance between the read/write head and the disk surface, so that smaller magnetized spots can be precisely written and then retrieved. Hence, these disk drives provide higher storage capacity with the same size disks and same number of disk surfaces. However, because of the sealed packaging, the disks are not removable from their disk drives. Hence, the storage capacity of these disk systems is limited.

## Disk Controller

A disk drive is connected to and controlled by a disk controller, which interprets the commands for operating the disk drive. Since disk is a direct access storage device, the disk controller typically supports only *Read* and *Write* commands. The disk address, consisting of surface number, cylinder/track number, and sector number, needs to be specified as parameters of the disk *Read* and *Write* commands. Often, a disk controller is connected to and controls more than one disk drive. In this case, the disk drive number must also be specified as a parameter of *Read* and *Write* commands, so that the read/write operation is carried out on the specified disk surface of the correct disk drive.

## Types of Magnetic Disks

All magnetic disks are round platters. They come in different sizes, different types of packaging, and can be made of rigid metal or flexible plastic. Based on these differences, there are many different types of magnetic disks available today. However, all of them may be broadly classified into two types – floppy disks and hard disks. Floppy disks are individually packaged in protective envelopes or plastic cases, whereas hard disks may be packaged individually or in multiples, in cartridges or contamination-free containers. Depending on the type of packaging, hard disks are further classified into Zip/Bernoulli disks, disk packs, and winchester disks. The broad classification of magnetic disks is shown in Figure 8.12. The four types of magnetic disks are described below.

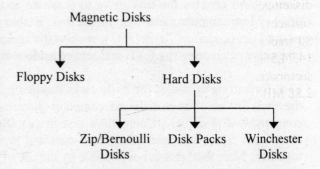

**Figure 8.12.** Broad classification of magnetic disks.

## Floppy Disks

A *floppy disk* is a round, flat piece of flexible plastic, coated with magnetic oxide. It is encased in a square plastic or vinyl jacket cover. The jacket gives handling protection to the disk surface. Moreover, it has a special liner, which provides a wiping action to remove dust particles, which are harmful for the disk surface and the read/write head. Floppy disks are so called because they are made of flexible plastic plates, which can bend, not hard plates.

They are also known as *floppies* or *diskettes*. They were introduced by IBM in 1972, and are now being produced in various sizes and capacities by many manufacturers.

### Floppy-disk drive

A *floppy-disk drive* is a device, which is used to read/write data from/to floppy disks. The drive has a spindle, which rotates the disk, and read/write heads, which can move in and out to position the read/write heads on any track of the disk surface. It is of the interchangeable magnetic disks type. That is, it allows the loading and unloading of magnetic disks, as and when they are needed, for reading/writing data on to them. A floppy disk can be very easily loaded into or unloaded from a floppy-disk drive, just by slipping the disk inside the drive's slot, or by pressing the eject button on the drive. The disks are loaded into the disk drive along with the jacket cover, and data are read/written through an aperture in the jacket. Unlike the hard-disk drives, the read/write heads of a floppy-disk drive make direct contact with the disk surface during the process of reading or writing. Hence, floppy disks are worn out with constant use. Manufacturers guarantee about 2 million reads of a floppy disk track. In case of currently used floppy-disk drives, the rotational speed of a floppy disk is of the order of 300 to 400 rpm, and the data transfer rate is of the order of 10 to 30 Kilobytes/second.

### 3½-inch floppy disk

The 3½-inch floppy disk is the most commonly used floppy disk today. Its diameter is 3½-inch. The disk is encased in a square, hard-plastic jacket cover. The jacket cover has a cutout (aperture) for the read/write head to make contact with the disk surface. This aperture is covered with a sliding metal piece (see Figure 8.13). When the diskette is inserted into the drive, the cover slides back to expose the disk surface to the read/write head.

All 3½-inch floppy disks are of double-sided type, and record data on both the disk surfaces. However, they come in three different capacities – double density, high density, and very high density. The double-density 3½-inch diskettes have 40 tracks, 18 sectors/track, and 512 bytes/sector, giving a total disk storage capacity of 2 (for two surfaces) × 40 × 18 × 512 = 7,37,280 bytes = 720 KB (approximately). The high-density 3½-inch diskettes have 80 tracks, 18 sectors/track, and 512 bytes/sector, giving a total disk storage capacity of 2 × 80 × 18 × 512 = 14,74,560 bytes = 1.4 MB (approximately). The very high-density 3½-inch diskettes have 80 tracks, 36 sectors/track, and 512 bytes/sector, giving a total disk storage capacity of 2 × 80 × 36 × 512 = 29,49,120 bytes = 2.88 MB (approximately).

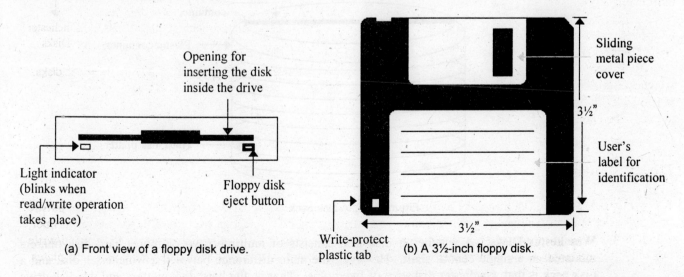

**Figure 8.13.** A 3½-inch floppy disk drive and disk.

Floppy disks are very cheap as compared to other secondary storage devices. They are also a convenient off-line storage medium for the small computer users. Hence, diskettes are currently one of the most popular, inexpensive secondary storage medium used in small computer systems.

## Hard Disks

Hard disks are the primary on-line secondary storage device for most computer systems today. Unlike floppy disks, which are made of flexible plastic or mylar, hard disks are made of rigid metal (frequently aluminium). The hard disk platters come in many sizes, ranging from 1 to 14-inch diameter.

### Types of hard disks

Depending on how they are packaged, hard disks are normally categorized into the following three types:

1. **Zip/Bernoulli Disks.** In this type, a single hard disk platter is encased in a plastic cartridge. A commonly used zip disk is of 3½ inch size, having a storage capacity of about 100 MB, depending on the formatting style used by a particular computer system. Its disk drive is called a *zip drive*. A zip drive may be of portable or fixed type. The fixed type is a part of the computer system, permanently connected to it. The portable type can be carried to a computer system, connected to it for the duration of use, and then can be disconnected and taken away when the work is done. The zip disks can be easily inserted into or removed from a zip drive, just as we insert and remove floppy disks in a floppy disk drive or a video cassette in a VCR.

2. **Disk Packs.** A disk pack consists of multiple (two of more) hard disk platters mounted on a single central shaft. Hence, all the disks of a disk pack revolve together at the same speed. As mentioned before, the disk drive of a disk pack has a separate read/write head for each disk surface, excluding the upper surface of the topmost disk, and the lower surface of the bottommost disk. These two surfaces are not used for data recording in a disk pack. When not in use, disk packs are stored in plastic cases, as shown in Figure 8.14. They are of removable/interchangeable type in the sense that they have to be mounted on the disk drive, before they can be used, and can be removed and kept off-line, when not in use. That is, different disk packs can be mounted on the same disk-pack drive at different instances of time. This gives virtually unlimited storage capacity to disk packs.

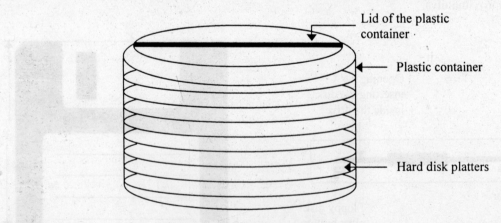

Figure 8.14. A disk pack.

3. **Winchester Disks.** A winchester disk also consists of multiple (two or more) hard disk platters mounted on a single central shaft. However, the main difference between a winchester disk and a disk pack is that winchester disks are of fixed type. That is, the hard disk platters and the disk drive

are sealed together in a contamination-free container, and cannot be separated from each other. Hence, as opposed to disk packs, which have virtually unlimited capacity, winchester disks have limited capacity. However, for the same number of disk platters of the same size, winchester disks can manage to have larger storage capacity than disk packs due to the following reasons:

– Because both the disk platters and the disk drive are sealed in a contamination-free container, and do not require to be separated later, all the surfaces of all the disk platters (including the upper surface of the topmost platter, and the lower surface of the bottommost platter) are used for data recording in case of winchester disks. That is, for a winchester disk with four platters, there are eight surfaces on which data can be recorded, as opposed to six surfaces, in case of a disk pack with four platters.

– The contamination-free environment allows winchester disks to employ much greater precision of data recording and accessing, resulting in greater density of data storage than the interchangeable disk packs.

Winchester disks were so named after the 30-30 Winchester rifle, because the early winchester disk systems had two 30-MB disks sealed together with the disk drive. The storage capacity of today's winchester disks is usually of the order of a few tens of megabytes to a few gigabytes ($10^9$ bytes).

# Advantages and Limitations of Magnetic Disks

## Advantages

1. Unlike magnetic tapes, which support sequential access of data, magnetic disks support direct access of data. Hence, they are more suitable for a wider range of applications.

2. Due to its random access property, magnetic disks are often used simultaneously by multiple users as a shared device. For example, winchester disks and disk packs are often used as on-line secondary storage devices, in which case they store data of multiple users of the computer system. A tape is not suitable for such type of usage, due to its sequential-access property.

3. Magnetic disks are suitable for both on-line and off-line storage of data. For example, winchester disks and disk packs are often used as on-line secondary storage devices, whereas floppy disks and zip disks are used as off-line secondary storage devices. In fact, the high-capacity winchester disks have made it possible for today's most personal computer users to enjoy the convenience of having all data and software readily accessible at all times.

4. Except for the fixed type winchester disks, the storage capacity of other magnetic disks is virtually unlimited, because as many disks as required can be used for storing very large data sets.

5. Due to their low cost and high data recording densities, the cost per bit of storage is low for magnetic disks. An additional cost benefit is that magnetic disks can be erased and reused many times.

6. Floppy disks and zip disks are compact and light in weight. Hence, they are easy to handle and store. Very large amount of data can be stored in a small storage space.

7. Due to their compact size and light weight, floppy disks and zip disks are also easily portable from one place to another. They are often used for transferring data and programs from one computer to another, which are not linked together.

8. Any information desired from a disk storage can be accessed in a few milliseconds, because it is a direct access storage device. This is not possible in case of a tape storage, which is a sequential access storage device.

9. Data transfer rate for a magnetic disk system is normally higher than a tape system.

10. Magnetic disks are less vulnerable to data corruption due to careless handling or unfavorable temperature and humidity conditions than magnetic tapes.

## Limitations

1. Although magnetic disks may be used for both types of applications (random as well as sequential data processing applications), for applications of the latter type, use of magnetic disks may be less efficient than magnetic tapes.

2. It is more difficult to maintain the security of information stored on magnetic disks, which are used as shared, on-line secondary storage devices, as compared to information stored on magnetic tapes or on other types of magnetic disks.

3. For winchester disks, a disk crash or drive failure often results in the loss of entire data stored on it. It is not easy to recover the lost data. Hence, suitable backup procedures are suggested for data stored on winchester disks.

4. Some types of magnetic disks, such as disk packs and winchester disks, are not so easily portable like magnetic tapes.

5. On a cost-per-bit basis, the cost of magnetic disks is low, but the cost of magnetic tapes is even lower.

6. They must be stored in a dust-free environment.

7. Floppy disks, zip disks and disk packs should be labeled properly to prevent erasure of useful data by mistake.

## Uses of Magnetic Disks

Magnetic disks are typically used for one or more of the following purposes:

1. For applications that are based on random data processing.

2. As a shared, on-line secondary storage device. Winchester disks and disk packs are often used for this purpose.

3. As a backup device for off-line storage of data, so that if by accident, the data on an on-line storage device is corrupted, it can be retrieved from the backup storage. Floppy disks, zip disks, and disk packs are often used for this purpose.

4. Archiving of data which are not used frequently, but which may be used once in a while. Floppy disks, zip disks, and disk packs are often used for this purpose.

5. Transferring of data and programs from one computer to another, which are not linked together. Floppy disks and zip disks are often used for this purpose.

6. Distribution of software by vendors. Originally sold software or software updates are often distributed by vendors on floppy disks and zip disks.

# OPTICAL DISK

As compared to magnetic tape and magnetic disk, optical disk is a relatively new secondary storage medium. During the last few years, it has proved to be a promising random access medium for high capacity secondary storage, because it can store extremely large amounts of data in a limited space.

An optical-disk storage system consists of a rotating disk, which is coated with a thin metal or some other material that is highly reflective. Laser beam technology is used for recording/reading of data on the disk. Due to the use of laser beam technology, optical disks are also known as *laser disks* or *optical laser disks*.

## Basic Principles of Operation

### Storage Organization

Unlike magnetic disks, which have several concentric tracks, an optical disk has one long track, which starts at the outer edge and spirals inward to the center (see Figure 8.15). This spiral track is ideal for reading large blocks of sequential data, such as music. However, it makes for slower random access time than the concentric tracks used by magnetic disks, whose sectors can be located faster, because they are always found on a given track at a fixed distance from the center.

Like a track on a magnetic disk, the track of an optical disk is split up into sectors, but with optical disks, each sector has the same length, regardless of whether it is located near the disk's center or away from the center. This type of data organization allows data to be packed at maximum density over the entire disk. However, it also requires a more complicated drive mechanism, because the rotation speed of the disk must vary inversely with the radius; the drive must slow down the disk's rotation speed to read sectors towards the outside of the disk, and speed it up to read sectors towards the center of the disk.

(a) Track pattern on an optical disk          (b) Track pattern on a magnetic disk

**Figure 8.15.** Difference in track patterns on optical and magnetic disks.

### Storage Capacity

The cost-per-bit of storage is very low for optical disks, because of their low cost and enormous storage density. They come in various sizes, ranging from 12-inch to 4.7-inch diameter. The most popular one is of 5.25 inch diameter, whose capacity is around 650 Megabytes. This storage capacity is equivalent to about 2,50,000 pages of printed text, or total capacity of 550 double-sided, high-density floppy disks of the same size. This tremendous storage capacity makes optical disks the most suitable storage media for multimedia applications (described in Chapter 19).

As optical disks have a single track, their storage capacity is a multiple of the number of sectors, and number of bytes per sector. That is,

*Storage capacity of an optical disk = Number of sectors × Number of bytes per sector*

The 5.25-inch optical disks typically have 3,30,000 sectors, each of 2352 bytes. That gives a total capacity of $3,30,000 \times 2352 = 776 \times 10^6$ bytes = 776 Megabytes. This is the unformatted capacity. The formatted capacity is about 650 Megabytes.

## Access Mechanism

Optical disks use laser beam technology for recording/reading of data on the disk surface. That is, the read/write head used in magnetic storage is replaced by two laser beam sources. One laser beam (of greater intensity) is used to write to the recording surface by etching microscopic pits on the disk surface, and another laser beam (of lesser intensity) is used to read the data from the light-sensitive recording surface. That is, data recording is done by focusing the stronger laser beam on the surface of the spinning disk. The laser beam is turned on and off at a varying rate, due to which tiny pits (visible only through a powerful microscope) are burnt into the metal coating of the disk along its tracks. To read the stored data, the less-powerful laser beam is focused on the disk surface. As shown in Figure 8.16, this beam is strongly reflected by the coated surface (known as a *land*), and weakly reflected by the burnt surface (known as a *pit*), producing patterns of on and off reflections, which are converted into electronic signals of binary 1s and 0s by a sensor. Note that, a mechanical read/write access arm is not needed in this case, because a light beam can be easily deflected to the desired place on the optical disk.

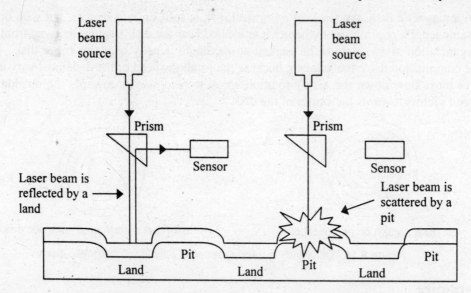

**Figure 8.16.** The surface of an optical disk consists of tiny lands and pits representing binary 1s and 0s respectively. The laser beam used for reading of stored information is strongly reflected by lands and weakly reflected (scattered) by pits.

## Access Time

Since a mechanical read/write access arm is not needed, the delay, which occurs in case of magnetic disks due to mechanical movements of the access arm, is not there in case of optical disks. Hence, you may think that data accessing from optical disks will be much faster (access time will be less) as compared to that from magnetic disks. However, this is not true. Optical disk drives are slower (have larger access time) than magnetic disk drives due to the following reasons:

1. We saw that the sectors of an optical disk are arranged on a continuous spiral track. This data organization results in a slower random access time than the concentric tracks used by magnetic disks, whose sectors can be located faster, because they are always found on a given track at a fixed distance from the center.

2. We also saw that in case of optical disks, each sector has the same length, regardless of whether it is located near the disk's center or away from the center. This data organization requires a more complicated drive mechanism, because the rotation speed of the disk must vary inversely with the radius; the drive must slow down the disk's rotation speed to read sectors towards the outside of the disk, and speed it up to read sectors towards the center of the disk. This access mechanism leads to slower data access (larger access time) as compared to magnetic disks, in which case the disks rotate at a constant speed, irrespective of the location of the data to be accessed.

Access times for optical disks are typically in the range of 100 to 300 milliseconds. Compare this with the access times of floppy disks, which are typically in the range of 100 to 200 milliseconds, and that of hard disks, which are in the range of 10 to 30 milliseconds.

## Optical Disk Drive

An optical disk has to be mounted on an optical disk drive, before it can be used for reading or writing of information. An optical disk drive contains all the mechanical, electrical and electronic components for holding an optical disk, and for reading or writing of information on to it. That is, it contains the tray on which the disk is kept, the read/write laser beams assembly, and the motor to rotate the disk. A typical optical disk drive is shown in Figure 8.17.

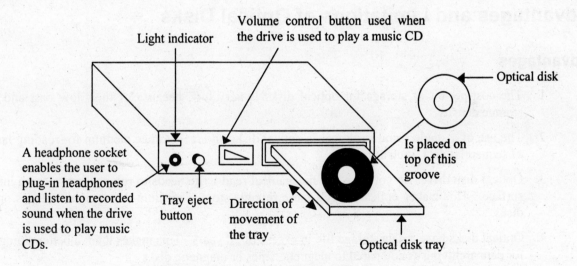

**Figure 8.17.** An optical disk drive and disk.

# Types of Optical Disks

All optical disks are round platters. They come in different sizes and capacities. The two most popular types of optical disks in use today are CD-ROM and WORM disks. They are described below.

## CD-ROM

CD-ROM stands for Compact Disk-Read-Only Memory. It is a spin-off of music CD technology, and works much like the music CDs used in music systems. In fact, if you have a soundboard and speakers connected to your computer, you can play music CDs with your computer.

The CD-ROM disk is a shiny, silver color metal disk of 5¼ inch (12 cm) diameter. It has a storage capacity of about 650 Megabytes. It is so called, because of its enormous storage capacity on a compact-size disk, and because it is a read-only storage medium. That is, these disks come pre-recorded, and the information stored on them cannot be altered.

## WORM Disk

WORM stands for *write-once, read-many*. WORM disks allow the users to create their own CD-ROM disks by using a CD-recordable (CD-R) drive, which can be attached to a computer as a regular peripheral device. WORM disks, which look like standard CD-ROM disks, are purchased blank and encoded using a CD-R drive. The information recorded on a WORM disk by a CD-R drive can be read by any ordinary CD-ROM drive. As the name implies, data can be written only once on a WORM disk, but can be read many times. That is, as with a CD-ROM disk, once data has been etched on to the surface of a WORM disk, it becomes permanent, which can be read, but never altered. Moreover, writing on a WORM disk cannot be done in multiple sessions, and all the data to be recorded have to be written on the disk surface in a single recording session. The same laser beam technology as discussed before is used for recording and reading of data.

# Advantages and Limitations of Optical Disks

## Advantages

1. The cost-per-bit of storage for optical disks is very low, because of their low cost and enormous storage density.

2. The use of a single spiral track makes optical disks an ideal storage medium for reading large blocks of sequential data, such as music.

3. Optical disk drives do not have any mechanical read/write heads to rub against or crash into the disk surface. This makes optical disks a more reliable storage medium than magnetic tapes or magnetic disks.

4. Optical disks have a data storage life in excess of 30 years. This makes them a better storage medium for data archiving as compared to magnetic tapes or magnetic disks.

5. Since data once stored on an optical disk becomes permanent, the danger of stored data getting inadvertently erased/overwritten is not there with optical disks.

6. Due to their compact size and light weight, optical disks are easy to handle, store, and port from one place to another.

7. Music CDs can be played on a computer having a CD-ROM drive along with a sound board and speakers. This allows computer systems to be also used as music systems, whenever desired.

## Limitations

1. It is a read-only (permanent) storage medium. Data once recorded, cannot be erased, and hence, the optical disks cannot be reused.

2. The data access speed for optical disks is slower than magnetic disks.

3. Optical disks require a more complicated drive mechanism than magnetic disks.

# Uses of Optical Disks

Optical disks are typically used for one or more of the following purposes:

1. For distributing large amounts of data at low cost. For example, a complete encyclopedia, dictionary, world atlas, dictionary of quotations, biographies of great people, information about all educational institutions of a particular type in a country, etc. are often distributed on CD-ROM disks.

2. For distribution of electronic version of conference proceedings, journals, magazines, books, product catalogs, etc.

3. For distribution of new or upgraded versions of software products by software vendors.

4. For storage and distribution of a wide variety of multimedia applications, such as video games.

5. For archiving of data, which are not used frequently, but which may be used once in a while.

6. WORM disks are often used by end-user companies to make permanent storage of their own proprietary information. For example, many banks use them for making a permanent record of their daily transactions.

# MASS STORAGE DEVICES

Mass storage devices are storage systems, which have storage capacity of several trillions of bytes of data. They use multiple units of the storage media being used (such as multiple disks, multiple tapes, multiple CD-ROMs, etc.) as a single secondary storage device. The three types of commonly used mass storage devices are:

1. Disk array, which uses a set of magnetic disks.

2. Automated tape library, which uses a set of magnetic tapes.

3. CD-ROM jukebox, which uses a set of CD-ROMs.

They are briefly described below.

The average access times of mass storage devices are measured in seconds, instead of milliseconds, because a transport mechanism must first move to retrieve the storage media (such as disk, tape or CD-ROM) upon which the desired data is stored. It requires several seconds to locate the storage media specified, and then few milliseconds are needed to transfer the data to the memory. Hence, an average access time of few seconds is common for these storage devices. However, a mass storage device has huge storage capacity, and a very small cost per bit stored.

Relatively slow access times limit the use of mass storage devices in many applications. However, mass storage devices are cost-effective alternative to on-line magnetic tape or disk storage in applications, which require huge storage capacity, and in which rapid access to data is not essential. When used for off-line storage, mass storage devices are often referred to as *archival storage*, because of the very large volumes of historical or backup data that they can store.

# Disk Array

A disk array, which first appeared on the market in 1993, is a set of hard disks, hard disk drives, and a controller, mounted in a single box. All the disks of a disk array form a single large storage unit. A disk array is commonly known as a *RAID* (*Redundant Array of Inexpensive Disks*). The term inexpensive comes from the fact that each of the medium-sized hard disks in the disk array is much less expensive than a single large hard disk.

Although RAID systems were originally developed to provide large secondary storage capacity with enhanced performance, today, they are also becoming popular due to enhanced reliability. Enhanced reliability is achieved in RAID units by taking advantage of the presence of multiple disks.

With more and more organizations relying on information technology to run their business, unscheduled interruptions have more serious consequences. As a result, today, many organizations are turning to the RAID as a safer way to store large amounts of data.

# Automated Tape Library

An automated tape library is a set of magnetic tapes, magnetic tape drives, and a controller, mounted in a single unit. The unit has one or more tape drives to read and write data on the tapes in the tape library. In case of units having multiple tape drives, it is possible to read/write data from/to multiple magnetic tapes simultaneously, resulting in faster data transfer rates. Multiple drives also lead to improved reliability of the storage unit, because if one of the drives fails, the unit can continue to function with other drives at a slower speed. The unit also has robotic arms to retrieve the appropriate tape from the tape library, and mount it on one of the tape drives for processing. The tape is automatically returned to the library at the end of the job. A large tape library can accommodate up to several hundred high capacity magnetic tapes, bringing the storage capacity of the storage unit to several terabytes (1 terabyte is equal to one trillion bytes).

Automated tape libraries are typically used for data archiving, and as an on-line data backup device for automated backup. They are mainly found in large computer centres.

# CD-ROM Jukebox

A CD-ROM jukebox is a set of CD-ROM disks, CD-ROM drives, and a controller, mounted in a single unit. The unit has one or more CD-ROM drives to read data from the CD-ROM disks in the jukebox. In case of units having multiple CD-ROM drives, it is possible to read data from multiple CD-ROM disks simultaneously, resulting in faster data transfer rates. Multiple drives also lead to improved reliability of the storage unit, because if one of the drives fails, the unit can continue to function with other drives at a slower speed. The unit also has robotic arms to retrieve the appropriate CD-ROM and mount it on one of the CD-ROM drives for processing. The CD-ROM is automatically returned to the appropriate slot at the end of the job. A large CD-ROM jukebox can accommodate up to several hundred CD-ROM disks, bringing the storage capacity of the storage unit to several terabytes.

CD-ROM jukeboxes are typically used for archiving read-only data, which needs to be accessed on-line, but where access time is not very critical.  For example, on-line museums, on-line digital libraries and on-line encyclopedia are a few systems, which may make use of this mass storage device in an effective manner.

# STORAGE HIERARCHY

We saw that different types of storages have different capacity, speed of access, and cost per bit stored.  Since a single type of storage is not superior in speed of access, capacity, and cost, most computer systems make use of a hierarchy of storage technologies.

A typical storage hierarchy pyramid is shown in Figure 8.18.  It includes cache memory, main memory, secondary storage and mass storage.  As we move up the pyramid, we encounter storage elements, which have faster access time, higher cost per bit stored, and less capacity.  A larger storage capacity, lower cost per bit stored, and slower access time are the results of moving down the pyramid. Hence, cache memory generally has the fastest access time, the smallest storage capacity, and the highest cost per bit stored.  The primary storage (main memory) falls next in the storage hierarchy list.  On-line, direct-access secondary storage devices, such as magnetic hard disks, make up the level of hierarchy just below main memory.  Off-line, direct-access and sequential-access secondary storage devices, such as magnetic tape, floppy disk, zip disk, WORM disk, fall next in the storage hierarchy. Mass storage devices, often referred to as archival storage, are at the bottom of the storage hierarchy.  They are cost-effective for the storage of very large quantities of data, when fast access time is not necessary.

Notice that, the use of a hierarchy of storage technologies shown in Figure 8.18, is a cost effective way of designing computer systems with very large storage capacities.

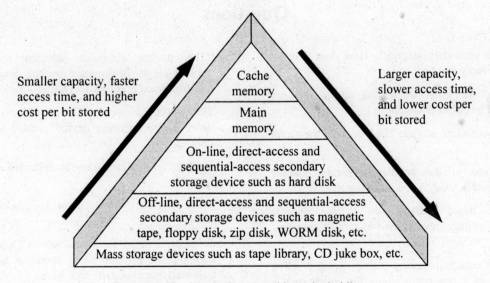

Smaller capacity, faster access time, and higher cost per bit stored

Larger capacity, slower access time, and lower cost per bit stored

Cache memory

Main memory

On-line, direct-access and sequential-access secondary storage device such as hard disk

Off-line, direct-access and sequential-access secondary storage devices such as magnetic tape, floppy disk, zip disk, WORM disk, etc.

Mass storage devices such as tape library, CD juke box, etc.

**Figure 8.18.**  A typical storage hierarchy ladder.

## Points to Remember

1.  The primary storage of a computer system has limited capacity, and is volatile.  Hence, additional memory, called auxiliary memory or secondary storage, is used with most computer systems.

2.  The *secondary storage* of a computer system is non-volatile, and has low cost per bit stored, but it generally has an operating speed far slower than that of the primary storage.

3. A *sequential-access storage device* is one in which the arrival at the location desired may be preceded by sequencing through other locations, so that access time varies according to location. On the other hand, a *random-access storage device* is one in which any location in the device may be selected at random, access to the information stored is direct, and approximately equal access time is required for each location.

4. *Magnetic tape* is the most popular sequential-access storage device. It consists of a plastic ribbon, usually ½ inch or ¼ inch wide, which is coated with a magnetizable recording material. The tape ribbon is stored in reels or a small cartridge or cassette.

5. *Magnetic disk* is the most popular direct-access storage device. It consists of a thin, circular plate made of metal or plastic, which is coated on both sides with a magnetizable recording material. The disk is stored in a specially designed protective envelope or cartridge, or several of them may be stacked together in a sealed, contamination-free container.

6. All types of magnetic disks may be broadly classified into two types – floppy disks and hard disks. *Floppy disks* are made of flexible plastic, whereas *hard disks* are made of rigid metal. Depending on the type of packaging, hard disks are further classified into zip disks, disk packs and winchester disks.

7. An *optical-disk* storage system consists of a rotating disk, which is coated with a thin metal or some other material, which is highly reflective. Laser beam technology is used for recording/reading of data on the disk.

8. The two most popular types of optical disks in use today are CD-ROM and WORM disks. *CD-ROM* disk is a read-only storage medium, whereas *WORM* disk is a write-once, read-many storage medium.

9. *Mass storage devices* use multiple units of a storage media to create a single secondary storage device. The three types of commonly used mass storage devices are disk array (also known as RAID), automated tape library, and CD-ROM jukebox.

10. As a single type of storage is not superior in speed of access, capacity and cost, most computer systems make use of a hierarchy of storage technologies, known as *storage hierarchy*. A typical storage hierarchy pyramid includes cache memory, main memory, secondary storage and mass storage.

# Questions

1. What is a secondary storage? How does it differ from a primary storage?

2. What are the main limitations of the primary storage of a computer system?

3. Why is secondary storage used in most computer systems?

4. Name some of the popular secondary storage devices used in today's computer systems.

5. Give the broad classification of the popular secondary storage devices used in today's computer systems.

6. What is a sequential-access storage device? Give examples of a few applications for which such a storage device is suitable.

7. What is a random-access storage device? Give examples of a few applications for which such a storage device is suitable.

8. Distinguish between a sequential access, a direct access, and a random access storage device. Give one example of each.

9. "The storage approach selected for a particular application is determined by the way the data are organized and processed." Discuss.

10. Differentiate between on-line and off-line storage of data. Name a storage device suitable for each type of data storage.

11. Explain how information is recorded on a magnetic tape.

12. What is a parity bit? How is it used for detecting errors?

13. What is a magnetic tape drive? Describe the main components, and the basic operation mechanism of a half-inch magnetic tape reel drive.

14. Define "data recording density" and "data transfer rate" for a magnetic tape drive. What is the data transfer rate for a magnetic tape system for which the tape density is 800 BPI and the tape speed is 200 inches per second?

15. In the context of magnetic tape storage, what is an inter-record gap? Why is it needed?

16. In the context of magnetic tape storage, what is an inter-block gap? Why is it needed?

17. In the context of magnetic tape, what is blocking? Explain how blocking helps in faster tape I/O operation.

18. In the context of magnetic tape storage, what is blocking factor? How is blocking factor generally decided?

19. What is a magnetic tape controller?

20. List out the main advantages of magnetic tapes as a secondary storage device.

21. List out the main limitations of magnetic tapes as a secondary storage device.

22. List out the main uses of magnetic tapes.

23. What is a magnetic disk? Explain how data are stored and organized on a magnetic disk.

24. In the context of magnetic disk storage, define the following terms and give the relationship among them (if any):
    (a) Track        (c) Cylinder
    (b) Sector       (d) Disk address

25. What will be the storage capacity of a double-sided disk, which has 400 tracks, 16 sectors per track and 512 bytes per sector?

26. What is a disk pack? Explain how data are organized and accessed from a disk pack.

27. What is a cylinder? A disk pack has 16 surfaces and 200 tracks on each surface. How many cylinders are there in this disk pack?

28. Explain how cylinder-based organization leads to faster access of data in a disk pack.

29. What factors determine the storage capacity of disks?

30. A disk pack consists of 6 disk plates. Each plate has 400 tracks and there are 50 sectors per track. If 512 bytes can be stored per sector, calculate the total number of bytes, which can be stored in this pack.

31. Describe the structure of the two commonly used types of access arms assembly in disk systems. List their relative advantages and disadvantages.

32. What is a head crash in case of a disk system? How does it affect a computer system?

33. Define the following terms in context of a disk storage:
    (a) Access time    (c) Latency
    (b) Seek time      (d) Transfer rate

34. Explain how do disk systems with multiple read/write heads per surface help in reducing seek time, as compared to those with single read/write head per surface.

35. What is transfer rate of a disk system? What are the two main parameters on which it depends?

36. The rotational speed of a disk system having a single recording surface is 300 rpm. It has 80 sectors/track and 512 bytes/sector. What is the transfer rate of this disk system?

37. Explain access time, seek time and latency for disk storage. What is the access time of a disk system, whose average seek time is 20 milliseconds and average latency is 7 milliseconds?

38. What is "flying-head?" How does it help in increasing the life of a disk storage?

39. Differentiate between direct and random access storage devices. In which category does a magnetic disk fall? Give reasons for your answer.

40. What is disk formatting? Why is it needed?

41. What is a magnetic disk drive? Differentiate between disk drives with interchangeable magnetic disks, and disk drives with fixed magnetic disks.

42. What is a disk controller? List out the typical commands supported by a disk controller, along with the parameters to be specified with each command.

43. List out the various types of magnetic disks commonly used in today's computer systems. Give some typical uses of each type of magnetic disk.

44. What is a floppy disk? Describe the basic principles of operation of a floppy disk drive.

45. What is a hard disk? Name three different types of hard disks. Give a typical usage of each type.

46. List out the advantages and limitations of magnetic disks as a secondary storage device.

47. List out the main advantages of magnetic disks as compared to magnetic tapes, as a secondary storage device.

48. List out the typical uses of magnetic disks.

49. What is an optical disk? How are data recorded/read from an optical disk?

50. Differentiate between the ways data are organized on a magnetic disk and an optical disk. Which data organization leads to faster random access time, and why?

51. What are the main parameters on which the storage capacity of an optical disk depends? Write the equation for calculating the storage capacity of an optical disk based on these parameters.

52. A 5¼-inch optical disk has 3,00,000 sectors, each of 2352 bytes. What is its total storage capacity?

53. Why are optical disk drives slower (have larger access time) than magnetic disk drives?

54. What are the two commonly used types of optical disks? What is the basic difference between the two?

55. Differentiate between a CD-ROM and a WORM disk. Give some typical uses of each.

56. What is a CD-ROM? Why is it so called?

57. What is a WORM disk? What limitation of a CD-ROM disk does it overcome? What limitation it still has?

58. What is meant by "data archiving"? Why is it done? Name some secondary storage media, which are used for data archiving.

59. List out the main advantages and limitations of optical disks as a secondary storage device.

60. List out the reasons why optical disks are a better storage medium for data archiving as compared to magnetic tapes and magnetic disks.

61. List out the typical uses of optical disks.

62. Write short notes on:
    (a) CD-ROM
    (b) WORM disk
    (c) Uses of optical disks
    (d) Advantages and limitations of optical disks

63. What are the three commonly used types of mass storage devices? What are the basic storage media components used in each type?

64. What is a disk array? How does it provide enhanced storage capacity and enhanced performance?

65. What is a RAID? Why is it so called? Explain how does it provide enhanced reliability.

66. What is an automated tape library? What are its main components? How are these components used together to provide a mass storage device? List out some typical uses of an automated tape library.

67. What is a CD-ROM jukebox? What are its main components? How are these components used together to provide a mass storage device? List out some typical uses of a CD-ROM jukebox.

68. Write short notes on:
    (a) Disk array
    (b) CD-ROM jukebox
    (c) Automated tape library

69. What is a storage hierarchy? Draw a typical storage hierarchy pyramid.

70. Write short notes on:
    (a) Magnetic tape          (c) Optical disk
    (b) Magnetic disk          (d) Storage hierarchy

71. Write the full form of the following abbreviations:
    (a) DAT          (e) CD-ROM
    (b) IRG          (f) WORM disk
    (c) IBG          (g) RAID
    (d) FAT

# Chapter 9

# Input-Output Devices

A computer system can be useful, only when it is able to communicate with its external environment (its users). As shown in Figure 9.1, the input-output devices (abbreviated *I/O devices*) provide the means of communication between the computer and the outer world. They are also known as *peripheral devices*, because they surround the CPU and the memory of a computer system. Input devices are used to enter data from the outside world into primary storage, and output devices supply the results of processing from the primary storage to the users. A wide variety of I/O devices are now available. For a particular application, one type may be more desirable than another. There are some devices, which are used for both input and output functions. The goal of this chapter is to familiarize you with the various types of I/O devices available for computer systems.

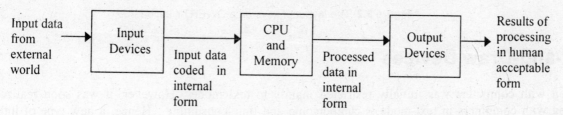

**Figure 9.1.** Illustrating the role of I/O devices in a computer system.

It is important to note that even the fastest of the I/O devices is very slow, when compared to the speed of primary storage and CPU. The main reason for this is that the speed of I/O devices in most cases depends upon mechanical movement, and the potential for improvement of such devices is limited. It has been difficult to produce I/O devices, which can match the processor and memory speeds, and there is a constant demand for faster and faster I/O devices.

# INPUT DEVICES

An *input device* is an electromechanical device, which accepts data from the outside world, and translates them into a form, which the computer can interpret. Several input devices are available today. They can be broadly classified into the following categories:

1. Keyboard devices
2. Point-and-draw devices
3. Data scanning devices
4. Digitizer

5. Electronic cards based devices
6. Voice recognition devices
7. Vision based devices

The various types of input devices along with their typical applications are described below.

## Keyboard Devices

Keyboard devices are the most commonly used input devices today. They allow data entry into a computer system by pressing a set of keys (labeled buttons), which are neatly mounted on a keyboard, which is connected to the computer system. The most popular keyboard used today is the 101-keys *QWERTY keyboard*. It is shown in Figure 9.2.

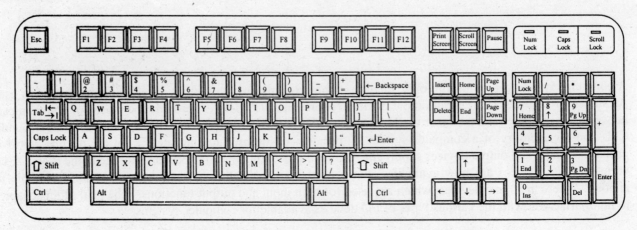

**Figure 9.2.** The layout of keys on a QWERTY keyboard.

## Point-and-Draw Devices

Interaction with computers was initially restricted mainly to text mode. However, it was soon realized that interacting with computers in text-mode is cumbersome and time-consuming. Hence, a new type of interface, called graphical user interface (GUI), was devised for interacting with computers. As shown in Figure 9.3, a GUI provides a screen full of graphic icons (small images on the screen) or menus to the user, and allows the user to make a rapid selection from the displayed icons or menus to give instructions to the computer. With such a user interface, the basic requirement is to have an input device, which can be used to rapidly point to and select a particular graphic icon or menu item from the multiple options displayed on the screen. The keyboard was found to be very inconvenient and unsuitable for this requirement. Hence, research efforts to find a suitable input device to meet this requirement, gave birth to several input devices like mouse, track ball, joystick, light pen and touch screen. Later it was realized that many of these devices, like mouse and light pen, could also be very effectively used to create graphic elements on the screen, such as lines, curves, and freehand shapes. With this **new ability,** these devices came to be known as point-and-draw devices. These input devices have made computers **a much** more easily usable tool, and have established the computer as a versatile tool for graphic designers. Some **of the** most commonly used point-and-draw devices are described below.

**Figure 9.3.** A graphical user interface (GUI) of Microsoft Windows desktop.

## Mouse

As of today, mouse is the most popular point-and-draw device. It has become a must-have input device on personal computers and workstations, which have a GUI-based user interface. As shown in Figure 9.4, a mouse is a small hand-held device, which can comfortably fit in a user's palm. It rolls on a small bearing, and has one or more buttons on the top. When a user rolls the mouse across a flat surface, such as on top of the table on which the computer is placed, the graphics cursor moves on the screen of the video display terminal in the direction of the mouse's movement. The *graphics cursor*, which is used to point and draw, is displayed on the screen as a variety of symbols, such as an arrow (◄), a wrist with a pointing finger (☛), etc. Depending on the application, the text and graphics cursor may be displayed on the screen at the same time.

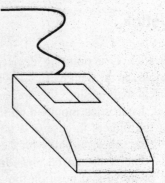

**Figure 9.4.** A mouse.

Since all movements of the mouse are reproduced by the graphics cursor on the screen, you can move the graphics cursor at a menu item or an icon by moving the mouse. For example, move the mouse away from you to move the cursor up on the screen, move the mouse towards you to move the cursor down on the screen, move the mouse right to move the cursor right on the screen, and move the mouse left to move the cursor left on the screen. In this way, the mouse can be used for quick positioning of the graphics cursor on the desired menu item or an icon. When positioned at a menu item or an icon, the graphics cursor is said to point to that menu item or icon. With a click of the mouse's button, the system can then be notified of this choice. Note that, notifying the system of a particular choice, out of the various options provided by the software, is much easier with a mouse than pressing various key combinations. With the proper software, a mouse can also be used to draw pictures on the screen and edit text.

## Trackball

A trackball is a pointing device, which is similar to a mouse. As shown in Figure 9.5, the ball, which is placed in the base of a mouse, is placed on the top along with the buttons, in case of a trackball. To move the graphics cursor around the screen, the ball is rolled with the fingers. Because the whole device is not moved for moving the graphics cursor, a trackball requires less space than a mouse for operation. Since it need not be moved for moving the graphics cursor, it is often attached to or built into the keyboard. Trackballs built into the keyboard are commonly used in laptop (notebook) computers, because a mouse is not practical for laptop users in a small space. Because the ball is fixed on the top, some people find it helpful to think of a trackball as an upside-down mouse.

A trackball comes in various shapes and forms with the same functionality. The three commonly used shapes are a ball, a button, and a square. In case of a ball, the ball is rolled with the help of fingers to move the graphics cursor. In case of a button, the button is pushed with a finger in the desired direction of the graphics cursor movement. In case of a square plastic, the finger is placed on top of it, and moved in the desired direction of the graphics cursor movement.

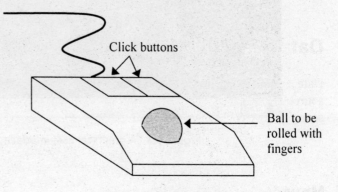

**Figure 9.5.** A trackball.

## Joystick

A joystick is a pointing device, which works on the same principle as a trackball. To make the movement of the spherical ball easier, the spherical ball, which moves in a socket, has a stick mounted on it (see Figure 9.6). Instead of using the fingers in case of a trackball, the user of a joystick moves the spherical ball with the help of the stick with his/her hand. The stick can be moved forward or backward, left or right, to move and position the graphics cursor at the desired position. Potentiometers are used to sense the movements. On most joysticks, a button on the top is provided to select the option, which is currently pointed to by the cursor. The button is clicked to make this selection. Typical uses of a joystick include video games, flight simulators, training simulators, and for controlling industrial robots.

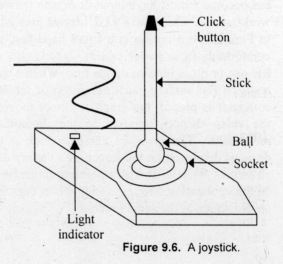

**Figure 9.6.** A joystick.

## Electronic Pen

Another point-and-draw device is an electronic pen. In a pen-based system, you hold the pen in your hand, and directly point with it on the screen to select menu items or icons; or directly draw graphics on the screen with it; or write with it on a special pad for direct input of the written information to the system.

## Touch Screen

Touch screen is the most simple, intuitive, and easiest to learn of all input devices. A touch screen enables the users to choose from available options by simply touching with their finger the desired icon or menu item displayed on the computer's screen.

Touch screens are the most preferred human-computer interface devices used in information kiosks. An *information kiosk* is an unattended system, which is used to store information of public interest, and allows common people to access the stored information as per their requirement. For example, information kiosks may be located

1. At an airport or a railway station to provide information to arriving passengers about hotels, restaurants, tourists spots, etc. in the city.

2. In large museums or zoos to guide the visitors to the locations of various attractions and facilities, and to caution them against things, which they are not supposed to do while inside.

# Data Scanning Devices

Data scanning devices are input devices, which are used for direct data entry into the computer system from source documents. Some of the data scanning devices are also capable of recognizing marks or characters. Data scanning devices typically have the following characteristics:

1. They eliminate some of the duplication of human effort required to get data into the computer. Human beings do not have to manually enter the data.

2. The reduction in human intervention improves data accuracy, and can increase the timeliness of the information processed.

3. Since scanners are direct data entry devices, they demand high quality of input documents. Documents that are poorly typed or have strikeovers or erasures are normally rejected.

4. With these devices, form design and ink specification may become more critical than is the case when people key in the data from the forms.

Data scanning devices are of many types. Some of the commonly used ones are described below.

## Image Scanner

An image scanner is an input device, which translates paper documents into an electronic format, which can be stored in a computer. The input documents may be typed text, pictures, graphics, or even handwritten material. This input device has been found to be very useful in preserving paper documents in electronic form. The copy of a document stored in a computer in this manner will never deteriorate in quality or become yellow with age, and can be displayed or printed, whenever desired. If the computer in which the scanned document is stored has the right kind of software (called *image-processing software*), the stored images can be altered and manipulated in interesting ways.

Image scanners come in various shapes and sizes. The two commonly used types are:

1. **Flatbed scanner.** As shown in Figure 9.7, a flatbed scanner is like a copy machine, which consists of a box having a glass plate on its top and a lid that covers the glass plate. The document to be scanned is placed upside down on the glass plate. The light source is situated below the glass plate, and moves horizontally from left to right when activated. After scanning one line, the light beam moves up a little, and scans the next line. The process is repeated for all the lines. It takes about 20 seconds to scan a document of size 21 cm × 28 cm.

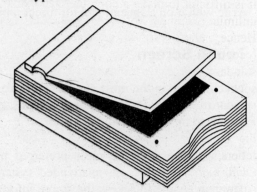

**Figure 9.7.** A flatbed scanner.

2. **Hand-held scanner.** As shown in Figure 9.8, a hand-held scanner has a set of light emitting diodes encased in a small case, which can be conveniently held in hand during operation. To scan a document, the scanner is slowly dragged from one end of the document to its other end, with its light on. The scanner has to be dragged very steadily and carefully over the document, otherwise the conversion of the document into its equivalent bit map will not be correct. Due to this reason, hand-held scanners are used only in cases where high accuracy is not needed. They are also used when the volume of documents to be scanned is low. They are also much cheaper as compared to flatbed scanners.

**Figure 9.8.** A hand-held scanner.

## Optical Character Recognition (OCR) Device

When image scanners are used for inputting text documents (typed or handwritten), they have the following two limitations:

1. Since the input document is stored as an image, instead of text, it is not possible to do any word processing of the document (the computer cannot interpret the stored document as letters, numbers and special characters).

2. The storage required for storing the document as an image is much more than that required for storing the same document as a text. For example, a page of printed text, having 2000 characters, can be stored as 2000 bytes by using the ASCII representation. A bit map image representation of the same document will require 10 to 15 times more storage, depending on the resolution (granularity) of grid points.

The OCR technology is used to overcome these limitations. In this case, the scanner is equipped with a character recognition software (called OCR software), which converts the bit map images of characters to equivalent ASCII codes. That is, the scanner first creates the bit map image of the document, and then the OCR software translates the array of grid points into ASCII text, which the computer can interpret as letters, numbers and special characters.

OCR software is extremely complex, because it is difficult to make a computer recognize an unlimited number of typefaces and fonts. Hence, these software are designed to recognize texts, which are written using standard type fonts (called OCR fonts). Two such standard fonts are OCR-A (American standard) and OCR-B (European standard). Figure 9.9 shows OCR-A fonts. Note that, if the document contains italics or bold face letters, or fonts other than that for which the OCR software has been designed, the OCR software will not work effectively.

**Figure 9.9.** OCR-A fonts.

## Optical Mark Reader (OMR)

These scanners are capable of recognizing a pre-specified type of mark made by pencil or pen. For example, many students might have appeared in objective type tests, in which they had to mark their answers to questions on a special pre-printed test scoring sheet by darkening a small square, circular, or oval shaped box by a pencil, to indicate their correct choice out of the various given options (see Figure 9.10). These answer sheets are directly fed to a computer for grading with the use of an optical mark reader.

*For each question, four options are given out of which only one is correct. Choose the correct option and mark your choice against the corresponding question number in the given answer sheet by darkening the corresponding circle with a lead pencil.*

1.  The binary equivalent of decimal 4 is:
    (a)  101
    (b)  111
    (c)  001
    (d)  100

2.  The full form of CPU is:
    (a)  Cursor Positioning Unit
    (b)  Central Power Unit
    (c)  Central Processing Unit
    (d)  None of the above

3.  Which is the largest unit of storage among the following:
    (a)  Terabyte
    (b)  Kilobyte
    (c)  Megabyte
    (d)  Gigabyte

Indicates direction in which the sheet should be fed to the OMR

1.  ○ a   ○ b   ○ c   ● d

2.  ○ a   ○ b   ● c   ○ d

3.  ● a   ○ b   ○ c   ○ d

(a) Question sheet                     (b) Pre-printed answer sheet

**Figure 9.10.** A sample question sheet of an objective test and its pre-printed answer sheet, which can be read by an OMR to grade the test.

The actual technique used by an OMR device for recognition of marks involves focusing a light on the page being scanned, and detecting the reflected light pattern from the marks. Pencil marks made with a soft lead pencil (high graphite content) reflect the light, enabling the reader to determine which responses are marked.

## Bar-Code Reader

Data coded in the form of small lines (known as bars) are known as bar codes. *Bar codes* represent alphanumeric data by a combination of adjacent vertical lines (bars) by varying their width and the spacing between them. They are particularly used for unique identification of all types of goods, books, postal packages, badges, tags, etc.

A bar-code reader is a device, which is used for reading (decoding) bar-coded data. It may be a hand-held scanner, or may be embedded in a stationary scanner. It scans a bar-code image, and converts it into an alphanumeric value, which is then fed to the computer to which the bar-code reader is connected, just as though the alphanumeric value had been typed on a keyboard.

A bar-code reader uses a laser-beam scanning technology. The laser beam is stroked across the pattern of bars of a bar code. Different bar codes, having different patterns of bars, reflect the beam in different ways, which is sensed by a light-sensitive detector. Reflected light patterns are converted into electrical pulses, and then transmitted to recognition logic circuits, which convert it into an alphanumeric value.

Just as there are a variety of internal bit encoding systems, there are a variety of bar-coding systems. The most widely known bar-coding system is the *Universal Product Code* (*UPC*), which now appears on almost all retail packages in USA. The UPC, originally used for supermarket items, is now being printed on other consumer goods also. The UPC bar-code patterns are decoded as 10 digits. The first 5 of these digits identify the manufacturer or supplier of the product, and the next 5 digits identify a specific product of the manufacturer (see Figure 9.11).

Bar code readers are commonly found in supermarkets and department stores. When a customer picks up a product for purchasing, and brings it to the cash counter for payment, the sales person at the counter uses a bar-code reader to scan the bar code printed on the product. The bar-code reader converts the bar code into an alphanumeric value, and feeds it to the computer, which looks up the price of the product, possibly updates inventory and sales records, and uses the price and description information to prepare a purchase bill for the customer. Postal delivery services also use bar codes to identify and track each packet. For example, Federal Express of USA uses a unique bar-coding system, and their employees can usually tell a customer, within a matter of minutes, the current location of any packet.

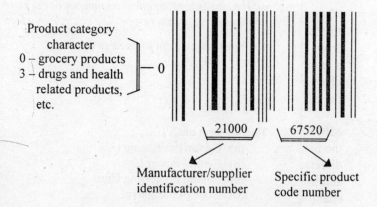

Figure 9.11. An example of UPC bar code.

## Magnetic-Ink Character Recognition (MICR)

MICR is similar to OCR, and is used by the banking industry for faster processing of the large volume of cheques being handled every day by this industry. Banks, which employ MICR technology, use a special type of cheque.

The bank's identification code (name, branch, etc.), account number, and the cheque number are pre-printed (encoded) by using characters from a special character set on all these cheques with a special ink, which contains magnetizable particles of iron oxide, before the cheques are given to the customers for use. A sample cheque, which employs MICR technology, is shown in Figure 9.12.

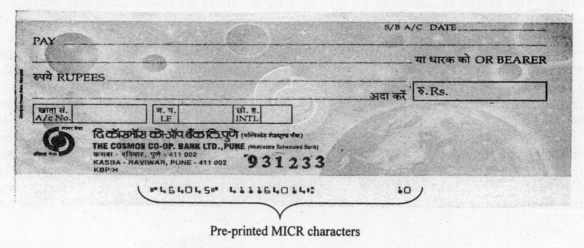

Pre-printed MICR characters

**Figure 9.12.** A bank cheque that employs MICR technology.

When a customer presents a filled-in cheque at a bank, a bank employee manually enters (keys in) the amount written on the cheque, in the lower right corner of the cheque by using an MICR inscriber, which prints the amount with the magnetic ink. The date of the transaction is automatically recorded for all cheques processed that day. This cheque is then processed by using an MICR reader-sorter, which can recognize magnetic ink characters. The MICR reader-sorter reads the data on the cheques, and sorts the cheques for distribution to other banks, or for further processing.

The most commonly used character set by MICR devices is known as E13B font, which consists of the numerals 0 to 9, and four special characters, as shown in Figure 9.13. Coded data in the form of these fonts are transferred from cheques to the computer by an MICR reader-sorter. As the cheques enter the reading unit, they pass through a magnetic field, which causes the particles in the ink to become magnetized. Read heads then interpret these characters by examining their shapes. The sorter is used to sort the cheques into different pockets, according to their identification code numbers.

MICR technology speeds up data input for the banking industry, because cheques can be directly fed into the input device, and automatically processed thereafter. Besides enabling faster processing of cheques, this technology also ensures accuracy of data entry, because most of the information is pre-printed on the cheque, and is directly fed to the computer. However, MICR has not been adopted by other industries, because the currently supported character set has only 14 symbols (10 digits and 4 special characters). No alphabetic characters are available.

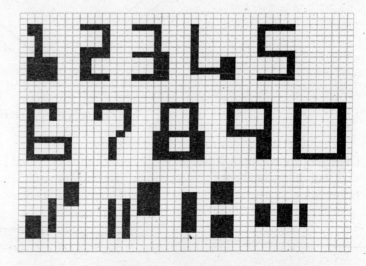

**Figure 9.13.** The E13B font (character set) used by MICR devices.

# Digitizer

A digitizer is an input device, which is used for converting (digitizing) pictures, maps and drawings into digital form for storage in computers. For example, the $x$ and $y$ coordinates of points in a drawing may be stored in digital form. This enables re-creation of the drawing from the stored information, and easy incorporation of changes in the drawing, as and when required.

As shown in Figure 9.14, a digitizer consists of a *digitizing tablet* (also known as *graphics tablet*) associated with a *stylus*. The digitizing tablet is a flat surface, which contains hundreds of fine copper wires forming a grid. Each copper wire receives electric pulses. The digitizing tablet can be spread over a working table, and is connected to a computer. The stylus is like a pen, or a lens-like cursor with a cross hair and button. The stylus is connected to the tablet, and can be pressed down at a point on the tablet to input the $(x, y)$ coordinates of the point. When the stylus is moved on the tablet, the cursor on the computer's screen moves simultaneously to a corresponding position on the screen to provide visual feedback to the operator. This enables the operator to draw sketches directly, or to input sketched drawings very easily. Inputting drawings or developing sketches by using a digitizer is further simplified by the fact that poorly sketched lines, arcs and other graphical objects are automatically input as mathematically precise objects, like straight lines and smooth curves.

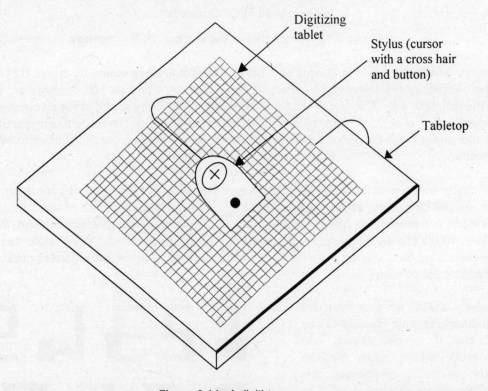

**Figure 9.14.** A digitizer.

Digitizers are commonly used in the area of Computer Aided Design (CAD) by architects and engineers to design cars, buildings, medical devices, robots, mechanical parts, etc. They are also used in the area of Geographical Information System (GIS) for digitizing of maps, which are available in paper form.

# Electronic-card Reader

Electronic cards and their associated readers offer another means of direct data entry into a computer system. Electronic cards are small plastic cards having encoded data, which are appropriate for the application for which they are used. An electronic-card reader, which is normally connected to a computer, is used to read the data encoded on an electronic card, and transfer it to the computer for further processing.

Electronic cards are often used by banks, and issued to the customers for use in *automatic teller machines* (*ATMs*). An ATM allows a customer to deposit or withdraw cash 24 hours a day, without the need to interact with a bank employee. It is an unattended machine, which may be located at any place (either inside the bank or away from the bank). It is normally connected to the bank's computer. The electronic card for use in an ATM has the customer's account number and credit limit (maximum amount that he/she can withdraw in a day) encoded on the card. An ATM has an electronic-card reader associated with it. When a customer inserts his/her card into the ATM (actually the electronic-card reader of the ATM), the reader reads the data encoded on the card, and transmits it to the bank's computer, which activates the customer's account. The customer can then carry out the desired transaction by following the instructions displayed on the screen of the ATM, and by pressing a few keys on the customized keyboard of the ATM.

# Voice Recognition Devices

Voice recognition devices are input devices, which allow a person to input data to a computer system by speaking to it. Hence, they make computers much easier to use. However, as a data input device, currently voice recognition systems have limited success, because correct interpretation by a machine of the large number of words in the vocabulary of a language is difficult. The major difficulty has been that people speak with different accents (pronounce differently) and intonations (with different tone or pitch of the voice), and the fact that the meaning of words can vary depending on the context in which they are used. Hence, today's voice recognition systems are limited to accepting few words within a relatively small domain, and can be used to enter only limited kinds and quantities of data.

Although in its infancy, voice recognition systems are already being used for a wide range of applications. Some of its typical applications are as follows:

1. For inputting data to a computer system by a person in situations where his/her hands are busy, or his/her eyes must be fixed on a measuring instrument or some other object. For example, doctors in an operation room can request certain information about a patient while operating.

2. For authentication of a user by a computer system based on voice input.

3. For limited use of computers by individuals with physical disabilities.

In addition to making input of data easier, voice recognition systems also provide tremendous freedom of movement to the operator, because the operator is free to stand up and move around, while inputting voice data to the system.

# Vision-Input System

A vision-input system allows a computer to accept input just by seeing an object. The input data in this case is normally an object's shape and features in the form of an image. The idea is to simulate the capability of a human vision system in a limited sense.

A computer with a vision-input device consists of a digital camera, and follows the following steps to recognize a given object:

1. The digital camera is focused on the input object to take a picture of the object.

2. The digital camera creates an image of the object in digital form (in 1s and 0s), so that it can be stored and interpreted by the computer.

3. The digitized image of the object is matched against similarly formed pre-stored images in the computer's image database.

4. Depending on whether a match is found or not, the system takes the appropriate action.

Vision-input devices are mainly used today in factories for designing industrial robots, which are used for quality control and assembly processes. For example, a robot used for quality control may inspect objects and separate those, which do not meet certain quality-control specifications. Another robot may be used to separate objects of different shapes in different bins.

## OUTPUT DEVICES

An *output device* is an electromechanical device, which accepts data from a computer and translates them into a form, which is suitable for use by the outside world (the users). Several output devices are available today. They can be broadly classified into the following categories:

1. Monitors
2. Printers
3. Plotters
4. Screen image projector
5. Voice response systems

The various types of output devices along with their typical applications are described below.

Output devices generate computer output, which can be broadly classified into the following two types:

1. **Soft-copy output.** A soft-copy output is an output, which is not produced on a paper or some material, which can be touched and carried for being shown to others. They are temporary in nature, and vanish after use. For example, output displayed on a terminal screen, or spoken out by a voice response system are soft-copy output.

2. **Hard-copy output.** A hard-copy output is an output, which is produced on a paper or some material, which can be touched and carried for being shown to others. They are permanent in nature, and can be kept in paper files, or can be looked later, when the person is not using the computer. For example, output produced by printers or plotters on paper are hard-copy output.

## Monitors

Monitors are by far the most popular output devices used today for producing soft-copy output. They display the generated output on a television like screen (see Figure 9.15). A monitor is usually associated with a keyboard, and together they form a *video display terminal* (*VDT*). A VDT (often referred to as just *terminal*) is the most popular input/output (I/O) device used with today's computers. That is, it serves as both an input and an output device. The keyboard is used for input to the computer, and the monitor is used to display the output from the computer. The name "terminal" comes from the fact that a terminal is at the terminal, or end, point of a communication path.

The two basic types of monitors used today are *cathode-ray-tube* (*CRT*) and *flat-panel*. The CRT monitors look much like a television, and are used with non-portable computer systems. On the other hand, the flat-panel monitors are thinner and lighter, and are commonly used with portable computer systems, like notebook computers.

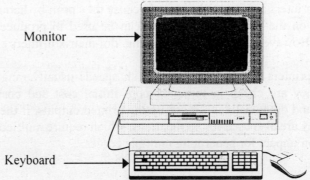

Monitor

Keyboard

**Figure 9.15.** A video display terminal consists of a monitor and a keyboard.

# Printers

Printers are the most commonly used output devices today for producing hard-copy output. The various types of printers in use today are described below.

## Dot-Matrix Printers

Dot-matrix printers are character printers, which print one character at a time. They form characters and all kinds of images as a pattern of dots. Figure 9.16 shows how various types of characters can be formed as a pattern of dots. A dot-matrix printer has a print head, which can move horizontally (left to right and right to left) across the paper. The print head contains an array of pins, which can be activated independent of each other to extend and strike against an inked ribbon to form a pattern of dots on the paper. To print a character, the printer activates the appropriate set of pins as the print head moves horizontally. For faster printing, many dot matrix printers are designed to print both while the print head moves from left to right, and while it moves from right to left, on return. Figure 9.17 shows a dot-matrix printer.

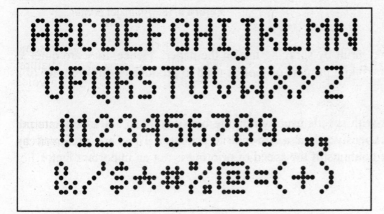

**Figure 9.16.** Formation of characters as a pattern of dots.

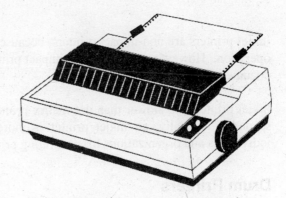

**Figure 9.17**. A dot-matrix printer.

Since dot matrix printers produce printed output as patterns of dots, they can print any shape of character, which a programmer can describe. This allows the printer to print many special characters, different sizes of print, and the ability to print graphics, such as charts and graphs.

Dot-matrix printers are impact printers, because they print by hammering the pins on the inked ribbon to leave ink impressions on the paper. Hence, they can be used to produce multiple copies by using carbon paper or its equivalent. However, due to impact printing, dot-matrix printers are noisy as compared to non-impact printers.

Dot-matrix printers are normally slow with speeds usually ranging between 30 to 600 characters per second. However, they are cheap in terms of both initial cost and cost of operation. Hence, they are preferred by individuals and organizations for generating printed outputs, if the speed and quality of printing are not important factors. They are also used for applications, which require multicopy output, such as shipping forms and invoices, which rely on impact for generating multiple copies.

## Inkjet Printers

Inkjet printers are character printers, which form characters and all kinds of images by spraying small drops of ink on to the paper. The print head of an inkjet printer contains up to 64 tiny nozzles, which can be selectively heated up in a few microseconds by an integrated circuit register. When the register heats up, the ink near it vaporizes, and is ejected through the nozzle, and makes a dot on the paper placed in front of the print head. To print a character, the printer selectively heats the appropriate set of nozzles as the print head moves horizontally. An inkjet printer is shown in Figure 9.18.

Inkjet printers produce higher quality output than dot-matrix printers, because they form characters by very tiny ink dots. A high-resolution inkjet printer has as many as 64 nozzles within height of 7mm, providing print resolution of around 360 dots per inch.

Since inkjet printers produce printed output as patterns of tiny dots, they can print any shape of characters, which a programmer can describe. This allows the printer to print many special characters, different sizes of print, and the ability to print graphics, such as charts and graphs.

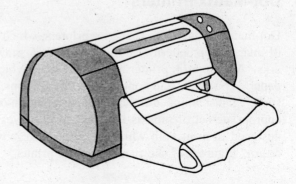

**Figure 9.18.** An inkjet printer.

Inkjet printers are non-impact printers, because they print by spraying ink on the paper. Hence, they are quiet in operation. However, like other non-impact printers, inkjet printers cannot be used to produce multiple copies of a document in a single printing.

Inkjet printers are slower than dot-matrix printers with speeds usually ranging between 40 to 300 characters per second. Typically, an inkjet printer is more expensive than a dot-matrix printer. They are preferred by individuals and organizations for generating printed outputs, if the speed of printing is not an important factor.

## Drum Printers

Drum printers are line printers, which print one line at a time. The print mechanism of a drum printer is shown in Figure 9.19. It consists of a solid cylindrical drum with characters embossed (raised characters) on its surface in the form of circular bands. Each band consists of all the printing characters supported by the printer in its character set, and the total number of bands is equal to the maximum number of characters (print positions) that can be printed on a line. Hence, a drum printer with 132 characters per line, and supporting a character set of 96 characters, will have altogether 12,672 (132×96) characters embossed on its surface.

In addition to the drum, the printer has a set of hammers mounted in front of the drum in a manner that an inked ribbon and paper can be placed between the hammers and the drum. The total number of hammers is equal to the total number of bands on the drum, that is, one hammer is located opposite to each band of the drum.

The drum rotates at a high speed, and a character at a print position is printed by activating the appropriate hammer, when the character embossed on the band at the print position passes below it. Hence, the drum would have to complete one full revolution to print each line of output. This means that all characters on a line are not printed at exactly the same time, but the time required to print an entire line is so fast that it appears as if one line is printed at a time.

The drum of a drum printer is expensive and cannot be changed often. Hence, drum printers can only print a pre-defined set of characters, in a pre-defined style, which is embossed on the drum. Due to this reason, drum printers do not have the ability to print any shape of characters, different sizes of print, and graphics, such as charts and graphs.

Drum printers are impact printers, because they print by hammering the paper and the inked ribbon against the characters embossed on the drum. Hence, they can be used to produce multiple copies by using carbon paper or its equivalent. However, due to impact printing, drum printers are noisy in operation, and often use a cover to reduce the noise level. Typical speeds of drum printers are in the range of 300 to 2000 lines per minute.

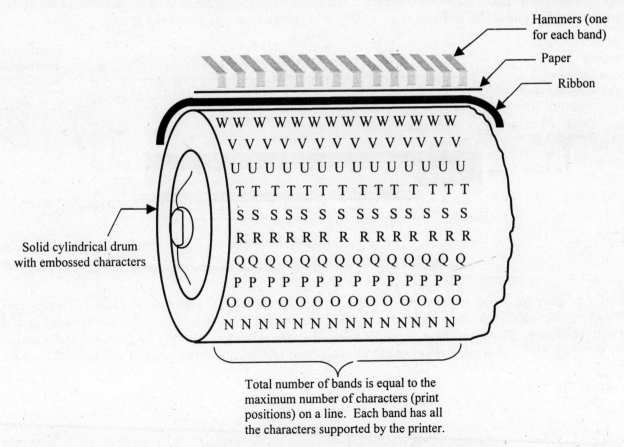

**Figure 9.19.** The printing mechanism of a drum printer.

## Chain/Band Printers

Chain/band printers are line printers, which print one line at a time. The print mechanism of a chain/band printer is shown in Figure 9.20. It consists of a metallic chain/band on which all the characters of the character set supported by the printer are embossed. A standard character set may have 48, 64 or 96 characters. In order to enhance the printing speed, the characters in the character set are embossed several times on the chain/band. For example, the chain/band of a 64 character set printer may have 4 sets of 64 characters each embossed on it. In this case, the chain/band will have altogether 256 (64×4) characters embossed on it.

In addition to the chain/band, the printer has a set of hammers mounted in front of the chain/band in a manner that an inked ribbon and paper can be placed between the hammers and the chain/band. The total number of hammers is equal to the total number of print positions. Therefore, if there are 132 print positions, the printer will have 132 hammers.

The chain/band rotates at a high speed, and a character at a print position is printed by activating the appropriate hammer, when the character embossed on the chain/band passes below it. Since the character set is repeated several times on the chain/band, it is not necessary to wait for the chain/band to make a complete revolution to position the desired character in the correct print position.

Unlike the drum of a drum printer, the chain/band of a chain/band printer can be easily changed. This allows the use of different fonts (styles of characters) and different scripts (languages) to be used with the same printer. However, just like drum printers, chain/band printers can only print pre-defined sets of characters, which are embossed on the chain/band used with the printer. Due to this reason, chain/band printers do not have the ability to print any shape of characters, different sizes of print, and graphics, such as charts and graphs.

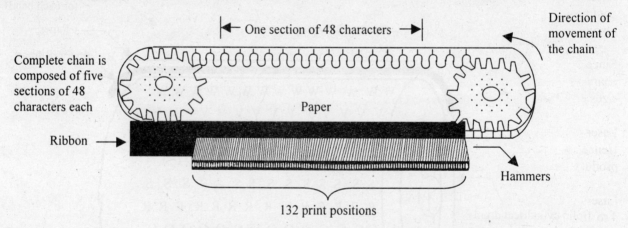

**Figure 9.20.** The printing mechanism of a chain/band printer.

Chain/band printers are impact printers, because they print by hammering the paper and the inked ribbon against the characters embossed on the chain/band. Hence, they can be used to produce multiple copies by using carbon paper or its equivalent. However, due to impact printing, chain/band printers are noisy in operation, and often use a cover to reduce the noise level. Typical speeds of chain/band printers are in the range of 400 to 3000 lines per minute.

## Laser Printers

Laser printers are page printers, which print one page at a time. The main components of a laser printer are a laser beam source, a multi-sided mirror, a photoconductive drum and toner (tiny particles of oppositely charged ink). To print a page of output, the laser beam is focused on the electro statically charged drum by the spinning multi-sided mirror. The mirror focuses the laser beam on the surface of the drum in a manner to create the patterns of characters/images to be printed on the page. As the drum is photoconductive, a difference in electric charge is created on those parts of the drum surface, which are exposed to the laser beam. As a result, the toner, which is composed of oppositely charged ink particles, sticks to the drum in the places, where the laser beam has charged the drum's surface. The toner is then permanently fused on the paper with heat and pressure to generate the printed output. The drum is then rotated and cleaned with a rubber blade to remove the toner sticking to its surface to prepare the drum for the next page printing. A laser printer is shown in Figure 9.21.

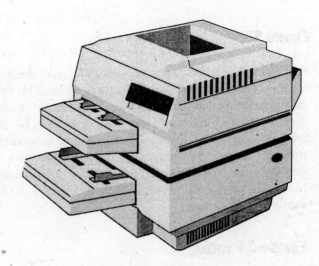

**Figure 9.21.** A laser printer.

Laser printers produce very high quality output, because they form characters by very tiny ink particles. The most common laser printers have resolution of 600 dpi (dots per inch), whereas some high-end laser printers have resolution of 1200 dpi. Because of their high resolution, these printers give excellent graphics art quality.

Since laser printers produce printed output as patterns generated by the laser beam, they can print any shape of characters, which a programmer can describe. This allows the printer to print many special characters, different sizes of print, and the ability to print graphics, such as charts and graphs.

Laser printers are non-impact printers, because they do not have hammers striking on an inked ribbon or paper. Hence, they are very quiet in operation. However, like other non-impact printers, laser printers cannot be used to produce multiple copies of a document in a single printing.

Laser printers are faster in printing speed than other printers discussed before. Low speed laser printers can print 4 to 12 pages per minute. Very high-speed laser printers are also available, which can print 500 to 1000 pages per minute. That is fast enough to print this entire book in about one minute. Because of their better print quality and printing speed, laser printers are more expensive than other printers.

# Plotters

We saw above that dot matrix, inkjet and laser printers are capable of producing graphics output. However, many engineering design applications, like architectural plan of a building, design of mechanical components of an aircraft or a car, etc., often require high-quality, perfectly-proportioned graphic output on large sheets. The various types of printers discussed above are not suitable for meeting this output requirement of such applications. A special type of output device, called *plotters*, is used for this purpose. Plotters are ideal output device for architects, engineers, city planners, and others who need to routinely generate high-precision, hard-copy, graphic.

output of widely varying sizes. The two commonly used types of plotters are drum plotter and flatbed plotter. They are briefly described below.

## Drum Plotter

In a drum plotter the paper, on which the design has to be made is placed over a drum, which can rotate in both clockwise and anti-clockwise directions to produce vertical motion. The mechanism also consists of one or more penholders mounted perpendicular to the drum's surface. The pen(s) clamped in the holder(s) can move left to right, or right to left to produce horizontal motion. The movements of the drum and the pen(s) are controlled by the graph-plotting program. That is, under computer control, the drum and the pen(s) move simultaneously to draw the designs and graphs on the sheet placed on the drum. The plotter can also annotate the designs and graphs so drawn by using the pen to draw characters of various sizes. Since each pen is program selectable, pens having ink of different colors can be mounted in different holders to produce multi-colored designs. Figure 9.22 shows a drum plotter.

## Flatbed Plotter

A flatbed plotter plots a design or graph on a sheet of paper, which that is spread and fixed over a rectangular flatbed table. In this type of plotter, normally the paper does not move, and the pen holding mechanism is designed to provide all types of motions necessary to draw complex designs and graphs. That is, under computer control, the pen(s) move in the required manner to draw the designs and graphs on the sheet placed on the flatbed table. The plotter can also annotate the designs and graphs so drawn by using the pen to draw characters of various sizes. Here also, provision is there to mount more than one pen in the pen(s) holding mechanism. Since each pen is program selectable, pens having ink of different colors can be mounted in different holders to produce multi-colored designs. The plot size is restricted by the area of the bed. Some may be as small as A4 size (8"×11" page), while some very large beds used in the design of cars, ships, aircrafts, buildings, highways, etc. can be up to 20 ft. by 50 ft. Some plotters are also designed to etch plastic or metal plates. In this case, the plastic or metal sheet is spread on the bed, and the drawing pen has a sharp-edged needle. Figure 9.23 shows a flatbed plotter.

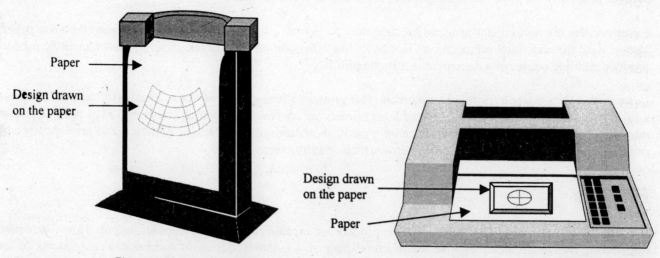

Paper

Design drawn on the paper

**Figure 9.22.** A drum plotter.

Design drawn on the paper

Paper

**Figure 9.23.** A flatbed plotter.

# Screen Image Projector

Screen image projector is an output device, which is used to project information from a computer on to a large screen (such as a cloth screen or a wall), so that it can be simultaneously viewed by a large group of people. This output device is very useful for making presentations to a group of people with the direct use of a computer. Before such an output device was available, the contents of a presentation were prepared using a computer, the presentation material was then printed on a printer, the printout was next reproduced on overhead projector transparency sheets by using a copy machine, and finally, the presentation was made by using an overhead projector. Special marker pens had to be used for marking certain portions of the contents on the transparency sheets during the presentation. A screen image projector greatly simplifies this job. It can be directly plugged to a computer system, and the presenter can make a presentation to a group of people by projecting the presentation material one after another on a large screen with the help of computer's keyboard or mouse. With this facility, the presenter can also directly point to, mark, or edit certain portions of the contents of the displayed material during the presentation to make the presentation more understandable. Additionally, a full-fledged multimedia presentation with audio, video, image and animation can be prepared and made by using this facility to make the presentation more lively and interesting, and also to greatly simplify the job of the presenter.

Screen image projectors have become a common presentation equipment today. They are commonly used with portable notebook computers to quickly setup a modern presentation facility at any place with great ease. Like monitors, screen image projectors provide a temporary, soft-copy output.

# Voice Response Systems

Just as a voice recognition system allows a user to talk to a computer, similarly, a voice response system enables a computer to talk to a user. A voice response system has an audio-response device, which produces audio output. Obviously, the output is temporary, soft-copy output. Voice response systems are of two types – voice reproduction system and speech synthesizer. They are briefly described below.

## Voice Reproduction System

A voice reproduction system produces audio output by selecting an appropriate audio output from a set of pre-recorded audio responses. The set of pre-recorded audio responses may include words, phrases or sentences spoken by human beings; music or alarms generated by musical instruments; or any other type of sound. The actual analog recordings of the pre-recorded sounds are first converted into digital data and then permanently stored on the computer's disk, or in its memory chip. When audio output is to be produced, the computer selects the appropriate sound from the set of pre-recorded sounds, the selected sound is converted back into analog form, which is then routed to a speaker to produce the audio output.

Voice reproduction systems are very useful in a wide range of applications. Their typical uses include:

1. Audio help for guiding how to operate a system. For example, banking industry uses voice reproduction systems in automatic teller machines to provide systematic guidance to customers on how to transact with the bank by using an ATM.

2. Automatic answering machines. For example, telephone enquiries for new telephone numbers in place of an old number, or vacancy status of a particular flight or train is often taken care of by an automatic answering machine.

3. Video games are made exciting and interesting by playing an event-based sound from a set of pre-recorded sounds.

4. Talking alarm clocks. For example, every hour the clock speaks out what is the time by selecting the appropriate voice message corresponding to that hour from the set of pre-recorded voice messages. Else the clock may speak "its time to wake up" at the time set for alarm.

5. Talking toys and home appliances also employ a voice reproduction system.

6. Often, personal computers with audio facility are used for automated multimedia presentations during exhibitions.

## Speech Synthesizer

A speech synthesizer converts text information into spoken sentences. To produce speech, these devices combine basic sound units, called *phonemes*. From a given text information, sequence of words are combined into phonemes, amplified, and output through the speaker attached to the system. Speech synthesizers are still in their infancy, because currently, they can produce only limited unique sounds with only limited vocal inflections and phrasing. However, they are very useful in a wide range of applications. Their typical uses include:

1. For reading out text information to blind persons. For example, a recently published book may be scanned using a scanner, converted into text using OCR software, and read out to blind persons using a speech synthesizer. This will allow blind persons to know the latest information published in a book, as soon as it is printed, rather than wait for the book to appear in Braille.

2. For allowing those persons, who cannot speak, to communicate effectively. For example, the person simply types the information, and the speech synthesizer converts it into spoken words.

3. For translation systems, which convert an entered text into spoken words in a selected language. For example, a foreigner coming to India may enter a text, which he/she wants to communicate to an Indian, and the speech synthesizer converts it into spoken words of the selected Indian language.

## Points to Remember

1. The input-output devices (abbreviated *I/O devices*) provide the means of communication between the computer and the outer world. They are also known as *peripheral devices*.

2. An *input device* is an electromechanical device, which accepts data from the outside world and translates them into a form, which the computer can interpret.

3. An *output device* is an electromechanical device, which accepts data from a computer and translates them into a form, which is suitable for use by the outside world (the users).

4. *Keyboard devices* are the most commonly used input devices today. They allow data entry into a computer system by pressing a set of keys (labeled buttons), which are neatly mounted on a keyboard, which is connected to the computer system.

5. *A graphical user interface* (*GUI*) provides a screen full of graphic icons (small images on the screen) or menus to the user, and allows the user to make a rapid selection from the displayed icons or menus to give instructions to the computer.

6. *Point-and-draw devices* are input devices, which can be used to rapidly point to and select a particular graphic icon or menu item from the multiple options displayed on the screen. Many of these devices can also be very effectively used to create graphic elements on the screen, such as lines, curves and freehand shapes. Some of the commonly used point-and-draw devices are mouse, trackball, joystick, electronic pen and touch screen.

7. *Data scanning devices* are input devices, which are used for direct data entry into the computer system from source documents. Some of the data scanning devices are also capable of recognizing marks or characters.

8. An *image scanner* is an input device, which translates paper documents into an electronic format, which can be stored in a computer. The input documents may be typed text, pictures, graphics, or even handwritten material.

9. An *optical character recognition* (*OCR*) *device* is a scanner equipped with a character recognition software.

It is used for inputting text documents and storing them in a form, which is suitable for doing word processing of the documents. That is, the computer can interpret the stored document as letters, numbers and special characters.

10. An *optical mark reader* (*OMR*) is a scanner, which is capable of recognizing a pre-specified type of mark made by pencil or pen. Any input data, which is of a choice or selection nature can be recorded for OMR input.

11. *Bar codes* represent alphanumeric data by a combination of adjacent vertical lines (called bars) by varying their width and the spacing between them. A *bar-code reader* is a scanner, which is used for reading (decoding) bar-coded data.

12. *Magnetic-ink character recognition* (*MICR*) technology is used by the banking industry for faster processing of the large volume of cheques. This technology also ensures accuracy of data entry, because most of the information is pre-printed on the cheque and is directly fed to the computer.

13. A *digitizer* is an input device, which is used for converting (digitizing) pictures, maps and drawings into digital form for storage in computers. This enables re-creation of the drawing from the stored information whenever required, as well as easy incorporation of changes in the drawing as and when required.

14. *Electronic cards* are small plastic cards having encoded data, which are appropriate for the application for which they are used. An *electronic-card reader*, which is normally connected to a computer, is used to read the data encoded on an electronic card, and transfer it to the computer for further processing.

15. *Voice recognition devices* are input devices, which allow a person to input data to a computer system by speaking to it.

16. A *vision-input system* allows a computer to accept input just by seeing an object. The input data in this case is normally an object's shape and features in the form of an image.

17. Computer output generated by output devices are of two types – soft-copy output and hard-copy output. *Soft-copy outputs* are temporary in nature, and vanish after use. *Hard-copy outputs* are permanent in nature, and can be kept in paper files, or can be looked at a later time, when the person is not using the computer.

18. *Monitors* are by far the most popular output device used today for producing soft-copy output. They display the generated output on a television like screen.

19. A monitor and a keyboard are usually associated together to form a *video display terminal* (*VDT*), which is often referred to as just *terminal*. A terminal serves as both an input and an output device, and is the most popular input/output (I/O) device used with today's computers.

20. *Printers* are the most commonly used output devices used today for producing hard-copy output.

21. *Dot-matrix printers* are character printers, which form characters and all kinds of images as a pattern of dots.

22. *Inkjet printers* are character printers, which form characters and all kinds of images by spraying small drops of ink on to the paper.

23. *Drum printers* are line printers, which print characters by striking a set of hammers on an inked ribbon and paper placed against a solid cylindrical drum with characters embossed on its surface in the form of circular bands.

24. *Chain/band printers* are line printers, which print characters by striking a set of hammers on an inked ribbon and paper placed against a metallic chain/band on which all the characters of the character set supported by the printer are embossed.

25. *Laser printers* are page printers, which produce very high quality output by forming characters and all kinds of images with very tiny ink particles.

26. *Plotters* are ideal output device for architects, engineers, city planners, and others, who need to routinely generate high-precision, hard copy graphic output of widely varying sizes. The two commonly used types of plotters are drum plotter and flatbed plotter.

27. *Screen image projector* is an output device, which is used to project information from a computer on to a large screen (such as a cloth screen or a wall), so that it can be simultaneously viewed by a large group of people.

28. *Voice response systems* enable computers to talk to their users. They are of two types – voice reproduction system and speech synthesizer. A *voice reproduction system* produces audio output by selecting an appropriate audio output from a set of pre-recorded audio responses. On the other hand, a *speech synthesizer* converts text information into spoken sentences.

# Questions

1. Why are I/O devices necessary for a computer system?

2. What are peripheral devices? Why are they so called?

3. Differentiate between an input device and an output device. Can a device be used as both an input device and an output device? If no, explain why. If yes, give an example of such a device.

4. Why are I/O devices very slow as compared to the speed of primary storage and CPU?

5. What is an input device? Name some of the commonly used input devices.

6. What are keyboard devices?

7. What are point-and-draw devices? Name some of the commonly used point-and-draw devices.

8. What is a mouse? Explain how is it used to notify the system of a particular user choice out of a given set of choices on the monitor's screen.

9. What is a trackball? How is it different from a mouse?

10. Explain how a trackball is used to notify the system of a particular user choice out of a given set of choices on the monitor's screen.

11. What is a joystick? How is it different from a trackball? Give some typical uses of a joystick.

12. Explain how an electronic pen is used as an input device.

13. What is a touch screen device?

14. Give some typical applications for which touch screen is most suitable as an input device.

15. What is an information kiosk? Give some typical uses of an information kiosk.

16. Write short notes on:
    - (a) Mouse
    - (b) Trackball
    - (c) Joystick
    - (d) Electronic Pen
    - (e) Touch screen
    - (f) Information kiosk

17. What are data scanning devices? How do they help in improving input data accuracy as compared to keyboard devices?

18. What is an image scanner?

19. Differentiate between a flatbed and a hand-held image scanner?

20. What are the limitations of an image scanner when it is used for inputting text documents? How does an OCR device overcome these limitations?

21. What is an OCR device? List out some of its advantages and limitations for inputting text documents.

22. What is an OMR device? What types of applications is it suitable for? Explain the technique used by it for recognition of marks.

23. What are bar codes? How does a bar-code reader read bar-coded data? Give a typical use of a bar-code reader.

24. What is the Universal Product Code (UPC)? Which input device is used for inputting data based on UPC?

25. What is an MICR device? Which industry is the primary user of MICR?

26. Explain how an MICR device helps in faster processing of bank cheques with greater accuracy.

27. What is the main limitation of MICR technology?

28. What is a digitizer? What are its two main components? What are its main areas of application?

29. Explain how a digitizer can be used to convert a drawing into digital form for storage in computers.

30. What is an electronic card? Give two applications where electronic cards can be effectively used.

31. What is a voice recognition device? Why do currently available voice recognition devices have limited success?

32. Give some typical applications of voice recognition systems.

33. What is a vision-input system? Give some typical applications of vision-input systems.

34. Write short notes on:
    - (a) Image scanner
    - (b) Bar-code reader
    - (c) Digitizer
    - (d) Electronic-card reader
    - (e) Vision-input systems
    - (f) Optical Mark Reader (OMR)
    - (g) Optical Character Recognition (OCR)
    - (h) Voice recognition devices
    - (i) Magnetic-Ink Character Recognition (MICR)

35. Write short notes on:
    (a) Keyboard devices
    (b) Point-and-draw devices
    (c) Data scanning devices

36. What is an output device? Name some of the commonly used output devices.

37. Differentiate between soft-copy and hard-copy outputs.

38. Name two output devices used for producing soft-copy output, and two output devices used for producing hard-copy output.

39. What is a computer terminal? Why is it so called?

40. What is a monitor device? Name the two basic types of monitors used today, along with their relative advantages and disadvantages.

41. What is a flat panel monitor? Where is it commonly used?

42. What is a printer? What are the commonly used types of printers?

43. Differentiate between impact and non-impact printers. Give their relative advantages and disadvantages. Name few printers of both types.

44. Explain the printing mechanism of dot-matrix printers.

45. List out the key features and limitations of dot-matrix printers.

46. Explain the printing mechanism of inkjet printers.

47. List out the key features and limitations of inkjet printers.

48. Explain the printing mechanism of drum printers.

49. List out the key features and limitations of drum printers.

50. Explain the printing mechanism of chain/band printers.

51. List out the key features and limitations of chain/band printers.

52. Explain the printing mechanism of laser printers.

53. List out the key features and limitations of laser printers.

54. Write short notes on:
    (a) Dot-matrix printers
    (b) Inkjet printers
    (c) Drum printers
    (d) Chain/band printers
    (e) Laser printers

55. What is a plotter? What types of users need it?

56. Explain the working mechanism of a drum plotter.

57. Explain the working mechanism of a flatbed plotter.

58. What is a screen image projector? What is it typically used for?

59. What is a voice response system? Give some of its typical applications.

60. What is a voice reproduction system? How does it function? Give some of its typical applications.

61. What is a speech synthesizer? How does it function? Give some of its typical applications.

62. Write short notes on:
    (a) Plotter
    (b) Screen image projector
    (c) Voice response systems
    (d) Voice reproduction system

63. Write the full forms of the following abbreviations:
    (a) GUI          (e) UPC
    (b) CAD          (f) MICR
    (c) OCR          (g) VDT
    (d) OMR          (h) CRT

# Chapter 10

# Computer Software

The terms hardware and software are frequently mentioned in connection with computers. *Hardware* is the term given to the machinery and the various individual pieces of equipment. It refers to the physical devices of a computer system. Hence, the input, storage, processing, control, and output devices are hardware. In fact, what we have described so far in the previous chapters is actually the hardware of computer systems. The term "software" will be introduced in this chapter, and will be discussed at length in the next few chapters.

## WHAT IS SOFTWARE?

A computer cannot do anything on its own. It must be instructed to do a desired job. Hence, it is necessary to specify a sequence of instructions, which a computer must perform to solve a problem. Such a sequence of instructions, written in a language, which can be understood by a computer, is called a *computer program*. It is the program, which controls the activity of processing by the computer, and the computer performs preciseiy what the program wants it to do. When a computer is using a program, we say, it is *running* or *executing* that program.

The term *software* refers to the set of computer programs, procedures, and associated documents (flowcharts, manuals, etc.), which describe the programs, and how they are to be used. To be precise, software means a collection of programs, whose objective is to enhance the capabilities of the hardware.

A *software package* is a group of programs, which solve a specific problem or perform a specific type of job. For example, a word-processing package may contain programs for text editing, text formatting, drawing graphics, spelling checking, etc. Hence, a multipurpose computer system has several software packages, one each for every type of job it can perform.

# RELATIONSHIP BETWEEN HARDWARE AND SOFTWARE

In order for a computer to produce useful output, its hardware and software must work together. Nothing useful can be done with the computer hardware on its own, and software cannot be utilized without supporting hardware.

To take an analogy, a cassette player and the cassettes purchased from market are hardware. However, the songs recorded on the cassettes are its software. To listen to a particular song, first of all that song has to be recorded on one of the cassettes, which should then be mounted on the cassette player, and played. Similarly, to get a particular job done by a computer, the corresponding software should be loaded in the hardware, before processing starts.

The following important points regarding the relationship between hardware and software are brought out by this analogy:

1. Both hardware and software are necessary for a computer to do useful job. Both are complementary to each other.

2. The same hardware can be loaded with different software to make a computer system perform different types of jobs, just as different songs can be played using the same cassette player.

3. Except for upgrades (like increasing the main memory and hard disk capacities, or adding speakers, modems, etc.), hardware is normally a one-time expense, whereas software is a continuing expense. Just as we buy new cassettes for the newly released songs, or for songs whose cassettes we do not have, similarly one buys new software to be run on the same hardware, as and when need arises or funds become available.

# TYPES OF SOFTWARE

Although, the range of software available today is vast and varied, most software can be divided into two major categories:

1. System software, and

2. Application software

## System Software

*System software* is a set of one or more programs, designed to control the operation and extend the processing capability of a computer system. In general, a computer's system software performs one or more of the following functions:

1. Supports the development of other application software.

2. Supports the execution of other application software.

3. Monitors the effective use of various hardware resources, such as CPU, memory, peripherals, etc.

4. Communicates with and controls the operation of peripheral devices, such as printer, disk, tape, etc.

Hence, system software makes the operation of a computer system more effective and efficient. It helps the hardware components work together, and provides support for the development and execution of application software (programs). The programs included in a system software package are called *system programs*, and the programmers who prepare system software are referred to as *system programmers*.

Some of the most commonly known types of system software are:

1. **Operating Systems.** Every computer has an operating system software, which takes care of the effective and efficient utilization of all the hardware and software components of the computer system. Operating system has been discussed in Chapter 14.

2. **Programming Language Translators.** Programming language translators are system software, which transform the instructions prepared by programmers in a programming language, into a form, which can be interpreted and executed by a computer system. Programming language translators have been discussed in Chapter 12.

3. **Communications Software.** In a network environment (where multiple computers are interconnected together by communications network), communications software enables transfer of data and programs from one computer system to another. Communications software has been described in Chapters 17 and 18.

4. **Utility Programs.** Utility programs (also known as *utilities*) are a set of programs, which help users in system maintenance tasks, and in performing tasks of routine nature. Some of the tasks commonly performed by utility programs include formatting of hard disks or floppy disks, taking backup of files stored on hard disk on to a tape or floppy disk, sorting of the records stored in a file in a particular order based on some key field(s), etc.

# Application Software

*Application software* is a set of one or more programs, designed to solve a specific problem, or do a specific task. For example, an application software for payroll processing produces pay slips as the major output, and an application software for processing examination results produces mark sheets as the major output along with some other statistical reports. Similarly, a program written by a scientist to solve his/her particular research problem is also an application software. The programs included in an application software package are called *application programs*, and the programmers who prepare application software are referred to as *application programmers*.

There are literally millions of application software available for a wide range of applications, ranging from simple applications, such as word processing, inventory management, preparation of tax returns, banking, hospital administration, insurance, publishing, to complex scientific and engineering applications, such as weather forecasting, space shuttle launching, oil and natural gas exploration, design of complex structures like aircrafts, ships, bridges, sky-rise buildings, etc. With so many applications available, it is not possible to categorize them all, and to cover them here. Some of the most commonly known application software are:

1. **Word-Processing Software.** A word-processing software enables us to make use of a computer system for creating, editing, viewing, formatting, storing, retrieving and printing documents (written material, such as letters, reports, books, etc.). This software has been discussed in Chapter 15.

2. **Spreadsheet Software.** A spreadsheet software is a numeric data analysis tool, which allows us to create a kind of computerized ledger. A manual ledger is a book having rows and columns, which accountants use for keeping a record of financial transactions, and for preparing financial statements. This software has been discussed in Chapter 15.

3. **Database software.** A *database* is a collection of related data stored and treated as a unit for information retrieval purposes. A *database software* is a set of one or more programs, which enable us to create a database, maintain it (add, delete and update its records), organize its data in desired

fashion (for example, sort its records alphabetically name-wise), and to selectively retrieve useful information from it (for example, get the telephone number of the person named Kashyap Rana from the address database, or get the names of all currently enrolled students from the student database whose birthdays fall today).

4. **Graphics Software.** A graphics software enables us to use a computer system for creating, editing, viewing, storing, retrieving and printing designs, drawings, pictures, graphs and anything else that can be drawn in the traditional manner.

5. **Personal Assistance Software.** A personal assistance software allows us to use personal computers for storing and retrieving our personal information, and planning and managing our schedules, contacts, financial and inventory of important items.

6. **Education Software.** Education software allows a computer system to be used as a teaching and learning tool. A few examples of such applications are those that teach young children to do (a) mathematics; (b) recognize alphabets; and (c) read whole words and sentences.

7. **Entertainment Software.** Entertainment software allows a computer system to be used as an entertainment tool. A good example of such an application is computer video games.

# LOGICAL SYSTEM ARCHITECTURE

The logical architecture of a computer system is shown in Figure 10.1. The architecture basically depicts the relationship among the hardware, system software, application software and users of a computer system. As shown in the figure, at the center of any computer system is the hardware, which comprises of the physical devices/components of the computer system. Surrounding the hardware is the system software layer, which constitutes the operating and programming environment of the computer system. That is, the software at this layer is designed to hide the hardware details of the system from application programmers, and to coordinate the operations of the various hardware devices for optimizing the performance of all the devices. Surrounding the system software is the application software layer, which consists of a wide range of software, which are designed to do a specific task, or solve a specific problem. The final layer is the layer of users who normally interact with the system via the user interface provided by the application software. Different application software usually provide different user interfaces. Hence, how a particular user interacts with the computer system, depends on which application he/she is using.

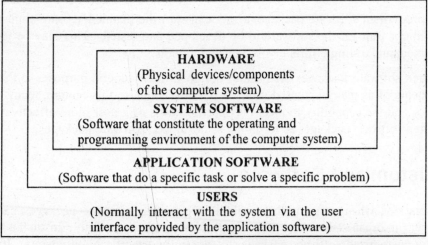

**HARDWARE**
(Physical devices/components
of the computer system)

**SYSTEM SOFTWARE**
(Software that constitute the operating and
programming environment of the computer system)

**APPLICATION SOFTWARE**
(Software that do a specific task or solve a specific problem)

**USERS**
(Normally interact with the system via the user
interface provided by the application software)

**Figure 10.1.** Relationship among the hardware, system software,
application software, and users of a computer system.

# ACQUIRING SOFTWARE

At one time, application and system software were included in the purchase price of the computer. Today, however, software is usually not included in the purchase price of the computer. For most computer manufacturers, the purchase price of a computer includes only the hardware, and a minimum of system software. The customer normally has to pay extra charges for additional system software and application software, which he/she may wish to purchase.

A desired software may be obtained today in one or more of the ways discussed below. The relative advantages and limitations of each way of obtaining software are also discussed below.

## Buying Pre-written Software

Thousands of pre-written software packages are available today. If you can find a software package, which meets your requirements, purchasing it is probably the best option. The following steps are typically followed in selecting and buying a pre-written software package by a user:

1. The user must first prepare a list of all available software packages, which are meant for performing the task(s) for which the user is looking for a software.

2. The second step is to select only those software packages, from the list prepared above, which will meet the requirements of the user. For example, compatibility with the user's available/planned hardware, I/O devices, operating system, etc.

3. The third step is to choose the best one (based on factors such as supported features, duration of warranty support, cost, etc.) from the list of selected ones.

4. The final step is to find out the source from where the finally chosen software can be purchased at the cheapest price. Different vendors normally offer different discount rates on the list price, and selecting the best vendor in terms of price and after-sale support is very important.

The following are the advantages and limitations of buying a pre-written software package:

1. A pre-written software package usually costs less, because its development and maintenance costs are shared by many customers.

2. With a pre-written software package, a user can start the planned activity almost immediately. The user need not wait for the software to be developed and tested. This may be very important, if the development and testing efforts involve several months.

3. Pre-written software packages are usually designed to be general purpose, so that they can meet the requirements of as many potential users as possible. Due to this feature, many times, the operating efficiency and the capability to meet the specific needs of a user more effectively is not as good for pre-written software packages as for in-house developed software packages.

## Ordering Customized Software

Often, there are situations when none of the available pre-written software packages can meet the specific requirements of a user (an organization or an individual), either partially or fully. In such a situation, it becomes necessary to create a customized software package, to satisfy the specific requirements. If the user has an in-house software development team, the software package can be created in-house. However, if such a team does not exist in-house, the user must get it created by another organization by placing an order for it. The following steps are typically followed for this:

1. The user has to first of all list out all its requirements very carefully.

2. The user then floats a tender for inviting quotations for the creation of the requisite software. Sometimes, the user may directly contact few software houses, instead of floating a tender for quotations.

3. After the quotations are received, the user shortlists a few of them for further interaction, based on the cost quoted by them, their reputation in the market, their submitted proposal, etc.

4. The user then personally interacts with the representative(s) of each of the shortlisted vendors. Based on this interaction, the user makes a final choice of the vendor, whom it wants to offer the contract for creation of the requisite software.

5. The selected vendor then creates the software package, and delivers it to the user. Often, the vendor has to very closely interact with the user, during the software development process.

Often, the user has to order for both the hardware and the software. In this case, the user may choose to place the order for both to a single vendor. The vendor develops the software on the chosen hardware, and delivers the software along with the hardware to the user. This is normally referred to as an *end-to-end solution* or a *turnkey solution*.

The following are the advantages and limitations of ordering a customized software package, rather than developing it in-house:

1. In case of ordering, the user need not maintain its own software development team. Maintaining and managing such a team is an expensive affair, and may not be justified for an organization, which does not need to develop software on a regular basis.

2. It is easier to carry out changes in the software, if it is developed by an in-house team. For ordered customized software, the user needs to always depend on the vendor for carrying out the changes, and the vendor may separately charge for every request for change.

## Developing Customized Software

If none of the available pre-written software packages can meet the specific requirements of an organization, and if the organization has an in-house software development team, the organization may very well choose to get a customized software package developed in-house for its requirements. The following steps are typically followed for the in-house development of a software package:

1. A project team is first constituted to carry out the development activity.

2. The team studies the requirements carefully, and plans the functional modules for the software.

3. It then analyzes which of the functional modules need to be developed, and which of the functional modules' requirements can be met with an existing pre-written software.

4. For the functional modules, which need to be developed, the team next plans their programs, and does the coding, testing, debugging and documentation for the planned programs.

5. All the modules are then tested in an integrated manner.

6. The software is then implemented, used and maintained.

The following are the advantages and limitations of developing a customized software package in-house rather than getting it developed by an outside party:

1. It is easier to carry out changes in the software, if it is developed in-house.

2. Developing software in-house means a major commitment of time, money and resources, because an in-house software development team needs to be maintained and managed.

## Downloading Public-domain Software

A *public-domain software* is a software, which is available free, or for a nominal charge, from the bulletin boards or user-group libraries on the Internet. Creators of these software obtain distribution for their products by supplying free copies to bulletin boards and user-group libraries. Their basic objective is to popularize their software to as many users as possible. Users are encouraged to copy these software and try them out. The software can be freely shared with other users. Hence, public-domain software are also referred to as *shareware* or *user-supported software*.

Often a user may find a public-domain software suitable for his/her requirements. In this case, he/she can obtain it by downloading it from the Internet.

The following are the advantages and limitations of downloading and using public-domain software packages:

1. They are normally free.

2. They can be downloaded and used immediately. The user need not wait for the software to be developed and tested, before the planned activity can be started.

3. They may not be properly tested before release, and their support is normally poor as compared to a commercial software. Hence, they may fail during operation, and bug fixing may not take place soon.

## SOFTWARE DEVELOPMENT STEPS

No matter whether a software is a pre-written software, or a customized software developed by a vendor or in-house, or a public-domain software, it has to be developed by someone in the first place. Developing a software and putting it to use is a complex process, which involves the following steps:

1. Analyzing the problem at hand, and planning the program(s) to solve the problem.
2. Coding the program(s).
3. Testing, debugging and documenting the program(s).
4. Implementing the program(s).
5. Evaluating and maintaining the program(s).

These steps have been covered in detail in the next few chapters. Chapter 11 deals with Step 1, Chapter 12 deals with Step 2, and Chapter 13 deals with Steps 3, 4 and 5.

## FIRMWARE

Computer software in conventional systems is supplied on storage media like CDs, floppies, tapes, disks, etc. However, with the advancement in technology, and the reduction in hardware cost, today, software is also being made available by many computer manufacturers on read-only memory (ROM) chips. These ROM chips can be easily plugged into the computer system, and they form a part of the hardware. Such programs (software), which are made available on hardware, are known as *firmware*. Firmware often refers to a sequence of instructions (software), which is substituted for hardware. For example, when cost is more important than performance speed, the computer system architect might decide not to use special electronic circuits (hardware) to multiply two numbers, but instead, write instructions (software) to cause the machine to accomplish the same function by repeated use of circuits already designed to perform addition. This software will be stored in a ROM chip of the computer, and will be executed (used) whenever the computer has to multiply two numbers. Hence, this software will be known as firmware. To be precise, firmware is software substituted for hardware, and stored in read-only memory.

Initially, only system software was supplied in the form of firmware. However, today, even application programs are being supplied in firmware. Dedicated applications are also programmed in this fashion, and made available in firmware. Because of the rapid improvements in memory technology, firmware is frequently a cost-effective alternative to wired electronic circuits, and its use in computer design has been gradually increasing. In fact, the increased use of firmware has today made it possible to produce smart machines of all types. These machines have microprocessor chips with embedded software.

## Points to Remember

1. The term *hardware* refers to the physical devices of a computer system. Hence, the input, storage, processing, control, and output devices are hardware.

2. The term *software* refers to a collection of programs. A *program* is a sequence of instructions written in a language, which can be understood by a computer.

3. A *software package* is a group of programs, which solve a specific problem, or perform a specific type of job.

4. The hardware and software of a computer must work together for the computer to produce useful output. Nothing useful can be done with the computer hardware on its own, and software cannot be utilized without supporting hardware.

5. Most software can be divided into two major categories – system software and application software. *System software* is a set of one or more programs, designed to control the operation and extend the processing capability of a computer system. *Application software* is a set of one or more programs, designed to solve a specific problem, or do a specific task.

6. A few examples of system software are operating systems, programming language translators, utility programs, and communications software.

7. A few examples of application software are word-processing software, spreadsheet software, database software, graphics software, personal assistance software, education software, and entertainment software.

8. Figure 10.1 shows the relationship among the hardware, system software, application software, and users of a computer system.

9. A user can acquire a desired software in one or more of the following ways:
   - By buying pre-written software
   - By ordering customized software
   - By developing customized software
   - By downloading public-domain software

   Each of these ways of acquiring software has its own advantages and limitations.

10. Developing a software and putting it to use is a complex process, which involves the following steps:
    - Analyzing the problem at hand, and planning the program(s) to solve the problem.
    - Coding the program(s).
    - Testing, debugging and documenting the program(s).
    - Implementing the program(s).
    - Evaluating and maintaining the program(s).

11. *Firmware* is software substituted for hardware, and stored in read-only memory.

# Questions

1. Define the terms hardware and software.

2. What is a computer program?

3. What is meant by running/executing a computer program?

4. What is a software package?

5. Hardware and software of a computer system are like two sides of a coin. Discuss.

6. Give an analogy to bring out the relationship between hardware and software of a computer system.

7. Hardware is normally a one-time expense, whereas software is a continuing expense. Elaborate.

8. How many types of software are there? Give three examples of each.

9. Define and distinguish between application software and system software.

10. Define the following terms:
    (a) System software
    (b) System program
    (c) System programmer
    (d) Application software
    (e) Application program
    (f) Application programmer

11. List out some of the key functions performed by the system software of a computer system.

12. Explain the importance of system software for a computer system.

13. What is a utility program? List out some of the tasks commonly performed by utility programs.

14. What is a communications software?

15. What is an education software? Give a few examples of such software.

16. What is an entertainment software? Give a few examples of such software.

17. Explain the relationship among the hardware, system software, application software, and users of a computer system.

18. How does a normal user interact with the hardware of a computer? Describe the various in-between layers.

19. What are the different ways of acquiring software? List out their relative advantages and limitations.

20. List out the relative advantages and disadvantages of creating a customized software in-house by an organization, versus getting it created by another organization.

21. What is a turnkey solution?

22. What is a shareware? What are the advantages and limitations of using a shareware?

23. List out the steps typically followed in developing a software and putting it to use.

24. Write short notes on:
    (a) Hardware
    (b) Software
    (c) Firmware

25. Write short notes on:
    (a) Types of software
    (b) Acquiring software
    (c) Software development steps
    (d) Relationship between hardware and software

26. Write short notes on:
    (a) System software
    (b) Application software
    (c) Relationship among the hardware, system software, application software, and users of a computer

27. What is firmware and what is its importance to the computer system architect?

28. Why is firmware gaining popularity?

29. Differentiate among hardware, software, and firmware.

# Chapter 11

# Planning the Computer Program

In Chapter 10, computer software has been described as a set of computer programs. In Chapter 10, we also saw that before writing a program for software, one must first plan the program. That is, to produce a correct and effective computer program, one must first plan the logic (the various steps) of the program. If one attempts to plan the logic, and write the program at the same time, he/she is likely to become so involved with the required instruction formats that program logic will suffer. Hence, before we learn how to write a program (in next chapter), we will first learn how to plan the logic of a computer program (in this chapter).

## PURPOSE OF PROGRAM PLANNING

If you are asked by your teacher to solve an arithmetic problem, and if you are not familiar with the steps involved in solving the problem, you will not be able to solve the problem. The same principle applies to writing computer programs also. A programmer cannot write the instructions to be followed by a computer, unless the programmer knows how to solve the problem manually.

If you know the steps to be followed for solving the given problem, but while solving the problem, you forget to apply some of the steps, or you apply the calculation steps in the wrong sequence, you will get a wrong answer. Similarly, while writing a computer program, if the programmer leaves out some of the instructions for the computer, or writes the instructions in the wrong sequence, the computer will calculate a wrong answer. Hence, to produce an effective computer program, it is necessary that the programmer writes every instruction in the proper sequence. However, the instruction sequence (logic) of a computer program can be very complex. Hence, in order to ensure that the program instructions are appropriate for the problem, and are in the correct sequence, programs must be planned, before they are written.

# ALGORITHM

## What is an Algorithm?

We saw above that planning a program involves defining its logic (the correct sequence of instructions needed to solve the problem at hand). The term *algorithm* is often used to refer to the logic of a program. It is a step-by-step description of how to arrive at the solution of the given problem. It may be formally defined as a sequence of instructions, designed in a manner that, if the instructions are executed in the specified sequence, the desired results will be obtained. In order to qualify as an algorithm, a sequence of instructions must possess the following characteristics:

1. Each and every instruction should be precise and unambiguous.

2. Each instruction should be such that it can be performed in a finite time.

3. One or more instructions should not be repeated infinitely. This ensures that the algorithm will ultimately terminate.

4. After performing the instructions, that is, after the algorithm terminates, the desired results must be obtained.

## Sample Algorithms

To gain insight into algorithms, let us consider some simple examples.

*Example 11.1.*

50 students in a class appeared in their final examination. Their mark sheets have been given to you. The division column of the mark sheet contains the division (FIRST, SECOND, THIRD or FAIL) obtained by the student. Write an algorithm to calculate and print the total number of students who passed in FIRST division.

*Algorithm:*

Step 1:   Initialize Total_First_Division and Total_Marksheets_Checked to zero.

Step 2:   Take the mark sheet of the next student.

Step 3:   Check the division column of the mark sheet to see if it is FIRST. If no, go to Step 5.

Step 4:   Add 1 to Total_First_Division.

Step 5:   Add 1 to Total_Marksheets_Checked.

Step 6:   Is Total_Marksheets_Checked = 50? If no, go to Step 2.

Step 7:   Print Total_First_Division.

Step 8:   Stop.

*Example 11.2.*

There are 100 employees in an organization. The organization wants to distribute annual bonus to the employees based on their performance. The performance of the employees is recorded in their annual appraisal forms. Every employee's appraisal form contains his/her basic salary, and the grade for his/her performance during the year. The grade is of three categories – 'A' for outstanding, 'B' for good, and 'C' for average performance. It has been decided that the bonus of an employee will be 100% of the basic salary for outstanding performance, 70% of the basic salary for good performance, 40% of the basic salary for average performance, and zero for all other cases. Write an algorithm to calculate and print the total bonus amount to be distributed by the organization.

*Algorithm:*

Step 1:   Initialize Total_Bonus and Total_Employees_Checked to zero.

Step 2:   Initialize Bonus and Basic_Salary to zero.

Step 3:   Take the appraisal form of the next employee.

Step 4:   Read the employee's Basic_Salary and Grade.

Step 5:   If Grade = A, then Bonus = Basic_Salary. Go to Step 8.

Step 6:   If Grade = B, then Bonus = Basic_Salary x 0.7. Go to Step 8.

Step 7:   If Grade = C, then Bonus = Basic_Salary x 0.4.

Step 8:   Add Bonus to Total_Bonus.

Step 9:   Add 1 to Total_Employees_Checked.

Step 10:  If Total_Employees_Checked < 100, then go to Step 2.

Step 11:  Print Total_Bonus.

Step 12:  Stop.

Programmers design algorithms like these to solve complex programming problems. It must be clear to the readers from these examples that even for very simple problems, the development of algorithms is not so simple as it might initially appear, and requires some thinking. It may also be noted from the given examples that to solve a given problem, every instruction must be strictly carried out in a particular sequence. It is this fact, which a beginner to problem solving by computers finds difficult to appreciate.

## Representation of Algorithms

There are various ways in which an algorithm can be represented. Programmers normally use one or more of the following ways to represent their algorithms:

1. As programs

2. As flowcharts

3. As pseudocodes

When an algorithm is represented in the form of a programming language, it becomes a program. Hence, any program is an algorithm, although the reverse is not true.

Besides represented as programs, algorithms are often represented as flowcharts and pseudocodes. These are the commonly used tools used by programmers for program planning, which can often be of immense help in developing an effective and correct algorithm for a program, before it is coded into a programming language.

These program-planning tools are described below. Programmers generally select one of these tools depending on their choice to plan their programs.

# FLOWCHARTS

## What is a Flowchart?

A *flowchart* is a pictorial representation of an algorithm. It is often used by programmers as a program-planning tool for organizing a sequence of steps necessary to solve a problem by a computer. It uses boxes of different shapes to denote different types of instructions. The actual instructions are written within these boxes using clear and concise statements. These boxes are connected by solid lines having arrow marks to indicate the flow of operation, that is, the exact sequence in which the instructions are to be executed. The process of drawing a flowchart for an algorithm is often referred to as *flowcharting*.

## Why Use Flowcharts?

Normally, an algorithm is first represented in the form of a flowchart, and the flowchart is then expressed in some programming language to prepare a computer program. The main advantage of this two-step approach in program writing is that, while drawing a flowchart, a programmer is not concerned with the details of the elements of programming language. Hence, he/she can fully concentrate on the logic of the procedure. Moreover, since a flowchart shows the flow of operations in pictorial form, any error in the logic of the procedure can be detected more easily than in the case of a program. Once the flowchart is ready, the programmer can forget about the logic, and can concentrate only on coding the operations in each box of the flowchart in terms of the statements of the programming language. This will normally ensure an error-free program.

Experienced programmers, sometimes, write programs without drawing the flowchart. However, for a beginner, it is recommended that a flowchart be drawn first to reduce the number of errors and omissions in the program. Moreover, it is a good practice to have a flowchart along with a computer program, because a flowchart often serves as a document for the computer program, and is very useful during the testing of the program, and while incorporating further modifications in the program.

## Flowchart Symbols

### Need for Flowchart Symbols

We have seen that a flowchart uses boxes of different shapes to denote different types of instructions. The communication of program logic through flowcharts is made easier by the use of symbols, which have standardized meanings. This is because, as long as everyone uses the same basic shapes, others can readily interpret the logic. For example, a diamond always means a decision. Hence, when a programmer looks at a flowchart, he/she can easily identify the decision points, because all are indicated by a diamond-shaped box.

## Basic Flowchart Symbols

Only a few symbols are needed to indicate the necessary operations in a flowchart. These basic flowchart symbols have been standardized by the American National Standards Institute (ANSI). They are shown in Figure 11.1, and their functions are discussed below.

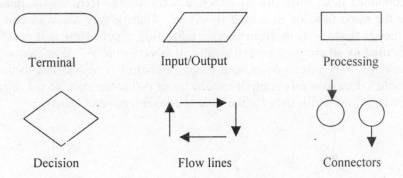

| Terminal | Input/Output | Processing |

| Decision | Flow lines | Connectors |

**Figure 11.1.** Basic flowchart symbols.

1. **Terminal.** The terminal symbol is used to indicate the beginning (*Start*), end (*Stop*), and pauses (*Halt*) in the program logic flow. It is the first symbol and the last symbol in the program logic. In addition, if the program logic calls for a pause in the program, the pause is also indicated with a terminal symbol. A pause is normally used in the program logic under some error conditions, or if forms had to be changed in the computer's line printer during the processing of that program.

2. **Input/Output.** The input/output symbol is used to denote any function of an input/output device in the program. If there is a program instruction to input data from a disk, tape, terminal, or any other type of input device, that step will be indicated in the flowchart with an input/output symbol. Similarly, all output instructions, whether it is output on a printer, magnetic tape, magnetic disk, terminal screen, or any output device, are indicated in the flowchart with an input/output symbol.

3. **Processing.** A processing symbol is used in a flowchart to represent arithmetic and data movement instructions. Hence, all arithmetic processes of adding, subtracting, multiplying and dividing are shown by a processing symbol. The logical process of moving data from one location of the main memory to another is also denoted by this symbol. When more than one arithmetic and data movement instructions are to be executed consecutively, they are normally placed in the same processing box, and they are assumed to be executed in the order of their appearance.

4. **Decision.** The decision symbol is used in a flowchart to indicate a point at which a decision has to be made, and a branch to one of two or more alternative points is possible. Figure 11.2 shows three different ways in which a decision symbol can be used. It may be noted from these examples that the criterion for making the decision should be indicated clearly within the decision box. Moreover, the condition upon which each of the possible exit paths will be executed should be identified, and all the possible paths should be accounted for. During execution, the appropriate path is followed depending upon the result of the decision.

5. **Flow lines.** Flow lines with arrowheads are used to indicate the flow of operation, that is, the exact sequence in which the instructions are to be executed. The normal flow of flowchart is from top to bottom and left to right. Arrowheads are required only when the normal top to bottom flow is not to be followed. However, as a good practice, and to avoid ambiguity, flow lines are usually drawn with an arrowhead at the point of entry to a symbol. Good practice also dictates that flow lines should not cross each other, and that such intersections should be avoided whenever possible.

6.  **Connectors.** Whenever a flowchart becomes complex enough that the number and direction of flow
    lines is confusing, or it spreads over more than one page, it is useful to utilize the connector symbol as
    a substitute for flow lines. This symbol represents an entry from, or an exit to another part of the
    flowchart. A connector symbol is represented by a circle, and a letter or digit is placed within the
    circle to indicate the link. A pair of identically labeled connector symbols is commonly used to
    indicate a continued flow, when the use of a line is confusing. Hence, two connectors with identical
    labels serve the same function as a long flow line. That is, they show an exit to some other chart
    section, or they indicate an entry from another part of the chart. How is it possible to determine if a
    connector is used as an entry or an exit point? It is very simple – if an arrow enters, but does not
    leave a connector, it is an exit point, and program control is transferred to the identically labeled
    connector, which does have an outlet. It may be noted that connectors do not represent any operation,
    and their use in a flowchart is only for the sake of convenience and clarity.

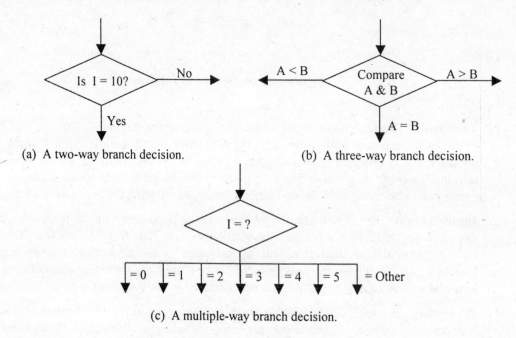

Figure 11.2. Examples of decision symbols.

# Sample Flowcharts

Describing an algorithm in the form of a flowchart is not very difficult. Only some common sense, and a little
practice are required. The art of flowcharting is introduced below with the help of some simple examples.

*Example 11.3.*

A student appears in an examination, which consists of total 10 subjects, each subject having maximum
marks of 100. The roll number of the student, his/her name, and the marks obtained by him/her in various
subjects, are supplied as input data. Such a collection of related data items, which is treated as a unit, is
known as a record. Draw a flowchart for the algorithm to calculate the percentage marks obtained by the
student in this examination, and to print it along with his/her roll number and name.

*Solution:*

The flowchart for the algorithm of this problem is shown in Figure 11.3. The first symbol is a terminal symbol labeled *"Start"*. It indicates the beginning of flowchart logic. It does not mean that the computer is to be turned on, or that anyone is to press a start button. The second symbol is an I/O symbol, which is labeled as "Read input data". This step will input the roll number, name, and marks obtained by the student from an input device into the main storage of the computer system. The third symbol is a processing symbol, which is labeled to indicate that at this step, the computer will add the marks obtained by the student in various subjects, and then store the sum in a memory location, which has been given the name *Total*. The fourth symbol is again a processing symbol. The label inside it indicates that the percentage marks obtained by the student is calculated at this stage by dividing *Total* by 10, and the result is stored in a memory location, which has been given the name *Percentage*. The fifth symbol is an I/O symbol that is labeled as "Write output data". This step will output the desired data (roll number, name and percentage marks obtained) on an output device, such as a printer. Note that, details such as the roll number, name and marks or percentage being input or output, are not a part of the logical steps of data input or data output operations. This information already appears in the system design documents, and will be included in the computer program as input and output descriptions. The sixth symbol is a terminal symbol labeled "Stop". It indicates the conclusion of the logic, that is, the conclusion of the computer program. The various symbols used in the flowchart are connected by directed flow lines to indicate the sequence in which the instructions are to be executed.

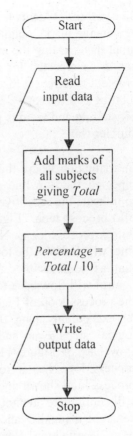

**Figure 11.3.** Flowchart for Example 11.3.

The logic depicted in Figure 11.3, therefore, will read the student's record, calculate the percentage marks obtained by him/her, print one line of output, and then stop. One would certainly not like to use a computer to solve a trivial problem, such as this. However, if we have to compute the percentage marks obtained by several students in the same examination, we may like to take the help of a computer. The next example illustrates how to do this.

**Example 11.4.**

50 students of a class appear in the examination of Example 11.3. Draw a flowchart for the algorithm to calculate and print the percentage marks obtained by each student, along with his/her roll number and name.

*Solution:*

Since all the students have appeared in the same examination, the process of calculating and printing the percentage marks obtained by each student will be the same. That is, the same process of reading the input data, adding the marks of all subjects, calculating the percentage, and then writing the output data has to be repeated for all the 50 students. Hence, an easy solution that comes to ones mind for this problem is to repeat the intermediate four symbols of Figure 11.3 fifty times. However, if that is done, a total of 202 (50 x 4 + 2) flowchart symbols will have to be drawn. Obviously, this will be a very time consuming and tedious job, and hence, is not desirable. We will now see how to solve this problem in a simpler way.

In a situation where the same logical steps have to be repeated, the flow line symbols are used in a flowchart to indicate the repetitive nature of the logic in the form of a process loop. Figure 11.4 illustrates a flowchart with a process loop. Note the arrowhead on the flow line, which forms the loop. It points upward indicating that as soon as the "Write" operation is over, the control will flow back to the "Read" operation. Hence, the process loop of Figure 11.4 solves the problem of an exceedingly long flowchart by reusing the same logical steps over and over again. However, the flowchart of Figure 11.4 is incomplete, because the process loop has introduced a new problem. The process loop shown does not have a logical ending. It will continue to attempt to repeat those four steps, until someone manually cancels the job. This is an example of an infinite loop. Hence, the flowchart of Figure 11.4 does not represent an algorithm, because an algorithm must terminate. Therefore, we have to find out a way of terminating the algorithm. This is done by the use of a decision symbol.

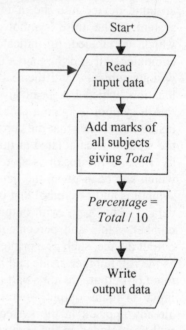

**Figure 11.4.** Flowchart for the solution of Example 11.4 with an infinite (endless) process loop.

Figure 11.5 shows a flowchart, which uses a decision step to terminate the algorithm. In this flowchart, another variable *Count* has been introduced, which is initialized to zero outside the process loop, and is incremented by 1, after processing the data for each student. Hence, the value of *Count* will always be equal to the number of students, whose data has already been processed. At the decision step, the value of *Count* is compared with 50, which is the total number of students who have appeared for the examination. The steps within the process loop are repeated, until the value of *Count* becomes equal to 50. When *Count* becomes equal to 50, the instruction at the decision step causes the control to flow out of the loop, and the processing stops, because a terminal symbol labeled *Stop* is encountered. Hence, the flowchart of Figure 11.5 is a complete and correct solution to the problem of Example 11.4.

Although the flowchart of Figure 11.5 is a correct solution to the given problem, it suffers from two major drawbacks. The first drawback is that for making the decision at the decision step, one must know the exact number of students who appeared in the examination. If the examination of Example 11.3 is a university examination in which the total number of students who appeared for the examination is too large (say more than ten thousand), the counting of the total number of input records (data for each student) becomes a tedious job. Even then, if we do stick to counting the input records manually, and supply the number of records to be compared against *Count* in the decision box, and if we make some error while counting, the logic will not work. If the supplied number is less than the actual number of input records, the computer will not process the data for last few students. On the other hand, if the supplied number is more than the actual number of input records, the computer will try to read more records than what is supplied, causing an error in the logic.

The second drawback is that the flowchart of Figure 11.5 is not a generalized solution to the given problem. If the examination is conduced every year, we will certainly like to use the same program every year to process the students' data. However, the number of students appearing in the examination may not remain the same every year. This year it may be 50, but next year it can be 55, or 60, or anything. Hence, if the computer program to solve this problem was based on the flowchart of Figure 11.5, the statement corresponding to the decision step in that program will have to be changed again and again to supply the exact number of students. This is not a good programming practice. A good algorithm (program) should be general in nature. For example, in this case, we should write a program, which need not be modified every time, even if the total number of students changes.

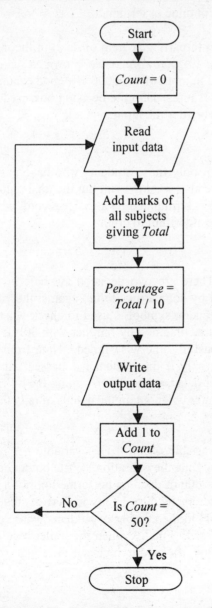

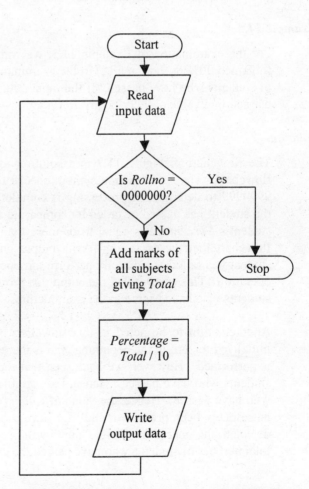

**Figure 11.5.** Flowchart for the solution of Example 11.4.

**Figure 11.6** Generalized flowchart for the solution of Example 11.4 using the concept of trailer record. Here the process loop is terminated by detecting a special non-data record.

The flowchart of Figure 11.5 suffers from these drawbacks, because in this flowchart the process loop is being controlled by counting. When the loop has been executed 50 times, the decision will cause execution to proceed to the "*Stop*", thus terminating processing. The reader should carefully step through the logic to ensure that the loop will be executed exactly 50 times, and not 49 or 51 times. To avoid these drawbacks, another method can be adopted to control the process loop. In this method, the end of input data is marked by a *trailer record.* That is, the last data record in the input is followed by a record whose sole purpose is to indicate that the end of the input data has been reached. For example, let us assume that the first 7 characters of the input record represent a student's roll number (*Rollno*). Since 0000000 is never used as a roll number, a value of 0000000 as the first 7 characters can be used to represent the trailer record. As each input record is processed, the *Rollno* can be compared with 0000000 to determine if processing is complete. The logic of this process is illustrated in the flowchart of Figure 11.6. It is important to recognize that the programmer would have to include instructions in the program, to compare the *Rollno* to 0000000, to determine whether to continue or terminate.

The concept of a trailer record is based on the notion of selecting a field (a particular item of data) in the input record, which will be used to indicate the end of data, and then selecting a *trailer value*, also known as *sentinel value*, which will never occur as normal data value for that field. The roll number of 0000000 is a good example. It may also be noted that when a trailer record is used to mark the end of input data, the decision box used for checking the trailer value should almost always be flowcharted immediately after the input symbol.

### Example 11.5.

For the examination of Example 11.3, we want to make a list of only those students who have passed (obtained 30% or more marks) in the examination. In the end, we also want to print out the total number of students who have passed. If the input data of all the students is terminated by a trailer record, which has sentinel value of 9999999 for *Rollno*, draw a flowchart for the algorithm to do this.

*Solution:*

The flowchart in Figure 11.7 is a solution to this problem. There are two decision symbols in this flowchart. The first decision symbol checks for a trailer record by comparing *Rollno* against the value 9999999 to determine if processing is complete. The second decision symbol is used to check whether the student has passed or failed by comparing the percentage marks obtained by him/her with 30. If the student's *Percentage* is equal to or more than 30, he/she has passed, otherwise failed. Note from the flowchart that the operation "Write output data" is performed, only if the student has passed. If the student has failed, we directly perform the operation "Read input data", without performing the "Write" operation. This ensures that the output list provided by the computer will contain the details of only those students who have passed in the examination.

Another point to be noted in this flowchart is the use of the variable *Count*. This variable has been initialized to zero in the beginning, and is incremented by 1, every time the operation "Write output data" is performed. However, we have seen that the operation "Write output data" is performed only for the students who have passed. Hence, the variable *Count* will be incremented by 1 only in case of students who have passed. Hence, the value of *Count* will always be equal to the number of students whose data has already been processed, and who have been identified as passed. Finally, when the trailer record is detected, the operation "Write Count" will print out the final value of *Count*, which will be equal to the total number of students who have passed the examination.

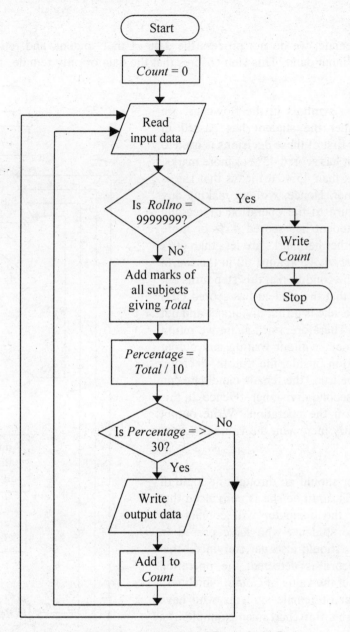

**Figure 11.7.** Flowchart for the solution of Example 11.5.

### Example 11.6.

The input data of each student for the examination of Example 11.3 also contains information regarding the sex of the candidate in the field named *Sexcode*, which can have values M (for male) or F (for female). We want to make a list of only those female students who have passed in second division (obtained 45% or more but less than 60% marks). In the end, we also want to print out the total number of such students. If the input data of all the students is terminated by a trailer record, which has a sentinel value of Z for *Sexcode*, draw a flowchart for the algorithm to do this.

### Solution:

The flowchart in Figure 11.8 is a solution to this problem. There are four decision symbols in this flowchart. The first one checks for a trailer record by comparing *Sexcode* against the value Z to determine if processing is complete. The second one is used to check whether the candidate is female or not by comparing the *Sexcode* of that candidate against F. Note that, if the *Sexcode* is not F, that is, the candidate is not a female, we do not process the data of that student, and return back to perform the operation of reading input data. This step ensures that the data of only female students will be taken for further processing.

The last two decision symbols in the flowchart are used to check whether the student has passed in second division. The first of these decisions is used to ensure that the student has scored 45% or more marks. If she has scored less than 45%, it means that she is not a second divisioner. Hence, without making any further check we return to the operation of reading input data. If the student has scored 45% or more marks, we check whether her marks are less than 60% by comparing the *Percentage* against 60 in the fourth decision symbol. If the condition at this step turns out to be false, it means that the student has scored 60% or more marks. Hence, she is a first divisioner and not a second divisioner. Therefore, once again we return back to read a new data without writing any output data. If the condition inside the fourth decision symbol turns out to be true, the female candidate can be classified to be a second divisioner. Hence, in this case only, we perform the operation "Write output data", and subsequently increment the value of *Count* by 1.

It is suggested that the reader should go through the logic of this flowchart again and again, until he/she is convinced that the output list provided by the computer will contain the details of only those female students who have passed in second division. The reader should also get convinced that finally, when the trailer record is detected, the operation "Write *Count*" would print out the value of *Count*, which will be equal to the total number of female students who have passed in second division. This flowchart is an example of a multiple-decision chart.

The flowchart of Figure 11.8 has been reproduced in Figure 11.9 to illustrate the use of connectors. There are four exit connectors having the label 1, all of which indicate a flow of control to the flowchart symbol having an entry connector labeled 1. This symbol is the input symbol in the flowchart. Similarly, the exit connector having a label 2 indicates a flow of control to the entry connector labeled 2. The reader should compare the flowcharts of Figure 11.8 and Figure 11.9, and should get convinced that both the flowcharts represent the same logic.

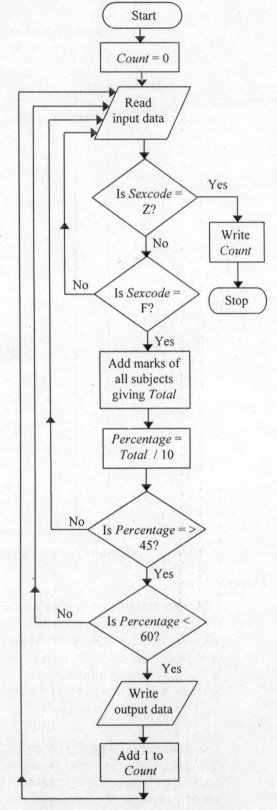

**Figure 11.8.** Flowchart for the solution of Example 11.6.

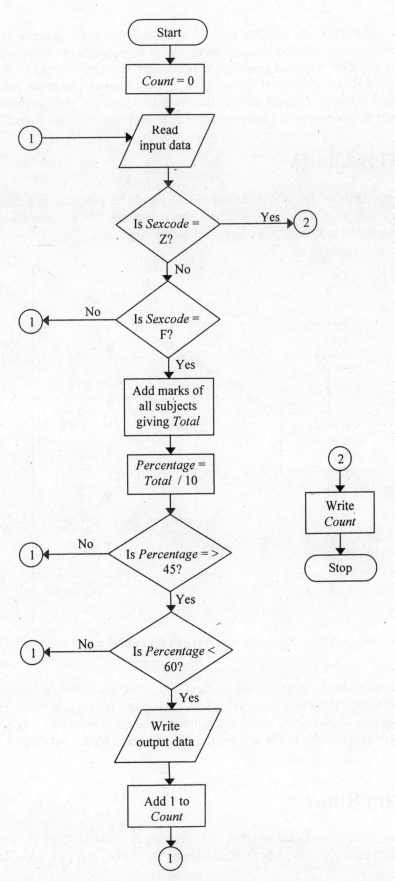

**Figure 11.9.** Flowchart of Figure 11.8 redrawn to illustrate the use of connectors.

A flowchart may seem simple to prepare, but you will find that much practice is needed to think through a problem in discrete, logical steps, to assume nothing, and to forget nothing. Moreover, not everyone will tackle a problem in exactly the same way, and hence, several different flowcharts could be drafted for the same problem. It may also be noted that a completed flowchart is not a complete computer program. It is only an aid to programming. For a given problem, it defines the procedure, and the logic involved. From the examples that have been discussed above, we are in a better position to understand what this "logic" means.

## Levels of Flowcharts

There are no set standards on the amount of detail that should be provided in a flowchart. A flowchart, which outlines the main segments of a program, or which shows less detail is a *macro flowchart*. On the other hand, a flowchart with more detail is a *micro flowchart*, or detailed flowchart.

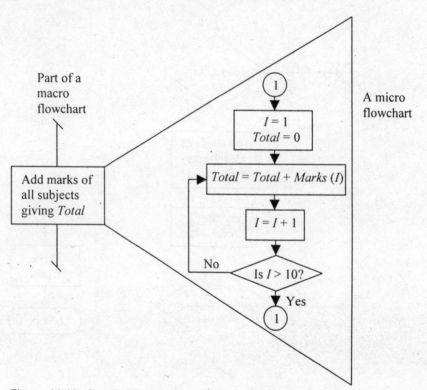

**Figure 11.10.** Detailed flowchart of add marks of all subjects giving *Total*.

For example, let us consider the examination problem, which we have already discussed. In all the flowcharts of the examination problem, there is a processing box having the instruction "Add marks of all subjects giving *Total*". To display how the value of *Total* is computed, a detailed flowchart can be drawn as shown in Figure 11.10. In a similar manner, the I/O boxes for the "Read" and "Write" operations can also be converted to a detailed flowchart.

## Flowcharting Rules

While programmers have a good deal of freedom in creating flowcharts, there are a number of general rules and guidelines, recommended by the American National Standards Institute (ANSI), to help standardize the flowcharting process. Various computer manufacturers and data processing departments usually have similar flowcharting standards. Some of these rules and guidelines are as follows:

1. First chart the main line of logic, then incorporate detail.

2. Maintain a consistent level of detail for a given flowchart.

3. Do not chart every detail, otherwise, the flowchart will only be a graphic representation, step-by-step, of the program. A reader, who is interested in greater detail can refer to the program itself.

4. Words in the flowchart symbols should be common statements, which are easy to understand. It is recommended to use descriptive titles written in designer's own language, rather than in machine-oriented language.

5. Be consistent in using names and variables in the flowchart.

6. Go from left to right, and top to bottom in constructing flowcharts.

7. Keep the flowchart as simple as possible. The crossing of flow lines should be avoided, as far as practicable.

8. If a new flowcharting page is needed, it is recommended that the flowchart be broken at an input or output point. Moreover, properly labeled connectors should be used to link the portions of the flowchart on different pages.

# Advantages and Limitations of Flowcharts

## Advantages

The following benefits may be obtained when flowcharts are used for the purpose of program planning:

1. **Better Communication.** A flowchart is a pictorial representation of a program. Hence, it is easier for a programmer to explain the logic of a program to some other programmer, or to his/her boss through a flowchart, rather than the program itself.

2. **Proper Program Documentation.** Program documentation involves collecting, organizing, storing, and otherwise maintaining a complete historical record of programs, and the other documents associated with a system. Good documentation is needed for the following reasons:

   – Documented knowledge belongs to an organization, and does not disappear with the departure (resignation/retirement) of a programmer.

   – If projects are postponed, documented work will not have to be duplicated.

   – If programs are modified in future, the programmer will have a more understandable record of what was originally done.

   Flowcharts often provide valuable documentation support.

3. **Efficient Coding.** Once a flowchart is ready, programmers find it very easy to write the corresponding program, because the flowchart acts as a road map for them. It guides them to go from the starting point of the program to the final point, ensuring that no steps are omitted. The ultimate result is an error-free program, developed at a faster rate.

4. **Systematic Debugging.** A flowchart is very helpful in detecting, locating, and removing mistakes (bugs) in a program in a systematic manner, because programmers find it easier to follow the logic of

the program in flowchart form. The process of removing errors (bugs) in a program is known as debugging.

5. **Systematic Testing.** Testing is the process of confirming whether a program will successfully do all the jobs for which it has been designed under the specified constraints. For testing a program, different sets of data are fed as input to that program to test the different paths in the program logic. For example, to test the complete logic of the program for Example 11.6, the following sets of data are necessary:

- Data for a male candidate.

- Data for a female candidate who has scored less than 45%.

- Data for a female candidate who has exactly scored 45%.

- Data for a female candidate who has scored more than 45%, but less than 60%.

- Data for a female candidate who has exactly scored 60%.

- Data for a female candidate who has scored more than 60%.

- Obviously, in the end, the trailer data having sentinel value.

A flowchart proves to be very helpful in designing the test data for systematic testing of programs.

## Limitations

In spite of their many obvious advantages, flowcharts have some limitations, which are as follows:

1. Flowcharts are very time consuming, and laborious to draw with proper symbols and spacing, especially for large complex programs. In this chapter, you have seen examples of small program flowcharts, developed for relatively small programs. You can very well imagine how difficult it would be to develop a detailed program flowchart for a program containing over 50,000 statements.

2. Owing to the symbol-string nature of flowcharting, any changes or modifications in the program logic will usually require a completely new flowchart. Redrawing a flowchart being a tedious task, many programmers do not redraw or modify the corresponding flowchart when they modify their programs. This leaves the program and its flowchart in an inconsistent state. That is, the logic used in the program, and that shown in its flowchart, do not match. This defeats the purpose of use of flowcharts as documentation support for programs. To take care of this problem, many companies use software tools, which automatically generate flowcharts directly from the program code. These software tools read the program's instructions and draw a flowchart of its logic. That is, this is a backward approach in which flowcharts are drawn from program codes mainly for documentation purpose.

3. There are no standards determining the amount of detail that should be included in a flowchart.

# PSEUDOCODE

# What is Pseudocode?

*Pseudocode* is another programming analysis tool, which is used for planning program logic. "Pseudo" means imitation or false, and "Code" refers to the instructions written in a programming language. Pseudocode, therefore, is an imitation of actual computer instructions. These pseudo-instructions are phrases written in ordinary natural language (e.g., English, French, German, etc.), which cannot be understood by the computer. Instead of using symbols to describe the logic steps of a program, as in flowcharting, pseudocode uses a structure, which resembles computer instructions. When pseudocode is used for program planning, a programmer can concentrate solely on developing the logic of the program, without worrying about the syntax for writing the program instructions, because pseudocode does not have any syntax rules for formulating instructions. Once the programmer is convinced that the program logic is sound, he/she can easily convert the pseudocode into a suitable programming language, which can be run on a computer. Since, pseudocode emphasizes the design of the program, it is also called *Program Design Language* (*PDL*).

## Pseudocodes for Basic Logic (Control) Structures

During the early days of program development, many programmers developed program logics for large programs with mazes of branches (jumps from one portion of the program to another), which altered the sequence of processing operations. Such programs are now referred to as "spaghetti code", because their program flowcharts appeared more like a plate of spaghetti than like logical analyses of programming problems. Understanding the logic of such programs was very difficult for someone other than the developer, and many times even for the developer after a lapse of few months. Hence, these programs were very difficult to modify for incorporating suggested enhancements, and quickly became nightmares for those responsible for their maintenance.

It was later discovered that any program logic, no matter how complex, could be expressed by using only the following three simple logic (control) structures:

1. Sequence logic,

2. Selection logic, and

3. Iteration (or looping) logic.

It was found that when programs are structured by using only these three logic structures, they can be read from top to bottom, and are easier to understand. That is, by conceptualizing the logic of a program in the form of these three logic structures, programmers can avoid writing spaghetti code, and produce programs, which are easy to understand and maintain. It was found that this also helped in reducing program errors, and the time spent in program testing. The use of these three basic control structures resulted in a more scientific approach to solving a programming problem, and was later termed as *structured programming* technique.

After realizing the advantages of structured programming technique, many organizations now impose the use of the three basic logic structures in all their programs. It is generally advised as good programming practices to develop program logics, and write programs using the three basic logic structures. Hence, in the discussion below, we will see the pseudocodes for the three basic logic structures (flowcharts of these logic structures have also been shown for those who are more comfortable with flowcharts).

## Sequence Logic

*Sequence logic* is used for performing instructions one after another in sequence. Hence, for sequence logic, pseudocode instructions are written in the order, or sequence, in which they are to be performed. The logic flow of psuedocode is from top to bottom. Figure 11.11 shows an example of sequence logic structure.

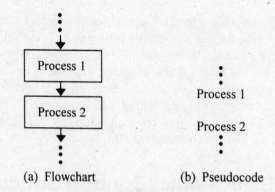

**Figure 11.11.** Flowchart and pseudocode for sequence structure.

## Selection Logic

*Selection logic*, also known as decision logic, is used for making decisions. It is used for selecting the proper path, out of two or more alternative paths, in a program logic. Selection logic is depicted as an IF...THEN...ELSE, or an IF...THEN, or a CASE structure. The flowcharts of Figures 11.12, 11.13 and 11.14 respectively illustrate the logic of these structures. Their corresponding pseudocodes are also given.

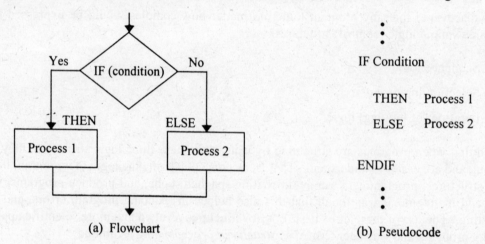

**Figure 11.12.** Flowchart and pseudocode for IF...THEN...ELSE selection structure.

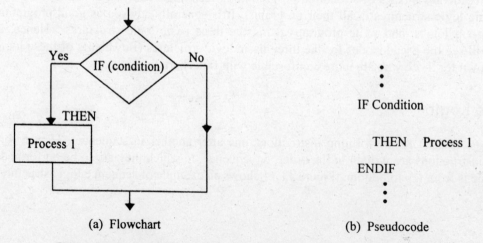

**Figure 11.13.** Flowchart and pseudocode for IF...THEN selection structure.

The IF…THEN…ELSE construct says that, if the condition is true, then do Process 1, else (if the condition is not true) do Process 2.  Hence, either Process 1 or Process 2 will be executed, depending on whether the specified condition is true or false.  However, if we do not want to choose between the two processes, and if we simply want to decide if a process is to be performed or not, the IF…THEN structure is used.   The IF…THEN structure says that, if the condition is true, then do Process 1, and if it is not true, then skip over Process 1.

The CASE structure is a multiple-way selection logic structure, which allows choosing from more than two control paths in a program logic.  It allows the selection of one of any number of statements, or statement groups. The CASE statement of Figure 11.14 says that, if the value of *Type* is equal to Type-1, execute Process 1, if it is equal to Type-2, execute Process 2, if it is equal to Type-3, execute Process 3, and so on.

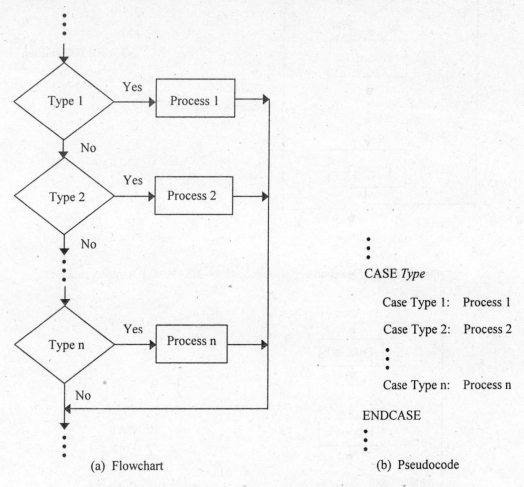

(a)  Flowchart                                                     (b)  Pseudocode

**Figure 11.14.**  Flowchart and pseudocode for CASE selection structure.

In all these structures, Process 1, Process 2, Process 3, etc. can actually be one or more processes.  They are not limited to a single process.  ENDIF is used to indicate the end of the IF…THEN and IF…THEN…ELSE decision structures, and ENDCASE is used to indicate the end of the CASE structure.

## Iteration (or Looping) Logic

*Iteration logic* is used to produce loops in program logic, when one or more instructions may be executed several times, depending on some condition.  It uses two structures called DO…WHILE and REPEAT…UNTIL.  They are illustrated by flowcharts in Figure 11.15 and Figure 11.16 respectively.  Their corresponding pseudocodes are also given. Both DO...WHILE and REPEAT...UNTIL are used for looping. In case of DO...WHILE, the looping will continue as long as the condition is true. The looping stops when the condition is not true. On the other hand, in case of REPEAT...UNTIL, the looping continues, until the condition becomes true. That is, the execution of the statements within the loop is repeated, as long as the condition is not true.

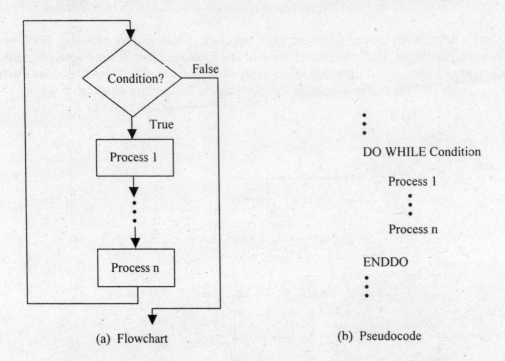

(a) Flowchart                                    (b) Pseudocode

**Figure 11.15.** Flowchart and pseudocode for DO...WHILE iteration structure.

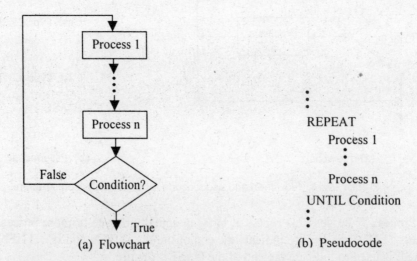

(a) Flowchart                                    (b) Pseudocode

**Figure 11.16.** Flowchart and pseudocode for REPEAT...UNTIL iteration structure.

Notice that, in case of DO...WHILE, the condition for looping is checked at the beginning of the loop. Hence, if the condition is found to be false when the loop is first encountered, the processes in the loop will not be executed at all (not even once). On the other hand, in case of REPEAT...UNTIL, the condition for looping is checked at the end of the loop. Hence, the processes inside the loop will be executed at least once.

In both DO...WHILE and REPEAT...UNTIL, the loop must contain a statement, which will change the condition that controls the loop. If it does not, the looping will continue without end, which is the case of an infinite loop. Remember that, no program should contain an infinite loop. Also, note that, the condition is tested at the top of the loop in DO...WHILE, and at the bottom of the loop in REPEAT...UNTIL. ENDDO marks the end of a DO...WHILE structure, and UNTIL followed by some condition marks the end of the REPEAT...UNTIL structure.

## Sample Pseudocode

The pseudocode version of the logic of the problem of Example 11.6, which was charted in Figure 11.8, is shown in Figure 11.17. In the pseudocode example, the first line initializes the value of *Count* to zero, and the second line reads the input data of the first student. The third line is the beginning of a loop using the DO...WHILE structure. It indicates that the loop will continue, as long as the trailer *Sexcode* is not equal to Z, that is, as long as the trailer record is not fond. In this example, a series of decisions followed by an instruction to read next student's record are included within the loop. The first statement within the DO...WHILE loop asks, "Is the *Sexcode* equal to F?" If the answer is yes, *Percentage* is calculated, and again the third statement within the loop asks, "Is *Percentage* equal to or greater than 45?" If it is, then "Is *Percentage* less than 60?" This is a series of three IF...THEN decision structures. Each one ends with an ENDIF vertically aligned below the appropriate IF.

```
Set Count to zero
Read first student record
DO WHILE Sexcode is not equal to Z
    IF Sexcode = F THEN
        Calculate Percentage
        IF Percentage = > 45 THEN
            IF Percentage < 60 THEN
                Write output data
                Add 1 to Count
            ENDIF
        ENDIF
    ENDIF
    Read next student record
ENDDO
Write Count
Stop
```

**Figure 11.17.** Pseudocode for the examination problem of Example 11.6.

```
Set Count to zero
Read first student record
DO WHILE Sexcode is not equal to Z
IF Sexcode = F THEN
Calculate Percentage
IF Percentage = > 45 THEN
IF Percentage < 60 THEN
Write output data
Add 1 to Count
ENDIF
ENDIF
ENDIF
Read next student record
ENDDO
Write Count
Stop
```

**Figure 11.18.** Non-indented version of the pseudocode of Figure 11.17.

The two instructions – "Write output data" and "Add 1 to *Count*" are performed only if all the three conditions (that of *Sexcode* being F, *Percentage* being equal to or more than 45, and *Percentage* being less than 60) are found to be true (answered yes). If any of the three conditions is not true, the logic path goes to the statement, which reads the next student's record. After the last student's record is processed, the trailer record, for which the value of *Sexcode* is Z, is encountered. This will cause the DO...WHILE loop to stop, because the condition (*Sexcode* not equal to Z) is no longer true. When the DO...WHILE condition is no longer true, the next logical step will be the instruction following the ENDDO. At this stage, the value of *Count* will be printed (Write *Count*), and finally the program execution will stop (Stop).

One important feature of pseudocode as a programming tool is the use of indentation. Each statement within the DO...WHILE loop is indented, to show that it is part of the loop. Similarly, the statements within each IF...THEN structure is indented properly to clearly specify the statements, which are part of each structure. The use of indentation in pseudocode is the same technique, which is used in the various programming languages. Its sole purpose is to clarify the logical structure of the program. With this technique, we can tell at a glance, which statements make up each of the logic structure of the total program logic. To fully appreciate this factor, the reader should compare the equivalent non-indented pseudocode of Figure 11.18 with that of Figure 11.17. The difference in clarity would be far greater, if this were a longer pseudocode covering, for instance, one or more pages.

# Advantages and Limitations of Pseudocode

## Advantages

1. Converting a pseudocode to a programming language is much more easier than converting a flowchart to a programming language.

2. As compared to a flowchart, it is easier to modify the pseudocode of a program logic, when program modifications are necessary.

3. Writing of pseudocode involves much less time and effort than drawing an equivalent flowchart. Pseudocode is easier to write than an actual programming language, because it has only a few rules to follow, allowing the programmer to concentrate on the logic of the program.

## Limitations

1. In case of pseudocode, a graphic representation of program logic is not available.

2. There are no standard rules to follow in using pseudocode. Different programmers use their own style of writing pseudocode. Hence, communication problem occurs due to lack of standardization.

3. For a beginner, it is more difficult to follow the logic of pseudocode, or write pseudocode, as compared to flowcharting.

## Points to Remember

1. To ensure that the program instructions are appropriate for the problem at hand, and in the correct sequence, programs must be planned before they are written.

2. The term *algorithm* refers to the logic of a program. It is a step-by-step description of how to arrive at a solution to the given problem.

3. When an algorithm is represented in the form of a programming language, it becomes a *program*. Hence, any program is an algorithm, although the reverse is not true.

4. Besides represented as programs, algorithms are often represented as flowcharts and pseudocodes.

5. A *flowchart* is a pictorial representation of an algorithm. It is often used by programmers as a program planning tool for organizing a sequence of steps necessary to solve a problem by a computer.

6. *Pseudocode* is a programming analysis tool, which allows programmers to plan program logic by writing the program instructions in an ordinary natural language, such as English.

7. *Structured Programming* is a more scientific approach to solving a programming problem by using only the three basic logic (control) structures namely, sequence logic, selection logic and iteration (or looping) logic.

8. Structured programming helps in producing programs, which are easy to understand and maintain. It also helps in reducing program errors, and the time spent in program testing.

9. *Sequence logic* is used for performing instructions one after another in sequence.

10. *Selection logic* is used for selecting the proper path, out of two or more alternative paths, in the program logic. It uses three control structures called IF...THEN, IF...THEN...ELSE and CASE.

11. *Iteration* (or *looping*) *logic* is used for producing loops in program logic, when one or more instructions may be executed several times, depending on some condition. It uses two control structures called DO...WHILE and REPEAT...UNTIL.

# Questions

1. Why is it advisable to plan the logic of a program, before writing it?

2. What is an algorithm? What are the characteristics necessary for a sequence of instructions to qualify as an algorithm?

3. What are the commonly used ways to represent algorithms? Which of these can be used for solving the corresponding problem on a computer?

4. Any program is an algorithm, although the reverse is not true. Discuss this statement.

5. What is a program planning tool? How is it useful? Name two commonly used program planning tools.

6. What is a flowchart?

7. How does a flowchart help a programmer in program development?

8. Can a flowchart be drawn for a task, if the person drawing the flowchart does not know how to perform the task manually? Discuss.

9. What are the various basic symbols used in flowcharting? Give their pictorial representation.

10. Describe the function of the various basic flowcharting symbols.

11. What is a record? A trailer record?

12. What is a sentinel value? Discuss its use.

13. What is a process loop? An infinite loop?

14. Why is it necessary to avoid infinite loops in program design?

15. "A loop consists of a body, a test for exit condition, and a return provision." Discuss this statement.

16. What is a generalized algorithm? Why should programs be general in nature?

17. Discuss the difference between loop control by counting, and loop control by the use of sentinel value. Which is preferable and why?

18. How can a counter be used to keep track of the number of times a loop has been executed?

19. Is it possible to have more than one flowchart for a given problem? Give reasons for your answer.

20. What is the difference between a macroflowchart and a microflowchart? Illustrate with an example.

21. What are the various guidelines to be followed while drawing a flowchart?

22. Discuss the advantages and limitations of flowcharting.

23. Why is proper documentation of a program necessary?

24. What are program bugs? What is debugging?

25. What is meant by testing a program? How is it done?

26. What is a pseudocode? Why is it so called? Give another name for pseudocode.

27. What are the three basic logic structures used in writing structured programs? Discuss the use of each.

28. What is structured programming? What are its main advantages?

29. Draw flowcharts for the two different structures used for selection logic.

30. What is the difference between the IF...THEN and the IF...THEN...ELSE structures?

31. Draw flowcharts for the two different structures used for iteration logic.

32. Both DO...WHILE and REPEAT...UNTIL are used for looping. Discuss the difference between the two structures.

33. What is the purpose of ENDIF and ENDDO statements?

34. What is indentation? Why is it used in writing pseudocodes?

35. Discuss the advantages and limitations of pseudocode.

36. Three numbers, denoted by the variables A, B, and C are supplied as input data. Draw a flowchart for the logic to pick and print the largest of the three numbers.

37. Draw a flowchart of the logical steps needed to produce a printed listing of all students over the age of 20 in a class. The input records contain the name and age of the students. Assume a sentinel value of 99 for the age field of the trailer record.

38. Draw a flowchart of the logical steps needed to print the name and age of the oldest, and the youngest student in a class. The input records contain the name and age of the students. Assume a sentinel value of 99 for the age field of the trailer record.

39. The first 20 records in a data set are to be read and printed. Draw a flowchart for the algorithm to do this job. Make sure that the processing stops after the twentieth record.

40. Input data regarding the information of employees of a company has been supplied. The first field of each input record contains the employee number (*EmployeeNo*). Assume that the input data of all the employees is terminated by a trailer record having a sentinel value of 99999 for *EmployeeNo*. Draw a flowchart for the logic to count and print the total number of input records, that is, the total number of employees.

41. For the employees problem of Question 40, we want to count and print the number of only male employees in the age group of 25 to 30. Assume that the input records contain *SexCode* and *Age* fields to provide this information. Draw a flowchart for the algorithm to perform this job.

42. A population survey has been carried out in a given city, and the information received from the survey has been stored in a computer, one record per citizen. That is, each record contains the name, address, sex, age, profession, etc., of one citizen. We want to print the details of all the adults (aged 18 years or more). Finally, we also want to print the total number of adults. Assume a suitable sentinel value for any field in the trailer record, and draw a flowchart for the algorithm to do this task.

43. A set of examination papers, which have been graded with scores from 0 to 100, is to be searched to find how many of them are above 90. The total has to be printed. Prepare a flowchart to do this job. Assume a suitable sentinel value for the trailer record.

44. Each paper in a set of examination papers includes a grade of A, B, C, D, or E. A count is to be made of how many papers have the grade of A, and how many have the grade of E. The total count of both types have to be printed at the end. Prepare a flowchart to perform this task. Assume a suitable sentinel value for the trailer record.

45. A shopkeeper wants to have a general program for his personal computer, which will prepare bills for each customer as and when he sells goods to them. His idea is that as soon as the customer purchases some goods from his shop, he will supply the description, unit price, and the quantity purchased for each item, as input to the computer. He wants that with this information, the computer should print each item along with its unit price, quantity purchased and the total price. Finally, the computer should also print the total cost of all the items purchased by the customer. Assuming a sentinel value of zero for the quantity purchased field in the trailer record, draw a flowchart for the logic to do this job.

46. An employer plans to pay bonus to each employee. Those earning Rs. 2000 or above are to be paid 10 percent of their salary; and those earning less than Rs. 2000 are to be paid Rs. 200. The input records contain the employee number, name, and salary of the employees. The output to be printed should contain the employee number, name, and the amount of bonus to be paid to each employee. Draw a flowchart for the algorithm to do this job. Assume a suitable sentinel value for any of the fields of the trailer record.

47. Each employee pay record includes the hours worked and the pay rate. The gross pay is to be determined as hours worked times pay rate, and is to be printed for each employee. For all hours worked in excess of 40, the overtime rate, which is 1.5 times the regular rate, is to be paid. Draw a flowchart for the problem logic to do this. Assume a suitable sentinel value for any of the input fields of the trailer record.

48. A data file contains a set of examination scores, and is followed by a trailer record with a value of -1. Draw a flowchart for the logic to calculate and print the average of the scores.

49. The data file of Question 48 is expanded to include several sets of data, each requiring calculation of its average. Each data set is followed by a trailer record with a value of -1; however, the last data set is followed by a trailer record with a value of -2. Draw a flowchart for the logic to perform this task.

50. Five numbers denoted by the variables A, B, C, D, and E are supplied as input. Draw a flowchart for the logic to print these numbers in descending order of magnitude.

51. Draw a flowchart to add up all the even numbers between 0 and 100. Before ending, print the result of the calculation.

52. Draw a flowchart for the logic to find out whether a given triangle ABC is isosceles. Assume that the angles of the triangle are supplied as input. Print the answer as yes or no.

53. Draw a flowchart for the logic to find out whether a given triangle ABC is a right angled triangle. Assume

that the sides of the triangle are supplied as input data. Print the answer as yes or no.

54. Draw a flowchart for the logic to find out whether a given quadrilateral ABCD is a rectangle. Assume that all the four angles and four sides of the quadrilateral are supplied as input data. Print the answer as yes or no.

55. Draw a flowchart for the logic to convert a number from base 10 to a new base using the division-remainder technique.

56. Draw a flowchart for the logic to convert a number to decimal from another base.

57. Write the pseudocode to solve the problem described in Question 37.

58. Write the pseudocode to solve the problem described in Question 38.

59. Write the pseudocode to solve the problem described in Question 41.

60. Write the pseudocode to solve the problem described in Question 44.

61. Write the pseudocode to solve the problem described in Question 45.

62. Write the pseudocode to solve the problem described in Question 46.

63. Write the pseudocode to solve the problem described in Question 47.

64. Write the pseudocode to solve the problem described in Question 51.

65. Write the pseudocode to solve the problem described in Question 52.

# Chapter 12

# Computer Languages

This chapter continues with the development of computer programs that was begun in Chapter 11. Once the planning for a computer program has been done, the next step in its development is to write the specific steps for solving the problem at hand in a language and form, which is acceptable to a computer system. A language that is acceptable to a computer system is called a *computer language* or *programming language*, and the process of writing instructions in such a language for an already planned program is called *programming* or *coding*. The goal of this chapter is to introduce some of the common computer languages, which are used for writing computer programs.

## ANALOGY WITH NATURAL LANGUAGES

A language is a means of communication. We use a natural language, such as English, to communicate our ideas and emotions to others. Similarly, a computer language is used by a programmer to instruct a computer what he/she wants it to do.

All natural languages (English, French, German, etc.) use a standard set of words and symbols (+, -, :, ;, <, >, etc.) for the purpose of communication. These words and symbols are understood by everyone using that language. We normally call the set of words allowed in a language, the *vocabulary* of the language. For example, the words we use in English form the vocabulary of English language. Each word has a definite meaning, and can be looked up in a dictionary. In a similar manner, all computer languages have a vocabulary of their own. Each word of the vocabulary has a definite unambiguous meaning, which can be looked up in the manual meant for that language. The main difference between a natural language and a computer language is that natural languages have a large vocabulary, but most computer languages use a very limited or restricted vocabulary. This is because a programming language, by its very nature and purpose, does not need to say too much. Every problem to be solved by a computer has to be broken down into discrete (simple and separate), logical steps, which basically comprise of four fundamental operations – input and output operations, arithmetic operations, movement of information within the CPU and memory, and logical or comparison operations.

Each natural language has a systematic method of using the words and symbols of that language, which is defined by the grammar rules of the language. Similarly, the words and symbols of a computer language must also be used as per set rules, which are known as the *syntax rules* of the language. In case of a natural language, people can use poor or incorrect vocabulary and grammar, and still make them understood. However, in the case of a computer language, we must stick to the exact syntax rules of the language, if we want to be understood correctly by the computer. Yet, no computer is capable of correcting and deducing meaning from incorrect instructions. Computer languages are smaller and simpler than natural languages, but they have to be used with great precision. Unless a programmer adheres exactly to the syntax rules of a programming language, even down to the punctuation marks, his/her instructions will not be understood by the computer.

Over the years, programming languages have progressed from machine-oriented languages, which use strings of binary 1s and 0s, to problem-oriented languages, which use common mathematical and/or English terms. However, all computer languages can be broadly classified into the following three categories:

1.  Machine Language

2.  Assembly Language

3.  High-level Language

We shall now examine the nature and characteristics of these three types of languages.

# MACHINE LANGUAGE

Although computers can be programmed to understand many different computer languages, there is only one language understood by the computer without using a translation program. This language is called the *machine language* of the computer. The machine language of a computer is normally written as strings of binary 1s and 0s. The circuitry of a computer is wired in a manner that it immediately recognizes the machine language instructions, and converts them into the electrical signals needed to execute them.

A machine language instruction normally has a two-part format, as shown in Figure 12.1. The first part of an instruction is the operation code, which tells the computer what function to perform, and the second part is the operand, which tells the computer where to find or store the data or other instructions, which are to be manipulated. Hence, each instruction tells the computer what operation to perform, and the length and locations of the data fields, which are involved in the operation. Every computer has a set of operation codes, called its instruction set. Each operation code (or opcode) in the instruction set is meant for performing a specific basic operation or function. Typical operations included in the instruction set of a computer are as follows:

1.  Arithmetic operations

2.  Logical operations

3.  Branch operations (either conditional or unconditional) for transfer of control to the address given in the operand field

4.  Data movement operations for moving data between memory locations and registers

5.  Data movement operations for moving data from or to one of the computer's input/output devices.

Figure 12.1 shows a typical single-address machine language instruction. Although, some computers are designed to use only single-address instructions, many computers use multiple-address instructions, which include the addresses of two or more operands. For example, the augend and addend may be the two operands of an addition operation.

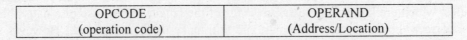

| OPCODE (operation code) | OPERAND (Address/Location) |
|---|---|

**Figure 12.1.** Instruction format.

We know that all computers use binary digits (0s and 1s) for performing internal operations. Hence, most computers' machine language instructions consist of strings of binary numbers. For example, a typical program instruction to print out a number on the printer might be

101100111111010011101100

The program to add two numbers in memory, and print the result might look something like the following:

```
00100000000000011001110011001
00110000000000010000100001
01100000000000111001011110
10100011111110111001011110
0000000000000000000000000000
```

This is obviously not an easy to use language, because it is difficult to read and understand, and also because it is written in a number system with which we are not familiar. However, some of the first programmers, who worked with the first few computers, actually wrote their programs in binary form as this one.

Since human programmers are more familiar with the decimal number system, most of them will prefer to write the computer instructions in decimal, and leave the input device to convert these to binary. In fact, without too much effort, a computer can be wired so that instead of using long strings of 1s and 0s, we can use the more familiar decimal numbers. With this change, the preceding program appears as follows:

```
10001471
14002041
30003456
50773456
00000000
```

This set of instructions, whether in binary or decimal, which can be directly understood by a computer without the help of a translating program, is called a machine code or machine language program. Hence, a machine language program need not necessarily be coded as strings of binary digits (1s and 0s). It can also be written using decimal digits, if the circuitry of the computer being used permits this.

## Advantages and Limitations of Machine Language

Programs written in machine language can be executed very fast by the computer. This is because machine instructions are directly understood by the computer, and no translation of the program is required. However, writing a program in machine language has several disadvantages, which are discussed below:

1. **Machine dependent.** Because the internal design of every type of computer is different from every other type of computer, the machine language also differs from computer to computer. Hence, after becoming proficient in the machine language of a particular computer, if a company decides to change to another computer, its programmers will have to learn a new machine language, and would have to rewrite all the existing programs.

2. **Difficult to program.** Although, machine language programs are directly and efficiently executed by the computer, it is difficult to program in machine language. It is necessary for the programmer either to memorize the dozens of operation code numbers for the commands in the machine's instruction set, or to constantly refer to a reference card. A programmer is also forced to keep track of the storage

locations of data and instructions. Moreover, a machine language programmer must be an expert who knows about the hardware structure of the computer.

3. **Error prone.** For writing programs in machine language, since a programmer has to remember the opcodes, and must keep track of the storage locations of data and instructions, it becomes very difficult for him/her to concentrate fully on the logic of the problem. This frequently results in programming errors.

4. **Difficult to modify.** It is difficult to correct or modify machine language programs. Checking machine instructions to locate errors is very difficult and time consuming. Similarly, modifying a machine language program later is so difficult that many programmers would prefer to code the new logic afresh, instead of incorporating the necessary modifications in the old program.

In short, writing a program in machine language is so difficult and time consuming that it is rarely used today.

# ASSEMBLY LANGUAGE

We saw above that programming in machine language is difficult and error-prone because:

1. A programmer needs to write numeric codes for the instructions in the computer's instruction set.

2. A programmer needs to write the storage locations of data and instructions in numeric form.

3. A programmer needs to keep track of the storage locations of data and instructions while writing a program.

Assembly language programming, which was introduced in 1952, helped in overcoming the above listed limitations of machine language programming in the following manner:

1. By using alphanumeric mnemonic codes, instead of numeric codes for the instructions in the instruction set. For example, using ADD instead of 1110 (binary) or 14 (decimal) for the instruction to add, using SUB instead of 1111 (binary) or 15 (decimal) for the instruction to subtract, and so on. With this feature, the instructions in the instruction set can be much easily remembered and used by the programmers.

2. By allowing storage locations to be represented in the form of alphanumeric addresses, instead of numeric addresses. For example, the memory locations 1000, 1001 and 1002 may be represented as FRST, SCND and ANSR respectively, in an assembly language program. With this feature, a programmer can much easily remember and use the storage locations of the data and instructions used in an assembly language program.

3. By providing additional instructions, called *pseudo-instructions*, in the instruction set, which are used for instructing the system how we want the program to be assembled inside the computer's memory. For example, there may be pseudo-instructions for telling the system things like:

```
START    PROGRAM   AT    0000
START    DATA      AT    1000
SET      ASIDE     AN    ADDRESS   FOR   FRST
SET      ASIDE     AN    ADDRESS   FOR   SCND
SET      ASIDE     AN    ADDRESS   FOR   ANSR
```

With this feature, a programmer need not keep track of the storage locations of the data and instructions while writing an assembly language program. That is, he/she need not even tell the computer where to place each data item, and where to place each instruction of a program.

A language, which allows instructions and storage locations to be represented by letters and symbols, instead of numbers, is called an *assembly language* or *symbolic language*. A program written in an assembly language is called an *assembly language program* or a *symbolic program*.

## Assembler

A computer can directly execute only machine language programs, which use numbers for representing instructions and storage locations. Hence, an assembly language program must be converted (translated) into its equivalent machine language program, before it can be executed on the computer. This translation is done with the help of a translator program, which is known as an *assembler*. The assembler of a computer system is a system software, supplied by the computer manufacturer, which translates an assembly language program into an equivalent machine language program of the computer. It is so called because, in addition to translating an assembly language program into its equivalent machine language program, it also, "assembles" the machine language program in the main memory of the computer, and makes it ready for execution.

The process of translating an assembly language program into its equivalent machine language program with the use of an assembler is illustrated in Figure 12.2. As shown in the figure, the input to the assembler is the assembly language program (often referred to as a *source program*), and its output is the machine language program (often referred to as an *object program*). Since the assembler translates each assembly language instruction into an equivalent machine language instruction, there is a one-to-one correspondence between the assembly language instructions of a source program, and the machine language instructions of its equivalent object program. Note that, during the process of translation of a source program into its equivalent object program by the assembler, the source program is not being executed. It is only being converted into a form, which can be executed by the computer's processor.

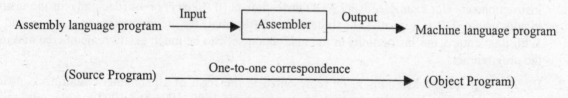

**Figure 12.2.** Illustrating the translation process of an assembler.

Notice that, in case of an assembly language program, the computer not only has to run the program to get the answer, but it also must first run the assembler (program) to translate the original assembly language program into its equivalent machine language program. This means that the computer has to spend more time in getting the desired answer from an assembly language program as compared to a machine language program. However, assembly language programming saves so much time and effort of the programmer that the extra time and effort spent by the computer is worth it.

Assembly language programming and translation of an assembly language program into its equivalent machine language program can be best illustrated with the help of an example. For this, let us assume that the computer uses the mnemonics given in Figure 12.3 for the operation codes mentioned against each. For simplicity, here we have considered only five operation codes, which will be used in writing our example program. Like this, there can be more than hundred operation codes available in the instruction set of a particular computer.

| Mnemonic | Opcode | Meaning |
|----------|--------|---------|
| HLT | 00 | Halt, used at the end of program to stop |
| CLA | 10 | Clear and add into A register |
| ADD | 14 | Add to the contents of A register |
| SUB | 15 | Subtract from the contents of A register |
| STA | 30 | Store A register |

**Figure 12.3.** A subset of the set of instructions supported by a computer.

We will write a simple assembly language program for adding two numbers and storing the result. The program is shown in Figure 12.4. To get an idea of how the assembler will convert this program into an equivalent machine language program, let us follow its instructions one-by-one. Notice that, the first five instructions of the program are pseudo-instructions for telling the assembler what to do. They are not part of the main program to add the two numbers.

```
START     PROGRAM    AT    0000
START     DATA       AT    1000
SET       ASIDE      AN    ADDRESS    FOR    FRST
SET       ASIDE      AN    ADDRESS    FOR    SCND
SET       ASIDE      AN    ADDRESS    FOR    ANSR
CLA       FRST
ADD       SCND
STA       ANSR
HLT
```

**Figure 12.4.** A sample assembly language program for adding two numbers and storing the result.

The first instruction of the assembly language program tells the assembler that the instructions for the main program (to add two numbers) should start at memory location 0000. Based on this directive, the assembler will load the first instruction of the main program (which happens to be CLA FRST in this example) at memory location 0000, and each following instruction will be loaded in the following address (that is, ADD SCND will be loaded at location 0001, STA ANSR at location 0002, and HLT at location 0003).

The second instruction of the assembly language program tells the assembler that the data of the program should start at memory location 1000. The next three instructions tell the assembler to set aside addresses for data items FRST, SCND and ANSR. Based on these four directives, the assembler sets up a mapping table somewhere in the computer memory, which looks something like the one shown in Figure 12.5. That is, the assembler picks up the first free address in the data area of the program, which is location 1000, and calls it FRST; it picks up the next free address in the data area, which is location 1001, and calls it SCND; and finally, it picks up the next free address in the data area, which is location 1002, and calls it ANSR.

| Symbolic name | Memory location |
|---------------|-----------------|
| FRST | 1000 |
| SCND | 1001 |
| ANSR | 1002 |

**Figure 12.5.** Mapping table set up by the assembler for the data items of the assembly language program of Figure 12.4.

The next instruction of the assembly language program is CLA FRST, which the assembler translates into 10 1000, by translating CLA into 10 with the help of Figure 12.3, and FRST into 1000 with the help of Figure 12.5. Similarly, the assembler will translate the instruction ADD SCND into 14 1001, and the instruction STA ANSR into 30 1002. Finally, it translates the next instruction HLT into 00, thus, providing the complete machine language program for the given assembly language program. Figure 12.6 shows the resulting machine language program.

| Memory | Contents | | Comments |
|--------|----------|--------|----------|
| location | Opcode | Address | |
| 0000 | 10 | 1000 | Clear and add the number stored at FRST to A register |
| 0001 | 14 | 1001 | Add the number stored at SCND to the contents of A register |
| 0002 | 30 | 1002 | Store the contents of A register into ANSR |
| 0003 | 00 | | Halt |
| - | | | |
| - | | | |
| - | | | |
| 1000 | | | Reserved for FRST |
| 1001 | | | Reserved for SCND |
| 1002 | | | Reserved for ANSR |

**Figure 12.6.** The equivalent machine language program for the assembly language program given in Figure 12.4.

# Advantages of Assembly Language over Machine Language

Assembly languages have the following advantages over machine languages:

1. **Easier to understand and use.** Due to the use of mnemonics, instead of numeric op-codes, and symbolic names for data locations, instead of numeric addresses, assembly language programs are much easier to understand and use as compared to machine language programs.

2. **Easier to locate and correct errors.** Due to the use of mnemonic op-codes and symbolic names for data locations, and also because programmers need not keep track of the storage locations of the data and instructions, fewer errors are made while writing programs in assembly language, and those that are made are easier to find and correct. Additionally, assemblers are designed to automatically detect and indicate errors for use of an invalid mnemonic op-code, or a name that has never been defined. For example, let us assume that an assembly language program instruction reads ADD AREA, and we forget to define AREA in the program. The assembler will look through its table, and not finding AREA in it, will indicate the error.

3. **Easier to modify.** Since they are easier to understand, it is easier to locate, correct, and modify instructions of an assembly language program than a machine language program. Moreover, insertion or removal of certain instructions from the program does not require change in the address part of the instructions following that part of the program. This is required in case of machine language.

4. **No worry about addresses.** An important advantage of assembly language is that programmers need not keep track of the storage locations of the data and instructions while writing an assembly language program. The importance of this advantage can be best illustrated with an example. Let us assume that we have written a long machine language program involving many instructions and several references to itself within the program, such as looping, branching, and so on. At the very end, we may suddenly discover that we have left out an instruction in the middle. If we insert that instruction, we will have to go through the entire program to check and modify (if necessary) all references to other instructions. This is certainly a tedious job. However, if we write the same program in assembly language, we merely add the extra instruction, and the assembler will take care of automatically modifying the references suitably.

5. **Easily relocatable.** The availability of pseudo-instructions for instructing the system how we want the program to be assembled inside the computer's memory makes assembly language programs easily relocatable, because their location can be easily changed merely by suitably changing the pseudo-instructions. This is not easily possible with machine language programming. This feature can be best illustrated with the help of an example. Let us assume that an assembly language program

starts at address 1000, and we suddenly find that we have another program to be used with this program, and this program also starts at location 1000. Obviously, one of the two programs will have to be rewritten to be moved to somewhere else. In machine language, this can be a complicated job. However, in case of assembly language, we merely have to suitably change the pseudo-instructions for assembling the program for one of the two programs. For example, we change the following pseudo-instructions for one of the programs:

> START PROGRAM AT 1000
> START DATA AT 2000

to the following pseudo-instructions:

> START PROGRAM AT 3000
> START DATA AT 4000

and run the assembly language program once again through the assembler. The equivalent machine language program will this time start at memory location 3000, instead of 1000, and there will be no conflict with the other program. In other words, assembly language programs can be easily moved from one section of the memory to another.

6. **Efficiency of machine language.** In addition to the above-mentioned advantages, an assembly language program also enjoys the efficiency of its corresponding machine language program, because there is one-to-one correspondence between the instructions of an assembly language program, and its corresponding machine language program. In other words, an assembly language program will be just as long as the resulting machine language program. Hence, leaving out the translation time required by the assembler, the actual execution time for an assembly language program, and its equivalent machine language program (written independently) will be the same.

## Limitations of Assembly Language

The following limitations of machine language are not solved by using assembly language:

1. **Machine dependent.** Since each instruction of an assembly language program is translated into exactly one machine language instruction, assembly language programs are machine dependent. That is, assembly languages differ from computer to computer, and an assembly language program can be executed only on the computer in whose assembly language it has been written. Hence, a decision to change to another computer will require learning a new language, and the conversion of all existing programs into the assembly language of the new computer.

2. **Knowledge of hardware required.** Since assembly languages are machine dependent, an assembly language programmer must have a good knowledge of the characteristics, and the logical structure of his/her computer to write good assembly language programs.

3. **Machine level coding.** In case of an assembly language, instructions are still written at the machine-code level. That is, one assembly language instruction is substituted for one machine language instruction. Hence, writing assembly language programs is still time-consuming and not very easy.

## Assembly Languages with Macro Instructions

In general, assembly languages are termed one-for-one in nature, that is, each assembly language instruction will result in one machine language instruction. However, quite often, a certain set of machine language or assembly language instructions have to be used repeatedly. For example, three instructions, one after the other, might be needed to print out a value on a particular computer. These three instructions, always in the same order, might be used repeatedly in the same program. Instead of forcing the programmer to write out the set of three instructions every time he/she wants to print a value, we might as well design the assembler (program) in such a way so as to take care of these instructions. Every time the programmer gave the PRINT instruction, for example, the assembler would translate it into three machine language instructions, instead of one, hence, supplying the complete set of instructions required for printing.

Any instruction, such as PRINT, which is translated into several machine language instructions, is called a *macro instruction*. There might be many such macro instructions permitted by a particular assembler. Hence, to speed up the coding process, assemblers were developed, which could produce a variable amount of machine language instructions for each macro instruction of the assembly language program.

The use of macro instructions adds much work to the computer, because the translation process becomes more than just changing each word into a number. The assembler must be able to supply the missing steps as well, but it means a tremendous saving of work for the programmer. The programmer gets relieved of the task of writing an instruction for every machine operation performed. Hence, the use of macro instructions, reduces the length of the programs, cuts down on errors, and simplifies programming.

The macro instruction capability was developed very early in the evolution of computer languages. In fact, it is this concept of multiple machine instructions from one macro instruction around which today's machine-independent, high-level languages are designed.

# HIGH-LEVEL LANGUAGE

We saw that both machine and assembly languages have the following limitations:

1. They are machine dependent. A machine language program, or an assembly language program, cannot be executed on any computer other than the one for which it is written.

2. They require the programmers to have a good knowledge of the internal structure of the computer being used.

3. It is difficult, error prone and time consuming to write programs in machine language or assembly language, because they deal with machine-level coding, requiring one instruction to be written for each machine-level operation.

Due to these limitations, machine and assembly languages are often referred to as *low-level programming languages*. High-level programming languages were designed to overcome these limitations of low-level programming languages. That is, high-level languages are characterized by the following features:

1. They are machine independent. That is, a program written in a high-level language can be easily ported and executed on any computer, which has the translator software for the high-level language.

2. They do not require the programmers to know anything about the internal structure of the computer on which the high-level language programs will be executed. In fact, since high-level languages are machine independent, a programmer writing a program in a high-level language may not even know on which computer will his/her program be executed. This allows the programmers to mainly concentrate on the logic of the problem, rather than be concerned with the details of the internal structure of the computer.

3. They do not deal with the machine-level coding. Rather, they deal with high-level coding, enabling the programmers to write instructions using English words and familiar mathematical symbols and expressions. Each statement of a high-level language is normally a macro instruction, which is translated into several machine language instructions. This is one-to-many translation, and not one-to-one as in the case of assembly language. For example, let us consider the same problem of adding two numbers (FRST and SCND), and storing the sum in ANSR. We have already seen that three low-level (machine/assembly) instructions are required for performing this job. However, if we use a high-level language, say FORTRAN for instance, to instruct the computer to do this job, only one instruction need be written:

$$ANSR = FRST + SCND$$

This instruction is obviously very easy to understand and write, because it resembles the familiar algebraic notation for adding two numbers: $a = b + c$.

The advent of high-level languages has enabled the use of computers to solve problems even by non-expert users. This has allowed many users, without any background in computer science and engineering, to become computer programmers. This, in turn, has resulted in the creation of a large number of computer applications in diverse areas, leading to the use of computers today in every occupation.

# Compiler

We saw that a computer can directly execute only machine language programs. Hence, a high-level language program must be converted (translated) into its equivalent machine language program, before it can be executed on the computer. This translation is done with the help of a translator program, which is known as a *compiler*. Hence, a compiler is a translator program (much more sophisticated than an assembler), which translates a high-level language program into its equivalent machine language program. A compiler is so called, because it compiles a set of machine language instructions for every program instruction of a high-level language.

The process of translating a high-level language program into its equivalent machine language program with the use of a compiler is illustrated in Figure 12.7. As shown in the figure, the input to the compiler is the high-level language program (often referred to as a *source program*), and its output is the machine language program (often referred to as an *object program*). Since high-level language instructions are macro instructions, the compiler translates each high-level language instruction into a set of machine language instructions, rather than a single machine language instruction. Hence, there is a one-to-many correspondence between the high-level language instructions of a source program, and the machine language instructions of its equivalent object program. Note that, during the process of translation of a source program into its equivalent object program by the compiler, the source program is not being executed. It is only being converted into a form, which can be executed by the computer's processor.

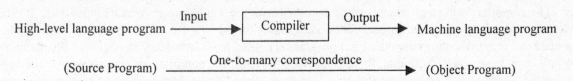

**Figure 12.7.** Illustrating the translation process of a compiler.

A compiler can translate only those source programs, which have been written in the language for which the compiler is meant. For example, a FORTRAN compiler is only capable of translating source programs, written in FORTRAN. Therefore, each computer requires a separate compiler for each high-level language that it supports. That is, to execute both FORTRAN and COBOL programs on a computer, the computer must have a FORTRAN compiler and a COBOL compiler. This is illustrated in Figure 12.8.

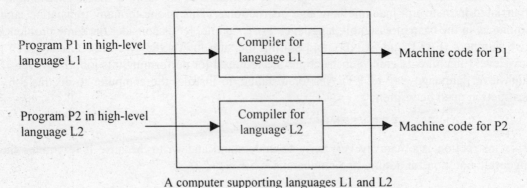

A computer supporting languages L1 and L2

**Figure 12.8.** Illustrating the requirement of a separate compiler for each high-level language supported by a computer.

Also, note that an object program for one computer will not be the same as the object program for another computer. Hence, it is necessary that each computer must have its own "personal" compiler for a particular language, say L1. Figure 12.9 illustrates how machine-independence is achieved by using different compilers to translate the same high-level language program to machine language programs of different computers.

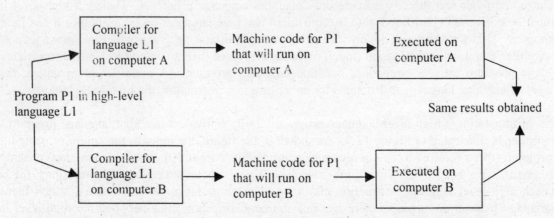

**Figure 12.9.** Illustrating the machine independence characteristic of a high-level language. Separate compilers are required for the same language on different computers.

Compilers are large programs, which reside permanently on secondary storage. When a source program is to be translated, the compiler and the source program are copied from secondary storage into the main memory of the computer. The compiler, being a program, is then executed with the source program as its input data. It generates the equivalent object program as its output, which is normally saved in a file on secondary storage. Whenever there is a need to execute the program, the object program is copied from secondary storage into the main memory of the computer and executed. Note that, there is no need to repeat the compilation process every time you wish to execute the program. This is because the object program stored on secondary storage is already in machine language. You simply have to load the object program from the secondary storage into the main memory of the computer, and execute it directly. Also, note that compilation is necessary whenever we need to modify the program. That is, to incorporate changes in the program, you must load the original source program from secondary storage into the main memory of the computer, carry out necessary changes in the source program, recompile the modified source program, and create and store an updated object program for execution.

In addition to translating high-level language instructions into machine language instructions, compilers also automatically detect and indicate certain types of errors in source programs. These errors are referred to as *syntax errors,* and are typically of the following types:

1.  Illegal characters
2.  Illegal combination of characters
3.  Improper sequencing of instructions in a program
4.  Use of undefined variable names

A source program containing one or more errors detected by the compiler will not be compiled into an object program. In this case, the compiler will generate a list of coded error messages indicating the type of errors committed. This error list is an invaluable aid to the programmer in correcting the program errors. As shown in Figure 12.10, the programmer uses this error list to re-edit the source program for removing the errors, and creates a modified source program, which is recompiled. As shown in the figure, the process of editing the source program to make necessary corrections, and recompiling the modified source program, is repeated, until the source program is free of all syntax errors. Also, notice from the figure that the compiler generates the object program only when there are no syntax errors in the source program.

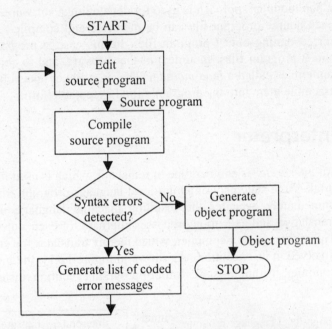

**Figure 12.10.** Illustrating recompilation of a source program, until it is free of all syntax errors.

A compiler, however, cannot detect *logic errors*. It can only detect grammatical (syntax) errors in the source program. It cannot know ones intentions. For example, if one has wrongly entered –25 as the age of a person, when he/she actually intended +25, the compiler cannot detect this. Programs containing such errors will be successfully compiled, and the object code will be obtained without any error message. However, such programs, when executed, will not produce correct results. Hence, logic errors are detected only after the program is executed, and the result produced does not tally with the desired result.

# Linker

A software often consists of several thousands, even several millions, of lines of program code. For software of this size, it is impractical to store all the lines of code in a single source program file due to the following reasons:

1.  The large size of the file would make it very difficult, if not impossible, to work with. For example, it might not be possible to load the file for compilation on a computer with limited main memory capacity. Again, while editing the file, it could be very tedious and time-consuming to locate a particular line of code.

2.  It would make it difficult to deploy multiple programmers to work concurrently towards the development of the software for completing it within a specified time limit.

3. Any change in the source program, no matter how small, would require the entire source program to be recompiled. Recompilation of large source programs is often a time-consuming process.

To take care of these problems, a modular approach is generally adapted to develop reasonably sized software. In this approach, the software is divided into functional modules and separate source programs are written for each module of the software. Often, there is no need to even write source programs for some of the modules, because there might be programs available in a program library, which offer the same functionality. These library programs are maintained in their object code form.

When modular approach is used for developing a software, the software consists of multiple source program files. Each source program file can be modified and compiled independent of other source program files to create a corresponding object program file. In this case, a program called a *linker* is used to properly combine all the object program files (modules) of the software, and to convert them into the final executable program, which is sometimes called a *load module*. That is, a linker takes object program files (modules), and fits them together to assemble them into the program's final executable form.

# Interpreter

An *interpreter* is another type of translator, which is used for translating programs written in high-level languages. It takes one statement of a high-level language program, translates it into machine language instructions, and then immediately executes the resulting machine language instructions. That is, in case of an interpreter, the translation and execution processes alternate for each statement encountered in the high-level language program. This differs from a compiler, which merely translates the entire source program into an object program, and is not involved in its execution. As shown in Figure 12.11, the input to an interpreter is the source program, but unlike a compiler, its output is the result of program execution, instead of an object program.

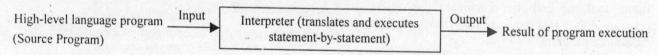

**Figure 12.11.** Illustrating the role of an interpreter.

After compilation of the source program, the resulting object program is permanently saved for future use, and is used every time the program is to be executed. Hence, repeated compilation (translation of the source code) is not necessary for repeated execution of a program. However, in case of an interpreter, since no object program is saved for future use, repeated interpretation (translation plus execution) of a program is necessary for its repeated execution. Note that, since an interpreter translates and executes a high-level language program statement-by-statement, a program statement must be reinterpreted (translated and executed) every time it is encountered during program execution. For example, during the execution of a program, each instruction in a loop will have to be reinterpreted, every time the loop is executed.

As compared to compilers, interpreters are easier to write, because they are less complex programs than compilers. They also require less memory space for execution than compilers.

The main advantage of interpreters over compilers is that a syntax error in a program statement is detected and brought to the attention of the programmer as soon as the program statement is interpreted. This allows the programmer to make corrections during interactive program development. Therefore, interpreters make it easier and faster to correct programs.

The main disadvantage of interpreters over compilers is that they are slower than compilers when running a finished program. This is because each statement is translated every time it is executed from the source program. In case of a compiler, each statement is translated only once and saved in the object program. The saved object program can be executed many times as and when needed, and no translation of any statement is required during the execution of the program. Because the interpreter does not produce an object program, it must perform the translation process each time a program is executed.

To combine the advantages of both interpreters and compilers, sometimes, the program development environment of a computer system provides both a compiler and an interpreter for a high-level language. In these cases, the interpreter is used to develop and debug programs. Then, after a bug-free state is reached, the programs are compiled to increase their execution speed. The object program produced by the compiler is subsequently used for routine processing.

Assemblers, compilers, and interpreters are also referred to as *language processors*, since they are used for processing a particular language instructions.

# Advantages and Limitations of High-level Languages

## Advantages of High-level Languages

High-level languages enjoy the following advantages over assembly and machine languages:

1. **Machine independence.** A program written in a high-level language can be executed on many different types of computers with very little, or practically no effort of porting it on different computers. This means that a company changing computers, even to one from a different manufacturer, will not be required to rewrite all the programs that it is currently using. This also means that a commercial software will have a larger market, because it need not be restricted to one type of computer. Hence, the time and effort spent on software development are better rewarded with high-level language programming.

2. **Easier to learn and use.** High-level languages are easier to learn, because they are very similar to the natural languages used by us in our day-to-day life. They are also easier to use, because a programmer need not know the internal details of the computer for programming in a high-level language.

3. **Fewer errors.** While programming in a high-level language, a programmer need not worry about how and where to store the instructions and data of the program, and need not write machine-level instructions for the steps to be carried out by the computer. This allows the programmer to concentrate more on the logic of the program under development. All these factors lead to fewer programming errors during program development. Furthermore, compilers and interpreters are designed to automatically detect and indicate syntax errors. Hence, syntax errors, if any, in the program can be easily located and corrected by the programmer.

4. **Lower program preparation cost.** Writing programs in high-level languages requires less time and effort, which ultimately leads to lower program preparation cost. Generally, the cost of all phases of program preparation (coding, debugging, testing, etc.) is lower with a high-level language than with an assembly language, or with a machine language.

5. **Better documentation.** The statements of a program written in a high-level language are very similar to the natural language statements used by us in our day-to-day life. Hence, they can be easily understood by a programmer familiar with the problem domain. As a result, very few, or practically

no separate comment statements are required in programs written in high-level languages. Due to this reason, high-level languages are also sometimes referred to as self-documenting languages.

6. **Easier to maintain.** Programs written in high-level languages are easier to maintain than assembly language or machine language programs. This is because they are easier to understand, and hence, it is easier to locate, correct, and modify instructions as and when desired. Insertion or removal of certain instructions from a program is also possible without any complication. Hence, major changes can be incorporated with very little effort.

## Limitations of High-level Languages

The two main limitations of high-level languages are as follows:

1. **Lower efficiency.** Generally, a program written in a high-level language has lower efficiency than one written in an assembly language, or a machine language, to do the same job. That is, programs written in high-level languages take more time to execute, and require more main memory space. Hence, when a program's efficiency is important, its performance critical parts are written in assembly language, and non-critical parts are written in a high-level language.

2. **Less flexibility.** Generally, high-level languages are less flexible than assembly languages, because they do not normally have instructions or mechanism to control the computer's CPU, memory and registers. An assembly language provides the programmers access to all the special features of the machine they are using. Certain types of operations, which are easily programmed using the machine's assembly language, are impractical to attempt using a high-level language. This lack of flexibility means that some tasks cannot be done in a high-level language, or can be done only with great difficulty.

In most cases, the advantages of high-level languages far outweigh the disadvantages. Most computer installations use a high-level language for most programs, and use an assembly language for doing special tasks, which cannot be easily done otherwise.

# OBJECT-ORIENTED PROGRAMMING LANGUAGES

Soon after the advent of first few programming languages, it was realized by the people working in the computer industry that programming is a difficult and time-consuming task. Hence, researchers have been continuously working towards developing better and better programming languages to make programming simpler, easier, and faster. The goal of the designers of every new programming language was to introduce some aspects or concepts in their programming language, which will help in achieving the above-mentioned objectives. *Object-Oriented Programming* (often referred to as OOP, pronounced "oop") is one such concept used in programming languages. The concept of OOP was first introduced in 1967 by the developers of a programming language named Simula-67. This concept started gaining popularity in 1980s with the development of another programming language named Smalltalk, which made extensive use of this concept. Today, this concept has been made part of almost all major programming languages, and is being used quite widely in software development.

The basic idea behind OOP is that programming languages are used for simulating real-world problems on computers. Since much of the real world is made up of objects, a simulation of such a world must include simulated objects. Hence, the essence of OOP is solving problems by identifying the real-world objects of the problem and the processing required of those objects, and then creating simulations of those objects, their processes, and the required communications between the objects.

# SOME HIGH-LEVEL LANGUAGES

A large number of high-level languages have been developed since the first ones in the early 1950s. By now, more than 1000 high-level languages have been developed, but many of them are no longer in use. Only a few have been truly significant, and even fewer have been widely used. In this section, we will briefly describe some popular high-level languages. Our primary objective here is to provide some insight into these languages, rather than to provide detailed knowledge required to write programs in these languages.

# FORTRAN

FORTRAN stands for **FOR**mula **TRAN**slation. It is one of the oldest high-level languages. It was designed to solve scientific and engineering problems, and is currently the most popular language amongst scientists and engineers. It was originally developed by John Backus and his team at IBM (International Business Machine) Corporation for its 704 computer in 1957. Since then, it has undergone several revisions, and has been evolving into a wider and more useful language with time.

The original version of FORTRAN, which was developed by John Backus and his team, was soon followed by a version, which was popular as FORTRAN II. The next popular advanced version was FORTRAN IV. In order to make FORTRAN language machine independent (that is, to allow a program, which was written for one computer system to be run on another computer system), FORTRAN IV was standardized by American National Standards Institute (ANSI) in the year 1966. With this, FORTRAN became the first standardized language. In 1977, an updated version of FORTRAN IV, called FORTRAN 77, was released and standardized by ANSI. This version was oriented towards structured programming approach, and had several new features for this. FORTRAN 90 is the latest version of FORTRAN standardized by ANSI. It again has many new features as compared to FORTRAN 77.

As FORTRAN language is oriented towards solving problems of a mathematical nature, it has been designed as an algebra-based programming language. Any formula or mathematical relationship, which can be expressed algebraically, can be easily expressed as a FORTRAN instruction. For example, $A = B + C - D$. To illustrate the nature of FORTRAN programs, a simple FORTRAN program to compute and print the sum of 10 numbers is shown in Figure 12.12.

```
C       FORTRAN PROGRAM TO COMPUTE
C       THE SUM OF 10 NUMBERS
        SUM = 0
        DO 50 I = 1, 10
        READ (5, 10) N
        SUM = SUM + N
50      CONTINUE
        WRITE (6, 20) SUM
10      FORMAT (F6.2)
20      FORMAT (1X, 'THE SUM OF GIVEN NUMBERS = ', F10.2)
        STOP
        END
```

**Figure 12.12.** A sample FORTRAN program.

It can be seen from the example of Figure 12.12 that a FORTRAN program consists of a series of statements for input/output, calculation, logic/comparison, etc. The words READ, WRITE, DO, CONTINUE, STOP, END, etc. in the statements mean exactly what one would expect.

In the given example, the first two lines, which begin with the character C, are comment statements. Comment statements are used in programs for the purpose of documentation, or explanation of the logic. Comments do not form a part of the program logic, and are ignored by the computer. In the third statement of the program, the value of SUM is initialized to zero. The next statement starts a DO loop. This loop ends in the line having label 50, which is a CONTINUE statement. Inside the loop, values of N are read and added to SUM one by one. After the computer loops 10 times, reading and accumulating the sum of 10 numbers, the computer goes out of the loop, and drops down to the next statement. This is the WRITE statement, which prints the message: THE SUM OF GIVEN NUMBERS = followed by the computed value of SUM. The next statement, which is a STOP statement, tells the computer to stop the execution of the program. Finally, the END statement tells the computer that there are no more instructions or statements in the program. The data for this program is contained in a separate file, and is not shown in the program.

# COBOL

COBOL stands for **CO**mmon **B**usiness **O**riented **L**anguage. As its name implies, it was designed for business data processing applications. Today, it is the most widely used programming language for business-oriented applications. Business data processing applications deal with storing, retrieving, and processing corporate accounting information, and to automate such functions as inventory control, billing, and payroll.

The initial work on the design of COBOL language was started in 1959 under the leadership of retired Navy Commodore and Mathematician Grace Hopper. The language specifications of COBOL were later worked out in 1959-1960 by a committee of the **CO**nference on **DA**ta **SY**stems **L**anguages (CODASYL) as a joint effort of computer users, manufacturers, and the United States Government. After the language specifications were defined by this committee, the various manufacturers wrote the COBOL compilers for their computers. An ANSI COBOL standard was first published in 1968. Revised versions of this standard were published by ANSI in 1974 and 1985, which were known as COBOL 74 and COBOL 85. As long as these standards are followed, a COBOL program can be run on any computer system with an ANSI COBOL compiler. Visual COBOL is an object-oriented version of the language. COBOL language continues to evolve even today. COBOL 2002 is the latest COBOL standard.

COBOL was designed to have the appearance and structure of a business report written in English. Hence, a COBOL program is constructed from sentences, paragraphs, sections and divisions. All COBOL programs must have the following four divisions:

1.  Identification Division, which specifies the program and its author.

2.  Environment Division, which specifies the computer and the peripherals used to compile and execute the program. If the program is to be processed on a different computer, this division will have to be rewritten.

3.  Data Division, which specifies the structure and format of the input and output data files, as well as all storage locations used to hold intermediate results and other values during processing.

4.  Procedure Division, which contains the sequence of operations to be performed by the program.

The nature of COBOL programs is illustrated in Figure 12.13 with the help of a simple COBOL program to compute and print the sum of given numbers. It can be easily seen from this example that COBOL programs are verbose, but easy to read. COBOL is often referred to as a self-documenting language. *Self-documenting languages* are those, which do not require much explanation to be understood by someone reading the program instructions. The self-documenting aspect of COBOL is made possible by its following features:

1.  Its English-like commands.

2.  Its English-like sentences and paragraph structure.

3.  Its very generous maximum symbolic field-name length of 30 characters. With a field-name length of up to 30 characters, the name can clearly identify the field, and its purposes. COBOL programmers should ensure that the used field-names are meaningful, so that the self-documenting feature of the language is not lost.

```
        IDENTIFICATION DIVISION.
        PROGRAM_ID.          SUMUP.
        AUTHOR.              P K SINHA.
    *  THIS PROGRAM COMPUTES AND PRINTS
    *  THE SUM OF GIVEN NUMBERS.

        ENVIROMENT DIVISION.
        CONFIGURATION SECTION.
        SOURCE_COMPUTER.          BURROUGHS_6700.
        OBJECT_COMPUTER.          BURROUGHS_6700.
        INPUT_OUTPUT SECTION.
        FILE_CONTROL.
              SELECT DATA_FILE              ASSIGN TO DISK.
              SELECT OUTPUT_FILE            ASSIGN TO PRINTER.

    DATA DIVISION.
    FILE SECTION.

    FD      DATA_FILE
            RECORD CONTAINS 80 CHARACTERS
            LABEL RECORD IS OMITTED
            DATA RECORD IS INPUT_DATA_ RECORD.

    01      INPUT_DATA_RECORD.
            05      N                       PICTURE 9(6)V99.
            05      FILLER                  PICTURE X(72).

    FD      OUTPUT_FILE
            RECORD CONTAINS 132 CHARACTERS
            LABEL RECORD IS OMITTED
            DATA RECORD IS OUTPUT_RECORD.

    01      OUTPUT_RECORD.
            05      FILLER                  PICTURE X.
            05      TITLE                   PICTURE X(25).
            05      SUM                     PICTURE 9(10)V99.
            05      FILLER                  PICTURE X(94).

    WORKING_STORAGE SECTION.
    77      MESSAGE                         PICTURE X(25)
                                            VALUE IS "THE SUM OF GIVEN NUMBERS=".

    PROCEDURE DIVISION.
    OPEN_FILES.
            OPEN INPUT DATA_FILE.
            OPEN OUTPUT OUTPUT_FILE.

    INITIALIZATION.
            MOVE SPACES TO OUTPUT_RECORD.
            MOVE ZERO TO SUM.

    PROCESS_LOOP.
            READ DATA_FILE AT END GO TO PRINT_PARA.
            ADD N TO SUM.
            GO TO PROCESS_LOOP.

    PRINT_PARA.
            MOVE MESSAGE TO TITLE.
            WRITE OUTPUT_RECORD.

    END_OF_JOB.
            CLOSE DATA_FILE.
            CLOSE OUTPUT_FILE.
            STOP RUN.
```

**Figure 12.13.**  A sample COBOL program.

The main drawback of COBOL is that it is a verbose language. Writing a COBOL program is somewhat tedious and time consuming, because of all the extra words needed in its statements. However, over the years, this drawback has been taken care of largely in the following manner:

1. A rich set of libraries of COBOL business applications modules and programs has been made available today by many vendors. COBOL programmers often make use of these library programs in their applications for faster development.

2. Automatic program generators for COBOL programs have also been developed and made available by some vendors. These software packages are capable of generating 70 to 80% of the code needed in a particular application program from the application's specifications. The programmer has to manually write only 20 to 30% of the code needed to tie the program elements together, and to create a customized problem solution for the application. The use of a COBOL program generator can significantly reduce the time and effort needed to code new COBOL programs.

# BASIC

BASIC stands for **B**eginners **A**ll-purpose **S**ymbolic **I**nstruction **C**ode. It was developed in the year 1964 by Professor John Kemeny and Thomas Kurtz at Darmouth College in the United States. They had the following objectives for developing a new programming language:

1. It should be an interactive language, which permits direct communication between the user and the computer, during the preparation and use of programs.

2. It must be easy for non-science students to learn and use the language.

To meet these objectives, the designers took the following approach in the design of BASIC language:

1. It was designed to use terminals as the method of computer access. Before this, most programs were entered into computers through either punched cards or paper tape.

2. It was designed to use an interpreter as the language translator, instead of a compiler (FORTRAN and COBOL use compilers), so that programmers could create, run, test and debug a program in interactive mode.

3. It was designed with very few statements and grammatical rules, so that it could be easily learnt and used by beginner programmers.

BASIC was the first high-level language to be implemented on personal computers when they were introduced. Today, BASIC is available in almost all personal computers, and even in some pocket calculators. This fact makes it one of the most widely installed computer languages in the world.

Though simple and easy to learn, BASIC is quite flexible and reasonably powerful. It can be used for both business and scientific applications. Users of BASIC range from school students to scientists and engineers to business managers. It is also used to teach programming concepts to beginners.

A minimal version of BASIC was standardized by ANSI in 1978. However, this standard is so simple that it has been extended in virtually every available BASIC dialect. Today, BASIC has many dialects including BASICA, QBASIC, and Visual Basic. Microsoft's Visual Basic supports object-oriented features. Furthermore, note that, although BASIC began as an interpreted language, several new dialects of BASIC have added compilers. Microsoft's QuickBASIC and Visual Basic produce compiled programs.

A BASIC program to compute and print the sum of 10 numbers is shown in Figure 12.14. It can be observed from this example that each statement of a BASIC program starts with a statement number and a key word, followed in most cases by some type of action. For example, in the statement, "40 LET S = S + N", 40 is the statement number, LET is the key word, and S = S + N is the action. The first two statements of the program, which are REM statements, are remarks being made for the purpose of explaining or documenting a program step. They have no effect on the program logic. A remark/comment statement must have a line number, the key word REM, and any

```
5       REM PROGRAM TO COMPUTE
6       REM THE SUM OF 10 NUMBERS
10      LET S = 0
20      FOR I = 1 TO 10
30      READ N
40      LET S = S + N
50      NEXT I
60      PRINT "THE SUM OF GIVEN NUMBERS = "; S
70      DATA 4, 20, 15, 32, 48
80      DATA 12, 3, 9, 14, 44
90      END;
```

**Figure 12.14.** A sample BASIC program.

remark that the programmer wishes to make. In our example, the remark statement was used to name the program. The two LET statements are assignment statements. The READ and PRINT statements read input data and print output result respectively. The FOR and NEXT statements control the loop, which is meant for adding the 10 numbers one-by-one. The two DATA statements in the program are used to furnish the input data. The END statement stops the program.

# Pascal

Named after the famous seventeenth-century, French mathematician, Blaise Pascal, this language was first developed in the year 1971 by Professor Nicklaus Wirth of Federal Institute of Technology in Zurich, Switzerland. His main objective was to develop a language, which can allow beginners to learn good problem solving and programming practices. To meet this objective, Pascal was developed based on the concepts associated with structured programming. That is, it was designed in a manner that complete Pascal programs could be written without the use of any GO TO statement. Special control statements for selection and looping structures were provided for this purpose. To make programs structured, Pascal programs are composed of blocks. Each block of statements starts with a *Begin* statement, and ends with an *End* statement.

Due to the above-mentioned features, Pascal is widely recognized as a language, which encourages programmers to write well-structured, modular programs, and instills good programming practices in a programmer. Hence, it is recognized as an educational language, and is used to teach programming to beginners.

Pascal was standardized by ANSI in 1983. Since then, several dialects of Pascal have been made available on different computer systems. An object-oriented version of Pascal is also available. Pascal is suitable for both scientific and business applications, because it has features to manipulate, not only numbers, but also vectors, matrices, strings of characters, sets, records, files and lists.

A Pascal program to compute and print the sum of 10 numbers is shown in Figure 12.15. The first line of the program contains the name of the program, which is SUMNUMS. This is followed by two comment lines. Any comment can be placed within the symbols (* and *). Then, all the variables are declared. The variables SUM and N are declared as real, and hence, they can be assigned any real number. Similarly, the variable I, which has been declared to be an integer variable, can be assigned any integer value. The heart of the program starts with the word BEGIN, and ends with the word END. First, the variable SUM is initialized to zero. The next statement starts a DO loop, which reads and computes the sum of the 10 numbers. Finally, the statement having WRITELN prints the result of the computation.

```
PROGRAM SUMNUMS (INPUT, OUTPUT);
(* PROGRAM TO COMPUTE THE SUM OF 10 NUMBERS *)

(* DECLARATION OF VARIABLES *)
VAR SUM, N : REAL;
VAR I : INTEGER;

(* MAIN PROGRAM LOGIC STARTS HERE *)
BEGIN
        SUM := 0;
        FOR I := 1 TO 10 DO
        BEGIN
                READ (N);
                SUM := SUM + N;
        END;
        WRITELN ('THE SUM OF GIVEN NUMBERS=', SUM);
END;
```

**Figure 12.15.** A sample Pascal program.

## SOME MORE HIGH-LEVEL LANGUAGES

The high-level programming languages, which were discussed above are not necessarily the most important or most popular languages. These languages were presented in some detail to give you a better understanding of computer programming, and nature of high-level languages in general. There are several other programming languages, which are equally important and popular. Some of these languages are described below.

## C and C++

C language was developed in 1972 at AT&T's Bell laboratories, USA by Dennis Ritchie and Brian Kernighan. Their objective was to develop a language, which will have the virtues of high-level programming languages (mainly machine independence) with the efficiency of an assembly language. To meet this objective, C language was designed to have the following features:

1. It was developed as a compiled language (uses compiler as its translator), so that C language programs could be easily ported to other computers equipped with a C compiler.

2. It supports pointers with pointer operations. This feature allows the programmers to directly access the memory addresses where variables are stored, and to perform bit-level manipulation of data stored in memory or processor registers.

3. It supports user-defined data types for greater flexibility in programming.

4. It supports modular and structured programming concepts. That is, while writing a C program to solve a problem, the problem may be broken down into smaller tasks, a function may be written (or used) to solve each task, and the C program may become a group of functions, which are linked together to produce the problem solution. It also supports a rich library of functions, which can be directly used by programmers for efficient coding of their applications.

5. It is a small and concise language providing only the bare essential features, so that a C language program can be translated by a language translator into an efficient machine language code.

Due to its features mentioned above, C soon became the language of choice of systems programmers who wanted to write portable systems software, and commercial software packages like operating systems, compilers, spreadsheet, word processing, and database management systems. In fact, the first major use of C was to write the UNIX operating system. Today, C is extensively used by all types of programmers for programming various different types of applications.

Although, conciseness and flexible use of pointers make C a very powerful language, they also make C a language, which is difficult to learn and comprehend. Beginner programmers often find it difficult to understand and use the flexibility offered by pointers in programming a solution. Moreover, its conciseness feature allows brief programs to be written for carrying out complex computations. Often, such programs are difficult to understand and modify, particularly when they make extensive use of pointers.

For several years after its development, the only standard for C was a book on C written by its developers Kernighan and Ritchie. An ANSI standard for C was produced in 1989. A new version of C, named C++ (pronounced "C plus plus"), was developed by Bjarne Stroustrup at Bell Labs in the early 1980s. The evolution of C++ continued during the first half of 1980, and the first widely available implementation appeared in 1985. C++ is so called because ++ is an operator in C, which increments a variable by 1. Therefore, the C language is incremented to its next level with C++.

C++ contains all the elements of the basic C language, but has been expanded to include numerous object-oriented programming features. The most essential part of support for object-oriented programming is the class/object mechanism, which is the central feature of C++. C++ provides a collection of predefined classes, along with the capability of user-defined classes.

C++ being a superset of C is an extremely powerful and efficient language. However, C++ is also more difficult to learn than C, because learning C++ means learning everything about C, and then learning object-oriented design and its implementation with C++.

Over the years, C++ has become a very popular language. It is said that in a few more years C++ may replace C, because more and more C programmers are migrating to C++. Another factor in favor of the future popularity of C++ is that it is almost completely downward compatible with C (meaning that C programs can be, for the most part, compiled as C++ programs), and in most implementations it is possible to link C++ code with C code.

# Java

Java is a language primarily used for Internet-based applications. Its development started at Sun Microsystems in 1991 by a team led by James Gosling. The language was formally announced in May 1995, and its first commercial release was made in early 1996.

The main objective of the developers of Java was to design a language with the following features:

1. The compiled code should be machine-independent (recall that the compiled code of other high-level languages is machine dependent).

2. The developed programs should be simple to implement and use, even in consumer electronics products like TV set-top boxes, hand-held devices, telephones, and VCRs.

Java was designed to have these features in the following manner:

1. Java uses the concept of *just-in-time compilation*, in which Java programs are typically compiled into machine-independent byte-code, which is interpreted by the Java runtime system at program execution time.

2. Java was developed as a small subset of C++ features to keep it simple and easy to use. Several of the complex features of C++, such as, pointer and multiple inheritance, are not part of Java. Hence, Java is considered to be a "clean" object-oriented language.

Before the innovation of Java, Internet applications were static in nature, because they offered visually static pages of information. The advent of Java and its use in Internet applications enabled the use of dynamic pages, which allow users to interact with what appears on the screen. Hence, Java brings animation and interactivity to Internet-based applications.

The use of Java is not only limited to Internet-based applications. It can also be used to develop anything from spreadsheets to tutorials to interactive games. It can also be used in embedded systems, as in consumer electronics products, such as hand-held devices, telephones, and VCRs.

Software developed to allow the user to observe and interact with Java programs has been named *HotJava*.

# RPG

RPG stands for **R**eport **P**rogram **G**enerator. As the name implies, it is a language designed to generate the output reports resulting from the processing of common business applications. The language was developed by IBM as a result of their customer requests for an easy and economic mechanism for producing reports. It was launched in the year 1961 for use on the IBM 1401 computer. The later version of RPG, called RPG II, greatly improved the language and gave it additional capabilities.

RPG is considered different from other programming languages. Instead of writing instructions or statements, the programmer uses very detailed coding sheets to write his/her specifications about input, calculations, and output. These sheets specify exactly what is to be done, and then the computer uses them to generate the necessary instructions to perform the desired applications. Hence, RPG is easier to learn and use as compared to COBOL. It is, therefore, well suited for applications where large files are read, few calculations are performed, and output reports are created. However, RPG has restricted mathematical capability, and cannot be used for scientific applications.

RPG is primarily used to process business applications on small computers.

# LISP

LISP stands for **LIS**t **P**rocessing. It was developed in 1959 by John McCarthy of MIT. His goal was to develop a language, which will be good at manipulating non-numeric data, such as symbols and strings of text. Such data handling capability is needed in compiler development, and in Artificial Intelligence (AI) applications, which deal with the idea of using computers for modeling human information storage and retrieval, along with other fundamental processes of the brain. This capability was provided in the form of list processing feature, which allows computers to process symbolic data in lists (collection of non-contiguous memory cells, which are chained together with pointers). A list having four data elements is shown in Figure 12.16.

LISP is a functional programming language, and is very different from other imperative languages like FORTRAN, COBOL, and Pascal. All computations in a functional programming language are accomplished by applying functions to arguments. There need not be assignment statements, or even variables, which are used the way those of the imperative languages (to store values, which change during program execution).

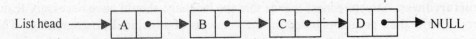

List head ⟶ A ⟶ B ⟶ C ⟶ D ⟶ NULL

**Figure 12.16.** A list with four data elements.

Due to its powerful list processing capability, LISP is extensively used in the areas of pattern recognition, artificial intelligence, and for simulation of games. It totally dominated AI applications area for almost a quarter of a century. Even today, it is the most widely used language for AI applications.

# SNOBOL

SNOBOL stands for **StriNg** **O**riented **symBOl**ic **L**anguage. It is another language used for non-numeric applications. As the name implies, the language was designed to manipulate strings of characters. It has powerful string manipulation features, which facilitate various types of operations on strings of characters, such as string comparisons, splitting of a string, combining two strings, etc. Hence, it has been widely accepted for applications in the area of text processing.

# CHARACTERISTICS OF A GOOD PROGRAMMING LANGUAGE

In the previous section, we saw that there are some high-level languages, which are very popular, and there are others, which could not become so popular in-spite of being very powerful. There might be many reasons for the success of a language, but one obvious reason is the characteristics of the language. Several characteristics believed to be important for making a programming language good are:

1. **Simplicity.** A good programming language must be simple and easy to learn and use. It should provide a programmer with a clear, simple, and unified set of concepts, which can be easily grasped. The overall simplicity of a programming language strongly affects the readability of the programs written in that language, and programs, which are easier to read and understand, are also easier to maintain. It is also easy to develop and implement a compiler or an interpreter for a programming language, which is simple. However, the power needed for the language should not be sacrificed for simplicity. For example, BASIC is liked by many programmers only because of its simplicity.

2. **Naturalness.** A good language should be natural for the application area, for which it has been designed. That is, it should provide appropriate operators, data structures, control structures, and a natural syntax to facilitate the users to code their problem easily and efficiently. FORTRAN and COBOL are good examples of scientific and business languages respectively, which posses high degree of naturalness.

3. **Abstraction.** Abstraction means the ability to define and then use complicated structures or operations in ways that allow many of the details to be ignored. The degree of abstraction allowed by a programming language directly affects its writability. For example, object-oriented languages support high degree of abstraction. Hence, writing programs in object-oriented languages is much easier. Object-oriented languages also support reusability of program segments due to this feature.

4. **Efficiency.** Programs written in a good programming language are efficiently translated into machine code, are efficiently executed, and acquire as little space in the memory as possible. That is, a good programming language is supported with a good language translator (a compiler or an interpreter), which gives due consideration to space and time efficiency.

5. **Structuredness.** Structuredness means that the language should have necessary features to allow its users to write their programs based on the concepts of structured programming. This property of a language greatly affects the ease with which a program may be written, tested, and maintained. Moreover, it forces a programmer to look at a problem in a logical way, so that fewer errors are created while writing a program for the problem.

6. **Compactness.** In a good programming language, programmers should be able to express intended operations concisely. A verbose language is generally not liked by programmers, because they need to write too much. COBOL is disliked by many programmers, because it is verbose in nature and lacks compactness.

7. **Locality.** A good programming language should be such that while writing a program, a programmer need not jump around visually as the text of the program is prepared. This allows the programmer to concentrate almost solely on the part of the program around the statement currently being worked with. COBOL lacks locality, because data definitions are separated from processing statements, perhaps by many pages of code.

8. **Extensibility.** A good programming language should also allow extension through simple, natural, and elegant mechanisms. Almost all languages provide subprogram definition mechanisms for this purpose, but there are some languages, which are rather weak in this aspect.

9. **Suitability to its Environment.** Depending upon the type of application for which a programming language has been designed, the language must also be made suitable to its environment. For example, a language designed for real time applications must be interactive in nature. On the other hand, languages used for data processing jobs like pay-roll, stores accounting, etc., may be designed to be operative in batch mode.

# SELECTING A LANGUAGE FOR CODING AN APPLICATION

One is often faced with the situation of selecting a programming language, out of the many options available for coding an application. The following factors generally influence the selection process:

1. **Nature of the application.** The language should be suitable for the application area. For example, FORTRAN is suitable for scientific and engineering applications, while COBOL is suitable for business applications.

2. **Familiarity with the language.** If there are multiple languages, which are found suitable for the application area, the language selected should be one that is best known to the programmers who are going to code the application.

3. **Ease of learning the language.** If there are multiple languages, which are found suitable for the application area, and if the programmers are not familiar with any of them, the language, which is easier to learn and use, should be selected.

4. **Availability of program development tools.** Before selecting a language, one must also find out whether the language is well supported with good program development tools like compiler, interpreter, debugger, linker, etc. The time and effort needed for coding the application can be greatly reduced, if the selected language is supported with good program development tools.

5. **Execution efficiency.** If the execution efficiency of the application is important, one many use an assembly language, instead of a high-level language for coding the application. This is because an assembly language program written by a clever programmer usually has a shorter production run time, and takes less storage space than does a program of the same application written in a high-level language.

6. **Features of a good programming language.** Finally, the features of a good programming language discussed in the previous section often influence the selection process.

# SUBPROGRAM

Let us assume that we are writing a program for solving a trigonometric problem, and we need to calculate the square root of three numbers at three different places in the program. We could, of course, write the steps required for the calculation of square root, each time we need them in the program. However, a much easier way of handling the problem would be to write these steps once, and then refer to them each time we need them. Every programming language provides a way to do this by defining subprograms. A *subprogram* is a program written in a manner that it can be brought into use in other programs and used whenever needed, without rewriting. A subprogram is referred to by different names in different programming languages. For example, other names used to refer to subprograms are *subroutines*, *subprocedures*, and *functions*.

The structure of a subprogram is shown in Figure 12.17. It consists of a header and a body. The *subprogram header*, which is the first line of a subprogram, provides a name for the subprogram, and it may optionally specify a list of parameters (also known as arguments). The *subprogram name* is used by other programs to refer to the subprogram when they want to use the subprogram. The parameters are specific variable names, numeric values, or other data, which you want the subprogram to use when it executes the instructions in its body. The list of parameters is optional, because there may be subprograms for which you do not need or want to pass any arguments. The *subprogram body* contains the set of instructions, which perform the intended task of the subprogram.

Once created, a subprogram can be used by other programs as often as needed. At whatever points in a program the function performed by the subprogram is required; a statement to call the subprogram is inserted by the programmer. Typically, the subprogram call statement contains the name of the subprogram, followed by the list of parameters enclosed within a pair of parentheses. If you do not need or want to pass any arguments to the subprogram, the empty parentheses are still required normally, to distinguish the statement as a subprogram call. For example, a statement to call the subprogram, which calculates the square root of a number, may be a = sqrt (b);  Different programming languages may have different syntax for writing the call statement for calling a subprogram.

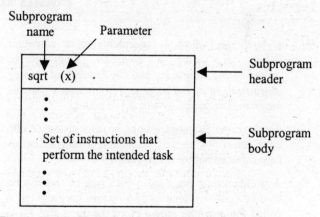

**Figure 12.17.** The structure of a subprogram.

While executing a program, which has one or more subprogram call statements, when the computer encounters a subprogram call statement, the control flow jumps to wherever the subprogram's code is, executes the statements in the subprogram body, then returns to that statement of the calling program, which is immediately after the call statement. The flow of control in case of a subprogram call is illustrated in Figure 12.18. Note that, the subprogram itself need never be written again, nor need it appear more than once in a program, no matter how often its services may be required.

Subprograms may be intrinsic or programmer-written. *Intrinsic subprograms* (commonly referred to as *built-in-functions*) are those provided with the language, so that the programmer need only call them in a program to have them automatically invoked. There are many functionalities, such as those for finding square roots, sines, cosines, logarithms, etc., which are used repeatedly by many programmers in their programs. Such functionalities are usually supplied along with a programming language in the form of built-in-functions. On the other hand, *programmer-written subprograms* are written and used as and when they are needed.

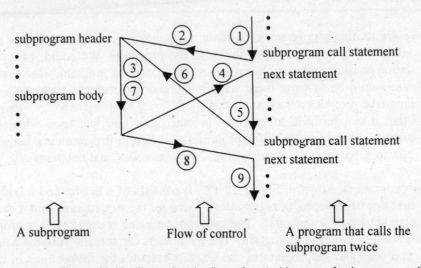

**Figure 12.18.** Illustrating the flow of control in case of subprogram calls.

# Points to Remember

1. A language, which is acceptable to a computer system, is called a *computer language* or *programming language*, and the process of writing instructions in such a language for an already planned program is called *programming* or *coding*.

2. All computer languages can be broadly classified into three categories, namely machine language, assembly language and high-level language.

3. A programming language, which can be understood by a computer without using a translation program, is called the *machine language* of the computer. It is normally written as strings of binary 1s and 0s.

4. A language, which allows instructions and storage locations to be represented by letters and symbols, instead of numbers, is called an *assembly language* or *symbolic language*. A program written in an assembly language is called an *assembly language program* or a *symbolic program*.

5. An *assembler* is a translator program, which translates (converts) an assembly language program (source program) into its equivalent machine language program (object program).

6. Machine and assembly languages are often referred to as *low-level programming languages*, because they are machine dependent, they require the programmers to have a good knowledge of the internal structure of the computer being used, and they deal with machine-level coding requiring one instruction to be written for each machine-level operation. *High-level programming languages* overcome these limitations of low-level programming languages.

7. A *compiler* is a translator program, which translates (converts) a high-level language program (source program) into its equivalent machine-language program (object program).

8. A *linker* is a software, which takes multiple object program files (modules) of a software, and fits them

together to assemble them into the program's final executable form, which is sometimes called a *load module*.

9. An *interpreter* is a translator program, which translates (converts) a high-level language program into its equivalent machine-language program. However, unlike a compiler, which merely translates the entire source program into an object program and is not involved in its execution, an interpreter takes one statement of the source program, translates it into machine language instructions, and then immediately executes the resulting machine language instructions, before taking the next statement for translation. No object program of the source program is generated by the interpreter.

10. *Object-oriented programming* (OOP) deals with solving problems by identifying the real-world objects of the problem and the processing required of those objects, and then creating simulations of those objects, their processes, and the required communications between the objects.

11. Today, many different high-level languages are in use because each was designed for different specific purposes. Some of these are FORTRAN, COBOL, BASIC, Pascal, C, C++, Java, RPG, LISP and SNOBOL.

12. Several characteristics believed to be important with respect to making a programming language good are simplicity, naturalness, abstraction, efficiency, structuredness, compactness, locality, extensibility, and suitability to its environment.

13. The factors that generally influence the process of selecting a programming language, out of the many options available for coding an application are, nature of the application, familiarity with the language, ease of learning the language, availability of program development tools, execution efficiency, and features of a good programming language.

14. A *subprogram* is a program written in a manner that it can be brought into use in other programs and used whenever needed, without rewriting. Other names used to refer to subprograms are *subroutines*, *subprocedures*, and *functions*.

# Questions

1. What is a programming language? Why is it so called?

2. What is meant by coding a program?

3. Discuss the analogy between a computer language and a natural language.

4. How does a computer language differ from a natural language?

5. What is meant by syntax rules of a programming language?

6. Name the three categories of computer languages in order of their ease of usage.

7. What is a machine language? Why is it required?

8. What are the advantages and limitations of machine language?

9. When is a computer language called machine dependent? What is the main disadvantage of such a language?

10. A machine language instruction has two-part format. Identify these parts and discuss the function of each.

11. What is a mnemonic? How is it helpful in case of computer languages?

12. What is an assembly language? What are its advantages over machine language?

13. What is an assembler?

14. What is the difference between a source program and an object program?

15. What is a macro instruction? How does it help in making a programmer's job easier?

16. Why are machine and assembly languages often referred to as low-level languages?

17. List out the main characteristic features of high-level languages. Name five high-level languages.

18. Why are high-level languages easier to learn and use?

19. What is a compiler? Why is it required? A computer supports five high-level languages. How many compilers will this computer have?

20. It is said that an assembly language is "one-for-one", but a high-level language is "many-for-one". Explain what this means.

21. Illustrate the machine independence characteristic of a high-level language.

22. Differentiate between syntax errors and logic errors found in computer programs. Which type of error is more difficult to detect and correct? Give reasons for your answer.

23. While writing a program, a programmer erroneously instructed the computer to calculate the area of a rectangle by adding the width to its length (that is, AREA = LENGTH + WIDTH), instead of multiplying the length and width. Would you expect the language processor to detect this error? Explain why.

24. A programmer eliminates all language processor errors from his/her program, and then runs it to get printed results. The programmer, therefore, concludes that the program is complete. Comment.

25. What type of errors in a program can be detected by a compiler? What type of errors cannot be detected?

26. What is a linker? Why is it required?

27. Explain the differences among assemblers, compilers, interpreters, and linkers.

28. What is an interpreter? How does it differ from a compiler?

29. What advantages do compilers have over interpreters?

30. What advantages do interpreters have over compilers?

31. When would you prefer to use a compiler than an interpreter?

32. When would you prefer to use an interpreter than a compiler?

33. What are the advantages and limitations of high-level languages as compared to machine and assembly languages?

34. What is object-oriented programming?

35. Briefly describe the development and use of the following programming languages:
    - (a) FORTRAN
    - (b) COBOL
    - (c) BASIC
    - (d) Pascal
    - (e) C
    - (f) C++
    - (g) RPG
    - (h) SNOBOL
    - (i) LISP
    - (j) Java

36. What is meant by standardization of a language? Why is it important?

37. What are comment statements? Why are they used in a program? How are they treated by a language processor?

38. Name the four divisions of a COBOL program. What is the purpose of each division?

39. What is a self-documenting language? Illustrate with an example?

40. Why is COBOL often referred to as a self-documenting language?

41. The main drawback of COBOL is that it is a verbose language. How has this drawback been largely taken care of now?

42. List out some of the program preparation techniques, which are often included under the term "structured programming".

43. In Java, the compiled code is machine independent. Explain how is this achieved.

44. What is HotJava?

45. What characteristics are desirable for a good programming language?

46. What factors generally influence the process of selecting a programming language out of the many options available for coding an application?

47. Would you be equally likely to choose FORTRAN or COBOL for programming a given problem? Why?

48. What is a subprogram? How do subprograms help in program writing?

49. What is a built-in-function? Give few examples of built-in-functions.

50. Illustrate with an example the flow of control in case of subprogram calls.

51. Give the full form of the following:
    - (a) FORTRAN
    - (b) COBOL
    - (c) BASIC
    - (d) RPG
    - (e) LISP
    - (f) SNOBOL
    - (g) OOP

# Chapter 13

# System Implementation and Operation

In the previous two chapters, we have discussed the analysis, design, and coding phases of software development. After the computer programs have been prepared, the developed software, along with the associated hardware, enters the implementation and operation phase. The goal of this chapter is to describe the main activities of the implementation and operation phase, which include testing and debugging of programs, complete documentation of the system, changeover to the new system, and system modification and maintenance.

## TESTING AND DEBUGGING

### Definition of Testing and Debugging

As long as computers are programmed by human beings, computer programs will be subject to errors. Program errors are known as *bugs*, and the process of detecting and correcting these errors is called *debugging*. In general, *testing* is the process of making sure that the program performs the intended task, and *debugging* is the process of locating and eliminating program errors. Testing and debugging are important steps in program development. They are also time-consuming steps. In fact, for large programs, the time spent in testing and debugging often exceeds the time spent in coding the program.

# Types of Program Errors

In general, there are two types of errors, which occur in a computer program. They are:

1. **Syntax Errors.** *Syntax errors* result when the rules or syntax of the programming language are not followed. Such program errors typically involve incorrect punctuation, incorrect word sequence, undefined terms, or misuse of terms. For example, the FORTRAN statement C = (A + B/2 has a syntax error, because of the missing closing parenthesis, which should be placed in the appropriate place, depending on the logic of the program. A program cannot be successfully compiled and executed, until all its syntax errors have been corrected.

2. **Logic Errors.** A *logic error* is an error in planning the program's logic. Such errors cause the program to produce incorrect output. That is, a program, which is free of syntax errors, but has one or more logic errors, will be successfully compiled and executed, but will not produce correct result. The problem is that, since the program contains logic errors, the logic being followed during its execution will not be correct. Hence, the program will not produce the desired results. For example, if a FORTRAN instruction should be "A = B + C", but has been coded as "A = B – C", it is an example of a logic error, because the result produced by the program will not be correct.

# Testing a Program

In case of a logic error, since no language rules have been violated, the computer does not know that an error has been made. Hence, it will not produce any error message for a logic error. Therefore, identifying logic errors in a program is the responsibility of the program development and testing team. The testing procedure involves running the program to process input test data, and comparing the produced results with the known correct results. If the results generated for the test data do not match with the known correct results, it is assumed that the program contains one or more logic errors.

Logic errors are typically due to either missing logic or incorrect logic. If the logic is incorrect, the results generated from the test data will be wrong. These errors are the easiest of the logic errors to find. Errors caused by missing logic result from logical situations, which the program was not designed to handle. As an example, let us assume that a numeric field is to be used in an arithmetic process, and the data entry operator enters a value for the field, which is not numeric. The program logic should determine that the data is not numeric, before attempting the arithmetic process. If this logic is missing, and nonnumeric data is used in an arithmetic operation, the program will fail. This type of logic error can be difficult to find. The only way for this error to occur is for nonnumeric data to be entered into a numeric field. It is possible for the program to be used for weeks, months, or years, before this happens and the error in program logic shows up.

In order to completely test the program logic, the test data must test each logical function of the program. Hence, the selection of proper test data is important in program testing. In general, the test data selected for testing a program should include:

1. All types of possible valid data. This will ensure that the program has been correctly designed to handle all types of input data, which falls within the scope of the program.

2. All types of possible invalid data (such as incorrect, incomplete, or inappropriate data). This is necessary to test the error-handling capabilities of the program (how the program reacts in case of abnormal and unusual input data). Good programs should be able to produce appropriate error messages, instead of hanging (not continuing with its execution) or generating meaningless output.

If a program runs successfully with the test data, and produces correct results, it is normally released for use. However, even at this stage, errors may still remain in the program. In case of a complex program, there may be thousands of different possible paths through the program, and it may not be practical, or even possible, to trace through all these paths during testing. There are certain errors in complex software systems, which remain dormant for months and years together. Hence, it is impossible to certify that such systems are free of all logic errors. Therefore, if a software is going to be sold commercially, instead of releasing it directly in the commercial market, it is first released to a selected set of users. This release version of the software is known as *beta version*. The selected set of users use the beta version of the software for an identified period of time, and report any bug found in the software to the company, which is developing the software. The use of beta version of the software by the selected set of users for identifying errors, which might have been overlooked during the regular testing phase, is known as *beta testing*. After beta testing, the reported bugs (if any) are fixed, and then the software is released to the commercial market. Note that, even at this stage, the software may contain certain errors.

## Debugging a Program for Syntax Errors

Syntax errors and logic errors are collectively known as *bugs*, and the process of eliminating these errors is known as *debugging*. As compared to logic errors, syntax errors are much easier to eliminate, because almost all language processors are designed to detect syntax errors. On the source listing of a program, the language processors indicate each program statement, which has one or more errors, and give hints as to the nature of the error. These error messages are very useful and are used by the programmers to rectify all syntax errors in their programs. Hence, it is a relatively easy task to detect and correct syntax errors.

It should be noted that in high-level languages, such as FORTRAN and COBOL, a single error often causes multiple error messages to be generated. There are two reasons for this. One is that high-level language instructions often require multiple machine instructions. The other reason is that symbolic instructions are often dependent upon other instructions, and if an instruction containing an error is one that defines a field name, all instructions in the program using that field name will be listed as errors. The error message will say that a field being used is not a defined name. In such a case, removal of the single error will result in the removal of all associated error messages.

## Debugging a Program for Logic Errors

Unlike syntax errors, the computer does not produce any error message for logic errors in a program. Hence, logic errors are more difficult to eliminate than syntax errors. However, once the testing of a program indicates the presence of logic error in it, one or more of the following methods may be used to locate and correct logic errors:

1. **Doing Hand Simulation of the Program Code.** One approach is to take a printout of the source code of the program, and go through its execution manually with the test data input, which produced incorrect results. In the manual execution, you follow the same sequence of paths, which the computer would have followed for the test data, keeping track of the changes in the values of the various variables, which you come across during the execution. The cause of the problem is very likely to be detected before you complete the manual execution. This method is normally used only for simple and small programs, because manual execution of a program is a tedious process.

2. **Putting Print Statements in the Program Code.** Another approach is to put several print or write statements at appropriate locations in the program, so that the values of different variables can be printed/displayed to indicate intermediate computations results. The program is re-compiled and executed with these statements. These statements print/display the values of intermediate computations telling you what is happening during the execution of the program. The cause of the

problem is very likely to be detected by doing a proper analysis of the printed/displayed intermediate results. Once the errors have been found and corrected, these print or write statements are removed from the program.

3. **Using a Debugger.** This is the most commonly used approach. A *debugger* is a software tool, which assists the programmer in following the program's execution step-by-step by allowing him/her to display intermediate calculation results and field values, whenever desired. In effect, a debugger helps the programmer in debugging the program logic much more easily than having to put (and later remove) print/write statements into the program's source code. Almost all modern programming language processors are supported with some kind of debugger.

4. **Using Memory Dump.** This approach is normally used when the program "hangs up" during a test run. In this approach, a printout of the contents of main memory and registers is taken at the time when the program hangs up. This printout is called a *memory dump* or *storage dump*. The memory dump lists the instructions and data held in the computer's main memory in their raw form, that is, their binary or equivalent hexadecimal or octal form. The cause of the problem is very likely to be detected by doing a proper analysis of this listing.

## Difference Between Testing and Debugging

Since both testing and debugging deal with program errors, many people often confuse between these two terms. The discussion above has clearly indicated that testing and debugging are two separate tasks. The points listed in Figure 13.1 further clarify the difference between the two.

| Sl. No. | Testing | Debugging |
|---|---|---|
| 1 | Testing is the process of validating the correctness of a program. Its objective is to demonstrate that the program meets its design specifications. | Debugging is the process of eliminating errors in a program. Its objective is to detect the exact cause of, and remove known errors in the program. |
| 2 | Testing is complete when all desired verifications against specifications have been performed. | Debugging is complete when all known errors in the program have been fixed. Note that, debugging process ends only temporarily, because it must be restarted whenever a new error is found in the program. |
| 3 | Testing is a definable process, which can and should be planned and scheduled properly. | Debugging, being a reactive process, cannot be planned ahead of time. It must be carried out as and when errors are found in a program. |
| 4 | Testing can begin in the early stages of software development. Although the test runs of a program can be done only after the program is coded, but the decision of what to test, how to test, and with what kind of data to test, can and should be done before the coding is started. | Debugging can begin only after the program is coded. The approach used for debugging largely depends on the personal choice of the programmer and the type of problem in the program. |

**Figure 13.1.** Difference between testing and debugging.

# DOCUMENTATION

## What is Documentation?

*Documentation* is the process of collecting, organizing, storing, and maintaining a complete historical record of programs, and other documents used or prepared during the different phases of the life cycle of a software. A software cannot be considered to be complete, until it is properly documented. In fact, documentation is an on-going process, which starts in the study phase of the software and continues, until its implementation and operation phase. Moreover, documentation is a process, which never ends throughout the life of the software. It has to be carried out from time to time, as and when the software is modified during its maintenance phase.

## Need for Documentation

Proper documentation of a software is necessary due to the following reasons:

1. It solves the problem of indispensability of an individual for an organization. Even if the person, who has designed or programmed the software, leaves the organization, the documented knowledge remains with the organization, which can be used for the continuity of the software.

2. It makes a software easier to modify and maintain in the future. The key to maintenance is proper and dynamic documentation. It is easier to understand the logic of a program from the documented records, rather than its code. System flowcharts, program flowcharts, or comments used within the programs prove to be very helpful in this regard.

3. It helps in restarting a software project, which was postponed due to some reason. The job need not be started from scratch, and the old ideas may still be easily recapitulated from the available documents, which avoids duplication of work, and saves lot of time and effort.

## Forms of Documentation

The three commonly used forms of documentation, for documenting a software, are comments, system manual and user manual. They are briefly described below. Note that all three forms of documentation are necessary to properly and completely document a software.

### Comments

Comments are natural language statements put within a program to assist anyone reading the source program listing in understanding the logic of the program. They do not contain any program logic, and are ignored (not translated) by the language processor. From maintenance point of view, comments are considered to be a must. All high-level languages provide the facility to write comments along with the source code of a program. It is suggested that programmers should liberally use this facility for proper documentation of their programs.

Comments should be used intelligently to improve the quality and understandability of the program. They should not be redundant, incorrect, incomplete, or written in a manner that cannot be understood by anyone else. For example, a redundant comment for the statement N = N + 1 would be "INCREMENT N BY 1". Useful comments are those, which describe the meaning of a group of statements, such as "READ AND ECHO PRINT THE INPUT DATA". In other words, comments should mediate between the program and the problem domain.

## System Manual

A good software must be supported with a standard system manual, which contains the following information:

1. A statement of the problem clearly defining the objectives of developing the software, and its usefulness to various categories of users.

2. A description of the software specifying the scope of the problem, the environment in which it functions, its limitations, its input data requirements, and the form and type of output required.

3. Specific program names along with their description and purpose.

4. Detailed system flow charts and program flow charts, cross-referenced to the program listing.

5. Description of the program listings, and the control procedures.

6. A source listing of all the programs, together with full details of any modifications made since.

7. Specifications of all input and output media required for the operation of various programs.

8. Specimen of all input forms and printed outputs.

9. File layout, that is, the detailed layout of input and output records.

10. The structure and description of test data and test results, storage dumps, trace program printouts, etc., used to debug the programs.

## User Manual

A good software package must be supported with a good user manual to ensure the smooth running of the package. It is the user who will perform the regular processing after the software is released, and not the programmer who has developed the package. Hence, the user manual must contain the following information:

1. Set up and operational details of each program.

2. Loading and unloading procedures.

3. Starting, running, and terminating procedures.

4. A description and example, of any control statements, which may be used.

5. All console commands along with errors and console messages, which could arise, their meaning, reply and/or operation action.

6. List of error conditions with explanations for their re-entry into the system.

7. List of programs to be executed before and after execution of each program.

8. Special checks (if any) and security measures, etc.

## Documentation Standard

The importance of software documentation cannot be over emphasized. There have been too many problems in the past with poorly documented software. The result is usually errors and problems with the software at a later date. It is very difficult to incorporate modifications in such software. Hence, they are very expensive to maintain. Several computer organizations have, therefore, developed strict documentation standards. These standards describe in detail how documentation is to be performed, how to choose meaningful program variable names, how to design the GUI for the software, how and up to what detail to include comments in program code, and what diagrams, charts, reports, outputs, etc. are necessary for documentation to be completed successfully.

# CHANGEOVER TO THE NEW SYSTEM

Once the software is thoroughly tested, and all known errors have been removed, the software, along with the associated hardware, is deployed at site for use by the intended users. At this stage, the old system (manual system in most cases), if any, is phased out and the new system is phased in.

## Changeover Operations

The changeover process normally involves the following operations:

1. Imparting system and user training to the members of the organization in which the new system is deployed. The system training is imparted to those members who will be responsible for managing and maintaining the system. The user training is imparted to those members who will be operating the system and/or using the results produced by the system. Anyone else who will be affected by the new system should also receive some training to become familiar with the changes.

2. Replacing all old operation procedures by new ones. This may involve discarding of old forms, manual registers, etc.

3. Replacing of all old input and output devices with those of the new system.

4. Defining the roles of different members, and assigning the responsibilities to them as per the requirements of the new system.

5. Converting data in all currently existing files into a form acceptable to the new system. This may involve inputting of data stored in manual registers and hard-copy files, through the input devices of the new system. It is important to consolidate the files and eliminate duplicate records in them, while converting them to the new form. File inconsistencies or any errors in existing files must also be detected and removed.

## Changeover Methods

The three normally followed methods to carry out the changeover process are immediate changeover, parallel run and phased conversion. Each of these methods has its own advantages and disadvantages. No single method is suitable for converting all types of systems, and the choice of a particular method largely depends upon the prevailing conversion circumstances. These methods are briefly described below.

### Immediate Changeover

As shown in Figure 13.2(a), in this method, a suitable cut-off date is decided, and the new system is put to operation from that day onwards, while the operation of the old system is completely abandoned from the cut-off date.

It has been found that most systems pose some problem during the changeover process. Hence, the method of immediate changeover is generally considered to be risky, because any failure in the new system during the changeover phase may cause total breakdown of those operations of the organization, which are related to the new and the old system. The work cannot progress at all, because the operation of the old system has already been stopped.

This method, however, is preferred in those situations where available manpower and changeover time is less, and the system is not so critical that some problem during the changeover process would lead to a disaster.

## Parallel Run

As shown in Figure 13.2(b), in this method, both the old and new systems are parallely operated with the same data for the initial three or four cycles. During this overlapping period of complete operation of the two systems, the results produced by the new system are compared with those produced by the old system to develop confidence in the new system. Some discrepancies may be discovered. Often, these are due to inaccuracies in the old system that were not recognized before as inaccuracies. Some discrepancies may also be due to missing program logic for which no programming was provided, or due to mistakes in the programming itself. These must be corrected by further debugging, before the conversion is complete.

This method is one of the safest ways to deploy a new system, because of the availability of old system as a backup. There is no interruption of work if there are problems with the new system, because the old system is still in operation, and the problems found in the new system can be corrected while the old system is still being used.

This method, however, is very expensive, because additional manpower is needed during the overlapping period for the operation of two systems in parallel. Due to the requirement of additional manpower, the organization is under considerable strain during the period of parallel operation, and organizational breakdowns tend to occur, if the period of parallel operation is long. Hence, parallel operation must not be carried on any longer than needed to establish confidence in the new system. Continuing them too long is a sign of weakness in the new system.

This method is not preferred in situations where manpower resource is scarce. It is also not used in situations where the new system differs to a great extent from the old system in its functions, and its input and output.

## Phased Conversion

As shown in Figure 13.2(c), in this method, the complete changeover to the new system takes place incrementally over a period of time. The new system is gradually implemented part by part, and the old system is gradually phased out. The results produced by each part of the new system are compared against the results of the old system. Any discrepancies or errors found are checked and removed. Once confidence is developed in a particular part of the new system, that part of the new system is phased in, and the corresponding part (operations) of the old system is phased out. This approach is continued for each and every part of the new system. Hence, over a period of time, the new system is gradually phased in, while the old system is gradually phased out.

This method is not as expensive as the parallel run method, because the changeover process being gradual can usually be handled with existing manpower. Moreover, there is no danger of interruption of work if there are problems with the new system, because the corresponding part of the old system is still in operation. The users also get sufficient time to become acquainted with the new system. Hence, they can confidently handle the new system when the complete system is handed over to them.

This method, however, cannot be used in situations where the time period supplied for conversion process is very less, or when the new system significantly differs from the old system.

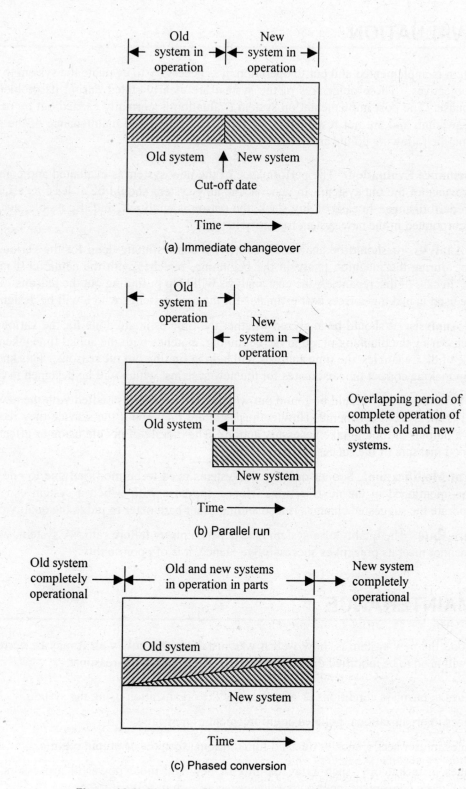

**Figure 13.2.** Methods of system changeover to the new system.

# SYSTEM EVALUATION

Once the new system is implemented and put to operation, it is necessary to evaluate the system to verify whether it is meeting its objectives. These objectives of the system are clearly stated during its problem analysis and system planning phase. The post implementation system evaluation is normally carried out by people who have an independent viewpoint, and are not responsible for the development and maintenance of the system. While evaluating a system, the following points are normally considered:

1. **Performance Evaluation.** The performance of the new system is evaluated and compared with the performance of the old system. In general, the new system should be at least as efficient as the old one in performance. In case of any slack, the reason is analyzed, and if possible, necessary changes are incorporated in the new system to rectify it.

2. **Cost Analysis.** It should be analyzed whether the cost estimate done for the various phases of the project, during the planning phase in the beginning, matches with the actual cost incurred in each phase. In case of discrepancies, the cost analysis will help in finding out the reasons. This knowledge can be used in making correct cost estimates for the new systems, which will be designed in future.

3. **Time Analysis.** It should be analyzed whether the time estimate done for the various phases of the project, during the planning phase in the beginning, matches with the actual time taken in each phase. In case of discrepancies, the time analysis will help in finding out the reasons. This knowledge can be used in making correct time estimates for the new systems, which will be designed in future.

4. **User Satisfaction.** It should be found out whether the users are satisfied with the new system. How useful is the system for them? How enthusiastic are they about the service they receive? Do they receive outputs in time to take necessary action? The morale of people using or affected by a system is a good measure of the success of the system.

5. **Ease of Modification.** Sooner or later, all systems need to be modified due to one or more of the reasons mentioned in the next section. Hence, the ease with which a system can be modified to incorporate the suggested changes is also an important parameter to judge the quality of the system.

6. **Failure Rate.** The quality of a system also depends on its failure rate. A system, which frequently fails cannot meet its objectives successfully. Hence, it is of poor quality.

# SYSTEM MAINTENANCE

No matter how good the new system is, how well it was installed, and how well it may be currently operating, sooner or later it will need to be modified due to one or more of the following reasons:

1. Changes in business conditions or operations of the organization using the system.

2. Changes in organizational policies or enforcement of new laws.

3. Changes in user needs, such as demand for additional features or output reports.

4. Changes in technology, such as availability of new and more powerful processors, more efficient storage, more convenient input/output devices, new system software, etc.

System maintenance is an important phase of the overall life cycle of a computerized system, and its importance should not be under estimated. In fact, several studies have shown that, on an average, the maintenance cost of a computerized system is two to four times more than the initial development cost. This means that more than half of the programming tasks in this world involve program maintenance. Due to this reason, in some organizations there are programmers who do nothing but maintain production programs.

Frequent change is disrupting and disturbing. Therefore, some control over changes is required. One method of achieving this is to have all requests for change evaluated by a change control board. This board should be made up of the principal users of the system, a system analyst, and data processing personnel who are familiar with the system. Normal maintenance operations need not be approved by the change control board, but these operations should be recorded and summarized for periodic reporting to the board. Examples of maintenance activities are modifying the format of a report, or rewriting a part of a computer program component to improve its efficiency. Major changes are those that significantly alter the system, or require extensive personnel, hardware, or software. An example of a major change would be conversion of a system from Unix to Windows environment.

When programs are modified, it is important to make sure that program documentation is also changed accordingly. Without the existence of proper documentation that is consistent with the programs, future changes would be very difficult and costly to accomplish.

# Points to Remember

1. *Testing* is the process of making sure that the program performs the intended task.

2. Program errors are known as *bugs*, and the process of detecting and correcting these errors is called *debugging*.

3. There are two types of errors, which occur in a computer program – syntax errors and logic errors. *Syntax errors* result when the rules or syntax of the programming language are not followed. *Logic errors* are errors in planning the program's logic. Such errors cause the program to produce incorrect result.

4. As compared to logic errors, syntax errors are easier to detect and correct, because the language processors are designed to detect syntax errors in a program.

5. The commonly used methods for locating and correcting logic errors are doing hand simulation of the program code, putting print statements in the program code, using a debugger, and using memory dump.

6. A *debugger* is a software tool, which assists the programmer in following the program's execution step-by-step by allowing him/her to display intermediate calculation results and field values, whenever desired.

7. *Documentation* is the process of collecting, organizing, storing, and maintaining a complete historical record of programs, and other documents used or prepared during the different phases of the life cycle of a software. The three commonly used forms of documentation, for documenting a software, are program comments, system manual and user manual.

8. Once the software is thoroughly tested, and all known errors have been removed, the software, along with the associated hardware, is deployed at site for use by the intended users. At this stage, a changeover from the old system to the new system takes place. The three normally followed methods (shown in Figure 13.2) to carry out the changeover process are immediate changeover, parallel run and phased conversion.

9. *System evaluation* is the process of evaluating a system (after it is put to operation) to verify whether it is meeting its objectives. The points normally considered for evaluating a system are performance evaluation, cost analysis, time analysis, user satisfaction, ease of modification and failure rate.

10. *System maintenance* is the process of incorporating changes in an existing system to enhance, update or upgrade its features.

# Questions

1. What are the two types of errors that can occur in a computer program? Give an example of each to illustrate their nature.

2. Differentiate between syntax errors and logic errors in computer programs.

3. Will a program run, if there are syntax errors in it? Give reasons for your answer.

4. Will a program run, if there are logic errors in it? Give reasons for your answer.

5. What is testing of a program? Why should a program be tested?

6. What are the different types of test data that should be selected for testing a program?

7. Why is it not possible for a very complex software system to certify that it is error free?

8. What is a beta version of a commercial software? What is beta testing?

9. How are syntax errors detected and corrected?

10. How are logic errors detected and corrected?

11. Is it easier to detect a syntax error or a logic error in a program? Give reasons for your answer.

12. What is a program bug? What is debugging?

13. Describe the various methods that may be used to locate and correct logic errors.

14. What is a debugger? How does it help a programmer?

15. What is a memory dump? How is it useful for a programmer?

16. Differentiate between testing and debugging.

17. What is software documentation? Why is it needed?

18. Describe the different types of documentation normally used for documenting a software system.

19. What are program comments? Why are they needed?

20. What is a system manual of a software system? What type of information does it typically contain?

21. What is a user manual of a software system? What type of information does it typically contain?

22. What is documentation standard? Why is it needed?

23. What type of operations is normally carried out in the system changeover process?

24. Describe the three different methods of system changeover along with their advantages and disadvantages.

25. Why is system evaluation needed? What are the main parameters normally used to evaluate a new system?

26. Why do we need to modify a system, if it is currently operating well?

27. Why is system maintenance considered an important process in the life cycle of a computerized system?

28. How can frequent program modifications be controlled?

# Chapter 14

# Operating Systems

In the last few chapters, we learnt about the planning, coding, operation, and maintenance of software systems. In the next few chapters, we will learn about some of the commonly used software. In this chapter, you will learn about operating system, which is a very important software that falls under the category of system software. In the next chapter, you will learn about some commonly used application software packages.

## WHAT IS AN OPERATING SYSTEM?

An *operating system* (often referred to as OS) is an integrated set of programs that controls the resources (the CPU, memory, I/O devices, etc.) of a computer system and provides its users with an interface or virtual machine that is more convenient to use than the bare machine. According to this definition, the two primary objectives of an operating system are:

1. **Making a computer system convenient to use.** An operating system is a layer of software on top of the bare hardware of a computer system, which manages all parts of the system, and presents to the user with an interface or *virtual machine,* which is easier to program and use. That is, the operating system hides the details of the hardware resources from the programmer and provides the programmer with a convenient interface for using the computer system. It acts as an intermediary between the hardware and its users, providing a high-level interface to low-level hardware resources, and making it easier for the programmer and other users to access and use those resources.

   The logical architecture of a computer system is shown in Figure 14.1. As shown in the figure, the hardware resources are surrounded by the operating system layer, which in turn is surrounded by a layer of other system software (such as compilers, editors, utilities, etc.) and a set of application programs (such as commercial data processing applications, scientific and engineering applications, entertainment and educational applications, etc.). Finally, the end users view the computer system in terms of the user interfaces provided by the application programs.

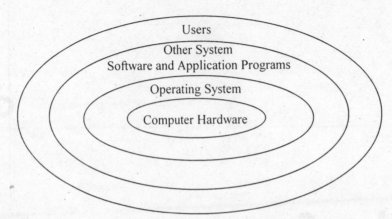

**Figure 14.1.** Logical architecture of a computer system. The operating system layer hides the details of the hardware from the programmer and provides the programmer with a convenient interface for using the system.

2. **Managing the resources of a computer system.** The second important objective of an operating system is to manage the various resources of the computer system. This involves performing such tasks as keeping track of who is using which resource, granting resource requests, accounting for resource usage, and mediating conflicting requests from different programs and users. The efficient and fair sharing of resources among users and/or programs is a key goal of most operating systems.

## Main Functions of an Operating System

The main functions performed by most operating systems of today are as follows:

1. **Process Management.** The process management module of an operating system takes care of the creation and deletion of processes, scheduling of various system resources to the different processes requesting them, and providing mechanisms for synchronization and communication among processes.

2. **Memory Management.** The memory management module of an operating system takes care of the allocation and deallocation of memory space to the various programs in need of this resource.

3. **File Management.** The file management module of an operating system takes care of file-related activities such as organization, storing, retrieval, naming, sharing, and protection of files.

4. **Security.** The security module of an operating system protects the resources and information of a computer system against destruction and unauthorized access.

5. **Command Interpretation.** The command interpretation module of an operating system takes care of interpreting user commands, and directing the system resources to handle the requests. With this mode of interaction with the system, the user is usually not too concerned with the hardware details of the system.

In addition to the above listed major functions, an operating system also performs few other functions such as keeping an account of which users (or processes) use how much and what kinds of computer resources, maintenance of log of system usage by all users, and maintenance of internal time clock.

## MEASURING SYSTEM PERFORMANCE

The efficiency of an operating system and the overall performance of a computer system are usually measured in terms of the following:

1. **Throughput.** *Throughput* is the amount of work that the system is able to do per unit time. It is measured as the number of processes that are completed by the system per unit time. For example, if $n$ processes are completed in an interval of $t$ seconds, the throughput is taken as $n/t$ processes per second during that interval. Throughput is normally measured in processes/hour. Note that the value of throughput does not depend only on the capability of a system, but also on the nature of jobs being processed by the system. For long processes, throughput may be one process/hour; and for short processes, throughput may be 100 processes/hour.

2. **Turnaround time.** From the point of view of an individual user, an important criterion is how long it takes the system to complete a job submitted by him/her. *Turnaround time* is the interval from the time of submission of a job to the system for processing to the time of completion of the job. Although, higher throughput is desirable from the point of view of overall system performance, individual users are more interested in better turnaround time for their jobs.

3. **Response time.** Turnaround time is usually not a suitable measure for interactive systems, because in an interactive system, a process can produce some output early during its execution and can continue executing while previous results are being output to the user. Hence, another measure used in case of interactive systems is *response time*, which is the interval from the time of submission of a job to the system for processing to the time the first response for the job is produced by the system.

In any computer system, it is desirable to maximize throughput and minimize turnaround time and response time.

# PROCESS MANAGEMENT

A *process* (also called *job*) is a program in execution. The main objective of the process management module of an operating system is to manage the processes submitted to the system in a manner to minimize the idle time of the various processors (CPU, I/O processors, etc.) of the computer system. In this section, we will learn about some of the mechanisms commonly used in modern operating systems to achieve this objective. We will also see how these mechanisms have gradually evolved from the early days of computers.

## Process Management in Early Systems

In early computer systems, a job was typically executed in the following manner:

1. A programmer would first write the program on paper.

2. It was then punched on cards or paper tape along with its data.

3. The deck of cards or the paper tape containing the program and data was then submitted at the reception counter of the computer centre.

4. An operator would then take the cards deck or paper tape and manually load it into the system from card reader or paper tape reader. The operator was also responsible for loading any other software resource (such as a language compiler) or setting hardware devices required for the execution of the job. Before loading of the job, the operator had to use the front panel switches of the computer system to clear the main memory to remove any data remaining from the previous job.

5. The operator would then set the appropriate switches in the front panel to run the job.

6. The result of execution of the job was then printed on the printer, which was brought by the operator to the reception counter for the programmer to collect it later.

The same process had to be repeated for every job to be executed by the computer. This method of job execution was known as the *manual loading mechanism* because the jobs had to be manually loaded one after another by the computer operator in the computer system. Notice that in this method, job-to-job transition was not automatic. The manual transition from one job to another caused lot of computer time to be wasted since the computer remained idle while the operator loaded and unloaded jobs and prepared the system for a new job. In order to reduce this idle time of the computer, a method of automatic job-to-job transition was devised. In this method, known as *batch processing*, when one job is finished, the system control is automatically transferred back to the operating system which automatically performs the housekeeping jobs (such as clearing the memory to remove any data remaining from the previous job) needed to load and run the next job. In case of batch processing systems, jobs were typically executed in the following manner:

1.  Programmers would prepare their programs and data on decks of cards or paper tapes, and submitted them at the reception counter of the computer centre.

2.  The operator would periodically collect all the submitted programs and would batch them together and then load them all into the input device of the system at one time.

3.  The operator would then give a command to the system to start executing the jobs.

4.  The jobs were then automatically loaded from the input device and executed by the system one-by-one without any operator intervention. That is, the system would read the first job from the input device, execute it, print out its result on the printer, and then repeat these steps for each subsequent job, until all the jobs in the submitted batch of jobs were over.

5.  When all the jobs in the submitted batch were processed, the operator would separate and keep the printed output of each job at the reception counter for the programmers to collect them later.

The batch processing mechanism helped in reducing the idle time of a computer system because transition from one job to another did not require any operator intervention. Another major time saving made possible by batch processing was reduction in set-up time by batching of similar jobs together by the operator. For example, if all FORTRAN compilation jobs are batched together, the system needs to load the FORTRAN compiler only once for processing all these jobs.

The obvious question is how the computer separates one job from another from a batch of jobs for automatic job-to-job transition. Moreover, how does the system know which compiler or what hardware devices are to be used by a particular job when there is no operator intervention? To facilitate all these, *control statements* and *job control languages* (JCLs) were introduced along with the concept of batch processing. The control statements are used by the operating system to identify a new job and to determine what resources are needed by the job during its execution. These control statements are written in a language known as the job control language. Hence, each program has, besides the program itself, a set of instructions called JCL instructions, which instruct the operating system on the identity and requirements of the job. JCL statements tell the operating system things such as the name of the job, the user's name and account number, the I/O devices to be used during processing, the assembler or compiler to be used if language translation is required, and so on. Figure 14.2 shows a sample deck of cards prepared for the compilation and execution of a COBOL program in a batch processing system.

Notice from the figure that in order to distinguish a control card from data or program cards, control cards are identified by a special character or pattern on the card. Several systems used the dollar-sign character ($) in the first column to identify a control card, while IBM's JCL used slash marks (//) in the first two columns. Other systems used some other characters or codes. The basic idea in selection of these special characters or codes was that no program or data card should have these characters or code.

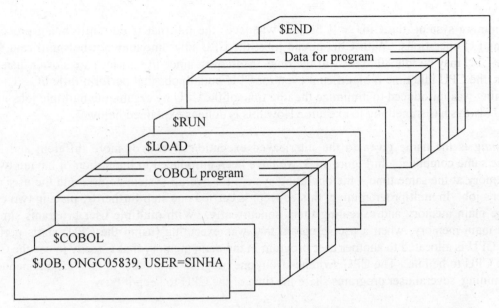

**Figure 14.2.** Illustrating the use of job control statements and the structure of a sample deck of cards submitted for processing in a batch processing system.

# Multiprogramming

In case of both manual loading and batch processing of jobs, the jobs are loaded into the system and processed one at a time. That is, once loaded, a job will remain in the main memory until its execution is completed and the next job will be loaded only after the completion of the previous job. As shown in Figure 14.3, in such a situation, the job, which is currently loaded and is being executed, will be the sole occupant of the user's area of the main memory (the operating system always resides in a part of the main memory) and it will have the CPU exclusively available for itself. The situation shown in Figure 14.3 is that of a *uniprogramming system* in which only one job is processed at a time and all the system resources are exclusively available for the job until it completes.

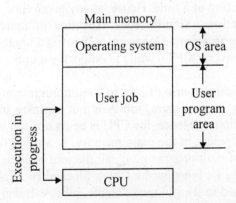

**Figure 14.3.** A uniprogramming system model in which only one job is processed by the system at a time and all the system resources are exclusively available for the job until it completes.

It was observed that a job does not need the CPU for the entire duration of its processing. This is because in addition to doing computation (for which CPU is needed), a job often needs to perform I/O operations (such as reading or writing some data to a tape or disk, waiting for some data to be input from the keyboard, and printing some results) during the course of its processing. In fact, depending on the CPU utilization during the course of processing, jobs are broadly classified into the following two types:

1. **CPU-bound jobs.** These jobs mostly perform numerical calculations, with little I/O operations. They are so called because they heavily utilize the CPU during the course of their processing. Programs used for scientific and engineering computations usually fall in this category of jobs.

2. **I/O-bound jobs.** These jobs perform very little computation and most of the time they perform I/O operations. Hence, their CPU utilization is very low. Programs used for commercial data processing applications usually fall in this category of jobs.

In a uniprogramming system, the CPU will be idle whenever the job that is currently being processed by the system performs I/O operations. With CPU-bound jobs, the CPU idle time may not be significant, but for I/O-bound jobs, the CPU may be idle 80 to 90% of the time. Moreover, since I/O devices are slower than the CPU by 20 to 100 times, the CPU idle time is significant even for CPU-bound jobs that perform little I/O. The concept of multiprogramming was introduced to minimize the idle time of the CPU by organizing multiple jobs in the system so that the CPU always has something to execute. How this is done is explained below.

*Multiprogramming* is the name given to the interleaved execution of two or more different and independent programs by the same computer. In Figure 14.3, we have been introduced to the notion of having two programs in the main memory at the same time – the operating system for overall system control and the user program for performing user's job. In multiprogramming, this concept is carried one step further by placing two or more user programs in the main memory and executing them concurrently. With multiple user programs simultaneously residing in the main memory, when a user program that was executing (using the CPU) starts performing I/O operations, the CPU is allocated to another user program in the main memory that is ready to use the CPU, instead of allowing the CPU to be idle. The CPU switches from one program to another almost instantaneously. Hence, in multiprogramming, several user programs share the time of the CPU to keep it busy.

It is important to note here that multiprogramming is not defined to be the execution of instructions from several programs simultaneously. Rather, it does mean that there are a number of programs available to the CPU (stored in the main memory) and that a portion of one is executed, then a segment of another, and so on. Although two or more user programs reside in the main memory simultaneously, the CPU is capable of executing only one instruction at a time. Hence, at any given time, only one of the programs has control of the CPU and is executing instructions. Simultaneous execution of more than one program with a single CPU is impossible. In some multiprogramming systems, only a fixed number of jobs can be processed concurrently (*multiprogramming with fixed tasks*) (MFT), while in others the number of jobs can vary (*multiprogramming with variable tasks*) (MVT).

A typical scenario of jobs in a multiprogramming system is shown in Figure 14.4. At the particular time instance shown in the figure, job A is not utilizing the CPU since it is busy writing output data on to the disk (I/O operations). Hence, the CPU is being utilized to execute job B, which is also present in the main memory. Job C, also residing in the main memory, is waiting for the CPU to become free. Actually, as shown in Figure 14.5, in case of multiprogramming, all the jobs residing in the main memory will be in one of the following three states – running (it is using the CPU), blocked (it is performing I/O operations) and ready (it is waiting for CPU to be assigned to it). In our example, jobs A, B and C are in blocked, running and ready states respectively. Since job C is in the ready state, as soon as the execution of job B is completed or job B requires doing I/O operation, the CPU will start executing job C. In the meanwhile, if job A completes its output operation, it will be in the ready state waiting for the CPU. Hence, in multiprogramming, the CPU will never be idle as long as there is always some job to execute. Note that although many jobs may be in ready and blocked states, only one job can be running at any instant.

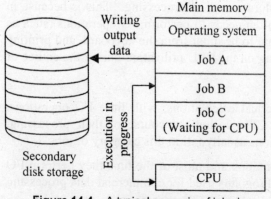

**Figure 14.4.** A typical scenario of jobs in a multiprogramming system.

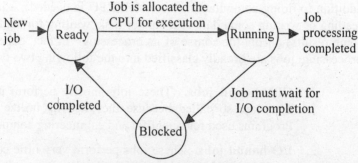

**Figure 14.5.** The three different states in which jobs may be after getting loaded in the main memory in a multiprogramming system.

The area occupied by each job residing simultaneously in the main memory is known as a *memory partition*. The actual number of partitions, and hence jobs, allowed in the main memory at any given time varies depending upon the operating system in use. Moreover, those jobs awaiting entry into main memory are queued on a fast secondary storage device such as a magnetic disk. The first job from this queue will be loaded into the main memory as soon as any one of the jobs already occupying the main memory is completed and the corresponding memory partition becomes free.

## Requirements of Multiprogramming Systems

Multiprogramming systems have better throughput than uniprogramming systems because the CPU idle time is drastically reduced. However, multiprogramming systems are sophisticated because they require the following additional hardware and software features:

1. **Large memory.** For multiprogramming to work satisfactorily, large main memory is required to accommodate a good number of user programs along with the operating system.

2. **Memory protection.** Computers designed for multiprogramming must provide some type of memory protection mechanism to prevent a job in one memory partition from changing information or instruction of a job in another memory partition. For example, in Figure 14.4 we would not want job A to inadvertently destroy something in the completely independent job B or job C. In a multiprogramming system, this is achieved by the memory protection feature, a combination of hardware and software, which prevents one job from addressing beyond the limits of its own allocated memory area.

3. **Job status preservation.** In multiprogramming, when a running job is blocked for I/O processing, the CPU is taken away from this job and given to another job that is ready for execution. Later, the former job will be allocated the CPU to continue its execution. Notice that this requires preserving of the job's complete status information when the CPU is taken away from it and restoring this information back, before the CPU is given back to it again. To enable this, the operating system maintains a *process control block* (PCB) for each loaded process. A typical process control block is shown in Figure 14.6. With this arrangement, before taking away the CPU from a running process, its status is preserved in its PCB, and before the process resumes execution when the CPU is given back to it later, its status is restored back from its PCB. Hence, the process can continue execution without any problem.

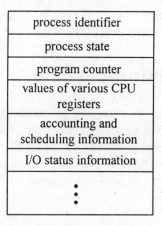

| process identifier |
| process state |
| program counter |
| values of various CPU registers |
| accounting and scheduling information |
| I/O status information |
| ⋮ |

**Figure 14.6.** A typical process control block (PCB).

4. **Proper job mix.** A proper mix of I/O-bound and CPU-bound jobs is required to effectively overlap the operations of the CPU and I/O devices. If all the loaded jobs need I/O at the same time, the CPU will again be idle. Hence, the main memory should contain some CPU-bound and some I/O-bound jobs so that at least one job is always ready to utilize the CPU.

5. **CPU scheduling.** In a multiprogramming system, often there will be situations in which two or more jobs will be in the ready state, waiting for CPU to be allocated for execution. When more than one process is in the ready state when the CPU becomes free, the operating system must decide which of the ready jobs should be allocated the CPU for execution. The part of the operating system concerned

with this decision is called the *CPU scheduler*, and the algorithm it uses is called the *CPU scheduling algorithm*.

# Multitasking

Technically speaking, multitasking is the same as multiprogramming. That is, *multitasking* is the system's capability to concurrently work on more than one task (job or process). This means that whenever a task (job or process) needs to perform I/O operations, the CPU can be used for executing some other task (job or process) that is also residing in the system and is ready to use the CPU.

Many authors do not distinguish between multiprogramming and multitasking because both the terms refer to the same concept. However, some authors prefer to use the term multiprogramming for multi-user systems (systems that are simultaneously used by many users such as mainframe and server class systems), and multitasking for single-user systems (systems that are used by only one user at a time such as a personal computer or a notebook computer). Note that even in a single-user system, it is not necessary that the system work only on one job at a time. In fact, a user of a single-user system often has multiple tasks concurrently processed by the system. For example, while editing a file in the foreground, a sorting job can be given in the background. Similarly, while compilation of a program is in progress in the background, the user may be reading his/her electronic mails in the foreground. In this manner, a user may concurrently work on many tasks. In such a situation, the status of each of the tasks is normally viewed on the computer's screen by partitioning the screen into a number of windows. The progress of different tasks can be viewed on different windows in a multitasking system.

Hence, for those who like to differentiate between multiprogramming and multitasking, multiprogramming is the concurrent execution of multiple jobs (of same or different users) in a multi-user system, while multitasking is the concurrent execution of multiple jobs (often referred to as tasks of same user) in a single-user system.

# Multiprocessing

Up to this point, we have considered systems with a single CPU. However, we have already seen that the use of I/O processors improves the efficiency of a computer system by making possible concurrent input, processing, and output operations. The CPU can perform arithmetic and logical operations on parts of one or more programs, while I/O operations are concurrently carried out by I/O processors on other parts of programs. Figure 14.7 shows the architecture of a computer with its CPU, memory and I/O processors.

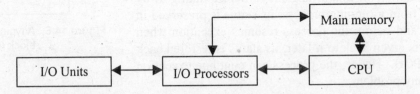

**Figure 14.7.** Architecture of a computer system showing its CPU, memory and I/O processors.

The idea to use I/O processors to improve the performance of a computer system was carried one step further by designing systems that make use of more than one CPU. Such systems are called multiprocessing systems. The term *multiprocessing* is used to describe interconnected computer configurations, or computers with two or more CPUs, which have the ability to simultaneously execute several programs. In such a system, instructions from different and independent programs can be processed simultaneously by different CPUs, or the CPUs may simultaneously execute different instructions from the same program. The basic organization of a typical multiprocessing system is shown in Figure 14.8.

Multiprocessing systems are of two types – tightly coupled systems and loosely coupled systems. In *tightly coupled systems*, there is a single system-wide primary memory, which is shared by all the processors. On the other hand, in *loosely coupled systems*, the processors do not share memory, and each processor has its own local memory.

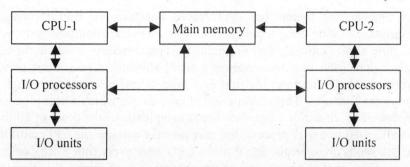

**Figure 14.8.** Basic organization of a typical multiprocessing system.

## Difference between Multiprogramming and Multiprocessing

Multiprogramming is the interleaved execution of two or more processes by a single-CPU computer system. On the other hand, multiprocessing is the simultaneous execution of two or more processes by a computer system having more than one CPU. To be more specific, multiprogramming involves executing a portion of one program, then a segment of another, etc., in brief consecutive periods. Multiprocessing, however, makes it possible for the system to simultaneously work on several program segments of one or more programs.

## Advantages and Limitations of Multiprocessing

Multiprocessing systems typically have the following advantages:

1.  **Better Performance.** Due to multiplicity of processors, multiprocessor systems have better performance (shorter response times and higher throughput) than single-processor systems. For example, if there are two different programs to be run, two processors are evidently more powerful than one because the programs can be simultaneously run on different processors. Furthermore, if a particular computation can be partitioned into a number of subcomputations that can run concurrently, in a multiprocessor system, all the subcomputations can be simultaneously run, with each one on a different processor (popularly known as parallel processing).

2.  **Better Reliability.** Due to multiplicity of processors, multiprocessor systems also have better reliability than single-processor systems. In a properly designed multiprocessor system, if one of the processors breaks down, the other processor(s) automatically takes over the system workload until repairs are made. Hence, a complete breakdown of such systems can be avoided.

Multiprocessing systems, however, require a very sophisticated operating system to schedule, balance, and coordinate the input, output, and processing activities of multiple processors. The design of such an operating system is a complex and time taking job. Moreover, multiprocessing systems are expensive to procure and maintain. In addition to the high charge paid initially, the regular operation and maintenance of these systems is also a costly affair.

# Time-sharing

*Time-sharing* is a mechanism to provide simultaneous interactive use of a computer system by many users in such a way that each user is given the impression that he/she has his/her own computer. It uses multiprogramming with a special CPU scheduling algorithm to achieve this.

A time-sharing system has many (even hundreds of) user terminals simultaneously connected to the same computer. Using these terminals, multiple users can simultaneously work on the system. The multiprogramming feature allows multiple user programs to simultaneously reside in the main memory. The special CPU scheduling algorithm, used in a time-sharing system, allocates a very short period of CPU time one-by-one to each user process, beginning from the first user process and proceeding through the last one, and then again beginning from the first one. This short period of time during which a user process gets the attention of the CPU is known as a *time slice*, *time slot*, or *quantum*, and is typically of the order of 10 to 100 milliseconds. That is, when the CPU is allocated to a user process, the user process will use the CPU until the allotted time slice expires (the system's clock sends an interrupt signal to the CPU after every time slice), or until the process needs to perform some I/O operation, or if the execution of the process is over during this time period. Notice here that in a time-sharing system, the CPU is taken away from a running process when the allotted time slice expires, even though the process can continue to run. Hence, the process state diagram of a time-sharing system is as shown in Figure 14.9 (compare this with the process state diagram of Figure 14.5).

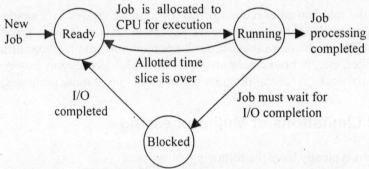

**Figure 14.9.** The process state diagram for a time-sharing system.

Now let us see how the CPU scheduling algorithm, mentioned above, gives an impression to each user that he/she has his/her own computer. Let us assume that the time slice of a time-sharing system is 10 milliseconds. That is, the CPU scheduling algorithm of this system allocates 10 milliseconds to each user process one-by-one in a circular fashion (when the last process is over, it comes back to the first process). Let the processing speed of the system's CPU be 500 million instructions per second. That is, it can execute $500 \times 10^6 \times 10^{-3} \times 10 = 5 \times 10^6 = 5$ million instructions in 10 milliseconds. This is large enough for substantial progress of a single user process. Let there be 100 user terminals and 100 simultaneous users using the system. If 10 milliseconds is allocated to each user process one-by-one, a particular user will get the CPU's attention once in every $10 \times 100$ milliseconds = 1 second. As human reaction time is normally of the order of a few seconds, a particular user will not notice any delay in executing his/her commands and will normally feel that he/she is the sole user of the system. In this manner, each user is given the impression that he/she has his/her own computer, whereas actually a single computer is shared among many users.

## Requirements of Time-sharing Systems

Time-sharing systems typically require the following additional hardware and software features:

1.  A number of terminals simultaneously connected to the system, so that multiple users can simultaneously use the system in interactive mode.

2.  A relatively large memory to support multiprogramming.

3.  Memory protection mechanism to prevent one job's instructions and data from other jobs in a multiprogramming environment.

4. Job status preservation mechanism to preserve a job's complete status information when the CPU is taken away from it, and restoring this information back, before the CPU is given back to it again.

5. A special CPU scheduling algorithm, which allocates the CPU for a very short period one-by-one to each user process in a circular fashion.

6. An alarm clock mechanism to send an interrupt signal to the CPU after every time slice.

## Advantages of Time-sharing Systems

Although time-sharing systems are complex to design, they provide several advantages to their users. The main advantages of time-sharing systems are as follows:

1. **Reduces CPU idle time.** The speed of thinking and typing of a user is much slower than the processing speed of a computer. Hence, during interactive usage of a system, while a particular user is engaged in thinking or typing his/her input, a time-sharing system can service many other users. In this manner, time-sharing systems help in reducing the CPU idle time, increasing the system throughput.

2. **Provides advantages of quick response time.** The special CPU scheduling algorithm used in time-sharing systems ensures quick response time to all users. This feature can be effectively used for interactive programming and debugging to improve programmers' efficiency. Multiple programmers can simultaneously work for, writing, testing and debugging of portions of their programs, or try out various approaches to a problem solution.

3. **Offers good computing facility to small users.** Small users can gain direct access to much more sophisticated hardware and software than they could otherwise justify or afford. In time-sharing systems, they merely pay a fee for resources used and are relieved of the hardware, software, and personnel problems associated with acquiring and maintaining their own installation.

# MEMORY MANAGEMENT

Other than the CPU, the main memory is an important resource of a computer system, which must be properly managed for the overall system performance. The memory management module of an operating system takes care of this requirement. Its job is to keep track of which parts of memory are in use and which parts are not in use, to allocate memory to processes when they need it, and deallocate when they are done. In this section, we will discuss about a number of different memory management schemes used in earlier and modern operating systems.

## Uniprogramming Memory Model

The uniprogramming memory model is used in uniprogramming systems in which only one job is processed by the system at a time, and all the system resources are exclusively available for the job, until it completes. As shown in Figure 14.10, in this memory management scheme, the operating system resides in one part of the memory and the entire remaining part of the memory is available for use by the currently active user process.

In this scheme, the operating system loads a program to be executed from disk into the user area of the memory and executes it. When the process finishes, the operating system cleans up the user area of the memory and then loads the next program to be executed.

Although this memory management scheme is simple and easy to implement, it does not lead to proper utilization of the available main memory resource. This is because whatever memory space is not occupied by the currently active user process, remains unused for the entire duration of the process's execution. Hence, this memory management scheme is now used only on very small or dedicated computer systems.

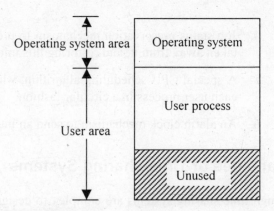

**Figure 14.10.** Uniprogramming memory model.

# Multiprogramming Memory Models

We saw that in a multiprogramming system, multiple user processes need to simultaneously reside in the main memory. The two memory management schemes used to facilitate this are multiprogramming with fixed number of memory partitions and multiprogramming with variable number of memory partitions. They are described below.

## Multiprogramming with Fixed Number of Memory Partitions

In this scheme, the user area of the memory is divided into a number of fixed-sized partitions. The partitions may be of equal or unequal size, but the size of each partition is fixed. Figure 14.11 shows a multiprogramming memory model with $n$ equal-sized partitions. Each partition may contain exactly one process. Hence, the degree of multiprogramming is bounded by the number of partitions. That is, at a time only $n$ processes can be loaded in the system.

All new jobs are put into an input queue. When a partition is free, the next job from the input queue is picked up and loaded into the free partition. When a process terminates, the partition occupied by it becomes free for use by another process. Note that if the system uses unequal-sized partitions, when a partition becomes free, the process closest to the front of the input queue that fits in it could be loaded into this partition.

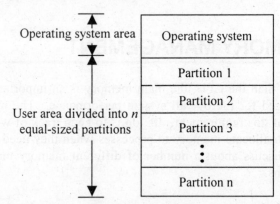

**Figure 14.11.** Multiprogramming memory model with fixed number of memory partitions (all partitions of equal size).

This scheme of memory management was used in IBM OS/360 mainframe systems for several years. It was called *MFT* (*Multiprogramming with a Fixed number of Tasks*). It is no longer in use.

## Multiprogramming with Variable Number of Memory Partitions

In the scheme described above, since the partitions are of fixed size, any space in a partition, which is in excess of the actual memory requirement of the process loaded into it, is lost (remains unused), until the process terminates. On an average, 50% of the memory may remain unused due to this reason. To overcome this problem of under utilization of memory, the scheme with variable number of memory partitions was introduced. In this scheme, the number, size, and location of the partitions vary dynamically as processes come and go.

This memory management scheme is illustrated in Figure 14.12 with an example. Initially, all memory in the user area is available for user processes. When a process arrives, only as much memory as needed by it is allocated to it, keeping the rest available to satisfy future requests. As processes come and go, memory partitions get allocated and deallocated, each partition being exactly of the size of the memory required by the process to which it is allocated. Since the memory requirement of different processes is generally different, as processes come and go, various sizes of free memory blocks are created in the memory. The operating system maintains a table to keep track of which parts of memory are free and which are occupied. When a new process arrives, the operating system searches for a free block that is large enough for this process. If the free block is too large, it is split into two parts. One part is large enough to meet the memory requirement of the process and is allocated to the process. The other part contains the remaining memory that is entered as a smaller free block in the operating system table. When a process terminates, it releases the partition allocated to it. If the released partition is adjacent to a free block or blocks, it is merged with the free block or blocks to create a larger free block. In this manner, the number, size, and location of the partitions vary dynamically as processes come and go.

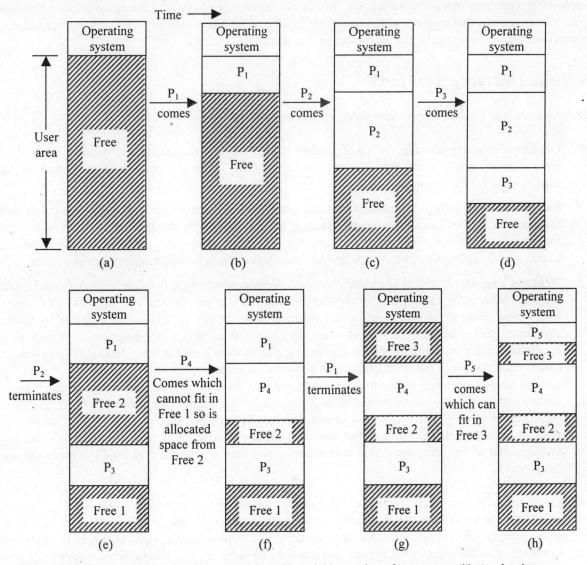

**Figure 14.12.** An example of multiprogramming with variable number of memory partitions. As shown, the number, size, and location of the partitions vary dynamically as processes come and go.

# Virtual Memory

## What is Virtual Memory?

Conventional memory management schemes, discussed until now, suffer from the following two main limitations:

1. A process cannot be loaded and has to keep waiting for its execution to start until sufficient free memory for loading the entire process becomes available. This may delay a process's turnaround time.

2. A process cannot be loaded (and hence executed) in a system whose main memory size is less than the total memory required by the process.

*Virtual memory* is a memory management scheme, which overcomes the above-mentioned limitations by allowing the execution of processes that might not be completely loaded in the main memory. That is, it does not require an entire process to be in memory, before its execution can start.

## How is Virtual Memory Realized?

The three basic concepts used for the realization of virtual memory are:

1. **On-line secondary storage.** It is a secondary storage device whose capacity is much larger than the main memory capacity and which is always kept on-line to the system. High-speed disk storage is usually used for this purpose.

2. **Swapping.** Swapping is the process of transferring a block of data from the on-line secondary storage to main memory or from main memory to the on-line secondary storage. When data is transferred from on-line secondary storage to main memory, it is called *swapping in* of data, and when data is transferred from main memory to on-line secondary storage, it is called *swapping out* of data.

3. **Demand paging.** In a virtual memory system, all processes are partitioned into pages and reside on the on-line secondary storage. The physical memory is also partitioned into page frames of the same size. Now, instead of swapping in the entire process before its execution can start, a swapping algorithm (called demand paging) is used, which swaps in only those pages of a process that are currently needed in the memory for continuing the process's execution. This idea is based on the observation that since the instructions of a program are executed one-by-one, all parts of the program are not needed simultaneously in the memory. When there is no free page frame in the memory to accommodate a page, which needs to be swapped in to continue the process's execution, a page-replacement algorithm is invoked to create one for the accessed page. It deals with the process of selecting a page that is residing in the memory, but is not currently being used. The selected page is swapped out to free the page frame it is occupying, which is then used to hold the accessed page of the process.

Based on the way virtual memory is realized, *virtual memory* is also often described as a hierarchy of two storage systems – one of them is a low cost, large capacity, low speed system (on-line disk storage), and the other is a high cost, small capacity, high speed system (main memory). The operating system manages the two storage systems in such a way that the users of the system feel that they have access to a single, large, directly addressable and fast main memory. That is, from the point of view of applications programmers, the effective (or virtual) size of the available main memory appears to be unlimited.

## Advantages and Disadvantages of Virtual Memory

### Advantages

1. It provides a very large virtual memory to programmers on a system having smaller physical memory. That is, the logical memory size is no longer constrained by the physical memory size of the system.

2. It enables the execution of a process on a system whose main memory size is less than the total memory required by the process.

3. It enables a process's execution to be started even when sufficient free memory for loading the entire process is not available. This helps in greatly improving the process's turnaround time. This feature can also be effectively used to simultaneously accommodate program segments of a large number of users in the main memory. This increases the degree of multiprogramming resulting in increased CPU utilization and system throughput.

4. It makes programming task much easier, since the programmer no longer needs to worry about the size limitations of the physical memory available, but can concentrate, instead, on the problem to be programmed.

5. An analysis of the execution of real programs shows that programs often do not execute all parts of their code during a typical execution run. For example, depending on the data, a large part of the code may be skipped on some condition check and may never be executed during that execution run. Similarly, certain options and features of a program, such as those for handling unusual error conditions, may be rarely used, and are generally not needed during most execution runs of the program. With virtual memory mechanism, since the parts of a program are loaded on demand, the parts that are not needed during a particular execution run of a program may never get loaded. This, in turn, leads to less I/O activity than in the case when the whole program is loaded before execution. With less I/O, each user program would run faster, resulting in better throughput, turnaround time, and response time.

### Disadvantages

1. It is difficult to implement because it requires algorithms to support demand paging.

2. If used carelessly, it may substantially decrease performance instead of increasing performance. This happens when page-fault rate is very high for a process. That is, the process spends more time in swapping out and swapping in of pages than in its execution.

# FILE MANAGEMENT

A *file* is a collection of related information. Every file has a name, its data, and attributes. The *name* of a file uniquely identifies it in the system and is used by its users to access it. A file's *data* is its contents. The contents of a file is a sequence of bits, bytes, lines, or records whose meaning is defined by the file's creator and user. The *attributes* of a file contain other information about the file, such as the date and time of its creation, date and time of last access, date and time of last update, its current size, its protection features (who can access the file and in what way), etc. The list of attributes maintained for a file varies considerably from one system to another.

The file management module of an operating system takes care of file-related activities, such as accessing, naming, sharing, and protection of files. In this section, we will discuss about the important concepts used for file management in various operating systems.

# File Access Methods

To use the information stored in a file, it must be accessed and read into computer memory. The two commonly supported file access methods at operating system level are sequential and random access. They are briefly described below.

1. **Sequential Access Files.** Sequential access files are normally used with sequential access storage media, such as magnetic tape. Information stored in a sequential access file can be accessed only sequentially. That is, a process can read the bytes or records in the file in the order in which they are stored, starting at the beginning. Reading of bytes or records randomly or out of order is not possible. A sequential file can, however, be rewound and read as often as needed.

2. **Random Access Files**. Random access files are normally used with random access storage media, such as magnetic or optical disks. Unlike a sequential access file, information stored in a random access file can be accessed randomly, irrespective of the order in which the bytes or records are stored. For example, a specific byte/record of the file can be directly accessed without the need to read all the bytes/records before it.

   Random access files are essential for many applications. For example, in a railway reservation system, the information about all the tickets booked on a particular train may be stored in a single file. If a customer wants to cancel an already booked seat, the reservation program must be able to access the specific record for that seat without having to read the records for hundreds of other booked seats first, so that the booking service can be fast enough.

All operating systems do not support both sequential and random access files. Some support only sequential access files, some support only random access files, while there are some which support both. Those, which support files of both types, normally require that a file be declared as sequential or random when it is created. Such a file can be accessed only in a manner consistent with its declaration. Most modern operating systems support only random access files.

# File Operations

An operating system provides a set of operations to deal with files and their contents. A typical set of file operations provided by an operating system may be as follows (the actual set varies from one operating system to another):

1. **Create.** Is used to create a new file.

2. **Delete.** Is used to delete an existing file, which is no longer needed.

3. **Open.** Is used to open an existing file, when a user wants to start using it.

4. **Close.** Is used to close a file, when the user has finished using it.

5. **Read.** Is used to read data stored in a file.

6. **Write.** Is used to write new data in a file.

7. **Seek.** Is used with random access files to first position the read/write pointer to a specific place in the file, so that data can be read from, or written to, that position.

8. **Get attributes.** Is used to access the attributes of a file.

9. **Set attributes.** Is used to change the user-settable attributes (such as, protection mode) of a file.

10. **Rename.** Is used to change the name of an existing file.

11. **Copy.** Is used to create a copy of a file, or to copy a file to an I/O device, such as a printer or a display.

# File Naming

When a file is created, it is given a name, which can be later used to access the file. The rules for naming files vary from one operating system to another. For instance, consider the following examples:

1. MS-DOS allows only up to 8 characters for a file name, Macintosh allows up to 31 characters, and Microsoft Windows allows up to 255 characters. With longer file names, users have greater flexibility in assigning more descriptive and meaningful names to their files.

2. Some operating systems allow only letters and numbers to be used in file names, whereas others also allow special characters (sometimes barring a few) to be used in file names. Hence, names like *letter3_from_Ram*, *reminder2_to_Sham* are often valid file names.

3. Some operating systems (such as Unix) distinguish between upper case letters and lower case letters, whereas others (such as MS-DOS) do not. Hence, the file names *Sinha*, *sinha* and *SINHA* will be treated as different and can be assigned to three different files in Unix, but they will be treated as same in MS-DOS and cannot be assigned to three different files.

4. Many operating systems support file names having two or more parts, with the different parts separated by a period. For example, MS-DOS supports two-part file names in which the first part can have 1 to 8 characters, and the optional second part can have 1 to 3 characters (such as *letter.txt*). In Unix, a file may have more than two parts, as in *prog.c.z*, where *.c* and *.z* are used to indicate that it is a C language program file, which has been compressed using the Ziv-Lempel compression algorithm. In such file names, the second and subsequent parts are called file extensions. *File extensions* usually indicate something about the file and are often used by applications to check for the intended type of file before operating on it. For example, a C language compiler may actually insist that the files it is to compile end in *.c*, and it may refuse to compile them if they do not. Some applications automatically supply their own extensions, such as *.doc* (for a Microsoft Word file) or *.wk4* (for a Lotus 1-2-3 file). Some typical file extensions and their meanings are shown in Figure 14.13.

# SECURITY

Security in computer systems deals with protecting the various resources and information of a computer system against destruction and unauthorized access. A total approach to computer security involves both external and internal security. *External security* deals with securing the computer system against external factors such as fires, floods, earthquakes, stolen disks/tapes, leaking out of stored information by a person who has access to the information, and so on. For external security, the commonly used methods include maintaining adequate backup copies of stored information at places far away from the original information, using security guards to allow the entry of only authorized persons into the computer center, allowing the access to sensitive information to only trusted employees/users, and so on.

| File extension | Its meaning |
|---|---|
| .bas | Basic source program file |
| .c | C source program file |
| .ftn | Fortran source program file |
| .pas | Pascal source program file |
| .obj | Object file (compiler output, not yet linked) |
| .bin | Executable binary program file |
| .lib | Library of .obj files used by the linker |
| .dat | Data file |
| .hlp | Text file for HELP command |
| .man | Online manual page file |
| .txt | General text file |
| .bak | Backup file |
| .doc | Microsoft word document file |
| .wav | Microsoft windows sound file |
| .wk4 | Lotus 1-2-3 spreadsheet file |
| .xls | Microsoft Excel spreadsheet file |
| .jpg | JPEG graphics file |
| .gif | GIF graphics file |

**Figure 14.13.** Some typical file extensions and their meaning.

*Internal security*, on the other hand, mainly deals with the following aspects:

1. **User authentication.** Once a user is allowed physical access to the computing facility, the user's identification must be checked by the system, before the user can actually use the facility. This requirement is taken care of by user authentication mechanisms.

2. **Access control.** A computer system contains many resources and several types of information. Obviously, not all resources and information are meant for all users. Therefore, even when a user passes the authentication phase and is allowed to use the computing facility, a way is needed to prohibit the user from accessing those resources/information that he/she is not authorized to access. This requirement is taken care of by access control mechanisms.

3. **Cryptography.** Even if a user somehow manages to gain access to some information, which he/she is not authorized to access, a way is needed to ensure that the user cannot make use of that information. This requirement is taken care of by cryptography mechanisms, which work on the idea that if it is not possible to ensure access control, it is better to prevent comprehension of information.

# COMMAND INTERPRETATION

The command interpretation module (known as *command interpreter*) of an operating system provides a set of commands using which the user can give instructions to the computer for getting some job done by it. The commands supported by the command interpretation module are known as *system calls*. When a user gives instructions to the computer by using these system calls, the command interpreter takes care of interpreting these commands and directing the system resources to handle the requests. Hence, the command interpreter provides a user interface to hide the hardware details of the system from the user. In this manner, it greatly contributes to the 'ease of use' objective of an operating system.

The two broad categories of user interfaces supported by various operating systems are:

1. **Command-line Interface.** This is the textual user interface in which the user gives instructions to the computer by typing commands. That is, to enter a command, the user uses the keyboard to type

words and symbols. For example, in Unix, the user has to type *"rm report.txt"* to delete the file named *report.txt*. If the user types a command incorrectly, the command interpreter will respond with a message indicating that it did not understand the command. When this happens, the user has to just retype the command correctly.

There is no problem in typing simple commands as illustrated in the example above. However, users often need to give detail instructions to the computer about their jobs when they submit them for execution. To facilitate this, systems, which support command-line interface, also support some type of *command language* (CL) or *job-control language* (JCL). Users can write codes in the JCL to give detail instructions to the system about their job. The command interpreter is designed to interpret the codes written in JCL and invoke appropriate system actions.

2. **Graphical User Interface.** *Graphical user interface* or GUI (pronounced "gooey") is much easier to learn and use than a command-line interface. Unlike command-line interface in which commands are textual, GUI commands are graphical (pictorial). As shown in Figure 9.3 (refer to Chapter 9), a GUI provides to the user, a screen full of graphic icons (small images on the screen) or menus, and allows the user to make a rapid selection from the displayed icons or menus to give instructions to the computer. A point-and-draw device is normally used to rapidly point to and select a particular graphic icon or menu item from the multiple options displayed on the screen. For example, we saw that in a system that uses command-line interface, to delete a file named *report.txt* we need to type a command like *"rm report.txt."* However, in a system that uses GUI, the same operation can be performed simply by using a mouse to drag the icon that represents the file, until it is superimposed on an icon shaped like a trashcan. Then releasing the mouse button that was used for dragging the file causes the file to disappear into the bulging trashcan.

# OS CAPABILITY ENHANCEMENT SOFTWARE

There are several tasks of a routine nature that many users often need to perform on their computer system. For example, program compilation, sorting of file contents in a particular order, and taking backup of important files are tasks of such nature. Not all computer users can write their own programs for performing these tasks. Even if they could write, it would clearly be wasteful, if each user spent a lot of time developing programs for these tasks. This gap between the functionality of an operating system and the needs of users for these frequently used routines created a market for a special category of software that enhance the capability of an operating system. These software are either supplied by the operating system vendor, or third-party software vendors, or may be a combination of both these sources. They are normally grouped into three categories – translating programs, library programs, and utility programs. They are briefly described below.

## Translating Programs

*Translating programs*, also known as language processors, are system programs, which translate a source program written by the user to an object program, which is meaningful to the hardware of the computer. These include the assembler and the various compilers and interpreters available with the system. Often the program development tools used for testing and debugging of programs are also included in this category of software.

## Library Programs

*Library programs* consist of frequently used functions and operations. For example, in the area of scientific applications, the commonly used library programs include those that compute mathematical functions, such as sine, cosine, square root, exponential, and logarithm of numbers; and those that perform mathematical operations, such as matrix multiplication, matrix inversion, statistical analysis, and conversion of numbers from one base to another (such as binary to decimal and decimal to binary). Similarly, in the area of string processing, the commonly used library programs include those that perform such operations as string comparison, string copy, string concatenation, and calculation of the length of a given string. Library programs commonly used for file manipulation include those that perform such operations as sorting the file contents to arrange its data in a specified sequence, merging the contents of two or more sorted files into one file containing all the items of all the original files in sorted order, concatenating of two files to create a single file out of their contents, searching for some specific data from a file, and file editing.

# Utility Programs

*Utility programs* assist the users with system maintenance tasks, such as disk formatting, data compression, data backup, and scanning the system for computer viruses. Few of the frequently used utility programs are briefly described below.

## Disk Formatting Utility

Whenever a new disk (which may be a hard disk, floppy disk, or optical disk) is to be used with a system, it must be formatted properly according to the requirements of the associated operating system. The disk formatting utility allows a user to perform this task with great ease.

## Data Compression Utility

This utility uses a compression algorithm to transform files into a fraction of their normal size, so that they occupy less storage space on disk, or can be transferred across a network in less time. The utility has an associated decompression algorithm, which is used to bring back a compressed file into its normal form and size when accessed by a user. Often the amount of disk space saved by using this technique is significant – it can effectively double the capacity of a disk.

## Data Backup Utility

Data stored in a computer system can be damaged or lost in several ways, such as a disk crash, a virus, a hardware malfunction, or simply an accidental erasure by its owner. Hence, it is always suggested to keep backup of important data. A backup utility is used to create copy of data on some storage media, such as floppy disk, CD-ROM, or magnetic tape, which can be stored off-line away from the computer system. When some data stored on-line is damaged or lost, it can be restored from the backup media. It is not necessary that the backup media is always kept off-line. In today's era of computer networks, some backup devices are kept on-line at a place away from the main computer system and the data backup is done automatically by the computer system on this device.

## Antivirus Utility

A *computer virus* is a piece of code attached to a legitimate program, which, when executed, infects other programs in the system by replicating and attaching itself to them. In addition to this replicating effect, a virus normally does some other damage to the system, such as corrupting/erasing files. Therefore, due to its spreading nature, a virus can cause severe damage to a system.

A typical virus works as follows. The intruder writes a new program, which performs some interesting or useful function (such as some game or utility) and attaches the virus to it in such a way that when the program is executed, the viral code is also executed. The intruder then sends this infected program by mail to other users of the system, or offers it free or for a nominal charge on floppy disks. Now, if anyone uses the infected program, its viral code is executed. When the viral code of the infected program executes, it randomly selects an executable file on the hard disk and checks to see if it is already infected. Most viruses include a string of characters, which acts as a marker showing that the program has been infected. If the selected file is already infected, the virus selects another executable file. When an uninfected program is found, the virus infects it by attaching a copy of itself to the end of that program and replacing the first instruction of the program with a jump to the viral code. When the execution of the viral code finishes, it executes the instruction that had previously been first and then jumps to the second instruction so that the program now performs its intended function. Notice that a virus spreads because every time an infected program is executed, it tries to infect more programs. Also, notice that a virus does not infect an already infected file in order to prevent an object file from growing ever longer. This allows the virus to infect many programs without noticeably increasing disk space usage.

When a computer system suffers from virus infection, it has to be cured. Antivirus utilities are often used to cure a computer from virus infection. These utilities first identify the virus type with which the computer is infected by matching its marker against the markers of well-known viruses. Once the type is known, the original programs are restored from their infected versions by applying a detailed knowledge of the infection method used by the virus. For example, in viruses that modify jump instructions at the beginning of the host program, recovering can be done simply by restoring the original jump to the start of the host program code. However, notice that these utilities can only cure known viruses. They cannot cure a newly encountered type of virus. A good antivirus utility can normally cure several hundred types of viruses and its power can be regularly improved by frequently updating it as new viruses are discovered.

# SOME POPULAR OPERATING SYSTEMS

## Unix

Unix is a multi-user, time-sharing operating system. Although it can be used on a wide variety of computers, ranging from notebook computers to super computers, it is especially prevalent on RISC workstations, such as those from Sun Mircosystems, Hewlett-Packard, IBM, and Silicon Graphics.

Unix was developed in the early 1970s at Bell Laboratories by Ken Thompson and Dennis Ritchie for a small PDP-11 computer. It was the first operating system to be written in a high-level language, C. The normal practice until then was to use assembly language for writing operating systems due to which operating systems were system dependent. That is, they were usable only on the system for which they were developed. However, since Unix was written in C language, moving it to a new machine, known as porting it, was much easier. This was an important reason for its large popularity and availability on a wide variety of systems.

## MS-DOS

MS-DOS stands for Microsoft Disk Operating System. It is a single-user operating system for IBM and IBM-compatible personal computers. It was introduced in 1981 jointly by Microsoft and IBM and was the most popular operating system for personal computers in the 1980s. Its popularity started reducing in the 1990s with the launch of Microsoft Windows operating system.

# Microsoft Windows

Microsoft Windows operating system was developed by Microsoft to overcome the limitations of its own MS-DOS operating system. The first successful version of this operating system was Windows 3.0, which was released in 1990. The subsequently released versions were Windows 95, Windows 98, and Windows 2000. The numbers associated with these released versions indicate their year of release. The main features of Microsoft Windows are as follows:

1. Its native interface is a GUI. Hence, it is easier for a new user to learn and use the system.

2. Microsoft Windows was designed to be not just an operating system, but also a complete operating environment. That is, all its programs conform to a standard way of working. For example, a Microsoft Windows word processor works similarly the way a Microsoft Windows spreadsheet (or any other type of Windows program) works. This means that the experience gained by learning one Windows program is useful while using any other Microsoft Windows program.

3. It is a single-user, multitasking operating system. That is, a user may run more than one program at a time. For example, while editing a file in the foreground, a sorting job can be given in the background. The monitor's screen can be partitioned into multiple windows and the progress of different programs can be viewed on different windows.

With these features, Microsoft Windows became an operating system of choice for most personal computer users after 1990.

# Microsoft Windows NT

Microsoft Windows NT is a multi-user, timesharing operating system developed by Microsoft. It was designed to have Unix-like features so that it can be used for powerful workstations, networks and database servers. Its main features are as follows:

1. Unlike Unix, its native interface is a GUI. The look and feel of Microsoft Windows NT's GUI is similar to that of Microsoft Windows' GUI.

2. It supports multiprogramming and is also designed to take advantage of multiprocessing on systems having multiple processors.

3. It has built-in networking and communications features, so that any computer with Microsoft Windows NT can be made to work as a network client or server.

4. It provides strict system security.

5. It has a rich set of tools for software development and system administration.

6. It can run Microsoft Windows applications and many Unix applications directly.

# Linux

Linux is an open-source operating system enhanced and backed by thousands of programmers worldwide. It is a multi-tasking operating system, which was originally designed to be used on personal computers. The name "Linux" is derived from its inventor Linus Torvalds. Linus was a student at the University of Helsinki, Finland in early 1990s when he wrote the first version of an Unix-like kernel as a toy project. He later posted the code on the Internet and asked programmers across the world to help him build it into a working system. The result was

Linux. Torvalds holds the copyright, but permits free distribution of the source code. That is, he oversees development of the kernel and owns its trademark. When someone submits a change or a feature, Torvalds and his core team of kernel developers review the merit of adding it to the source code.

# Points to Remember

1. An *operating system* (often referred to as OS) is an integrated set of programs that controls the resources (the CPU, memory, I/O devices, etc.) of a computer system and provides its users with an interface or virtual machine that is more convenient to use than the bare machine.

2. The main functions performed by most modern operating systems are process management, memory management, file management, security and command interpretation.

3. The efficiency of an operating system and the overall performance of a computer system are usually measured in terms of its throughput, turnaround time, and response time.

4. A *process* (also called *job*) is a program in execution. The main objective of the process management module of an operating system is to manage the processes submitted to the system in such a manner to minimize the idle time of the various processors (CPU, I/O processors, etc.) of the computer system.

5. In a *uniprogramming system,* only one job is processed by the system at a time and all the system resources are exclusively available for the job until it completes.

6. *Multiprogramming* is the name given to the interleaved execution of two or more different and independent programs by the same computer.

7. *Multitasking* is the concurrent execution of multiple jobs (often referred to as *tasks* of same user) in a single-user system.

8. The term *multiprocessing* is used to describe interconnected computer configurations, or computers with two or more CPUs, which have the ability to simultaneously execute several programs. In such a system, instructions from different and independent programs can be processed simultaneously by different CPUs, or the CPUs may simultaneously execute different instructions from the same program.

9. *Time-sharing* is a mechanism to provide simultaneous interactive use of a computer system by many users in such a way that each user is given the impression that he/she has his/her own computer. It uses multiprogramming with a special CPU scheduling algorithm to achieve this.

10. The memory management module of an operating system manages the main memory of the system. Its job is to keep track of which parts of memory are in use and which parts are not in use, to allocate memory to processes when they need it and deallocate when they are done.

11. In a *multiprogramming memory model*, multiple user processes can simultaneously reside in the main memory. The two memory management schemes used to facilitate this are multiprogramming with fixed number of memory partitions and multiprogramming with variable number of memory partitions.

12. *Virtual memory* is a memory management scheme that allows the execution of processes, which might not be completely loaded in the main memory. The three basic concepts used for the realization of virtual memory are on-line secondary storage, swapping and demand paging.

13. A *file* is a collection of related information. Every file has a name, its data and attributes.

14. The file management module of an operating system takes care of file-related activities such as structuring, accessing, naming, sharing and protection of files.

15. Security in computer systems deals with protecting the various resources and information of a computer system against destruction and unauthorized access. The commonly used approaches for this are user authentication, access control and cryptography.

16. The command interpretation module (known as *command interpreter*) of an operating system serves as an interface for the user to communicate with the computer via its operating system. The two broad categories of user interfaces supported by various operating systems are command-line interface and graphical user interface.

17. The gap between the functionality of an operating system and the needs of users for frequently used routines is often bridged by a special category of software known as *OS capability enhancement software*. These software are normally grouped into three categories – translating programs, library programs, and utility programs.

18. Some popular operating systems are Unix, MS-DOS, Microsoft Windows, Microsoft Windows NT and Linux.

# Questions

1. What is an operating system? Why is it necessary for a computer system?

2. What are the two primary objectives of having an operating system in a computer system? Explain how an operating system helps in meeting these objectives.

3. Draw the logical architecture diagram of a computer system. Explain the role of an operating system in this architecture.

4. Explain the role of an operating system as a resource manager of a computer system.

5. "The operating system tends to isolate the hardware from the users". Discuss this statement.

6. List out the various functions normally performed by an operating system.

7. Explain the role of an operating system with respect to the following functions:
   (a) Process management
   (b) Memory management
   (c) File management
   (d) Security
   (e) Command interpretation

8. What are the main parameters normally used for measuring the performance of a computer system?

9. Define the following terms:
   (a) Throughput
   (b) Turnaround time
   (c) Response time

10. What is a process in a computer system? What is the main objective of the process management module of an operating system?

11. How was a job typically executed in early computer systems? What was the major drawback in this approach of job execution?

12. What is batch processing? How are jobs typically executed in a batch processing system?

13. What are control statements? Why are they needed?

14. Do all computers use the same types of JCL statements? Why?

15. You want to compile and execute a FORTRAN program. In plain English, list out the necessary JCL statements you will prepare for this job.

16. What is the difference between a uniprogramming system and a multiprogramming system? What are their relative advantages and disadvantages?

17. Define multiprogramming. Explain how multiprogramming ensures effective utilization of main memory and CPU.

18. Differentiate between I/O-bound and CPU-bound jobs.

19. List out some of the hardware and software requirements for a multiprogramming system to work satisfactorily.

20. What is a memory partition?

21. What is a process control block? Why is it needed? What does it typically contain?

22. What is multitasking? What are the similarities and differences (if any) between multiprogramming and multitasking?

23. What is multiprocessing? Draw the basic organization diagram of a typical multiprocessing system.

24. Differentiate between tightly coupled and loosely coupled multiprocessing systems.

25. How is multiprocessing different from multiprogramming?

26. Discuss the advantages and limitations of multiprocessing systems.

27. What is time-sharing? What is a time-slice?

28. In a timesharing system, explain how each user feels that he/she is the sole user of the computer system.

29. What are the three different states in which all users of a timesharing system fall? Illustrate how a particular user switches from one state to another.

30. List out some of the hardware and software requirements of a time-sharing system.

31. List out some of the main advantages of time-sharing systems.

32. Why are timesharing systems considered most suitable for program development and testing?

33. Multiprogramming and timesharing both involve multiple user processes in the computer concurrently. What is the basic difference between the two concepts?

34. Differentiate among the following terms:
   (a) Multiprogramming  (c) Multiprocessing
   (b) Multitasking       (d) Timesharing

35. What is the main objective of the memory management module of an operating system?

36. Differentiate between uniprogramming and multiprogramming memory models. What are their relative advantages and disadvantages?

37. Differentiate between multiprogramming with fixed number of memory partitions and multiprogramming with variable number of memory partitions.

38. What is a virtual memory? Why is it so called? How is it useful?

39. Explain the three basic concepts used for the realization of virtual memory.

40. What is swapping? How does it help in memory management?

41. List out the advantages and disadvantages of virtual memory.

42. What is a file? Differentiate between a file's data and its attributes.

43. What is a file name? Why is it used?

44. What are the typical jobs performed by the file management module of an operating system?

45. Differentiate between sequential access and random access files.

46. List out some of the typical file operations provided by an operating system and mention what each operation is used for.

47. What is a file extension in a file name? What are file extensions typically used for? List out some typical file extensions and their meaning.

48. What are the typical jobs performed by the security module of an operating system?

49. Differentiate between external security and internal security requirements of a computer system.

50. What are the various security aspects that an operating system normally needs to deal with as part of the internal security of a computer system?

51. Differentiate between user authentication and access control requirements of a computer system.

52. What is cryptography? How does it help in improving the security of a computer system?

53. What are the typical jobs performed by the command interpretation module of an operating system?

54. What is a command interpreter? How does it contribute to the 'ease of use' objective of an operating system?

55. What are system calls? How are they used?

56. Differentiate between command-line interface and graphical user interface. List out their relative advantages and disadvantages.

57. What is a job control language (JCL)? Why is it needed?

58. What are OS capability enhancement software? Name a few types of software that fall in this category.

59. What are translating programs? Name a few types of software that fall in this category.

60. What are library programs? Give a few examples of such programs.

61. What are utility programs? Give a few examples of frequently used utility programs.

62. Write short notes on:
    (a) Disk formatting utility   (d) Data backup utility
    (b) Data compaction utility   (e) Antivirus utility
    (c) Data compression utility

63. What is a computer virus? How does a typical virus works? When a computer system suffers from virus infection, how is it cured?

64. Name four popular operating systems. Describe the main features of any two of them.

65. Write short notes on the following:
    (a) Objectives of an operating system
    (b) Functions of an operating system
    (c) Parameters for measuring system performance

66. Write short notes on the following:
    (a) Batch processing       (d) Multiprocessing
    (b) Multiprogramming       (e) Timesharing
    (c) Multitasking           (f) Virtual memory

67. Write short notes on the following:
    (a) File access methods
    (b) File naming
    (c) File operation
    (d) Uniprogramming memory model
    (e) Multiprogramming memory model

68. Write short notes on the following:
    (a) User authentication
    (b) Access control
    (c) Cryptography

69. Write short notes on the following:
    (a) Translating programs   (c) Utility programs
    (b) Computer virus         (d) Library programs

# Chapter 15

# Application Software Packages

This chapter provides greater detail of some of the most commonly known application software packages, which were introduced in Chapter 10. Out of the ones discussed in Chapter 10, we have chosen to provide additional details of the following application software because they are readily available as pre-written software packages and are most widely used packages:

1. Word-processing package

2. Spreadsheet package

3. Graphics package

4. Personal assistance package

Each of these pre-written software packages is available from multiple vendors. However, the features of a particular type of software package are more or less same, irrespective of the vendor. Only their mode of operation may vary from one vendor's package to that of another. Hence, in this chapter, we will mainly concentrate on the general features of the packages, rather than their mode of operation. Once you are familiar with the features, the mode of operation can be easily learnt for the specific software package, which you have to use by using its operation manual.

## WORD-PROCESSING PACKAGE

### What it is?

*Word-processing* is a term, which describes the use of hardware and software to create, edit, view, format, store, retrieve and print documents (written material such as letters, reports, books, etc.). A word-processing package enables us to do all these on a computer system.

# Commonly Supported Features

Today's word-processing packages normally support the features described below.

## Entering Text

This feature allows you to enter text with the computer's keyboard. Every character typed on the keyboard is immediately displayed on the computer's screen. While entering text, you need not worry about moving to the next line as your text approaches the end of the current line. The *word wrap* feature of word-processing software determines when the current line is full, and the text that follows is automatically moved to the next line. Since the software recognizes when to begin a new line and automatically moves words to the next line, the only time you have to press the Enter key is at the end of a paragraph. This feature is very useful for people with fast typing speed, because they can go on entering text at their speed, without the need to keep track of where to end a line.

## Editing Text

This feature allows you to make changes in an already entered document. Changes that might have required extensive retyping with a typewriter, can now be made on the screen with a few keystrokes with a word-processing package.

While editing, you can use either insert mode or typeover mode. In *insert mode*, new characters typed are inserted in the text at the position of the cursor. That is, characters to the right of the cursor move to the right to make room for the new characters, as they are typed. In *typeover mode*, the new characters typed, replace (type over) the existing characters at the position of the cursor.

While editing, you can also delete unwanted text. Few characters or words at the cursor position are normally deleted with the use of Delete key (to delete characters to the right of the cursor) or Backspace key (to delete characters to the left of the cursor). However, a block of text (say a few lines, or a few sentences, or an entire paragraph or page) is deleted by first selecting (highlighting) it with the use of a mouse or a combination of keys, and then deleting it all at once by pressing the Delete key. Whenever some text is deleted, the text following the deleted text is automatically moved over to fill the space generated by the deleted text.

Text editing feature also supports *cut-and-paste* facility, which allows you to move a block of text from one place to another within a document, or even between documents. Sometimes, a block of text may be used at several locations in a document, or in several documents. In such situations, a slightly modified version of this facility, known as *copy-and-paste* facility, is used in which the block of text is copied at desired positions, but not deleted from its original position.

## Formatting Page Style

This feature allows you to define the page layout format for a document. Definition of a page layout format may include things such as:

1. Space to be left for left, right, top, and bottom page margins.

2. The default spacing between two lines (such as single space, double space, 1.5 space, etc.).

3. Automatic numbering of pages with page number style (such as 1, 2, 3, ..., or 1/10, 2/10, 3/10, ..., or 1 of 10, 2 of 10, 3 of 10, ...; etc.) and page number position (top center, top left and right, bottom center, bottom left and right, etc.).

4. Automatic placement of header and footer labels on each page (such as the header labels in this book).

5. Setting text in multiple columns, on a single page. The multi-column option is frequently used in newsletter and newspaper printing.

It is also possible to create and store multiple standard page format styles (called *style sheets*) for different categories of documents like memos, letters, reports, books, etc. Most word-processing software come with a few pre-stored style sheets. The basic idea is to save time and effort of re-creating a page format, every time you have to create a new document. When you create a new document, you simply choose a style sheet from the list of pre-stored style sheets, depending on the document type. All the page format specifications defined in the chosen style sheet automatically apply to the new document. You can even modify a few specifications of a style sheet, which you want differently from the standard specifications in the style sheet. This can be done much faster than defining all the format specifications afresh.

The beauty of a word-processing package is that you can change page format specifications as often as needed. There is no need to re-type the document if it is to be printed with a different page format. For example, a document prepared with multi-column page format can be converted to a single-column page format just by changing the page format style. The document is printed according to the most-recent format specifications.

## Formatting Text

This feature allows you to format portions of text to improve the general appearance and readability of a document. It normally includes things such as:

1. Selection of an appropriate font. A *font* is a complete set of characters with the same style and size. A word-processing package comes with several standard fonts, such as Times, Helvetica, Palatino, etc. Different fonts may be applied to different portions of the same document. For example, chapter heading, section heading and the running text of a book may use three different fonts. A particular font should be used only if your word-processing package and your printer support that font. Figure 15.1 shows a few font types.

2. Selection of an appropriate font size. Font size is measured in *points*. A point is 1/72 of an inch, and the size refers to the distance from the top of the tallest character to the bottom of the character that extends the lowest (such as $y$, $p$ or $q$). Different font sizes may be applied to different portions of the same document. For example, chapter heading, section heading and the running text of a document usually use three different font sizes. Figure 15.2 shows a few font sizes.

3. Selecting an appropriate font style. Commonly used font styles are *italic*, **bold** and underline. They are normally used to highlight individual words or phrases or portions of text in a document. Figure 15.3 illustrates their use in a document.

> This sentence is written in Times New Roman font.
>
> **This sentence is written in Helvetica font.**
>
> This sentence is written in Palatino font.
>
> `This sentence is written in Courier New font.`
>
> **This sentence is written in Antique Olive font.**

**Figure 15.1.** A few examples of font types.

This sentence is written in 10 point Times New Roman font.

This sentence is written in 12 point Times New Roman font.

This sentence is written in 16 point Times New Roman font.

This sentence is written in 24 point Times New Roman font.

This sentence is written in 36 point Times New Roman font.

**Figure 15.2.** A few examples of font sizes.

*This sentence is written in italic style.*

**This sentence is written in bold style.**

This sentence is written in underline style.

You can even make individual words *italic*, **bold**, or underline.

**Figure 15.3.** A few examples of font styles.

4. Selecting an appropriate justification. *Justification* is the alignment of text on the left or the right margin, or on both margins. In case of *left-justification*, beginnings of lines are aligned with the left margin of the page. This style is also known as *ragged right* because the ends of lines at the right edge just end where the last word ends. In case of *right-justification*, ends of lines are aligned with the right margin of the page. In case of *full-justification*, all the lines are properly aligned with both the left and right margins of the page. A world-processing software accomplishes this by making micro adjustment of space between the words, and sometimes even between the characters on a line. In case of *center-justification* of a particular line, it is placed at the center of a line with equal spacing both on its left and right ends. Center-justification is commonly used for titles or headings. Figure 15.4 illustrates the use of various types of justification of text.

5. Indenting text appropriately wherever desired, such as at the beginning of a paragraph, or to set aside some portion of text from the main text in a document, or to enter text in tabular form. Tab stops are normally used for indentation. *Tab stops* are typically pre-defined at every fourth or fifth character, or at every ½-inch from the left margin of a page layout. Most word-processing packages allow you to change or define new tab stop positions. The Tab key on the keyboard allows you to move the cursor to the next tab stop while entering text. Figure 15.5 illustrates a few uses of indentation.

6. Creating numbered or bulleted list of items. As shown in Figure 15.6, this feature allows descriptive items to be presented as a numbered or bulleted list for better comprehension and readability. Each item in the list has a separate number or bullet or some other symbol attached to its beginning. The numbers or symbols are automatically inserted by the word-processing software as soon as you press the Enter key.

The term *hardware* refers to the physical devices of a computer system. Hence, the input, storage, processing, control, and output devices are hardware. The term *software* refers to a collection of programs. A *program* is a sequence of instructions written in a language that can be understood by a computer. It is the program, which controls the activity of processing by the computer and the computer performs precisely what the program wants it to do.

(a) Example of left-justified (ragged-right) text.

The term *hardware* refers to the physical devices of a computer system. Hence, the input, storage, processing, control, and output devices are hardware. The term *software* refers to a collection of programs. A *program* is a sequence of instructions written in a language that can be understood by a computer. It is the program, which controls the activity of processing by the computer and the computer performs precisely what the program wants it to do.

(b) Example of right-justified text.

The term *hardware* refers to the physical devices of a computer system. Hence, the input, storage, processing, control, and output devices are hardware. The term *software* refers to a collection of programs. A *program* is a sequence of instructions written in a language that can be understood by a computer. It is the program, which controls the activity of processing by the computer and the computer performs precisely what the program wants it to do.

(c) Example of full-justified text.

### Introduction to Hardware and Software

The term *hardware* refers to the physical devices of a computer system. Hence, the input, storage, processing, control, and output devices are hardware. The term *software* refers to a collection of programs. A *program* is a sequence of instructions written in a language that can be understood by a computer. It is the program, which controls the activity of processing by the computer and the computer performs precisely what the program wants it to do.

(d) Example of centered text heading.

**Figure 15.4.** A few examples of various types of justification of text.

A software package is a group of programs, which solve a specific problem or perform a specific type of job. For example, a word-processing package may contain programs for text editing, text formatting, drawing graphics, spelling checking, etc. Hence, a multipurpose computer system has several software packages, one each for every type of job it can perform.

(a) Example of paragraph indentation.

A software package is a group of programs, which solve a specific problem or perform a specific type of job.

For example, a word-processing package may contain programs for text editing, text formatting, drawing graphics, spelling checking, etc.

Hence, a multipurpose computer system has several software packages, one each for every type of job it can perform.

(b) Example of indenting some portion of text to set it aside from the main text.

| Sl. No. | Name | Age | % of Marks obtained |
|---------|---------|-----|---------------------|
| 1. | Srirang | 25 | 85% |
| 2. | Manikant | 27 | 65% |
| 3. | Jaipal | 26 | 80% |

(c) Example of use of indentation for entering text in tabular form.

**Figure 15.5.** Examples illustrating a few uses of indentation.

> Some of the typical features found in a grammar checker are:
> 1. It highlights the use of double words (such as *for for*).
> 2. It highlights phrases with redundant words (such as very highest).
> 3. It highlights the misuse of capital letters (such as PraDeep or PradeeP).
>
> (a) Example of numbered list of items.
>
> ---
>
> In general, a computer's system software performs one or more of the following functions:
> - Supports the development of other application software.
> - Supports the execution of other application software.
>
> (b) Example of bulleted list of items.

**Figure 15.6.** Example illustrating the use of numbered or bulleted list of items.

## Entering Mathematical Symbols

Several scientific and engineering documents often use mathematical symbols. This feature allows you to enter complex mathematical equations using mathematical symbols. Figure 15.7 shows the use of a few mathematical symbols.

$$\left\{ t^{(2)} \middle| R(t) \wedge \left[ \exists u^{(u)} \right] \left( S(u) \wedge \neg u[1] = u[2] \right) \right\}$$

$$\left\{ <a,b,c> \middle| \exists <a,b> \left( <a,b> \in r \wedge <a,c> \in s \right) \right\}$$

**Figure 15.7.** Example of a few mathematical symbols.

## Displaying Documents

This feature allows you to display the contents of the document, you are currently working on, on the screen of the computer's monitor. For editing the displayed text, the text cursor can be moved to any position in the document. In case of a large document, which cannot completely fit on the screen, you can browse through the document by *scrolling* a line at a time, a screen at a time, or a page at a time, by using suitable keys on the keyboard.

Based on this feature, word-processing packages are of two types — one with WYSIWYG (pronounced "wiz-ee-wig") facility, and the other one with ordinary text display facility. *WYSIWYG* is an acronym for *"What You See Is What You Get"*, and word-processing packages with this facility can display a document on the screen in a form that closely resembles what the printed document will look like. These word-processing packages employ high-resolution graphics. On the other hand, word-processing packages with ordinary text display facility can display only ordinary text. Hence, the embedded codes that the user has supplied for formatting the text are also displayed along with the document's contents as ordinary text. That is, the result of formatting is not visible on the screen and appears only on the printed document. However, such word-processing packages normally provide *preview facility*, which permits you to see what the document will look like (almost, if not exactly) when it is printed. Today, most of the popular word-processing packages are of WYSIWYG type.

## Saving, Retrieving and Deleting Documents

This feature allows you to save a document on a secondary storage and to retrieve it later at any time for reuse. At the time of saving a document for the first time, you must specify a file name for the document. The document is later retrieved for reuse by specifying its file name. You may even permanently remove the document from the secondary storage by deleting it, when you feel that it is no more useful for you, or when you have created and saved a new version of it.

When you are editing a document, you should save it at frequent intervals so that you do not lose the updates made to it in case of a power failure. This is because, any power failure wipes out all work that has not been saved. To take care of this problem, some word-processing packages offer an automatic save feature, which saves the document you are currently working on after every few minutes.

## Printing Documents

This feature allows you to print your documents on a printer for generating their hard copies. Some of the commonly supported printing facility in almost all modern word-processing packages and printers are:

1.  Selective printing of a single page, specific pages, a range of pages, or the whole document.

2.  Single-sided or double-sided printing. Single-sided printing prints only on one side of a paper, while double-sided printing prints on its both sides.

3.  Portrait and landscape modes of printing. In *portrait mode*, the printed lines are parallel to the shorter edge of the paper (like in this book), whereas in *landscape mode*, the printed lines are parallel to the longer edge of the paper.

4.  Previewing a document before printing it. This facility shrinks down the pages of your document so that an entire page or even facing pages can be displayed on the screen at once in almost the same form as it will appear when printed. This avoids wastage of paper by allowing you to see how margin and other settings will finally appear in your document, without having to print the document first.

## Importing Text, Graphics and Images

This feature allows you to import text, graphics and images from some other document into a document that you are currently working on. It often helps in saving tremendous time and effort because the user need not spend time in creating a piece of text, diagram, graph or image, which can be easily obtained from somewhere else. In addition to importing, many word-processing packages also have document conversion facility, which enables an imported document, which was prepared using a different word-processing package, to be converted into a document compatible with the user's word-processing package.

## Searching and Replacing Text String

This feature enables you to quickly search for all occurrences of a specific word, phrase, or groups of characters in a document. For example, you might have used the month November at several places in your document. If you want to ensure that the current month name appears at all places in the document, you can use the search facility to enable you to do this quickly.

In addition to providing this simple search capability, word-processing packages also support search-and-replace facility. This facility enables you to perform selective or global replacement of a specific word, phrase, or groups of characters with a new set of characters. For example, suppose a document contains the name *Pradip* at several places. If we realize later that this is the wrong spelling of the name and it should be *Pradeep* instead of *Pradip*, we can use the search-and-replace facility to change all occurrences of *Pradip* to *Pradeep* in the document.

## Checking Spelling

Most modern word-processing packages come with an electronic dictionary and a spell checker to allow you to ensure that your document does not contain any mis-spelled word. A spell checker looks up every word in your document against the pre-stored words in the electronic dictionary and alerts you if no match is found for a particular word in the dictionary. In such a situation, the spell checker highlights the word and waits for your action. You may choose to do either of the following:

1. You can correct the spelling.

2. If you do not know the correct spelling, you can ask the spell checker to give you a list of words with similar spelling and choose the correct word from the list.

3. If the word is spelt correctly, but has been highlighted simply because it is not present in the electronic dictionary (for example, names of people and companies, abbreviations, acronyms, etc.), you can instruct the spell checker to ignore the word, or to add it to the dictionary.

Unfortunately, spell checkers are not yet smart enough to check for the improper use of correctly spelt words. For example, it will not flag "form" when the word should be "from".

## Checking Grammar and Style

Similar to a spell checker, some advanced word processing packages come with a grammar checker, which enables you to correct grammatical mistakes and use of improper writing styles in your document. Some of the typical features found in a grammar checker are:

1. It highlights the use of double words (such as *for for*).

2. It highlights phrases with redundant words (such as *very highest*).

3. It highlights the misuse of capital letters (such as *PraDeep* or *PradeeP*).

4. It highlights text having subject and verb mismatches (such as *she were*).

5. It highlights punctuation errors (such as , .).

6. It highlights sentences written in the passive voice rather than the active voice (such as "*The book was given by Mohan*" is in passive voice whereas "*Mohan gave the book*" is in active voice).

# SPREADSHEET PACKAGE

# What it is?

A *spreadsheet package* is a numeric data analysis tool, which allows us to create a kind of computerized ledger. A manual ledger is a book having rows and columns, which accountants use for keeping a record of financial transactions and for preparing financial statements. Accountants use the manual ledger with pencil, erasure and hand calculator to prepare financial statements. This is a tedious task and often takes a long time due to several iterations of formula calculations to come out with an acceptable and satisfactory financial statement. A spreadsheet package offers considerable ease of performing such tasks by automating all arithmetic calculations, and making it easier to change certain numeric values and immediately seeing the effect of these changes across the worksheet (ledger). With spreadsheet software in place, we are no longer confined to using pencils, erasers, and hand calculators for dealing with any task that requires numeric data analysis.

Whereas paper ledgers were tools for accountants, spreadsheet packages are tools for anyone who needs to record, organize, or analyze numbers as rows and columns of data. Some typical uses of spreadsheet packages are:

1.  For maintaining and analyzing inventory, payroll, and other accounting records by accountants.
2.  For preparing budgets and bid comparisons by business analysts.
3.  For recording grades of students and carrying out various types of analysis of the grades by educators.
4.  For analyzing experimental results by scientists and researchers.
5.  For tracking stocks and keeping records of investor accounts by stockbrokers.
6.  For creating and tracking personal budgets, loan payments, etc. by individuals.

This list is by no means exhaustive and is given here only to give an idea of how flexible and versatile tool is a spreadsheet package.

# Commonly Supported Features

An example of a sample spreadsheet is shown in Figure 15.8. Some of the key features of spreadsheet packages are explained below with the help of this example.

## Rows and Columns

A spreadsheet is organized in a tabular form with rows and columns. The rows are identified by numbers, whereas the columns are identified by letters. Single letters are used to identify the first 26 columns and double letters are used for subsequent columns (A, B, ..., Z; AA, AB, ..., AZ; BA, BB, ..., BZ; ...). A large spreadsheet may have hundreds of rows and hundreds of columns.

## Cells

The intersection of a row and a column is called a *cell*. A cell is identified by its address, which is a combination of its column letter and row number (such as F4, C18). Data are stored in cells.

## Range of Cells

Many spreadsheet operations involve a range of cells instead of a single cell. For instance, in Figure 15.8, the contents of cell E5 is equal to the sum of the contents of cells B5, C5 and D5, which is a range of three cells in a row. A range of cells may involve many cells and entering every individual cell for an operation to be performed on them may be cumbersome and time taking. To take care of this problem, all spreadsheet packages allow the use of following types of cell ranges:

1.  **Row Range.** It is used to include a set of adjacent cells in the same row. For example, the range B5..D5 refers to the cells B5, C5 and D5.

2. **Column Range.** It is used to include a set of adjacent cells in the same column. For example, the range C5..C9 refers to the cells C5, C6, C7, C8 and C9.

3. **Block Range.** It is used to include a set of adjacent cells in a rectangular group of cells. For example, the range B5..D9 refers to the cells B5, B6, B7, B8, B9, C5, C6, C7, C8, C9, D5, D6, D7, D8 and D9.

Notice that a particular range is indicated by the addresses of the endpoint cells separated by two periods (B5..D9) or a colon (B5:D9).

## Cell Contents

Different types of data can be entered into a cell. The four commonly used types of cell data are:

1. **Label.** A label is any string of alphanumeric text. Labels are used either to enter alphanumeric values in cells (such as in cells A5 to A9 of Figure 15.8) or to enter descriptive data or titles to make the contents easier to understand (such as in the cells in rows 1 and 3 of Figure 15.8). Notice from the figure that the label in cell B1 extends across columns C, D, E and F. This is possible when the adjacent cells are blank, otherwise the text gets truncated after the column width.

2. **Numeric Value.** A numeric value is a number on which the spreadsheet can perform calculations. For example, in the spreadsheet of Figure 15.8, cells B5..D9 contain numeric values.

3. **Formula.** A formula may include numbers, mathematical operators (such as +, -, *, /, etc.), mathematical functions supported by the spreadsheet (such as SUM, AVG, MIN, MAX, etc.), and cell addresses. For example, cell E9 contains the formula @SUM(B9..D9), which means that the sum of the numeric values of cells B9, C9 and D9 should be displayed in cell E9. The same result could have also been obtained by entering the formula B9+C9+D9 in cell E9. Cell F9 of the spreadsheet of Figure 15.8 also contains a formula, which is E9/3 and calculates the percentage marks obtained by the student named J. Smith. Notice that in case of formula entry, the contents displayed in the cell is not the formula itself, but the result of formula calculation.

4. **Date and Time.** Although not used in the spreadsheet of Figure 15.8, the date and/or time contents type is normally used in a spreadsheet to display the actual date and time, whenever the spreadsheet is opened for use, or if calculations are to be made based on date or time. For example, in case of a spreadsheet used for interest calculation, it is required to figure out the number of days between two dates. Cell entries with data type as date are helpful for such applications.

## Relative and Absolute Cell Addresses

When a formula entered in a cell has references to other cells (contains cell addresses), by default, the references are relative to the cell with the formula in it. For example, cell E5 contains the formula @SUM(B5..D5), which adds the contents of cells B5, C5 and D5. This formula can be entered once in cell E5, and then copied in cells E6, E7, E8 and E9. Because the cell address is relative, this copying will result in cell E6 having the formula @SUM(B6..D6), cell E7 having the formula @SUM(B7..D7), and so on. Similarly, the formula +E5/3 can be entered once in cell F5, and then copied in cells F6, F7, F8 and F9. Notice that the facility of relative cell addressing can be of great help in creating a spreadsheet quickly by entering the formulas once and copying them to other cells as in the example of Figure 15.8.

If a formula requires a cell address, which should not change even when the formula is copied to other cells, you can use absolute cell addressing to accomplish this. Depending on the requirement, a cell reference can be made fully or partially absolute as follows:

1. Precede both the column letter and the row number of the cell with a dollar sign ($) to make both column and row references absolute. For example, $A$2 is a reference to cell A2, which is absolute as to both row and column. When copied at any other cell location, it will always reference the cell A2.

2. Precede only the column letter of the cell with a dollar sign ($) to make only the column reference absolute. For example, $A2 is a cell reference, which is absolute as to column only. When copied at any other cell location, it will reference the cell in column A of the current row. That is, if a formula entered in cell A2 containing $A2 is copied in cell E12, this cell reference in the formula in cell E12 will refer to cell A12.

3. Precede only the row number of the cell with a dollar sign ($) to make only the row reference absolute. For example, A$2 is a cell reference, which is absolute as to row only. When copied at any other cell location, it will reference the cell in row 2 of the current column. That is, if a formula entered in cell A2 containing A$2 is copied in cell E12, this cell reference in the formula in cell E12 will refer to cell E2.

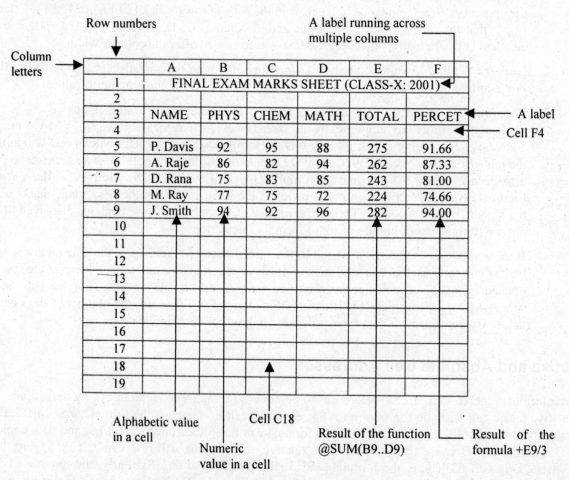

**Figure 15.8.** A simple example of a spreadsheet.

## Spreadsheet Commands

All spreadsheet packages come with a set of commands to enable you to perform many different operations. For example, *copy* and *move* commands enable you to copy/move the contents of one or more cells to some other cells. *Insert* and *delete* commands enable you to add/remove a column or row anywhere in your spreadsheet. *Format* commands enable you to control the way cell contents are displayed. Formatting features include specifying the width of columns, the number of decimal places in a non-integer numerical value, automatic insertion of a dollar sign and commas to separate thousands for currency amounts (such as $6,852), the use of right- or left-justified values or labels, etc. *Save* and *retrieve* commands enable you to store the format and data of an already created spreadsheet on a disk, and to retrieve it later for updates and analyses. *Print* command enables you to generate a hard copy of all or part of a spreadsheet.

## Spreadsheet Graphics

Most spreadsheet packages come·with presentation graphics feature, which enables you to create graphs and charts from numerical data stored in a spreadsheet. As shown in Figure 15.9, the most popular types of graphs and charts supported for graphical representation of numerical data are line graphs, bar charts and pie charts. This feature is very useful in presenting spreadsheet data in easier to understand visual forms, because most people find it difficult to interpret a table of numbers.

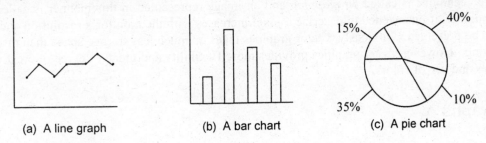

(a) A line graph          (b) A bar chart          (c) A pie chart

**Figure 15.9.** Examples of a line graph, a bar chart and a pie chart.

# GRAPHICS PAKCAGE

## What it is?

Graphics packages enable us to use a computer system for creating, editing, viewing, storing, retrieving and printing designs, drawings, pictures, graphs and anything else that can be drawn in the traditional manner.

## Commonly Supported Features

Today's graphics packages normally support the feature described below.

### Draw Designs

This feature enables users to draw graphics objects, such as lines, circles, rectangles, arcs, etc., to create diagrams and designs. Users need not worry about drawing straight lines or exact circles. The system automatically makes the lines, circles, arcs, etc. smooth and properly connected to each other. The system also allows users to move, copy, delete, rotate, tilt, flip horizontally or vertically, increase or decrease the size of the graphic objects. With all these facilities, users can draw complex designs with great ease.

In fact, *computer-aided design* (*CAD*) is an area that is mainly based on this feature of graphics software. CAD systems are used by architects and engineers to create architectural drawings, product designs, landscaping plans, and many different types of engineering drawings. They enable designers to work much faster than they once worked in the era of manual drafting, creating those designs in few hours, which used to take several days.

## Paint Drawings and Pictures

This feature enables users to create and modify drawings and pictures in the form of images. Unlike the draw feature (discussed above), which uses vector graphics for composing graphic objects, the paint feature uses raster graphics for composing graphic images. In *vector graphics*, the design is composed of patterns of lines, points, circles, arcs, and other geometric shapes (vectors), which can be easily represented by few geometric parameters (for example, a line is represented by recording the *x* and *y* coordinates of two points, and a circle is represented by recording the *x* and *y* coordinates of a point and the radius of the circle). On the other hand, in *raster graphics*, the image is composed of patterns of dots called pixels (picture elements). That is, a painting software creates an image by turning individual screen pixels on or off. Because the image is mapped on to the screen based on binary bits, this technique is called *bit mapping* and an image represented in this manner is called a *bit-mapped image*. The number of bits needed to describe a pixel increases with the monitor's resolution and the number of colors that can be presented. Obviously, vector graphics takes up much less storage space than raster graphics for the same drawing. However, raster graphics provides more flexibility and greater degree of creativity in drawing complex shapes and use of colors.

## Present Graphs

This feature enables users to create graphs and charts from numerical data. The numerical data to be converted into a graph or chart may be imported from another software, such as a spreadsheet or a database. Among the most popular types of graphs and charts used for graphical representation of numerical data are line graphs, bar charts and pie charts (see Figure 15.9). *Line graphs* contain one or more lines connecting data points plotted on a horizontal and vertical axes. *Bar charts* use one or more bars on a horizontal and vertical axes to show values by the lengths of the bars. Sometimes, a bar is divided into component parts, and the sum of all the parts equals the total length of the stacked bar. *Pie charts* use one or more circles divided into sectors to show the component parts of a whole. Presentation graphics software is very useful for analysts and decision makers, because it allows them to gain a better understanding of the relationships, changes, and trends that are buried in their numeric data. This helps them in making more informed decisions.

## Drag-and-drop Objects

This feature enables the users to create their overall designs and pictures much faster by allowing them to use ready-made graphic objects or images, supplied with the software. For example, the drawing software comes with a set of ready-made shapes like line, rectangle, circle, etc., which the user can use in his/her design as per the requirement. The user can select a desired object from the set of given objects, and drag it to the desired position on the drawing area, and then drop it there to add it to the overall design. The drag feature also allows the user to suitably change the size or the shape of the object to match with the overall design. It also enables the user to glue multiple objects together, so that they stay connected and move together if one of them is moved on the drawing area. Similarly, the painting software comes with a *clip art library* of stored images. The user can select a desired image from the clip art library, drag it to the desired position on the drawing area, and then drop it there to add it to the overall picture being created. The user can also change the size, color, texture, etc. of the image to match with the overall picture. With this feature, the user need not spend time in creating an image, which is readily available in the clip art library.

## Import Objects

This feature further enables the users to create their overall designs and pictures much faster by allowing them to use not only the graphic objects or images supplied with the software, but even those graphic objects or images that are stored in files created by some other software or means. For example, a photograph may be scanned, and the scanned image may be imported into and included in an overall picture, which the user is currently creating. Similarly, a graphics object or image received from someone through electronic mail can be imported in a drawing from the mail file. With this feature, the user need not spend time in creating an image or an object, which can be readily obtained from somewhere else.

## Screen Capture

This feature enables the users to take a snapshot of a screen display and to convert it into an image, which can be stored in a file and later imported into a document. This feature is very useful while writing books or manuals, which need to include screen images as illustrations. A screen is captured as a bit-mapped image. Once stored in a file, it can be imported into any document at any time and even manipulated with a paint program.

# PERSONAL ASSISTANCE PACKAGE

## What it is?

Personal assistance packages allow individuals to use personal computers for storing and retrieving their personal information, and planning and managing their schedules, contacts, finances and inventory of important items.

## Commonly Supported Features

Today's personal assistance packages normally support the features described below.

### Calendar

This feature enables users to record their appointments and plan their schedules on a yearly, monthly, weekly, daily and even hourly basis. Unlike a hard-copy calendar, which can also be used by individuals for this purpose, a calendar software is designed to automatically alert a user prior to a scheduled meeting with an audible alarm or a pop-up message on the display, warn the user of possible schedule conflicts when a new appointment is recorded, and automatically schedule tasks of recurring nature. It also allows users to view or print the highlights of past or future events at the desired level of granularity (yearly, monthly, weekly, hourly, etc.).

### To-do List

This feature enables users to record, prioritize and manage the things to do. A user can dynamically keep entering the tasks to do as and when they come up, and at any point of time the user can instruct the system to display or print the tasks by project, deadline date, or priority. The software also allows users to add or delete tasks to update the to-do list, or to include additional information against a task to record its current status or any other information related to the execution of the task.

## Address Book

This feature enables users to record the names, addresses, telephone numbers, affiliations, date of births, etc. of their friends, relatives, clients, and other contact persons. The entries in the address book can be made as and when they come up, and at any point of time the user can ask the system to provide details of a particular person, or to display or print a list of persons having something in common. For example, from the address book, a user can easily obtain a list of persons living in a particular city, persons whose date of birth falls on a particular date, persons affiliated to a particular organization, etc.

## Investments Book

This feature enables users to maintain a record of their investments or loans, such as long-term and short-term deposits in banks, stocks, bonds, housing loan, car loan, life insurance, medical insurance, etc. The software automatically alerts a user prior to the maturity of a term deposit, or prior to the due date of the premium payment for a loan or insurance with an audible alarm or a pop-up message on the display. It also allows users to view or print the summary or details of their investments or liabilities at any instance of time. The software can also be fed with the information of an individual's daily, weekly, or monthly income and expenditure statements, which, when clubbed with the investments and liabilities information, helps in effective financial planning by the individual.

## Inventory Book

This feature enables users to maintain a record of their household goods along with associated information for each item, such as when and from where was it purchased, what is the duration of its warranty period, is it insured or not, etc. In addition to making the list of all available items in a house readily available, this feature also enables the user to find out the details of an item when there is a break down in it or when it is stolen.

# Points to Remember

1. A *word-processing package* enables us to create, edit, view, format, store, retrieve and print documents on a computer system.

2. Some of the commonly supported features found in modern word-processing packages are entering text; editing text; formatting page style; formatting text; entering mathematical symbols; displaying documents; saving, retrieving and deleting documents; printing documents; importing text, graphics and images; searching and replacing text string; checking spelling; and checking grammar and style.

3. A *spreadsheet package* is a numeric data analysis tool, which allows us to create a kind of computerized ledger. It is useful for any numerical analysis problem whose data can be organized as rows and columns.

4. Some of the key features of modern spreadsheet packages are support for a large number of cells, support for addressing a range of cells by the addresses of the endpoint cells, support for different types of cell data (such as, label, numeric value, formula, and date and time), support for use of relative and absolute cell addresses in formula, support for a wide range of commands, and support for displaying numeric data in the form of graphs and charts.

5. A *graphics package* enables us to use a computer system for creating, editing, viewing, storing, retrieving and printing designs, drawings, pictures, graphs and anything else that can be drawn in the traditional manner.

6. Some of the commonly supported features found in modern graphics packages are drawing designs, painting drawings and pictures, presenting graphs and charts, dragging-and-dropping graphic objects, importing graphic objects, and capturing screen snapshots.

7. *Computer-aided-design* (*CAD*) deals with the integration of computers and graphics design packages for the purpose of automating the design and drafting process.

8. A *personal-assistance package* allows individuals to use personal computers for storing and retrieving their personal information, and planning and managing their schedules, contacts, finances and inventory of important items.

9. Some of the commonly supported features found in modern personal-assistance packages are calendar, to-do-list, address book, investments book and inventory book.

# Questions

1. What is a word-processing package? List out some of the key features supported by modern word-processing packages.

2. Differentiate between the insert and typeover modes of text entry in a word-processing package.

3. Differentiate between the cut-and-paste and copy-and-paste facilities of a word-processing package.

4. What is a style sheet in a word-processing application? How is it useful?

5. What is a font? What is meant by font size and font style?

6. Differentiate between left- and right-justified text.

7. What is meant by WYSIWYG facility? How is it useful?

8. What is print-preview facility? How is it useful?

9. Differentiate between portrait and landscape modes of printing.

10. What is meant by text, graphics and image importing facility? How is it useful?

11. Explain the search-and-replace facility of a word-processing package.

12. What is a spell checker in a word-processing package? How does it work?

13. What is a grammar checker in a word-processing package? List out some of its typical features found in a modern word-processing package.

14. What is a clip art library? Describe how it helps in document preparation with a word processor.

15. List out any five features of a word-processing package. Explain how each of these five features is helpful in document preparation.

16. What is meant by word-wrap feature? How is it useful?

17. Give an example of a situation when the global search-and-replace command of a word-processing package will prove useful.

18. What options does a spell checker typically present to the user when it encounters an unidentified word in a document?

19. A spell checker cannot check for the improper use of correctly spelt words. Explain why?

20. What is a spreadsheet package? List out some of its typical uses.

21. Think of an application for which a spreadsheet package is useful. Now draw a sample spreadsheet for the application.

22. What is a cell in a spreadsheet? How is a single cell identified? How is a range of cells identified?

23. Differentiate among row range, column range and block range of cells in a spreadsheet.

24. List out the four commonly used types of cell data found in a spreadsheet along with the need for each type.

25. Differentiate between relative and absolute cell addresses in a spreadsheet. Explain the need for these two types of cell addresses.

26. Explain how a cell address can be made fully or partially absolute when used in a formula.

27. List out some of the formatting features supported in a modern spreadsheet package.

28. Explain about the graphics feature of modern spreadsheet packages. How is it useful?

29. What is a graphics software? List out some of the features normally supported in a graphics software.

30. What is the major difference between the paint and the draw features of a graphics software?

31. What is a CAD system? List out some of its typical uses.

32. Differentiate between vector graphics and raster graphics. Give their relative advantages and disadvantages.

33. What is a bit-mapped image? Why is it so called?

34. Explain how the following features of a graphics software are useful:
    (a) Present graphs
    (b) Drag-and-drop objects
    (c) Import objects
    (d) Screen capture

35. What is a personal assistance package? List out some of the features normally supported by it. Explain the usefulness of each of these features.

36. Write short notes on:
    (a) Spreadsheet package
    (b) Graphics package
    (c) Word-processing package
    (d) Personal assistance package

37. Write short notes on:
    (a) Computer Aided Design (CAD)
    (b) Vector graphics

    (c) Raster graphics

38. Write short notes on the following features of a word-processing package:
    (a) Word-wrap
    (b) Text editing
    (c) WYSIWYG
    (d) Print preview
    (e) Page formatting
    (f) Text formatting
    (g) Search-and-replace
    (h) Import text, graphics and image

39. Write short notes on the following with reference to a spreadsheet package:
    (a) Cell contents
    (b) Range of cells
    (c) Graphics feature
    (d) Relative and absolute cell addresses

# Chapter 16

# Business Data Processing

In this chapter, which deals with the basic concepts of business data processing, you will learn about the following:

1. Difference between data and information, and how data processing converts data into information.

2. The data storage hierarchy commonly used to facilitate data processing.

3. The standard methods of organizing data.

4. The basic concepts of database systems.

## WHAT IS DATA PROCESSING?

*Data* is a collection of facts – unorganized, but able to be organized into useful information. A collection of sales orders, employee time sheets, and class attendance cards are a few examples. Data can be manipulated to produce output, such as bills, employee salary slips, and student attendance reports. This output, which can be used to help people make decisions, is called *information*. That is, information is data arranged in an order and form that is useful to the people who receive it.

*Processing*, in general terms, is a series of actions or operations that converts some input into useful output. When we speak of data processing, the input is data, and the output is useful information. Hence, *data processing* is defined as a series of actions or operations, which convert data into useful information. It consists of three sub-activities – capturing the input data, manipulating the data, and producing the output results. A *data processing system* includes the resources, such as people, procedures, and devices, which are used to accomplish the processing of data for producing desirable output.

Hence, data is the raw material of information, and just as raw materials are transformed into finished products by a manufacturing process, raw data is transformed into information by data processing.

# DATA STORAGE HIERARCHY

In data processing, storage of data is often conceptualized as a *data storage hierarchy*, which normally consists of the following six levels (see Figure 16.1):

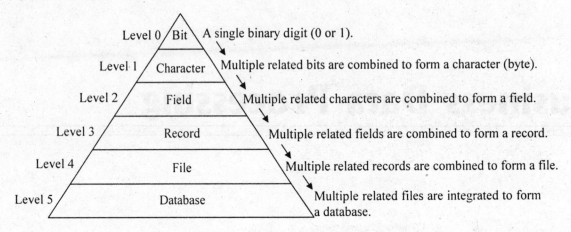

**Figure 16.1.** Data storage hierarchy used in data processing.

1. **Bit.** The smallest item of data is a single binary digit (a bit), either a 0 or 1.

2. **Character.** Multiple related bits are combined to form a character (or byte). For example, the letter M, the number 8, and the special character $ are characters. A bit is the basic unit of primary and secondary storage, and a character is the basic unit for human perception.

3. **Field.** Multiple related characters are combined to form a field. For example, if we are processing employees' data of a company, we may have an employee-code field, an employee-name field, an hours-worked field, an hourly-pay-rate field, a tax-rate-deduction field, etc. A *field* is a meaningful collection of related characters. It is the smallest logical data entity, which is treated as a single unit in data processing. Note that a field may sometimes have a single character, such as sex code may be represented as M or F.

4. **Record.** Multiple related fields are combined to form a record. For example, an employee record will contain the fields containing the data of an employee, such as the employee's code, name, hours worked, pay-rate, tax-rate deduction, and so forth. Similarly, a student record will contain the fields containing the data of a student. Hence, a record is a collection of related fields, which are treated as a single unit.

5. **File.** Multiple related records are combined to form a file. For example, a collection of all the employee records of a company would be an employee file. Similarly, a collection of all the inventory records of a company forms an inventory file. Hence, a *file* is a number of related records, which are treated as a unit. Notice that every record in a file has the same set of fields. Each record in a file is identified, for storage and retrieval purposes, by a *key field* whose contents are unique for each record in a file. In case of our employee file, employee-code field may serve as the key field.

6. **Database.** Multiple related files are integrated to form a database. For example, an employee database of an organization may integrate the records of multiple employee files, such as employee salary file containing details of salary and taxation information of all employees, employee personnel

information file containing details of personnel information of all employees, and employee skill-set file containing details of various types of skills of all employees. In a database, the data from multiple files are integrated in a manner that data redundancy is minimized. For example, in case of the above example of three different employee files, if in each file an employee record contains an employee address field, and if an employee changes his/her residence, the address must be changed in all the three files. In a database, the three files will be integrated in a manner that an employee's address data is stored only once and made available to all applications. Therefore, only one update will be needed in case of change of address of an employee. In essence, a database is a collection of logically related data elements from multiple files.

Figure 16.2 illustrates the relationship among character, field, record, and file with the help of an example.

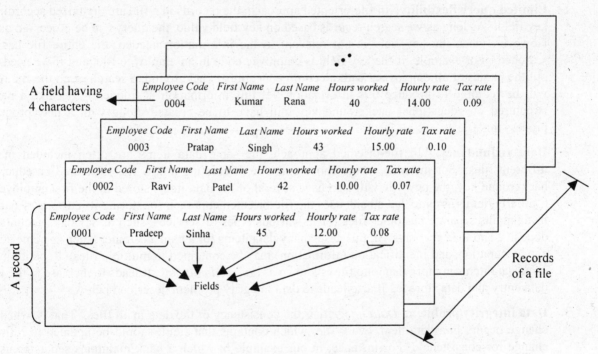

**Figure 16.2.** Illustrating the relationship among character, field, record, and file.

# STANDARD METHODS OF ORGANIZING DATA

The two standard methods used in data processing for organizing data are file-oriented approach and database-oriented approach. The file-oriented approach was the traditional method used in early days of data processing and has largely been replaced today by the database-oriented approach. However, several applications, dealing with simple and small data sets, use the file-oriented approach, even today. Hence, both these methods are discussed below.

## File-oriented Approach

In this method, an application's data is organized into one or more files and the application program processes the data stored in these files to generate the desired output. For example, it is customary to set up a *master file* of permanent (and, usually, the latest) data, and to use *transaction files* containing data of a temporary nature. For instance, in a payroll processing application, the master payroll file will contain not only all the permanent details about each employee, his/her name, address, employee code, pay-rate, income tax rate, and so forth, but also the current gross-pay-to-date total and the tax-paid-to-date total. The transaction payroll file will contain details of hours worked this week, normal and overtime, and if piecework is involved, the quantity of goods made. When the payroll program is processed, both files will have to be consulted to generate this week's pay-slips, and the master file updated in readiness for the following week.

# Database-oriented Approach

The file-oriented method of organizing data for data processing applications is simple, inexpensive, and usually easy to use. However, it suffers from the following limitations:

1. **Limited query flexibility.** In file-oriented approach, the records in a file are organized according to a key field. As long as we search records based on key field value, the query can be processed quickly. However, when the key field is not relevant to the information needed, the entire file has to be searched. For example, if the key field is employee code in an employee file, and if we need to list out the names of all employees with a certain educational background, a search of all the file records will be required to produce this information. If this information is frequently needed, a new file structured on educational background key will have to be created along with a new program to process this file.

2. **Data redundancy.** In file-oriented approach, the same data items are often included in many different files. For instance, in the above example of creating a new file structured on educational background key, the new file will also have several of the data items stored in the first employee file. Similarly, let us assume that a bank uses the file-oriented approach for storing its customers' data, and it maintains separate customer files for its various types of services, such as savings accounts, term deposits, and loan accounts. In this case, many data items for a bank customer (such as home address, age, occupation, and identification information) may be contained in multiple files. Repetition of the same data items in more than one file is known as *data redundancy*. It leads to increase in the cost of data entry and data storage. It also leads to data integrity problem described below.

3. **Data integrity problem.** *Data integrity* is the consistency of the data in all files. That is, when some change occurs in a data item, every file, which contains that field, should be updated to reflect the change for consistency. For instance, in our example in which a bank maintains separate customer files for each type of account, when a customer moves to a new address, his/her address field must be updated in all the customer files in which this customer's record is present. Integrity of data is necessary to avoid confusions, which may result when one file is updated while others are not. For example, when a data item changes, if all the files containing the data item are not updated correctly, there may be frequent discrepancies among reports produced from different files, causing confusion.

4. **Lack of program/data independence.** In file-oriented approach, the application programs usually contain data format statements that precisely define each data field to be processed. This often results in different files having the same data item stored using different data formats. *Data dependence* occurs when the data is dependent on the application. Due to data dependence problem, whenever there is a need to add, delete, or change data formats, the application program must also be changed. Data dependence problem also causes incompatibility among data files from different applications due to which these data files cannot be linked, if such a need arises.

5. **Limited data security flexibility.** A file-oriented approach normally offers file-level data security feature. That is, data access restrictions can be enforced only for an entire file, not for a record or a field of data item.

Dissatisfied with these limitations of the file-oriented approach of organizing data, researchers began looking for a better method of organizing data to consolidate activities. Their efforts resulted in the database-oriented approach for organizing data. In this approach, data from multiple related files are integrated together in the form of a database, which has the following properties:

1. It provides greater query flexibility.

2. It reduces data redundancy.

3. It solves data integrity (inconsistency) problem.

4. It makes data independent of the application programs. That is, fields can be added, changed, and deleted from the database without affecting existing programs.

5. It also includes data security features at database level, record level, and even at field level to provide greater flexibility of restricted data access.

# FILE MANAGEMENT SYSTEM

In the file-oriented approach of organizing data, a set of programs is provided to facilitate the users in organizing, creating, deleting, updating, and manipulating their files. All these programs together form a *File Management System* (*FMS*). The commonly supported features in a typical file management system are described below.

## File Types

Data files are categorized according to the way the application uses them. A file management system typically supports the following types of files:

1. **Transaction File**. A *transaction file* is used to store input data until it can be processed. For example, in a payroll processing application for generating pay slips of employees on a weekly basis, the transaction file will contain weekly data of each employee, such as details of hours worked this week, normal and overtime, and if piecework is involved, the quantity of goods made.

2. **Master File**. A *master file* contains all the current data relevant to an application. For example, in the payroll processing application mentioned above, the master file will contain the permanent details about each employee (his/her name, address, employee code, pay-rate, income tax rate, and so forth), and also the current gross-pay-to-date total and the tax-paid-to-date total. When the payroll program is processed, both the master file and the current week's transaction file are consolidated to generate this week's pay-slips, and the master file is updated in readiness for the following week.

3. **Output File**. Some applications use multiple programs for data processing. In such applications, often the output produced by one program is used as input to another program. Hence, the produced output by the former program is stored in a file known as *output file*, which is later on used by the latter program.

4. **Report File**. A *report file* holds a copy of a report generated by a data processing application in computer-accessible form, until it is convenient to print it. It is often advantageous to keep report files instead of paper documents because the files are easier to store and carry.

5. **Backup File**. A *backup file* is a copy of a file created as a safety precaution against loss of data, which may be caused due to corruption or inadvertent deletion of the original file. Regular creation of backup files is extremely important.

# File Organizations

File organization deals with the physical organization of the records of a file for the convenience of storage and retrieval of data records. System designers choose to organize, access, and process the records of various files in different ways, depending on the type of application and needs of the users. The three commonly used file organizations in business data processing applications are sequential, direct/random and indexed sequential.

The selection of a particular file organization depends upon the type of application. The best organization to use in a given application is the one that meets the application's data access and processing requirements in the most effective and economical manner. Hence, an application designer must evaluate the strengths and weaknesses of each file organization, before making a choice of the type of file organization to be used for the application.

File organization requires the use of some *key field* or unique identifying value, which is found in every record in the file. The key value must be unique for each record of the file because duplications would cause serious problems. In the payroll example, the employee code field may be used as the key field.

## Sequential Files

In a sequential file, records are stored one after another in an ascending or descending order determined by the value of the key field of the records. In payroll example, the records of the employee file may be organized sequentially by employee code sequence. The principal storage medium for sequential files is magnetic tape.

The computer processes a sequential file in the order in which data is stored in the file. That is, the first record is read and processed first, then the second record is read and processed, and so on. For instance, to locate a particular record in a sequential file, the computer reads each record in sequence from the beginning of the file and compares its key field value to the one that is needed. The search ends only when the desired key value matches with the key field value of the currently read record. Notice that with this processing mechanism, if only a single record has to be processed, on an average, about half the file has to be searched to retrieve the desired record for processing. Hence, sequential files are not suitable for applications that process only one or a few records at a time.

Sequential file organization is the most efficient and economical file organization in case of applications in which there is a large number of file records to be updated at regularly scheduled intervals. That is, when the *activity ratio* (the ratio of the total number of records in transaction file and the total number of records in master file) is very high. This can be ensured by using the idea of batch processing, in which transactions of a similar type are accumulated into batches, then these batches are sorted into sequence with respect to the key field values of the records, and then the entire batch of records is processed in a single pass through the file. Applications such as payroll processing and monthly bill processing are processed in this manner.

### Advantages of Sequential Files

1.  They are conceptually simple to understand and use.

2.  They are also easy to organize and maintain.

3.  They need relatively inexpensive I/O media and devices for their storage and processing.

4.  They are most efficient and economical to use in applications in which the activity ratio is high (most records are changed during update runs).

## Disadvantages of Sequential Files

1. They are very inefficient and uneconomical for applications in which the activity ratio is very low.

2. Since an entire sequential file may need to be read just to retrieve and update few records, accumulation of transactions into batches is recommended before processing them. Hence, the use of sequential files is limited to a batch-processing environment.

3. Because of the need to accumulate transactions into batches before processing them, sequential processing precludes the possibility of up-to-the-minute data.

4. Sequential processing requires the files to be sorted before processing. That is, both the transaction and master files must be sorted and placed in the same sequence before processing.

5. Sequential processing often leads to data redundancy problem, since the same data may be stored in several files sequenced on different keys.

# Direct Files

Many applications require up-to-the-minute timeliness of data. The users of such applications cannot afford to wait for the transactions to be accumulated in batches and then processed together. Such applications require a transaction to be processed immediately as and when it occurs. A few examples of such applications are airline or railway reservation systems, teller facility in banking applications, systems for enquiring whether a certain item is in stock in a store, etc. Note that, since only one transaction is processed at a time, the activity ratio is very low in these applications, making the use of sequential files very inefficient and uneconomical. For such applications, the use of *direct/random file organization* is recommended, in which the desired record pertaining to the current transaction at hand can be directly located by its key field value, without having to search through a sequence of other records. For example, when a passenger makes a reservation request for a train, the computer can directly access the record for the train and update its seats position for the specified journey date. Obviously, direct/random files need to be stored on a direct access storage device to enable direct access of records. The principal storage medium for direct/random files is magnetic/optical disk.

The obvious question that arises is, how are the records in a direct file physically organized, so that it becomes possible to directly access a record, given its key field value, from a number of records stored in the file. To enable this, direct file organization uses an address generating function to convert a record key value into a storage address on the disk on which the file is stored. Each record in the file is stored at the location to which the address generating function maps the record's key field value. The process is known as *hashing* and the address generating function is called a *hashing algorithm*.

Although the hashing algorithm is selected in a manner to generate a unique address for each record key value, but in practice, the hashing algorithm sometimes maps the key values of two or more records to the same storage address. This problem is known as *collision*. When a collision occurs, it may be taken care of in many ways. One method is to use a pointer at the address calculated by the hashing algorithm. This pointer points to a linked list of addresses, which contains the physical addresses of all records whose key values map to the address calculated by the hashing function.

To search a record, given its key value, the computer applies the hashing algorithm on the given key to generate its corresponding address. If the record is found at the calculated address, the search is over. Otherwise, the computer traverses the linked list pointed to by the pointer stored at the calculated address, accesses the addresses stored in the linked list and the corresponding records one-by-one, and compares the given key with the key of the accessed record. The search process finishes as soon as the record with the matching key is found.

If required, the records of a direct file may also be processed sequentially in ascending or descending sequence of key field value. However, if a large number of records need to be processed sequentially (that is, if the activity ratio is high), direct files prove to be very inefficient as compared to sequential files, because the computer has to use the hashing algorithm and reposition the read/write head of the disk for every record that has to be processed.

### Advantages of Direct Files

1. Given the key, any record can be quickly located and retrieved directly, without the need for a sequential search of the file.

2. Transactions need not be sorted and placed in sequence before processing.

3. Accumulation of transactions into batches is not required before processing them. They may be processed as and when generated.

4. It can support interactive online applications, which need to provide up-to-the-minute information in response to inquiries from users.

5. If required, it is also possible to process direct file records sequentially in a record key sequence.

### Disadvantages of Direct Files

1. They require relatively expensive hardware and software resources because they must be stored on a direct-access storage device, such as a disk.

2. Due to address generation overhead involved, they are less efficient and economical than sequential files for use in sequential applications with high activity ratio.

3. Special security measures are often necessary for online direct files, which are simultaneously accessible from multiple online stations.

## Indexed Sequential Files

We are all familiar with the concept of an index. For example, the display board containing the names and room numbers of the various occupants at the entrance lobby of a large multistoried building is an index, which helps us locate a particular person's room within the building. For instance, to find the room of Dr. Sharma within the building, we would look up his name in the directory (index) and read the corresponding floor number and room number. This idea of scanning a logically sequenced table is preferable to searching door-by-door for the particular name. Similarly, if we wished to read the section in this book about printers, we would not begin on page 1 and read every page until we came across the topic of interest. Rather, we would find the subject in the contents (which serves as an index) or the index at the back of the book to locate the page number, and then turn directly to that page to begin reading.

Indexed sequential files use exactly the same principle. As shown in Figure 16.3, in indexed sequential file organization, there are actually two files for every data file – the *data file*, which contains the records stored in the file, and the smaller *index file*, which contains the key and disk address of each record stored in the data file. The records of the file can be stored in random sequence, but the index table is in sorted sequence on the key value. This provides the user with a very powerful tool. Not only can the file be processed randomly, but it can also be processed sequentially. A request for a particular record is first directed to the smaller, more accessible index file, which in turn, points to the physical location of the desired record on the direct access storage device, such as a disk. For instance, to locate the record of an employee (in the example of Figure 16.3) whose employee code is 0004, the computer first searches the index file for this employee code key and obtains the address value 1002 corresponding to it. It then directly accesses the record stored at the address location 1002 of the storage device.

This technique of file management is commonly referred to as the *Indexed Sequential Access Method* (*ISAM*) and the files of this type are called *ISAM* files.

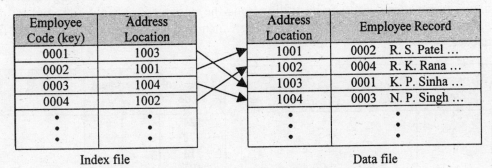

| Employee Code (key) | Address Location |
|---|---|
| 0001 | 1003 |
| 0002 | 1001 |
| 0003 | 1004 |
| 0004 | 1002 |
| ⋮ | ⋮ |

| Address Location | Employee Record | |
|---|---|---|
| 1001 | 0002 | R. S. Patel ... |
| 1002 | 0004 | R. K. Rana ... |
| 1003 | 0001 | K. P. Sinha ... |
| 1004 | 0003 | N. P. Singh ... |
| ⋮ | ⋮ | ⋮ |

Index file                                                   Data file

**Figure 16.3.** Organization of an indexed sequential file.

## Advantages of Indexed Sequential Files

1. They can be quite efficiently used for sequential processing of high activity ratio applications.

2. They can also be used quite efficiently for direct access processing of low activity ratio applications.

## Disadvantages of Indexed Sequential Files

1. They require relatively expensive hardware and software resources because they must be stored on a direct-access device, such as a disk.

2. They require more storage space than other types of files because of the need for index file.

3. When used for direct access online applications, access to records may be slower than direct files.

# File Utilities

File utilities are routines, which perform generalized operations on data files. Normally, they are quite general in nature in the sense that they can operate on any data format and even on data files stored on different types of storage medium. The operations performed by some of the commonly used file utilities are described below.

## Sorting

A file sorting utility is used to arrange the records of a file in some defined sequence. This sequence is determined by the ordering of certain specified fields (known as *keys*) within the record. The simplest case of sorting is an ordering of the records in a file on a single key. For example, the records of an employee file may be sequenced by ascending order of employee code, as shown in Figure 16.4. A more complex ordering may be produced by introducing a further key in the sorting process. For example, if each record of the employee file also contains a field for department code to which the employee belongs, a desired order of sorting may be employee code within department code. This means that all records for the lowest department code are presented for each employee belonging to that department in ascending sequence of employee code, then all records for the next department code, and so on. This is shown in Figure 16.5. Out of the two keys used in this sorting example, department code is called the *primary key*, and employee code is called the *secondary key*, because the order of sorting is employee code within department code.

The size of keys, the number of keys, and the type of ordering (ascending, descending), which can be specified as input parameters, varies from one sorting utility to another. These parameters decide the extent and sophistication of sorting utilities. A sorting utility enables users to specify their particular sequencing requirements for a file by means of simple parameters. The sorting utility reads the unsequenced input file, and by means of various copying techniques, ultimately produces an output file, which contains the records of the input file ordered in the required sequence.

| Employee Code | Department Code | Other fields (Name, Address, Qualification, Basic Salary, etc.) |
|---|---|---|
| 101 | 2 | --- |
| 123 | 3 | --- |
| 124 | 1 | --- |
| 176 | 2 | --- |
| 178 | 1 | --- |
| 202 | 3 | --- |
| 213 | 1 | --- |

**Figure 16.4.** Sorting on one key in ascending employee code sequence.

| Employee Code | Department Code | Other fields (Name, Address, Qualification, Basic Salary, etc.) |
|---|---|---|
| 124 | 1 | --- |
| 178 | 1 | --- |
| 213 | 1 | --- |
| 101 | 2 | --- |
| 176 | 2 | --- |
| 123 | 3 | --- |
| 202 | 3 | --- |

**Figure 16.5.** Sorting on two keys. Ascending employee code (secondary key) within ascending department code (primary key).

## Searching

A file searching utility is used to find a particular record from a file. The searching is carried out with respect to certain specified fields (known as *keys*) within the record. For example, in the employee file of Figure 16.4, the user can specify the value 202 for the employee code field to request the computer to search the corresponding employee's record.

The efficiency of a search algorithm depends on the file organization. For example, to search a particular record in a sequential file, the file is scanned sequentially, beginning with the first record, and the specified key is compared one-by-one with the key field of each record. The search process terminates when the record with the matching key is found. On the other hand, direct or index sequential file organizations enable immediate access to the desired record with the help of either the hashing algorithm (in case of direct file organization) or the index file (in case of index sequential file organization). The user needs to only specify the file and the key, and the searching utility searches through the file and produces the desired record. Normally the time required for searching a particular record from a direct or index sequential file is much less as compared to the time required to search it from a sequential file.

## Merging

A file merging utility is used to combine the records of two or more ordered (sorted) files into a single ordered file. Each of the constituent files must be in the same order, although the record layout of files need not be identical. The output file produced by the merging utility has the records in the same order as the input files, placing records from each in their correct relative order. Figure 16.6, illustrates the merging of two input files A and B to produce an output file C.

## Copying

A file copying utility is used to produce an exact copy of a file, either from one unit of a storage device on to another similar unit (such as from one tape reel to another, or from one floppy disk to another), or from one storage medium to another (such as from tape to hard disk, or from CD-ROM to hard disk).

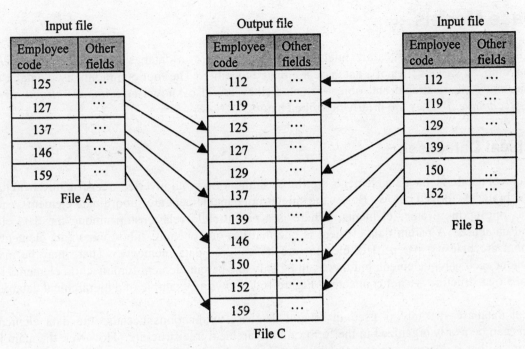

**Figure 16.6.** Merging of files A and B to produce file C.

File copying utilities are often used for taking back-up copies of files. For example, a file may be copied from a hard disk to a tape or floppy for back-up purpose. File copying utilities are also known as *peripheral interchange programs* since they may be used to copy a file from one peripheral device on to another peripheral device.

## Printing

A file printing utility is used to print a file on a printer to produce hard copy of its contents. Printing utilities often provide the facility to print file contents in different formats. They often provide some selection and editing facilities to enable printing of parts of files (such as specified number of records and only certain fields of records). Special printing facilities are often provided to print files that contain program instructions rather than data.

## Maintenance

A file maintenance utility is used to selectively copy the data of one or more files into a new file, or to selectively update a file's contents. For example, facilities provided in a file maintenance utility may include the combining of data from more than one file into a single file, the deletion of records identified by record key or record count within a file, and the selection of specific fields of records to be copied from an existing file into a new file.

# DATABASE MANAGEMENT SYSTEM

In the database-oriented approach of organizing data, a set of programs is provided to facilitate the users in organizing, creating, deleting, updating, and manipulating their data in a database. All these programs together form a *Database Management System* (*DBMS*). The commonly supported features in a typical database management system are described below.

# Database Models

We saw that multiple related files are integrated together to form a database. A *database model* defines the manner in which the various files of a database are linked together. The four commonly used database models are hierarchical, network, relational and object-oriented (they are also known as *database structures* or *database structuring techniques*). They are briefly described below.

## Hierarchical Databases

In a hierarchical database, the data elements are linked in the form of an inverted tree structure with the root at the top, and the branches formed below. Below the single-root data element are subordinate elements, each of which, in turn, has one or more other elements. There is a parent-child relationship among the data elements of a hierarchical database. A parent data element is one that has one or more subordinate data elements. The data elements that are below a parent data element are its children data elements. There may be many children elements under each parent element, but there can be only one parent element for any child element. Note that the branches in a tree structure are not connected. Figure 16.7 shows an example of a hierarchical database.

Hierarchical database structure is used in several database applications because the data elements of many applications can be neatly organized in the form of a hierarchical tree structure. However, the main limitation of this structure is that it does not support flexible data access, because the data elements can be accessed only by following the path down the tree structure. Hence, it is important to determine all types of relationships among the data elements and map them properly in the form of a hierarchical tree structure when the database is first designed. For instance, let us take the example of Figure 16.7, which shows a hierarchical database of an organization's employees. Employees are categorized by the department in which they work, and within a department, they are categorized by their job function, such as managers, engineers, technicians, and support staff. If the personnel department has a shortage of support staff one day, producing a list of all support staff, to take a decision for using some support staff from other departments for this department, would not be directly possible. Instead, the support staff assigned to each department would have to be determined department-by-department.

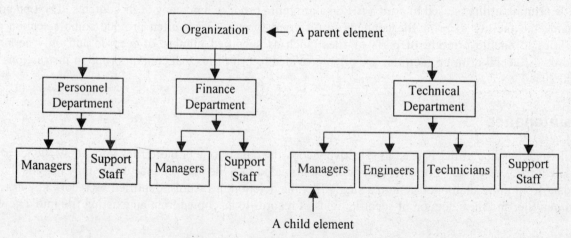

**Figure 16.7.** An example of a hierarchical database.

## Network Databases

A network database structure is an extension of the hierarchical database structure. In this model also, the data elements of a database are organized in the form of parent-child relationships, and all types of relationships among the data elements must be determined when the database is first designed. In a network database, however, a child data element can have more than one parent element or no parent at all. Moreover, in this type of database, the database management system permits the extraction of the needed information by beginning from any data element in the database structure, instead of starting from the root data element.

Figure 16.8 shows an example of a network database, which maintains the relationships among the courses offered and the students enrolled for each course in a college. As can be seen from the example, the parent and child elements can have many-to-many relationships in a network database structure. That is, each student may be enrolled for several courses, and each course may have a number of students enrolled for it. With this database structure used for this example, it is easily possible to produce both a course-wise students report (a report showing all students enrolled for each course) and a student-wise courses report (a report showing all courses taken by each student). For example, it is easy to tell from the database structure that in this semester, Maths course has been taken by Seeta, Geeta, Ram and Sohan. It is also easy to tell that in this semester, Geeta has taken the courses Hindi, Maths and Computer Science. The example also shows a child element that has no parent element (the student named Raju – he might be a research student who has not taken any course in this semester).

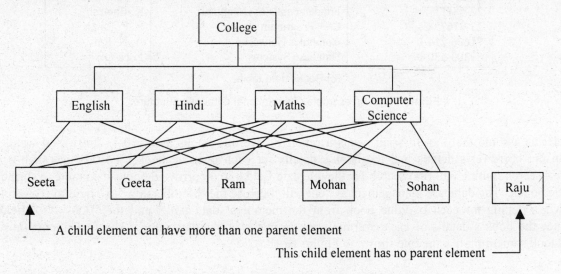

**Figure 16.8.** An example of a network database.

## Relational Databases

In a relational database, the data elements are organized in the form of multiple tables with rows and columns. Each table of the database is stored as a separate file. Each table column represents a data field, and each row a data record (also known as a *tuple*). The data in one table (or file) is related to data in another table with a common field.

Figure 16.9 shows an example of a relational database structure in which a sample library database is comprised of three tables. The first table contains the data of library members, the second table contains the data of borrowed books, and the third table contains the data of books in the library. Each new member is assigned a membership number and issued a library card with this number on it. The member's name, address, and membership number are added to the first table. When a member borrows a book, the membership number of the borrower, the book's ISBN number (which serves as the unique identification number for a book), and the due date for returning the book are added to the second table. The first and second tables are related by the 'Membership No.' common field, and the second and third tables are related by the "Book No.' common field.

| Membership No. | Member's name | Member's Address |
|---|---|---|
| 83569 | K. N. Raina | C-15, Sarita Vihar, Pune-7 |
| 62853 | D. P. Singh | A-22, Anand Park, Pune-5 |
| 12859 | R. Pandey | D-18, Vrindavan, Pune-7 |
| 32228 | R. S. Gupta | A-12, Nandanvan, Pune-2 |
| 23466 | S. K. Ray | B-05, Royal Villa, Pune-3 |
| 11348 | P. K. Sen | B-16, Anand Park, Pune-5 |
| 16185 | T. N. Murli | A-11, Vrindavan, Pune-7 |

(a) Members data table.

| Borrower (Membership No.) | Book No. (ISBN) | Due Date (DD-MM-YYYY) |
|---|---|---|
| 12859 | 27-21675-2 | 10-12-2001 |
| 11348 | 89303-530-0 | 08-11-2001 |
| 32228 | 13-201702-5 | 10-11-2001 |
| 16185 | 22-68111-7 | 05-12-2001 |
| 12859 | 71606-214-0 | 06-11-2001 |
| 62853 | 13-48049-8 | 15-11-2001 |
| 11348 | 18-23614-1 | 12-11-2001 |

(b) Borrowed books data table.

| Book No. (ISBN) | Book Title | Author |
|---|---|---|
| 13-201702-5 | Concepts of Physics | H. C. Verma |
| 13-48049-8 | Concepts of Chemistry | S. S. Dubey |
| 18-23614-1 | Astrology for You | N. K. Sharma |
| 22-68111-7 | Fundamentals of Computers | K. Ramesh |
| 27-21675-2 | C++ Programming | R. P. Rajan |
| 71606-214-0 | Computer Networks | A. N. Rai |
| 89303-530-0 | Database Systems | P. N. Dixit |

(c) Books data table.

**Figure 16.9.** An example of a relational database structure.

Now, let us assume that the librarian wants a report of overdue books as of 10-11-2001, and wants the list to contain the borrower's details and the book's details for each overdue book. To produce such a report, the database search routine will first search for the due date field in the borrowed books data table to surface the three overdue books. The database management system will then use the 'Membership No.' field to cross-reference the borrower's details for each overdue book from the members' data table, and the 'Book No.' field to cross-reference the book's details of each overdue book from the books data table. The final report thus produced, would look something like the one shown in Figure 16.10.

**List of overdue books as on 10-11-2001**

| Membership No. | Member's Name | Member's Address | Due Date | Book No. | Book Title | Book Author |
|---|---|---|---|---|---|---|
| 11348 | P. K. Sen | B-16, Anand Park, Pune-5 | 08-11 | 89303-530-0 | Database Systems | P. N. Dixit |
| 32228 | R. S. Gupta | A-12, Nandanvan, Pune-2 | 10-11 | 13-201702-5 | Concepts of Physics | H. C. Verma |
| 12859 | R. Pandey | D-18, Vrindavan, Pune-7 | 06-11 | 71606-214-0 | Computer Networks | A. N. Rai |

**Figure 16.10.** A report of overdue books as of 10-11-2001 from the sample database of Figure 16.9.

The relational database model provides greater flexibility of data organization and future enhancements in the database as compared to the hierarchical and network database models. For many applications, the data elements can be organized in a relational database in a manner that is identical to the actual relationships that exist between the data elements. Hence, many users find the relational database model to be closer to their intuitive model of the real-life situation, making this model easier to understand and use. Moreover, if new data is to be added to an existing relational database, it is not necessary to redesign the database afresh. Rather, new tables containing the new data can be added to the database, and then these tables can be related to the existing tables with common key fields. Data can also be reorganized, when necessary, to create new tables by selecting certain rows or specific columns from other tables, or by joining columns and rows from two separate tables.

## Object-oriented Databases

The hierarchical, network, and relational database models (henceforth referred to as conventional database models) were developed for the conventional business data processing applications, such as inventory control, payroll, accounts, employee information systems, and so on. Attempts to make use of these database models in a wide variety of other types of applications, exposed several serious shortcomings of these database models. These applications include computer-aided design (CAD), computer-aided engineering (CAE), computer-aided manufacturing (CAM), computer-aided software engineering (CASE), expert systems, and multimedia systems. Some of the key features, required for effective modeling of these applications, which are absent in conventional database models are:

1. Ability to model complex nested entities, such as design and engineering objects, and multimedia documents. Conventional database models do not provide mechanisms, such as configuration management, to represent and manage such entities.

2. Support for general data types found in object-oriented programming languages. Database management systems based on conventional database models support only a limited set of atomic data types, such as integer, string, etc. They do not even allow the storage and retrieval of long unstructured data, such as images, audio, and textual documents.

3. Support for proper match between object-oriented programming languages and database languages. A database application is normally implemented by using some conventional programming language (such as COBOL, PASCAL, C, or C++), and some database languages (data definition language, data manipulation language, query language), which are part of the database management system. With the popularity of object-oriented paradigm, the use of object-oriented programming languages for implementing applications has become a common practice. However, database languages used in database management systems for conventional database models do not use object-oriented concepts for implementing applications. This mismatch between object-oriented programming languages and database languages used in database management systems for conventional database models, makes database implementation of many applications inconvenient.

The object-oriented database model was introduced to overcome the above listed shortcomings of conventional database models. An *object-oriented database* is a collection of objects whose behavior and state, and the relationships are defined in accordance with object-oriented concepts (such as object, class, class hierarchy, etc.). An *object-oriented database management system* is one, which allows the definition and manipulation of an object-oriented database.

Figure 16.11 shows an example of an object-oriented database structure. The class *Vehicle* is the root of a class-composition hierarchy, which includes the classes *VehicleSpecs*, *Company*, and *Employee*. The class *Vehicle* is also the root of a class hierarchy involving the classes *TwoWheeler* and *FourWheeler*. The class *Company* is, in turn, the root of a class hierarchy with subclasses *DomesticCompany* and *ForeignCompany*. It is also the root of a class-composition hierarchy involving the class *Employee*.

For the database structure of Figure 16.11, a typical query may be "list out the President's and Company's names for all the companies located in Pune, India, which manufacture two-wheeler vehicles."

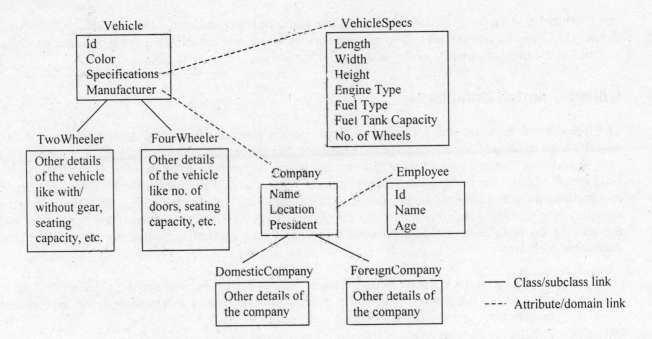

**Figure 16.11.** An example of an object-oriented database structure.

# Main Components of a DBMS

A DBMS frees the users of a database from the need to worry about the organization and location of data. It allows users to organize, process, and retrieve selected data from a database, without the need to know about the underlying database structure. The four major components of a DBMS are:

1.  Data Definition Language (DDL),

2.  Data Manipulation Language (DML)

3.  Query Language, and

4.  Report Generator.

They are briefly described below.

## Data Definition Language (DDL)

The *data definition language* (*DDL*) is used to define the structure of a database. The database structure definition (also commonly known as *database schema*) typically includes the following:

1.  Defining all data elements to be included in the database.

2.  Defining the organization of the data elements (fields) into records (or tuples), tables, etc.

3.  Defining a name, field length, and field type for each data element. A field name is used to refer to the corresponding data element while accessing it. Field length is used to define the maximum size of the data element (such as an employee name field, may have a maximum size of 30 characters). Common field types are numeric (can contain only the digits 0 to 9, a decimal point, and a + or − sign), alphanumeric (can contain a combination of alphabetic characters, special symbols, and digits),

logical (can contain one of two possible values – Yes/No or True/False), date (can contain a single date), and memo (can be used to hold any type of reminder that the user might like to type).

4. Defining controls for fields that can have only selective values. For example, in an employee database, the sex field can have controls to accept only the values M or F. Similarly, the age field can have controls to accept only the values 18 or more and less than 70. Such controls ensure the correctness of entered data to some extent.

5. Defining access controls to the various tables, records, and fields for different categories of users to protect the privacy of sensitive data items from unauthorized users.

6. Defining the logical relationships among the various data elements of the database.

In short, virtually everything about the database structure is included in its schema. It is possible to generate a complete description of a database from its schema. This description, in turn, can be used by systems analysts in defining new applications on the database.

Database systems are typically installed and coordinated by an individual called the *database administrator*. He/she has the overall authority to establish and control data definitions and standards. He/she is responsible for determining the relationships among data elements, and for designing the database security system to guard against unauthorized use. He/she also trains and assists applications programmers in the use of the database. A *data dictionary* is developed and used in a database to document and maintain the data definitions. It is automatically created/updated by the DDL module of the DBMS as the database schema is defined or changed.

## Data Manipulation Language (DML)

Once the structure of a database (database schema) has been defined, the database is ready for the entry and manipulation of data. The *data manipulation language (DML)* includes the commands, which enable the users to enter and minipulate the data. With these commands, the user can do such things as, add new records to the database, navigate through the existing records, view the contents of the various fields of a record, modify the contents of one or more fields of a record, delete an existing record, and sort the records in a desired sequence.

In some DBMS, the data definition language and the data manipulation language are combined together, while in others, they are supported as separate DBMS components.

## Query Language

Although it is possible to navigate through a database one record at a time to extract the desired information from the data stored in the database, this approach can be very inefficient and frustrating when there are thousands of records and several files in the database. Hence, all database management systems provide a *query language*, which enables users to define their requirements for extracting the desired information from the database in the form of queries. For example, from an inventory database, a user may be interested in such information as "list out the item description and vendor name for all items whose current inventory level is less than 20 units", or "list out the stock number and item description for all items with a profit margin greater than 25%".

Earlier, each database management system had its own query language. In this approach, queries developed for one DBMS could not be used with other DBMSs. However, eventually one query language, called SQL (pronounced "S-Q-L"), emerged as an industry standard. It was originally developed by IBM and was based on an earlier query language called SEQUEL, which is an acronym for "Structured English QUEry Language". Today, SQL is the standard query language used in many DBMSs.

A query language can be easily learnt by a non-programmer. This enables normal users of a database to access the database for desired information without the help of any programmer.

## Report Generator

A *report* is the presentation of inforamtion extracted from a database. The *report generator* enables the users of a database to design the layout of a report in the desired format. This means that the user can specify proper spacing between the data items to be presented in a report, and can also include suitable report titles and subtitles, column heading, page numbers, separation lines, and other elements, which make a report more readable and presentable. The report generator can also be instructed to perform arithmetic operations (such as calculating subtotals and totals) on the data found in numeric fields to make a report more meaningful and useful.

A user can define the layout of a report and then store it for later use. This facility is often used for generating periodic reports. For example, this facility is found to be very useful for generation of employee pay-slips from an employee database every month, or generation of consumer bills every month, for the consumers of a service. The report layout format remains the same every month, only the data changes.

# Creating and Using a Database

In this section, we will take a closer look at how a database is created and used. Large databases on large computer systems are normally created and maintained by professional programmers. The users of these databases, however, need not be programmers. They can be easily used by non-programmers to access the data and produce reports. On the other hand, many database management systems, designed for personal computer systems, enable non-programmers to not only use, but even to create their own databases. These databases are normally simple in structure and small in size.

## Creating a Database

Creation of a database is a three steps process:

1. Defining its structure (schema),
2. Designing forms (custom screens) for displaying and entering data, and
3. Entering the data into it.

These steps are briefly described below.

### Schema Definition

The first thing we do to set up a database is to define its structure (schema definition). This is done by identifying the characteristics of each field in it. A good way to begin defining the schema of a database is to list down on paper all the fields, which are to be included in the database, and then to determine the name, type, and size of each field. This information is then captured into the system by using a tool called *schema builder*. The schema builder enables a user to define a database schema interactively by prompting the user to enter the field name, field type, field size, and so on, for each field.

While defining the schema of a database, it is important to consider possible future needs and the needs of all types of users of the database. That is, all possible fields that may be needed, should be included in the database structure while defining it. Although it is possible to modify the database structure at any time, making such modifications is a time-consuming process. Hence, it is always better to design a database carefully in the first instance, and minimize the need to modify the database structure.

## Designing Forms

After defining the structure of a database, the next step is to design the forms (custom screens), which permit convenient data entry. Each form displays a set of fields of the database structure with appropriate amount of blank spaces against each to enable data entry for those fields. A typical form is shown in Figure 16.12.

To facilitate easier data entry, forms are often designed with several fancy features, such as:

1. A list box for a field, which lists several options on it from which the user can select a choice. For example, in the form of Figure 16.12, the SEX field may have a list box, which lists the options "Male" and "Female" on it, and the user simply selects the appropriate option for an employee. Depending on the user's selected option, the system automatically enters "M" or "F" in the SEX field. Similarly, the STATE field may have a list box, which lists all the states on it, from which the user can select the appropriate option for an employee's address.

2. Simple validation checks defined for a field to ensure correctness of entered data to some extent. For example, in the form of Figure 16.12, a validation check may be defined for the POSTAL CODE field to accept only six numeric characters. With this, the field will not accept less than or more than six characters. Similarly, a validation check may be defined for the AGE field to accept values only in the range of 18 to 70 (both inclusive). Validation checks can also be used to force a certain character position of a field to be a letter or numeral.

3. Automatic conversion of typed characters to upper- or lower-case. For example, in the form of Figure 16.12, this feature may be used with the STATE field. Hence, the system will accept "mh", "Mh", "mH" or "MH" for the state code of Maharashtra, and will automatically convert the entry to "MH". This feature can greatly ease data entry and ensure the uniformity of data.

4. Automatic formatting of certain fields. For example, in the form of Figure 16.12, this feature can be used with the TELEPHONE NO. field to automatically display the value of this field in the specified format (with the parentheses, space, and hyphen). That is, to enter the telephone number "(020) 5680-489", the user only needs to type "0205680489", and the system automatically causes the form to display "(020) 5680-489".

## Entering Data

After the forms have been designed, the database is ready for entry of data. Data is entered one record at a time. To enter the data, the user issues a command, which calls up and displays the appropriate form with blank fields. The user then keys in the data for each field in the appropriate spaces. In this manner, the user enters the data for the first record, then for the second record, and so on. In most database systems, the records are automatically assigned a number as they are entered.

While entering data into the fields, the tab key or enter key is usually used to move to the next field. Pressing enter or tab key in the last field on the form saves the record in the database and moves to a new, blank form for the next record to be entered. In addition to using the tab or enter key to move forward through fields, one can directly go to any field on the form at any time by clicking on it with the mouse.

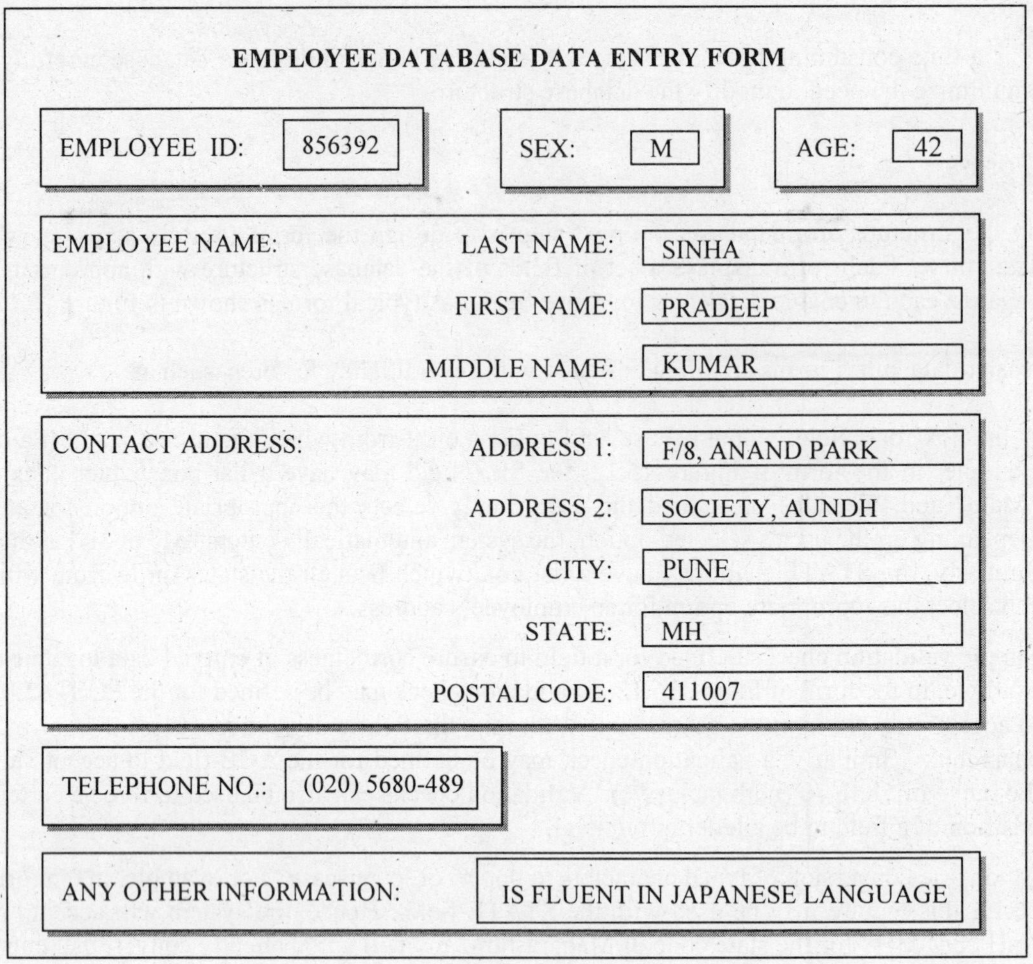

**EMPLOYEE DATABASE DATA ENTRY FORM**

EMPLOYEE ID:    856392          SEX:    M          AGE:    42

EMPLOYEE NAME:              LAST NAME:    SINHA

                           FIRST NAME:    PRADEEP

                           MIDDLE NAME:    KUMAR

CONTACT ADDRESS:            ADDRESS 1:    F/8, ANAND PARK

                           ADDRESS 2:    SOCIETY, AUNDH

                                CITY:    PUNE

                               STATE:    MH

                         POSTAL CODE:    411007

TELEPHONE NO.:    (020) 5680-489

ANY OTHER INFORMATION:          IS FLUENT IN JAPANESE LANGUAGE

**Figure 16.12.** A typical database form used for data entry.

## Viewing, Modifying, Deleting and Adding Records

All database systems provide commands to view, modify, delete, or add the records of an already established database. The command for viewing a record enables the user to display the data in the various fields of a record in the same screen format as that used for data entry. The user can specify the record to be displayed by specifying its key field value. The database system usually also provides the flexibility to the user to move between records for viewing different records, such as "go to the first record", "go to the previous record", "go to the next record", and "go to the last record".

Many database systems also provide a facility to set up a *filter*, which allows the user to browse through and view only those records, which meet some criterion. For example, in the employee database created by using the form of Figure 16.12, if the user wants to view the records of only female employees, the user can set a filter for the "Sex" field, and only the records, which contain "F" in that field will be displayed. Note that while a filter is set, the user cannot access the records that do not meet the filter criteria. Filters provide a quick and convenient way to narrow down the number of records the user has to work with.

The command for modifying a record enables the user to not only view, but also to update the data in the various fields of a record. To modify the contents of a particular field of a record, the record is first displayed, then the cursor is positioned in the field at the appropriate character position where the change is to be made by clicking the mouse there, and then the contents of the field is appropriately edited. The data in any other field of the record can be similarly edited. Finally, the enter key has to be pressed for the changes to take effect. Some database systems may prompt the user to confirm the changes, before effecting the changes and allowing the user to move to another record.

The command for deleting a record enables the user to remove the selected record from the database. To delete a record, the user first selects the record, either by specifying its key field value, or by using the facility to move between records just as is done in the case of viewing a record. The user then uses the delete command, and the record is deleted. Most database systems prompt the user to confirm the deletion of the record before deleting it. This feature prevents deletion of a record by mistake.

The command for adding a record enables the user to add new records to the database. When this command is enabled, the system displays a blank form and waits for the user to enter data. The user then keys in the data for each field in the appropriate spaces, and finally presses enter or tab key, after keying the data in the last field to save the record. On doing this, the system displays a new blank form for the next record to be entered. If no more records are to be added, the user can use the mouse to select the option to terminate the data entry process for adding new records.

## Searching for Desired Information

A database management system derives much of its power from the ease with which its users can search for the desired information from the large volume of data stored in a database. The commonly supported features in modern database systems for this are:

1.  Find command,
2.  Query language, and
3.  Query By Example (QBE)

These features are briefly described below.

### Find Command

The Find command is used for simple database queries, like searching for records having a particular string pattern in a field. For example, in the employee database created by using the form of Figure 16.12, the Find command may be used to list out the records of all employees whose last name is "SINHA". Similarly, it may be used to list out the records of all employees who belong to the city of "PUNE".

To use Find, the user has to type the string pattern to be searched and then has to indicate which field to search in. For instance, in the above example, the user has to type "SINHA" and indicate that this string has to be searched in the "LAST NAME" field. The user can specify either a single field or all fields.

The Find command cannot be used for creating an elaborate set of criteria for complex queries. Furthermore, it can operate on only one table at a time, and the user cannot save a specified criteria for future use.

### Query Language

For handling complex quieries, all database systems support a query language. Most of these query languages conform to the SQL standard. In SQL, the user has to specify the criteria for search along with the fields and table (or tables) with which to work with. The criteria for search can be built by using the relational operators (= [equal to], > [greater than], < [less that], and combinations of these operators), and the logical operators (AND, OR, and NOT). For example, to list out the names of all employees whose last name starts with the letter "S", who belong to "PUNE", and whose age is more than 40 years, the SQL query will look as follows:

SELECT [LAST NAME], [FIRST NAME], [MIDDLE NAME]

FROM Employee

WHERE ([LAST NAME] = "S..") AND (CITY = "PUNE") AND ([AGE > 40])

The keywords SELECT, FROM, and WHERE tell the SQL engine how to interpret each part of the query statement. The SELECT keyword tells SQL which fields are to be displayed for the records that match the criteria. The FROM keyword tells SQL which table(s) to work with. The WHERE keyword tells SQL the criteria for selecting the records (search criteria). The brackets [...] around some of the field names are needed in the above example because these field names contain spaces, and the brackets help the database to interpret each field name correctly.

A query language can be easily learnt and used even by a non-programmer, because the complexity of a query language statement is normally more or less of the same order as given in the above SQL statement. Furthermore, a query language uses only a few keywords, which are easy to remember and use. In fact, SQL has only a few dozen or so basic keywords.

Other advantages of using a query language are that a query statement can be used for creating an elaborate set of criteria for complex queries, it can operate on multiple tables at a time, and a specified criteria can be saved for future use.

### Query By Example (QBE)

Although query languages are easy to learn and use, many database developers further simplify the job of database users of specifying search criteria by providing front ends for the query language, which collect the facts about a query from the user and compose query language statements internally. The front end usually consists of a form (called *QBE form*), and the user simply specifies the search criteria by inputting values into the fields of this form. Again the values may be input either by typing them or by selecting an option from a set of options provided for a particular field, depending on how the front end has been designed to work.

The QBE form is designed to collect all necessary information from the user for composing query language statement(s) for the search criteria. Once the user completes the QBE form, the QBE engine automatically converts the user inputs into suitable query language statement(s) for search processing. Hence, the user is relieved of remembering the query language keywords and using them with the correct syntax to form queries. This front-end feature is called *query by example (QBE)*. It has been found to be very userful for many database users, especially the beginners.

## Creating Reports

The user of a database system can use the report generator of the database system to assemble the output of a database query in the desired format. For this, the user creates a report specifying the layout of the display (or printout) of the fields requested by the user in the query. The user can also specify the titles and subtitles for the report, the column headings for the various fields, and other elements, to make the output appear more presentable. Furthermore, the user can even specify the output to be sorted with respect to one or more fields in the output. When the sorting is on more than one field, the user has to specify the primary, secondary, and tertiary key fields. A created report can be saved and used later for generating similar reports whenever required.

Figure 16.13 shows a sample output of a report created for the employee database whose data entry form is shown in Figure 16.12. The report is used to display (or print) the list of employees who belong to the city of PUNE. The report contains the last name, first name, address-1, address-2, and telephone number of all such employees. The report is sorted to present the list of employees in alphabetical order of their last name.

**LIST OF EMPLOYEES WHO BELONG TO PUNE**
**DATE: DECEMBER 15, 2001**

| LAST NAME | FIRST NAME | ADDRESS-1 | ADDRESS-2 | TELEPHONE NUMBER |
|-----------|------------|-----------|-----------|------------------|
| Gupta | Rajiv | A-12, Nandanvan | M. G. Road | 4623-489 |
| Murli | Tapan | A-11, Vrindavan | Pashan Road | 5863-490 |
| Pandey | Rupa | D-18, Vrindana | Pashan Road | 5865-323 |
| Raina | Pushpa | C-15, Sarita Vihar | Aundh Road | 5755-832 |
| Ray | Suhas | B-05, Royal Villa | M. G. Road | 4685-635 |
| Sen | Prakash | B-16, Anand Park | Aundh Road | 5762-333 |
| Singh | Deepak | A-22, Anand Park | Aundh Road | 5728-628 |

**Figure 16.13.** A sample output of a report to generate a list of employees who belong to Pune. The report is sorted to present the list in alphabetical order of their last name.

Many database developers further simplify the job of database users by creating commonly anticipated reports, storing them, and providing a simple graphical user interface to select from the available reports. In this case, the user has to only select one of the reports from the available options while outputting query results. The user needs to create a new report only when none of the available options meet his/her requirement. The newly created report can then be added to the list of available options for future use.

# Points to Remember

1. *Data processing* is defined as a series of actions or operations, which convert data into useful information. Hence, data is the raw material of information, and just as raw materials are transformed into finished products by a manufacturing process, raw *data* is transformed into *information* by data processing.

2. A *data processing system* includes the resources, such as people, procedures, and devices, which are used to accomplish the processing of data for producing desirable output.

3. In data processing, storage of data is often conceptualized as a *data storage hierarchy*, which normally consists of bit, character, field, record, file and database.

4. Multiple related bits are combined to form a character, multiple related characters are combined to form a field, multiple related fields are combined to form a record, multiple related records are combined

to form a file, and multiple related files are integrated to form a database.

5. The two standard methods used in data processing for organizing data are file-oriented approach and database-oriented approach.

6. In the file-oriented approach of organizing data, an application's data is organized into one or more files and the application program processes the data stored in these files to generate the desired output. A set of programs is provided to facilitate the users in organizing, creating, deleting, updating, and manipulating their files. All these programs together form a *File Management System* (*FMS*).

7. In the database-oriented approach of organizing data, data from multiple related files are integrated together in the form of a database, which has the following properties:
   - It provides greater query flexibility.
   - It reduces data redundancy.

- It solves data integrity (inconsistency) problem.
- It makes data independent of the application programs. That is, fields can be added, changed, and deleted from the database without affecting existing programs.
  - It also includes data security features at database level, record level, and even at field level to provide greater flexibility of restricted data access.

A set of programs is provided to facilitate the users in organizing, creating, deleting, updating, and manipulating their data in a database. All these programs together form a *Database Management System (DBMS)*.

8. *File organization* deals with the physical organization of the records of a file for the convenience of storage and retrieval of data records. The three commonly used file organizations in business data processing applications are sequential, direct/random, and indexed sequential.

9. *File utilities* are routines, which perform a variety of generalized operations on data files. The operations performed by some of the commonly used file utilities are sorting, searching, merging, copying, printing and maintenance.

10. A *database model* defines the manner in which the various files of a database are linked together. The four commonly used database models are hierarchical, network, relational, and object-oriented.

11. The four major components of a database management system are data definition language (DDL), data manipulation language (DML), query language and report generator.

12. The *data definition language* (*DDL*) is used to define the structure of a database. The database structure definition is commonly known as *database schema*.

13. The *data manipulation language* (*DML*) includes all the commands that enable the users to enter and manipulate the data.

14. The *query language* enables users to define their requirements for extracting the desired information from the database in the form of queries.

15. The *report generator* enables the users of a database to design the layout of a report in the desired format.

# Questions

1. What is the difference between data and information?

2. What is meant by data processing?

3. What is a data processing system?

4. In data processing, storage of data is often conceptualized as a data storage hierarchy. Describe the various levels of this hierarchy.

5. Give an example to illustrate the relationship among a character, a field, a record, and a file.

6. What is a database? How is it different from a file?

7. What are the two standard methods used in data processing systems for organizing data? Explain their relative advantages and disadvantages.

8. Describe three drawbacks of traditional information processing systems that use separate, unrelated files.

9. What is the difference between a master file and a transaction file?

10. What is a key field? How is it useful?

11. What is data redundancy? Explain with an example. Now explain how the database-oriented approach of data organization helps in reducing data redundancy as compared to the file-oriented approach.

12. What is data integrity problem? Explain how the database-oriented approach of data organization helps in solving this problem.

13. What is a file management system?

14. Describe the various types of files commonly supported in a typical file management system.

15. What is the difference between an output file and a report file?

16. What is a backup file? Why is regular creation of backup files important?

17. What is meant by file organization? What are the three commonly used file organizations in business data processing? How do we decide to use a particular file organization for an application?

18. What is a sequential file? What is the principal storage medium used for storing sequential files? Give examples of few applications, which will benefit from the use of sequential files.

19. What is activity ratio in file processing? What type of file organization is suitable for (a) an application that has high activity ratio, (b) an application that has low

activity ratio? Give an example of each type of application.

20. How is a sequential file organized? How are records in a sequential file accessed? How are these records processed?

21. What is a direct file? What is the principal storage medium used for storing direct files? Give examples of few applications, which will benefit from the use of direct files.

22. How is a record stored in a direct file? How is it retrieved and processed?

23. Explain how are the records in a direct file physically organized so that it becomes possible to directly access a particular record, given its key field value.

24. What is hashing? How is it useful in direct file organization? What is a collision? How can it be handled?

25. If the activity ratio is high, the use of direct files proves to be very inefficient as compared to sequential files. Explain why.

26. Explain the basic principle used in indexed sequential file organization. Explain the roles of data file and index file in indexed sequential file organization.

27. How are records stored in an indexed sequential file? How are they retrieved and processed?

28. Explain how can indexed sequential files be used quite efficiently for both sequential and direct access processing.

29. Discuss the advantages and limitations of the sequential, direct, and indexed sequential file organizations.

30. What are file utilities?

31. Differentiate between the process of sorting and merging of files.

32. Explain the use of the following file utilities: copying, searching, printing, and maintenance.

33. What is a database management system?

34. What is a database model? Name the four commonly used database models and describe any two.

35. Write short notes on:
    (a) Hierarchical database model
    (b) Network database model
    (c) Relational database model
    (d) Object-oriented database model

36. Explain the relational database model with the help of an example. List out its main advantages as compared to the hierarchical and network database models.

37. If new type of data is to be added to an existing relational database, it is not necessary to redesign the database afresh. Discuss this statement. Give an example to illustrate this.

38. List out some of the key features found in the object-oriented database model that are absent in conventional database models.

39. Why is the object-oriented database model preferred for database applications such as CAD, CAM, CAE, CASE, expert systems and multimedia systems?

40. Explain the object-oriented database model with the help of an example.

41. What are the four major components of a database management system (DBMS)? Describe the roles of each of these components in the overall design and usage of a database.

42. What is a data definition language (DDL)? What is its role in the overall design and/or usage of a database?

43. What is a data manipulation language (DML)? What is its role in the overall design and/or usage of a database?

44. What is a query language? What is its role in the overall design and/or usage of a database?

45. What is the difference between the data manipulation language and the query language with respect to what each enables the user to do?

46. What is a report generator? What is its role in the overall design and/or usage of a database?

47. A report generator can be instructed to perform arithmetic operations on the data found in numeric fields to make a report more meaningful and useful. Discuss this statement. Give an example to illustrate this.

48. What is a database schema? What all does it typically include about a database?

49. What are the jobs and responsibilities of a database administrator?

50. What is a data dictionary? How is it created/updated?

51. What is SQL? How is it useful?

52. List out, in proper sequence, the three basic steps involved in creating a database? Describe these steps.

53. What are forms? List out a few features that may be incorporated into a form to facilitate easier data entry.

54. What is a filter? Explain with an example.

55. List out the three commonly supported features in modern database systems that may be used for searching for desired information from a database.

56. Explain with an example how "Find" command can be used for making a database query? What are the limitations of "Find" command?

57. Explain with an example how a query language can be used for making a database query? What are the advantages of using a query language against "Find" command?

58. What is query by example (QBE)? How does it make the job of querying a database simpler?

59. A DBMS derives much of its power from the ease with which its users can search for the desired information from the large volume of data stored in a database. Discuss this statement.

60. What is a report? How is it created and used? Give an example of a sample report.

61. Write short notes on:
    (a) Data storage hierarchy
    (b) Output versus report files
    (c) Backup files
    (d) Master versus transaction files
    (e) File-oriented versus database-oriented approaches of organizing data

62. Write short notes on:
    (a) Sequential file organization
    (b) Direct file organization
    (c) Indexed sequential file organization

63. Write short notes on:
    (a) Sorting          (d) Copying
    (b) Searching        (e) Printing
    (c) Merging          (f) Maintenance

64. Write short notes on:
    (a) Database models
    (b) Database schema
    (c) Components of a DBMS
    (d) Query features in database systems

# Chapter 17

# Data Communications and Computer Networks

It is not the processing power of computers, but the power of communication among computers that has revolutionized the information age. The marriage of computing and data communication technologies (means and methods by which data is transferred from one location to another) is one of the most exciting developments in today's information age. This development has given birth to computer networks. A *computer network* is a network of geographically distributed multiple computers connected in a manner to enable meaningful transmission and exchange of information among them. Sharing of information, sharing of resources (both hardware and software), and sharing of processing load are some of the major objectives of a computer network.

The goal of this chapter is to introduce the various aspects of data communications technology, and to discuss how this technology is combined with computer technology to form computer networks. Following are some of the important concepts, which you will learn in this chapter:

1. Basic elements of a communication system.

2. Techniques, channels and devices used to transmit data between distant locations.

3. Various types of computer networks.

4. Communication protocols, which are rules and procedure for establishing and controlling the transmission of data from one computer to another.

5. Characteristics and advantages of distributed computing systems.

# BASIC ELEMENTS OF A COMMUNICATION SYSTEM

Communication is the process of transferring messages from one point to another. As shown in Figure 17.1, the three basic elements of any communication system are:

1. A *sender* (source), which creates the message to be transmitted.

2. A *medium*, which carries the message.

3. A *receiver* (sink), which receives the message.

For example, when you speak to your friend on the telephone, you are the sender, the telephone line, through which your voice is transmitted, is the medium, and your friend is the receiver. This is a simple example of voice communication. The same concept holds good for data communication also. Data communication is the function of transporting data from one point to another. In this case, the sender and receiver are normally machines, in particular, computer devices (computers, terminals, peripheral devices like printers, plotters, disks, etc.), and the transmission medium may be telephone lines, microwave links, satellite links, etc. However, the messages that are transmitted are data, not voice conversations. Hence, the electronic systems, which transfer data from one point to another, are called *data communication systems*. Unlike computers, which process and rearrange data, data communication systems transmit data from one point to another without any change.

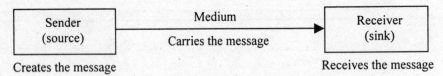

**Figure 17.1.** Basic elements of a communication system.

# DATA TRANSMISSION MODES

There are three ways, or modes, of transmitting data from one point to another. As shown in Figure 17.2, these are simplex, half duplex, and full duplex.

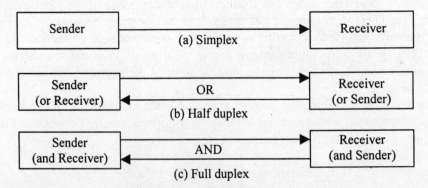

**Figure 17.2.** Modes of data transmission.

1. **Simplex.** If transmission is simplex, communication can take place in only one direction. Devices connected to such a circuit are either a send-only or a receive-only device. For example, a data collection terminal on a factory floor (send only), or a printer (receive only). At first thought, that might appear adequate for many types of applications in which flow of information is unidirectional. However, in almost all data processing applications, communication in both directions is required.

Even for a "one-way" flow of information from a terminal to a computer, the system will be designed to allow the computer to signal the terminal that data has been received. Without this capability, the remote user might enter data and never know that it was not received by the computer (due to some problem somewhere). Hence, simplex circuits are seldom used because a return path is generally needed to send acknowledgement, control, or error signals.

2. **Half Duplex.** A half duplex system can transmit data in both directions, but only in one direction at a time. Hence, a half duplex line can alternately send and receive data. It requires two wires. This is the most common type of transmission for voice communication because only one person is supposed to speak at a time. It is also used to connect a terminal with a computer. The terminal might transmit data and then the computer responds with an acknowledgement.

3. **Full Duplex.** In a half duplex system, the line must be "turned-around" each time the direction is reversed. This involves a special switching circuit and requires a small amount of time (approximately 150 milliseconds). With high-speed capabilities of the computer, this turn-around time is unacceptable in many instances. Also, some applications require simultaneous transmission in both directions. In such cases, a full duplex system is used, which allows information to flow simultaneously in both directions on the transmission path. Use of a full duplex line improves efficiency, because the line turn-around time required in a half duplex arrangement is eliminated. It requires four wires.

# DATA TRANSMISSION SPEED

A term used to describe the data-handling capacity of a communication system is bandwidth. *Bandwidth* is the range of frequencies that is available for the transmission of data. A narrow bandwidth in a communication system is analogous to a narrow road. The flow of information in such a system – its data transfer rate – is limited, just as is the flow of traffic in a narrow road. Wider bandwidths permit more rapid information flow. Hence, the wider the bandwidth of a communication system, the more data it can transmit in a given period.

When dealing with computer input/output devices, we think in terms of characters per second. However, in case of data transmission, we talk in terms of bits per second. The ASCII code uses 7 data bits per character plus a parity bit. For data communication, additional bits are added to control the process. Although the number of bits depends upon the communication system used, commonly encountered systems use a total of either 10 or 11 bits per character. Hence, a terminal having a speed of 30 characters per second would probably be used with a communication system, which transmits at the rate of 300 bits per second.

The communication data transfer rate is measured in a unit called *baud*. In general usage, baud is identical to bits per second. For instance, a rate of 300 baud is 300 bits per second. Therefore, a 30 characters per second terminal would be said to operate at 300 baud. However, technically, baud refers to the number of signal (state) changes per second. Hence, using more sophisticated coding techniques; 1 baud can represent 2 or even 3 bits per second. However, with most communication systems, 1 baud represents only one signal change per second, and is equivalent to 1 bit per second.

Depending on their transmission speeds, communication channels (paths) are grouped into the following three basic categories:

1. **Narrowband.** Narrowband or subvoice grade channels range in speed from 45 to 300 baud. They are used for handling low data volumes, and are adequate for low-speed devices. They are used mainly for telegraph lines and low speed terminals.

2. **Voice band.** Voice band channels handle moderate data volumes, and can transmit data at speeds up to 9600 baud. They are so called because their major application is for ordinary telephone voice communication. They are also used for data transmission from slow I/O devices to CPU or vice versa. Moreover, most remote terminals are connected to computers through voice band channels.

3. **Broadband.** Broadband or wideband channels are used when large volumes of data are to be transmitted at high speed. These systems provide data transmission rates of 1 million baud or more. A company might use a broadband facility for high-speed computer-to-computer communication, or for simultaneous transmission of data to several different devices.

As might be expected, the cost of the data transmission service increases with speed. Hence, a thorough analysis of the business needs and associated costs is necessary in making a proper choice.

# DATA TRANSMISSION MEDIA

The sender-medium-receiver concept has actually been with us for a very long time. For example, shouting to another person involves voice transmission over a distance via the medium air, which carries the sound wave. The use of telephone lines, as a transmission medium, considerably enhances the possible distance. Like telephone lines, there are several types of physical channels (communication media) through which data can be transmitted from one point to another. Some of the most common data transmission media are briefly described below.

## Twisted-Pair Wire

A twisted-pair wire consists of two bunches of thin copper wires, each bunch enclosed separately in a plastic insulation, then twisted around each other to reduce interference by adjacent wires (see Figure 17.3). It is also called *unshielded twisted-pair* (UTP) cable because other than the plastic coating around the two individual bunches of copper wires, nothing shields it from outside interference.

UTP cables are commonly used in local telephone communication and short distance (up to about 1 km) digital data transmission. They are normally used to connect terminals to the main computer, if they are placed at a short distance from the main computer. Data transmission speed of up to 9600 bits per second (or 9600 baud) can be achieved, if the distance is not more than 100 meters. However, for longer distance data transmission, local telephone lines are used. In this case, typical speed of digital signal transmission is 1200 bits per second.

UTP cables are an inexpensive medium of data transmission. They are easy to install and use. However, their use is limited because they easily pick up noise signals, which results in high error rates when the line length extends beyond 100 meters.

**Figure 17.3.** A twisted-pair wire (UTP cable).

## Coaxial Cable

Coaxial cables are groups of specially wrapped and insulated wire lines, which are able to transmit data at high rates. As shown in Figure 17.4, they consist of a central copper wire surrounded by a PVC insulation over which a sleeve of copper mesh is placed. The metal sleeve is again shielded by an outer shield of thick PVC material. The signal is transmitted by the inner copper wire, and is electrically shielded by the outer metal sleeve.

Coaxial cables offer much higher bandwidths than UTP cables, and are capable of transmitting digital signals at rates of 10 mega bits per second. They are extensively used in long distance telephone lines and as cables for cable TV. They are also used by telephone companies to transmit data. In many cases, several coaxial cables are packaged into a very large cable, which can handle over 40,000 telephone calls simultaneously. Furthermore, coaxial cables have much higher noise immunity, and can offer cleaner and crisper data transmission without distortion or loss of signal.

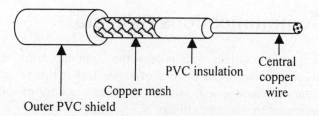

**Figure 17.4.** A coaxial cable.

# Microwave System

Another popular transmission media is microwave. This is a popular way of transmitting data, since it does not incur the expense of laying cables. Microwave systems use very high frequency radio signals to transmit data through space. However, at microwave frequencies, the electromagnetic waves cannot bend or pass obstacles like hill. Hence, it is necessary for microwaves transmission to be in a line-of-sight. In other words, the transmitter and receiver of a microwave system, which are mounted on very high towers, should be in a line-of-sight. This may not be possible for very long distance transmission. Moreover, the signals become weaker after traveling a certain distance and require power amplification.

In order to overcome the problems of line-of-sight and power amplification of weak signals, microwave systems use repeaters at intervals of about 25 to 30 kms in between the transmitting and receiving stations (see Figure 17.5). The first repeater is placed in line-of-sight of the transmitting station and the last repeater is placed in line-of-sight of the receiving station. Two consecutive repeaters are also placed in line-of-sight of each other. The data signals are received, amplified, and retransmitted by each of these stations.

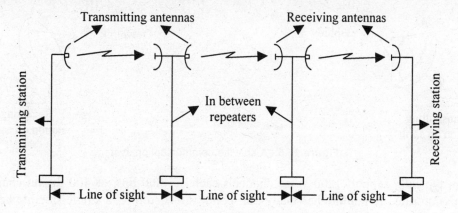

**Figure 17.5.** A microwave communication system.

Microwave systems permit data transmission rates of about 16 Giga (1 Giga = $10^9$) bits per second. Furthermore, it can carry literally thousands of voice channels at the same time. The link can support 250,000 voice channels. The initial installation cost of microwave links being very high, they are mostly used to link big cities with heavy telephone traffic between them.

# Communications Satellite

The main problem with microwave communication is that the curvature of the earth, mountains, and other structures often block the line-of-sight. Due to this reason, several repeater stations are normally required for long distance transmission, which increases the cost of data transmission between two points. This problem is overcome by using satellites.

A communication satellite is basically a microwave relay station placed in outer space. These satellites are launched either by rockets or space shuttles, and are precisely positioned 36,000 kms above the equator with an orbit speed, which exactly matches the earth's rotation speed. Since a satellite is positioned in a geosynchronous orbit, it is stationary relative to earth, and always stays over the same point on the ground. This allows a ground station to aim its antenna at a fixed point in the sky. Each satellite can receive and retransmit signals to slightly less than half of the earth's surface. Therefore, at least three satellites are needed in geosynchronous orbit to provide worldwide data transmission service. Hundreds of satellites are now in orbit to handle international and domestic data, voice, and video communications needs. The INSAT series of Indian satellites are positioned in outer space in a manner to be accessible from any place in India.

As shown in Figure 17.6, in satellite communication, microwave signal at 6 GHz or 14 GHz (read as gigahertz = $10^9$ Hz) is transmitted from a transmitter on earth to the satellite positioned in space. By the time this signal reaches the satellite, it becomes weak due to 36,000 kms travel. A transponder, which is mounted on the satellite, amplifies the weak signal and transmits it back to the earth at a frequency of 4 GHz or 11 GHz. This signal is received at the receiving station on the earth. It may be noted that the retransmission frequency is different from the transmission frequency to avoid the interference of the powerful retransmission signal with the weak incoming signal.

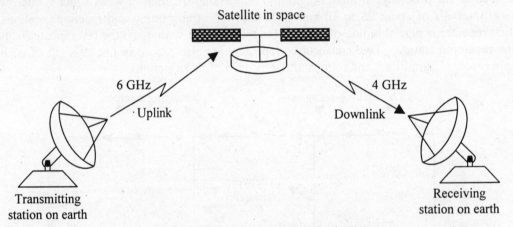

**Figure 17.6.** A satellite communication system.

A transponder can typically support 1200 voice channels each of 4800 bps, or 400 digital channels each of 64 Kbps data transmission rate. A satellite has many transponders. Therefore, a single satellite has enormous data communication capability.

The use of 4 GHz to 6 GHz band of frequencies for transmission and retransmission of microwave signals in a satellite communication system is called the *C-band transmission*. On the other hand, the use of 11 GHz to 14 GHz band of frequencies is called the *$K_u$-band transmission*.

To enable a large number of users to benefit from satellite communication, it was realized that the size and cost of the receive-transmit earth stations has to be considerably reduced, so that one can easily install a private earth station. To meet this requirement, smaller dish antennas, having lower power transmitters and receivers, have been built for installation at users' sites. These dish antenna systems are popularly known as *VSATs* (*Very Small Aperture Terminals*). The aperture refers to the diameter of the dish antenna, which is about 1 to 2 meters.

Satellite communication systems have the following advantages:

1. A satellite, which is essentially a microwave relay station visible from any point of a very large area, can be used for data transmission between any two randomly chosen points in that area.

2. Data transmission costs are independent of the distance between two points as long as the two points are within the area covered by the satellite.

3. A satellite having many transponders has enormous data communication capability.

4. Error detection is trivial in a satellite communication system because a transmitting station can receive back its own transmission and check whether the satellite has transmitted the information correctly. If not, it can retransmit the data.

A satellite communication system, however, suffers from the following disadvantages:

1. The initial cost of placing a satellite into its orbit is very high.

2. Owing to the travel of microwave signal from the sending earth station to the satellite and then back to the receiving earth station, there is a 270 msec propagation delay between the sender and receiver of any information.

3. The manner in which a satellite communication system works, any data sent to the satellite for transmission, automatically gets broadcast to all receiving stations within the satellite's range. Hence, special security measures are needed to prevent unauthorized tampering of information.

4. Atmospheric disturbances, like thunder and lightening, affect the $K_u$-band transmission of a satellite communication system. Hence, C-band transmission is recommended during bad weather.

# Optical Fibers

Optical fibers are hair-thin threads of glass or plastic, which can serve as a data transmission medium as copper wires or coaxial cables. The basic difference is that optical fibers transmit light signals instead of electrical signals. Because light travels much faster than electricity, optical fibers can transmit data at much higher speed than copper wires or coaxial cables, and also with no significant loss of intensity over very long distances.

Optical fibers are made of glass, plastic or silica. Plastic fibers are least efficient, but tend to be cheaper and more rugged. Glass or silica fibers are much smaller, and their lower attenuation makes them more suited for very high capacity channels.

Physically, a fiber-optic cable consists of three concentric layers – the inner core, a cladding around it, and the outer protective coating. The inner core, which has a diameter of 8 to 200 micrometers, consists of a bunch of optical fibers. The cladding around it is made of plastic or glass, and has a refractive index less than that of the core. The characteristics of light propagation depend primarily on the fiber size, its construction, the refractive index profile, and the nature of the light source. The outer protective coating is made up of plastic.

The main components of an optical fiber communication system are shown in Figure 17.7. Towards its source side is a converter, which converts electrical signals into light waves. The converter uses either a light-emitting diode (LED) or a laser diode to convert electric signals into light signals. These light waves are then transmitted over the optical fiber to the receiver's end. At the receiver's end, another converter is placed, which detects the light waves and converts them back to electrical signals. It uses photoelectric diodes for this purpose. These electric signals are then amplified using an amplifier, and sent to the receiver.

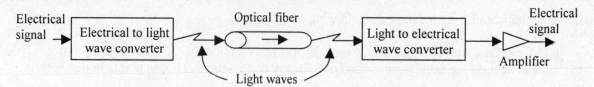

Figure 17.7. An optical fiber communication system.

Optical fibers have the following advantages:

1. **Large bandwidth.** Optical fibers can transmit massive amounts of data at very high speed and long distances. They can have 10 to 100 times greater bandwidths than the best coaxial cables. Their bandwidths are typically in the range of 200 MHz per Km to 3 GHz per Km. A fiber-optic cable consisting of a bunch of 10 optical fibers can accommodate more than 200,000 voice channels.

2. **Low loss.** As compared to electrical signals, light signals can travel at very high speed with no significant loss of intensity over long distances. In case of use of data transmission medium, which use electrical signals for transmitting data, such as copper wires or coaxial cables, electrical signals have to be intercepted and amplified by repeaters at short intervals along the way. Light signals flowing through a fiber-optic cable also must be amplified, but much less as compared to that of electrical signals. The implication is that signal repeaters need not be placed so close together, which reduces the cost of an optical fiber communication system.

3. **Immunity to electromagnetic interference.** Because they are made of insulators, optical fiber transmissions are not affected by magnetic or electrical interference, which can cause errors in other media, especially in twisted-pair wire. Consequently, optical fiber communication systems have the potential for reducing costs associated with complex error checking and correction mechanisms, which must be used with media that are affected by electromagnetic interference.

4. **Small size and lightweight.** Fiber optic cables are much smaller in size and lighter in weight than copper wires or coaxial cables. For example, a fiber optic cable with a core and cladding of 0.125 mm diameter and 3.5 mm outer protective coating has the same information carrying capacity as 900 twisted copper wire pairs with an 8 cm outer diameter and weighing 100 times as much. Size and weight are important factors when considering conduits running under overcrowded city streets. In some large cities there simply is no room for additional bulky copper wires. In this case, the use of smaller and lighter fiber optic cables is very effective.

5. **Security.** Optical fiber offers increased security against unauthorized tampering of information, since it is extremely difficult and expensive to tap optical signals.

6. **Safety and electrical insulation.** Optical fibers, being insulators, provide electrical isolation between the source and the destination. Hence, they present no electrical spark hazards and can be safely used in those places where it is unsafe to use electrical conductors.

7. **Analog and digital signals transmission.** Both analog and digital signals can be transmitted by the use of optical fibers. In analog transmission the light intensity is varied continuously. On the other hand, in digital transmission the light source is turned on or off.

Optical fibers, however, suffer from the following disadvantages:

1. Optical fibers, being fragile, cannot be turned at sharp corners. They can turn only those corners, which have radius of at least a few inches. This creates problem in the physical laying of the fiber optic cable.

2. Aligning and joining two fiber optic cables is not so simple and easy as for twisted copper wire pairs or coaxial cables. It requires special equipment to do so.

Optical fibers are already being widely used for data transmission among computers. Their advantages are making them the transmission medium of choice for many applications, which involve telephones, televisions and computers.

# DIGITAL AND ANALOG DATA TRANSMISSION

Data is propagated from one point to another by means of electrical signals, which may be in digital or analog form. As shown in Figure 17.8(a), in an analog signal, the transmitted power varies over a continuous range, for example, sound, light and radio waves. The amplitude (v) of analog signals is measured in volts and its frequency (f) in hertz (Hz). The higher is the frequency of the signal, the more number of times it crosses the time axis. However, a digital signal is a sequence of voltage pulses represented in binary form (see Figure 17.8(b)).

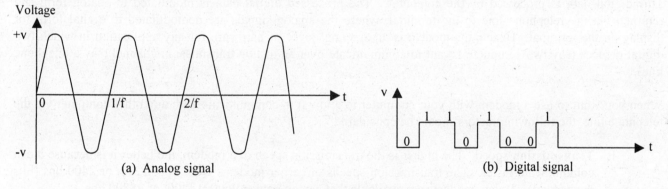

**Figure 17.8.** Analog and digital signals.

Computer generated data is digital, whereas the telephone lines used for data communication in computer networks are usually meant for carrying analog signals. When digital data is to be sent over an analog facility, the digital signals must be converted to analog form. The technique by which a digital signal is converted to its analog form is known as *modulation*. The reverse process, that is, the conversion of analog signal to its digital form, at a destination device, is called *demodulation*.

## Modulation Techniques

Modulation is most often used for superimposing digital data on analog waves. There are three forms of modulation – amplitude, frequency and phase modulation. They are discussed below.

1. **Amplitude Modulation (AM).** Two binary values (0 and 1) of digital data are represented by two different amplitudes of the carrier signal, keeping the frequency and phase constant. On voice grade lines, it is used up to 1200 bits per second. However, amplitude modulated signals are sensitive to impulse noises, which arise due to electrical sparks near the transmission line.

2. **Frequency Modulation (FM).** Two binary values of digital data are represented by two different frequencies, while the amplitude and phase are kept constant. Also known as *frequency shift keying* (FSK), this method is less susceptible to error than amplitude modulation. Another advantage of this method is that it is easier to design devices based on FSK because discrimination between two frequencies is simpler than detecting phase changes. Hence, for medium speed communications (1200 to 2400 bits per second), the FSK scheme is preferred.

3. **Phase Modulation (PM).** Two binary values or digital data are represented by the shift in phase of the carrier signal. That is, a sine wave with phase $= 0^0$ represents a digital 1, and a sine wave with phase $= 180^0$ represents a digital 0. This technique is more noise resistant and efficient than both amplitude modulation and frequency modulation. For higher speed transmission of 9600 bits per second, phase modulation is more reliable and is preferred to other methods.

# Modems

The process of modulation and demodulation, that is, the conversion of digital data to analog form and vice-versa, is carried out by a special device called a *modem* (**mo**dulator/**dem**odulator). Hence, when an analog facility is used for data communication between two digital devices (say a terminal and a computer), two modems are required, one near each digital device. As shown in Figure 17.9, the digital signal generated at the terminal is converted to analog form by the modulator of the modem placed near it. The analog signal is transmitted through the telephone line, which is converted to digital form by the demodulator of the modem placed near the computer. This digital data is processed by the computer. The processed digital data is modulated to analog form and returned via the telephone line to the terminal, where the analog signals are demodulated to digital form for display on the terminal. Hence, the modem is an essential piece of hardware for any application in which two digital devices (say two computers) want to communicate over an analog transmission channel (say a telephone line).

When you want to use a modem with your computer to allow it to communicate with any other computer via the telephone line, the following factors should be considered:

1. **Transmission speed.** The higher is the transmission speed of a modem, the better it is because it can communicate faster. The transmission speeds of earlier modems were 300, 1200, or 2400 bps (bits per second). Today, modems are available that can operate at 9600, 14400, or 28800 bps.

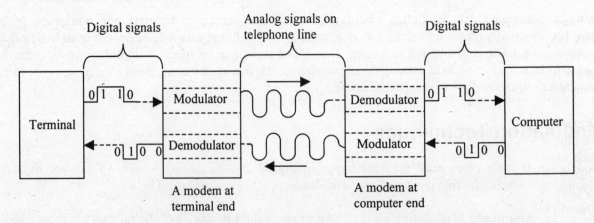

**Figure 17.9.** Illustrating the use of modems in data communications.

2. **Internal versus external.** Modems are of two kinds, internal and external. An internal modem is an optional add-on circuit board, which plugs into one of the computer's expansion slots. It gets its power from the computer's expansion bus. It is manufactured and supplied by the computer manufacturer itself. An external modem, on the other hand, is a separate box, which contains the circuitry and logic to modulate data signals. It has its own power supply, on/off switch, and front-panel LCDs to indicate its status. For this reason, external modems are slightly more expensive. An external modem is connected to the computer via a serial port.

3. **Facsimile facility.** Some modems, known as *FAX modems*, are capable of emulating a FAX machine in addition to performing the functions of a regular modem. A computer equipped with a FAX modem can send/receive text and images as a FAX to/from a remote FAX machine, or another computer equipped with a FAX modem. FAX modems can be of external or internal type.

## Analog versus Digital Transmission

If data is sent over long distances, the analog signal can become weak and distorted. To avoid this, *amplifiers* are used along communication lines between modems. An amplifier used in a communication system is similar to the amplifier used in a home stereo system – it strengthens or amplifies a weak signal.

Today, signals are also sent in digital mode. In this case, modems are not needed. When digital mode of transmission is used over long distances, a *repeater* is used to receive and then transmit the signal. Like an amplifier, the purpose of a *repeater* is to strengthen a weak digital signal over long distances.

Digital transmission of digital data is preferred to analog transmission of digital data due to the following reasons:

1. Lower cost,

2. No modems required,

3. Higher transmission speeds possible, and

4. Lower error rate (higher reliability).

# DATA TRANSMISSION SERVICES

We saw that there are many different types of data transmission media, which may be used for transmission of data from one point to another. In practice, transmission of data from one computer system to another often involves several data transmission media, which together constitute the data transmission path between the sender and receiver computers. For example, the data transmission path between two computers, which are located far away from each other, might be constituted of copper wire, fiber optic cable and communication satellite.

Organizations may afford to lay their own communication channels in a smaller geographical area, such as within a building or a campus. However, it becomes impractical for organizations to do so in a larger geographical area, such as between two cities or two countries. It is also impractical for them to set their own satellites in orbit. Therefore, organizations hire the services of data transmission service providers (popularly known as *common carriers*) for their data communications needs. VSNL (Videsh Sanchar Nigam Limited), BSNL (Bharat Sanchar Nigam Limited) and MTNL (Mahanagar Telephone Nigam Limited) are a few such common carriers in India, whereas AT&T, MCI, Western Union and GTE are a few such common carriers in the USA. The various types of services offered by the common carriers are:

1. **Dial-up line.** Dial-up line (also known as *switched line*) is a service, which operates in a manner similar to a telephone call. That is, a user of a computer willing to communicate with a remote computer first makes a connection request by dialing up the remote computer. A circuit is then established between the two computers via the telephone company's switching system. The modem attached to the user's computer then sends and receives data over the telephone line. Just as in the case of a telephone call, the charge for data transmission service in this case depends on the duration of communication (circuit establishment), and the distance between the two computers.

2. **Leased line.** Leased line (also known as *private line* or *dedicated line*) is a special conditioned telephone line, which directly and permanently connects two computers. It can be used for both voice and data transmissions. Hence, if an organization has two offices in two different cities, it is often cheaper for the organization to acquire its own leased line between the two offices, which can be used by the organization for all its voice (telephone calls) and data transmissions between the two offices. The charges for a leased line are often based on channel capacity (bps) and distance (air miles).

3. **Integrated Services Digital Network (ISDN).** The ISDN is a telephonic system, which provides digital (not analog) telephone and data services. As it supports digital services (including digitized voice), the ISDN telephone users enjoy noise-free, CD-quality, sound. Moreover, with the ISDN, no modem is necessary because it supports digital transmission of all types of data (including voice). This also results in very short call set-up time between two ISDN subscribers.

   The main factor that led to the development of the ISDN was the adoption of digital transmission by many public telephone systems. Voice traffic in such networks is encoded using pulse-code modulation at 64 Kbps. Naturally, these networks could also carry data, resulting in integrated digital networks (IDN).

   Based on the transmission and switching capabilities, the ISDNs are currently of two types – narrowband ISDN and broadband ISDN. *Narrowband ISDN* is based on 64 Kbps bit-streams that are combined into higher-capacity "trunks" using time-division multiplexing. For example, 32 64-Kbps channels can be combined into one 2-Mbps channel. The narrowband ISDN, however, cannot support the requirements of several types of data services, especially those needed for multimedia applications. For example, the bandwidth required for full-definition digital video is in the 100 Mbps range. To handle this sort of traffic, as well as bursts of data traffic from computers, *broadband ISDN* (often referred to as B-ISDN) was introduced. B-ISDN is based on optical fibers and asynchronous time-division multiplexing. The advantage of asynchronous time-division multiplexing over conventional time-division multiplexing is that it allows the total bandwidth available to be divided between contending activities in a much more flexible way.

   ISDN has become so popular that a term to describe the standard analog service has been coined: *Plain Old Telephone Service* (*POTS*).

4. **Value Added Network (VAN).** Some companies specialize in providing value added data transmission service. The value added over and above the standard services of the common carriers may include electronic mail, data encryption/decryption, access to commercial databases, and code conversion for communication between incompatible computers. These companies normally lease dedicated lines of a common carrier, do value addition to enhance the communication facilities, and then sell that enhanced service. This type of service is popularly known as *value-added network* (*VAN*) service.

# COMMUNICATION PROCESSORS

In a data communications network, the task of network designers is to select and coordinate the network components in a manner to move the necessary data to the right place, at the right time, with a minimum of errors, and at the lowest possible cost. A number of communication processors (typical micro- or mini- computers) are used by network designers to achieve these goals. The functions of some of the commonly used communication processors are briefly described below.

## Multiplexers

There are many applications in which several terminals are connected to a computer. If each terminal is operating at 300 bits per second over a communication line (channel), which can operate at 9600 bits per second, we see a very inefficient operation. It has been found that the capacity of a channel exceeds that required for a single signal. A channel is an expensive resource. Hence, for its optimal utilization, the channel can be shared to simultaneously transmit multiple signals over it. The method of dividing a physical channel into multiple logical channels to enable a number of independent signals to be simultaneously transmitted on it is known as *multiplexing*. The electronic device, which performs this task is known as a *multiplexer*.

A multiplexer takes several data communication lines or signals, and converts them into one data communication line or signal at the sending location. For example, as shown in Figure 17.10, there may be 4 terminals connected to a multiplexer. The multiplexer takes the signals from the 4 terminals, and coverts them into one

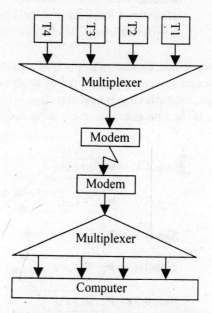

**Figure 17.10.** A multiplexed system.

large signal, which can be transmitted over one communication line. Then, at the receiving location, a multiplexer takes the one large signal, and breaks it into the original 4 signals. Without multiplexers, you would have to have 4 separate communication lines.

Hence, with multiplexing it is possible for a single transmission medium to concurrently transmit data between several transmitters and receivers. There are two basic methods of multiplexing channels. They are frequency-division multiplexing and time-division multiplexing.

1. **Frequency-Division Multiplexing (FDM).** In FDM, the available bandwidth of a physical medium is split up (divided) into several smaller, disjoint logical bandwidths. Each of the component bandwidths is used as a separate communication line (channel). Figure 17.11 illustrates the process of FDM.

   The best example of FDM is the way we receive various stations in a radio. Each radio station is assigned a frequency range within a bandwidth of radio frequencies. Several radio stations may be transmitting speech signals simultaneously over the physical channel, which is "ether" in this case. A radio receiver antenna receives signals transmitted by all the stations. Finally, the tuning dial in the radio is used to isolate the signal of the station tuned. In FDM, the signals to be transmitted must be analog signals. Hence, digital signals must be converted to analog form, if they are to use FDM.

2. **Time-Division Multiplexing (TDM).** In TDM, the total time available in the channel is divided between several users, and each user of the channel is allotted a time slice (a small time interval), during which he/she may transmit a message. That is, multiple data streams belonging to different users are interleaved into one data stream at the sending end of the channel. At the receiving end, a demultiplexer is used to reassemble individual chunks of messages, sent by the users, into full messages. Figure 17.12 shows multiplexing of three different signals using TDM. The same idea may be extended for multiplexing several signals.

Although TDM may be used to multiplex digital or analog signals, its usage is more appropriate for digital data transmission. It is also very much suitable for communication between computers because such communications occur in short fast bursts. Besides this, TDM is generally more efficient as more subchannels can be derived. It is up to the network designers to allocate time slots to different channels. It is common to have 32 low-speed terminals connected to one high-speed line.

Whether or not to use multiplexing usually depends upon economics. The cost of high-speed modems and multiplexers is very high compared to the cost of low-speed lines. However, if line costs are high due to long distances, multiplexing is cost effective. One serious disadvantage with multiplexing relates to a transmission line failure. If the line goes out, everything is dead. With individual lines, only one terminal is likely to be lost.

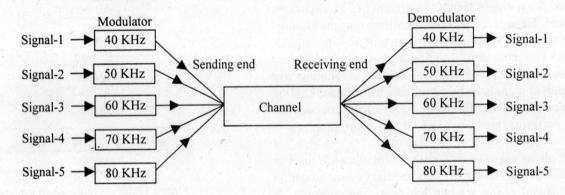

**Figure 17.11.** Illustrating frequency-division multiplexing.

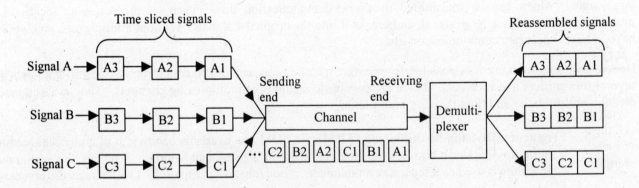

**Figure 17.12.** Illustrating time-division multiplexing.

# Concentrators

A concentrator performs the same function as a multiplexer, but concentrators have the ability to actually reduce the number of signals. For example, 100 signals from different devices coming into the concentrator could leave as only 70 or 80 signals. The signals are concentrated to form a fewer number of signals. This requires intelligence. This intelligence normally takes the form of microprocessors or even minicomputers. Hence, a concentrator is an intelligent multiplexer.

The advantage of using a concentrator is that devices of varying speeds and types are connected to the concentrator, which in turn is connected to the host computer by high-speed lines. Concentrators are especially useful where data communication cost is high, such as long-distance international communications. In general, concentrators are more expensive than multiplexers.

## Front-End Processors (FEP)

If information is to be moved from point-to-point in a computer network, some type of control is necessary. Network processing (also known as communications processing) is the control of information movement between the various locations of a network. This is a substantial task.

In the early network days, the communications-processing job was handled by the main computer. This began to place heavy additional loads on the CPU. Hence, the ability of the computer to do information processing, i.e., the job for which it was intended, was seriously degraded. Front-end processors were designed to solve this problem (see Figure 17.13).

A front-end processor is usually installed in the same location as the main computer. Its primary purpose is to offload communications processing task from the main computer, thereby, the main computer can be dedicated to applications and data processing jobs. It virtually acts like an intelligent terminal, or like a secretary/receptionist to the main computer.

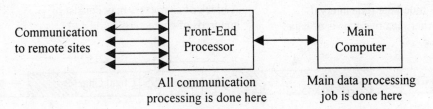

**Figure 17.13.** Illustrating the use of a front-end processor.

## ASYNCHRONOUS AND SYNCHRONOUS TRANSMISSION

Data transmission on a communication line is normally carried out in two different modes – asynchronous and synchronous. In *asynchronous* transmission, data is transmitted character by character at irregular intervals. That is, the sender can send a character at any convenient time, and the receiver will accept it. This is the characteristic of many terminals. When a terminal is connected to a computer, and an operator manually presses keys on the terminal, the time spent between successive keystrokes would vary.

In order to enable the receiver to recognize a character when it arrives, the transmitter "frames" each character. Preceding the character is a *start bit*, and following the character will be one or two (depending upon the system) *stop bits*. Hence, for the 7-bit ASCII code, for each character the transmitter transmits the seven character bits, one parity bit, one start bit, and one or two stop bits, for a total of either 10 or 11 bits. The concept of the character framed by start-stop bits is illustrated in Figure 17.14(a). Note that in asynchronous transmission, the time between transmitting any two characters can be zero or of any length. Hence, the computer might send a continuous stream of characters to the terminal, or characters keyed in by a terminal operator can be sent to the computer as and when the operator keys in a new character.

Asynchronous transmission is well suited to many keyboard type terminals. The advantage of this method is that it does not require any local storage at the terminal or the computer, because transmission takes place character by character. Hence, it is cheaper to implement. However, since the transmission line is idle during the time intervals between transmitting characters, the idle time of the transmission line may be a matter of concern, if the line cost is high. Even though less efficient than synchronous transmission, it is also used with devices such as printers, simply to reduce cost.

*Synchronous* mode of data transmission involves blocking a group of characters in somewhat the same way records are blocked on magnetic tape. Each block is then framed by header and trailer information. The header consists of synchronization information, which is used by the receiving device to set its clock in synchronism with the sending end clock. The header also contains information to identify the sender and receiver. Following the header is a block of characters, which contains the actual message to be transmitted [see Figure 17.14(b)]. The number of characters in a block may be variable, and may consist of hundreds of characters. The message characters in the block are terminated by a trailer. The trailer contains an end of message character, followed by a check character to aid detection of any transmission error. Hence, with synchronous transmission, entire blocks of characters are framed and transmitted together.

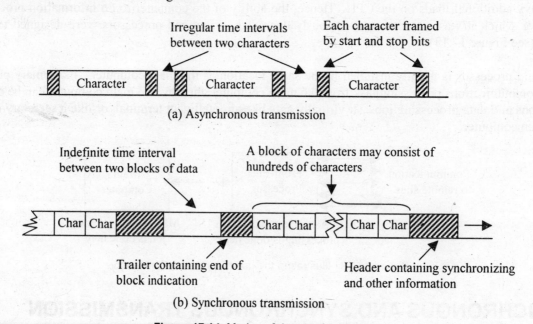

**Figure 17.14.** Modes of data transmission.

Synchronous transmission is well suited to remote communication between a computer and such devices as buffered terminals and printers. Here the logical data block length would be 80 or 132 characters. It is also used for computer-to-computer communication.

The primary advantage of synchronous transmission is its efficiency. It enables the use of much higher data rates than with asynchronous transmission, because it eliminates the need for individual start-stop bits on each character. The main disadvantage of synchronous transmission is the need for local buffer storage at the two ends of the line to assemble blocks, and the need for accurately synchronized clocks at both ends. As a result, synchronous equipment usually costs more.

# SWITCHING TECHNIQUES

In its simplest form, data communication takes place between two devices, which are directly connected by some form of transmission medium – twisted wires, coaxial cables, microwave and satellite links. Often however, it is impractical or uneconomical for two devices to be directly connected. Instead, communication is achieved by transmitting data from source to destination through a network of intermediate nodes. These nodes provide a switching facility, which moves data from node to node until the destination is reached. There are three different methods of establishing communication links between the sender and receiver in a communication network, namely, circuit switching, message switching and packet switching. They are briefly described below.

## Circuit Switching

It is the simplest method of data communication in which a dedicated physical path is established between the sending and receiving stations through the nodes of the network. This method is used to connect two subscribers for a telephone conversation. Computers and terminals connected through a telephone network also use this method of establishing communication path among them.

The method of circuit switching is illustrated in Figure 17.15. Each rectangle represents a switching node of the communication network. When a message is to be communicated, a physical path is established between the sending station and receiving station by physically connecting the incoming and outgoing line of each of the intermediate switching nodes, which fall on the path. Once a circuit is established between the two stations, it is exclusively used by the two parties, and the dedicated physical link between both ends continues to exist, until the connection is terminated either by the sender or the receiver. As soon as the connection is terminated by one of the two stations, the dedicated resources are deallocated and can now be used by other stations also.

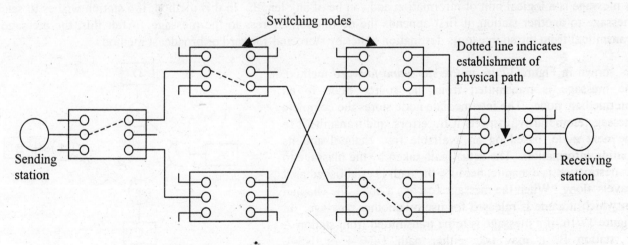

**Figure 17.15.** Illustrating the method of circuit switching.

Hence, circuit switching involves three phases – circuit establishing, data transfer and circuit disconnection. It is used in the Public Switched Telephone Network (PSTN).

## Advantages

1. Once the circuit is established, data is transmitted with no delay other than the propagation delay, which is negligible (typically of the order of 6 msec per 1000 kms).

2. It is suitable for low-speed communication between a terminal and a computer, because the method is simple and requires no special facilities.

3. Since a dedicated continuous transmission path is established, the method is suitable for long continuous transmissions.

4. Since the full capacity of the circuit is available for exclusive use by the connected pair of nodes, the transmission time required to send a message can be known and guaranteed after the circuit has been established. Hence, it is the preferred method for transmission of voice and real-time data.

## Disadvantages

1. Before actual data transfer, the time required to establish a physical link between the two stations is of the order of 10 secs or more, depending on the distance. For many computer applications, such as point of sale verification, this elapse time is too large and unsuitable.

2. Since the physical link is a dedicated one, the channel capacity is dedicated to one source for the entire duration of a connection. Hence, the network resources are not properly utilized.

3. Since communications between computers occur in short fast bursts with long silent periods in between (during which the communication line is not used), the method proves to be very uneconomical when used for communication between computers, which are connected using expensive, high-speed transmission lines.

# Message Switching

A message is a logical unit of information and can be of any length. In this method, if a station wishes to send a message to another station, it first appends the destination address to the message. After this, the message is transmitted from the source to its destination either by store-and-forward or broadcast method.

As shown in Figure 17.16, in the *store-and-forward* method, the message is transmitted from the source node to an intermediate node. The intermediate node stores the complete message temporarily, inspects it for errors, and transmits it to the next node, based on an available free channel and its routing information. The actual path taken by the message to its destination is dynamic, because the path is established as it travels along. When the message reaches a node, the channel on which it came is released for use by another message. In Figure 17.16, if a message is to be transmitted from station A to station B, it may take either path 1-2-3-4 or 1-5-4, depending on the availability of a free output path at that particular moment.

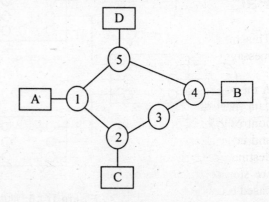

**Figure 17.16.** Illustrating store-and-forward method of message switching.

As shown in Figure 17.17, in the *broadcast* method, the message is broadcast over a common medium, which is known as broadcast channel. All the stations check the destination address of each message as they pass by, and accept only those addressed to them. The routing delays inherent in store-and-forward method are eliminated in this method. However, this method requires that all stations must be connected to the broadcast channel.

## Advantages

1. In message switching, no physical connection is required between the source and the destination as required in case of circuit switching.

2. As channels are used only when messages are transmitted, this method uses the channels very effectively.

## Disadvantages

1. As the message length is unlimited, each switching node must have sufficient storage to buffer messages. In many cases, this storage space may be under-utilized.

2. In message switching, a message is delayed at each node for the time required to receive the message, plus a queuing delay while waiting for an opportunity to retransmit the message to the next node.

3. The method is too slow for interactive/real-time applications. Hence, it is used when message delays are not critical.

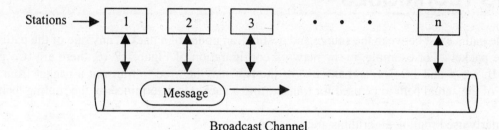

**Figure 17.17.** Illustrating broadcast method of message switching.

# Packet Switching

This method works in a similar fashion as message switching. However, it overcomes the disadvantages of message switching technique, because in this method routing is done on 'packet' basis, not on 'message' basis.

A message is split up into 'packets' of a fixed size (of the order of one or few thousand bits). Besides the block of data (part of a message) to be sent, a packet has a header, which contains the destination and source addresses, control information, message number, number of current and last packet, synchronization bits, acknowledgement and error checking bytes, etc. Like message switching, the packets may be routed from the sender node to the destination node either by store-and-forward or broadcast method. In the store-and-forward method, the packets are stored temporarily at the intermediate nodes for error recovery purposes, and are routed to the next node, based on an available free channel. The actual path taken by the packet to its destination is dynamic, because the path is established as it travels along. Hence, it is possible that different packets of the same message can be routed across different paths leading to the same destination, depending upon line availability and congestion.

Packet switching is used in the X.25 public packet network and the Internet.

## Advantages

1. Unlike messages, packets are of small and fixed size. Hence, the storage requirement for buffering the packets at intermediate nodes is minimal.

2. Since the routing is done on packet basis, the intermediate nodes do not have to wait for the entire message. Hence, the transmission is very fast.

3. The method is fast enough for interactive/real-time applications.

4. It is suitable for "bursty" communication among computers, and is widely used in wide area networks.

## Disadvantages

1. Due to the need to buffer each packet at every intermediate node, and to reassemble the packets at the destination node, the overhead incurred per packet is large.

2. There is no guarantee of how long it takes a message to go from its source node to its destination node, because the time taken for each packet depends on the route chosen for that packet, along with the volume of data being transferred along that route.

# ROUTING TECHNIQUES

When multiple paths exist between the source and destination nodes of a packet, any one of the paths may be used to transfer the packet. For example, in the network configuration of Figure 17.16, there are two paths between nodes A and B: 1-5-4 and 1-2-3-4, and any one of the two may be used to transmit a packet from node A to B. The selection of the actual path to be used for transmitting a packet is determined by the routing technique used.

The two popularly used routing algorithms are:

1. **Source routing.** In this method, the source node selects the entire path before sending the packet. That is, all intermediate nodes, via which the packet will be transferred to its destination, are decided at the source node of the packet, and this routing information is included along with the packet.

2. **Hop-by-hop routing.** In this method, each node along the path decides only the next node for the path. That is, each node maintains information about the status of all its outgoing channels and the adjacent nodes, and then selects a suitable adjacent node for the packet and transmits it to that node. The routing decisions are typically based on the channel availability and the readiness of the adjacent nodes to receive and relay the packet.

# NETWORK TOPOLOGIES

The term *network topology* refers to the way in which the nodes (computers or other devices that need to communicate) of a network are linked together. It determines the data paths, which may be used between any pair of nodes in the network. Although the number of possible network topologies is seemingly limitless, the four major ones are star network, ring network, completely connected network, and multi-access bus network.

The choice of network topology for installing a computer network depends upon a combination of factors, such as:

1. The desired performance of the system.

2. The desired reliability of the entire system.

3. Size (number of nodes and their geographical distribution) of the system.

4. Expandability of the system.

5. Cost of the components and services required to implement the network.

6. Availability of communication lines.

7. Delays involved in routing information from one node to another.

# Star Network

Figure 17.18 shows the star arrangement of a computer network, in which multiple computers are connected to a host computer. That is, the computers in the network are not linked directly to each other and can communicate only via the host computer. The routing function is performed by the host computer, which centrally controls communication between any two other computers by establishing a logical path between them.

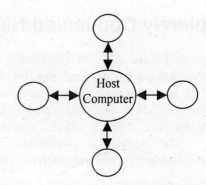

**Figure 17.18.** A star configuration of computer network.

## Advantages

1. Star topology has minimal line cost because only *n-1* lines are required for connecting *n* nodes.

2. Transmission delays between two nodes do not increase by adding new nodes to the network, because any two nodes may be connected via two links only.

3. If any of the local computers fails, the remaining portion of the network is unaffected.

## Disadvantage

1. The system crucially depends on the central node. If the host computer fails, the entire network fails.

# Ring Network

Figure 17.19 shows the circular or ring arrangement of a computer network, in which each computer has communicating subordinates, but there is no master computer for controlling other computers. A node receives data from one of its two adjacent nodes. The only decision a node has to take is whether the data is for its own use. If it is addressed to it, it utilizes it. Otherwise, it merely passes it on to the next node.

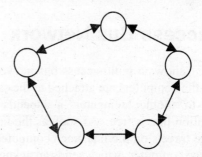

**Figure 17.19.** A ring configuration of computer network.

## Advantages

1. The ring network works well where there is no central-site computer system.

2. It is more reliable than a star network because communication is not dependent on a single host computer. If a link between any two computers breaks down, or if one of the computers breaks down, alternate routing is possible.

## Disadvantages

1. In a ring network, communication delay is directly proportional to the number of nodes in the network. Hence, addition of new nodes in the network increases the communication delay.

2. The ring network requires more complicated control software than star network.

# Completely Connected Network

As shown in Figure 17.20, a completely connected network has a separate physical link for connecting each node to any other node. Hence, each computer of such a network has a direct dedicated link, called a point-to-point link, with all other computers in the network. The control is distributed with each computer deciding its communication priorities.

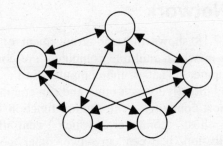

**Figure 17.20.** A completely connected computer network.

## Advantages

1. This type of network is very reliable, as any link breakdown will affect only communication between the connected computers.

2. Each node of the network need not have individual routing capability.

3. Communication is very fast between any two nodes.

## Disadvantage

1. It is the most expensive network from the point of view of link cost. If there are $n$ nodes in the network, $n(n-1)/2$ links are required. Hence, the cost of linking the system grows with the square of the number of nodes.

# Multi-access Bus Network

Figure 17.21 shows a multi-access bus network, in which a single transmission medium is shared by all nodes. That is, all the computers are attached to the same communication line (channel). When a computer wants to send a message to another computer, it appends the destination address to the message and checks whether the communication line is free. As soon as the line becomes free, it broadcasts (places) the message on the line. As the message travels on the line, each computer checks whether it is addressed to it. The message is picked up by the addressee computer, which sends an acknowledgement to the source computer and frees the line. This type of network is also known as 'multipoint' or 'multidrop' or 'broadcasting' network. It is appropriate for use in a local area network where a high-speed communication channel is used and computers are confined to a small area. It is also appropriate when satellite communication is used, because one satellite channel may be shared by many computers at a number of geographical locations.

## Advantages

1. It helps in reducing the number of physical lines.

2. The failure of a computer does not affect the communication among other computers in the network.

3. Addition of new computers to the network is easy.

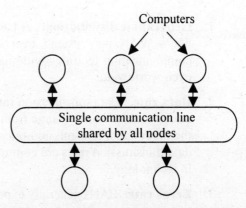

**Figure 17.21.** A multi-access bus network.

## Disadvantages

1. All computers in the network must have good communication and decision-making capability.

2. If the communication line fails, the entire system breaks down.

# Hybrid Network

Different network configurations have their own advantages and limitations. Hence, in reality, a pure star or ring or completely connected network is rarely used. Instead, an organization will use some sort of hybrid network, which is a combination of two or more different network topologies. The exact configuration of the network depends on the needs and the overall organizational structure of the company involved. In some cases, the hybrid network may have components of star, ring, and completely connected networks. A typical hybrid network of this type is shown in Figure 17.22.

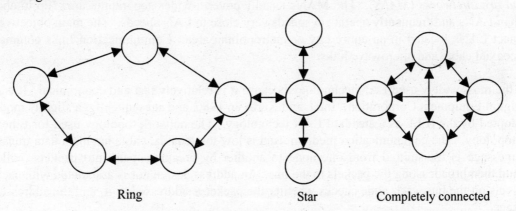

Ring                                        Star                    Completely connected

**Figure 17.22.** A typical hybrid network having a combination of ring, star, and completely connected network configurations.

# NETWORK TYPES (LAN, WAN AND MAN)

Networks are broadly classified into two types: *local-area networks* (*LANs*) and *wide-area networks* (*WANs*). The WANs are also referred to as *long haul networks*. The key characteristics, which are often used to differentiate between these two types of networks, are as follows:

1. **Geographic distribution.** A LAN is restricted to a limited geographic coverage of a few kilometers, but a WAN may extend over several thousand kilometers. Therefore, LANs typically provide communication facilities within a building or a campus, whereas WANs may operate nationwide or even worldwide.

2. **Data rate.** Data transmission rates are usually much higher in LANs than in WANs. Transmission rates in LANs usually range from 10 Megabit per second (Mbps) to 1 Gigabit per second (Gbps). On the other hand, transmission rates in WANs usually range from 1200 bits per second to 2 Mbps. The data transmission rates are continuously increasing for both LANs and WANs with the advancements in technology.

3. **Error rate.** LANs generally experience fewer data transmission errors than WANs do. Typically, bit error rates are in the range of $10^{-8}$ to $10^{-12}$ with LANs as opposed to $10^{-5}$ to $10^{-7}$ with WANs.

4. **Communication link.** The most common communication links used in LANs are twisted pair, coaxial cable, and fiber optics. On the other hand, since the sites in a WAN are physically distributed over a large geographic area, typical communication links used in WANs are telephone lines, microwave links, and satellite channels.

5. **Ownership.** A LAN is typically owned by a single organization because of its limited geographic coverage. A WAN, however, is usually formed by interconnecting multiple LANs each of which may belong to a different organization.

6. **Communication cost.** The cost to transmit data in a LAN is negligible, since the transmission medium is usually owned by the user organization. However, with a WAN, this cost may be very high because the transmission media used are leased lines or public communication systems, such as telephone lines, microwave links, and satellite channels.

Networks that share some of the characteristics of both LANs and WANs are sometimes referred to as *metropolitan area networks* (*MANs*). The MANs usually cover a wider geographic area (up to about 50 km in diameter) than LANs and frequently operate at speeds very close to LAN speeds. The main objective of MANs is to interconnect LANs located in an entire city or metropolitan area. Communication links commonly used for MANs are coaxial cable and microwave links.

*Ethernet* is the most widely used LAN technology because it is relatively fast and economical. It was introduced by DEC (Digital Equipment Corporation), Intel, and Xerox in 1980, and subsequently, a slightly modified version of it was adopted by the IEEE as a standard LAN technology. The network topology used for Ethernet is multi-access bus topology. The communication medium used is low-loss coaxial cable having a data transfer rate of 10 Mbps. A message is transmitted from one node to another by breaking it up into packets (called *frames* in Ethernet), and then broadcasting the packets to the bus. An address designator is associated with each packet. As a packet travels on the bus, each node checks whether the packet is addressed to it, and the addressee node picks up the message.

The *ARPANET* of the Advanced Research Projects Agency of the U.S. Department of Defense was the first WAN. It connected about 40 universities and research institutions throughout the United States and Europe with about 50 computers, ranging in size from mini-computers to supercomputers. *ERNET* (**E**ducation and **R**esearch **NET**work) is a WAN, which links several education and research institutions in India. *NICNET* (**N**ational **I**nformatics **C**entre's **NET**work) is a WAN, which links several offices of NIC (National Informatics Centre) of India up to district headquarters. Indian Railways also has its own WAN, which links its booking offices across the nation, facilitating the passengers to book tickets on most major trains from anywhere in India. Similarly, international airlines worldwide also link their computers to form a WAN, which facilitates booking of flight tickets on international flights. *SWIFT* is a WAN, which interconnects the computers of International banks to reconcile their accounts and for electronic funds transfer. The Internet (described in the next chapter) is a WAN, which encompasses many LANs and computers across the world.

# COMMUNICATION PROTOCOLS

A *protocol* is a set of formal operating rules, procedures, or conventions that govern a given process. A *communication* or *network protocol*, therefore, describes the rules that govern the transmission of data over communication networks. These rules provide a method for orderly and efficient exchange of data between the sender and receiver, and for the proper interpretation of controls and data, which are transmitted as raw bits and bytes. These rules are embedded in the data communication software.

## Roles of a Communication Protocol

In any computer network, a communication protocol normally performs the following functions for the efficient and error-free transmission of data. It has a separate set of rules (implemented in software) for performing each of these functions.

1.  **Data sequencing.** It refers to breaking a long message into smaller packets of fixed size. Data sequencing rules define the method of numbering (or sequencing) packets to detect loss or duplication of packets, and to correctly identify packets, which belong to the same message.

2.  **Data routing.** Routing algorithms are designed to find the most efficient paths between the source and destination nodes of a message. They can handle varying degree of traffic on the present network configuration with optimal time utilization.

3.  **Data formatting.** Data formatting rules define which group of bits or characters within a packet constitutes data, control, addressing, or other information.

4.  **Flow control.** A communication protocol also prevents a fast sender from overwhelming a slow receiver. It ensures resource sharing and protection against traffic congestion by regulating the flow of data on the communication lines.

5.  **Error control.** These rules are designed to detect errors in messages and to ensure transmission of correct messages. The most common method for correcting errors is to retransmit the erroneous message block. This method requires coordination between the sender and receiver nodes, so that the block having error is discarded by the receiver node and is retransmitted by the sender node.

6.  **Precedence and order of transmission.** These rules ensure that all nodes get a chance to use the communication lines and other resources of the network based on the priorities assigned to them.

7.  **Connection establishment and termination.** These rules define how connections are established, maintained and terminated when two nodes of a network want to communicate with each other.

8.  **Data security.** Providing data security and privacy is also built into most communication software packages. It prevents access of data by unauthorized users.

9.  **Log information.** Several communication software are designed to develop log information, which consists of all jobs and data communications tasks that have taken place. Such information may be used for charging the users of the network based on their usage of the network resources.

# Concept of Layered Protocols in Network Design

Modern computer networks are designed in a modular fashion for easy and efficient handling of the system. They are normally split up into a series of modules, and are logically composed of a succession of layers. Each layer offers certain services to the higher layers, shielding those layers from the details of how the offered services are actually implemented. Each layer has its own set of protocols. A particular layer of one machine communicates only with the corresponding layer of another machine by using the protocols of this layer.

The main reasons for using the concept of layered protocols in network design are as follows:

1.  The protocols of a network are fairly complex. Designing them in layers makes their implementation more manageable.

2.  Layering of protocols provides well-defined interfaces between the layers, so that a change in one layer does not affect an adjacent layer. That is, the various functionalities can be partitioned and implemented independently, so that each one can be changed as technology improves without the other ones being affected. For example, a change in a routing algorithm of a network control program should not affect the functions of message sequencing, which is located in another layer of the network architecture.

3.  Layering of protocols also allows interaction between functionally paired layers in different locations. This concept aids in permitting the distribution of functions to remote nodes.

The terms *protocol suite*, *protocol family*, or *protocol stack* are used to refer to the collection of protocols (of all layers) of a particular network system.

# Network Interface Cards

*Network interface card*, often referred to as *NIC* or *network card*, is a hardware device, which allows a computer to be connected to a network, both functionally and physically. The NIC is a printed circuit board, which is installed on to one of the expansion slots of the computer, and provides a port on the back of the computer to which the network cable is attached. It is one of the several add-on cards (expansion boards) that the computer may have.

As the NIC is connected directly to the computer's I/O bus, the design of a NIC is specific to the computer's I/O bus hardware, the computer's operating system, and the network's communication protocol. The network's communication protocol is embedded in the NIC's ROM. Hence, there are different NICs for different networks, even for the same computer. For example, if a computer is to be connected to an Ethernet LAN, it must be equipped with an Ethernet network card, and if it is to be connected to an ATM network, it must be equipped with an ATM network card.

# The OSI Model

The initial computer networks had their own set of standards and conventions that were quite hardware oriented. Each manufacturer used to develop its own communication protocols for its networks. For example, IBM launched SNA (Systems Network Architecture) in 1974. Similarly, DEC (Digital Equipment Corporation) launched its network in 1980 for use on the DEC range of computers. The architecture of DECNET (Digital Equipment Corporation Network) is known as DNA (Digital Network Architecture). Like SNA, it is a private network architecture oriented only to DEC hardware. Other telecommunication protocols are BNA (Burroughs Network Architecture) by Burroughs Incorporation, DSN (Distributed Systems Network) by Hewlett Packard,

PRIMENET (Prime Computers Network) by Prime Incorporation, etc. Hence, the data communication protocols of one network were not compatible with any other network. Moreover, standards of the same network architecture also kept changing from time to time. For example, earlier versions of SNA were not compatible with its subsequent versions. Such incompatibilities started creating bottleneck in the efficient and proper utilization of network resources.

This problem was recognized by the International Standards Organization (ISO), which established a subcommittee to develop an international standard on network architectures. The result was the *Open System Interconnection* (OSI) model, which is a framework for defining standards for linking heterogeneous computers in a packet switched network. Hence, the standardized OSI protocols made it possible for any two heterogeneous computer systems, located anywhere in the world, to easily communicate with each other.

The OSI model is also designed in a highly structured way. Its architecture is shown in Figure 17.23. It is a seven-layer architecture in which a separate set of protocols is defined for each layer. Hence, each layer has an independent function and deals with one or more specific aspects of the communication. The roles of the seven layers are briefly described below.

In actual implementation of the seven layers, the first three layers are likely to be in hardware, the next two layers in the operating system, the presentation layer in library subroutines in the user's address space, and the application layer in the user's program.

## Physical Layer

The physical layer is responsible for transmitting raw bit streams between two nodes. That is, it may convert the sequence of binary digits into electric signals, light signals, or electromagnetic signals, depending on whether the two nodes are on a cable circuit, fiber-optic circuit, or microwave/radio circuit, respectively. Even electrical details, such as how many volts to use for 0 and 1, how many bits can be sent per second, and whether transmission can take place only in one direction or in both directions simultaneously, are decided by the physical layer protocols. In addition, the physical layer protocols also deal with the mechanical details, such as the size and shape of the connecting plugs, the number of pins in the plugs, and the function of each pin. RS232-C is a popular physical layer standard for serial communication lines.

## Data-Link Layer

The physical layer simply transmits the data from the sender's node to the receiver's node as raw bits. It is the responsibility of the data-link layer to detect and correct any errors in the transmitted data. Since the physical layer is only concerned with a raw bit stream, the data-link layer partitions it into frames, so that error detection and correction can be performed independently for each frame. The data-link layer also performs flow control of frames between two sites to ensure that a sender does not overwhelm a receiver by sending frames at a rate faster than the receiver can process.

## Network Layer

The network layer is responsible for setting up a logical path between two nodes for communication to take place. It encapsulates frames into packets, which can be transmitted from one node to another by using a high-level addressing and routing scheme. That is, routing is the primary job of the network layer, and the routing algorithm forms the main part of the network layer protocols. Two popular network layer protocols are the *X.25 Protocol* and the *Internet Protocol* (called *IP*).

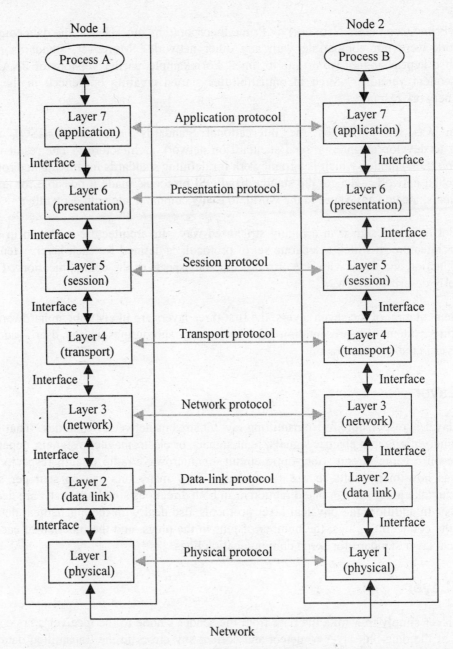

**Figure 17.23.** Layers, interfaces, and protocols in the OSI model. [Reproduced, with permission, from the book titled *Distributed Operating Systems: Concepts and Design* by Pradeep K. Sinha. © 1997 IEEE].

## Transport Layer

The transport layer accepts messages of arbitrary length from the session layer, segments them into packets, submits them to the network layer for transmission, and finally reassembles the packets at the destination. Some packets may be lost on the way from the sender to the receiver, and depending on the routing algorithms used in the network layer, packets may arrive at the destination in a sequence that is different from the order in which they are sent. The transport layer protocols include mechanisms for handling lost and out-of-sequence packets. For this, the transport layer records a sequence number in each packet, and uses the sequence numbers for detecting lost packets and for ensuring that messages are reconstructed in the correct sequence. The two most popular transport layer protocols are the *Transport Control Protocol* (*TCP*) and the *User Datagram Protocol* (*UDP*).

## Session Layer

The session layer provides means of establishing, maintaining and terminating a dialogue or a session between two end users. It allows the two parties to authenticate each other before establishing a dialog session between them. It specifies dialog type – one way, two way alternate, or two way simultaneous – and initiates a dialog session, if the message is a connection request message. It also provides priority management service, which is useful for giving priority to important and time-bound messages over normal, less-important messages.

## Presentation Layer

The presentation layer provides facilities to covert message data into a form, which is meaningful to the communicating application layer entities. For this, the presentation layer may perform such transformations as encoding and decoding, code conversion, compression and decompression, encryption and decryption, on the message data.

## Application Layer

The application layer provides services that directly support the end users of the network. It is a collection of miscellaneous protocols for various commonly used applications, such as electronic mail, file transfer, remote login, remote job entry, and schemas for distributed databases. Some popular application layer protocols are X.400 (Electronic Mail Protocol), X.500 (Directory Server Protocol), FTP (File Transfer Protocol), and rlogin (Remote Login Protocol).

# Example of Message Transfer in the OSI Model

To illustrate the functions of the various layers of the OSI model, let us consider a simple example of message transmission. With reference to Figure 17.24, let us assume that a process at the sending node wants to send a message $M$ to a process at the receiving node. The sending node's process builds the message $M$ and passes it to the application layer (7) on its machine. The application layer software adds a header ($H_7$) to $M$ and passes the resulting message to the presentation layer (6), via the interface between layers 7 and 6. The presentation layer software performs text compression, code conversion, security encryption, and so on, on the received message, and after adding a header ($H_6$) to it, it passes the resulting message on to the session layer (5). Depending on the type of dialog, the session layer software establishes a dialog between the sender and the receiver processes. It also regulates the direction of message flow. A header ($H_5$) is added to the message at this layer, and the resulting message is passed on to the transport layer (4). The transport layer software now splits the message into smaller units ($M_1$ and $M_2$), called packets, and adds a header ($H_4$) to each packet. These headers contain the sequence numbers of the message packets. The packets are then passed on to the network layer (3). The network layer software makes routing decisions for the received packets, and sets up a logical path between the sending and receiving nodes for transmission of the packets. It then adds a header ($H_3$) to each packet and passes them on to the data-link layer (2). The data-link layer software adds a header ($H_2$) and a trailer ($T_2$) to each of these packets. The trailers contain the checksum of the data in the corresponding packets. The resulting message units are called frames, which are passed on to the physical layer (1). The physical layer software simply transmits the raw bits from the sender's machine to the receiver's machine by using the physical connection between the two machines.

On the receiver's machine, the message data traverses up from the physical layer to the application layer. As the message data traverses to higher-level layers, each layer performs the functions assigned to it, and strips off the headers or trailers added by its peer layer at the sending node. For example, the data-link layer at the receiving machine performs error detection by recalculating the checksum for each frame and comparing it with the checksum in the trailer of the frame. It strips off the header ($H_2$) and the trailer ($T_2$) from the frames, before passing them on to the network layer. The application layer of the receiver's machine finally passes on the message in its original form to the communicating process on the receiver's node. Notice that the software of a particular layer on the sending machine conceptually communicates only with its peer layer on the receiving machine, although physically it communicates only with the adjacent layers on the sending machine. This abstraction is crucial to network design.

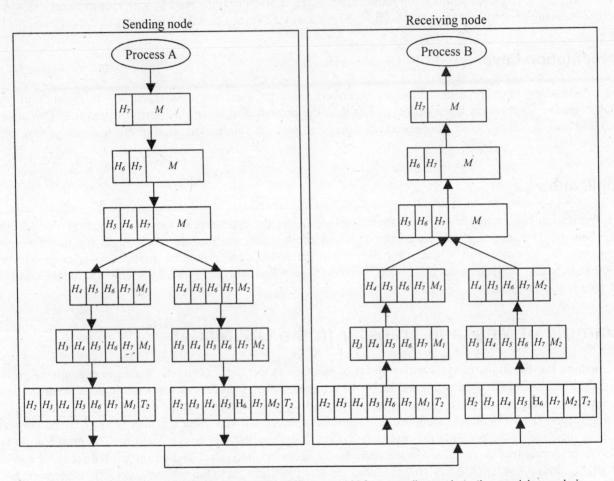

**Figure 17.24.** An example illustrating transfer of message M from sending node to the receiving node in the OSI model: $H_n$, header added by layer n; $T_n$, trailer added by layer *n*. [Reproduced, with permission, from the book titled Distributed Operating Systems: Concepts and Design by Pradeep K. Sinha. © 1997 IEEE].

# INTERNETWORKING TOOLS

Interconnecting two or more networks to form a single network is called *internetworking*, and the resulting network is called an *internetwork*. Therefore, a WAN of multiple LANs is an internetwork.

Internetworks are often heterogeneous networks composed of several network segments, which may differ in topology and protocol. For example, an internetwork may have multiple LANs, some of which may have multi-access bus topology while others may have ring topology; some of these LANs may be using Ethernet technology while others may be using Token Ring technology; and some segments of the network may be using the IP suite while others may be using IBM's SNA (System Network Architecture) protocol suite. Internetworking allows these relatively unrelated networks to evolve into a single working system. That is, the goal of internetworking is to hide the details of different physical networks, so that the resulting internetwork functions as a single coordinated unit.

Internetworking tools are used to interconnect two or more networks to form a single network. The three commonly used internetworking tools are:

1. **Bridges.** Bridges operate at the bottom two layers of the OSI model (physical and data link). Therefore, they are used to connect networks, which use the same communication protocols above the data-link layer, but may or may not use the same protocols at the physical and data-link layers. For example, bridges may be used to connect two networks, one of which uses fiber-optic communication medium and the other uses coaxial cable; or one of which uses Ethernet technology and the other uses Token Ring technology. However, both networks must use the same high-level protocols (e.g., TCP/IP or XNS) to communicate.

2. **Routers**. Routers operate at the network layer of the OSI model. Therefore, routers do not care what topologies or access-level protocols the interconnected network segments use. Since routers use the bottom three layers of the OSI model, they are usually used to interconnect those networks, which use the same high-level protocols above the network layer. Note that the protocols of data-link and physical layers are transparent to routers. Therefore, if two network segments use different protocols at these two layers, a bridge must be used to connect them.

   Unlike bridges, routers do not view an internetwork from end to end. That is, bridges know the ultimate destination of a data, but routers only know which is the next router for the data being transferred across the network. However, routers are smarter than bridges in the sense that they not only copy a data from one network segment to another, but they also choose the best route for the data by using information in a routing table to make this decision. That is, managing traffic congestion is a big plus of routers; they employ a flow control mechanism to direct traffic on to alternative, less congested paths.

3. **Gateways.** Gateways operate at the top three layers of the OSI model (session, presentation, and application). They are the most sophisticated internetworking tools and are used for interconnecting dissimilar networks, which use different communication protocols. That is, gateways are used to interconnect networks, which are built on very different communications architectures. For instance, a gateway may be used to interconnect two networks, one of which uses the IP suite and the other uses the SNA protocol suite. Since networks interconnected by a gateway use dissimilar protocols, protocol conversion is the major job performed by gateways. Additionally, gateways sometimes also perform routing functions.

# WIRELESS NETWORKS

One of the most challenging and interesting recent trends in the computer and communications industries is the integration of wireless communications and computing. The resulting network is referred to as a *wireless computing system*. A wireless computing system enhances the functionality of computing equipment by freeing communication from the location constraints of the wired computing systems.

Wireless computing systems can be broadly classified into the following two categories:

1. **Fixed wireless systems.** These wireless computing systems support little or no mobility of the computing equipment associated with the wireless network. For example, a LAN can be set up using wireless technology to get rid of the hassles of laying cables. The LAN will work as a conventional wired LAN except for the difference that it does not need any cabling to be carried out.

2. **Mobile wireless systems.** These wireless computing systems support mobility of the computing equipment, which the users use to access the resources of the wireless network. In turn, these systems support mobility of users and allow the mobile users to access information from anywhere and at anytime. The resulting computing environment, which is often called *mobile computing* or *nomadic computing*, no longer requires a user to maintain a fixed position in the network, and enables almost unrestricted user mobility. Typical computing equipment used in mobile wireless systems include smart phones, personal digital assistants (PDAs), and pagers with Internet access.

# DISTRIBUTED COMPUTING SYSTEMS

*A distributed computing system* is a configuration in which many independent computer systems (which may be geographically far apart) are connected by a communication network, and in which messages, processing task, programs, data, and other resources are transmitted between cooperating computer systems. Such an arrangement, enables the sharing of many hardware and software resources, as well as information, among several users who may be sitting far away from each other. It also increases the usability of computers by bringing them closer to the end users, and by integrating them into daily business activities at the locations at which these activities take place. The individual computers of a distributed computing system are often referred to as *nodes*.

It is obvious that distributed computing systems are much more complex and difficult to build than traditional centralized systems. The increased complexity is mainly due to the following reasons:

1. The system must be designed in a manner to effectively use and manage a very large number of distributed resources.

2. The system must be designed to enable communication among the various nodes of the system. Special software is usually needed to handle loss of messages during transmission across the network, or to prevent overloading of the network.

3. Special security measures are needed to protect the widely distributed shared resources and services against intentional or accidental violation of access control and privacy constraints.

Despite the increased complexity and the difficulty of building distributed computing systems, the installation and use of distributed computing systems is rapidly increasing. This is mainly because the advantages of distributed computing systems outweigh their disadvantages. The major advantages that have led to the emergence and popularity of distributed computing systems are as follows:

1. **Inherently distributed applications.** Several applications require a distributed computing system for their realization. A few examples of such applications are electronic mail facility, a computerized worldwide airline reservation system, and a computerized banking system in which a customer can deposit/withdraw money from his or her account from any branch of the bank.

2. **Information sharing among distributed users.** In a distributed computing system, information generated by one of the users can be easily and efficiently shared by the users working at other nodes of the system. For example, a project can be performed by two or more users who are geographically far off from each other, but whose computers are part of the same distributed computing system. In this case, although the users are geographically separated from each other, they can work in cooperation, for example, by transferring the files of the project, logging on to each other's remote computers to run programs, and exchanging messages by electronic mail to coordinate the work.

3. **Resource sharing.** Information is not the only thing that can be shared in a distributed computing system. Sharing of software resources, such as software libraries and databases, as well as hardware

resources, such as printers, hard disks, and plotters can also be done in a very effective way among all the computers and the users of a single distributed computing system.

4. **Shorter response times and higher throughput.** Multiple processors of a distributed computing system can be utilized properly for providing shorter response times and higher throughput than a single-processor centralized system. For example, if a computation can be partitioned into a number of subcomputations that can run concurrently, all the subcomputations can be simultaneously run with each one on a different processor of a distributed computing system. Distributed computing systems with very fast communication networks are increasingly being used as parallel processing systems to solve single complex problems rapidly. Another method often used in distributed computing systems for achieving better overall performance is to distribute the load more evenly among the multiple computers by moving jobs from currently overloaded ones to lightly loaded ones.

5. **Higher reliability.** A reliable system prevents loss of information even in the event of component failures. The multiplicity of storage devices and processors in a distributed computing system allows the maintenance of multiple copies of critical information within the system, and the execution of important computations redundantly to protect them against catastrophic failures. With this approach, if one of the processors fails, the computation can be successfully completed at the other processor, and if one of the storage devices fails, the information can still be used from the other storage device.

6. **Extensibility and incremental growth.** It is possible to gradually extend the power and functionality of a distributed computing system by simply adding additional resources (both hardware and software) to the system, as and when the need arises. For example, additional processors can be easily added to the system to handle the increased workload of an organization, which might have resulted from its expansion. Incremental growth is a very attractive feature, because for most existing and proposed applications, it is practically impossible to predict future demands of the system.

7. **Better flexibility in meeting users' needs.** Different types of computers are usually more suitable for performing different types of computations. For example, computers with ordinary power are suitable for ordinary data processing jobs, whereas high-performance computers are more suitable for complex mathematical computations. In a centralized system, the users have to perform all types of computations on the only available computer. However, a distributed computing system may have a pool of different types of computers, in which case, the most appropriate one can be selected for processing a user's job, depending on the nature of the job.

# Points to Remember

1. A *computer network* is a network of geographically distributed multiple computers, connected in a manner to enable meaningful transmission and exchange of information among them. Sharing of information, sharing of resources (both hardware and software), and sharing of processing load, are some of the major objectives of a computer network.

2. The three basic elements of any communication system are a sender (source), which creates the message to be transmitted, a medium, which carries the message, and a receiver (sink), which receives the message.

3. The three modes of transmitting data from one point to another are simplex, half duplex, and full duplex. In *simplex* mode of transmission, communication can

take place in only one direction. A *half duplex* system can transmit data in both directions, but only in one direction at a time. A *full duplex* system allows information to flow simultaneously in both directions.

4. *Bandwidth* is the range of frequencies that is available for the transmission of data. The wider the bandwidth of a communication system, the more data it can transmit in a given period of time.

5. The data transfer rate is measured in a unit called *baud*, which is identical to bits per second.

6. There are several types of physical channels (communication media) through which data can be transmitted from one point to another. Some of the most common data transmission medium are wire pairs,

coaxial cable, microwave system, communications satellite and optical fibers.

7. The technique by which a digital signal is converted to its analog form is known as *modulation*. The reverse process, that is, the conversion of analog signal to its digital form is called *demodulation*.

8. The process of modulation and demodulation, that is, the conversion of digital data to analog form and vice-versa is carried out by a special device called a *modem* (**mod**ulator/**dem**odulator).

9. Data transmission service providers are popularly known as *common carriers*. The various types of services offered by the common carriers are dial-up line, leased line, Integrated Services Digital Network (ISDN), and Value Added Network (VAN).

10. The method of dividing a physical channel into many logical channels, to enable a number of independent signals to be simultaneously transmitted on it, is known as *multiplexing*. The electronic device, which performs this task, is known as a *multiplexer*.

11. The two modes of data transmission on a communication line are asynchronous and synchronous. In *asynchronous transmission*, the sender can send data at any convenient time and the receiver will accept it. On the other hand, in *synchronous transmission*, the sender and receiver must synchronize with each other to get ready for the data transmission before it takes place.

12. The three different methods of establishing communication links between the sender and receiver in a communication network are *circuit switching*, *message switching* and *packet switching*.

13. The selection of the actual path to be used to transmit a packet in a WAN is determined by the *routing* strategy used.

14. The term *network topology* refers to the way in which the nodes of a network are linked together. Although the number of possible network topologies is seemingly limitless, the four major ones are star network, ring network, completely connected network, and multi-access bus network.

15. Based on characteristics such as geographic distribution of nodes, data rate, error rate, and communication cost, networks are broadly classified into two types: LAN and WAN. Networks that share some of the characteristics of both LANs and WANs are sometimes referred to as MANs.

16. A *communication* or *network protocol* describes the rules for transmission of data over communication networks. These rules provide a method for orderly and efficient exchange of data between the sender and receiver, and for the proper interpretation of controls and data, which are transmitted as raw bits and bytes.

17. *Network Interface card*, often referred to as *NIC* or *network card*, is a hardware device, which allows a computer to be connected to a network, both functionally and physically.

18. Computer networks are implemented using the concept of layered protocols. The *OSI model* provides a standard for layered protocols for WANs. The seven layers of the OSI model are physical, data-link, network, transport, session, presentation, and application. Of the available protocol suites for network systems, the Internet Protocol (IP) suite is the most popular and widely used.

19. Interconnecting two or more networks to form a single network is called *internetworking*, and the resulting network is called an *internetwork*. The goal of internetworking is to hide the details of different physical networks, so that the resulting internetwork functions as a single coordinated unit. Tools such as bridges, routers, and gateways are used for internetworking. The Internet is the best example of an internetwork.

20. A *wireless computing system* enhances the functionality of computing equipment by freeing communication from the location constraints of the wired computing systems.

21. Wireless computing systems are of two types – *fixed wireless systems*, which support little or no mobility of the computing equipment associated with the wireless network, and *mobile wireless systems,* which support mobility of the computing equipment, which the users use to access the resources of the wireless network.

22. A *distributed computing system* is a configuration in which many independent computer systems (which may be geographically far apart) are connected by a communication network, and in which messages, processing task, programs, data, and other resources are transmitted between cooperating computer systems. Such an arrangement enables the sharing of many hardware and software resources, as well as information, among several users who may be sitting far away from each other.

# Questions

1. What is a computer network? How is it useful?

2. Identify the basic elements of a communication system and the purpose of each.

3. Differentiate among simplex, half duplex, and full duplex modes of data transmission.

4. Which mode of data transmission is suitable for communication between a terminal and a computer?

5. "A full duplex line is faster since it avoids the delay that occurs in a half duplex circuit." Explain.

6. Explain the terms "bandwidth" and "baud".

7. Differentiate among narrowband, voice band, and broadband communication channels. Give a practical application of each.

8. What is a wire pair? In what situations are they suitable for use in data transmission?

9. What is a coaxial cable? Give some of its practical uses.

10. Explain how microwave systems can be used for communication between two distant stations.

11. How are communications satellites used? What are the possible advantages and limitations of using a communications satellite?

12. What is an optical fiber? How is it used for data communications? What are its advantages?

13. Differentiate between analog and digital transmission of data. Give their advantages and disadvantages.

14. What do you understand by modulation and demodulation?

15. Why is modulation used in signal transmission? Describe the three different forms of modulation.

16. What are modems? What purpose do they serve in data communication systems?

17. Describe some of the common factors to be considered while selecting a modem.

18. What is a repeater? How is it different from an amplifier?

19. When are public telephone lines used to connect a terminal to a computer? Are modems required for this purpose? Why?

20. Explain about the following types of services offered by the common carriers:

    (a) Dial-up line
    (b) Leased line
    (c) Integrated Services Digital Network (ISDN)
    (d) Value Added Network (VAN)

21. What is ISDN? Differentiate between narrowband and broadband ISDN.

22. What is a Value Added Network (VAN)?

23. What is a multiplexer? Explain its function with the help of a diagram.

24. Describe the two basic methods of multiplexing. Give uses of both the methods.

25. List out the differences between FDM and TDM. Which method is suitable for communication between computers and why?

26. What is a concentrator? Justify its use in a data communication system.

27. What is FEP? Illustrate its use.

28. Describe the asynchronous and synchronous modes of data transmission.

29. List out the relative advantages and disadvantages of asynchronous and synchronous modes of data transmission.

30. Explain how circuit switching is used to link the sender and receiver in a communication network. What are the advantages and disadvantages of this method of switching?

31. Explain the store-and-forward method of message switching. Give the advantages and disadvantages of this message switching technique.

32. What is packet switching? Why is this method used for digital data communication between computers?

33. What is routing? Differentiate between source routing and hop-by-hop routing methods.

34. What is meant by network topology? Describe three commonly used network topologies with their relative advantages and disadvantages.

35. What is a hybrid network? Why are they used?

36. Write a short note on multi-access bus network.

37. What is a LAN? What are its main objectives?

38. What is WAN? What is a MAN?

39. Differentiate between a LAN and a WAN. Give one example of each.

40. What is a communication protocol? What are the normal functions performed by these protocols?

41. Why are communication protocols needed in a computer network?

42. What is a network interface card? Explain its usage in a computer system.

43. Why is layering used in the design of communication networks?

44. Describe the layering concepts in the OSI model of network architecture with the functions of each layer.

45. What is meant by internetworking? What are the main issues in internetworking? Explain the difference among the following terms:
    (a) Bridge
    (b) Router
    (c) Gateway

46. What is a wireless computing system? How is it useful?

47. Differentiate between fixed wireless systems and mobile wireless systems.

48. What is a distributed computing system? Why are distributed computing systems gaining popularity?

49. List out the advantages and limitations of a distributed computing system.

50. Write short notes on:
    (a) Data transmission modes
    (b) Data transmission speed

    (c) Data transmission media
    (d) Data transmission services

51. Write short notes on:
    (a) Microwave system
    (b) Communications satellite
    (c) Optical fibers

52. Write short notes on:
    (a) Network interface card
    (b) ISDN
    (c) Value Added Network (VAN)
    (d) Dial-up line
    (e) Leased line

53. Write short notes on:
    (a) Modem
    (b) Multiplexer
    (c) Concentrator
    (d) Front-end processor

54. Write short notes on:
    (a) Switching techniques
    (b) Routing techniques
    (c) Network topologies
    (d) Asynchronous and synchronous transmission

55. Write short notes on:
    (a) LAN versus WAN
    (b) Communication protocols
    (c) Ethernet

56. Write short notes on:
    (a) The OSI model
    (b) Internetworking tools
    (c) Distributed computing systems

# Chapter 18

# The Internet

## DEFINITION (WHAT IT IS?)

The *Internet* is a huge network of computers, which links many different types of computers all over the world. It is a network of networks, which share a common mechanism for addressing (identifying) computers, and a common set of communication protocols for communications between two computers on the network.

## BRIEF HISTORY

The Internet has its root in the ARPANET system of the Advanced Research Project Agency of the U.S. Department of Defense. ARPANET was the first WAN and had only four sites in 1969. The Internet evolved from the basic ideas of ARPANET for interconnecting computers, and was initially used by research organizations and universities to share and exchange information. In 1989, the U.S. Government lifted restrictions on the use of the Internet, and allowed it to be used for commercial purposes as well. Since then, the Internet has rapidly grown to become the world's largest network. It now interconnects more than 30,000 networks, allowing more than 10 million computers, and more than 50 million computer users in more than 150 countries around the world to communicate with each other. The Internet continues to grow at a rapid pace.

## ITS BASIC SERVICES

There are basically four types of services provided by the Internet to its users. These are described below.

# Electronic Mail

The electronic mail service (known as *e-mail* in short) allows an Internet user to send a mail (message) to another Internet user in any part of the world in a near-real-time manner. The message takes anywhere from a few seconds to several minutes to reach its destination, because it must be passed from one network to another, until it reaches its destination.

E-mail service has many similarities with the postal mail service, which all of us are familiar with. All Internet users have an e-mail address, just like all of us have a postal address. Each Internet user has a logical mailbox just like each one of us has a mailbox in our house. When sending a mail to another user, the sender specifies the e-mail address of the receiver just as we write the postal address of the receiver in the postal mail system. The e-mail service delivers an already sent mail into the receiver's mail box. The receiver extracts the mail from the mailbox and reads it at his/her own convenient time just like in a postal mail system. After reading the message, the receiver can save it, delete it, pass it on to someone else, or respond by sending another message back.

Messages in e-mail service can contain not only text documents, but also image, audio and video data. The only restriction is that the data to be sent must be digitized, that is, converted to a computer-readable format.

With e-mail service, the Internet has proved to be a rapid and productive communication tool for millions of users. As compared to paper mail, telephone, and fax, e-mail is preferred by many because of its following advantages:

1. It is faster than paper mail.

2. Unlike the telephone, the persons communicating need not be available at the same time.

3. Unlike fax documents, e-mail documents can be stored in a computer, and can be easily edited using editing programs.

# File Transfer Protocol

The File Transfer Protocol service (known as *FTP* in short) allows an Internet user to move a file from one computer to another on the Internet. A file may contain any type of digital information – text document, image, artwork, movie, sound, software, etc. Hence, anything that can be stored on a computer can be moved with FTP service. Moving a file from a remote computer to ones own computer is known as *downloading* the file, and moving a file from ones own computer to a remote computer is known as *uploading* the file.

By using the FTP service, a file transfer takes place in the following manner:

1. A user executes the *ftp* command on his/her local computer, specifying the address of the remote computer as a parameter.

2. An FTP process running on the user's computer (called FTP client process) establishes a connection with an FTP process running on the remote computer (called FTP server process).

3. The user is then prompted for login name and password to ensure that the user is allowed to access the remote computer.

4. After successful login, the desired file(s) are downloaded or uploaded by using *get* (for downloading) and *put* (for uploading) commands. The user can also list directories, or move between directories of the remote computer, before deciding the file(s) to be transferred.

Notice from the discussion presented above that a user could transfer files to/from a remote computer, only if he/she has access rights for the remote computer. With this restriction, it is almost impossible to provide access rights to the vast number of the users of the Internet to a computer that contains sharable information. The concept of anonymous FTP site is used to overcome this problem. An *anonymous FTP site* is a computer, which allows a user to log in with a username of *anonymous* and a password that is the user's e-mail address. The user can then download files from the computer, which have been stored on it for sharing. Such sites are called *publicly accessible sites* because they can be accessed by any user on the Internet.

Of course, FTP service is also used for more secure file transfer operations. In such cases, a user needs a valid username and password to access a particular computer. This is common; for example, for organizations that wish to let only certain people access their computer.

# Telnet

The telnet service allows an Internet user to log in to another computer somewhere on the Internet. That is, a user can execute the *telnet* command on his/her local computer to start a login session on a remote computer. This action is also called "remote login."

To start a remote login session, the user types the command *telnet* and the address of the remote computer on the terminal of his/her local computer. The user then receives a prompt asking to enter a login name (user ID) and a password to ensure that the user has the access rights for accessing the remote computer. If the user specifies a correct login name and password, he/she gets logged in to the remote computer. Once the login session is established with the remote computer, telnet enters the input mode, and anything typed on the terminal of the local computer by the user is sent to the remote computer for processing.

Some of the common uses of the telnet service are:

1. Using the computing power of the remote computer. The local computer may be an ordinary personal computer and the remote computer may be a powerful super computer.

2. Using a software on the remote computer. The software that the user wants to use may not be available on the local computer.

3. Accessing remote computer's database or archive. The information archive, such as the public database or library resources may be available on the remote computer.

4. For logging in to ones own computer from another computer. For example, if the user is attending a conference in another city and has access to a computer on the Internet, he/she can telnet to his/her own computer and read his/her electronic mails.

# Usenet News

The usenet service allows a group of Internet users to exchange their views/ideas/information on some common topic, which is of interest to all the members belonging to the group. Several such groups exist on the Internet and are called *newsgroups*. For example, the newsgroup named *comp.security.misc* consists of users having interest in computer security issues.

A newsgroup is like a large notice board, which is accessible to all the members belonging to the group. A member, who wants to exchange his/her views/ideas/information with other members, sends a specially formatted message, which is processed and interpreted as a notice to be posted on the notice board by the member's computer, which has an appropriate software running for this purpose. After the processing of the message is over, it can be read (seen) from any member's computer just like a notice posted on a notice board can be read by anyone having access to the notice board.

There are two types of newsgroups – moderated and nonmoderated. In a *moderated newsgroup*, only selected members have the right to directly post (write) a message to the virtual notice board, whereas in a *nonmoderated newsgroup*, any member can directly post a message to the virtual notice board. In a moderated newsgroup, a message sent by an ordinary member first goes to the computer of one of the selected members having the right to directly post a message to the notice board. The message is then checked by this member who decides whether the message is appropriate for being posted, and does any editing that might be required to improve the quality of the message. This member then posts the message on the notice board. After this only, the message becomes readable to (can be seen by) other members.

The main idea of a moderated newsgroup is to ensure the quality of the newsgroup. As no one moderates the quality of the messages of a nonmoderated newsgroup, anyone can post anything. However, members of such newsgroups should be careful in posting a message, because other members may react angrily by sending a flaming message in response to an ill mannered message. To address this issue, the concept of *netiquette* (network etiquette) has arisen, which deals with rules of framing messages that will not hurt others.

# The World Wide Web

The *World Wide Web* (called *WWW* or *W3* in short) is the most popular and promising method of accessing the Internet. The main reason for its popularity is the use of a concept called *hypertext*. Hypertext is a new way of information storage and retrieval, which enables authors to structure information in novel ways. An effectively designed hypertext document can help users rapidly locate the desired type of information from the vast amount of information on the Internet. Hypertext documents enable this by using a series of *links*. A link can be shown on the screen in multiple ways, such as a labeled button, highlighted text, or different color text than normal text if your computer has a color display, or author-defined graphic symbols. A link is a special type of item in a hypertext document, which connects the document to another document that provides more information about the linked item. The latter document can be anywhere on the Internet (in the same document in which the linked item is, in the same computer in which the former document is, or in another computer, which is at the other end of the world). By "connect" we mean that a user simply selects the linked item (using a mouse or key command) and the user almost immediately sees the other document on his/her computer terminal.

The concept of hypertext can be best illustrated with the help of an example. Let us assume that the screen of your computer terminal has the following hypertext document currently displayed on it:

> Pradeep K. Sinha has been involved in the research and development of distributed systems for almost a decade. At present, Dr. Sinha is working at the **Centre for Development of Advanced Computing (C-DAC)**, Pune, India. Before joining C-DAC, Dr. Sinha worked with the **Multimedia Systems Research Laboratory (MSRL) of Panasonic** in Tokyo, Japan.

This hypertext document has the following two links, which are shown on the screen as highlighted (bold and underlined) texts:

1.  Centre for Development of Advanced Computing (C-DAC). Let us assume that this link connects the current document to another document, which gives detailed information about C-DAC, and is located on a computer system at C-DAC in Pune, India.

2.  Multimedia Systems Research Laboratory (MSRL) of Panasonic.  Let us assume that this link connects the current document to another document, which gives detailed information about MSRL of Panasonic, and is located on a computer system at MSRL of Panasonic in Tokyo, Japan.

Now, if you use your mouse to click anywhere on the link ***Multimedia Systems Research Laboratory (MSRL) of Panasonic*** of the displayed document, within a few seconds you will find yourself connected to the computer at MSRL of Panasonic in Tokyo, and displayed on your computer screen will be the document, which gives detailed information about MSRL of Panasonic.

Hypertext documents on the Internet are known as *Web Pages*.  Web Pages are created by using a special language called *HyperText Markup Language (HTML* in short).  HTML is a subset of the more generalized language called *Standard Generalized Markup Language (SGML* in short), which is a powerful language for linking documents for easier electronic access and manipulation.  HTML is becoming a de-facto industrial standard for creating Web Pages.

The WWW uses the client-server model, and an Internet Protocol called *HyperText Transport Protocol (HTTP* in short) for interaction between the computers on the Internet.  Any computer on the Internet, which uses the HTTP protocol, is called a *Web Server*, and any computer, which can access that server, is called a *Web Client*.  The use of the client-server model and the HTTP allows different kinds of computers on the Internet to interact with each other.  For example, a Unix workstation may be the web server and a Windows PC may be the web client, if both of them use the HTTP protocol for transmitting and receiving information.

# WWW BROWSERS

To be used as a web client, a computer needs to be loaded with a special software tool, which is known as *WWW browser* (or *browser* in short).  Browsers normally provide the following navigation facilities to help users save time when they are jumping from server to server while Internet surfing (the process of navigating the Internet to search for useful information):

1.  Unlike FTP and Telnet, browsers do not require a user to remotely log in to a server computer, and then to log out again when the user has finished accessing information stored on the server computer.

2.  Browsers allow a user to specify an URL address of a server computer to facilitate the user to directly visit the server computer's site, and to access information stored on it.  *URL* stands for *Uniform Resource Locator*.  It is an addressing scheme used by WWW browsers to locate sites on the Internet.

3.  Browsers allow a user to create and maintain a personal *hotlist* of favorite URL addresses of server computers, which the user is likely to frequently visit in future.  A user's hotlist is stored on his/her local web client computer.  Browsers provide hotlist commands to allow the user to add, delete, update URL addresses in the hotlist, and to select an URL address of a server computer from the hotlist, when the user wants to visit that server computer.

4.  Many browsers have a "history" feature.  These browsers maintain a history of the server computers visited in a surfing session.  That is, they save (cache) in the local computer's memory, the URL addresses of the server computers visited during a surfing session, so that if the user wants to go back to an already visited server later on (in the same surfing session), the link is still available in the local computer's memory.

5.  Browsers allow a user to download (copy from a server computer to the local computer's hard disk) information in various formats (i.e., as a text file, as an HTML file, or as a PostScript file).  The downloaded information can be later (not necessarily in the same surfing session) used by the user.

For example, downloaded information saved as a PostScript file can be later printed on a PostScript-compatible printer, where even the graphics will be properly reproduced.

# USES OF THE INTERNET

The worldwide scope of the Internet makes it perhaps, the single most valuable tool for use in many significant ways by both non-profit and commercial organizations. Some of the important current strategic uses of the Internet are listed below:

1. **On-line communication.** The electronic mail service on the Internet is extensively used today by computer users around the world to communicate with each other. With this facility, the Internet has proved to be a rapid and productive communication tool for millions of users.

2. **Software sharing.** The Internet provides access to a large number of shareware software development tools and utilities. A few examples of such available shareware tools are compilers, code libraries, mail servers, and operating systems. For example, a set of such shareware tools is available via *ftp* from the Internet site *sunsite.unc.edu*. The Free Software Foundation also provides a wealth of GNU software tools on the Internet, which that can be downloaded free of charge. For more details on the software tools offered by the Free Software Foundation, you can anonymous *ftp* to the Internet site *prep.at.mit.edu*, and look in the directory */pub/GNU*.

3. **Exchange of views on topics of common interest.** The Internet has a number of news groups. Each news group allows a group of users to exchange their views on some topic of common interest. For example, the news group *comp.os.os2.advocacy* contains views about the OS/2 operating system.

4. **Posting of information of general interest.** The Internet is also being extensively used as a large electronic bulletin board on which information of general interest can be posted to bring it to the attention of interested users around the world. Some commonly posted information includes career opportunities, conference and event announcements, and calls for papers for conferences and journals.

5. **Product promotion.** Several commercial organizations are effectively using the Internet services for promoting their products. These organizations make use of WWW server sites, which are focused on disseminating timely information about corporate happenings, product announcements, recent strategic alliances, press releases, and other information of potential interest to existing and prospective customers. For example, *comp.sys.sun.announce* news group contains information about Sun Microsystem's latest product announcements.

6. **Feedback about products.** Commercial organizations are also using the Internet to gather information about user satisfaction of existing products, market opportunities of new products, and ideas for potential new products. This is usually accomplished by putting up an interactive survey application by the organization on a WWW site on the Internet.

7. **Customer support service.** Many organizations are also using the Internet to provide timely customer support. The combined electronic mail, ftp, and other services on the Internet provide all of the enabling tools necessary to provide such first-rate customer support. For example, bugs in fielded software products can be reported to an organization via electronic mail, and bug fixes, minor releases, workarounds, known problems and limitations, and general advice about a product can be made available by an organization to its customers via an *ftp* server.

8. **On-line journals and magazines.** The Internet now has literally thousands of electronic subscriptions, which can be found both for free and low cost. There are many WWW sites on the Internet, which deal with electronic versions of many journals and magazines. For example, the Internet edition of the Times of India newspaper is available at the Internet site

*http://www.timesofindia.com.* Researchers are working in the direction to extend this idea to support full-fledged electronic libraries on the Internet.

9.  **On-line shopping.** The Internet has also facilitated the introduction of a new market concept, which consists of virtual shops. These shops remain open 24 hours all the year round, and are accessible to purchasers all around the world. They provide information about products or services for sale through WWW servers. Using the Internet services, customers submit specific product queries and request specific sales quotes. Through a well-defined authorization and authentication scheme, the Internet services are then used to accept orders placed by the customers, to handle order payments, and to track orders to fulfillment. For example, the Internet site *amazon.com* is a WWW-based bookshop on the Internet, where information on all types of International books can be found and books can be ordered on-line.

10. **Worldwide video conferencing.** Worldwide video conferencing is an emerging service on the Internet, which allows a group of users located around the globe to talk and interact with each other as if they were sitting and discussing in a single room. The parties interacting can see each other talking on their computer screens and can hear each other's voice through a special audio-device fixed in their computers. The CU-SeeMe system developed at Cornell University is an example of an Internet-based video conferencing system. For information on CU-SeeMe, you can *ftp* to the Internet site *gated.cornell.edu* and look in the directory */pub/video/CU-SeeMe.FAQ.76.txt.*

# Points to Remember

1.  The *Internet* is a huge network of computers, which links many different types of computers all over the world. It is a network of networks, which share a common mechanism for addressing (identifying) computers, and a common set of communication protocols for communications between two computers on the network.

2.  The four basic services provided by the Internet to its users are electronic mail, file transfer protocol, telnet, and usenet news.

3.  The *electronic mail* service (known as *e-mail* in short) allows an Internet user to send a mail (message) to another Internet user in any part of the world in a near-real-time manner.

4.  The *File Transfer Protocol* service (known as *FTP* in short) allows an Internet user to move a file from one computer to another on the Internet.

5.  The *telnet* service allows an Internet user to log in to another computer somewhere on the Internet.

6.  The *usenet* service allows a group of Internet users to exchange their views/ideas/information on some common topic, which is of interest to all the members belonging to the group.

7.  The WWW uses a concept called hypertext. *Hypertext* documents on the Internet are known as *Web Pages*. Web Pages are created by using a special language called *HyperText Markup Language* (HTML), which is a powerful language for linking documents for easier electronic access and manipulation.

8.  To be used as a web client, a computer needs to be loaded with a special software tool that is known as a *browser*. Browsers normally provide several navigation facilities to help users save time when they are doing Internet surfing.

# Questions

1.  What is the Internet? How did it evolve?

2.  List out three main characteristic features of the Internet that may be used to define it.

3.  Name some of the basic services provided by the Internet. Explain how each of these services helps the Internet users.

4. In what manner is e-mail service similar to postal mail service? In what manner are the two different from each other?

5. List out some of the advantages and disadvantages of e-mail service against fax service.

6. List out some of the advantages and disadvantages of e-mail service against telephone service.

7. What is an electronic mail (e-mail)? Why is it preferred by many to paper mail, telephone and fax services?

8. What is the file transfer protocol (FTP)? List out the steps involved in downloading/uploading a file by using the FTP service.

9. Explain how is it ensured that only authorized users can access resources of a remote computer in case of FTP and Telnet services.

10. Explain the difference between "downloading" and "uploading" of information.

11. List out some of the common uses of the telnet service offered by the Internet.

12. What is an anonymous FTP site? Why is it used?

13. What is a newsgroup? How is it useful?

14. Differentiate between moderated and nonmoderated newsgroups.

15. What is hypertext? How is it useful?

16. Define the following terms with respect to the Internet:
    (a) HTML          (d) Web client
    (b) HTTP          (e) Web browser
    (c) Web server

17. What is a WWW browser? What types of navigation facilities are typically supported by modern browsers to help users save time while Internet surfing?

18. Describe some of the typical uses of the Internet.

19. Write short notes on:
    (a) Electronic mail
    (b) File transfer protocol
    (c) Telnet service
    (d) Usenet news

20. Give the full form of:
    (a) FTP          (d) SGML
    (b) WWW          (e) HTTP
    (c) HTML          (f) URL

# Chapter 19

# Multimedia

In Chapter 1, we saw that modern computers are not only used as a fast calculating machine, but also as a device, which operates upon data. We also saw that data comes in various shapes and sizes, depending on the type of computer application. In fact, the increasing popularity and usage of computers over the years is mainly due to their capability to handle different types of data. This capability of computers makes them suitable for a wide range of applications and users. Hence, this chapter will deal with the different types of data that modern computer systems can process, and the issues involved in processing these data types.

This chapter starts with an introduction to multimedia and multimedia computer systems. It then describes the commonly used media in computer systems along with the issues in handling each one of them. Some key multimedia applications are then described to allow the readers to appreciate the various uses of multimedia.

## WHAT IS MULTIMEDIA?

A medium (plural media) is something, which can be used for presentation of information. There are two basic ways to present some information:

1.  **Unimedium presentation.** In this case, a single medium is used to present information. For example, a stereo system is a unimedium device, because it presents information by using only sound medium. Similarly, a book having only text (no diagrams) is also a unimediaum device, because it presents information by using only text medium.

2.  **Multimedia presentation.** In this case, more than one medium is used to present information. For example, a TV system is a multimedia device, because it presents information by using sound and video media. Similarly, a book having both text and diagrams is also a multimedia device, because it presents information by using text, graphics and images.

Obviously, multimedia presentation of any information greatly enhances the comprehension capability of the user of the information because it involves the use of more of our senses. For example, students in a class can understand a lecture better, if the lecturer draws illustrative diagrams on the board while delivering his/her lecture (multimedia presentation), instead of using only voice explanation (unimedium presentation).

In case of computer systems, the commonly used media for the purpose of storage, access and transmission of information are:

1. Text (alphanumeric characters)

2. Graphics (line drawings and images)

3. Animation (moving images)

4. Audio (sound)

5. Video (Videographed real-life events)

Hence, in the computer world, multimedia refers to the use of more than one of the above listed media for information presentation to the computer users – such as text and sound.

## WHAT IS A MULTIMEDIA COMPUTER SYSTEM?

A multimedia computer system is a computer system, which has the capability to integrate two or more types of media (text, graphics, image, audio, and video) for the purpose of generation, storage, representation, manipulation and access of multimedia information. In general, the data size for multimedia information is much larger than textual information, because representation of graphics, animation, audio or video media in digital form requires much larger number of bits than that required for representation of plain text. Due to this, multimedia computer systems require:

1. Faster CPU (for quicker processing of large amount of data),

2. Larger storage devices (for storing large data files),

3. Larger main memory (for running programs with large data size),

4. Good graphics terminals (for displaying graphics, animation and video), and

5. I/O devices required to play any audio associated with a multimedia application program.

All multimedia computer systems need not have all the features listed above. For example, a computer system, which does not have the capability to handle audio and video media can still be called a multimedia computer system, because it can still handle multiple media (text and graphics). However, a full-fledged multimedia computer system must be capable of handling all types of media discussed above, and hence, must have all the features listed above.

## MULTIMEDIA COMPONENTS

## Text

Alphanumeric characters are used to present information in text form. Computers are widely used for text processing.

## Hardware Requirements for Text

Text processing, with the use of computers, generally involves the following hardware devices (see Chapter 9 for a description of some of these I/O devices):

1. Keyboards are most commonly used to input text data.

2. OCRs (Optical Character Recognizers) are used for direct input of printed text to computers.

3. Computer screens are used to display text information.

4. Printers are most commonly used to output text in hard copy form.

## Software Requirements for Text

The following text processing capabilities are highly desirable in a multimedia computer system for better presentation and use of textual information:

1. **Text editing.** Text editors and word processing packages are used to generate, edit and properly layout a text document.

2. **Text style.** Presentation of text information can be made more effective by using text of various sizes, fonts and styles (bold, italics, shadow, etc.). For example, newspapers use a good combination of all these styles to better highlight more important news than less important ones. Similarly, in a book like the one you are now reading, a combination of various text styles are used to put more emphasis on certain words or phrases than the remaining text.

3. **Text searching.** Usage of text information can be greatly enhanced by text searching feature. This feature allows the user to enter a word or phrase, and the computer quickly finds and displays that part of the text where the word or phrase appears in the textual information, with the word or phrase highlighted.

4. **Hypertext.** Both presentation and use of textual information can be greatly enhanced by using hypertext feature. This feature provides great flexibility of structuring and accessing computer-based text information. It generalizes the concepts of "footnote" and "cross reference" of traditional information (or document) organization, and allows users to obtain information by clicking on an anchor (a word or phrase linked to another document) within a document. An anchor is often called a "hotword". This means, if the user wants more information about a particular hotword, he/she can select that hotword (usually with a mouse pointer), and open a window with additional text explaining that word or phrase.

5. **Text importing and exporting.** The task of creating a textual document can often be greatly simplified, if the document preparation software has text-importing feature. This is because some of the text you want to incorporate in your document may already exist as a file created by a word processor or a database file. The file (partly or fully) can be simply imported into the new document at the desired location, instead of retyping the entire text again. If the imported file is large, it will result in enormous saving of time and effort required to prepare the new document. Similarly, text exporting feature is very useful in allowing other packages to use an existing document (partly or fully).

# Graphics

Computer graphics deals with the generation, representation, manipulation and display of pictures with the aid of a computer. Graphics is an important component of multimedia because a picture is a powerful way to illustrate information. For example, in a multimedia application meant for educating small children, displaying the photograph of a horse along with its textual description, makes the illustration much more effective. Without the photograph, it will be very difficult to explain, using only text, how a horse looks like. Similarly, displaying the photograph of an employee, along with his/her name, address, sex, age, etc. from a company's database of employees, makes the employee information much more effective.

## Graphics Types

The pictures used in computer graphics can be broadly classified into two types:

1. **Line drawings.** These are drawings and illustrations in the form of 2D and 3D pictures, which are created from mathematical representation of simple objects, like lines, circles, arcs, etc. Simple object types are used to create complex objects. For example, the picture of a chair can be drawn using lines and arcs. Numerical results obtained from computations can also be transformed to graphics forms, like bar graphs or pie charts, by using simple objects.

   The area of computer graphics, which deals with this type of pictures, is known as *generative graphics*. Generative graphics is extensively used in creating illustrative diagrams. For example, most of the figures in this book have been created by using this technique. Two very important applications of generative graphics are CAD (Computer Aided Design) and CAM (Computer Aided Manufacturing). Nowadays, CAD packages are extensively used in designing models for aircraft, ship, and building structures, layout of printed circuit boards, and chemical plant pipelines, etc. Based on these drawings, manufacturing information, such as parts list, subassembly list, etc., are automatically generated and used by CAM packages. The greatest advantage of using CAD and CAM packages for such applications is that design ideas may be quickly checked and graphically conceptualized interactively. Moreover, design changes may be quickly modified, immediately creating accurate assembly drawings and associated parts and subassembly lists.

2. **Images.** These are pictures and photographs, which are composed of a collection of pixels (short form of "picture element," which is a unit of measurement across a computer screen). As shown in Figure 19.1, the pixels of an image are arranged as a two-dimensional matrix. This two-dimensional (or spatial) representation is called the image resolution. Since the storage representation of images is a direct translation of the image, pixel by pixel, no concept of a line, arc, or circle exists.

   As shown in the figure, each pixel consists of three components: red (R), green (G), and blue (B). On a display screen, each component of a pixel corresponds to a phosphor. A phosphor glows when excited by an electron gun. Various combinations of different RGB intensities produce different colors.

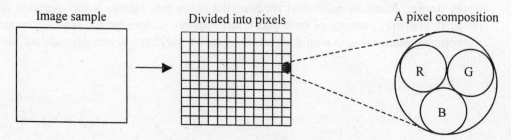

**Figure 19.1.** An image composition.

The area of computer graphics, which deals with this type of pictures, is known as *cognitive graphics*. Cognitive graphics, along with image processing techniques (like image compression and decompression, cleaning of noisy or blurred images, image editing, etc.), is extensively used in applications, which deal with recognition and classification of pictures. For example, an image database containing images of peoples' fingerprints is commonly used nowadays in criminal investigation. Another similar application is classification of images of ECG patterns, X-rays of different parts of the body, etc. to perform medical diagnosis of patients by using computers.

## Hardware Requirements for Graphics

Computer graphics generally involves the following hardware devices (see Chapter 9 for a description of some of these I/O devices):

1. A locating device (such as a mouse, a joystick, or a stylus) attached to a video display terminal along with a drawing software is often used to directly draw pictures on computer screen from scratch for generative graphics applications.

2. A flatbed or rectangular-coordinate digitizer is also used as an input device for generative graphics applications for inputting existing line drawings (such as a map) to a computer.

3. Scanners (optical scanners, image-scan digitizers, etc.) are most commonly used as input devices for capturing photographs and drawings as digital images for cognitive graphics applications.

4. Digital images are also captured directly by a digital camera or a frame capture hardware, such as a video capture board interfaced to some standard video source, like video camera or video cassette recorder (VCR).

5. Computer screens with graphics display capability are used to display graphics.

6. Laser printers are most commonly used to output graphics in hard copy form.

7. Plotters are also used to output graphics in hard copy form.

## Software Requirements for Graphics

The following graphics processing capabilities are highly desirable in a multimedia computer system for better presentation and use of graphics information:

1. **Painting or drawing software.** This software allows the user to create graphics from scratch by using a mouse and various simple objects, such as lines, circles, and polygons with various supporting colors. It also allows the user to modify and enhance graphic images produced by using a scanner or screen capture software. All these features make this software very useful for creating desired graphics in a multimedia application.

2. **Screen capture software.** Often we need to incorporate images from computer screen displays in some document. Screen capture software packages are used in such cases to capture the display of a computer screen as a graphic image.

3. **Clip art.** Clip art is a library of commonly used graphic images or objects, such as a personal computer, printer, aeroplane, telephone, flower, building, etc. These images can be directly imported from the library and used in a multimedia application, saving the time and effort, which might otherwise be required to create or search and capture a similar image object. This is also helpful, if one does not have a scanner or some other means of inputting graphics into the computer. A clip art library often provides the facility to add new objects or delete an existing object from the library.

4. **Graphics importing.** The task of creating a multimedia application incorporating graphics can often be greatly simplified, if the application software can import graphic images in some standard formats. Common graphic formats include .BMP, .GIF, and .PCX.

# Animation

Computer animation deals with the generation, sequencing, and display (at a specified rate) of a set of images (called *frames*) to create an effect of visual change or motion, similar to a movie film (video). Animation is an important component of multimedia, because just as a picture is a powerful way to illustrate information, a small animation clip is even more powerful and useful for illustrating concepts, which involve movement. For example, in the multimedia application meant for educating small children (our previous example), an animation clip will be very effective in illustrating the difference in movement of a horse during a gallop versus a walk. Without animation, it will be very difficult to explain such concepts by using only still images and/or text. Similarly, in a multimedia application meant for teaching swimming, the proper way to swing hands for swimming can be more effectively illustrated with an animation as compared to images and/or textual description.

Animation is often confused with video (described later in this chapter) may be because both deal with the display of a sequence of images (frames) to generate an effect of motion. However, animation is commonly used in those instances where videography is not possible, or animation can better illustrate the concept than video. For example, collision between two stars, or movement of planets around sun, cannot be video graphed, and hence, can be best illustrated with the help of an animation clip. Similarly, flow of blood in our arteries and veins, and pumping of blood by our heart can be best illustrated with the help of an animation clip. Animation is also very commonly used in advertisements, cartoon films, video games, and virtual reality applications. *Virtual reality* is a relatively new computer technology, using which, the user can put on a pair of goggles and a glove and tour a three-dimensional world that exists only in the computer, but appears realistic to the user.

Animation deals with displaying a sequence of images at a reasonable speed to create an impression of movement. For a jerk-free full motion animation, 25 to 30 frames have to be displayed per second.

## Hardware Requirements for Animation

Computer animation generally involves the following hardware devices:

1. Image generation tools and devices, such as scanners, digital camera, and video capture board interfaced to some standard video source, like video camera or video cassette recorder (VCR), are used to generate images to be used in animation.

2. Computer monitors with image display capability is the minimum requirement for outputting (displaying) animation. In addition, multimedia computer systems capable of handling animation also require a graphics accelerator board, which not only controls the resolution and number of colors of display, but also speeds up the refresh rate. *Refresh rate* is the time taken to paint the computer screen with a new image frame, replacing the previous image frame. Increased speed, due to the use of graphics accelerator board, smoothes out the movement (avoids flickering of animated sequences) because subsequent frames, which make up the animation can be displayed quicker.

## Software Requirements for Animation

The following software capabilities are highly desirable in a multimedia computer system with animation facility:

1. **Animation creation software.** It allows the user to create animation sequences from scratch by using a mouse and various simple objects, such as lines, circles and polygons, with various supporting colors. For example, an animation sequence to illustrate bouncing of a ball can be created as follows:

   - select a circle object and fill it with red color;

   - then start the recorder of the animation creation software;

   - then select the colored circle and drag it around the screen by using a mouse, recording several positions for it on the screen (each time you release the mouse button, you record the object's position on the screen);

   - finally, stop the recorder and use save command to save the animation.

   Now, to test the recorded animation, start the player of the animation creation software and click on the colored ball. The ball will bounce across the screen according to the positions recorded during the recording phase. The same bouncing sequence will repeat every time you click on the ball.

2. **Screen capture software.** It is used to capture the displays of a computer screen as graphic images, which can be used in animation.

3. **Animation clips.** This is a library of animation clips from which one can select and directly import an animation clip and use it in a multimedia application, saving the time and effort, which might otherwise be required to create a similar animation clip. This is also useful, if one does not have an animation creation software. An animation clips library often provides the facility to add a new animation clip or delete an existing animation clip from the library.

4. **Animation file importing.** The task of creating a multimedia application incorporating animation can often be greatly simplified, if the application software can import animation files in some standard formats. Common animation file formats include .FLI and .FLC.

5. **Software support for high resolution.** If the animation sequences of a multimedia application are made up of very high quality images, it is important to have not only the necessary hardware, but also software support for displaying high resolution images, which have many colors to maintain the high quality of animation display.

6. **Recording and playback capability.** It allows the user to control the recording and display of an animation sequence. For example, it provides the user with options to 'pause' and 'replay' the animation sequence.

7. **Transition effects.** Animation can be even more interesting, if it is enhanced with transition effects, such as fade-in and fade-out, layering, zooming, and rotation of objects.

# Audio

Computer audio deals with synthesizing, recording, and playback of audio or sound with the aid of a compu . Audio is another very important component of multimedia, because in many cases sound can substant y reinforce our understanding of information presented in other ways, and in some cases sound is the only wa to provide the desired information. For example, in the multimedia application meant for educating small children (our previous example), voice explanation can be added to the animation clip for describing what is being shown, and pointing out what to look for that makes a horse's gallop different from a horse's walk. Similarly, an animation clip can show the horse neighing and neighing sound can be added to effectively convey the type of sound horses make. Note that, it is nearly impossible to provide an accurate description of a horse's neigh, a lion's roar, or a bird's chirp using text, and graphics is of no help in these cases. Hence, sound is the only medium that can accurately provide such information.

## Analog and Digital Audio

Audio information travels in natural medium in the form of sound waves, which are analog in nature. For the computer to be able to understand audio information, sound waves must be converted from analog to digital form. *Transducer* is a device capable of changing signals from one form to another. For example, microphone is an example of a transducer, which converts sound waves into electrical signals. Conversely, loudspeaker is an example of a transducer, which converts electrical signals into sound waves.

Information can be represented as analog signals or digital signals. Analog signals exhibit a continuous tone of smooth fluctuations, while digital signals are composed of discrete values represented by numbers. The transformation between analog and digital signals is achieved by A/D (Analog-to-Digital) conversion and D/A (Digital-to-Analog) conversion. A/D conversion transforms an analog input (such as voltage) into a series of numeric representation by digitization. D/A conversion is the reverse process, which transforms a sequence of discrete numbers back into continuous analog signal.

## Hardware Requirements for Audio

Computer audio generally involves the following hardware devices:

1. A sound board (or sound card), which is equipped with A/D and D/A converters.

2. Some type of input device (such as a microphone) is used for audio input to record a human voice or music or any type of sound in a computer. The A/D converter of the sound board takes care of digitizing the input sound.

3. Some type of output device (such as speakers or headphones) is used for audio output to listen to a recorded sound. The D/A converter of the sound board takes care of converting the sound from its digital to analog form.

4. Synthesized sound can also be generated on a computer by using keyboard (as interaction device) and sound sequencer software.

5. Sound editors are used to cut and paste sound sequences, to add special effects, and to create new sound sequences from existing sound sequences.

6. Audio mixers are used to combine multiple channels of sound with controls like synchronization points.

## Software Requirements for Audio

The following software capabilities are highly desirable in a multimedia computer system with audio facility:

1. **Audio clips.** This is a library of audio clips (pre-made sound effects, music, and narrations) from which one can select and directly import an audio clip, and use it in a multimedia application. This saves enormous time and effort, which might otherwise be required to create a similar audio clip. This is also useful, if one does not have the facility to create sound sequences. An audio clips library often provides the facility to add a new audio clip or delete an existing audio clip from the library.

2. **Audio file importing.** The task of creating a multimedia application incorporating audio can often be greatly simplified, if the application software can import audio files in some standard formats. Common audio file formats include .WAV (Windows files), .MID (MIDI files), .VOC, and .INS.

3. **Software support for high quality sound.** If a multimedia application uses very high quality audio, to reproduce the sound effectively, it is important to have not only the necessary hardware, but also software support for both recording and playback of high quality audio.

4. **Recording and playback capability.** It allows the user to control the recording and playback of an audio sequence. For example, it provides the user with options to "pause" and "replay" the sound sequence.

5. **Text-to-speech conversion software.** It is used to convert written text into corresponding sound.

6. **Speech-to-text conversion software.** It is used to convert speech into corresponding text.

7. **Voice recognition software.** It is used to identify the speaker of a given voice by matching the voice with a set of voices stored in a database along with the details of the speaker of each voice.

# Video

Like animation, computer video deals with the recording and display of a sequence of images at a reasonable speed to create an impression of movement. Each individual image of a sequence of images is called a *frame*. For a jerk-free full motion video, 25 to 30 frames have to be displayed per second. Like animation, video is also an important component of multimedia because it is very useful for illustrating concepts that involve movement. Although, both animation and video deal with the display of a sequence of images to generate an effect of motion, video typically deals with recording of a real-life event produced by a device, such as a digital video recorder.

Video information travels in natural medium in the form of light waves, which are analog in nature. For computer usage of video information, light waves must be converted from analog to digital form. Video camera is a transducer, which is commonly used to convert light waves into electrical signals. Conversely, monitor is a transducer, which is commonly used to convert electrical signals into light waves. Like audio, in case of video also, the transformation between analog and digital signals is achieved by A/D and D/A conversions.

## Hardware Requirements for Video

The following hardware devices are generally required in a computer system capable of handling video (see Chapter 9 for a description of some of these I/O devices):

1. A video camera is the most commonly used input device for capturing video data.

2. A video monitor (TV monitor or computer monitor) is the most commonly used output device for displaying video data.

3. A video board (or video card), which is equipped with A/D and D/A converters. In addition to performing the basic function of A/D and D/A conversions of video signals, a video board also has connectors for video camera and video monitor. Note that the video camera, the video monitor, and the video board must be compatible with each other.

4. Video editors are used to cut and paste video sequences, to add special effects, and to create new video sequences from existing video sequences. They also allow superimposing of text and audio on a video sequence.

## Software Requirements for Video

The following software capabilities are highly desirable in a multimedia computer system with video facility:

1. **Video clips.** This is a library of video clips from which one can select and directly import a video clip, and use it in a multimedia application, saving the time and effort, which might otherwise be required to create a similar video clip. A video clip library often provides the facility to add a new video clip or delete an existing video clip from the library.

2. **Recording and playback capability.** It allows the user to control the recording and display of a video sequence. For example, it provides the user with options to 'pause' and 'replay' the video sequence.

# MULTIMEDIA APPLICATIONS

The capability of computers to handle different types of media makes them suitable for a wide range of applications and users. Below we discuss some multimedia applications to enable the readers to appreciate the use of multimedia and to visualize its other applications.

## Multimedia Presentation

We saw that multimedia applications can present information in a variety of forms (text, graphics, animation, audio, video) involving the use of more of our senses. Hence, multimedia presentation can be used to better explain a subject matter to the students, because it enhances the comprehension capability of the students. It is extremely effective in getting across new ideas and concepts. Moreover, it helps in making a presentation more interesting, and has the inevitable effect of grabbing and holding a person's attention.

## Foreign Language Learning

Using a book for learning a foreign language is difficult because one is not sure how to pronounce the words written in textual form. The book can have an accompanying audio tape to solve this problem, but it is inconvenient for the learner to keep rewinding the tape to find specific information. Moreover, the learner also does not have the flexibility to quickly hear the pronunciation for a specific word. Using a multimedia program, which incorporates text and sound, the learner can see words and phrases on the screen as they are pronounced by the computer program. The learner also has the flexibility to request the computer to pronounce any word displayed on the screen by selecting that word (say by clicking over it). Additional features may be incorporated in the program to assist in faster learning process. For example, if the learner does not understand the meaning of a word or phrase, he/she may point to it to display a translation for it in his/her native language.

## Video Games

With the advent of multimedia, there has been a boom in the different types of video games available on computer systems. Sound and animation have been particularly important in these applications to make the games thrilling and exciting for the user. Because the sequence of events in such games depends on the actions of the player, these programs are very interactive in nature.

## Special Effects in Films

Several movies now contain many visual tricks, which could never be accomplished without the aid of computers. For example, in the Hindi movie, Chachi 420, the hero is shown being transformed from man to woman by the use of a computer graphics technique called morphing. In the English movie, Jurassic Park, the dinosaurs were shown as living creatures (although they are extinct and no more exist) by the use of multimedia technology only. Similarly, a number of very successful films, including Titanic, Star Wars, Superman, Spiderman, have used multimedia technology for providing special effects.

## Multimedia Kiosk

A multimedia kiosk generally has a touch-screen monitor with a very user-friendly graphical user interface for ease of operation by general public. Multimedia kiosks are often used in public places as information providers, in place of help desks with an attendant. For example, a multimedia kiosk placed at an airport might provide the travellers with information on tourist attractions, restaurants, and hotels, along with graphic images and maps showing how to get there. A kiosk at a large museum may be used to provide the visitors with information on what types of displays are in which parts of the museum. A kiosk at a cosmetic counter in a supermarket may provide customers with information on makeup for particular skin types and colors.

## Animated Advertisements

For sales promotion, companies often advertise their products and services on television. Most of the TV programmes are sponsored by one or more companies, and in turn, they get time slots for advertising their products during the programme. Several of these advertisements use computer animation to effectively communicate the usefulness of the products or services. For example, if you carefully watch the advertisements for detergent soaps/powders, toothpastes, insecticides for mosquitoes and cockroaches, etc., you will see few scenes in them, which cannot be videographed. These scenes are produced by using computer animation.

## Multimedia Conferencing

Multimedia conferencing, also known as video conferencing, refers to a system that simulates face-to-face interactions among participating users, located far from each other, as if they were sitting and discussing in a single room. In this system, each participating user has a PC (or a workstation) on his/her working desk, which has a video camera and mike attached to it. The PCs of all these users are interconnected together through a high-speed network. The network is used to transmit audio, video and other data from one participant's PC to the PCs of other participants. A user willing to communicate with other users, talks in front of his/her PC. The audio-visual equipment attached to his/her PC captures the information, which is then transmitted to the PCs of other users. The coordination support software coordinates the proceeds of the conference, and resolves any conflicts when multiple users want to communicate simultaneously.

## Points to Remember

1. *Multimedia* refers to the use of more than one of the following media for information presentation:
   - Text (alphanumeric characters)
   - Graphics (line drawings and images)
   - Animation (moving images)
   - Audio (sound)
   - Video (videographed real-life events)

2. A *multimedia computer system* is a computer system, which has the capability to integrate two or more types of media (text, graphics, animation, audio, and video) for the purpose of generation, storage, representation, manipulation and access of multimedia information.

3. In general, the data size for multimedia information is much larger than textual information. Because of this, multimedia computer systems require:
   - Faster CPU (for quicker processing of large amount of data),
   - Larger storage devices (for storing large data files),
   - Larger main memory (for running programs with large data size),
   - Good graphics terminals (for displaying graphics, animation and video), and
   - I/O devices required to play any audio associated with a multimedia application program.

4. *Computer graphics* deals with the generation, representation, manipulation and display of pictures (line drawings and images) with the aid of a computer.

5. *Computer animation* deals with the generation, sequencing, and display (at a specified rate) of a set of images (called frames) to create an effect of visual change or motion, similar to a movie film (video). Animation is commonly used in those instances where videography is not possible, or animation can better illustrate the concept than video.

6. *Computer audio* deals with synthesizing, recording, and playback of audio or sound with the aid of a computer.

7. *Transducer* is a device capable of changing signals from analog to digital form or vice-versa.

8. *Computer video* deals with the recording and display of a sequence of images at a reasonable speed to create an impression of movement. Each individual image of such a sequence is called a *frame*.

# Questions

1. What is multimedia? Explain with the help of some examples.

2. Tell which ones of the following are unimedium and which ones are multimedia devices (give justification for your answers):
   (a) TV system
   (b) Stereo system
   (c) Telephone system
   (d) A book having only text (no diagrams)
   (e) A book having both text and diagrams
   (f) A modern personal computer

3. List out the commonly used media types generally used in modern computer systems and explain how each one helps in information presentation.

4. What is a multimedia computer system? What are it typical characteristics? Do all multimedia systems need to have all these characteristics?

5. You have a printed document of 100 pages. Give two different ways in which this textual data can be input to a computer system.

6. Name two output devices, which can be used with a computer system to output text information. Give their relative advantages and disadvantages.

7. What is a "hypertext?" Explain how it helps in presentation and use of information.

8. What is meant by "text importing" and "text exporting"? Explain how these features help in the creation of a document.

9. What is computer graphics? Give a few examples to explain its uses in multimedia applications.

10. Explain the difference between "generative graphics" and "cognitive graphics". Give two uses of each.

11. What is a "pixel"? Explain how an image is composed and displayed on a computer screen.

12. Name two input devices for generative graphics applications. Describe a practical use of each.

13. Name two input devices for cognitive graphics applications. Describe a practical use of each.

14. Name three output devices that may be used with a computer system to output graphics data. Describe a practical use of each of these devices.

15. What is a painting/drawing software? Describe two uses of this software in creating multimedia applications.

16. What is a screen capture software? Describe a typical use of this software.

17. What is a clip art? How does it help in the creation of multimedia applications?

18. What is meant by "graphics importing"? Explain how this feature helps in the creation of multimedia applications.

19. Name some of the common graphics file formats.

20. What is computer animation? Give a few examples to explain its uses in multimedia applications.

21. Differentiate between "animation" and "video". Explain the difference with the help of few examples.

22. What is an animation creation software? Describe with the help of a typical example how this software can be used to create an animation sequence.

23. What is an animation clips library? How does it help in the creation of multimedia applications?

24. Name some of the common animation file formats.

25. Name some of the transition effects features, which may be used to make animation more interesting.

26. What is computer audio? Give a few examples to explain its use in multimedia applications.

27. What is a transducer? Name three devices that can be categorized as a transducer.

28. Explain the role of analog-to-digital and digital-to-analog converters in the acquisition and playback of analog signals by a computer system.

29. What is a sound board card in a multimedia computer system? What are its basic functions?

30. What is an audio clips library? How does it help in the creation of multimedia applications?

31. Name some of the common audio file formats.

32. What is computer video? Give a few examples to explain its uses in multimedia applications.

33. Give examples of two transducers, which deal with video data.

34. Give examples of two transducers, which deal with audio data.

35. What is the role of a video board card in a multimedia computer system?

36. Give some examples of multimedia applications in education.

37. Give some examples of multimedia applications in entertainment.

# Chapter 20

# Classification of Computers

General purpose computers come in many sizes and capabilities. Traditionally, computers were classified by their size, processing speed and cost. Based on these factors, computers were classified as microcomputers, minicomputers, mainframes and supercomputers. However, with the rapidly changing technology, this classification is no more relevant. The problem is that, computer technology is changing so fast that, just after few months of introduction of a new computer in the market, new models of computers are introduced, which have much higher performance and cost less. Hence, a recently introduced small system can outperform the large models of a few years ago, and a new minicomputer can do the work of an earlier mainframe, at a much lower cost. Hence, today computers are classified based on their mode of use. According to this classification scheme, computers are classified as notebook computers, personal computers, workstations, mainframe systems, supercomputers, and clients and servers. In this chapter, you will learn about these types of computers.

## NOTEBOOK COMPUTERS

Notebook computers are portable computers, which are mainly meant for use by people who need computing power wherever they go. As the name implies, notebook computers are approximately of the size of an 8½ x 11 inch notebook, and can easily fit inside a briefcase. Since they have to be carried along, they are also light in weight, weighing around 2 Kg. They are also known as laptop PCs (laptop personal computers), because they are as powerful as a PC, and their size and weight allows them to be used by comfortably placing them on ones lap.

As shown in Figure 20.1, a notebook computer uses an almost full-size keyboard, a small flat screen liquid crystal color display, and a trackball (instead of a mouse, because notebook computers are often used without a desk). They also have a hard disk, a floppy disk drive, and a CD-ROM drive. The display screen is foldable in a manner that, when not in use, it can be folded to flush with the keyboard, to convert the system into notebook form. When in use, the display screen is folded open, as shown in the figure. Many models of notebook computers can be plugged into a "dock" on a docking station (a personal computer or a workstation), to take advantage of the larger machine's big monitor, storage space, and other peripherals, such as a printer. Many models of notebook computers can also be connected to a network, to enable them to download data (read files) from other computers on the network, as and when such a need arises, or to access the Internet. Since notebook computers are meant to be mobile and used from anywhere, efforts are being made to provide wireless connectivity to these systems with other stationary computers.

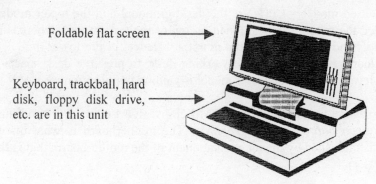

Foldable flat screen ⟶

Keyboard, trackball, hard disk, floppy disk drive, etc. are in this unit ⟶

**Figure 20.1.** A notebook computer.

Notebook computers are designed to be used even at places where there is no power point available to connect them with a power source (for example while traveling in a train or aeroplane). Hence, they are designed to operate with chargeable batteries. With a fully charged battery, a notebook computer can be used for a few hours.

Notebook computers normally run MS-DOS or WINDOWS operating system. They are mostly used for word processing, spreadsheet computing, data entry, and preparing presentation materials, while a person is traveling. They are also used for making presentations, by plugging them into an LCD (liquid crystal display) projection system, when presentations are to be made at a location away from ones office.

The processing capability of a notebook computer is normally as good as an ordinary PC (personal computer) because both use the same type of processor, such as an Intel Pentium processor. However, a notebook computer generally has lesser hard disk storage than a PC, to keep its total weight to around 2 Kg. Notebook computers are typically more expensive (2 to 3 times) than a normal PC.

# PERSONAL COMPUTERS (PCs)

A PC is a non-portable, general-purpose computer, which can easily fit on a normal size office table (leaving some writing space to keep writing pads and other office stationary), and is generally designed to be used by one person at a time (single-user-oriented). As the name implies, PCs were mainly designed to meet the personal computing needs of individuals, either in their working places or at their homes. In fact, PCs have changed the work culture and work habits of numerous organizations and individuals. An increasing proportion of office work now involves the use of computers. Hence, today PCs are found on the working desks of several employees, in any organization. PCs are also providing employees with flexible working environments. Those employees, who could not work during traditional office hours due to personal reasons, can now work part of the time in the office and the remainder of the time at home, by having a PC in their homes. Several individuals also keep a PC in their homes to run a business in their homes. PCs are also used, both by children and adults, for education and entertainment. Hence, PCs are now very common everywhere, and can be found in offices, classrooms, homes, hospitals, shops, clinics, etc.

The configuration of PCs varies from one PC to another, depending on their usage. However, the most commonly used configuration consists of a system unit, a monitor (display screen), a keyboard, and a mouse. The system unit, which is in the form of a box, consists of the main circuit board (consisting of CPU, memory, etc.), the hard disk storage, the floppy disk drive, the CD-ROM drive, any special add-on cards (such as network interface card), and ports for connecting peripheral devices (such as printer).

The two most commonly used models of PCs are the desktop model and the tower model. As shown in Figure 20.2, in the desktop model, the monitor is positioned on top of the system unit, whereas in the tower model, the system unit is designed to stand by the side of the monitor. Hence, in the tower model, the system unit can be positioned even on the floor beside or under the working desk, to preserve desk space. Although the desktop model was more popular few years ago, the tower model is gaining popularity now.

A PC generally employs several chips (CPU chip, RAM chips, ROM chips, I/O handling chips, etc.) on a main circuit board, called a *system board*, or *motherboard*. The motherboard is what distinguishes one PC from another. Often PCs are distinguished by the main component of the motherboard, that is the microprocessor chip, which is used as their CPU.

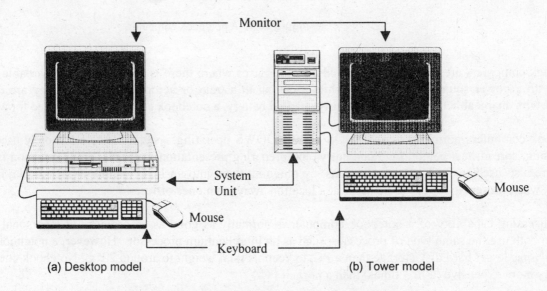

**Figure 20.2.** The two most commonly used models of PCs.

The popular operating systems for PCs are MS-DOS, MS-Windows, Windows-NT, Linux and Unix. An OS called OS/2 was also used on IBM PCs few years ago, and the Apple's Macintosh PCs run the Apple's propriety OS called Macintosh OS, and Apple's version of Unix called A/UX. Most of these operating systems enable the user to switch between tasks. This capability is known as *multitasking* – a single-user variation of the multiprogramming concept. Multitasking eases user operation and saves lots of time, when a user has to switch between two or more applications, while performing a job. For example, let us assume that a user is using a word processor to create an annual report, and he/she needs to do some arithmetic calculations on the computer, and include the calculated results in the report. Without multitasking, the user would have to close the annual report file and the word processing application, open the calculator application, make the necessary calculations, write down the results, close the calculator application, and reopen the word processing application and the annual report file. With multitasking, the user simply opens the calculator application, makes the necessary calculations, and switches back to the annual report file, to continue working on it.

PCs generally cost from a few tens of thousands to about a lakh of rupees, depending on the configuration. A few of the major PC manufacturers are IBM, Apple, Compaq, Dell, Zenith, Siemens, Toshiba, and Hewlett-Packard.

# WORKSTATIONS

A workstation is a powerful desktop computer, which is designed to meet the computing needs of engineers, architects, and other professionals, who need greater processing power, larger storage, and better graphics display facility than what PCs provide. For example, workstations are commonly used for computer-aided design (CAD), simulation of complex scientific and engineering problems, visualization of the results of simulation, and for multimedia applications, such as for creating special audio-visual effects for television programmes and movies.

A workstation looks very much like a PC, and is typically used by only one person at a time, just like a PC. The following characteristics are often used to differentiate between the two:

1. **Processing power.** The processing power of a workstation is several times (typically 5 to 10 times) more than that of an average power of a PC.

2. **Storage capacity.** Workstations have larger main memory (typically 0.5 GB to a few GB) as compared to PCs, which have few tens or hundreds of MB of main memory. The hard disk capacity of a workstation is also much more (typically several tens of GB) as compared to that of PCs (typically few GB).

3. **Display facility.** Most workstations have a large-screen (21 inch or more) monitor capable of displaying high-resolution graphics. Hence, the color and graphics adapter card, which is optional for PCs, is available by default in workstations. PCs normally use monitors having smaller screen (19 inch or less).

4. **Processor design.** PCs normally use CPUs based on CISC technology, whereas workstations use CPUs based on RISC technology. Popular RISC processors used in workstations are ALPHA (used in DEC-ALPHA workstations), RIOS (used in IBM workstations), SPARC (used in SUN workstations), and PA-RISC (used in HP workstations).

5. **Operating system.** Unlike PCs which can run any of the five major OSs – MS-DOS, MS-Windows, Windows-NT, Linux and Unix, all workstations generally run the Unix operating system or a variation of it, such as AIX (used in IBM workstations), Solaris (used in SUN workstations), and HP-UX (used in HP workstations). Also, unlike most operating systems for PCs, which are single-user oriented, a workstation's operating system is designed to enable it to support a multiuser environment.

6. **Network interface card.** Most workstations have built-in hardware to connect to a Local Area Network (LAN). This facility is normally optional in case of a PC.

Workstations generally cost from a few lakhs to few tens of lakhs of rupees, depending on the configuration. The biggest manufacturer of workstations is Sun Microsystems. Other manufacturers of workstations include IBM, DEC, Hewlett-Packard (HP), and Silicon Graphics.

# MAINFRAME SYSTEMS

There are several organizations, such as banks, insurance companies, hospitals, railways, etc., that need on-line processing of large number of transactions, and require computer systems, which have massive data storage and processing capabilities. Mainframe systems are computer systems, which are mainly used for handling the information processing needs of such organizations. They are also used in such environments, in which a large number of users need to share a common computing facility, such as in research groups, educational institutions, engineering firms, etc.

By its very nature of usage, a mainframe system is housed in a central location, with several user terminals connected to it. The user terminals act as access stations, and may or may not be located in the same building, in which the mainframe system is located. A typical configuration of a mainframe system consists of the following components (see Figure 20.3):

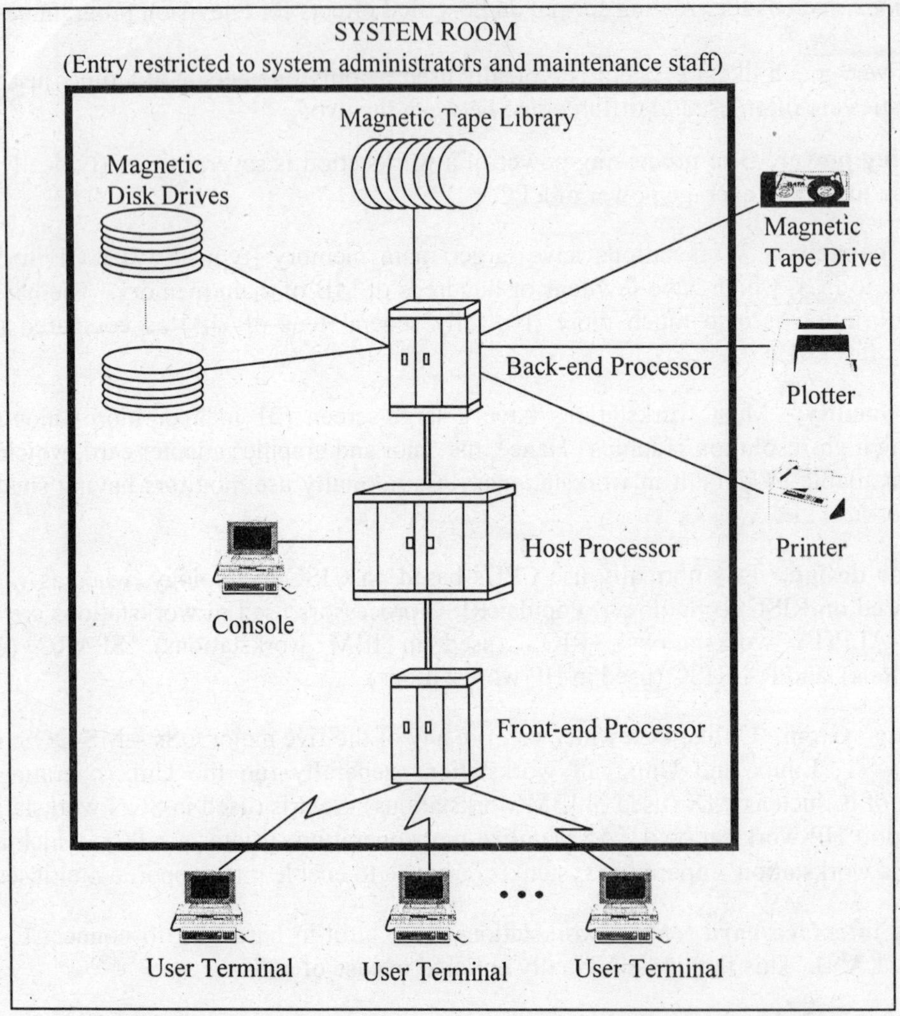

USERS ROOM
(Entry restricted to authorized users)

SYSTEM ROOM
(Entry restricted to system administrators and maintenance staff)

Magnetic Tape Library

Magnetic Disk Drives

Magnetic Tape Drive

Back-end Processor

Plotter

Host Processor

Printer

Console

Front-end Processor

User Terminal        User Terminal    ...    User Terminal

**Figure 20.3.** A typical configuration of a mainframe computer system.

1. **Host, front-end, and back-end computers.** A mainframe computer system is usually composed of several computers (subordinate computers), in addition to the mainframe, or host computer. The host computer carries out most of the computations, and has direct control over all the other computers. The other computers relieve the host computer of certain routine processing requirements. For example, a front-end computer is used for handling communications to and from all the user terminals connected to the computer system, thus relieving the host computer of communications-related processing requirements. Similarly, a back-end computer is used to handle data I/O operations, thus relieving the host computer of locating a particular I/O device and transferring data to or from it. As shown in the figure, the host and other computes are located in the systems room, to which entry is restricted to system administrators and maintenance staff.

2. **Console(s).** One or more console terminals are also located in the systems room. These terminals are directly connected to the host computer, and are mainly used by the system administrators to monitor the health of the system, or to perform some system administration activities, such as changing the configuration of the system, installing new software on the system, taking system backup, etc.

3. **Storage devices.** For large volume data storage, a mainframe system has several magnetic disk drives (located in the systems room), which are directly connected to the back-end computer. All data, to and from these magnetic disks, are accessed by the host computer, via the back-end computer. In addition, a mainframe system also has a few tape drives and a magnetic tape library, for restoration or backup of data, from or to magnetic tapes. The tape library is located in the systems room, and is used by the system administrators, to take regular backups of the data from magnetic disks on to magnetic tapes. The tape drives are located in the users room, so that users who bring their input data on tape or want to take their output data on tape, can have access to the tape drives.

4. **User terminals.** User terminals, which act as access stations, are used by the users to work on the system. In the figure, although all the user terminals are shown to be located in the user room, some of them may be located at geographically distributed locations. Since mainframe systems allow multiple users to simultaneously use the system (through the user terminals), their operating systems support multiprogramming with timesharing. This enables all the users to get good response time, and an illusion that their jobs are being attended to by the system.

5. **Output devices.** The user terminals serve the purpose of soft copy output devices. However, for hard copy outputs, a mainframe system usually has several printers and one or more plotters, connected to the back-end computer. These output devices are also located in the user room, so that they are accessible to the users, for taking their outputs.

It is unlikely that you would find two mainframe systems configured in exactly the same way. The configuration of a mainframe system depends a lot on the type of usage and the kind of users it is meant for. The example of Figure 20.3 is just one possible configuration.

Mainframe systems are much bigger and several times more expensive than workstations. A typical mainframe system looks like a row of large file cabinets, and needs a large room, with closely monitored humidity and temperature. A mainframe system may cost anywhere from a few tens of lakhs to a few crores of rupees, depending on the configuration. A mainframe system having smaller configuration (slower host and subordinate computers, lesser storage space, and fewer user terminals) is often referred to as a *minicomputer system*. However, there is no well-defined boundary for differentiating between the two. Two major vendors of mainframe systems are IBM and DEC.

# SUPERCOMPUTERS

Supercomputers are the most powerful and expensive computers available at a given time. They are primarily used for processing complex scientific applications, which require enormous processing power. Some of the supercomputing applications (applications that need supercomputers for processing) are as follows:

1. Petroleum industry uses supercomputers to analyze volumes of seismic data, which are gathered during oil-seeking explorations, to identify areas where there is possibility of getting petroleum products inside the earth. This helps in more detailed imaging of underground geological structures, so that the expensive resources for drilling oil wells and extraction of petroleum products from them, can be more effectively channelized to those areas, where the analysis results show better possibility of getting petroleum deposits.

2. Aerospace industry uses supercomputers to simulate airflow around an aircraft at different speeds and altitude. This helps in producing an effective aerodynamic design, to develop aircrafts with superior performance.

3. Automobile industry uses supercomputers to do crash simulation of the design of an automobile, before it is released for manufacturing. Doing crash simulation of an automobile on computer screen is less expensive, more revealing, and safer than crashing a real model of the automobile. This helps in producing better automobile designs, which are safer to ride.

4. Structural mechanics industry uses supercomputers to solve complex structure engineering problems, which designers of various types of civil and mechanical structures need to deal with, to ensure safety, reliability, and cost effectiveness. For example, the designer of a large bridge has to ensure that the bridge must work in various atmospheric conditions and pressures from wind, velocity, etc., and under different load conditions. Actual construction and testing of such expensive structures is prohibitive in most cases.

5. Meteorological centers use supercomputers for weather forecasting. In weather forecasting, weather data supplied by a worldwide network of space satellites, airplanes, and ground stations are fed into supercomputers. These data are analyzed by a series of computer programs to arrive at forecasts. This analysis involves solving of complex mathematical equations, which model the atmosphere and climate processes.

There are many more supercomputing applications. It is not possible to cover all of them here. All these applications are impractical, if not impossible, on mainframe systems.

Supercomputers use *multiprocessing* and *parallel processing* technologies to solve complex problems faster. That is, they use multiple processors, and parallel processing enables a complex problem to be divided into smaller problems, which can be assigned to different processors of the system and processed in parallel. A *parallel program* is written in a manner to break up the original problem into smaller computational modules, which can be allocated to different processors, and multiple processors can work independently and cooperate to solve the problem. Hence, if the original problem takes 100 hours to process on a single-processor system, and if it can be broken into 100 smaller computational modules, it can be theoretically solved in about 1 hour by using a supercomputer, which has 100 processors. Since modern supercomputers employ parallel processing technology, they are also known as *parallel computers* or *parallel processing systems*. Moreover, modern supercomputers employ hundreds of processors, and are also known as *massively parallel processors*.

Like mainframe systems, supercomputers also support multiprogramming, which allows simultaneous access of the system by multiple users. However, the main difference between these two types of systems is that supercomputers primarily address processor-bound applications, whereas mainframe systems are oriented to input/output-bound applications. In *processor-bound applications*, the amount of work that can be performed by the computer system is limited primarily by the speed of the CPU(s), whereas in *I/O-bound applications*, the amount of work that can be performed by the computer system is limited primarily by the speeds of the I/O devices. Supercomputers are rarely used for processing input/output-intensive applications, such as payroll processing, accounting, or record-keeping applications. To do so would waste an expensive and relatively rare resource.

Leaders in the development of supercomputers include Cray Research Company, IBM, Silicon Graphics, Fujitsu, and Intel. Realizing the importance of supercomputers in the advancement of a nation, some national efforts of building supercomputers indigenously have also been initiated. This has resulted in the development of PARAM series of supercomputers by the Centre for Development of Advanced Computing (C-DAC), Anupam series of supercomputers by the Bhabha Atomic Research Centre (BARC), and PACE series of supercomputers by the Defence Research and Development Organization (DRDO), Hyderabad. The PARAM 10000 supercomputer (shown in Figure 20.4) has been developed by C-DAC.

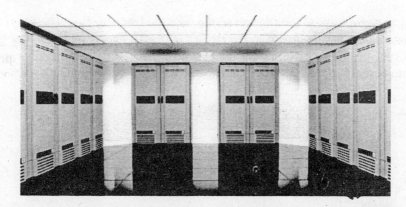

**Figure 20.4.** C-DAC's PARAM 10000 supercomputer [reproduced with permission from C-DAC].

Because computer technology changes so quickly, the advanced capabilities of a supercomputer today, may become the standard features next year, and next year's supercomputer will be vastly more powerful than today's. Supercomputers can typically cost from few tens of lakhs to few tens of crores of rupees, depending on their processing capability and configuration.

# CLIENTS AND SERVERS

This is a purely role-based classification of computer systems. With the increased popularity of computer networks, it has become possible to interconnect several computers, which can communicate and interact with each other over the network. In such a computing environment, there are several resources/services, which can be shared among multiple users for cost-effective usage, and can be best managed/offered centrally. A few examples of such resources/services are:

1. **File server.** It provides a central storage facility, to store files of several users on the network.

2. **Database server.** It manages a centralized database, and enables several users on the network to have shared access to the same database.

3. **Print server.** It manages one or more printers, and accepts and processes print requests from any user in the network.

4. **Name server.** It translates names into network addresses, enabling different computers on the network to communicate with each other.

In these cases, it is usual to have one process, which "owns" the resource or service and is in charge of managing it. This process accepts requests from other processes, which want to use the resource or service. The process that owns the resource and does this management is called a *server process*, and the computer on which the server process runs is called a *server computer*, because it services requests for use of the resource. Other processes, which send service requests to the server, are called *client processes*, and the computers on which the client processes run are called *client computers*. Note that there may be multiple client computers, which send service requests to the same server computer. A generic client-server computing environment is shown in Figure 20.5.

In a client-server computing environment, it is common for one server to use the services of another server, and hence, to be both a client and a server at the same time. For example, let us assume that a client-server computing environment has clients, a file server, and a disk block server. Any client can send a file access request to the file server. On receiving such a request, the file server checks the access rights, etc. of the user, but does not actually read/write the file blocks itself. Instead, it sends a request to the disk block server for accessing the requested data blocks. The disk block server returns to the file server, the requested data blocks. The file server then extracts the actual data from the data blocks and returns it to the client. In this scenario, the file server is both a server and a client. It is a server for the clients, but a client for the disk block server. Hence, the concept of client and server computers is purely role-based, and may change dynamically, as the role of a computer changes.

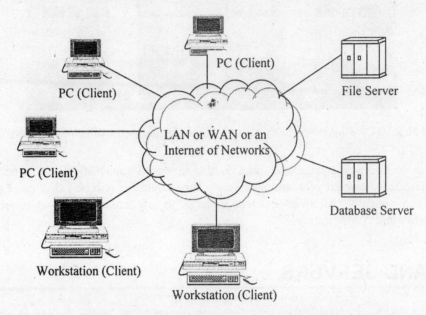

**Figure 20.5.** A generic client-server computing environment.

Figure 20.6 summarizes and presents a relative comparison of different types of computers, based on some key features.

# Points to Remember

1. Traditionally, computers were classified by their size, processing speed and cost. Based on these factors, computers were classified as microcomputers, minicomputers, mainframes and supercomputers. However, with the rapidly changing technology, this classification is no more relevant.

2. Today, computers are classified based on their mode of use. According to this classification scheme, computers are classified as notebook computers, personal computers, workstations, mainframe systems, supercomputers, and clients and servers.

3. *Notebook computers* are portable computers, which are small enough to fit inside a briefcase, light enough to be easily carried around, and are designed to operate with chargeable batteries, to enable them to be used even at places where there is no power point

available. They normally run MS-DOS or WINDOWS operating system, and are mostly used for word processing, spreadsheet computing, data entry, preparing presentation materials, and making presentations.

4. A *personal computer* is a non-portable, general-purpose computer, which can easily fit on a normal size office table, and is generally designed to be used by one person at a time. PCs are mainly used to meet the personal computing needs of individuals, either in their working places or at their homes. They are also used both by children and adults for education and entertainment. They normally run MS-DOS, MS-Windows, Windows-NT, Linux, or Unix operating system, and support multitasking, which eases user operation and saves lots of time, when a user has to switch between two or more applications while performing a job.

| Types of computers / Key features | Notebook | Personal Computer | Workstation | Mainframe system | Supercomputer | Client | Server |
|---|---|---|---|---|---|---|---|
| Size | Very small (can be placed on ones lap) | Small (can be placed on an office table) | Medium (Slightly larger than PC) | Large (needs a large room) | Large (needs a large room) | Generally small (may be large if it also plays the role of a server) | Generally large |
| Processing power | Low | Low | High | Higher | Highest | Generally low | Generally high |
| Main memory capacity | Low | Low | High | Higher | Highest | Generally low | Generally high |
| Hard disk storage capacity | Low | Low | High | Highest | Higher | Generally low | Generally high |
| Has its own monitor, keyboard, and mouse for user interface | Yes | Yes | Yes | Generally no | Generally no | Yes | Generally no |
| Display facility | Foldable flat screen small display | Medium size display screen | Large-screen color monitor, which can display high-resolution graphics | Generally not available | Generally not available | Medium to large screen monitor | Generally not available |
| Single/multiple processors | Single | Generally single | Generally multiple | Multiple | Multiple | Generally single | Generally multiple |
| Single/multiple - User oriented | Single | Single | Generally single | Multiple | Multiple | Single | Multiple |
| Popular operating systems | MS-DOS, MS-Windows | MS-DOS, MS-Windows, Windows-NT, Linux, Unix | Unix or a variation of it | A variation of Unix, or proprietary | A variation of Unix, or proprietary | MS-DOS, MS-Windows, Windows-NT, Linux, Unix | Windows-NT, Unix or its variation, or proprietary |
| Popular usage | Word processing; Spreadsheet; Data Entry; Preparing presentation materials; and Making presentations | Personal computing needs of individuals either in their working places or at their homes; and Education and entertainment of children and adults | Computing needs of engineers, architects, designers; Simulation of complex scientific and engineering problems and visualizing the results of simulation; and Multimedia applications | Data and information processing of I/O-bound applications | Large processor-bound applications, like complex scientific simulations | Provide highly user-friendly interface in a client-server computing environment | Manage a shared resource and provide a set of shared user services in a client-server computing environment |
| Major vendors | IBM, Compaq, Siemens, Toshiba | IBM, Apple, Compaq, Dell, Zenith, Siemens, Toshiba, Hewlett-Packard | Sun Microsystems, IBM, DEC, Hewlett-Packard, Silicon Graphics | IBM, DEC | Cray, IBM, Silicon Graphics, Fujitsu, Intel, C-DAC | Same as PC and Workstation vendors | Same as Workstation, Mainframe System, and Supercomputer vendors |

**Figure 20.6.** Relative comparison of different types of computers based on some key features.

5. A *workstation* is a powerful desktop computer, which is designed to meet the computing needs of engineers, architects, and other professionals, who need greater processing power, larger storage, and better graphics display facility than what PCs provide. Workstations are commonly used for computer-aided design, multimedia applications, and simulation of complex scientific and engineering problems and visualization of the results of simulation. Workstations generally run the Unix operating system or a variation of it. A workstation's operating system is generally designed to support a multiuser environment.

6. *Mainframe systems* are computer systems, which are mainly used for handling the bulk of data and information processing of such organizations as banks, insurance companies, hospitals, railways, etc. They are also used in such environments, in which a large number of users need to share a common computing facility, such as in research groups, educational institutions, engineering firms, etc. A typical configuration of a mainframe system consists of a host computer, a front-end computer, a back-end computer, one or more console terminals, several magnetic disk drives, a few tape drives, a magnetic tape library, several user terminals, several printers, and one or more plotters. A typical mainframe system looks like a row of large file cabinets and needs a large room. A mainframe system having smaller configuration (slower host and subordinate computers, lesser storage space, and fewer user

terminals) is often referred to as a *minicomputer system*.

7. *Supercomputers* are the most powerful and expensive computers available at a given time. They are primarily used for processing complex scientific applications, which require enormous processing power. Some of the well known supercomputing applications include analysis of large volumes of seismic data, simulation of airflow around an aircraft, crash simulation of the design of an automobile, solving complex structure engineering problems, and weather forecasting. Like mainframe systems, supercomputers also support multiprogramming. However, the main difference between these two types of systems is that supercomputers primarily address processor-bound applications, whereas mainframe systems are oriented to input/output-bound applications.

8. Supercomputers use multiprocessing and parallel processing technologies to solve complex problems faster, and hence, they are also known as *parallel computers* or *parallel processing systems*. Moreover, modern supercomputers employ hundreds of processors and are also known as *massively parallel processors*.

9. In a client-server computing environment, a *client* is generally a single-user PC or workstation, which provides a highly user-friendly interface to the end user. It runs client processes, which send service requests to the server. A *server* is generally a relatively large computer, which manages a shared resource and provides a set of shared user services to the clients. It runs the server process, which services client requests for use of the resource managed by the server.

# Questions

1. List out some of the parameters that were traditionally used to classify computers. What were the major types of computers based on this classification scheme? Why is this classification scheme no more valid?

2. On what basis are computers classified today? How many types of computers are there based on this classification scheme?

3. What is a notebook computer? Why is it so called? What are its main uses?

4. What is a laptop personal computer? Why is it so called? Describe a typical configuration of a laptop PC.

5. Notebook computers can be used even while traveling in a train or airplane. Discuss this statement.

6. What operating systems do notebook computers normally use?

7. What features make a notebook computer portable?

8. What is a personal computer? Describe its typical uses.

9. Describe a typical configuration of a PC.

10. Which are the two commonly used models of PCs? How are they different?

11. How are a microprocessor, a motherboard, and a personal computer related?

12. What operating systems do PCs normally use?

13. What is a workstation? What are its common uses?

14. List out the major differences between a PC and a workstation.

15. What operating systems do workstations normally use?

16. What is a mainframe system? What are its typical uses?

17. Describe a typical configuration of a mainframe system.

18. Differentiate among the host computer, front-end computer, and back-end computer of a mainframe system.

19. What is the purpose of a console in a mainframe system?

20. What are the various types of storage devices normally used in a mainframe system?

21. What are the various types of input/output devices normally used in a mainframe system?

22. What is a minicomputer system?

23. Discuss how the subordinate computers of a mainframe system help in improving the overall performance of the system.

24. What is a supercomputer? What are its primary uses?

25. Give examples of at least three supercomputing applications. Explain why do these applications require a supercomputer.

26. What is parallel processing? Explain with an example how parallel processing can help solve a complex problem faster.

27. Why are modern supercomputers also known as massively parallel processors?

28. What is the main difference between a supercomputer and a mainframe system?

29. Give three examples of resources/services that can best be handled by a server in a client-server computing environment.

30. In a client-server computing environment, is it possible for a computer to be both a client and a server at the same time? If no, explain why? If yes, give an example of such a scenario.

31. Write short notes on:
    (a) Workstations
    (b) Mainframe systems
    (c) Supercomputers
    (d) Notebook computers
    (e) Personal computers
    (f) Client and server computers

# Glossary

The purpose of this glossary is to present definitions of some of the terms that are often used in the field of computers and data processing.

## A

**Access control** Deals with the policies and mechanisms to prohibit a user/process from accessing those resources/information, which he/she/it is not authorized to access.

**Access time** The time interval between the instant at which data is called for from a storage device and the instant delivery begins.

**Accumulator Register (A)** A register, which holds the initial data to be operated upon, the intermediate results, and also the final results of processing operations.

**Activity ratio** The ratio of the total number of records in transaction file and the total number of records in master file.

**Adder** A logic circuit capable of forming the sum of two or more quantities.

**Address** An identification, represented in the form of a name, label, or number, for designating a particular location in storage area.

**Address register** A local storage register, which contains the address of the next instruction to be executed.

**Algorithm** A sequence of precise and unambiguous instructions for solving a problem in a finite number of operations.

**Alphabetic** Pertaining to a character set, which contains the letters A to Z and the blank character.

**Alphanumeric** Pertaining to a character set, which contains letters, digits, and usually other special characters, such as comma, dollar sign, plus sign, etc.

**American National Standards Institute (ANSI)** A U.S. based national organization, which establishes uniform standards in several fields.

**American Standard Code for Information Interchange (ASCII)** A standard coding system for computers.

ASCII-7 is a 7-bit code, and its extended version, ASCII-8, is an 8-bit code.

**Analog computer** A computer, which operates on data, which is in the form of continuously variable physical quantities, such as electrical current.

**Anonymous ftp site** On the internet, a computer, which allows a user to log in with a username of anonymous and then a password, which is the user's e-mail address.

**Antivirus utility** A program used to cure a computer from virus infection.

**Application programmer** A programmer who prepares application software.

**Application software** A set of one or more programs designed to solve a specific problem or do a specific task, such as pay calculation, processing of examination results, stores accounting and inventory control, etc.

**Architecture** The organization and interconnection of the various components of a computer system.

**Archiving** The process of storing old data files on separate disks or tapes to make room for new files on the hard disk of a computer.

**Arithmetic Logic Unit (ALU)** The unit of a computing system, which performs all mathematical and logical operations. It is one of the components of the central processing unit (CPU) of the computer.

**Artificial intelligence** A branch of computer science, which deals with computers, which possess reasoning, learning, and thinking capabilities that resemble those of humans.

**Assembler** A computer program, which translates an assembly language program to its machine language equivalent.

**Assembly language** A programming language, which allows instructions and storage location to be represented by letters and symbols instead of numbers. Also known as symbolic language.

**Assembly program** A program written in an assembly language. Also known as symbolic program.

**Asynchronous communication** Data transmission mode in which the sender can send data at any convenient time and the receiver will accept it.

**Automated tape library** A mass storage device, which uses a set of magnetic tapes and tape drives with a controller mounted in a single unit. All the tapes of an automated tape library form a single large storage unit. They are typically used for data archiving and as an on-line data backup device for automated backup.

**Automatic Teller Machine (ATM)** An unattended machine used in banks, which allows a customer to deposit or withdraw cash by the use of an electronic card without the need to interact with a bank employee.

**Auxiliary memory** A storage, which supplements the main memory of a computer. Often referred to as secondary storage, this section of the computer's memory is non-volatile and has low cost per bit stored, but it generally has an operating speed far slower than that of the primary storage.

## ß

**Backbone** The main trunk lines of a computer network, which facilitates the interconnection of other computers and computer networks on the same network.

**Background processing** The automatic execution of lower-priority (background) computer programs, when higher-priority (foreground) programs are not using the system resources.

**Backup** Alternate facilities of programs, data files, hardware equipment, etc., which are used in case the original one is destroyed, lost, or fails to operate.

**Backup file** A copy of a file, created as a safety precaution against loss of data caused due to corruption, or inadvertent deletion of the original file.

**Band printers** See chain printers.

**Bandwidth** The range of frequencies available for data transmission. The wider the bandwidth of a communications system, the more data it can transmit in a given period of time.

**Bar codes** Representation of alphanumeric data by a combination of adjacent vertical lines (called bars) by varying their width and the spacing between them. A *barcode reader* is a scanner, which is used for reading (decoding) bar-coded data.

**Base** The total number of digits (symbols) available to represent numbers in a positional number system.

**Batch processing** The running of several computer programs one after another without the need of a human operator to run each program individually.

**Baud** A unit for measuring data transmission speed. It is used to describe the capacity of a carrier. In general usage, a baud is identical to bits per second.

**Beginners All-Purpose Symbolic Instruction Code (BASIC)** An easy-to-learn, high-level, interactive programming language, which is frequently used with personal computers, and in timesharing environments.

**Bernoulli disk** A magnetic disk-based storage medium in which a single hard disk platter is encased in a plastic cartridge.

**Beta testing** The use of beta version of a software by a selected set of users for identifying errors, which might have been overlooked during the regular testing phase.

**Beta version** The version of a software, which is released to a selected set of users for testing, before its actual release.

**Binary** A characteristic or property involving a selection, choice, or condition, in which there are two possibilities.

**Binary Coded Decimal (BCD)** One of the early coding systems, which is based on the idea of converting each digit of a decimal number into its binary equivalent, rather than converting the entire decimal value into a pure binary form. For example, the decimal number 42 is represented by 0100 0010 in 8-4-2-1 BCD notation.

**Binary number system** A number system with a base of two. It consists of two digits : 0 and 1.

**Biometric device** A device used for user authentication, which verifies some physical characteristic of a user, such as the person's appearance, fingerprints, hand geometry, voice, or signature.

**Bit** Acronym for binary digit, which stands for one binary piece of information. This can be either 0 or 1.

**Bitmap** A method of displaying graphic images on a monitor by altering the color (or turning on or off) of individual dots (pixels) on the coordinate system.

**Block** A group of related items (records, characters, etc.) handled as a unit during input and output. A section of program code treated as a unit.

**Blocking factor** The process of grouping two or more records together to form a block, and the number of records put together in each block is called a blocking factor.

**Boolean algebra**   An algebra, which deals with logical propositions, which are either true or false. This algebra is suitable for use with binary number system, and is very useful in designing logic circuits, which are used by the processors of computer systems.

**Boolean function**   A mathematical function in Boolean algebra. For example, $w = x + y \cdot z$.

**Boolean variable**   A variable used in Boolean algebra. It can assume a value true or false.

**Booting**   The process of automatic loading of the operating system to primary storage, and readying a computer system for use.

**Branch instruction**   An instruction, which transfers program control to a non-consecutive instruction.

**Bridge**   An internetworking tool, which is used to connect networks that use the same communication protocols above the data-link layer, but may not use the same protocols at the physical and data-link layers.

**Broadband channel**   Communication channels, which are capable of data transfer rates of 1 million baud (bits/second) or more. They are used to handle high volumes of data, and for high-speed computer to computer communication, or for simultaneous transmission of data to several different devices.

**Browser**   A software tool, which provides several navigation facilities to help users do Internet surfing easily and effectively.

**Buffer**   A small storage area used to store information on a temporary basis for compensating the difference in rates of flow of data between various computer devices. For example, when data flows from an I/O device to the CPU, it passes through a buffer.

**Bug**   An error in a computer program.

**Built-in-functions**   Subprograms, which are provided with the language so that the programmer need only call them in a program to have them automatically invoked. Also known as intrinsic subprograms.

**Bundled**   The inclusion of software with the hardware of a computer system as part of the system's total price.

**Byte**   A fixed number of adjacent bits, which represent a particular character or symbol. Normally a byte consists of eight bits.

## C

**C**   A programming language, which was designed to have the virtues of high-level programming languages (mainly machine independence) with the efficiency of an assembly language.

**C++**   A programming language, which contains all the elements of the basic C language, but has been expanded to include numerous object-oriented programming features.

**Cache memory**   A small high speed memory, which is used to increase the speed of processing by making current programs and data available to the CPU at a rapid rate.

**Call statement**   A program statement, which transfers program control to a subroutine.

**Canonical form**   A Boolean function whose terms contain all variables (or their complements). This is the unreduced form of the Boolean function in minterm or maxterm form.

**Carrier**   Any device, which is used to transmit data from one location to another.

**Cathode Ray Tube (CRT)**   An electronic tube with a TV like screen upon which information may be displayed.

**C-band transmission**   The use of 4 GHz band of frequencies for transmission and retransmission of microwave signals in a satellite communication system.

**CD-ROM jukebox**   A mass storage device, which uses a set of CD-ROM disks, disk drives, and a controller mounted in a single unit. All the CD-ROM disks of a CD-ROM jukebox form a single large storage unit. They are typically used for archiving read-only data.

**Cell**   The intersection of a row and column in a spreadsheet. A user enters text, number, or formula in a cell.

**Central Processing Unit (CPU)**   The control unit and the arithmetic logic unit of a computer system are jointly known as the CPU. It is the brain of any computer system in which all calculations and comparisons performed by a computer are carried out. The CPU is also responsible for activating, and controlling operations of other units of a computer system.

**Chain printers**   Line printers, which print characters by striking a set of hammers on an inked ribbon and paper placed against a metallic chain on which all the characters of the character set supported by the printer are embossed.

**Channel**   (1) A path for carrying signals between a source and a destination. (2) A track on a magnetic tape, or a band on a magnetic drum.

**Character addressable storage**   A storage device, in which each character has one unique location with its own address. Another name for character addressable storage is variable-word-length storage.

**Character printer**   A printer with a print mechanism, which prints one character at a time.

**Charge-Coupled Device (CCD)** A completely electronic storage device fabricated on semiconductor chips. It stores data as pockets of charge in a semiconductor.

**Chip** A thin wafer of silicon on which integrated electronic components are deposited.

**Circuit switching** The simplest method of data communication in which a dedicated physical path is established between the sending and the receiving stations through the nodes of the network for the complete duration of information exchange.

**Client computer** In a client-server computing environment, a computer, which is used by an end user to interact with the server computer. It runs client processes, which send service requests to the server.

**Client-server computing** A network of computers, which consists of a server computer (such as, file server, database server, print server, name server), and multiple client computers, which share programs and data from the server.

**Clip art library** A collection of graphic images stored on disk, which can be readily used in word processing or desktop publishing documents, or in presentation graphics, or for other purposes.

**Clock speed** The number of times the built-in electronic clock of a computer system pulses in one second.

**Coaxial cable** A cable made up of a single wire in the center of an insulator wrapped in mesh. It is often used as a medium to transmit data between computers, and between computers and peripheral devices.

**Code** (1) The statements of a computer program. (2) A set of rules outlining the way in which data may be represented (like BCD, EBCDIC, ASCII).

**Code generator** A very high-level programming language in which programmers specify through an interactive dialog with the system, the design specifications of a system (which tasks are to be performed), and it automatically generates (produces) the program source code for the system.

**Coding** The process of writing computer instructions in a programming language.

**Collate** To combine items from two or more sequenced files into a single one.

**Collating sequence** An ordering assigned to the characters of a character set to be used for sequencing purposes. A commonly encountered collating sequence involves the special characters, letters, and digits, in that order.

**Combinational circuit** A group of logic gates interconnected to form a logic circuit.

**Command interpreter** The part of an operating system, which serves as an interface for the user to communicate with the computer via its operating system.

**Command-line interface** A textual user interface in which the user gives instructions to the computer by typing commands using the keyboard.

**Comment** An entry in a computer program for the purpose of documentation or explanation. Comments are used within a program to assist anyone reading the source program listing. They do not contain any program logic, and are ignored (not translated) by the language processor.

**COmmon Business Oriented Language (COBOL)** A high-level programming language developed for business data processing applications.

**Common carriers** Data transmission service providers.

**Communication protocol** A set of rules and procedures established to interconnect and communicate between computers. It provides a method for orderly and efficient exchange of data by establishing rules for the proper interpretation of controls and data transmitted as raw bits and bytes.

**Communications processor** A processing unit, which coordinates networks and data communications. Within a computer network, it ensures that data flows to and from different computer systems correctly and efficiently.

**Communications satellite** A microwave relay station precisely positioned 36000 kms. above the equator with an orbit speed that exactly matches the earth's rotation speed. It is used for data transmission between any two randomly chosen points in a very-very large area.

**Communications software** Software that enables transfer of data and programs from one computer system to another in a network of computers.

**Compact Disk-Read-only Memory (CD-ROM)** A shiny, silver color metal disk of 5¼-inch (12 cm) diameter having a storage capacity of about 650 Megabytes. It is so called, because of its enormous storage capacity on a compact-size disk, and because it is a read-only storage medium.

**Compile** To translate a program written in a high-level language into its equivalent machine language program. Usually a single source statement yields more than one machine instruction.

**Compiler** A translator program (software package), which translates a high-level language program into its equivalent machine language program.

**Complement** For a number, which has n digits in it, a complement is defined as the difference between the number and the base raised to the $n^{th}$ power minus one.

For example, complement of $37_{10} = 10^2 - 1 - 37 = 62_{10}$. In Boolean algebra, the complement of a variable is the reverse (NOT) of its value. For example, complement of A is $\bar{A}$.

**Completely connected network**  A network in which there is a separate physical link for connecting each node to any other node in the network.

**Complex Instruction Set Computer (CISC) Architecture**  An architecture of CPUs with large instruction set, variable-length instructions, and a variety of addressing modes.

**Computer**  An electronic device, which can automatically accept and store input data, process them, and produce output results by interpreting and executing programmed instructions.

**Computer Aided Design (CAD)**  Use of computers to automate design and drafting operations.

**Computer Aided Manufacturing (CAM)**  Use of computers to automate manufacturing operations.

**Computer animation**  The area of computer science, which deals with the generation, sequencing, and display (at a specified rate) of a set of images (called frames) to create an effect of visual change òr motion, similar to a movie film (video). Animation is commonly used in those instances where videography is not possible, or animation can better illustrate the concept than video.

**Computer audio**  The area of computer science, which deals with synthesizing, recording, and playback of audio or sound with the aid of a computer.

**Computer graphics**  The area of computer science, which deals with the generation, representation, manipulation and display of pictures (line drawings and images) with the aid of a computer.

**Computer literacy**  Having sufficient computer knowledge, so that an individual can work and live in a computerized society.

**Computer network**  A distributed data processing system in which multiple computers are linked together for the purpose of data communication and resource sharing.

**Computer system**  The various components (input and output devices, storage, CPU) of a computer integrated together to perform the steps called for in the program being executed.

**Computer video**  The area of computer science, which deals with the recording and display of a sequence of images at a reasonable speed to create an impression of movement.

**Computer-Based Training (CBT)**  Using computer technologies for training and education. The use of

computers helps in making tutoring programs, which are tailored to the student's level of subject mastery, and can provide immediate feedback.

**COnference on DAta SYstems Languages (CODASYL)**  A committee of computer users, manufacturers, and the United States government, which helps to establish programming standards for various programming languages.

**Console**  In a mainframe system, the terminal, which is directly connected to the host (main computer), and is mainly used by the system administrators to monitor the health of the system, or to perform some system administration activities.

**Constant**  A value, written into a program instruction, which does not change during the execution of the program.

**Control program**  An operating system program, which controls the operations and management of resources of a computer system. The control program's major functions are job scheduling, input/output scheduling, and program monitoring.

**Control unit**  The unit of a computer system, which manages and coordinates the operations of all the other components of the computer system. It is one of the components of the central processing unit (CPU) of the computer.

**Counter**  A device, register or storage location for storing integers, which is suitably incremented or decremented to represent the number of occurrences of an event.

**CPU scheduler**  The part of an operating system, which is concerned with deciding which of the ready jobs should be allotted the CPU for execution.

**CPU-bound jobs**  Jobs which heavily utilize the CPU operations during the course of their processing.

**Crash**  A hardware or software failure that causes a computer system to stop functioning.

**Cryptography**  A means of protecting private information against unauthorized access in those situations where it is difficult to ensure access control. The basic idea behind this security technique is that, if it is not possible to ensure access control, it is better to prevent comprehension of information.

**Cursor**  A highlight on the screen of a monitor, which indicates the location of the next keyed-in character on the display screen. It can appear as a small rectangular object, line, arrow, or I-beam pointer, or in a spreadsheet, as a large block covering an entire cell.

**Cybernatics**  The use of computers coupled with automatic machinery to carry out complex operations.

**Cyberspace** The world-wide network of computers.

**Cycle time** The time interval between the instant at which a read/write command is given to a memory, and the instant when the next such instruction can be issued to the memory (also known as memory cycle time).

**Cylinder** In a disk pack, a set of corresponding tracks on all the surfaces is called a cylinder. All tracks of a cylinder are accessible by a single movement of the access mechanism.

# D

**Daisy wheel printer** A letter-quality printer, which uses a printing head with the appearance of daisy and/or a wheel. Each petal of the daisy wheel has a character embossed on it.

**Data** A collection of facts in raw form, which become information after proper organization or processing.

**Data Base Management System (DBMS)** A set of programs provided to facilitate the users in organizing, creating, deleting, updating, and manipulating their data in a database.

**Data Definition Danguage (DDL)** A language used to define the structure of a database.

**Data dependence** Dependency of data on the application.

**Data dictionary** A document, which maintains the data definitions of a database. It is automatically created/updated by the DDL as the database schema is defined or changed.

**Data element** A meaningful collection of related characters. Also called a field or data item.

**Data entry** The conversion of human readable data into a form, which a computer system can interpret. This is also called data preparation.

**Data integrity** Consistency of data in all files.

**Data Manipulation Language (DML)** A language used to enter and manipulate the data in a database.

**Data processing** See processing.

**Data processing system** A system that accomplishes data processing. It includes the necessary resources, which are people, procedures and devices needed to process the data.

**Data redundancy** Repetition of the same data items in more than one file.

**Data storage hierarchy** In data processing, organization of data into growing hierarchy for easy manageability. A typical data storage hierarchy consists of bits, characters, fields, records, files and database.

**Data transfer rate** The speed at which data is transferred from main memory to another medium on which data are recorded. For magnetic tape, the data transfer rate is equal to the product of the tape speed and recording density. In a network environment, it refers to the speed of transfer of data from one computer to another on the network.

**Database** A collection of data files integrated and organized into a single comprehensive file system, which is arranged to minimize duplication of data, and to provide convenient access to information within that system to satisfy a wide variety of user needs.

**Database administrator** One who is responsible for defining, updating, and controlling access to a data base.

**Database model** The manner in which the various files of a database are linked together. The four commonly used database models are hierarchical, network, relational, and object-oriented.

**Database schema** The database structure definition.

**Database software** A set of programs, which enables users to create a database, maintain it (add, delete and update its records), organize its data in desired fashion, and to selectively retrieve useful information from it.

**De Morgan's theorem** A theorem in Boolean algebra, which states how to complement a Boolean expression.

**Debugger** A software tool, which helps the programmer in debugging the logic of a program by allowing him/her to follow the program's execution step-by-step, and to display intermediate calculation results and field values whenever desired.

**Debugging** The process of finding and correcting program errors (bugs).

**Decimal number system** A number system with a base of 10. The ten allowable digits are 0, 1, 2, 3, 4, 5, 6, 7, 8, and 9. It is used in our day-to-day life.

**Decision logic** A selection logic.

**Decoder** The part of CPU, which has the necessary circuitry to decode and interpret the meaning of every instruction supported by the CPU.

**Dedicated line** See leased line.

**Design phase** A phase in the life-cycle of software system during which the detailed design of the system selected in the study phase occurs.

**Desktop Publishing (DTP)** An application software package, which allows a user to perform design, typesetting, and paste-up functions, and to produce high-quality, camera-ready printed pages of the documents so prepared on a high-quality printer.

**Development phase**  A phase in the life-cycle of a software system during which a system is constructed to meet the requirements specified in the design phase.

**Diagnostic routines**  Programs used to print error messages by a computer to indicate system problems, and improper program instructions.

**Dial-up line**  A data transmission service, which operates in a manner similar to a telephone call.  Also known as switched line.

**Digital Computer**  A computer, which works with discrete quantities.  It uses numbers to simulate real-time processes.  Compare with analog computer.

**Digitizer** An input device used for converting (digitizing) pictures, maps and drawings into digital form for storage in computers.  This enables re-creation of the drawing from the stored information whenever required, and easy incorporation of changes in the drawing as and when required.

**Direct file** A file organization in which the desired record (piece of information) can be directly located by its key field value without having to search through a sequence of other records.  Also known as random file.

**Direct/leased-line connection**  A method of connecting a computer to the Internet by using a dedicated (leased) telephone line.

**Directory**  A mapping table, which is used by operating systems to map file names to their corresponding file attributes and file data, and also to provide greater flexibility to users in file naming.

**Disk**  A flat, circular plate coated with a magnetic material on which data can be stored by magnetization of portions of the flat surface.

**Disk array**  A mass storage device, which uses a set of hard disks, hard disk drives, and a controller mounted in a single box.   All the disks of a disk array form a single large storage unit.  Also known as Redundant Array of Inexpensive Disks (RAID).

**Disk drive** A devise used for storage and retrieval of data stored on disk.

**Disk pack**  A removable direct-access storage medium containing multiple magnetic disks mounted vertically on a single shaft.

**Diskette** A low-cost, thin, flexible magnetic disk storage device used on small computer systems.  Also called a floppy disk.

**Distributed computing system**  A computer system consisting of interconnected, multiple computers.

**Distributed database** Seamless integration of multiple databases located on different computers. A distributed database management system functions in a manner that the multiple distributed databases managed by it appear as a single, centralized database to the end users.

**Documentation** Documentation of a software system involves collecting, organizing, storing, and maintaining a complete historical record of programs, and other documents used or prepared during the different phases of the system.

**Dot-matrix printers**  Character printers, which form characters and all kinds of images as a pattern of dots.

**Dots Per Inch (DPI)**  A measurement of the quality for printed output.  It refers to the number of dots, which can be printed per linear inch, horizontally or vertically.

**Downloading**  Moving a file from a remote computer to ones own computer in a network environment.

**Downtime**  The period during which a computer is malfunctioning or not operating correctly due to machine failures.

**Drum printers** Line printers, which print characters by striking a set of hammers on an inked ribbon and paper placed against a solid cylindrical drum with characters embossed on its surface in the form of circular bands.

**Dumb terminal**  A terminal, which has no local processing capability.

**Dynamic Data Exchange (DDE)**  A technique for linking applications, which allows a user to move data from one application into another, such as from a spreadsheet into a word-processor.  Changes made in one application are automatically reflected in linked applications.

**Dynamic RAM (DRAM)**  A type of RAM, which uses an external circuitry to periodically "regenerate" or refresh the storage charge to retain the stored data.

**E**

**Edit**  To modify the form or format of the data by inserting or deleting characters where needed.

**Editor**  A software used to interactively review and modify text materials and other program instructions.

**Education software**  Software, which allows computer systems to be used as a teaching and learning tool.

**Electrically EPROM (EEPROM)** An EPROM chip in which the stored information is erased by using high voltage electric pulses.  Also known as flash memory.

**Electronic card** A small plastic card having encoded data appropriate for the application for which it is used.  An electronic-card reader, which is normally connected to a computer, is used to read the data encoded on an electronic card, and transfer it to the computer for further processing.

**Electronic Data Interchange (EDI)** The use of computers and data communications to transmit data electronically between companies.

**Electronic Data Processing (EDP)** Pertaining to data processing equipment, which is predominantly electronic, such as an electronic digital computer.

**Electronic Funds Transfer (EFT)** A general term referring to a cashless approach used to pay for goods and services. Electronic signals between computers are often used to adjust the accounts of the parties involved in a transaction.

**Electronic mail** A service on the Internet, which allows an Internet user to send a mail (message) to another Internet user in any part of the world in a near-real-time manner.

**Electronic pen** An input device, which serves as an effective point-and-draw device.

**Electrostatic printer** A high-speed printer, which uses charged pins to form character matrices on chemically treated paper.

**Electrothermal printer** A high-speed printer, which uses heated elements to create characters as matrices of small dots on heat-sensitive paper.

**Elementary data item** A data item, which is not broken down into smaller units.

**E-Mail** See electronic mail.

**Emulator** A program, which permits one computer to execute the machine-language instructions of another computer of different make.

**Encryption** The process of transforming an intelligible information into an unintelligible form.

**End user** Any individual who uses the information generated by a computer based system.

**End-of-tape (EOT) marker** A reflective marker, which indicates the end of the usable tape.

**End-to-end solution** A computerized solution offered to a user in which a single vendor takes the responsibility of supplying all the hardware and software components of the solution.

**Entertainment software** Software, which allows computer system to be used as an entertainment tool.

**Erasable Programmable Read Only Memory (EPROM)** A memory chip in case of which it is possible to erase information stored in it, and the chip can be reprogrammed to store new information.

**Ethernet** The most widely used LAN technology.

**Execution time** The total time required to execute a program on a particular system is called its execution time for that computer system.

**Explicitly Parallel Instruction Computing (EPIC)** A technology, which is fast emerging as the technology for next-generation processors. The three key features used in this technology for improved processor performance are explicit parallelism, predication and speculation.

**Extended Binary Coded Decimal Interchange Code (EBCDIC)** An 8-bit coding system, developed by IBM, which is used to represent characters in many computers.

# F

**Facsimile (FAX)** Transmission of pictures, texts, maps, graphs, etc., over transmission lines, phone lines, and other carriers between geographically separated points. An image is scanned at a transmitting point, and duplicated at a receiving point.

**Feasibility study** A study to determine whether the proposed solution is technically and economically feasible in all respect.

**Field** In a record, a meaningful collection of one or more related characters treated as a unit.

**Fifth-generation computers** Computers built since 1989 till now. They use ultra large-scale integrated circuits, very fast and large main memory and disk storage, and very powerful programming languages and operating systems.

**File** A collection of related information.

**File Management System (FMS)** A set of programs provided to facilitate the users in organizing, creating, deleting, updating, and manipulating their files.

**File Transfer Protocol (FTP)** An application level protocol, which allows a user to move a file from one computer to another in a network environment.

**File utilities** A set of routines, which perform a variety of generalized operations (such as, sorting, searching, merging, copying, printing and maintenance) on data files.

**Firewall** A software, which usually runs on the proxy server of an organization, and controls the flow of incoming and outgoing messages from within an organization for providing better security to the organization.

**Firmware** A sequence of instruction (software), which is substituted for hardware, and stored in read-only memory (ROM).

**First-generation computers**  Computers built between 1942 and 1955, which used vacuum tubes, and were programmed in assembly language.  Few examples are ENIAC, EDVAC and EDSAC.

**Fixed-wireless system**  A wireless computing system, which supports little or no mobility of the computing equipment associated with the wireless network.

**Fixed-head magnetic disk**  A magnetic disk system, which that eliminates the use of an access mechanism by distributing all the read/write heads over the disk surfaces.

**Flash memory**  See Electrically EPROM (EEPROM).

**Flip-flop**  An electronic circuit, which can be placed in one out of two stable states.  Each state may be used to represent a binary digit.

**Floating-point numbers**  Signed numbers held in a fraction-exponent format.  For example, 3216 would be represented as $0.3216 \times 10^4$ in floating-point notation.

**Floppy disk**  See diskette.

**Flowchart**  A pictorial representation, which uses predefined symbols to describe either the logic of a computer program (program flowchart), or the data flow and processing steps of a system (system flowchart).

**Flowcharting**  The process of drawing a flowchart for an algorithm.

**Font**  A complete set of characters with the same style and size.

**Foreground processing**  Automatic execution of high-priority (foreground) jobs by preempting resources held by low-priority (background) jobs.  Contrast with background processing.

**FORmula TRANslation (FORTRAN)**  A high-level, programming language used for scientific and engineering applications.

**Fourth-generation computers**  Computers built between 1975 and 1989.  They used large-scale integrated circuits, semiconductor memories, and powerful high-level languages and operating systems.

**Frequency Division Multiplexing (FDM)**  A method used to concurrently transmit data between several transmitters and receivers over a single transmission medium.  The available bandwidth of a physical medium is divided into smaller, disjoint, logical bandwidths, and each of the component bandwidths is used as a separate communications line (channel).

**Front-end processor**  A processor designed specifically to handle the communications processing task.  Its main purpose is to off-load communications processing task from the host computer, thereby the host computer can be dedicated for applications and data processing jobs.

**Full adder**  An adder, which adds three binary digits and outputs a result bit and a carry bit.

**Full duplex**  A data transmission mode in which data signals can be transmitted between a source and a destination in both directions simultaneously.

**Function**  A subprogram, which returns a single value.

## G

**Garbage-In-Garbage-Out (GIGO)**  Refers to computer errors caused due to incorrect input data, or unreliable programs.

**Gateway**  (1) A computer, which is connected to the Internet by using a dedicated (leased) telephone line, and is used to provide Internet connectivity to other computers via it.  (2) An internetworking tool, which is used to interconnect dissimilar networks that use different communication protocols.

**Generation**  In computer talk, it is a step in technology. It provides a framework for the growth of the computer industry.

**Gigabytes (GB)**  Memory storage equal to 1,073,741,824 ($2^{30}$) bytes in a computer.

**Gigaflop**  $10^9$ floating-point arithmetic operations per second.

**Graphical User Interface (GUI)**  An interface for computer users, which provides icons (pictures) and menus (list of choices), which users can select with a mouse for telling the computer what they want it to do for them.

**Graphics software**  Software, which enables users to use a computer system for creating, editing, viewing, storing retrieving and printing designs, drawings, pictures, graphs, and anything else, which can be drawn in a traditional manner.

**Gray scales**  The number of shades of a color that can be presented on a monochrome (black and white) monitor's screen, or on a monochrome printer's output.

**Groupware**  See computer supported co-operative working (CSCW).

## H

**Hacker**  A computer enthusiast who uses the computer as a source of recreation by pushing its capabilities to its limits (performance, security, storage, etc.).

**Half adder**  An adder, which adds two binary digits, and outputs a result bit and a carry bit (if any).

**Half duplex**  A communication system in which data can be transmitted between a source and a destination in both directions, but only in one direction at a time.

**Hard disk**  A magnetic disk storage device, which uses disks made of rigid metal (frequently aluminium). The hard disk platters come in many sizes ranging from 1 to 14- inch diameter.

**Hard-copy output**  A computer output, which is permanent in nature and can be kept in paper files, or can be looked at a later time, when the person is not using the computer. For example, output produced by printers or plotters on paper.

**Hardware**  The physical components of a computer system, such as electronic, magnetic, and mechanical devices.

**Hashing**  The process of using an address generating function (called hashing algorithm) to map a record's key field value to its storage address.

**Hertz**  One cycle per second.

**Hexadecimal number system**  A number system with a base of 16. Its digits range from 0 to F. It is commonly used as a shortcut notation for groups of four binary digits.

**Hierarchical database**  A database model in which the data elements are linked in the form of an inverted tree structure with the root at the top and the branches formed below.

**Hierarchical network**  A communications network in which computers or processors are connected in a tree-like structure.

**High-level language**  A programming language whose structure is application oriented, and is independent of the structure of the computer. Each statement of such a language is translated into many machine language statements.

**Hotlist**  A personal list of favorite URL addresses, which an Internet user is likely to frequently visit in future. A user's hotlist is automatically created and stored on his/her local web client computer by a browser.

**Hybrid network**  A network, which is a combination of two or more different network topologies.

**Hydra printers**  Multifunctional devices, which perform the functions of two or more of the following office equipment – printer, fax machine, copy machine and scanner.

**Hypertext**  Documents that are prepared by using special linking facility for easier electronic access and manipulation.

**HyperText Markup Language (HTML)**  A powerful language used for creating hypertext documents.

**HyperText Transport Protocol (HTTP)**  An Internet Protocol for interaction between the computers on the Internet.

## I

**I/O ports**  Sockets used to plug-in I/O devices to a computer system.

**I/O-bound jobs**  Jobs whose CPU utilization is very low. They mostly perform I/O operations during the course of their processing.

**Icon**  A graphical object displayed on a visual display screen, which is used in place of words or phrases to allow users to select program options, when selected with a mouse or other pointing device.

**Impact printer**  A printer, which prints characters by causing hammers to strike against the paper on which information is to be printed.

**Indexed Sequential Access Method (ISAM)**  See indexed sequential file.

**Indexed sequential file**  A file organization in which an index (directory) file is used to have both sequential and random access to the records of the file. Also known as the Indexed Sequential Access Method (ISAM).

**Information**  Processed data obtained as the output of data processing. It is used by people to enhance understanding and to achieve specific purposes.

**Inkjet printers**  Character printers, which form characters and all kinds of images by spraying small drops of ink on to the paper.

**Input**  Data and instructions entered into a computer for processing purposes.

**Input device**  A device used to enter data and instructions into a computer. Examples are keyboard, mouse, trackball, joystick, scanner, digitizer, voice recognition system, and vision input system.

**Input/Output (I/O)**  Pertaining to the techniques, media, and devices used for man-machine interaction.

**Input/Output Register (I/O)**  A register, which is used to communicate with the input/output devices.

**Instruction**  A command or order given to a computer. It normally consists of a code to indicate the operation to be performed, and address(es) in memory where the operand(s) would be found.

**Instruction Register (I)**  A register, which holds the current instruction that is being executed.

**Instruction Set**  A set of machine instructions that the CPU has built-in ability to execute.

**Integrated Circuits (ICs)** Circuits consisting of several electronic components like transistors, resistors, and capacitors grown on a single chip of silicon, eliminating wired interconnection between components.

**Integrated Services Digital Network (ISDN)** A telephonic system, which provides digital (not analog) telephone and data services.

**Intelligent terminal** A terminal having extensive local processing capability. It has a built-in microcomputer, which can be programmed by users.

**Inter Block Gap (IBG)** When several records are in one block, these gaps separate the blocks of records on magnetic tape.

**Inter Record Gap (IRG)** Blank space between two consecutive records on a tape.

**Interface** Electronic circuit used to interconnect I/O devices to a computer's CPU or memory.

**Internal storage** The addressable storage in a digital computer, which is directly under the control of the CPU.

**Internet** A network of networks of computers, which links many different types of computers all over the world.

**Internet search engine** An application available on the WWW, which helps users locate the web sites containing useful information and references to such information.

**Internet Service Provider (ISP)** An organization, which maintains one or more gateway computers, and provides Internet access facility to other users by allowing them to connect their computers to its own gateway computer(s) by using a modem.

**Internet surfing** The process of navigating the Internet to search for useful information.

**Internetworking** Interconnecting of two or more networks to form a single network. The resulting network is called an internetwork.

**Interpreter** A language processor, which translates a statement of a high-level language, and immediately executes it before translating the next source language statement. It is the most common language processor for BASIC.

**Iteration logic** A program construct, which is used to produce loops in program logic, when one or more instructions may be executed several times depending on some condition. Also known as looping logic.

## J

**Java** A programming language, which was designed to have machine-independent compiled code. It is primarily used for Internet-based applications.

**Job** See process.

**Job Control language (JCL)** A special purpose language, which is used to describe to a computer's operating system the resource requirements of a job fed to the computer for processing.

**Joystick** An input device, which serves as an effective pointing device for applications, such as video games, flight simulators, training simulators, and for controlling industrial robots.

**Jump instruction** An instruction or signal, which, conditionally or unconditionally, specifies the location of the next instruction, and directs the computer to that instruction. A jump instruction is used to alter the normal sequence of control of the computer.

**Justification** The alignment of text at the left margin, the right margin, or both margins.

## K

**Kernel** The central controlling part of an operating system, which implements the most primitive of the system's functions. It is the only part of an operating system, which a user cannot replace or modify.

**Key field** A unique field in a record, which is used to distinguish one record from another.

**Keyboard** An input device, which enables data entry into a computer by pressing a set of keys (labeled buttons), which are neatly mounted on a keyboard connected to the computer system.

**Key-to-tape** A device used to enter data onto a magnetic tape.

**Kilobytes (KB)** Memory storage equal to 1024 ($2^{10}$) bytes in a computer.

**Kiosk** An unattended system, which is used to store information of public interest, and allows common people to access the stored information as per their requirement.

**K$_u$-band transmission** The use of 11 GHz to 14 GHz band of frequencies for transmission and retransmission of microwave signals in a satellite communication system.

## L

**Label** One or more characters used to identify a statement, an instruction, or a data field in a computer program.

**Label record** A machine-readable record, which is used to identify a data file. It is the first record of the file.

**Landscape mode** A mode of printing in which the printed lines are parallel to the longer edge of the paper.

**Language processor** A software used to convert source program instructions to object or machine language instructions. Few examples are assembler, compiler and interpreter.

**Large Scale Integration (LSI)** Integration of over 30,000 electronic components on a single chip.

**Laser disk** See optical disk.

**Laser printers** Page printers, which produce very high quality output by forming characters and all kinds of images with very tiny ink particles. They use a combination of laser-beam and electrophotographic techniques to create printed outputs.

**Latency** In case of disk storage, the relational delay time for the desired data (sector) to come under the read/write head positioned over that track. Maximum latency time equals the time taken by disk to rotate once.

**Leased line** A data transmission service in which a special conditioned telephone line directly and permanently connects two computers. A leased line can be used for both voice and data transmission. Also known as private line or dedicated line.

**Library routine** A tested routine maintained in a library of programs.

**Light pen** A pen shaped device, which is used as an input device to input data into computers by writing or sketching on the screen of a cathode ray tube.

**Linker** A program, which is used to properly combine all the object program files (modules) of a software, and to convert them into the software's final executable form.

**Linux** An open-source operating system enhanced and backed by thousands of programmers world-wide. It is a multi-tasking operating system, which was originally designed to be used on personal computers.

**LISt Processing (LISP)** A programming language suitable for manipulating non-numeric data, such as symbols and strings of text. It is used in the areas of pattern recognition, artificial intelligence, and for simulation of games.

**Load module** The final executable form of a software produced by a linker.

**Local Area Network (LAN)** A computer network, which interconnects computers and other peripheral devices within a limited geographical area of a few kilometers.

**Logic circuit** See combinational circuit.

**Logic error** An error, which occurs when the actual logic of a program is different from the desired logic. Such errors cause the program to produce incorrect output.

**Logic gate** An electronic circuit, which operates on one or more input signals to produce standard output signals. For example, AND, OR and NOT gates. Logic gates are the building blocks of all the circuits in a computer.

**Logical operators** Symbols used to show a logical relationship between two data items. Examples in FORTRAN are .EQ. for equal, and .GT. for greater than.

**Logo** An easy-to-learn programming language, which is commonly used to teach problem-solving skills to children.

**Loop** A sequence of instructions, which is executed repeatedly, until a terminal condition occurs.

**Looping logic** See iteration logic.

**Low-level languages** Programming languages, which normally translate from one source instruction to one object instruction. These languages are machine dependent.

## M

**Machine language** A low-level language, which is directly understandable by the computer system. Each model of a computer has a unique machine language.

**Macro** A sequence of frequently used operations, or keystrokes bundled together as a single command, or keystroke by software, so that the invocation of the single command or keystroke leads to the invocation of all the operations/keystrokes in the specified sequence. This helps speed user interaction with the system.

**Macro flowchart** A flowchart, which outlines the main segments of a program, or shows less detail.

**Macro instruction** An instruction in a source language, which is equivalent to a specified sequence of machine instructions.

**Magnetic core** Tiny rings made of magnetic material, which can be polarized to represent a binary 1 or 0.

**Magnetic disk** See disk.

**Magnetic Ink Character Recognition (MICR)** A technology used by the banking industry for faster processing of the large volume of cheques. This technology also ensures accuracy of data entry, because most of the information is pre-printed on the cheque and is directly fed to the computer.

**Magnetic storage** Storage devices such as disks, drums, tapes, cores, etc., which utilize the magnetic properties of materials to store data.

**Magnetic tape** A secondary storage device, which uses a long plastic strip coated with a magnetic material as a recording medium.

**Magneto-optical disk** A storage disk, which integrates optical and magnetic disk technologies to enable rewritable storage with laser-beam technology.

**Main memory** See primary storage.

**Mainframe system** A computer system, which is mainly used for handling the bulk of data and information processing of such organizations as banks, insurance companies, hospitals, railways, etc. They are also used in such environments where a large number of users need to share a common computing facility, such as in research groups, educational institutions, engineering firms, etc.

**Management Information System (MIS)** An organized collection of people, procedures, and devices used to provide the right information to the right person at the right time for proper decision-making.

**Manufacturer-programmed ROM** A ROM in which data is burnt in by the manufacturer of the electronic equipment in which it is used.

**Mass storage** Storage systems, which provide access to several terabytes of stored data. They use multiple units of storage media (such as multiple disks, multiple tapes, multiple CD-ROMs) as a single secondary storage device.

**Massively Parallel Processing (MPP)** An approach to designing supercomputers in which thousands of processors are integrated within a single computer, so that the supercomputer can perform thousands of tasks simultaneously.

**Master file** A file containing relatively permanent data. This file is often updated by records in a transaction file.

**Maxterm** A Boolean quantity consisting of all terms (in its normal form or complement form) ORed together. Any combination ($2^n$ for n variables) of terms and complements is permissible, provided all are included in the term.

**Medium Scale Integration (MSI)** A circuit with about 100 transistors fabricated on a single chip.

**Megabytes (MB)** Memory storage equal to 1,048,576 ($2^{20}$) bytes in a computer.

**Memory** A device or medium, which can accept data, hold them, and deliver them on demand at a later time.

**Memory Address Register (MAR)** A register, which holds the address of the active memory location and loaded from the program control register when an instruction is read from memory.

**Memory Buffer Register (MBR)** A register, which holds the contents of the memory word read from, or written in, memory.

**Memory dump** Contents of memory duplicated on another storage device or printed on a printer.

**Memory partition** In a multiprogramming system, the area occupied by each job residing simultaneously in the main memory.

**Menu** A list of processing choices displayed on the screen from which a user may select.

**Menu bar** A menu in which the options are displayed on a horizontal bar (usually at the tope of the display screen) displayed across the screen.

**Merging** The combining of records from two or more ordered files into a single ordered file.

**Message switching** A data communication method in which the data (message) to be sent is first appended with the destination address, and then sent across the network to its destination.

**Metropolitan Area Network (MAN)** Networks, which share some of the characteristics of both LANs and WANs. They usually interconnect computers spread over a geographical area of about 50 kilometers.

**Micro flowchart** A flowchart with more details. It is also called a detailed flowchart.

**Microcode** The very basic directions, which tell the CPU how to execute an instruction; located in the control unit.

**Microcomputer** The smallest category of computer fabricated using a microprocessor, and other integrated circuits, namely a ROM, RAM, and I/O interface chips.

**Microkernel** Technology, which allows operating systems to be modeled and designed in a modular fashion.

**Microprocessor** An IC chip, which contains all the circuits needed to perform arithmetic logic and control functions, the core activities of all computers, on a single chip.

**Microprogram** Firmware programs residing in read-only memory (ROM). They deal with low-level machine functions, and are essentially substitutes for additional hardware.

**Microsecond** One-millionth of a second.

**Millisecond** One-thousandth of a second.

**Minterm** A Boolean quantity consisting of all terms (in its normal form or complement form) ANDed together. Any combination ($2^n$ for n variables) of terms and complements is permissible, provided all are included in the term.

**MIPS** Millions of Instructions Per Second.

**Mnemonic** Any kind of mental trick we use to help us remember. For example, a computer may be designed to interpret the machine code of 1111 (binary) as the subtract operation, but it is easier for a human being to remember it as SUB.

**Mobile computing** A wireless computing system, which supports mobility of the computing equipment, which the users use to access the resources associated with the wireless network. It allows mobile users to access information from anywhere and at anytime. Also known as nomadic computing.

**Modulation** The technique by which a digital signal is converted to its analog form for transmission over an analog facility.

**MOdulator-DEModulator (Modem)** Devices used to convert digital signals (to be communicated over an analog channel, such as telephone line) to analog form at the sending end, and back to digital form at the receiving end.

**Monitor** A popular output device used for producing soft-copy output. It displays the output on a television like screen.

**Motherboard** The main circuit board of a computer system. It has the CPU chip, RAM chips, ROM chips, I/O handling chips, etc. mounted on it. Also known as system board.

**Mouse** A small, hand-held input device, which serves as an effective point-and-draw device in today's computers.

**MS-DOS** Stands for Microsoft Disk Operating System. A single-user operating system, which was popularly used for personal computers in the 1980s.

**Multi-access bus network** A network in which a single transmission medium is shared by all nodes.

**Multimedia** Use of more than one media (such as text, graphics, animation, audio and video) for information presentation.

**Multimedia computer system** A computer system, which has the capability to integrate two or more types of media (text, graphics, animation, audio, and video) for the purpose of generation, storage, representation, manipulation and access of multimedia information.

**Multiplexing** The method of dividing a physical channel into many logical channels, so that a number of independent signals may be simultaneously transmitted on it.

**Multiprocessing** A term used to describe interconnected computer configurations, or computers with two or more independent CPUs, which have the ability to simultaneously execute several programs.

**Multiprocessor** A computer system consisting of two or more CPUs under a common control.

**Multiprogramming** Interleaved execution of two or more different and independent programs by the same computer.

**Multitasking** Concurrent execution of multiple jobs (often referred to as *tasks* of same user) in a single-user system.

# N

**Nanosecond** One-billionth ($10^{-9}$) of a second.

**Narrowband channel** Communication channels, which handle low volumes of data, typically from 45 to 300 baud. They are used mainly for telegraph lines and low speed terminals.

**Netiquette** Deals with the rules of framing messages while interacting with other Internet users.

**Network** See computer network.

**Network database** A database model in which the data elements are organized in the form of parent-child relationships.

**Network Interface Card (NIC)** A hardware device, which allows a computer to be connected to a network, both functionally and physically.

**Network topology** The structure of interconnection of nodes of a computer network.

**Newsgroup** A group of Internet/Intranet users, who use the usenet facility of the Internet to exchange their views/ideas/information on some common topic, which is of interest to all the group members.

**Node** An end point of a branch in a network, or a common junction of two or more network branches.

**Nomadic computing** See mobile computing.

**Nonimpact printer** A printer, which performs some type of operation to the paper, instead of physically striking it (as in the case of an impact printer). To print characters with nonimpact printers, the paper can be sprayed with ink, magnetized, electrically charged, heated, placed under pressure, or struck by laser beams.

**Non-positional number system** A number system in which each symbol represents the same value, regardless of its position in the number, and the symbols are simply added to find out the value of a particular number. It is very difficult to perform arithmetic with such a number system.

**Non-volatile storage** A storage medium, which retains its contents when the power is turned off or interrupted.

**Notebook computer** A small, portable computer mainly for use by people who need computing power wherever they go.

**Numeric** Pertaining to a character set, which contains the numbers 0 to 9.

# O

**Object Linking and Embedding (OLE)** A feature found in application software packages, which allows joining of documents in different applications, so that changes in either document are reflected in the other document.

**Object program** A fully compiled or assembled program, which is ready to be loaded into the computer. It results from the translation of a source program by a language processor.

**Object-oriented database** A database model, which captures object-oriented concepts, such as class hierarchy, inheritance, and methods.

**Object-Oriented Programming (OOP)** A programming methodology, which deals with solving problems by identifying the real-world objects of the problem and the processing required of those objects, and then creating simulations of those objects, their processes, and the required communications between the objects.

**Object-oriented programming languages** Programming languages, which encapsulate data and sequences of operations into abstract entities called objects, providing a stronger encapsulation mechanism than procedure. Hence, object-oriented programming provides a more powerful modeling tool than procedure-oriented programming.

**Octal number system** A number system with a base of 8. The octal digits range from 0 to 7. It is commonly used as a shortcut notation for groups of three binary digits.

**Off-line** A device or system not directly under the control of a computer system.

**Off-line data entry devices** Input devices through which data is recorded on some media, such as floppies or tapes, and then entered later into the computer from the media for processing.

**On-line** A device or system directly connected to and under the control of a computer system.

**On-line data entry devices** Input devices, which are connected directly to the computer on which the entered data is processed.

**Operand** The part of a machine level instruction, which tells the central processor the location of the data to be manipulated.

**Operating system** An integrated set of programs, which controls the resources of a computer system, and provides its users with an interface or virtual machine, which is more convenient to use than the bare machine.

**Operation code (op code)** The part of a machine level instruction which tells the central processor what has to be done.

**Operation phase** The life-cycle phase during which the system constructed in the development phase is used.

**Optical bar-code reader** An input device, which is able to interpret combinations of marks (bars), which represent data.

**Optical Character Recognition (OCR) device** An input device (a scanner) equipped with a character recognition software. It is used for inputting text documents, and store them in a form suitable for doing word processing of the documents.

**Optical disk** A storage medium, which consists of a rotating disk, which is coated with a thin metal or some other material that is highly reflective. Laser beam technology is used for recording/reading of data on the disk. Also known as laser disks.

**Optical fiber** Hair-thin threads of glass or plastic used as a data transmission medium. They use light signals for data transmission.

**Optical Mark Reader (OMR)** An input device (a scanner), which is capable of recognizing a pre-specified type of mark made by pencil or pen. Any input data, which is of a choice or selection nature can be recorded for OMR input.

**OSI protocol** A communication protocol to interconnect geographically dispersed heterogeneous computers. This protocol has been standardized by the International Standards Organization (ISO).

**Output** The information generated as a result of processing by a system.

**Output device** A device used in a computer system to supply information and results of computation to the outside world. Examples are monitor, printer, plotter, screen image projector, and voice response system.

# P

**Packed decimal format** A modified form of zoned decimal number, which places two decimal digits into each byte of the field with the exception of the rightmost byte, which contains one digit and the sign of the field.

**Packet switching** A data communication method in which the data (message) to be sent is first split up into packets of fixed size; each packet is then appended with source and destination addresses, and some control information; and then the packets are sent across the network to their destination. At the receiver end, the packets are reassembled to recreate the message.

**Page** A program segment, which is loaded into the main memory only when it is needed for execution.

**Page printer** A high-speed printer with a mechanism, which appears to print an entire page at one time.

**Palmtop computer** A battery-operated computer with personal assistance tools. It is small-enough to fit in ones pocket, and operated by keeping it on ones palm.

**Parallel binary adder** An adder in which all the bits of the two binary numbers are added simultaneously.

**Parallel processing** A technology in which a multi-processor system is used to solve complex problems faster by breaking the problem into sub-problems, and allowing different sub-problems to be processed simultaneously by different processors of the multi-processor system.

**Parity bit** An extra bit added to a string of bits, which enables the computer to detect internal errors in the transmission of binary data.

**Pascal** A high-level programming language named after Blaise Pascal, which facilitates the use of structured programming techniques.

**Password** A code by which a user gains access to a computer system. It is used for security purposes.

**Patch** A modifications of a software carried out between its two released versions. A patch (modification) is created to fix a newly discovered bug. All the patches are incorporated in a new release version of the software.

**Peripherals** The various input/output devices and auxiliary storage units of a computer system.

**Personal assistance software** Software, which enables users to use personal computers for storing and retrieving personal information, and planning and managing personal schedules, contacts, finances, and inventory of important items.

**Personal Computer (PC)** A small and inexpensive computer used by individuals for carrying out personal jobs, or for applications, such as entertainment, home management, and hobbies.

**Personal Digital Assistant (PDA)** A pocked-sized computer having facilities, such as calendar, calculator, notepad, etc.

**Phase modulation** A form of modulation in which two binary values of digital data are represented by the shift in phase of the carrier signal. That is, a sine wave with phase $= 0^0$ represents a digital 1, and a sine wave with phase $= 180^0$ represents a digital 0.

**Picosecond** One trillionth of a second.

**Pixel** A picture element. It is used to represent one point in a raster scan display device.

**Plotter** An ideal output device, which is often used by architects, engineers, city planners, and others who need to routinely generate high-precision, hard-copy, graphic output of widely varying sizes.

**Point-and-draw devices** Input devices, which can be used to rapidly point to, and select a particular graphic icon, or menu item from the multiple options displayed on the screen. Many of these devices can also be very effectively used to create graphic elements on the screen, such as lines, curves and freehand shapes. Some of the commonly used point-and-draw devices are mouse, trackball, joystick, electronic pen and touch screen.

**Point-Of-Sale (POS) device** An I/O device capable of immediately updating sales and inventory records at a central CPU, and producing a printed sales transaction receipt.

**Portrait mode** A mode of printing in which the printed lines are parallel to the shorter edge of the paper.

**Positional number system** A number system in which there are only a few symbols called digits, and these symbols represent different values, depending on the position they occupy in the number. The value of each digit in such a number is determined by the digit itself, the position of the digit in the number, and the base of the number system.

**Preview** A feature of a word-processing package, which permits the users to see what the document will look like (almost, if not exactly) when it is printed.

**Primary storage** A temporary storage area, which is built into the computer hardware, and in which instructions and data of a program reside mainly when the program is being executed by the CPU.

**Printer** An output device used to produce hard-copy output.

**Private line** See leased line.

**Procedure** A subprogram, which performs an action but returns no value.

**Process** A program in execution. Also known as a job.

**Processing** Performing a series of actions, or operations on data to convert them into useful information.

**Processor** A unit of a computer system, which interprets instructions and executes them.

**Program** A set of sequenced instructions (written in a language that can be understood by a computer) used to direct and control the operations of the computer to solve a problem, or to perform a particular task.

**Program Control (PC) Register** A register, which holds the address of the next instruction to be executed.

**Program Design Language (PDL)**  See pseudocode.

**Program library**  A collection of complete programs, subroutines, and program modules, which have already been developed, tested, and documented, usually as a result of other programming projects.

**Programmable Read-Only Memory (PROM)**  Similar to read only memory with the exception that these chips can be reprogrammed by using special external equipment.

**Programmer**  One who designs, writes, tests, and maintains computer programs.

**Programming language**  A language used to express algorithms in computer understandable form.

**Protocol**  See communication protocol.

**Prototyping**  The process of developing a small working model of a final operational system to demonstrate the concepts, look, and feel of the final system.

**Pseudocode**  A programming analysis tool, which is used for planning program logic.  It is an imitation of actual computer instructions written in a natural language, such as English.  Also known as Program Design Language (PDL).

**Public-domain software**  A software, which is available free, or for a nominal charge from the bulletin boards, or user-group libraries on the Internet.  Also known as shareware or user-supported software.

**Quantum**  See time slice.

**Query By Example (QBE)**  A software tool, which enables database users to specify search criteria by providing a front end for the query language, which collects the facts about a query from the user, and composes query language statements internally.

**Query language**  A language, which enables users to define their requirements for extracting the desired information from the database in the form of queries.

**Radix**  Same as base.  See base.

**Random Access Memory (RAM)**  A memory in which the time to retrieve stored information is independent of the address where it is stored.

**Random file**  See direct file.

**Random/direct-access storage device**  A storage device in which access to any stored information is direct, and approximately equal access time is required for accessing any information irrespective of its location.  Magnetic,

optical and magneto-optical disks are typical examples of such a storage device.

**Raster graphics**  Graphic objects composed of patterns of dots called pixels.

**Read-Only Memory (ROM)**  A non-volatile memory chip in which data are stored permanently, and cannot be altered by the programmer.

**Record**  A collection of related items of data treated as a unit.

**Record length**  A measure of the size of a record, usually specified in units, such as characters.

**Reduced Instruction Set Computer (RISC) Architecture**  An architecture of CPUs with a small instruction set, fixed-length instructions, and reduced references to memory to retrieve operands.

**Redundant Array of Inexpensive Disks (RAID)**  See disk array.

**Registers**  Small, high-speed storage units, which are used to hold the information on a temporary basis when there is an interpretation and execution of instructions by the CPU.  Data stored in a specific register have a special meaning to the CPU.

**Relational database**  A database model in which the data elements are organized in the form of multiple tables, and the data in one table is related to data in another table through the use of a common field.

**Remote access**  Accessing a computer from a distant station using communication facilities.

**Report file**  A file, which holds a copy of a report generated by a data processing application in computer-accessible form, until it is convenient to print it.

**Report generator**  A software, which enables the users of a database to design the layout of a report, so that it can be presented in the desired format.

**Report Program Generator (RPG)**  A business oriented, general purpose programming language designed to generate the output reports resulting from the processing of common business applications.

**Response time**  The elapsed time between submission of a job to the system for processing, and the first response produced by the system for the job.

**Ring network**  A computer network in which there is no host computer for controlling other computers, and each computer in the network has communicating subordinates.

**Router**  An internetworking tool, which is used to interconnect those networks, which use the same high-level protocols above the network layer.

**Routing**  The selection of actual path to be used to transmit a message in a wide-area network environment.

**RS-232-C interface**  A standard interface used for interconnecting user terminals to computers.  It was defined by the Electronics Industrial Association (USA).

**Run time**  The time required to complete a single, continuous, execution of an object program.

## S

**Scanner**  An input device used for direct data entry into the computer system from source documents.

**Schema builder**  A software tool, which enables a user to define a database schema interactively by prompting the user to enter the field name, field type, field size, and so on for each field.

**Screen image projector**  An output device, which is used to project information from a computer on to a large screen (such as a cloth screen or a wall), so that it can be simultaneously viewed by a large group of people.

**Scrolling**  Using program-specified ways (by the use of keys or mouse) to move the items displayed in a window up or down, or left or right to see parts of the file that extend past the bottom or top or sides of the window.

**Second-generation computers**  Computers built during the period 1955 and 1964.  They used transistors in CPU, and magnetic cores for main memory.  On software front, they used high-level languages like FORTRAN and COBOL for programming, and batch operating systems.

**Secondary storage**  See auxiliary memory.

**Sector**  The smallest unit with which any disk can work. Disk drives are designed to access only whole sectors at a time.

**Security**  Policies and mechanisms, which deal with protecting the various resources and information of a computer system against destruction and unauthorized access.

**Seek time**  In a disk system, the time required for a read/write head to move to the track where the data to be read or written is stored.  Maximum seek time equals the time taken for the head to move from the outermost track to the innermost track.

**Selection logic**  A program construct, which is used for selecting the proper path out of two or more alternative paths in the program logic.  Also known as decision logic.

**Self-documenting languages**  Programming languages, which do not require much explanation to be understood by someone reading the program instruction.  For example, COBOL language.

**Semiconductor storage**  A storage device whose storage elements are formed as solid-state electronic components on an integrated circuit chip.

**Sequence logic**  A program construct, which is used for performing instructions one after another in sequence.

**Sequential file**  A file in which records are stored one after another in an ascending or descending order determined by the value of the key field of the records.

**Sequential processing**  A technique in which a number of similar items or transactions to be processed are grouped together and processed in a designated sequence.

**Sequential-access storage device**  A storage device in which information can only be retrieved in the same sequence in which it is stored.  Magnetic tape is a typical example of such storage device.

**Server computer**  In a client-server computing environment, a computer, which manages a shared resource and provides a set of shared user services to the clients.  It runs the server process, which services client requests for use of the resource managed by the server.

**Shareware**  See public-domain software.

**Simplex**  A data transmission mode in which data can flow only in one direction.

**Simulation**  To represent and analyze properties or behavior of a physical or hypothetical system by the behavior of a system model.

**Single In-line Memory Module (SIMM)**  A memory board with memory chips on it.  Memory chips can be added on the board to increase the computer's main memory capacity.

**Small Scale Integration (SSI)**  Integration of only about ten to twenty electronic components on a single chip.

**Smart card**  An electronic card having a built-in microprocessor chip.  Data to be encoded on the card is permanently stored in the memory of the chip.

**Smart terminal**  A terminal having local data editing capability, and the ability to consolidate input data, before sending them to the main computer.  It has a microprocessor, some internal storage, and I/O capabilities.

**Soft-copy output**  A computer output, which is temporary in nature, and vanishes after use.  For example, output displayed on a terminal screen, or spoken out by a voice response system.

**Software**  A set of computer programs, procedures, and associated documents (flowcharts, manuals, etc.) related to the effective operation of a computer system.

**Software package** A group of programs, which solve a specific problem, or perform a specific type of job. For example, a word-processing package.

**Software piracy** The illegal copying or use of software.

**Solid state** Electronic components, whose operation depends on the control of electric or magnetic phenomena in solids, such as transistors and diodes.

**Sort** The process of arranging data into a desired sequence.

**Source program** A program written in a symbolic or high-level language, such as assembly language, COBOL, BASIC, etc.

**Special character** A graphic character, which is neither a letter, a digit, nor a space character. For example, the dollar sign, comma, period, etc.

**Special purpose computer** A computer, which is meant for doing only a particular type of jobs.

**Speech synthesizer** A voice response system, which converts text information into spoken sentences.

**Spreadsheet** A numeric data analysis tool (software package), which allows users to create a kind of computerized ledger.

**SQL** A standard query language for relational databases.

**Stack** A memory in which information, which is stored last is on top, and is retrieved first. Also known as LIFO (Last-in-first-out) storage.

**Stand-alone** In a distributed data processing system, it refers to a computer system, which has an independent (from a central-site computer) processing and storage capability.

**Star network** A network in which multiple computers are connected to a central host computer. These computers are not linked directly to each other, and can communicate only via the host computer.

**Statement** In programming, an expression or generalized instruction in a source language.

**Storage** See memory.

**Storage hierarchy** A hierarchy of storage technologies (such as cache memory, main memory, secondary storage and mass storage) used in a computer system. This is usually done because a single type of storage is not superior in speed of access, capacity, and cost.

**Stored program computer** A computer where the program to solve a problem, and the necessary data are stored in its memory.

**Structured design** A system design approach in which a difficult problem is broken into smaller problems, which is small enough to manage, but independent enough to solve separately.

**Structured programming** An organized approach to programming involving the use of the three basic control structures – sequence, selection, and iteration, and the use of top-down concepts to decompose main functions into lower-level components for modular coding purposes.

**Study phase** A system life-cycle phase during which a problem is identified, alternative solutions are studied, and the most feasible solution is selected.

**Subprocedure** See subroutine.

**Subprogram** See subroutine.

**Subroutine** A standardized program written in a manner that it can be used as part of another program whenever necessary. A subroutine is normally invoked through other programs by the use of CALL statements. Also known as subprogram and subprocedure.

**Supercomputer** Computer systems characterized by their very high processing speeds. They are generally used for complex scientific applications.

**Swapping** Storing programs on disk, and then transferring these programs into main storage as and when they are needed. The technique is used to process large programs, or several programs with limited memory.

**Symbolic language** See assembly language.

**Symbolic program** See assembly program.

**Synchronous communication** Data transmission mode in which the sender and receiver must synchronize with each other to get ready for data transmission, before it takes place.

**Syntax** A set of rules of a programming language, which define the pattern or structure of the word order and punctuation of an instruction. It is analogous to rules of grammar in English language.

**Syntax errors** Errors in computer programs, which typically involve incorrect punctuation, incorrect word sequence, undefined terms, or misuse of terms. These errors are automatically detected, and pointed out by language processors.

**System** A group of integrated parts (people, methods, machines, and materials), which have a common purpose of achieving some objective(s).

**System analysis** A detailed step-by-step investigation of related procedures to see what must be done, and the best way of doing it.

**System analyst** The individual responsible for planning a computer data processing system. He/she utilizes tools, such as flowcharts, decision tables, program design language, etc. These plans are then passed to the computer programmer.

**System commands** Commands used to communicate with the operating system of the computer.

**System programmer** A programmer who prepares system software.

**System software** A set of one or more programs designed to control the operation, and extend the processing capability of a computer system.

## T

**Tape density** The amount of data, which can be placed over a given length of tape. The density is usually expressed in bytes or characters per inch.

**Tape drive** A device used for storage and retrieval of data stored on magnetic tape medium.

**Telecommunications** Transmission of data between computer system and/or terminals at different locations through telephone facilities.

**Telnet** An application level protocol, which allows a user to log in to another computer from his/her current computer in a network environment.

**Template** A standard format used to quickly create new documents in the same format.

**Terabytes (TB)** Memory storage equal to about one trillion ($10^{12}$) bytes.

**Teraflop** $10^{12}$ floating-point arithmetic operations per second.

**Terminal** See Video Display Terminal (VDT).

**Testing** The process of making sure that the program performs the intended task.

**Thermal printer** A printing device, which utilizes paper that is sensitive to heat.

**Third-generation computers** Computers built between 1964 and 1975, which used integrated circuits in CPU, high speed magnetic core main memories, powerful high-level languages, and time sharing operating system.

**Throughput** The total amount of useful processing carried out by a computer system within a given time period. It is measured as the number of processes, which are completed by the system per unit time.

**Time division multiplexing** A method of sharing a communication channel in which the total time available in the channel is divided between several users and each user of the channel is allotted a time slice during which he/she may transmit a message. The channel capacity is fully utilized by interleaving a number of data streams belonging to different users into one data stream.

**Time log** A log documentation automatically maintained by many computer systems, which describes in detail how the computer system was used during the day.

**Time slice** The short period of time during which a user process gets the attention of the CPU in a time-sharing system. Also known as time slot or quantum.

**Time slot** See time slice.

**Time-sharing** A mechanism to provide simultaneous, interactive use of a computer system by many users in a manner that each user is given the impression that he/she has his/her own computer. It uses multiprogramming with a special CPU scheduling algorithm to achieve this.

**Top-down approach** A disciplined approach to system design or program design in which top-level functions are decomposed into a hierarchy of understandable lower-level modules for better management and easy handling.

**Touch screen** A simple, intuitive, and easy to learn input device, which enables the users to choose from available options by simply touching with their finger the desired icon or menu item displayed on the computer's screen.

**Track** In case of magnetic disk, one of many circular concentric rings used for storing data. In case of magnetic tape, a horizontal strip, or channel, running the full length of the tape, and used for recording data.

**Trackball** An input device, which serves as an effective pointing device.

**Transaction file** A file in which current data are stored for subsequent processing usually in combination with a master file.

**Transducer** A device capable of changing signals from analog form to digital form, or vice-versa.

**Transistor** A controlled electronic switch fabricated using a semiconductor. It is extensively used in the design of various electronic equipment.

**Transponder** A device mounted on a communication satellite, which receives, amplifies and retransmits signals from earth stations.

**Truth table** A table, which gives the output values for the varies input combinations in case of a logical expression.

**Tuple** A group of related fields (a row of a table) in a relational databases.

**Turnaround time** The elapsed time between the submission of a job to a computer system for processing, and the completion of the job.

**Turnkey solution** See end-to-end solution.

**Twisted-pair cable** A simple, inexpensive, and slow wired transmission medium.

# U

**Ultra Large Scale Integration (ULSI)** Integration of about ten million electronic components on to a single chip.

**Ultra Voilet EPROM (UVEPROM)** An EPROM chip in which the stored information is erased by exposing the chip for some time to ultraviolet light.

**Unbundled** A term, which means that the application software is priced separately from the computer hardware.

**Unconditional transfer** A program instruction, which causes the program control to flow out of normal sequence unconditionally.

**Uniform Resource Locator (URL)** An addressing scheme used by WWW browsers to locate sites on the Internet.

**Uninterrupted Power Supply (UPS)** A battery-supported power unit between an external power source and a computer system, which supplies clean and continuous power even during power failures.

**Universal gate** A logic gate, which is alone sufficient to implement any Boolean function. For example, NAND and NOR gates.

**Universal Product Code (UPC)** A universal or standardized optical bar code, which normally appears on retail packages, and which is read by a laser beam scanner.

**Unix** A multi-user, time-sharing operating system. It is a very popular operating system, and can be used on a wide variety of computers, ranging from notebook computers to super computers.

**Uploading** Moving a file from ones own computer to a remote computer in a network environment.

**Uptime** The time duration when the computer system is in operation.

**Upward compatible** The ability of hardware or software to function with all of the same equipment and software with which its predecessors could function.

**Usenet** A service on the Internet, which allows a group of Internet users to exchange their views/ideas/information on some common topic, which is of interest to all the members belonging to the group.

**User authentication** Deals with the problem of verifying the identity of a user (person or program), before permitting access to the requested resource.

**User-friendly** A program or computer system designed in a manner that even individuals who lack computer experience can easily use the system without much training.

**User-programmed ROM** A PROM in which the user can load and store "read-only" programs and data.

**User-supported software** See public-domain software.

**Utilities** A set of programs, which help users in performing system maintenance and other tasks of routine nature.

# V

**Value Added Network (VAN)** Enhanced data transmission service provided by doing value addition to the standard services of the common carriers. Added value may include features, such as electronic mail, data encryption/decryption, access to commercial databases, and code conversion for communication between incompatible computers.

**Variable name** In a program, the name assigned to a data field, which can assume any of a given set of values.

**Vector graphics** Graphic objects composed of patterns of lines, points, circles, arcs, and other geometric shares (vectors), which can be easily represented by few geometric parameters.

**Very Large Scale Integration (VLSI)** An electronic circuit with about 10,000 transistors fabricated in a single silicon chip.

**Very Small Aperture Terminals (VSATs)** Smaller disk antennas having lower power transmitters and receivers, which can be installed at users' sites. It enables a large number of users to benefit from satellite communication.

**Video conferencing** A system in which persons sitting at CRT screens see and talk to each other via a computer-communications network. It saves traveling cost and the valuable time of executives.

**Video Display Terminal (VDT)** A monitor and a keyboard used together as both an input and an output device. Also known as terminal.

**Virtual machine** The concept of adding the operating system layer on top of the bare hardware to manage all parts of the system, and present the users with an interface, which is easier to program and use.

**Virtual memory** A memory management scheme, which allows the execution of processes, which might not be completely loaded in the main memory. The three basic concepts used for the realization of virtual memory are on-line secondary storage, swapping and demand paging.

**Virus** A computer virus is a piece of code attached to a legitimate program, which, when executed, infects other programs in the system by replicating and attaching itself to them. In addition to this replicating effect, a virus normally does some other damage to the system, such as corrupting/erasing files.

**Vision input system** An input device, which allows a computer to accept input by seeing an object. The input data in this case is normally an object's shape and features in the form of an image.

**Visualization** Deals with exploring data and information graphically for better comprehension.

**Voice recognition device** An input device, which allows a person to input data to a computer by speaking to it.

**Voice reproduction system** A voice response system, which produces audio output by selecting appropriate audio output from a set of pre-recorded audio responses.

**Voice response system** An output device, which enables a compute to talk to its users.

**Voiceband** Data communications system, which handles moderate volumes of data, typically from 300 to 9600 bauds. Phone lines, which we use to talk to other people is an example.

**Volatile storage** A storage medium, which loses its contents when power fails, or when power is switched off.

## W

**Web client** Any computer on the Internet, which can access web servers.

**Web page** A hypertext document on the Internet.

**Web server** Any computer on the Internet, which uses the HTTP protocol.

**Wide Area Network (WAN)** A computer network, which interconnects computers spread over a large geographical area. It may also enable LANs to communicate with each other. This type of network may be developed to operate nationwide or worldwide, and the transmission medium used are normally public systems, such as telephone lines, microwave and satellite links.

**Wildcard (character)** A special character, usually a ? or an *, which is used in software commands as a generic reference to any character, or any combination of characters, respectively.

**Winchester disk** Medium-sized, non-interchangeable metal disks permanently housed in sealed, contamination-free containers, with built-in read/write heads.

**Window** A rectangular portion of a computer screen, which is dedicated to specific activity or application. The display screen can be separated into several windows to simultaneously show the status of the different applications at any instance of time.

**Windows** An operating system developed by Microsoft for use on personal computers. Its various release versions are Windows 3.0, Windows 95, Windows 98, Windows 2000 and Windows XP.

**Windows NT** A multi-user, timesharing operating system developed by Microsoft, which has Unix-like features. It is designed to be used for powerful workstations, and network and database servers.

**Wireless computing system** A computer network, which uses wireless communication technologies. It enhances the functionality of computing equipment by freeing communication from the location constraints of the wired computing systems.

**Word** A group of bits or characters considered as an entity, and capable of being stored in one storage location. Also fixed-size storage areas, which form the primary memory of a computer system.

**Word length** A measure of the size of a word, usually specified in units, such as characters or bits. Each location of a computer system can store a fixed number of characters or bits, called its word length.

**Word processing** The use of computers to create, view, edit, format, store, retrieve, and print text materials.

**Word wrap** A word processing feature, which automatically moves words down to the beginning of the next line, if they extend beyond the right margin.

**Word-addressable storage** Storage designed to store a fixed number of characters (equal to its word-length in bytes). For such a storage device, storage space is always allocated in multiples of word-length. Its another name is fixed-word-length storage.

**Workstation** A powerful desktop computer designed to meet the computing needs of engineers, architects, and other professionals, who need greater processing power, larger storage, and better graphics display facility than what PCs provide.

**World Wide Web (WWW or W3)** Network of computers across the world interconnected together on the Internet, and using the concept of hypertext to link Internet sites and information on the Internet.

**Worm** A computer virus designed to erase/alter the data/program from a computer system's memory/disk.

**Write-Once, Read-Many (WORM) disk** An optical disk, which looks like a standard CD-ROM disk, but allows the user to record his/her own information on it by using a CD-Recordable (CD-R) drive.

**WYSIWYG** Stands for What You See Is What You Get. This feature of a word-processing package allows the users to display a document on the screen in a form, which closely resembles what the printed document will look like.

## Z

**Zip disk** See Bernoulli disk.

**Zoned decimal number** Any numeric character coded in the Extended Binary Coded Decimal Interchange Code (EBCDIC). Each decimal digit occupies one byte of storage.

# Index

### ◆ AUTOCAD 2000

| ISBN | Title | Author | Price |
|---|---|---|---|
| 81-7656-080-4 | AutoCAD 2000 - No Experience Required | David | 270/- |
| 81-7656-404-4 | Introduction to AutoCAD 2000 | Roberts | 75/- |
| 81-7635-422-8 | Inside AutoCAD 2000 | Burchard | 450/- |

### ◆ ALGORITHMS & DATA STRUCTURE

| ISBN | Title | Author | Price |
|---|---|---|---|
| 81-7635-186-5 | Data Structure & Algorithms in Java | Lafore | 360/- |
| 81-7635-706-X | Data Structure Through C | Kanetkar | 165/- |
| 81-7656-707-8 | Data Structure Through C++ | Kanetkar | 165/- |

### ◆ ADVANCE COMPTUER ARCHITECTURE

| ISBN | Title | Author | Price |
|---|---|---|---|
| 81-7656-523-7 | Computer Organization and Architecture | Jain,S | 135/- |

### ◆ COMPUTER GRAPHICS & IMAGE PROCESSING

| ISBN | Title | Author | Price |
|---|---|---|---|
| 81-7656-602-0 | Computer Graphics - An Object-Oriented Approach with C++ | Pokorny | 270/- |
| 81-7029-397-9 | Computer GRAPHICS Secrets & Solutions | Corrigan | 120/- |
| 81-7029-515-7 | Image Processing in C | Phillips | 350/- |

### ◆ COMPUTER ARCHITECTURE

| ISBN | Title | Author | Price |
|---|---|---|---|
| 81-7656-523-7 | Computer Organization and Architecture | Jain,S | 135/- |
| 81-7656-549-0 | Computer Organization and System Software | Jain,S | 180/- |

### ◆ COMPUTER ARCHITECTURE & NETWORKING LAB

| ISBN | Title | Author | Price |
|---|---|---|---|
| 81-7656-523-7 | Computer Organization and Architecture | Jain,S | 135/- |
| 81-7656-197-5 | Network + LAB Manual | Evanson | 99/- |
| 81-7656-715-9 | Networking Complete | Sybex | 270/- |
| 81-7635-356-6 | Peter Norton's Complete guide to Networking | Norton | 270/- |

### ◆ DISCRETE MATHEMATICS

| ISBN | Title | Author | Price |
|---|---|---|---|
| 81-7656-639-X | Discrete Mathematics | Vinay Kumar | 150/- |

### ◆ DATA BASE MANAGEMENT SYSTEMS

| ISBN | Title | Author | Price |
|---|---|---|---|
| 81-7635-626-3 | Absolute Beginner's Guide to Databases | Peterson | 135/- |
| 81-7029-994-2 | DATA Processing and Information Technology | French | 135/- |
| 81-7656-638-1 | Introduction to Database Management | Jain,S | 165/- |
| 81-7656-711-6 | Relational DATABASE - Theory & Practice | Occardi | 99/- |
| 81-7656-551-2 | Teach Yourself Database Technologies | Bayross | 240/- |
| 81-7656-927-5 | Data Mining | BPB | 150/- |
| 81-7656-928-3 | Data Warehousing | BPB | 135/- |

### ◆ E-COMMERCE

| ISBN | Title | Author | Price |
|---|---|---|---|
| 81-7656-414-1 | Instant E-Commerce | Chase | 180/- |
| 81-7635-435-X | Teach Yourself E-Commerce Programming with ASP in 21 Days | Walther | 210/- |

### ◆ ELECTRONIC / DATA COMMUNICATION AND NETWORKS

| ISBN | Title | Author | Price |
|---|---|---|---|
| 81-7656-609-8 | Computer Networks | Jain,S | 150/- |
| 81-7656-571-7 | DATA COMMUNICATION: Network & Systems | Bartee,T | 225/- |
| 81-7656-608-X | Principles of Electronics - Analog & Digital | Jain,S | 150/- |
| 81-7635-319-1 | Understanding Data Communications (Covers PDA's, ISDN, SNMP, TCP/IP) | Held | 180/- |

### ◆ GENERAL COMPUTING

| ISBN | Title | Author | Price |
|---|---|---|---|
| 81-7635-680-8 | Encyclopedia of Technology Terms | Whatis.com | 570/- |

### ◆ INTERNET APPLICATIONS DEVELOPMENT

| ISBN | Title | Author | Price |
|---|---|---|---|
| 81-7029-911-X | ABCs of the INTERNET | Crumlish | 150/- |
| 81-7656-397-8 | Introduction to Computers and the Internet - Training Guide | Rain | 75/- |
| 81-7029-721-4 | INTERNET Instant Reference | Hoffman | 90/- |
| 81-7635-437-6 | How The Internet Works | Gralla | 540/- |
| 81-7029-744-3 | Learning to use the INTERNET | Ackermann | 180/- |

### ◆ INTERNET & INTRANET

| ISBN | Title | Author | Price |
|---|---|---|---|
| 81-7029-911-X | ABCs of the INTERNET | Crumlish | 150/- |
| 81-7635-437-6 | How The Internet Works | Gralla | 540/- |
| 81-7029-875-X | ABCs of INTRANETS | Dyson | 120/- |
| 81-7635-563-1 | How To Use The Internet -Visually | Cadenhead | 120/- |
| 81-7656-309-9 | INTERNET Complete | Sybex | 225/- |
| 81-7635-023-0 | Intranets Unleashed | Garret | 499/- |

### ◆ LABORATORY COURSE IN MICROCOMPTUER, BUSINESS AND OFFICE APPLICAITONS

| ISBN | Title | Author | Price |
|---|---|---|---|
| 81-7656-464-8 | BPB Computer Course | Wray | 120/- |
| 81-7635-436-8 | How Computers Work | White | 599/- |
| 81-7635-609-3 | How To Use Computers | Biow | 99/- |
| 81-7656-262-9 | Learn MS Office 2000 | Stultz | 240/- |
| 81-7656-095-2 | MS OFFICE 2000 Complete | Sybex | 270/- |
| 81-7656-500-8 | SQL Server and ADO Programming Complete | Sybex | 225/- |
| 81-7029-644-7 | Understanding SQL | Gruber | 225/- |

### ◆ MANAGEMENT INFORMATION SYSTEMS

| ISBN | Title | Author | Price |
|---|---|---|---|
| 81-7029-999-3 | Management Information System | Lucey | 120/- |

### ◆ MCA - LOGIC PROGRAMMING

| ISBN | Title | Author | Price |
|---|---|---|---|
| 81-7029-104-6 | Introduction to Turbo Prolog | Townsend | 150/- |
| BPB 1009 | Illustrated Turbo Prolog | Mcallister | 120/- |

### ◆ MULTIMEDIA SYSTEMS

| ISBN | Title | Author | Price |
|---|---|---|---|
| 81-7635-604-2 | Inside Flash 5 | Keating | 399/- |
| 81-7029-441-X | Multimedia on the PC | Sinclair | 120/- |
| 81-7029-972-1 | Multimedia Magic | Gokul,S | 270/- |
| 81-7635-614-X | Maya 4 Fundamentals | Lammers | 210/- |
| 81-7635-638-7 | Macromedia Director 8.5 Shockwave Studio for 3D- T. F. S. | Gross | 399/- |
| 81-7635-641-7 | Maya 4 - Visual Quickstart Guide | Riddell | 150/- |

### ◆ NETWORK SECURITY AND CRYPTOLOGY

| ISBN | Title | Author | Price |
|---|---|---|---|
| 81-7635-258-6 | How Network Works | Derfler | 390/- |
| 81-7029-957-8 | NT Network Security | Matthew | 450/- |
| 81-7635-358-2 | Peter Norton's Network Security Fundamentals | Norton | 150/- |
| 81-7656-789-2 | Security Complete | Sybex | 270/- |

### ◆ NETWORKING TECHNOLOGY & TCP/IP

| ISBN | Title | Author | Price |
|---|---|---|---|
| 81-7635-630-1 | Absolute Beginner's Guide To Networks | Habraken | 165/- |
| 81-7635-258-6 | How Network Works | Derfler | 390/- |

### ◆ NETWORKING TECHNOLOGY & TCP/IP

| | | | |
|---|---|---|---|
| 81-7635-060-5 | Inside TCP/IP | Siyan | 300/- |
| 81-7656-715-9 | Networking Complete | Sybex | 270/- |
| 81-7635-094-X | Networking Essentials Unleashed | Sportack | 399/- |
| 81-7635-356-6 | Peter Norton's Complete guide to Networking | Norton | 270/- |
| 81-7656-148-7 | TCP/IP 24seven | Govanus | 180/- |
| 81-7635-615-5 | TCP/IP Unleashed | Parker | 399/- |
| 81-7635-418-X | Understanding the Network | Michael | 180/- |

### ◆ OBJECT ORIENTED PROGRAMMING

| | | | |
|---|---|---|---|
| 81-7029-447-9 | Object-Oriented Programming with C++ | Parsons | 120/- |
| 81-7635-608-5 | Object-Oriented Programming in C++ | Lafore | 450/- |
| 81-7029-840-7 | Object-Oriented Programming: A New Way of Thinking | Donald | 90/- |
| 81-7656-863-5 | Introduction To Object-Oriented Programming and C++ | Kanetkar | 150/- |
| 81-7656-857-0 | Object Oriened Programming with C++ | BPB | 180/- |

### ◆ OPERATING SYSTEMS

| | | | |
|---|---|---|---|
| 81-7656-019-7 | Operating Systems | Ritchie | 120/- |

### ◆ ORACLE

| | | | |
|---|---|---|---|
| 81-7656-272-6 | Learn Oracle 8i | Ramalho | 225/- |
| 81-7656-541-5 | Mastering Oracle 8i | Freeman | 450/- |
| 81-7635-352-3 | Migrating to Oracle 8i | Thakkar | 270/- |
| 81-7656-577-6 | OCA/OCP: Introduction to Oracle 9i SQL Study Guide (Exam 1Z0-007) | Thomas | 330/- |
| 81-7656-584-9 | OCA/OCP: Oracle 9i DBA Fundamentals I Study Guide (Exam 1Z1-031) | Thomas | 330/- |
| 81-7656-604-7 | OCP: Oracle 9i DBA Fundamentals II Study Guide (Exam 1Z1-032) | Thomas | 330/- |
| 81-7656-632-2 | OCP: Oracle 9i Performance Tuning Study Guide (Exam 1Z1-033) | Thomas | 390/- |

### ◆ PRINCIPLES OF PROGRAMMING LANGUAGE

| | | | |
|---|---|---|---|
| 81-7656-752-3 | Computer Fundamentals - 3rd Revised Edition | Sinha | 150/- |
| 81-7656-663-2 | Foundation of Computing | Sinha | 297/- |
| 81-7656-621-7 | Let Us C - 4th Revised Edition | Kanetkar | 180/- |
| 81-7635-608-5 | Object-Oriented Programming in C++ | Lafore | 450/- |
| | The Handbook of Programming Language - HPL (4 Vol. Set) | | |
| 81-7635-122-9 | Vol. I - Object-Oriented Programming Language | Salus | 399/- |
| 81-7635-123-7 | Vol. II - Imperative Programming Languages | Salus | 240/- |
| 81-7635-124-5 | Vol. III - Little Languages & Tools | Salus | 300/- |
| 81-7635-125-3 | Vol. IV - Functional, and Logic Prog. Languages | Salus | 210/- |

### ◆ PROGRAMMING, LABORATORY COURSE IN C, C++

| | | | |
|---|---|---|---|
| 81-7656-375-7 | Data Structures Through C Language | DOEACC | 210/- |
| 81-7656-706-X | Data Structures Through C | Kanetkar | 165/- |
| 81-7656-621-7 | Let Us C - 4th Revised Edition | Kanetkar | 180/- |
| 81-7656-707-8 | Data Structures Through C++ | Kanetkar | 165/- |
| 81-7656-621-7 | Let Us C++ | Kanetkar | 180/- |
| | Let Us C++ (Multimedia CBT) CD-ROM | Kanetkar | 399/- |
| 81-7635-608-5 | Object-Oriented Programming in C++ | Lafore | 450/- |
| 81-7656-358-7 | Understanding Pointers in C | Kanetkar | 195/- |
| 81-7029-301-4 | Working With C (For DOEACC - 'A' & 'B' Level) | Kanetkar | 195/- |

### ◆ SYSTEM ANALYSIS AND DESIGN

| | | | |
|---|---|---|---|
| 81-7029-627-7 | Introducing SYSTEMS ANALYSIS | Skidmore | 90/- |
| 81-7656-601-2 | Introducing SYSTEMS DESIGN | Skidmore | 90/- |

### ◆ VISUAL BASIC, VISUAL C & VISUAL FOXPRO PROGRAMMING

| | | | |
|---|---|---|---|
| 81-7029-689-7 | FOXPRO 2.5 Made Simple | Taxali | 240/- |

### ◆ VISUAL BASIC, VISUAL C++ & VISUAL FOXPRO PROGRAMMING

| | | | |
|---|---|---|---|
| 81-7656-031-6 | Mastering VISUAL BASIC 6 | Petroutsos | 480/- |
| 81-7029-129-1 | Mastering FOXPRO 2.5 & 2.6 | Siegel | 345/- |
| 81-7029-499-1 | Programming in VISUAL BASIC | McBride | 99/- |
| 81-7656-622-5 | Programming in Visual Basic 6 | Bayross | 150/- |
| 81-7635-139-3 | Teach Yourself More Visual Basic 6 in 21 Days | Mauer | 240/- |
| 81-7635-150-4 | Teach Yourself Visual Basic 6 in 21 Days | Perry | 360/- |
| 81-7029-864-4 | Teach Yourself Visual FoxPro 5.0 for Win | King | 270/- |
| 81-7635-135-0 | Teach Yourself Visual C++ 6 in 21 Days | Chapman | 360/- |
| 81-7656-567-9 | Visual Basic Projects | Dasgupta | 135/- |
| 81-7656-078-2 | VISUAL BASIC 6 Complete | SYBEX | 270/- |
| 81-7029-971-3 | VISUAL C++ Programming | Kanetkar | 240/- |
| 81-7656-552-0 | VC++ Gems | Kanetkar | 270/- |
| 81-7656-279-3 | Visual FoxPro 6 Enterprise Development | Paddock | 299/- |
| 81-7635-146-6 | Visual Basic 6 - Unleashed | Thayer | 375/- |
| 81-7635-467-8 | Visual C++ 6 Unleashed | Williams | 499/- |

### ◆ WEB AUTHORING TOOLS, JAVA, PERL AND C# PROGRAMMING

| | | | |
|---|---|---|---|
| 81-7656-472-9 | C# - The Basics | Mukhi | 180/- |
| 81-7656-420-6 | C# Made Simple | BPB | 240/- |
| 81-7635-586-0 | C# Unleashed | Mayo | 450/- |
| 81-7635-304-3 | JAVA 2 Platform Unleashed | Jaworski | 499/- |
| 81-7635-616-6 | J2EE Unleashed | Bambara | 450/- |
| 81-7656-692-9 | Java 2, J2SE 1.4 - Complete | Sybex | 270/- |
| 81-7656-618-7 | Mastering JAVA 2 (J2SE 1.4) | Zukowski | 499/- |
| 81-7656-065-0 | Mastering PERL 5 | Herrmann | 399/- |
| 81-87105-70-4 | PERL 5 How - To : Waite Group | Glover | 399/- |
| 81-87105-51-8 | PERL 5 Interactive Course : Waite Group | Orwant | 495/- |
| 81-7635-462-7 | Presenting C# - Sharp | Wille | 150/- |
| 81-7635-263-2 | Teach Yourself PERL in 21 Days | Lemay | 240/- |
| 81-7635-579-8 | Teach Yourself C# in 21 Days | Jones | 297/- |
| 81-87105-95-X | Web Authoring Desk Reference | Weiss | 450/- |

### ◆ WEB SITE DEVELOPMENT & WEB CLIENT PROGRAMMING

| | | | |
|---|---|---|---|
| 81-7635-063-X | Designing Interactive Websites | Szeto | 270/- |
| 81-7656-415-X | Effective Web Design | Navarro | 270/- |
| 81-7656-308-0 | HTML Complete | Sybex | 270/- |
| 81-87105-42-9 | Macromedia Web Publishing - Unleashed | Darnell | 450/- |
| 81-7656-245-9 | The Complete Website Upgrade & Maintenance Guide | Schmeiser | 570/- |
| 81-7656-536-9 | Teach Yourself Web Technologies - Part I | Bayross | 270/- |
| 81-7656-543-1 | Teach Yourself Web Technologies - Part II | Bayross | 360/- |
| 81-7635-400-7 | Teach Yourself To Create Web Pages in 24 Hours - Starter Kit | Snell | 165/- |
| 81-7656-274-2 | Web Enabled Commercial Application Development Using HTML, DHTML, JavaScript, Perl CGI | Bayross | 390/- |